QUALITY MANAGEMENT FOR ORGANIZATIONAL EXCELLENCE

Introduction to Total Quality

Seventh Edition

David L. Goetsch

Stanley B. Davis

Boston   Columbus   Indianapolis   New York   San Francisco   Upper Saddle River
Amsterdam   Cape Town   Dubai   London   Madrid   Milan   Munich   Paris   Montreal   Toronto
Delhi   Mexico City   São Paulo   Sydney   Hong Kong   Seoul   Singapore   Taipei   Tokyo

Editorial Director: Vernon R. Anthony
Acquisitions Editor: David Ploskonka
Editorial Assistant: Nancy Kesterson
Director of Marketing: David Gesell
Executive Marketing Manager: Derril Trakalo
Senior Marketing Coordinator: Alicia Wozniak
Marketing Assistant: Les Roberts
Senior Managing Editor: JoEllen Gohr
Associate Managing Editor: Alexandrina Benedicto Wolf
Production Project Manager: Maren L. Miller
Production Manager: Laura Messerly
Art Director: Jayne Conte
Cover Designer: Suzanne Behnke
Image Permission Coordinator: Mike Lackey
Cover Art: Fotolia
Full-Service Project Management: Jogender Taneja/Aptara®, Inc.
Composition: Aptara®, Inc.
Printer/Binder: Edwards Brothers Malloy
Cover Printer: Lehigh-Phoenix Color Corp.
Text Font: Minion, 10/12 pt

Credits and acknowledgments for material borrowed from other sources and reproduced, with permission, in this textbook appear on the appropriate page within the text.

Library of Congress Cataloging-in-Publication Data

Goetsch, David L.
  Quality management for organizational excellence : introduction to total quality / David L. Goetsch, Stanley B. Davis. — 7th ed.
    p. cm.
  ISBN-13: 978-0-13-255898-3
  ISBN-10: 0-13-255898-X
  1. Total quality management.   I. Davis, Stanley, 1931-   II. Title.
  HD62.15.G64 2013
  658.4'013—dc23
                                          2011038639

10 9 8 7 6

ISBN 10:   0-13-255898-X
ISBN 13: 978-0-13-255898-3

PREFACE

BACKGROUND

At one time in history, Great Britain was the world's leader in commerce and industry. Eventually, the United States emerged as a major friendly competitor. Then, following World War II, the United States took over as the undisputed world leader of commerce and industry. During these postwar years, while the United States was enjoying unparalleled prosperity, Japan and Germany were rebuilding from the ashes of the war. With a great deal of help from the United States, Japan was able to rebound and during the 1970s began to challenge the United States in such key manufacturing sectors as automobiles, computers, and consumer electronics. By 1980, Japan had emerged as a world-class competitor and a global leader in selected areas of commerce and industry. German industry had also reemerged by this time. By 2000, Korea, China, and the Pacific Rim nations had also emerged as global competitors.

As a result, the United States found itself losing market share in economic sectors it had dominated (and taken for granted) for decades. At first, industrialists in the United States turned their backs on the lesson their counterparts in other industrialized nations had learned. This lesson was that the key to competing in the international marketplace was to simultaneously improve quality and productivity on a continual basis. However, as more and more market share slipped away, the message started to sink in for the United States. This belated awareness gave rise to a quality movement that began to take hold. Its progress was slow at first. However, an approach to doing business known as quality management has caught on and is now widely practiced as a way to achieve organizational excellence. Organizational excellence is a combination of peak performance, superior quality, and continual improvement.

This book advocates an approach to doing business that focuses all the resources of an organization on the continual and simultaneous improvement of quality and productivity. The purpose of this approach is to continually improve the organization's performance and, in turn, competitiveness.

WHY WAS THIS BOOK WRITTEN AND FOR WHOM?

This book was written in response to the need for a practical teaching resource that encompasses all of the various elements of quality management, including Lean, Six Sigma, and Lean Six Sigma, and pulls them together in a coherent format that allows the reader to understand both the big picture and the specific details of quality management. It is intended for use in universities, colleges, community colleges, corporate environments, and any other settings in which people want to learn to be effective agents of quality management. Students enrolled in technology, engineering, and management programs will find this book both valuable and easy to use. Practitioners in corporate settings will find it a valuable guide in understanding and implementing quality management.

The direct, straightforward presentation of material focuses on making the theories and principles of quality management practical and useful in a real-world setting. Up-to-date research has been integrated throughout in a down-to-earth manner.

ORGANIZATION OF THIS BOOK

The text consists of 22 chapters, organized in two parts. Part 1 explains the philosophy and concepts of quality management. Part 2 covers the tools and techniques of quality management. A standard format is used throughout the book. Each chapter begins with a list of major topics and provides a comprehensive summary. Key terms and concepts, factual review questions, a critical thinking activity, discussion assignments, and endnotes are found at the end. The endnotes provide readers with comprehensive lists of additional reading and research material that can be pursued at the discretion of the student and/or the instructor. The other materials encourage review, stimulate additional thought, promote discussion, and facilitate additional research.

HOW THIS BOOK DIFFERS FROM OTHERS

Most books in the market deal with one of the several elements of quality management, such as teamwork, just-in-time manufacturing, scientific measurement (SPC or quality tools), continual improvement, and employee involvement. Many of the books available were developed with the advanced-level practitioner in mind rather than the beginner. Few of the books in the market were formatted for use in a classroom setting. This book was written to provide both comprehensive and in-depth coverage of quality management. All the elements of quality management are covered, including several that receive little or no attention in other quality management books (e.g., peak performance, continual improvement, superior value, partnering, manufacturing networks, quality culture, and how to implement total quality). These subjects are covered in sufficient depth to allow a beginner to learn everything necessary to understand and implement total quality without having to look to any other source of information.

New in the Seventh Edition

The seventh edition contains major improvements that reflect the evolution of quality management, Lean, and Six Sigma; changes in the global marketplace; and feedback from customers. These include the following:

- Eliminated all old Quality Cases and replaced them with new cases. Quality Cases now appear in all odd-numbered chapters. In order to be selected as the subject of a Quality Case, an organization had to be a winner of the Baldrige Award, the Shingo Quality Prize from Japan, or the European Quality Award.
- Updated or replaced Quality Tips as appropriate.
- Updated all time-sensitive endnoted material.
- Updated all time-sensitive Discussion Assignments.
- Added new sections and new material on numerous topics, including quality certifications, quality management responsibilities of supervisors, product innovation following before leading, team facilitation, customer retention, and ISO 9000.
- Added a 100-year timeline showing the evolution of quality.
- Replaced the chapter on Quality Function Deployment (QFD) with a new chapter on the subject that focuses on not just what it is but how to use the concept.
- Updated and expanded the chapter on statistical process control.

- Updated and expanded the chapter on continual improvement methods.
- Updated and expanded the chapter on benchmarking.
- Updated and expanded the chapter on just-in-time/lean including all new discussion assignments.

Download Instructor Resources from the Instructor Resource Center

To access supplementary materials online, instructors need to request an instructor access code. Go to www.pearson-highered.com/irc to register for an instructor access code. Within 48 hours of registering, you will receive a confirming e-mail including an instructor access code. Once you have received your code, locate your text in the online catalog and click on the Instructor Resources button on the left side of the catalog product page. Select a supplement, and a login page will appear. Once you have logged in, you can access instructor material for all Pearson textbooks. If you have any difficulties accessing the Web site or downloading a supplement, please contact Customer Service at http://247pearsoned.custhelp.com/.

ACKNOWLEDGMENTS

The authors would like to thank the following reviewers for the helpful insights: Otha C. Hawkins, Alamance Community College; and Daniel S. Marrone, Farmingdale State College (SUNY).

ABOUT THE AUTHORS

David L. Goetsch is vice president of Northwest Florida State College and provost of the College's Joint Campus with the University of West Florida in Fort Walton Beach, Florida, where he also serves as professor of quality and safety management. He also administers Florida's Center for Manufacturing Competitiveness, which is located on this campus, and is president of The Institute for Continual Improvement, a private company dedicated to the continual improvement of quality, productivity, and competitiveness. Dr. Goetsch is cofounder of The Quality Institute, a partnership of the University of West Florida, Northwest Florida State College, and the Okaloosa Economic Development Council. He currently serves on the executive board of the institute.

Stanley B. Davis was a manufacturing executive with Harris Corporation until his retirement in 1992. He was founding managing director of The Quality Institute and is a well-known expert in the areas of total quality management and its implementation, statistical process control, just-in-time manufacturing, Six Sigma, benchmarking, quality management systems, and environmental management systems. He currently serves as professor of quality at the institute and heads his own consulting firm, Stan Davis Consulting, which is dedicated to assisting private industry and public organizations throughout North America achieve world-class performance and competitiveness.

BRIEF CONTENTS

CONTENTS

PART

1

PHILOSOPHY AND CONCEPTS

THE TOTAL QUALITY APPROACH TO QUALITY MANAGEMENT: ACHIEVING ORGANIZATIONAL EXCELLENCE

There are really only three types of people: those who make things happen, those who watch things happen, and those who say, "What happened?" —***Ann Landers***

MAJOR TOPICS
- **What Is Quality?**
- **The Total Quality Approach Defined**
- **Two Views of Quality**
- **Key Elements of Total Quality**
- **Total Quality Pioneers**
- **Keys to Total Quality Success**
- **The Future of Quality Management in the Twenty-First Century**
- **Quality Certifications**

The total quality concept as an approach to doing business began to gain wide acceptance in the United States in the late 1980s and early 1990s. However, individual elements of the concept—such as the use of statistical data, Six Sigma, Lean, teamwork, continual improvement, customer satisfaction, and employee involvement—have been used by visionary organizations for years. It is the pulling together and coordinated use of these and other previously disparate elements that gave birth to the comprehensive concept known as *total quality*. This chapter provides an overview of that concept, laying the foundation for the study of all remaining chapters.

WHAT IS QUALITY?

To understand total quality, we must first understand *quality*. Customers that are businesses will define quality very clearly using specifications, standards, and other measures. This makes the point that quality can be defined and measured. Although few consumers could define *quality* if asked, all know it when they see it. This makes the critical point that quality is in the eye of the beholder. With the total quality approach, customers ultimately define quality.

People deal with the issue of quality continually in their daily lives. We concern ourselves with quality when we are grocery shopping, eating in a restaurant, and making a major purchase, such as an automobile, a home, a television, or a personal computer. Perceived quality is a major factor by which people make distinctions in the marketplace. Whether we articulate them openly or keep them in the back of our minds, we all apply a number of criteria when making a purchase. The extent to which a purchase meets these criteria determines its quality in our eyes.

One way to understand quality as a consumer-driven concept is to consider the example of eating at a restaurant. How will you judge the quality of the restaurant? Most people apply such criteria as the following:

- Service
- Response time
- Food preparation
- Environment or atmosphere
- Price
- Selection

This example gets at one aspect of quality—the *results* aspect. Does the product or service meet or exceed customer expectations? This is a critical aspect of quality, but it is not the only one. *Total quality* is a much broader concept that encompasses not just the results aspect but also the quality of people and the quality of processes.

Quality has been defined in a number of different ways by a number of different people and organizations. Consider the following definitions:

- Fred Smith, CEO of Federal Express, defines quality as "performance to the standard expected by the customer."[1]
- The General Services Administration (GSA) defines quality as "meeting the customer's needs the first time and every time."[2]

- Boeing defines quality as "providing our customers with products and services that consistently meet their needs and expectations."[3]
- The U.S. Department of Defense (DOD) defines quality as "doing the right thing right the first time, always striving for improvement, and always satisfying the customer."[4]

In his landmark book *Out of the Crisis*, quality pioneer W. Edwards Deming has this to say about quality:

> Quality can be defined only in terms of the agent. Who is the judge of quality? In the mind of the production worker, he produces quality if he can take pride in his work. Poor quality, to him, means loss of business, and perhaps of his job. Good quality, he thinks, will keep the company in business. Quality to the plant manager means to get the numbers out and to meet specifications. His job is also, whether he knows it or not, continual improvement of leadership.[5]

Although Deming's landmark book is now dated, his thoughts on quality are still valid and insightful. Deming makes the point that quality has many different criteria and that these criteria change continually.[6] To complicate matters even further, different people value the various criteria differently. For this reason, it is important to measure consumer preferences and to remeasure them frequently. Deming gives an example of the criteria that are important to him in selecting paper:[7]

- It is not slick and, therefore, takes pencil or ink well.
- Writing on the back does not show through.
- It fits into a three-ring notebook.
- It is available at most stationery stores and is, therefore, easily replenished.
- It is reasonably priced.

Each of these preferences represents a variable the manufacturer can measure and use to continually improve decision making. Deming is well-known for his belief that 94% of workplace problems are caused by management and especially for his role in helping Japan rise up out of the ashes of World War II to become a major industrial power. Deming's contributions to the quality movement are explained in greater depth later in this chapter.

Although there is no universally accepted definition of quality, enough similarity does exist among the definitions that common elements can be extracted:

- Quality involves meeting or exceeding customer expectations.
- Quality applies to products, services, people, processes, and environments.
- Quality is an ever-changing state (i.e., what is considered quality today may not be good enough to be considered quality tomorrow).

With these common elements extracted, the following definition of *quality* can be set forth:

> *Quality* is a dynamic state associated with products, services, people, processes, and environments that meets or exceeds expectations and helps produce superior value.

Consider the individual elements of this definition: The *dynamic state* element speaks to the fact that what is considered quality can and often does change as time passes and circumstances are altered. For example, gas mileage is an important criterion in judging the quality of modern automobiles. However, in the days of 20-cent-per-gallon gasoline, consumers were more likely to concern themselves with horsepower, cubic inches, and acceleration rates than with gas mileage.

The *products, services, people, processes, and environments* element is critical. It makes the point that quality applies not just to the products and services provided, but also to the people and processes that provide them and the environments in which they are provided. In the short term, two competitors who focus on continual improvement might produce a product of comparable quality. But the competitor who looks beyond just the quality of the finished product and also focuses on the continual improvement of the people who produce the product, the processes they use, and the environment in which they work will win in the long run and, most frequently, in the short run. This is because quality products are produced most consistently by quality organizations.

The *superior value* element acknowledges that quality is a key element in providing superior value (i.e., superior quality, cost, and service).

Quality, Value, and Organizational Excellence

It is important for quality professionals to understand how quality fits into the bigger picture of providing superior value to customers. Organizations survive and thrive in a globally competitive marketplace by providing superior value to customers. Achieving organizational excellence is about developing the ability to consistently provide superior value to customers over the long term. Superior value has three basic elements: superior quality, superior cost, and superior service.

QUALITY TIP ▼

Ishikawa's Definition of Quality

Any discussion of the Japanese quality gurus must include Kaoru Ishikawa. Ishikawa defines quality as follows: (1) quality and customer satisfaction are the same thing and (2) quality is a broad concept that goes beyond just product quality to also include the quality of people, processes, and every other aspect of the organization.

Source: www.businessballs.com/ retrieved on January 15, 2011.

In order to achieve organizational excellence—the level of performance necessary for long-term success in a global environment—it is necessary to consistently provide superior value to customers. Quality is obviously one of the key elements in providing superior value. But total quality is even more than that. Total quality is a broad-based approach that encompasses all three of the elements of superior value. Continually improving the quality of products, processes, services, and costs is what total quality is all about—hence the name *total quality*. Organizations that effectively apply the total quality approach to management are the ones most likely to achieve organizational excellence.

THE TOTAL QUALITY APPROACH DEFINED

Just as there are different definitions of *quality*, there are different definitions of *total quality*. For example, the DOD defines the total quality approach as follows:

> Total quality consists of the continual improvement of people, processes, products (including services), and environments. With total quality anything and everything that affects quality is a target for continual improvement. When the total quality concept is effectively applied, the end results can include organizational excellence, superior value, and global competitiveness.

An easy way to grasp the concept of total quality is to consider the analogy of a three-legged stool, as shown in Figure 1–1. The seat of the stool is customer focus. This means with total quality the customer is in the "driver's seat"

as the primary arbiter of what is acceptable in terms of quality. Each of the three legs is a broad element of the total quality philosophy (i.e., measures, people, and processes). The "measures" leg of the stool makes the point that quality can and must be measured. The "people" leg of the stool makes the point that quality cannot be inspected into a product or service. Rather, it must be built in by people who are empowered to do their jobs the right way. The "processes" leg of the stool makes the point that processes must be improved, continually and forever. What is considered excellent today may be just mediocre tomorrow. Consequently, "good enough" is never good enough.

Another way to understand total quality as a concept is shown in Figure 1–2. Notice that the first part of the definition in Figure 1–2 explains the *what* of total quality; the second part explains the *how*. In the case of total quality, the *how* is important because it is what separates this approach to doing business from all of the others.

The *total* in *total quality* indicates a concern for quality in the broadest sense—what has come to be known as the "Big Q." Big Q refers to quality of products, services, people, processes, and environments. Correspondingly, "Little Q" refers to a narrower concern that focuses on the quality of one of these elements or individual quality criteria within an individual element.

How Is Total Quality Different?

What distinguishes the total quality approach from traditional ways of doing business can be found in how it is achieved. The distinctive characteristics of total quality are these: customer focus (internal and external), obsession with

Measures
- Statistical process control
- Benchmarking
- Quality tools

People
- Quality is built in
- Quality is expected, not inspected
- Employees are empowered

Processes
- Continual improvement
- "Good enough" is never good enough

FIGURE 1–1 Three-Legged Stool of Total Quality

What It Is
Total quality is an approach to doing business that attempts to maximize the competitiveness of an organization through the continual improvement of the quality of its products, services, people, processes, and environments.

How It Is Achieved
The total quality approach has the following characteristics:
- Strategically based
- Customer focus (internal and external)
- Obsession with quality
- Scientific approach to decision making and problem solving
- Long-term commitment
- Teamwork
- Continual improvement of people, processes, products, services, and environments
- Education and training
- Freedom through control
- Unity of purpose
- Employee involvement and empowerment
- Peak performance as a top priority

FIGURE 1–2 Total Quality: What It Is and How It Is Achieved

quality, use of the scientific approach in decision making and problem solving, long-term commitment, teamwork, continual process improvement, bottom-up education and training, freedom through control, unity of purpose, and employee involvement and empowerment, all deliberately aimed at supporting the organizational strategy. Each of these characteristics is explained later in this chapter.

The Historic Development of Total Quality

The total quality movement had its roots in the time and motion studies conducted by Frederick Taylor in the 1920s. Table 1–1 is a timeline that shows some of the major events in the evolution of the total quality movement since the days of Taylor. Taylor is now known as "the father of scientific management."

The most fundamental aspect of scientific management is the separation of planning and execution. Although the division of labor spawned tremendous leaps forward in productivity, it virtually eliminated the old practice of one highly skilled individual performing all the tasks required to produce a quality product. In a sense, that individual was CEO, production worker, and quality controller all rolled into one. Taylor's scientific management did away with this by making planning the job of management and production the job of labor. To keep quality from falling through the cracks, it was necessary to create a separate quality department. Such departments had shaky beginnings, and just who was responsible for quality became a clouded issue.

As the volume and complexity of manufacturing grew, quality became an increasingly difficult issue. Volume and complexity together gave birth to quality engineering in the 1920s and reliability engineering in the 1950s. Quality engi-

neering, in turn, resulted in the use of statistical methods in the control of quality, which eventually led to the concepts of *control charts* and *statistical process control*, which are now fundamental aspects of the total quality approach.

Reliability engineering emerged in the 1950s. It began a trend toward moving quality control away from the traditional after-the-fact approach and toward inserting it throughout the design and production processes. However, for the most part, quality control in the 1950s and 1960s involved inspections that resulted in nothing more than cutting out bad parts.

World War II had an impact on quality that is still being felt. In general, the effect was negative for the United States and positive for Japan. Because of the urgency to meet production schedules during the war, U.S. companies focused more on meeting delivery dates than on quality. This approach became a habit that carried over even after the war.

Japanese companies, on the other hand, were forced to learn to compete with the rest of the world in the production of nonmilitary goods. At first, their attempts were unsuccessful, and "Made in Japan" remained synonymous with poor quality, as it had been before World War II. Around 1950, however, Japan decided to get serious about quality and establishing ways to produce quality products.

Japanese manufacturers overcame a reputation for producing cheap, shabby products and developed a reputation as world leaders in the production of quality products. More than any other single factor, it was the Japanese miracle—which was not a miracle at all but the result of a concerted effort that took 20 years to really bear fruit—that got the rest of the world to focus on quality. When Western companies finally realized that quality was the key factor in global competition, they responded. Unfortunately, their first responses were the opposite of what was needed.

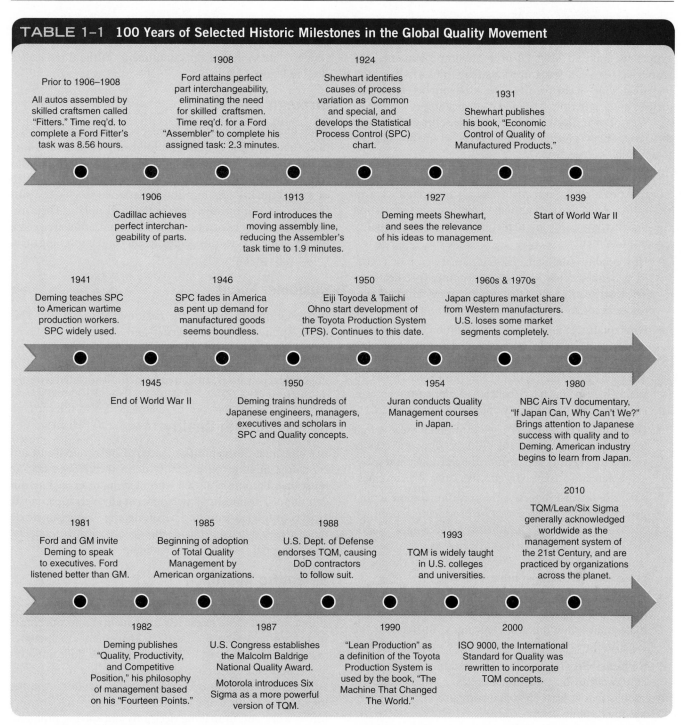

TABLE 1-1   100 Years of Selected Historic Milestones in the Global Quality Movement

Prior to 1906–1908
All autos assembled by skilled craftsmen called "Fitters." Time req'd. to complete a Ford Fitter's task was 8.56 hours.

1908
Ford attains perfect part interchangeability, eliminating the need for skilled craftsmen. Time req'd. for a Ford "Assembler" to complete his assigned task: 2.3 minutes.

1924
Shewhart identifies causes of process variation as Common and special, and develops the Statistical Process Control (SPC) chart.

1931
Shewhart publishes his book, "Economic Control of Quality of Manufactured Products."

1906
Cadillac achieves perfect interchangeability of parts.

1913
Ford introduces the moving assembly line, reducing the Assembler's task time to 1.9 minutes.

1927
Deming meets Shewhart, and sees the relevance of his ideas to management.

1939
Start of World War II

1941
Deming teaches SPC to American wartime production workers. SPC widely used.

1946
SPC fades in America as pent up demand for manufactured goods seems boundless.

1950
Eiji Toyoda & Taiichi Ohno start development of the Toyota Production System (TPS). Continues to this date.

1960s & 1970s
Japan captures market share from Western manufacturers. U.S. loses some market segments completely.

1945
End of World War II

1950
Deming trains hundreds of Japanese engineers, managers, executives and scholars in SPC and Quality concepts.

1954
Juran conducts Quality Management courses in Japan.

1980
NBC Airs TV documentary, "If Japan Can, Why Can't We?" Brings attention to Japanese success with quality and to Deming. American industry begins to learn from Japan.

2010
TQM/Lean/Six Sigma generally acknowledged worldwide as the management system of the 21st Century, and are practiced by organizations across the planet.

1981
Ford and GM invite Deming to speak to executives. Ford listened better than GM.

1985
Beginning of adoption of Total Quality Management by American organizations.

1988
U.S. Dept. of Defense endorses TQM, causing DoD contractors to follow suit.

1993
TQM is widely taught in U.S. colleges and universities.

1982
Deming publishes "Quality, Productivity, and Competitive Position," his philosophy of management based on his "Fourteen Points."

1987
U.S. Congress establishes the Malcolm Baldrige National Quality Award.
Motorola introduces Six Sigma as a more powerful version of TQM.

1990
"Lean Production" as a definition of the Toyota Production System is used by the book, "The Machine That Changed The World."

2000
ISO 9000, the International Standard for Quality was rewritten to incorporate TQM concepts.

In spite of these early negative reactions, Western companies began to realize that the key to competing in the global marketplace was to improve quality. With this realization, the total quality movement finally began to gain momentum.

TWO VIEWS OF QUALITY

The total quality philosophy introduced a whole new way of looking at quality. The traditional view of quality measured process performance in defective parts per hundred produced. With total quality, the same measurement is thought of in terms of defective parts per million produced. The traditional view focused on after-the-fact inspections of products. With total quality, the emphasis is on continual improvement of products, processes, and people in order to prevent problems before they occur. The traditional view of quality saw employees as passive workers who followed orders given by supervisors and managers. It was their labor, not their brains, that was wanted. With total quality, employees are empowered to think and make recommendations for continual improvement. They are also shown the control boundaries within which they must work and are given freedom to make decisions within those boundaries.

The traditional view of quality expected one improvement per employee per year. Total quality organizations expect to make at least 10 or more improvements per employee per year. Organizations that think traditionally focus on short-term profits. The total quality approach focuses on long-term profits and continual improvement.

The following statements summarize some of the major differences between the traditional view of quality and the total quality perspective:

- **Productivity versus quality.** The traditional view is that productivity and quality are always in conflict. You cannot have both. The total quality view is that lasting productivity gains are made only as a result of quality improvements.

- **How quality is defined.** The traditional view is that quality is defined solely as meeting customer specifications. The total quality view is that quality means satisfying customer needs and exceeding customer expectations.

- **How quality is measured.** The traditional view is that quality is measured by establishing an acceptable level of nonconformance and measuring against that benchmark. The total quality view is that quality is measured by establishing high-performance benchmarks for customer satisfaction and then continually improving performance.

- **How quality is achieved.** The traditional view is that quality is inspected into the product. The total quality view is that quality is determined by product and process design and achieved by effective control techniques.

- **Attitude toward defects.** The traditional view is that defects are an expected part of producing a product. Measuring defects per hundred is an acceptable standard. The total quality view is that defects are to be prevented using effective control systems and should be measured in defects per million (Six Sigma).

- **Quality as a function.** The traditional view is that quality is a separate function. The total quality view is that quality should be fully integrated throughout the organization—it should be everybody's responsibility.

- **Responsibility for quality.** The traditional view is that employees are blamed for poor quality. The total quality view is that at least 85% of quality problems are management's fault.

- **Supplier relationships.** The traditional view is that supplier relationships are short term and cost driven. The total quality view is that supplier relationships are long term and quality oriented.

KEY ELEMENTS OF TOTAL QUALITY

The total quality approach was defined in Figure 1–2. This definition has two components: the *what* and the *how* of total quality. What distinguishes total quality from other approaches to doing business is the *how* component of the

definition. This component has 11 critical elements, each of which is explained in the remainder of this section and all of which relate to one of the components of the three-legged stool in Figure 1–1.

Strategically Based

Total quality organizations have a comprehensive strategic plan that contains at least the following elements: vision, mission, broad objectives, and activities that must be completed to accomplish the broad objectives. The strategic plan of a total quality organization is designed to give it a *sustainable competitive advantage* in the marketplace. The competitive advantages of a total quality organization are geared toward achieving world-leading quality and improving on it, continually and forever.

Customer Focus

In a total quality setting, the customer is the driver. This point applies to both internal and external customers. External customers define the quality of the product or service delivered. Internal customers help define the quality of the people, processes, and environments associated with the products or services.

Obsession with Quality

In a total quality organization, internal and external customers define quality. With quality defined, the organization must then become obsessed with meeting or exceeding this definition. This means all personnel at all levels approach all aspects of the job from the perspective of "How can we do this better?" When an organization is obsessed with quality, "good enough" is never good enough.

Scientific Approach

Total quality detractors put off by such concepts as employee empowerment sometimes view total quality as nothing more than another name for "soft" management or "people" management. Although it is true that people skills, involvement, and empowerment are important in a total quality setting, they represent only a part of the equation. Another important part is the use of the scientific approach in structuring work and in making decisions and solving problems that relate to the work. This means that hard data are used in establishing benchmarks, monitoring performance, and making improvements.

Long-Term Commitment

Organizations that implement management innovations after attending short-term seminars often fail in their initial attempt to adopt the total quality approach. This is because they look at total quality as just another management innovation rather than as a whole new way of doing business that requires an entirely new corporate culture. Too few organizations begin the implementation of total quality with the long-term commitment to change that is necessary for success.

Teamwork

In traditionally managed organizations, the best competitive efforts are often among departments within the organization. Internal competition tends to use energy that should be focused on improving quality and, in turn, external competitiveness.

Continual Process Improvement

Products are developed and services delivered by people using processes within environments (systems). To continually improve the quality of products or services—which is a fundamental goal in a total quality setting—it is necessary to continually improve systems.

Education and Training

Education and training are fundamental to total quality because they represent the best way to improve people on a continual basis. It is through education and training that people who know how to work hard learn how to also work smart.

Freedom Through Control

Involving and empowering employees is fundamental to total quality as a way to simultaneously bring more minds to bear on the decision-making process and increase the ownership employees feel about decisions that are made. Total quality detractors sometimes mistakenly see employee involvement as a loss of management control, when in fact control is fundamental to total quality. The freedoms enjoyed in a total quality setting are actually the result of well-planned and well-carried-out controls. Controls such as scientific methodologies lead to freedom by empowering employees to solve problems within their scope of control.

Unity of Purpose

Historically, management and labor have had an adversarial relationship in U.S. industry. One could debate the reasons

---

QUALITY TIP ▼

Continually Improving People, Processes, and Products

The total quality approach seeks to improve everything all the time forever. This means that it encompasses continually improving (1) how well people are able to do their jobs, (2) how well processes perform, and (3) the quality of products and services provided by the people and processes. To achieve total quality, it is necessary to focus more on solving problems and continually improving and less on blaming individuals for problems.

---

behind management–labor discord *ad infinitum* without achieving consensus. From the perspective of total quality, who or what is to blame for adversarial management–labor relations is irrelevant. What is important is this: To apply the total quality approach, organizations must have unity of purpose. This means that internal politics have no place in a total quality organization. Rather, collaboration should be the norm.

A question frequently asked concerning this element of total quality is "Does unity of purpose mean that unions will no longer be needed?" The answer is that unity of purpose has nothing to do with whether unions are needed. Collective bargaining is about wages, benefits, and working conditions, not about corporate purpose and vision. Employees should feel more involved and empowered in a total quality setting than in a traditionally managed situation, but the goal of total quality is to enhance competitiveness, not to eliminate unions. For example, in Japan, where companies are known for achieving unity of purpose, unions are still very much in evidence. Unity of purpose does not necessarily mean that labor and management will always agree on wages, benefits, and working conditions, but it does mean that *all* employees work toward the common goal.

Employee Involvement and Empowerment

Employee involvement and empowerment is one of the most misunderstood elements of the total quality approach and one of the most misrepresented by its detractors. The basis for involving employees is twofold. First, it increases the likelihood of a good decision, a better plan, or a more effective improvement by bringing more minds to bear on the situation—not just any minds but the minds of the people who are closest to the work in question. Second, it promotes ownership of decisions by involving the people who will have to implement them.

Empowerment means not just involving people but also involving them in ways that give them a real voice. One of the ways this can be done is by structuring work that allows employees to make decisions concerning the improvement of work processes within well-specified parameters. Should a machinist be allowed to unilaterally drop a vendor if the vendor delivers substandard material? No. However, the machinist should have an avenue for offering his or her input into the matter.

Should the same machinist be allowed to change the way she sets up her machine? If by so doing she can improve her part of the process without adversely affecting someone else's, yes. Having done so, her next step should be to show other machinists her innovation so that they might try it.

Peak Performance

When effectively practiced, total quality allows every aspect of an organization to operate at peak levels. This means that all personnel and processes are operating at their best. Peak performance is essential to organizations that operate in a global environment where competition is intense, constant, and unforgiving.

TOTAL QUALITY PIONEERS

Total quality is not just one individual concept. It is a number of related concepts pulled together to create a comprehensive approach to doing business. Many people contributed in meaningful ways to the development of the various concepts that are known collectively as *total quality*. The three major contributors are W. Edwards Deming, Joseph M. Juran, and Philip B. Crosby. To these three, many would add Armand V. Feigenbaum and a number of Japanese experts, such as Shigeo Shingo.

Deming's Contributions

Of the various quality pioneers in the United States, the best known is W. Edwards Deming. According to Deming biographer Andrea Gabor:

> Deming also has become by far the most influential proponent of quality management in the United States. While both Joseph Juran and Armand V. Feigenbaum have strong reputations and advocate approaches to quality that in many cases overlap with Deming's ideas, neither has achieved the stature of Deming. One reason is that while these experts have often taken very nuts-and-bolts, practical approaches to quality improvement, Deming has played the role of visionary, distilling disparate management ideas into a compelling new philosophy.[9]

Deming came a long way to achieve the status of internationally acclaimed quality expert. During his formative years, Deming's family bounced from small town to small town in Iowa and Wyoming, trying in vain to rise out of poverty. These early circumstances gave Deming a lifelong appreciation for economy and thrift. In later years, even after he was generating a substantial income, Deming maintained only a simple office in the basement of his modest home out of which he conducted his international consulting business.

Working as a janitor and at other odd jobs, Deming worked his way through the University of Wyoming, where he earned a bachelor's degree in engineering. He went on to receive a master's degree in mathematics and physics from the University of Colorado and a doctorate in physics from Yale.

His only full-time employment for a corporation was with Western Electric. Many feel that what he witnessed during his employment there had a major impact on the direction the rest of his life would take. Deming was disturbed by the amount of waste he saw at Western Electric's Hawthorne plant. It was there that he pioneered the use of statistics in quality.

Although Deming was asked in 1940 to help the U.S. Bureau of the Census adopt statistical sampling techniques, his reception in the United States during these early years was not positive. With little real competition in the international marketplace, major U.S. corpora-

Autoliv Queretaro: Quality in Automotive Safety Systems

Autoliv Inc. is the world leader in automotive safety systems. The company's plant in Queretaro, Mexico employees approximately 5,000 of the company's 42,000 personnel and produces airbag cushions, airbag modules, and steering wheels for the North American automotive market. The Queretaro plant's customers include Chrysler, Ford, General Motors, Honda, Hyundai, Nissan, Mazda, Mitsubishi, Toyota, Volkswagen, and Volvo. Autoliv Queretaro received the prestigious Shingo Prize for quality by applying the principles of total quality.

The company's mission is to create, manufacture, and sell state-of-the art automotive safety systems. Its mission is to substantially reduce traffic accidents, fatalities, and injuries. Autoliv's strategy is to be the vehicle manufacturer's first-choice supplier of safety systems through technological leadership, complete system capabilities, highest-value safety system solutions, cost efficiency, quality excellence, global presence, highest level of service and engagement, and dedicated/motivated employees.

Maintaining superior quality is at the heart of Autoliv's success. The company is committed to a *zero defects* philosophy which it maintains by applying the following strategies: (1) managing all new products using a five-checkpoint process, (2) using a global supplier manual that defines a mandatory supplier collaboration process, (3) requiring the company's suppliers to comply with ISO/TS 16949, and (4) incorporating the principles of the Autoliv Production System into all production and support processes. The company's commitment to quality earned its Queretaro plant the prestigious Shingo prize for Excellence in Manufacturing.

When the Queretaro plant was selected for the Shingo Prize, it had achieved the following quality improvements: (1) improved production efficiency by 75%, (2) reduced changeover time by 20%, (3) boosted inventory turnover from 14 to 24, (4) increased units produced per week by 94%, (5) and maintained a 100% on-time delivery rate for four consecutive years.

Source: www.reliableplant.com/Articles/Print/4697

tions felt little need for his help. Corporations from other countries were equally uninterested. However, World War II changed all this and put Deming on the road to becoming, in Andrea Gabor's words, "the man who discovered quality."[10]

During World War II, almost all of Japan's industry went into the business of producing war materials. After the war, those firms had to convert to the production of consumer goods, and the conversion was not very successful. To have a market for their products, Japanese firms had to enter the international marketplace. This move put them in direct competition with companies from the other industrialized countries of the world, and the Japanese firms did not fare well.

By the late 1940s, key industrial leaders in Japan had finally come to the realization that the key to competing in the international marketplace is quality. At this time, Shigeiti Mariguti of Tokyo University, Sizaturo Mishibori of Toshiba, and several other Japanese leaders invited Deming to visit Japan and share his views on quality. Unlike their counterparts in the United States, the Japanese industrialists accepted Deming's views, learned his techniques, and adopted his philosophy. So powerful was Deming's impact on industry in Japan that the most coveted award a company there can win is the Deming Prize. In fact, the standards that must be met to win this prize are so difficult and so strenuously applied that it is now being questioned by some Japanese companies.

By the 1980s, leading industrialists in the United States were where their Japanese counterparts had been in the late 1940s. At last, Deming's services began to be requested in his own country. By this time, Deming was over 80 years old. He had not been received as openly and warmly in the United States as he was in Japan. Deming's attitude toward corporate executives in the United States can be described as cantankerous at best.

Gabor gives the following example of Deming's dealings with the U.S. executives from Ford Motor Company:

> The initial contacts were unsettling for Ford. Instead of delivering a slick presentation on how the automaker could solve its quality problems—the sort of thing that became the stock in trade of U.S. quality experts during the 1980s—Deming questioned, rambled, and seemed to take pleasure in making a laughingstock of his listeners. During the first meeting, wearing one of his signature timeworn three-piece suits, Deming glowered at the car executives with steely blue eyes.[11]

Deming's contributions to the quality movement would be difficult to overstate. Many consider him the founder of the movement. The things for which he is most widely known are the Deming Cycle, his Fourteen Points, and his Seven Deadly Diseases.

The Deming Cycle   Summarized in Figure 1–3, the Deming Cycle was developed to link the production of a product with consumer needs and focus the resources of all departments (research, design, production, marketing) in a cooperative effort to meet those needs. The Deming Cycle proceeds as follows:

1. Conduct consumer research and use it in planning the product (plan).
2. Produce the product (do).
3. Check the product to make sure it was produced in accordance with the plan (check).
4. Market the product (act).
5. Analyze how the product is received in the marketplace in terms of quality, cost, and other criteria (analyze).

Deming's Fourteen Points   Deming's philosophy is both summarized and operationalized by his Fourteen Points, which are contained in Figure 1–4. Deming modified the specific wording of various points over the years, which accounts for the minor differences among the Fourteen Points as described in various publications. Deming stated

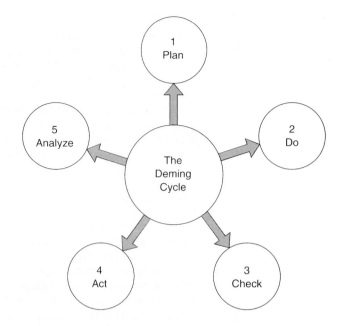

FIGURE 1–3 The Deming Cycle

repeatedly in his later years that if he had it all to do over again, he would leave off the numbers.

Deming's Seven Deadly Diseases   The Fourteen Points summarize Deming's views on what a company must do to effect a positive transition from business as usual to world-class quality. The Seven Deadly Diseases summarize the factors that he believed can inhibit such a transformation (see Figure 1–5).

The description of these factors rings particularly true when viewed from the perspective of U.S. firms trying to compete in the global marketplace. Some of these factors can be eliminated by adopting the total quality approach, but three cannot. This does not bode well for U.S. firms trying to regain market share. Total quality can eliminate or reduce the impact of a lack of consistency, personal review systems, job hopping, and using only visible data. However, total quality will not free corporate executives from pressure to produce short-term profits, excessive medical costs, or excessive liability costs. These are diseases of the nation's financial, health care, and legal systems, respectively.

By finding ways for business and government to cooperate appropriately without collaborating inappropriately, other industrialized countries have been able to focus their industry on long-term rather than short-term profits, hold down health care costs, and prevent the proliferation of costly litigation that has occurred in the United States. Excessive health care and legal costs represent non-value-added costs that must be added to the cost of products produced and services delivered in the United States.

Juran's Contributions

Joseph M. Juran ranks near Deming in the contributions he has made to quality and the recognition he has received as

1. Create constancy of purpose toward the improvement of products and services in order to become competitive, stay in business, and provide jobs.
2. Adopt the new philosophy. Management must learn that it is a new economic age and awaken to the challenge, learn their responsibilities, and take on leadership for change.
3. Stop depending on inspection to achieve quality. Build in quality from the start.
4. Stop awarding contracts on the basis of low bids.
5. Improve continuously and forever the system of production and service, to improve quality and productivity, and thus constantly reduce costs.
6. Institute training on the job.
7. Institute leadership. The purpose of leadership should be to help people and technology work better.
8. Drive out fear so that everyone may work effectively.
9. Break down barriers between departments so that people can work as a team.
10. Eliminate slogans, exhortations, and targets for the workforce. They create adversarial relationships.
11. Eliminate quotas and management by objectives. Substitute leadership.
12. Remove barriers that rob employees of their pride of workmanship.
13. Institute a vigorous program of education and self-improvement.
14. Make the transformation everyone's job and put everyone to work on it.

FIGURE 1–4 Deming's Fourteen Points

1. Lack of constancy of purpose to plan products and services that have a market sufficient to keep the company in business and provide jobs.
2. Emphasis on short-term profits; short-term thinking that is driven by a fear of unfriendly takeover attempts and pressure from bankers and shareholders to produce dividends.
3. Personal review systems for managers and management by objectives without providing methods or resources to accomplish objectives. Performance evaluations, merit ratings, and annual appraisals are all part of this disease.
4. Job hopping by managers.
5. Using only visible data and information in decision making with little or no consideration given to what is not known or cannot be known.
6. Excessive medical costs.
7. Excessive costs of liability driven up by lawyers that work on contingency fees.

FIGURE 1–5 Deming's Seven Deadly Diseases

a result. His Juran Institute Inc., in Wilton, Connecticut, is an international leader in conducting training, research, and consulting activities in the area of quality management (see Figure 1–6). Quality materials produced by Juran have been translated into 14 different languages.

Juran holds degrees in both engineering and law. The emperor of Japan awarded him the Order of the Sacred Treasure medal, in recognition of his efforts to develop quality in Japan and to promote friendship between Japan and the United States. Juran is best known for the following contributions to the quality philosophy:

- Juran's Three Basic Steps to Progress
- Juran's Ten Steps to Quality Improvement
- The Pareto Principle
- The Juran Trilogy

Juran's Three Basic Steps to Progress Juran's Three Basic Steps to Progress (listed in Figure 1–7) are broad steps that, in Juran's opinion, companies must take if they are to achieve world-class quality. He also believes there is a point of diminishing return that applies to quality and competitiveness.

Juran's Ten Steps to Quality Improvement
Examining Juran's Ten Steps to Quality Improvement (in Figure 1–8), you will see some overlap between them and

---

Research and Development
We dedicate ourselves to identifying proven roads that lead to enviable results, and to creating products and services that reflect the experience of successful quality efforts.

Consulting Services
Our quality professionals counsel and assist managers in assessing needs, developing strategies, and applying specific methods for achieving quality goals.

Seminars and Workshops
Juran courses are comprehensive and practical, addressing a full spectrum of needs, industries, and functions. Courses are presented worldwide at client organizations and as public offerings.

Training and Support Materials
Juran videos, workbooks, texts, and reference books are more widely used and translated than those of any other source.

FIGURE 1–6 Juran Institute Inc., Quality-Related Services Provided Worldwide

Source: Juran Institute Inc., www.juran.com, 2011.

---

1. Achieve structured improvements on a continual basis combined with dedication and a sense of urgency.
2. Establish an extensive training program.
3. Establish commitment and leadership on the part of higher management.

FIGURE 1–7 Juran's Three Basic Steps to Progress

Source: Juran Institute Inc., www.juran.com, 2011.

Deming's Fourteen Points. They also mesh well with the philosophy of quality experts whose contributions are explained later in this chapter.

The Pareto Principle The Pareto principle espoused by Juran shows up in the views of most quality experts, although it often goes by other names. According to this principle, organizations should concentrate their energy on eliminating the vital few sources that cause the majority of problems. Further, both Juran and Deming believe that systems that are controlled by management are the systems in which the majority of problems occur.

---

1. Build awareness of both the need for improvement and opportunities for improvement.
2. Set goals for improvement.
3. Organize to meet the goals that have been set.
4. Provide training.
5. Implement projects aimed at solving problems.
6. Report progress.
7. Give recognition.
8. Communicate results.
9. Keep score.
10. Maintain momentum by building improvement into the company's regular systems.

FIGURE 1–8 Juran's Ten Steps to Quality Improvement

Source: Juran Institute Inc., www.juran.com, 2011.

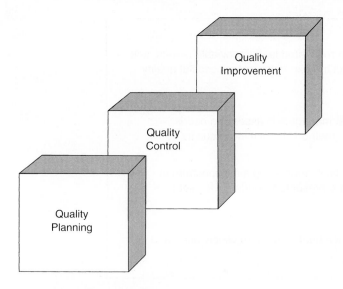

FIGURE 1–9 The Juran Trilogy

Source: The Juran Trilogy® is a registered trademark of Juran Institute Inc. (Southbury, Connecticut), www.juran.com.

The Juran Trilogy   The Juran Trilogy (Figure 1–9) summarizes the three primary managerial functions. Juran's views on these functions are explained in the following sections.

Quality Planning   Quality planning involves developing the products, systems, and processes needed to meet or exceed customer expectations. The following steps are required:

1. Determine who the customers are.
2. Identify customers' needs.
3. Develop products with features that respond to customer needs.
4. Develop systems and processes that allow the organization to produce these features.
5. Deploy the plans to operational levels.

QUALITY TIP ▼

The Pareto Principle

The Pareto principle, named after economist Vilfredo Pareto, is more commonly known in quality circles as the 80/20 rule. This rule is used variably to contend that 80% of the quality issues in an organization are caused by 20% of the problems or that 80% of the problems can be traced to a few critical sources (the 20%). Joseph Juran is credited with applying what was originally an economic principle to management and quality. He advised organizations to focus the bulk of their improvement efforts on identifying and eliminating these few critical sources of problems.

Quality Control   The control of quality involves the following processes:

1. Assess actual quality performance.
2. Compare performance with goals.
3. Act on differences between performance and goals.

Quality Improvement   The improvement of quality should be ongoing and continual:

1. Develop the infrastructure necessary to make annual quality improvements.
2. Identify specific areas in need of improvement, and implement improvement projects.
3. Establish a project team with responsibility for completing each improvement project.
4. Provide teams with what they need to be able to diagnose problems to determine root causes, develop solutions, and establish controls that will maintain gains made.

Crosby's Contributions

Philip B. Crosby started his career in quality later than Deming and Juran. His corporate background includes 14 years as director of quality at ITT Corporation (1965–1979). He left ITT in 1979 to form Philip Crosby Associates, an international consulting firm on quality improvement, which he ran until 1992, when he retired as CEO to devote his time to lecturing on quality-related issues. More recently, Crosby had once again entered the business arena as a quality consultant until his death in 2001.

Crosby, who defined quality simply as conformance, is best known for his advocacy of zero-defects management and prevention as opposed to statistically acceptable levels of quality. He is also known for his Quality Vaccine and Crosby's Fourteen Steps to Quality Improvement.

Crosby's Quality Vaccine consists of three ingredients:[12]

1. Determination
2. Education
3. Implementation

His Fourteen Steps to Quality Improvement are listed in Figure 1–10.

KEYS TO TOTAL QUALITY SUCCESS

Organizations that succeed never approach total quality as just another management innovation or, even worse, as a quick fix. Rather, they approach total quality as a new way of doing business. What follows are common errors organizations make when implementing total quality. The successful organizations avoid these errors.

1. Make it clear that management is committed to quality for the long term.
2. Form cross-departmental quality teams.
3. Identify where current and potential problems exist.
4. Assess the cost of quality and explain how it is used as a management tool.
5. Increase the quality awareness and personal commitment of all employees.
6. Take immediate action to correct problems identified.
7. Establish a zero defects program.
8. Train supervisors to carry out their responsibilities in the quality program.
9. Hold a Zero Defects Day to ensure all employees are aware there is a new direction.
10. Encourage individuals and teams to establish both personal and team improvement goals.
11. Encourage employees to tell management about obstacles they face in trying to meet quality goals.
12. Recognize employees who participate.
13. Implement quality councils to promote continual communication.
14. Repeat everything to illustrate that quality improvement is a never-ending process.

FIGURE 1–10 Crosby's Fourteen Steps to Quality Improvement

Source: Philip Crosby Associates, www.philipcrosby.com, 2011.

- **Senior management delegation and poor leadership.** Some organizations attempt to start a quality initiative by delegating responsibility to a hired expert rather than applying the leadership necessary to get everyone involved.

- **Team mania.** Ultimately teams should be established, and all employees should be involved with them. However, working in teams is an approach that must be learned. Supervisors must learn how to be effective coaches, and employees must learn how to be team players. The organization must undergo a cultural change before teamwork can succeed. Rushing in and putting everyone in teams before learning has occurred and the corporate culture has changed will create problems rather than solve them.

- **Deployment process.** Some organizations develop quality initiatives without concurrently developing plans for integrating them into all elements of the organization (i.e., operations, budgeting, marketing, etc.).

- **Taking a narrow, dogmatic approach.** Some organizations are determined to take the Deming approach, Juran approach, or Crosby approach and use only the principles prescribed in them. None of the approaches advocated by these and other leading quality experts is truly a one-size-fits-all proposition. Even the experts encourage organizations to tailor quality programs to their individual needs.

- **Confusion about the differences among education, awareness, inspiration, and skill building.** In order for people to do their part in making the total quality approach work effectively, they must have the skills to apply the fundamental tools of quality. Making them aware of quality and inspiring them to accept it at a philosophical level are good and necessary steps in the right direction. But helping them develop the actual skills necessary to implement the concept must also be part of the transformational process.

THE FUTURE OF QUALITY MANAGEMENT IN THE TWENTY-FIRST CENTURY

There are several trends that will shape the future of quality management. These trends are as follows:

- **Increasing global competition.** More and better competition from emerging industrialized nations will be an ongoing part of life for organizations.

QUALITY TIP ▼

Crosby's Four Absolutes of Quality Management

Philip B. Crosby's contributions to quality are legion, ranging from his best-selling books on quality-related subjects to his Quality College. An enduring contribution from Crosby is a set of four *absolutes* of quality management. These absolutes are as follows: (1) quality must be defined as conformance to requirements—not just as a good thing to do; (2) the best way to ensure quality is prevention, not inspection; (3) the standard for quality must be zero defects, not "close is good enough"; and (4) quality is measured by nonconformance, not indexes.

Source: www.businessballs.com, retrieved on January 15, 2011.

- **Increasing customer expectations.** Today's global customer is interested in not just the quality of a product provided but also the quality of the organization that backs it up. Customers want an excellent product or service from an organization that also provides accurate billing, reliable delivery, after-purchase support, and social responsibility.

- **Opposing economic pressures.** The global marketplace exerts enormous, unrelenting pressure on organizations to continually improve quality while simultaneously reducing the prices they charge for goods and services. The key to achieving higher quality and lower prices for customers is the reduction of the expenses associated with satisfying unhappy customers—expenses that amount to as much as 25% of the cost of sales in many companies.

- **New approaches to management.** Companies that succeed in the global marketplace have learned that *you manage budgets, but lead people*. The old approach of providing an occasional seminar or motivational speech for employees without making any fundamental changes in the way the organization operates will no longer work.

Quality Management Characteristics for the Future

To succeed in the global marketplace for now and in the future, organizations need to operate according to the principles of quality management. Such companies will have the following characteristics:

- A total commitment to continually increasing value for customers, investors, and employees

- A firm understanding that *market driven* means that quality is defined by customers, not the company

- A commitment to *leading* people with a bias for continuous improvement and communication

- A recognition that sustained growth requires the simultaneous achievement of four objectives continually forever: (a) customer satisfaction, (b) cost leadership, (c) effective human resources, and (d) integration with the supplier base

- A commitment to fundamental improvement through knowledge, skills, problem solving, and teamwork

- A commitment to fast-paced, constant learning, and an ability to respond quickly to changes in the competitive environment

- A commitment to achieving end-to-end collaboration using web-based, on-demand tools that are fully integrated throughout the supply chain

- A commitment to maintaining an environment in which creativity, critical thinking, and innovation are not just encouraged and supported, but demanded

As long as the concept of competition exists, there will be a need for quality management. In the twenty-first century, globalization will only intensify the level of competition businesses face. That is why the book you are now reading has been translated into Korean and Indonesian. The concept of quality management is being adopted globally and, as a result, will continue to be applied and refined through this century.

Companies that develop the characteristics listed above will be those that fully institutionalize the principles of quality management. Quality management as both a practice and a profession has a bright future. In fact, in terms of succeeding in the global marketplace, quality management is the future. Consequently, more and more companies are making quality management the way they do business, and more and more institutions of higher education are offering quality management courses and programs.

QUALITY CERTIFICATIONS

In a competitive work environment, one of the ways that quality professionals can distinguish themselves, enhance their credibility, and improve their career potential is to become certified in an appropriate quality discipline. The American Society for Quality (ASQ) offers certifications in a variety of disciplines, including Manager of Quality/Organizational Excellence, Quality Engineer, Reliability Engineer, Software Quality Engineer, Quality Auditor, Six Sigma Black Belt, Six Sigma Green Belt, Quality Technician, Calibration Technician, Quality Improvement Associate, Quality Inspector, Quality Process Analyst, Hazard Analysis and Critical Point Auditor, Biomedical Auditor, and Pharmaceutical GMP Professional.

The requirements for all of these certifications are available at the ASQ's Web site: www.asq.org/certification. At this Web site, there is a list of the various certifications available through the ASQ. Simply click on the certification of interest, and all relevant information pertaining to that certification will be available. In addition, the ASQ provides assistance to potential examinees who are preparing for certification examinations: They may find the help they need under the heading "Prepare for the exam" at the applicable page on the ASQ's certification Web site address (www.asq.org/certification). The requirements and body of knowledge relating to the most pertinent of these certifications—Manager of Quality/Organizational Excellence, Quality Engineer, and Quality Technician—are summarized in the following paragraphs.

Manager of Quality/Organizational Excellence[13]

This certification is for managers who lead and champion continual process-improvement initiatives, facilitates and leads team efforts to establish and monitor customer and supplier relations, supports strategic planning and deployment efforts, assists in the development of measurement systems, motivates staff, evaluates staff, manages projects, manages human resources, analyzes budgets and finances, evaluates risk, and uses management tools and techniques.

Education and Experience Requirements In order to sit for the Manager of Quality/Organizational Excellence examination, individuals must have ten years of experience in one or more of the following areas: leadership, strategic plan development and deployment, management elements and methods, quality management tools, customer focus, supply chain management, and training and development. At least five of the ten years of experience in one or more of these areas of expertise must be at the decision-making level. Education waivers of up to five years are allowed for individuals who have completed a diploma or degree from an institution accredited by the ASQ. The waivers apply as follows: (1) one year for a technical diploma, (2) two years for an associate degree, (3) four years for a baccalaureate degree, and (4) five years for a master or doctorate degree.

Examination Topics The ASQ offers a practice examination that helps prospective examinees determine what the test covers and what areas or topics they might need to review more thoroughly. The body of knowledge covered on the examination for certification as a Manager of Quality/Organizational Excellence is as follows:

Leadership. Organizational structures and culture, leadership challenges, team and team processes, and the ASQ Code of Ethics.

Strategic Plan Development and Deployment. Strategic planning models, business environment analysis, and strategic plan deployment.

Management Elements and Methods. Management skills and abilities, communication skills and abilities, project management, quality systems, and quality models and theories.

Quality Management Tools. Problem-solving tools, process management, and measurement/metrics.

Customer-Focused Organizations. Customer identification, segmentation, and relationship management.

Supply Chain Management. Supplier selection, supplier communications, supplier performance, supplier improvement, supplier certification/partnerships/alliances, and supplier logistics.

Training and Development. Training plans, needs analysis, training material/curriculum development and delivery, and training effectiveness/evaluation.

Quality Engineer[14]

The Quality Engineer certification is for individuals who develop and operate quality control systems, apply and analyze testing and inspection procedures, use metrology and statistical systems to diagnose and correct quality problems, understand human factors and motivation, understand quality cost techniques, develop and administer management information systems, and audit quality systems for identifying deficiencies and correcting them.

Education and Experience Requirements In order to sit for the Quality Engineer certification examination, individuals must have a minimum of eight years of work experience in one or more of the following disciplines: management and leadership, the quality system, product and process design, product and process control, and continuous improvement. Waivers of part of the experience requirement are available to individuals who have completed a diploma or degree from an institution accredited by the ASQ as follows: (1) one year for a technical diploma, (2) two years for an associate degree, (3) four years for a baccalaureate degree, and (4) five years for a masters or doctorate degree.

Examination Topics The ASQ provides a practice examination that helps prospective examinees find out what the test covers and what areas or topics they might need to review more thoroughly. The body of knowledge covered on the examination for certification as a Quality Engineer is as follows:

Management and Leadership. Topics include quality philosophies and foundations, the quality management system, the ASQ Code of Ethics, leadership principles and techniques, facilitation principles and techniques, communication skills, customer relations, supplier management, and barriers to quality.

The Quality System. Topics include elements of the quality system, documentation of the quality system, quality standards and other guidelines, quality audits, cost of quality, and quality training.

Product and Process Design. Topics include classification of quality characteristics, design inputs and review, technical drawings and specifications, design verification, and reliability/maintainability.

Product and Process Control. Topics include tools, material control, acceptance sampling, measurement and testing, metrology, and measurement analysis.

Continuous Improvement. Topics include quality control tools, quality management planning tools, continuous improvement techniques, corrective action, and preventive action.

Quantitative Methods and Tools. Topics include collecting and summarizing data, quantitative concepts, probability distributions, statistical decision making, relationships between variables, statistical process control, process and performance capability, and design and analysis of experiments.

Quality Technician[15]

This certification is for paraprofessionals who—under the direction of quality engineers and managers—analyze and solve quality problems, prepare inspection plans and instructions, select applications for sampling plans, prepare procedures, train inspectors, perform audits, analyze quality data, analyze quality costs, and apply basic statistical methods for process control.

Education and Experience Requirements In order to sit for the Quality Technician examination, individuals must have at least four years of higher education and/or work experience in one or more of the following disciplines: quality concepts and tools, statistical techniques, metrology and calibration, inspection and testing, quality audits, and preventive/corrective action. Education waivers of up to three years are allowed for individuals who have completed a certification program or degree from an institution accredited by the ASQ. The waivers apply as follows: (1) one year for certification through the Quality Technology program of a community college or technical school, (2) two years for an associate degree, and (3) three years for a baccalaureate, masters, or doctorate degree.

Examination Topics The ASQ offers a practice examination that helps prospective examines find out what the test covers and what topics they might need to review more thoroughly. The body of knowledge covered on the examination for certification as a Quality Technician is as follows:

Quality Concepts and Tools. Topics include quality concepts, quality tools, and team functions.

Statistical techniques. Topics include general concepts, calculations, and control charts.

Metrology and Calibration. Topics include measurement and test equipment and calibration.

Inspection and Testing. Topics include blueprint reading and interpretation, inspection concepts, inspection techniques and processes, and sampling.

Quality Audits. Topics include audit types, audit components, and tools/techniques.

Preventive and Corrective Action. Topics include preventive action, corrective action, and nonconforming material.

For more detail concerning the certification examinations, readers are encouraged to visit the certification pages of the ASQ's Web site: www.asq.org/certification. Details concerning study materials, costs, examination dates, and application procedures are provided on these pages.

SUMMARY

1. *Quality* has been defined in a number of different ways. When viewed from a consumer's perspective, it means meeting or exceeding customer expectations.

2. Total quality is an approach to doing business that attempts to maximize an organization's competitiveness through the continual improvement of the quality of its products, services, people, processes, and environments.

3. Key characteristics of the total quality approach are as follows: strategically based, customer focus, obsession with quality, scientific approach, long-term commitment, teamwork, continual process improvement, bottom-up education and training, freedom through control, unity of purpose, employee involvement and empowerment, and peak performance.

4. The rationale for total quality can be found in the need to compete in the global marketplace. Countries that are competing successfully in the global marketplace are seeing their quality of living improve. Those that cannot are seeing theirs decline.

5. W. Edwards Deming is best known for his Fourteen Points, the Deming Cycle, and his Seven Deadly Diseases.

6. Joseph M. Juran is best known for Juran's Three Basic Steps to Progress, Juran's Ten Steps to Quality Improvement, the Pareto Principle, and the Juran Trilogy.

7. Common errors made when starting quality initiatives include senior management delegation and poor leadership; team mania; the deployment process; a narrow, dogmatic approach; and confusion about the differences among education, awareness, inspiration, and skill building.

8. Trends affecting the future of quality management include increasing global competition, increasing customer expectations, opposing economic pressures, and new approaches to management.

KEY TERMS AND CONCEPTS

Bottom-up education and training

Continual process improvement

Crosby's Fourteen Steps to Quality Improvement

Crosby's Quality Vaccine

Customer focus

Deming Cycle

Deming's Fourteen Points

Deming's Seven Deadly Diseases

Employee involvement and empowerment

Freedom through control

Global customer

The Juran Trilogy

Long-term commitment

Obsession with quality

Pareto Principle

Peak Performance

Quality

Quality control

Quality improvement

Quality planning

Scientific approach

Teamwork

Total quality

TQC (Total Quality Control)

TQL (Total Quality Leadership)

TQM (Total Quality Management)

Unity of purpose

FACTUAL REVIEW QUESTIONS

1. Define the term *quality*.

2. What is total quality?

3. List and explain the key elements of total quality.

4. Explain the rationale for the total quality approach to doing business.

5. Describe the following concepts:
   - Deming's Fourteen Points
   - The Deming Cycle
   - Deming's Seven Deadly Diseases

6. List and explain Juran's main contributions to the quality movement.

7. Why do some quality initiatives fail?

8. For what contributions to the quality movement is Philip B. Crosby known?

9. Summarize the most common errors made when starting quality initiatives.

10. Explain the trends that are affecting the future of quality management.

CRITICAL THINKING ACTIVITY

Have We Spoiled Customers?

"If you want to understand how the worldwide quality movement has benefited consumers, just look at automobiles. What used to be considered a luxury option is now just standard," said one quality manager. "That is precisely the problem," said another quality manager, "We have spoiled the consumer. Now customers will never be happy no matter what we do." Join this debate. What is your opinion concerning the following questions?

1. What features in the modern automobile are customer driven?

2. Henry Ford once said something to the effect that the customer can have any color Model T he wants, as long as it's black. How did the world evolve from Henry Ford's attitude toward customers to the modern attitude of customer-driven quality?

3. Are global consumers spoiled and unrealistic in their expectations, or are they finally demanding their rights in the marketplace?

4. How has the worldwide demand for quality driven the concept of innovation? How has innovation changed your life?

DISCUSSION ASSIGNMENT 1–1

Winning and Longevity

A professional baseball team set its sights on winning the World Series. The team owner wanted to win big and win fast. Consequently, the team sank all of its resources into trading for the best players in the league. It was able to obtain enough of them that within two seasons the team was the World Series champion. However, the team had committed such a high percentage of its financial resources to players' salaries that other important elements of the team began to suffer. Its stadium quickly fell into such a state of disrepair that fans began to stay home. Training facilities also began to suffer, which caused discontent among the players. The money left over to pay the salaries of coaches wasn't enough to hold onto the good ones, most of whom accepted better offers from other teams. In short, by focusing so intently on the desired end result, this organization neglected other important aspects of building a competitive team. As a result, the team's World Series championship was a short-lived once-in-a-lifetime victory. The very next season the team's crumbling infrastructure sent it tumbling to the bottom of its division. Without the people, processes, and environment to turn the situation around, the team was eventually sold at a loss and moved to another city.

DISCUSSION QUESTIONS

Discuss the following questions in class or outside of class with your fellow students:

1. Why would a company that is turning out a satisfactory product want to continually examine its processes and the work environment? What happened to the old adage "If it's not broke, don't fix it"?

2. Create a manufacturing, processing, or service sector parallel for this activity. Discuss how this assignment would apply to a company.

DISCUSSION ASSIGNMENT 1–2

How Japan Caught Up with the United States and How the United States Caught Up with Japan Again

Immediately following World War II, the quality of products produced by Japanese companies was not good enough to compete in the international marketplace. The only advantage Japanese companies had was price. Japanese goods, as a rule, were cheap. For this reason, Western manufacturers, particularly those in the United States, saw the Japanese threat as being rooted in cost rather than quality.

Reading the future more accurately, albeit belatedly, Japanese companies saw quality as the key to success and, in 1950, began doing something about it. While Japanese companies were slowly but patiently and persistently creating a quality-based infrastructure (people, processes, and facilities), American companies were still focusing on cost, shifting the manufacture of labor-intensive products offshore and, at the same time, neglecting infrastructure improvements.

By the mid-1970s, the quality of Japanese manufactured goods in such key areas as automobiles and consumer electronics products was better than that of competing American firms. As a result, Japanese exports increased exponentially, while those of Western countries experienced corresponding decreases.[16]

This explains how Japan rose up out of the ashes of World War II to become a world-leading industrial nation. But the story does not end there. After losing market share to the Japanese for more than two decades, companies in the United States began to embrace the principles of quality management. As a result, by the mid-1990s companies in the United States had reasserted themselves in the global marketplace.

Now, the two countries are like well-matched heavyweight boxers who slug it out every day in the world of global business. On any given day, either can win the global business battle. There are no longer any automatic winners. Regardless of whether they are Japanese or American, those companies that adhere to the principles of quality management and continually improve are the ones that will win in today's marketplace.

DISCUSSION QUESTION

Discuss the following question in class or outside of class with your fellow students:

1. Why do you think that companies in the United States were slow to adopt the quality management principles Japanese companies had used to gain market share worldwide?

ENDNOTES

1. *Quality Management Seminar*, Northwest Florida State College, Leadership Institute, January 2011, 2.

2. Ibid.

3. Ibid.

4. Ibid.

5. W. Edwards Deming, *Out of the Crisis* (Cambridge: Massachusetts Institute of Technology Center for Advanced Engineering Study, 1986), 168.

6. Ibid., 169.

7. Ibid.

8. *Quality Management Seminar*, 3.

9. Andrea Gabor, *The Man Who Discovered Quality* (New York: Times Books, Random House, 1990), 16.

10. Ibid., 1.

11. Ibid., 136.

12. Retrieved from www.philipcrosby.com on January 4, 2011.

13. American Society for Quality, "Manager of Quality/Organizational Excellence." Retrieved from www.asq.org/certification/manager-of-quality/index.html on March 24, 2012.

14. *Quality Engineer Certification*. Retrieved from www.asq.org/certification/quality-engineer/index.html on March 24, 2012.

15. *Quality Technician Certification*. Retrieved from www.asq.org/certification/quality-technician/index.html on March 24, 2012.

16. Retrieved from www.juran.com on January 10, 2008.

QUALITY AND GLOBAL COMPETITIVENESS

I'm surprised how many people think you can throw a hand grenade at a competitor and expect he'll stand there and enjoy it. —**Frank Lorenzo**

MAJOR TOPICS

- **The Relationship Between Quality and Competitiveness**
- **Cost of Poor Quality**
- **Competitiveness and the U.S. Economy**
- **Factors Inhibiting Competitiveness**
- **Comparisons of International Competitors**
- **Human Resources and Competitiveness**
- **Characteristics of World-Class Organizations**
- **Management-by-Accounting: Antithesis of Total Quality**
- **U.S. Companies: Global Strengths and Weaknesses**
- **Quality Management Practices in Asian Countries**

One of the results of World War II combined with subsequent technological advances was the creation of the global marketplace. Following the war, industrialized countries began looking for markets outside their own borders. Although the war gave the world a boost in this regard, it was advances in technology that really made the global marketplace possible. Advances in communications technology have made people from all over the world electronic neighbors and electronic customers.

Advances in transportation technology allow raw materials produced in one country to be used in the manufacture of products in a second country that are, in turn, sold to end users in a third country. For example, leather produced in Australia might be shipped as raw material to Italy, where it is used in the manufacture of shoes and purses that are sold in the United States, France, and Japan. At the same time, leather produced in South America is sent to shoe manufacturers in Indonesia. These manufacturers, like their Italian counterparts, sell their shoes in the United States, France, and Japan. This means the manufacturers in

Italy compete with the manufacturers in Indonesia. This simple example demonstrates the kind of competition that takes place on a global scale every day. Such competition has become the norm, and it can be intense.

It used to be only large corporations and multinational corporations that faced global competition; now even small companies are affected. Today no company is immune to the effects of global competition.

THE RELATIONSHIP BETWEEN QUALITY AND COMPETITIVENESS

The relationship between quality and competitiveness is best illustrated by an example from the world of athletics. Consider track star Juan Arballo. In high school, he was his track team's best sprinter. Competing at the district level, Juan easily topped the competition in such events as the 100-, 200-, and 400-meter runs and several relays in which he was the anchor. He did well-enough in high school to win a college scholarship. However, at the college level the competition was of a higher quality, and Juan found he had to train harder and run smarter to win. This he did, and although he no longer won every race, Juan did well-enough to pursue a spot on the U.S. Olympic team. In the Olympic Trials, the quality of the competition was yet again better than that to which Juan was accustomed. He made the Olympic team but only in two events: the 200-meter dash and the 4 × 100 relay.

In the preliminary events at the Olympics, Juan Arballo found the quality of his competitors to be even better than he had imagined it would be. Some competitors had preliminary times better than the best times he had ever run in meets. Clearly, Juan faced the competitive challenge of his career. When his event was finally run, Juan, for the first time in his life, did not place high enough to win a medal. The quality of the global competition was simply beyond his reach.

In this example, at each successive level of competition the quality of the competitors increased. A similar phenomenon happens to businesses in the marketplace. Companies that used to compete only on a local, regional, or national level now find themselves competing against companies from throughout the world. Like Juan Arballo, some of these companies find the competition to be more intense than any they have ever encountered. Only those who are able to produce world-class quality can compete at this level. In practical terms, it is extremely important for a country's businesses to be able to compete globally. When they can't, jobs are lost and the quality of life in that country declines correspondingly.

COST OF POOR QUALITY

Many business executives adopt the attitude that ensuring quality is good thing to do until hard times set in and cost cutting is necessary. During tough times, quality initiatives are often the first functions to go. Companies that take this approach are those that have never integrated continual quality improvement as a normal part of doing business. Rather, they see it as a stand-alone, separate issue. What executives in such companies fail to calculate or to even understand is the costs associated with poor quality. This ironic dilemma is best illustrated with an example of two companies.

A Tale of Two Companies

Two companies, ABC Inc. and XYZ Inc., both need to compete in the global marketplace in order to survive. As might be expected, over the years competition has become increasingly intense. In order to be more competitive, ABC's executives undertook a major company-wide cost-cutting initiative. They eliminated quality audits; changed from trusted, proven suppliers to low-bid suppliers; purchased new computer systems; cut back on research and development; and reduced customer service staff.

These cost-cutting strategies did have the desired effect of decreasing the company's overhead, but they also had the unplanned consequences of disrupting the company's ability to satisfy customers and reducing the company's potential to develop new business in the future. The net outcome of all this was unhappy customers, disenchanted employees, and a decline in business. To make matters even worse, the company was still struggling with the poor performance record that caused its executives to want to cut costs in the first place.

The executives of XYZ Inc. also needed to make some changes in order to stay competitive, but they decided to take a different approach. XYZ's management team set out to identify all of the costs that would disappear if their company improved its performance in key areas. The costs identified included those associated with the following: late deliveries to customers, billing errors, scrap and rework, and accounts payable errors. In other words, XYZ's executives decided to identify the costs associated with poor quality. Having done

so, they were able to begin improvement projects in the areas identified without making cuts in functions essential to competitiveness (e.g., product quality, research and development, customer service).

Cost of Poor Quality and Competitiveness

Few things affect an organization's ability to compete in the global marketplace more than the costs associated with poor quality. When an organization does what is necessary to improve its performance by reducing deficiencies in key areas (cycle time, warranty costs, scrap and rework, on-time delivery, billing, etc.), it can reduce overall costs without eliminating essential services, functions, product features, and personnel. Reducing the costs associated with poor quality is mandatory for companies that hope to compete in the global marketplace. Reducing such costs is one of the principal drivers behind the total quality concept of continual improvement.

Figure 2–1 summarizes both the traditional and the hidden costs of poor quality. The key principle to understand when examining the hidden costs shown in Figure 2–1 is that if every activity in an organization is performed properly every time, these costs simply disappear.

Interpreting the Costs of Poor Quality

Once activities have been identified that exist only or primarily because of poor quality, improvement projects can be undertaken to correct the situation. It is important at this stage to select those projects that have the greatest potential to yield the highest return. The following steps can be used to measure the costs of poor quality so that selected improvement projects have the highest priority:

1. Identify all activities that exist only or primarily because of poor quality.

2. Decide how to estimate the costs of these activities.

Traditional Costs	
√ Waste	√ Customer returns
√ Rejects	√ Inspection
√ Testing	√ Recalls
√ Rework	

Hidden Costs	
√ Excessive overtime	√ Handling complaints
√ Pricing errors	√ Expediting
√ Billing errors	√ System costs
√ Excessive turnover	√ Planning delays
√ Premium freight costs	√ Late paperwork
√ Development cost of the failed product	√ Lack of follow-up
√ Field service costs	√ Excess inventory
√ Overdue receivables	√ Customer allowances
	√ Unused capacity

FIGURE 2–1 Factors to Consider When Quantifying the Costs of Poor Quality

3. Collect data on these activities and make the cost estimates.

4. Analyze the results and take necessary corrective actions in the proper order of priority.

Reducing the cost of poor quality reduces all other costs—product costs, the cost of doing business, and so on. This, in turn, improves the superior value equation: quality, cost, and service.

COMPETITIVENESS AND THE U.S. ECONOMY

The United States came out of World War II as the only major industrialized nation with its manufacturing sector completely intact. A well-oiled manufacturing sector and the availability of abundant raw materials helped the United States become the world leader in the production and export of durable goods. This resulted in a period of unparalleled prosperity and one of the highest standards of living ever experienced by any country.

While the United States was enjoying its position as the world's preeminent economic superpower, the other industrialized nations of the world, particularly Japan and Germany, were busy rebuilding their manufacturing sectors. As Japanese and German manufacturers rebuilt, two things became apparent to them:

1. To succeed, they would have to compete globally.

2. To compete globally, they would have to produce goods of world-class quality, which meant producing better goods but at reasonable, competitive prices.

Basking in their prosperity, U.S. manufacturers were slow to catch on that the game had changed from mass production with acceptable levels of waste to quality production with things done right the first time every time to provide superior value for customers. The old game was best cost. The new game had become best cost *and* best quality. When foreign companies—through a combination of better training, better technology, and better management—began to eat away at markets, U.S. companies, mistakenly seeing cost rather than quality as the issue, began sending work offshore to hold down labor costs. By the time U.S. companies learned that quality and value were key to success in the global marketplace, Japan, Germany, Taiwan, and Korea had made major inroads into global markets previously dominated by U.S. manufacturers (i.e., steel, automobiles, computers, and consumer electronics). In a relatively short period of time, the United States went from the world's leading lender and exporter to the world's biggest debtor, with a huge balance-of-trade deficit. By 1980, the United States was consuming more than it produced and the trend continues to this day.

Impact of Competitiveness on Quality of Life

A nation's ability to compete in the global marketplace has a direct bearing on the quality of life of its citizens. Because

> ### QUALITY TIP ▼
>
> **The United States and the Global Marketplace**
> Companies in the United States have had to learn the hard way that the key to winning in the global marketplace is consistently providing superior value for customers. Superior value consists of superior quality, cost, and service. By the time this realization set in, the U.S. companies in such sectors as automobiles and consumer electronics had lost substantial market share to their competitors in Japan, Korea, and such emerging industrial nations as China and Indonesia. The companies, regardless of their country of origin, that will survive and thrive in the global marketplace are those that can (1) achieve consistent peak performance from people, processes, suppliers, management systems, and all other factors that can effect their ability to deliver superior value and (2) continually improve what passes for peak performance.

the ability to compete translates into the ability to do a better job of producing quality goods, it is critical that nations and individual organizations within them focus their policies, systems, and resources in a coordinated way on continually improving both quality and competitiveness.

The United States began the first decade of the new century poised on the precipice of a growing gap between the haves and the have-nots. While Canada, France, Germany, Italy, Japan, Sweden, and Great Britain have taken steps to link economics, education, and labor market policy in ways that promote competitiveness, the United States is still debating the need for an industrial policy and struggling to reverse the decline of its public schools.

During the 1980s, the United States improved productivity by putting more people to work. Other countries improved their productivity by making the individual worker more efficient. Most new entrants into the workforce during the 1970s and 1980s were people who had not worked previously, primarily women. This influx of new workers helped the United States maintain its traditionally high level of productivity. However, by the 1990s, the gains that could be made by increasing the number of people in the workforce had been made.

From 2010 to the foreseeable future, the number of people in the prime working-years age groups in the United States will be on the decline.[1] As the size of the workforce continues the downward trend that began in the early 1990s, the only way to improve productivity will be to do what other industrialized countries have done—concentrate on improving the efficiency of individual workers. In other words, businesses in the United States will need to get more work out of fewer workers. As some businesses have already learned, the best way to do this is to adopt the total quality philosophy.

Figure 2–2 contains several vignettes relating to the quality of life in the United States. This figure presents either a bleak picture of bad times to come or an unprecedented national challenge. To meet the challenge, companies in the

FIGURE 2–2 Quality of Life
Issues in the United States

- Many of the higher paying manufacturing jobs are being exported to foreign countries.
- The number or people having to work at more than one job to maintain their quality of life has increased continually since the 1960s.
- The most financially rewarding work years have historically been those between ages 40 and 50. In the 1950s, people in this age bracket experienced a 36% increase in real income. By 2008, their counterparts had experienced a decline in real income and the trend continues.
- The gap between the haves and have-nots in America is growing.

United States will have to produce world-class value, which will require a commitment to superior quality, cost, and service.

FACTORS INHIBITING COMPETITIVENESS

Improving competitiveness on a national scale is no simple matter. Much can be done at the level of the individual company, where the total quality approach can be applied to great advantage, but competitiveness on a national scale requires more than just total quality. Students of quality management must understand this point. Failure to understand the limits of total quality has caused some business leaders to expect too much too soon. This, as a result, has turned them into detractors.

This section describes factors that can inhibit competitiveness but are beyond the scope of total quality. They are socioeconomic and sociopolitical in nature and are indigenous to the United States. In the age of global competition, managers should apply the principles of total quality to help make their individual organizations more competitive. Simultaneously, they should work through the political and social systems as private citizens and community leaders to help level the playing field among nations by correcting the inhibitors explained in this section. These inhibitors fall into the following categories: business- and government-related factors, family-related factors, and education-related factors.

Business- and Government-Related Factors

Those U.S. companies trying to compete in the global marketplace are rowing upstream while dragging an anchor. Actually, they drag three anchors. This was pointed out many years ago by W. Edwards Deming when he first set forth his Seven Deadly Diseases. His second, sixth, and seventh deadly diseases are as follows:[2]

- Emphasis on short-term profits fed by fear of unfriendly takeover attempts and pressure from lenders or shareholders
- Excessive medical costs
- Excessive costs of liability inflated by lawyers working on contingency fees

Each of these diseases adds cost to a company's products without adding value. Nothing could be worse when viewed from the perspective of competitiveness. A company might equal all competitors point for point on all quality and productivity criteria and still lose in the marketplace because it is a victim of deadly diseases that drive up the cost of its product.

Excessive medical costs and litigation, primarily related to workers' compensation, have also slanted the playing field in favor of foreign competitors. The annual cost of workers' compensation to U.S. businesses is almost $30 billion. This is a non–value-added cost that increases the price these businesses must charge for their products. Litigation and the associated legal costs have made tort reform an issue in the U.S. Congress and in the legislatures of most states. However, intense lobbying by trial lawyers has prevented any significant tort reform.

Overcoming these business-related inhibitors will require business and government to work together in a positive, constructive partnership to enact policies that will reduce these non–value-added costs to a minimum. To accomplish this goal, the United States will have to undertake major restructuring of its financial, legal, and medical systems.

Family-Related Factors

Human resources are a critical part of the competitiveness equation. Just as one of the most important factors in fielding a competitive athletic team is having the best possible players, one of the most important factors in fielding a competitive company is having the best possible employees. Consequently, the quality of the labor pool is important. The more knowledgeable, skilled, motivated, and able to learn members of the labor pool are, the better.

Well-educated, well-trained, motivated members of the labor pool quickly become productive employees when given jobs. Although providing ongoing training for employees is important in the age of global competitiveness, the type of training provided is important. Organizations that can offer training that has immediate and direct application spend less than those that have to begin by providing basic education for functionally illiterate employees. Since the 1970s, U.S. businesses have had to devote increasing amounts of money to basic education efforts, whereas foreign competitors have been able to provide advanced training that very quickly translates into better quality and productivity.

Many factors account for this difference. Some of these can be traced directly to the family. If the family unit, regardless of how it is constituted, is the nation's most important human resource development agency, the labor pool from which U.S. companies must draw their employees cannot match that in competing countries.

Single parents who must work full-time have little or no time to help their children excel in school. Children with parents who do not value education are unlikely to value it themselves. If the family has a strong influence—positive or negative, by design or by default—on the attitudes of children toward learning and work, the United States faces deep-seated problems that must be solved if its companies are going to compete in the global marketplace.

Education-Related Factors

The transition from classroom to workplace has never been easy, but in the age of global competition it has only become more difficult. The needs of employers have increased markedly. Unfortunately, the academic performance of students in the United States has not kept pace with changes in the global marketplace. High school graduation rates in the United States rank near the bottom when compared with those in other leading industrialized nations—nations America must compete with. In addition, the performance of those students who do graduate from high school is markedly lower than that of their contemporaries in competing industrialized countries.

On international tests of academic performance in such key areas as reading, mathematics, science, and problem solving, American students lag well behind their contemporaries in other countries. This is bad news for employers in the United States that must compete in an increasingly global environment. Human performance is one of the key ingredients in quality, productivity, value, organizational excellence, and all of the other factors that affect global competitiveness. Students who enter the workplace unable to perform at competitive levels in reading, mathematics, science, and problem solving just handicap their employers.

Figure 2–3 compares annual expenditures per pupil for leading industrialized countries. Of the top seven, the United States spends the most, whereas Korea spends the least. Figure 2–4 compares the number of school days required of students annually in the leading industrialized countries. With this criterion, the order is reversed when comparing the United States and Japan.

Figures 2–5, 2–6, 2–7, and 2–8 show the actual rankings of student performance on international tests of reading, mathematics, science, and problem solving as tracked by the Organization for Economic Cooperation and Development (OECD). Figure 2–5 shows the relative performance rankings of students in mathematics literacy. The average score of students from the United States is well below the international average (474 versus 498). Figure 2–6 shows similar

Country	Annual Funding ($)
United States	**7,560**
Italy	6,783
Japan	5,771
Germany	4,237
France	4,777
United Kingdom	4,416
Korea	3,714

FIGURE 2–3 Comparison of Per-pupil Funding in Selected Industrialized Countries

Source: The Management Institute, *Global Update* (January 2011), 13.

Country	Average School Days
Japan	240
Korea	222
Taiwan	222
Israel	215
Scotland	191
Canada	188
United States	**178**

FIGURE 2–4 Comparison of School Days per Year in Selected Industrialized Countries

Source: The Management Institute, *Global Update* (January 2011), 14.

results in science literacy. Figure 2–7 shows that students from the United States scored an average of 495 on reading while the average international score was 500. Figure 2–8 shows that students from the United States scored an average of 477 while the international average was 500. These scores do not bode well for the United States or for its employers who must compete in the global arena. In fact, what the scores mean is that if global competition were a footrace, the United States would be starting 100 yards behind in a 200-yard race.

U.S. Manufacturers and Global Competition

The most important sectors in determining the quality of life in a country are manufacturing and agriculture. The United States has led the world in agricultural production for many years and still does. The United States also led the world in manufacturing productivity for many years. Beginning with the 1960s, however, this lead began to slip. The decline continued and accelerated through the 1980s to the point that the U.S. manufacturing sector entered the 1990s struggling uphill to regain ground. In the mid-1990s, however, the United States began to reemerge as a world-class competitor. No longer is the United States, or any other country, the clear-cut leader in terms of manufacturing productivity. With the

Mean Achievement in Math Literacy	
Country	**Math Literacy**
Hong Kong	550
Finland	544
Korea	542
Netherlands	538
Liechtenstein	536
Japan	534
Canada	532
Belgium	529
Macao	527
Switzerland	527
Australia	524
New Zealand	523
Czech Republic	516
Iceland	515
Denmark	514
France	511
Sweden	509
Austria	506
Germany	503
Ireland	503
Slovak Republic	498
Norway	495
Luxembourg	493
Poland	490
Hungary	490
Spain	485
Latvia	483
United States	**483**

FIGURE 2–5 Mean Achievement Scores in Math Literacy
Source: www.oced.org, January 2011.

Mean Achievement in Science Literacy	
Country	**Science Literacy**
Finland	548
Japan	548
Hong Kong	539
Korea	538
Liechtenstein	525
Australia	525
Macao	525
Netherlands	524
Czech Republic	523
New Zealand	521
Canada	519
Switzerland	513
France	511
Belgium	509
Sweden	506
Ireland	505
Hungary	503
Germany	502
Poland	498
Slovak Republic	495
Iceland	495
United States	**491**

FIGURE 2–6 Mean Achievement Scores in Science Literacy
Source: www.oced.org, January 2011.

dawning of the new millennium, Japan, the United States, Germany, and Korea became increasingly competitive.

Figure 2–9 compares the productivity of automobile manufacturers in Japan, the United States, and Europe. In this chapter, the term *productivity* is used several times. In this context, the term should be viewed as "total factor productivity" (ratio of outputs to inputs from labor, capital, materials, and energy). The graph compares the average hours required by the most productive plants to produce one automobile. Japanese plants located in Japan are able to produce an automobile in an average of 15 hours. European manufacturers require more than twice that much time. Such U.S. manufacturers as General Motors, Ford, and Chrysler require an average of 20 hours per automobile. Japanese manufacturers with assembly plants in the United States using U.S. workers, such as Mazda, average 19 hours per automobile. Because hourly wages in Europe tend to be higher than those in Japan

and the United States, European firms operate at a double competitive disadvantage. European and U.S. firms are nibbling away at these productivity differences to the point that the gap between the best and worst producers is slowly but steadily closing.

Another area in which Japanese firms have gained a competitive advantage is product development. The *product development cycle*—the time it takes to turn an idea into a finished product—is typically shorter in Japan than in the United States and Europe. This allows Japanese firms to get new products to the market faster. Japanese automobile manufacturers take an average of 2 years to complete the product development cycle compared with more than 3 years for their competitors in the United States and Europe.

Another basis for comparison among automobile manufacturers is quality. Productivity gained at the expense of quality yields no competitive advantage. Figure 2–10 compares the major automobile-producing nations in terms of the average number of defects per 100 vehicles manufactured. The quality comparisons follow the same trends found in the earlier productivity comparisons. Japanese manufacturers average the fewest defects; European manufacturers average the most. American manufacturers find it difficult to compete in the global marketplace when their productivity and quality are

Mean Achievement in Reading Literacy	
Country	**Reading Literacy**
Finland	543
Korea	534
Canada	528
Australia	525
Liechtenstein	525
New Zealand	522
Ireland	515
Sweden	514
Netherlands	513
Hong Kong	510
Belgium	507
Norway	500
Switzerland	499
Japan	498
Macao	498
Poland	497
France	496
United States	**495**

FIGURE 2–7 Mean Achievement Scores in Reading Literacy

Source: www.oced.org, January 2011.

Advanced Problem-Solving Skills
• Korea..............................70% plus
• Japan............................70% plus
• Finland...........................70% plus
• Germany.........................58%
• Czech Republic.................58%
AVERAGE 52%
• Ireland...........................51%
• Russia............................43%
• United States....................42%

FIGURE 2–8 Percent of Students with Advanced Problem-Solving Skills

Source: www.oced.org, January 2011.

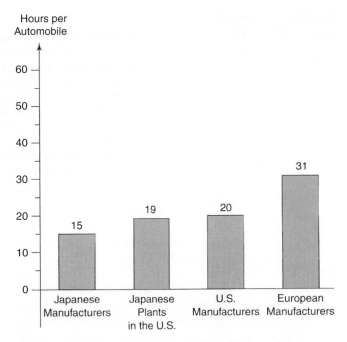

FIGURE 2–9 Comparative Productivity of Automobile Manufacturers (Most Productive Plants)

Source: Congress of the United States, Office of Technology Assessment, 2011.

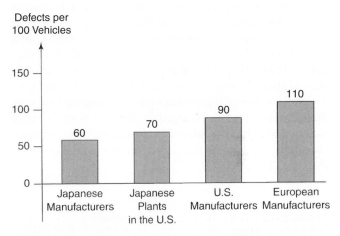

FIGURE 2–10 Comparative Defect Frequency among Automobile Manufacturers

Source: Congress of the United States, Office of Technology Assessment, 2011.

not up to international standards—a situation that must be reversed if the United States is to regain the preeminent position it has historically enjoyed in the world community.

Even a cursory examination of key economic indicators raises concerns. The ability of a country to compete in the manufacturing arena is a direct determinant of its quality of life. Manufacturing created the great American middle class. If the manufacturing sector dwindles because it cannot compete globally, the middle class dwindles correspondingly. Figure 2–11 contains a number of facts that indicate what has happened to the U.S. economy during the years since World War II. These are the years in which U.S. manufacturers have steadily lost ground to foreign competition.

Do these comparisons mean that U.S. manufacturers cannot compete? The answer is no. American manufacturers were slow to respond to the international quality revolution. However, in the 1980s and into the new millennium, the realization that quality coupled with productivity

FIGURE 2–11 Selected
Economic Indicators

Source: The Management Institute,
Global Update (May 2011), 12–13.

- Today 29% of children born in the United States will live in poverty. Forty years ago it was approximately 12%.
- The top 1% of income earners in the United States accounted for 60% of the total income increase realized in 2010.
- In 2010, the top 1% of the wealthiest U.S. citizens had as many assets as 93% of the poorest U.S. citizens.
- The real hourly wage of a worker in the United States today is 17% less than it was in 1979.
- Today the United States has the most unequal distribution of wealth of any industrialized country in the world.

was the key to winning global competition caused many U.S. firms to begin adopting the approach set forth in this book while simultaneously pushing for change in areas beyond their control (i.e., cost of capital, industrial policy, etc.). As the total quality approach continues to gain acceptance, companies in the United States are closing the competitiveness gap.

COMPARISONS OF INTERNATIONAL COMPETITORS

According to a report published by the World Economic Forum, the United States has reclaimed its place as the most competitive country in the world community.[3] This is good news, since the United States had slipped to fifth place during the 1990s. This means that in spite of the poor performance of students in the United States when compared with the performance of students in other industrialized nations, the United States has managed to improve in the areas of standard of living, manufacturing productivity, investment, and trade, which are critical indicators of national competitive status (Figure 2–12).

HUMAN RESOURCES AND COMPETITIVENESS

The point is made continually throughout this book that the most valuable resources for enhancing competitiveness are human resources. The truth of this point becomes apparent if one studies the approach taken by Germany and Japan to rebuild from the rubble of World War II. Both countries were devastated. Being left with only one real resource, the human resource, Germany and Japan were forced to adopt an approach that used this resource to the greatest possible advantage.

The German and Japanese systems are not perfect, nor are they infallible. They are examples of approaches that work as well as any other two systems can in a continually changing and unsure global marketplace. Further, they make wise and effective use of human resources.

Business, government, and labor leaders in the United States could learn a great deal from Germany and Japan. People often respond to suggestions that such study might be helpful by claiming that the culture of the United States is so different that what works in these countries won't

FIGURE 2–12 Critical Indicators of National Competitive Status

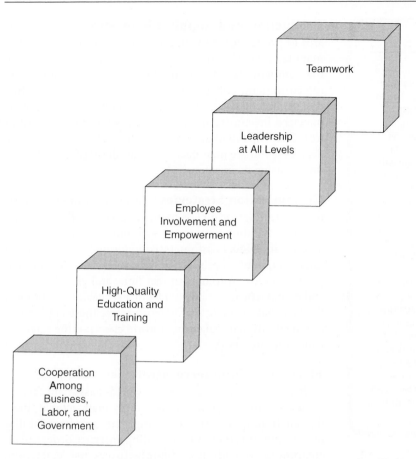

FIGURE 2–13 Strategies for Human Resource Competitiveness in Japan and Germany

Teamwork

Leadership at All Levels

Employee Involvement and Empowerment

High-Quality Education and Training

Cooperation Among Business, Labor, and Government

work in the United States. Such thinking misses the point entirely: few countries could be more different from one another than Japan and Germany, yet the approaches to competitiveness adopted by these countries are strikingly similar (see Figure 2–13).

CHARACTERISTICS OF WORLD-CLASS ORGANIZATIONS

It is often said that only "world-class" organizations can compete in the global marketplace. But what is a world-class organization? In an attempt to answer this question, the American Management Association (AMA) conducted a global survey.[4] According to this survey, the following are the top 15 areas in which organizations are concerned about doing well as they attempt to compete in the global marketplace:

1. Customer service
2. Quality control and assurance
3. Research and development/new product development
4. Acquiring new technologies
5. Innovation
6. Team-based approach (adopting and using effectively)
7. Best practices (study and use of)
8. Manpower planning
9. Environmentally sound practices
10. Business partnerships and alliances

11. Reengineering of processes
12. Mergers and acquisitions
13. Outsourcing and contracting
14. Reliance on consulting services
15. Political lobbying

Of the 15 areas listed in the survey, several are directly associated with the larger issue of quality. Customer service, quality control and assurance, innovation, team-based approach to work, partnerships and alliances, and reengineering of processes are all topics that figure prominently in any discussion of total quality.

In addition to these issues, the AMA survey found that respondents were concerned about a number of human resources topics. The 10 most important of these are as follows:

1. Worker productivity (improvement)
2. Employee training and development
3. Open communication between management and employees
4. Employee benefits and perquisites
5. Codes of workplace conduct
6. Conflict resolution
7. Employee satisfaction
8. Flextime arrangements
9. Management–employee–union relations
10. Child care

Once again, the AMA survey identified numerous quality-related concerns and functions that organizations must do well if they hope to compete globally. Worker productivity, employee training and development, codes of workplace conduct, conflict resolution, employee satisfaction, and management–employee–union relations are all total quality–related topics that are addressed at various points in this text.

World-Class Manufacturing: What It Takes

Organizations in business sectors ranging from banking to commercial transportation attempt to compete on a global scale. The most prominent of these come from the manufacturing sector. World-class manufacturers are those that consistently provide superior value (quality, cost, and service) for customers. The methods of world-class manufacturers are summarized in the following subsections:

Competitive Analysis Strategies In the area of competitive analysis, world-class manufacturers use the following methods to compare themselves with the competition for the purpose of improving their own performance: cost efficiencies in operations, speed to market, research and development supremacy, rapid delivery from suppliers, first-class delivery logistics, zero defects, real-time order management, seamless integration with sales and marketing, close to zero inventory, and networked or collaborative operations. By applying these criteria to themselves and their competitors, world-class manufacturers determine where their performance is and where it needs to be in order to compete globally.

Production and Supply Chain Strategies In the area of production and supply chain strategies, world-class manufacturers use the following methods to stay ahead of the competition: collaborative planning, forecasting, and replenishment; collaborative manufacturing and product design; direct delivery of materials to point of use; supplier-managed inventory; and use of channel-assembly distributors. Other manufacturers also use these strategies to varying degrees. Ultimate manufacturers stay ahead of the competition by using them extensively.

Customization Strategies In the area of customization strategies, world-class manufacturers use the following methods: building to order, mass production that is configured for individual customers, configuring to order (linking sales operations to production schedules), one-to-one customization for customers in real time, and global sourcing and manufacturing. As with the other strategies, it is not just the fact that ultimate manufacturers use these customization methods that makes them world class; it is the extent to which they use them.

Electronic Commerce Strategies In the area of electronic commerce strategies, world-class manufacturers use the following methods: supply management, buying, auctioning, Internet ordering, status and availability tracking by Internet, and accepting Internet orders from customers. World-class manufacturers use electronic commerce strategies almost twice as often as their competitors. In addition, these world-class organizations are on track to increase their use of electronic commerce over the next 5 years at a rate well beyond the projected rates of competitors.

Compensation Systems In the area of compensation systems, world-class manufacturers use the following methods as benchmarks for rewarding and recognizing managers and employees: product profitability, inventory levels, manufactured/delivered costs per unit, worker productivity, level of customer satisfaction, manufacturing cycle time, cost efficiencies in operations, employee retention rates, speed of response to market demands, percent of revenues from new products, total delivered cost per unit, zero defects, percent of costs saved from strategic outsourcing, integration of functions across the organization, economic value added, and percent of products from strategic alliances. Figure 2–14 contains a brief checklist of minimum performance benchmarks that manufacturers must be able to meet in order to compete in the global marketplace.

MANAGEMENT-BY-ACCOUNTING: ANTITHESIS OF TOTAL QUALITY

In too many businesses, accounting trumps quality. Often, managerial accounting becomes the tail that wags the dog—a questionable approach to doing business in a highly

Performance Measures	World-Class Benchmarks
Quality Rejects per Million Parts	< 10
Utilized Capacity	90%
Breakdown Losses	1%
On-Schedule Production	Targeted
Design Producibility	100%
Design Meets Cost Target	95%
Engineering Change Process Response Time	1 day
Annual Training Days per Employee	20

FIGURE 2–14 To Compete in the Global Marketplace, Manufacturers Must Consistently Exceed These Benchmarks

Source: International Finance Center, Washington, DC.

competitive environment. When managerial accounting becomes management-by-accounting, quality inevitably suffers. Management-by-accounting amounts to focusing solely on an organization's financial performance rather than managing the factors that most affect financial performance (e.g., people, process, and product quality).

The most obvious problem with management-by-accounting is that it leads to short-term thinking and short-term decision making. According to this approach, one of the fastest ways to improve financial performance in the short run is to ignore investing in continual improvement that are necessary to remain competitive in the long run. The practices like (1) keeping people trained and well-equipped; (2) employing best practices to keep processes operating at peak performance levels; and (3) maintaining world-class quality in all aspects of an organization's operations cost money in the short run but pay off in the long run. In other words, total quality is a long-term concept while management-by-accounting is a short-term concept.

One of the many reasons why companies fall into the management-by-accounting trap is that many CEOs come from a finance-related background, the most common college degree among the American CEOs being an MBA—a degree with a strong finance orientation. To avoid such ideological pitfalls, all business-related degrees need to include a more thorough study of quality. It is also why more quality professionals need to put themselves on the "CEO track" in their professions. Consider the following problems that result from the application of management-by-accounting:

- Management-by-accounting leads to decision making by analysis of financial spreadsheets rather than by consideration of the factors that lead to organizational excellence and world-class quality.

- Management-by-accounting encourages short-term cost cutting instead of long-term improvements to quality, value, and competitiveness.

- Management-by-accounting leads to narrowly-focused leadership of companies based solely on short-term financial considerations rather than broader thinking that encompasses all factors that contribute to organizational excellence and make a company competitive.

The master's of business administration degree, or MBA, is an excellent credential. So are the various other under-graduate and graduate degrees available from colleges and universities in the United States. It is the concept of focusing excessively on the score rather than the game—management-by-accounting—that is being questioned by quality advocates, not any specific degree. Management-by-accounting is an approach to management, not an academic credential.

As anyone knows, both the game and the score are important. We advocate a blending of the principles of quality management with the curricula of business, engineering, technology, and management programs. Students pursuing a degree in any of these disciplines should learn the principles of quality management set forth in this book as well as their traditional curriculum content. This will ensure that they know how to continually improve both performance and the score.

U.S. COMPANIES: GLOBAL STRENGTHS AND WEAKNESSES

As business continues the current trend toward globalization, how are companies in the United States faring? A business trying to compete in the global marketplace is like an athlete trying to compete in the Olympics. Nowhere is the competition tougher. Correspondingly, no country in the world gives its businesses such a solid foundation from which to work. The following factors account for a country's ability to compete in the international marketplace:

1. An economy that is open to foreign investment and trade

2. A government that minimizes controls on business but does a good job of supervising financial institutions

3. A judicial system that works well and helps reduce corruption

4. Greater transparency and availability of economic information

5. High labor mobility

6. Ease of entry by new businesses

In varying degrees, the United States meets all of these criteria. Of course, how well these criteria are fulfilled is a matter of debate between and among various interest groups and stakeholders. Nonetheless, when compared with other countries competing in the global marketplace, the United States fares well in all of these key areas. This being the case, a key advantage of American firms trying to compete in the global marketplace is these six factors working in their favor. Other advantages and disadvantages are summarized in the following sections.

Global Advantages of U.S. Companies

In the global marketplace, the United States is the world leader in the following industries: aerospace, airlines, beverages, chemicals, computer services, electrical products, entertainment, general merchandise, motor vehicles, office equipment, paper products, pharmaceuticals, photographic and scientific equipment, semiconductors, soap and cosmetics, and tobacco. Some of the reasons the United States is able to lead the world in these key industries include

1. Strong entrepreneurial spirit
2. Presence of a "small capitalization" stock market for small- and mid-sized companies
3. Rapidly advancing technologies
4. Comparatively low taxes
5. Low rate of unionization
6. World-class system of higher education (colleges and universities)

The United States leads the world in new business start-ups. This is because the entrepreneurial spirit is an integral part of the American persona. The presence of a small capitalization stock market allows small- and mid-sized companies to start up and expand without having to use all of their own capital or to take out higher-interest loans from banks, as is often the case in other countries. The United States leads the world in the development, transfer, diffusion, and use of technology. This helps ensure a continual stream of new products on the one hand and improved productivity on the other. Americans complain constantly about taxes (as they are entitled to do in exercising their rights as free citizens). But when compared with other industrialized nations, the United States has a low tax burden. Tension between labor and management can harm productivity and, in turn, decrease a company's ability to compete in the global marketplace. The amount of tension that exists between labor and management can typically be demonstrated by the level of union activity: the more the tension, the more the union activity. Compared with other industrialized nations, union activity in the United States is low.

The United States also provides the world's best higher education system. The number of top-notch colleges and universities in the United States is so much greater than those in other countries that comparisons are irrelevant. The cost of higher education in America, although viewed as high by U.S. citizens, is inexpensive when compared with that of other industrialized nations. In addition, financial aid is so readily available that almost any person with the necessary academic ability can pursue a college education in the United States.

Global Disadvantages of U.S. Companies

In spite of the many strengths companies in the United States can bring to the global marketplace, and in spite of this country's world-leading position in several key industries, there are still some disadvantages with which companies have to deal. The primary global disadvantages of U.S. companies are these:

1. Expanding government regulation
2. A growing "underclass" of have-nots
3. A weak public school system (K–12)
4. A poorly skilled labor force and poor training opportunities
5. An increasing protectionist sentiment (to restrict imports)
6. Growing public alienation with large institutions (public and private)

Regardless of which major political party has controlled Congress over the past 40 years, the general trend has been toward increasing government regulation of business. Regulating business is a difficult balancing act. On the one hand, businesses cannot be allowed to simply pursue profits, disregarding the potential consequences to the environment and other national interests. On the other hand, too much regulation or unnecessary regulation can make it impossible to compete globally. The growing divide between haves and have-nots in the United States might lead to the establishment and perpetuation of a permanent economic and social underclass. This is precisely what happened in Russia when Czar Nicholas II was overthrown by the Communists in the early 1900s. People who lose hope might very well respond in ways that threaten the peace, stability, and social fabric of the United States. One of the key factors in the establishment of a social and economic underclass is the failure of America's public school system (K–12). Even with the best system of higher education in the world, America cannot overcome the shortcomings of its K–12 system. In fact, if drastic improvements are not made, over time those shortcomings will begin to erode the quality of our higher education system.

The most fundamental problem with the public school system from the perspective of global competition is that most of the jobs in companies that need to compete globally require less than a college education. These jobs must be performed by high school graduates who, if they cannot read, write, speak, listen, think, and calculate better than their counterparts in other countries, will be outperformed. Poorly skilled workers are an outgrowth of the failure of the nation's public school system, in which the overwhelming majority of Americans are educated. Ideally, every high school graduate should be fully prepared to either go to work or go on to college. When this is not the case, as it certainly is not, American companies must try to compete with a less-skilled labor force. This is like a baseball coach trying to win with a team of players who cannot pitch, catch, run, or hit.

One of the factors that contributed to the Great Depression of the 1930s was global protectionism. Americans wanted their farmers and their manufacturers to be "protected" from their counterparts in other countries. Protectionism hurts everyone and never really protects anyone. But as other countries (principally Japan, Korea, and China) have entered U.S. markets, the jobs of American workers have been threatened. A natural but ill-informed response is to call for protectionist measures and to adopt slogans such as "Buy American." Economists are quick to point out, however, that the only valid reason to "buy American" is that American products are the best made. If they are not, buying them makes little sense and is nothing more than misguided patriotism. The better approach is to ask why the American products are not the best and then to do what is necessary to make them the best.

The final factor that gives U.S. companies a disadvantage is the growing tendency of the public to see big organizations as the "bad guys." This is displayed in many different ways. Disgruntled employees will sometimes pretend injuries and file fraudulent workers' compensation claims. Employees will cheat and steal from their employers. Of course, the most common way animosity toward big business is acted out is by employees giving less than their best on the job. Another expression is when the public at large supports antibusiness legislation and unnecessary regulations.

QUALITY MANAGEMENT PRACTICES IN ASIAN COUNTRIES

Companies in the United States compete for market share every day with companies all over the world. Global competition has become a way of life for business and industry. Some of the most intense competition comes from Asia, where companies have effectively adopted many of the quality management practices set forth in this book. The most intense competition for companies in the United States now comes from Japan, Korea, and China. Most students of quality are familiar with the strides Japanese

companies have made since beginning to adopt quality management practices after World War II. But what is less known is that many other Asian companies are following Japan's lead as a way to compete effectively at the global level. These countries include Bangladesh, Brunei, India, Indonesia, Malaysia, the Philippines, Singapore, South Korea, and Thailand.

Industrialization in these Asian countries began to gain a foothold in the 1960s and developed rapidly through the 1980s. In the 1980s, companies in these countries began to form quality control circles as a way to gain employee input for continually improving processes and products. By the 1990s, companies in these Asian countries were well along in the adoption and effective application of the principles of total quality management including ISO 9000 registration. By the late 1990s, many companies in these countries had refined their total quality techniques and had begun to emphasize not just the product quality but the service quality, too.

The dawning of the new century saw Asian companies adopting ISO 14000 as a way to ensure effective environmental management. National quality awards similar to the Baldrige Award in the United States and the Deming Prize in Japan were adopted by several of these Asian countries. As of now, the leading companies throughout Asia are applying global best practices to maximize performance, value, and quality.

The globalization of the marketplace has transformed doing business into an enterprise similar to competing in the Olympics. In the global arena, only the best of the best survive and thrive, the intensity of the competition only increases, what was considered outstanding performance yesterday won't even make the grade tomorrow, and even the smallest countries can produce world-class performers.

Companies in the United States that used to compete only locally or regionally now find themselves battling daily against companies from not just Japan but also India, Brunei, Bangladesh, Thailand, Korea, Singapore, Malaysia, Indonesia, and the Philippines. What's more, companies from these countries have learned the value of effectively adopting and applying the principles set forth in this book.

SUMMARY

1. The relationship between quality and competitiveness can be summarized as follows: In a modern global marketplace, quality is the key to competitiveness.

2. The costs of poor quality include the following: waste, rejects, testing, rework, customer returns, inspection, recalls, excessive overtime, pricing errors, billing errors, excessive turnover, premium freight costs, development cost of the failed product, field service costs, overdue receivables, handling complaints, expediting, system costs, planning delays, late paperwork, lack of follow-up, excess inventory, customer allowances, and unused capacity.

3. The United States came out of World War II as the only major industrialized nation with its manufacturing sector completely intact. Germany and Japan were devastated by damage during the war. They rebuilt their manufacturing bases on the assumption that to compete globally they would have to produce goods of

world-class quality. That strategy helped them recover and become world leaders in manufacturing.

4. Several factors can inhibit competitiveness, including those related to business and government, family, and education.

5. When making comparisons among internationally competing countries, the following indicators are used: standard of living, trade and export growth, investment, and manufacturing productivity.

6. The most important key in maximizing competitiveness is the human resource. Following World War II, this was the only resource that Germany and Japan had to draw on. Consequently, they built economic systems that encourage private employers to make business decisions that emphasize improved productivity and quality rather than price.

KEY TERMS AND CONCEPTS

Competitive analysis strategies
Competitiveness
Cost of poor quality
Customization strategies
Education-related factors
Export growth
Family-related factors
Global integration
Investment
Manufacturing productivity
Product development cycle
Quality of life
Research and development

FACTUAL REVIEW QUESTIONS

1. Explain the relationship between quality and competitiveness.

2. Explain how the costs of poor quality can affect competitiveness.

3. Describe the evolution of the rebuilding effort undertaken by Japan and Germany following World War II.

4. Explain the actions of U.S. manufacturers during the period in which Japan and Germany were rebuilding following World War II.

5. How does a nation's ability to compete affect its quality of life?

6. Explain how education-related factors can inhibit competitiveness.

7. Compare investment and manufacturing productivity in the United States with investment and manufacturing productivity in Japan.

8. List and briefly explain the basic philosophical constructs underlying the human resource aspects of the competitiveness of Japan and Germany.

CRITICAL THINKING ACTIVITY

Two quality managers meet for lunch every Friday to discuss common problems, compare notes, and make suggestions to each other. Today their discussion has turned into a debate. The topic is the impact of competitiveness on the quality of life in America. "I think you are taking the issue of competitiveness too far. Sure it's important to my company and to yours, too. But I don't think it has that much of an effect on the overall quality of life in America," said the first quality manager. "I could not disagree with you more," responded his colleague. "The quality of life we enjoy in this country is tied directly to the ability of U.S. companies to compete in the global marketplace." Take one side or the other in this debate and complete one of the following activities:

1. Debate the issue in class with your fellow students.

2. Make a list of the ways competitiveness can affect the quality of life.

3. Write a position paper explaining your opinions in this debate.

DISCUSSION ASSIGNMENT 2–1

Technology Adoption by Small Manufacturers

"The Office of Technology Assessment (OTA) reports that only 11 to 15 percent of all machine tools in the U.S. are automated; the majority of those automated are found in large companies."

"A Census Bureau study found that half of the small manufacturers surveyed don't use any of 17 technologies cited by experts as critical to competitiveness and didn't plan to do so in the next five years. Among firms that used one of the technologies, 60 percent had no plans to adopt other technologies."

DISCUSSION QUESTIONS

Discuss the following questions in class or outside of class with your fellow students:

1. Why don't more small companies in the United States adopt modern technologies?

2. How can modern technologies be justified from a cost perspective in a small company?

DISCUSSION ASSIGNMENT 2–2

Pennsylvania's Industrial Resource Centers

Pennsylvania's Department of Community and Economic Development maintains a network of industrial resource centers (IRCs) that are operated as nonprofit corporations managed by the private sector but with financial support from the state. These IRCs all have a similar mission: to help small and medium-sized manufacturers adopt world-class technologies and techniques—technologies and techniques that will lead to organizational excellence. The principles of total quality are the heart of the IRCs' purpose.

Typical of these IRCs is the Northwest Industrial Resource Center (NWIRC) which serves an area consisting of 13 primarily rural counties that encompass approximately 2,000 manufacturing enterprises. Services provided fall into two broad categories: (1) business growth services and (2) manufacturing excellence services. Business growth services include those that help small and medium-sized manufacturers grow their principle product line (e.g., strategic planning, sales and marketing, new product development, and succession planning). Manufacturing excellence services, such as lean manufacturing, value-stream mapping, ISO support, and continual quality improvement, include those that help improve quality and productivity.

DISCUSSION QUESTIONS

Discuss the following questions in class or outside of class with your fellow students:

1. What kind of non-technology-oriented help might be needed by a small manufacturer?

2. How could the IRC model be applied to the service sector and other nonmanufacturing companies?

ENDNOTES

1. U.S. Bureau of Labor Statistics. Retrieved from www.bls.gov on January 3, 2011.

2. Retrieved from www.managementwisdom.com, January 4, 2011.

3. World Economic Forum. Retrieved from www.weforum.org on January 3, 2011.

4. American Management Association. Retrieved from www.amanet.org, on January 3, 2011.

STRATEGIC MANAGEMENT: PLANNING AND EXECUTION FOR COMPETITIVE ADVANTAGE

A mission statement is "a long, awkward sentence that demonstrates management's inability to think clearly." —Scott Adams (Author of Dilbert)

MAJOR TOPICS
- **What Is Strategic Management?**
- **Competitive Strategy**
- **Core Competencies and Competitive Advantage**
- **Components of Strategic Management**
- **Strategic Planning Overview**
- **Creative Thinking in Strategic Planning**
- **Conducting the SWOT Analysis**
- **Developing the Vision**
- **Developing the Mission**
- **Developing the Guiding Principles**
- **Developing Broad Strategic Objectives**
- **Developing Specific Tactics (Action Plan)**
- **Executing the Strategic Plan**
- **Strategic Planning in Action: A "Real-World" Case**

In today's global business arena, even small companies can find themselves being challenged by competitors from all over the world. Never has the world of business been so intensely competitive as it is now. Consequently, it is important for business leaders to think strategically, to plan for gaining and sustaining competitive advantage, and to effectively execute their plans. This chapter explains the concept of strategic management, explains why this concept is so important, and demonstrates how to plan and execute the strategy to gain and sustain competitive advantage.

WHAT IS STRATEGIC MANAGEMENT?

To understand strategic management, one must first understand the concept of organizational strategy. Strategies are defined as follows:

> Organizational strategies are the approaches adopted by organizations to ensure successful performance in the marketplace. These approaches are typically set

forth in a comprehensive document called the *strategic plan.*

Strategic management is management that bases all actions, activities, and decisions on what is most likely—within an ethical framework—to ensure successful performance in the marketplace. From the strategic manager's perspective, resources are wasted unless they contribute to success in the marketplace, and the more direct the contribution, the better.

COMPETITIVE STRATEGY

To survive and thrive in a globally competitive marketplace, organizations must adopt a broad strategy that gives them a sustainable competitive advantage. All such strategies fall into one or more of the following categories:

- **Cost leadership strategies.** Strategies in this category seek to improve efficiency and control costs throughout an organization's activity-cost chain (supplier activity costs, in-house activity costs, and distribution activity costs).
- **Differentiation strategies.** Strategies in this category seek to add value, as defined by customers, to the organization's products or services. Such strategies typically involve gaining technological superiority over competitors, continually outperforming competitors in the area of quality, providing more and better support services to customers, and providing customers more value for their money.
- **Market-niche strategies.** Strategies in this category focus on a narrowly defined segment of the market (market niche) and attempt to make the organization in question the market leader in that niche. Leadership can be achieved by adopting cost leadership or differentiation strategies or both designed to appeal specifically to the target market.

Total quality relates to strategic management in that it enhances an organization's ability to gain a sustainable competitive advantage in the marketplace. Handled properly, total quality can be the most effective cost leadership or differentiation strategy an organization can adopt. This is because the total quality approach is the best way to continually improve efficiency and cut costs throughout an organization's activity-cost chain while simultaneously continually improving the features of the product or service that differentiate it in the marketplace. Total quality can also improve an organization's chances of becoming a leader in a given market niche.

CORE COMPETENCIES AND COMPETITIVE ADVANTAGE

One task to be accomplished as part of the strategic planning process is identifying the organization's core competencies. This task is generally completed as part of the SWOT (strengths, weaknesses, opportunities, and threats) analysis, since an organization's core competencies should be part of its strengths. A core competency is something an organization does so well that it can be viewed as a competitive advantage. A competitive advantage is any aspect of the organization that (1) contributes directly and significantly to increasing customer demand by achieving superior value (i.e., superior quality, cost, and service) and (2) is difficult for competitors to replicate.

An organization's core competencies might be based on its ability to achieve economy of scale, proprietary access to a given technology, expertise in a given area that cannot be replicated, ability to maintain world-class performance from critical processes, market proximity, high-performance corporate culture, research and development expertise, or ability to respond rapidly to market research or in any other factors that contribute directly and significantly to the organization's ability to provide superior value consistently over time.

It is important that organizations understand their core competencies. Too many organizations give in to the temptation to pursue business that is outside the realm of their core competencies rather than finding new marketers for their core products and services. This approach typically leads to quality and productivity problems that invariably undermine the value of the organization's new products and services.

Perhaps the best way to understand what happens when companies decide to operate outside the realm of their core competencies is to consider a sports analogy. There have been several examples in which professional athletes whose core competencies were in one sport attempted to cross over and play another sport. Two that come immediately to mind are Michael Jordan, one of the greatest basketball players in the history of the National Basketball Association, and Dion Sanders, a Hall of Fame–caliber defensive back in football. Both of these gifted athletes left their core competencies relating to basketball and football behind and attempted to play professional baseball.

It was not that these two high-profile athletes were not good at baseball—they were; but they were just not good enough to compete with other professionals whose core competencies were in baseball. As a result, both had a measure of success playing baseball, but neither had a stellar career. They simply could not perform in this new "market" at the world-class level that they could in their core sports. This same type of thing often happens to companies that try to operate outside the realm of their core competencies.

COMPONENTS OF STRATEGIC MANAGEMENT

Strategic management consists of two interrelated activities: (a) strategic planning and (b) strategic execution. These two primary components of strategic management are described in the following sections.

Strategic Planning

Strategic planning is the process by which an organization answers such questions as the following: Who are we? Where are we going? How will we get there? What do we hope to accomplish? What are our strengths and weaknesses? What are the opportunities and threats in our business environment? Strategic planning involves developing a written plan that has the following components: an organizational vision; an organizational mission; guiding principles; broad strategic objectives; and specific tactics, projects, and activities for achieving the broad objectives. Specific tactics, projects, and activities are often referred to as the "action plan."

Strategic Execution

Strategic execution involves implementing strategies set forth in strategic planning, monitoring progress toward their achievement, and adjusting the plans and strategies as necessary. Strategic execution is implementation that achieves maximum efficiency and effectiveness.

Monitoring involves constantly checking actual performance against performance benchmarks. Strategic monitoring answers such questions as these: Are we achieving our objectives? This is the *effectiveness* question. Are we performing as well as we need to perform? This is the *efficiency* question. Adjusting as necessary involves making corrections when the specific strategies or tactics adopted are not producing the desired results. Such adjustments can involve a minor tweaking of plans, a search for ways to overcome unexpected barriers that are encountered, or even the adoption of a whole new set of specific strategies.

STRATEGIC PLANNING OVERVIEW

Strategic planning, as described previously, is the process whereby organizations develop a vision, a mission, guiding principles, broad objectives, and specific strategies for achieving the broad objectives. Before even beginning the planning process, an organization should conduct a SWOT analysis. SWOT is the acronym for *strengths, weaknesses, opportunities,* and *threats*. A SWOT analysis answers the following

SWOT Analysis (Environmental Assessment)	Step 1
Develop the Vision	Step 2
Develop the Mission	Step 3
Develop the Guiding Principles	Step 4
Develop the Broad Strategic Objectives	Step 5
Develop the Specific Tactics (Action Plan)	Step 6

FIGURE 3–1 The Strategic Planning Process

questions: What are this organization's strengths? What are this organization's weaknesses? What opportunities exist in this organization's business environment? What threats exist in this organization's business environment?

The steps in the strategic planning process (Figure 3–1) should be completed in this particular order because each successive step grows out of the preceding one. The SWOT analysis provides a body of knowledge that is needed to undertake strategic planning. The mission grows out of and supports the vision. The guiding principles, which represent the organization's value system, guide the organization's behavior as it pursues its mission. The broad objectives grow out of the mission and translate it into measurable terms. Specific strategies tie directly to the broad objectives. Typically, there will be two to five tactical goals for each objective, but this is a general guideline, not a hard and fast rule.

CREATIVE THINKING IN STRATEGIC PLANNING

In the age of global competition, it is even more important than ever to think creatively when developing strategic plans. Should we attempt to find new markets that take advantage of our core competencies? Should we undertake an acquisition that will give our organization a new and additional core competency? Should we adopt a local, regional, or global strategy? Part of the purpose of strategic planning is to ferret out things that are done the same way year after year simply because that is always what the organization has done or how it has done it.

In a speech given in Sandestin, Florida, author and business consultant Robert Kriegel labeled as "sacred cows" these things that organizations keep doing simply because they have always done them.[1] This concept is the basis for his book *Sacred Cows Make the Best Burgers.* According to Kriegel, organizations should make a point of periodically identifying and eliminating costly sacred cows because they make it difficult to provide superior value. An excellent time to identify sacred cows, new approaches, and better ways to be more competitive is during the strategic planning process. But doing this requires creative thinking.

Following are some strategies for promoting creative thinking as part of the strategic planning process: (1) begin by telling a couple of stories about creative ideas that changed everything for a few selected organizations (e.g., Nokia's idea to produce digital cellular telephones when Motorola had a lock on the market for analog phones), (2) challenge participants to see who can suggest the most ridiculous idea and record all ideas (this will break the ice and remove inhibitions that might otherwise cause participants to think their ideas have no merit), (3) do not allow naysayers to put down or criticize the ideas of others or use the "that's already been tried" tactic, (4) challenge all existing approaches (they might be sacred cows), and (5) allow time for ideas to germinate—do not try to complete the planning process too quickly.

CONDUCTING THE SWOT ANALYSIS

The rationale for conducting a SWOT analysis before proceeding with the development of the strategic plan is that the organization's plan should produce a good fit between its internal situation and its external situation. An organization's internal situation is defined by its strengths and weaknesses. An organization's external situation is defined by the opportunities and threats that exist in its business environment. The strategic plan should be designed in such a way that it exploits an organization's strengths and opportunities while simultaneously overcoming, accommodating, or circumventing weaknesses and threats.

Identifying Organizational Strengths

An organizational strength is any characteristic or capability that gives the organization a competitive advantage. The following are examples of common organizational strengths:

- Financial strength
- Good reputation in the marketplace
- Strategic focus
- High-quality products and services
- Proprietary products and services
- Cost leadership
- Strong management team
- Efficient technological processes

- Talented workforce
- Faster time to market

These are just some of the strengths an individual organization may have; many others are possible. The key is accurately defining an organization's strengths before beginning to develop its strategic plan.

Identifying Organizational Weaknesses

An organizational weakness is any characteristic or capability that puts the organization at a competitive disadvantage. These are examples of common organizational weaknesses:

- Strategic confusion or lack of direction
- Obsolete facilities
- Obsolete processes
- Weak management team
- Insufficient skills or capabilities in the workforce
- Poorly defined operating procedures
- Too narrow a product line
- Products with decreasing demand
- Too diverse a product line
- Poor image in the marketplace
- Weak distribution system
- Weak financial position
- High unit costs compared with those of competitors
- Poor quality in products and services

These are just a few of many weaknesses an organization may have. The main thing is to identify an organization's weaknesses accurately before undertaking the strategic planning process.

Identifying External Opportunities

External opportunities are opportunities in the organization's business environment that represent potential avenues to grow and gain a sustainable competitive advantage. The following are examples of external opportunities that organizations may have:

- Availability of new customers
- Expanding market for existing or potential or planned products
- Ability to diversify into related products and services
- Removal of barriers that inhibit growth
- Failures of competitors
- New online technologies that enhance productivity or quality

Of course, other external opportunities might be available to an organization besides these. You need to identify all such opportunities accurately before undertaking the strategic planning process.

Identifying External Threats

An external threat is a phenomenon in an organization's business environment that has the potential to put the organization at a competitive disadvantage. Such external threats might include the following:

- Entry of lower-cost competitors
- Entry of higher-quality competitors
- Increased sales of substitute products and services
- Significant slowdown in market growth
- Introduction of costly new regulatory requirements
- Poor supplier relations
- Changing tastes and habits of consumers
- Potentially damaging demographic changes

Many other external threats might confront an organization. Accurately identifying every potential external threat before you begin the strategic planning process is a must.

DEVELOPING THE VISION

An organization's guiding force, the dream of what it wants to become, and its reason for being should be apparent in its vision. A vision is like a beacon in the distance toward which the organization is always moving. Everything about the organization—its structure, policies, procedures, and allocation of resources—should support the realization of the vision.

In an organization with a clear vision, it is relatively easy to stay appropriately focused. If a policy does not support the vision, why have it? If a procedure does not support the vision, why adopt it? If an expenditure does not support the vision, why make it? If a position or even a department does not support the vision, why keep it? An organization's vision must be established and articulated by executive management and understood by all employees. The first step in articulating an organizational vision is writing it down. This is called the *vision statement.*

Writing the Vision Statement

A well-written vision statement, regardless of the type of organization, has the following characteristics (Figure 3–2). It

- Is easily understood by all stakeholders
- Is briefly stated, yet clear and comprehensive in meaning
- Is challenging, yet attainable
- Is lofty, yet tangible
- Is capable of stirring excitement for all stakeholders
- Is capable of creating unity of purpose among all stakeholders
- Is not concerned with numbers
- Sets the tone for employees

From these characteristics, it can be seen that crafting a worthwhile vision statement is a challenging undertaking.

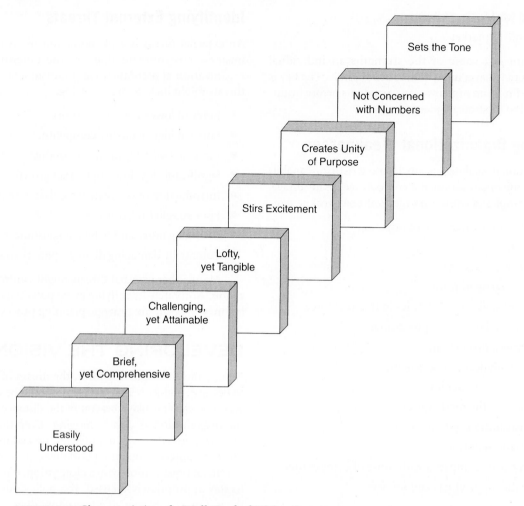

FIGURE 3–2 Characteristics of a Well-Crafted Vision Statement

Following are three vision statements—two for service providers and one for a manufacturer—that satisfy the criteria set forth in Figure 3–2.

- The Institute for Corporate Competitiveness (ICC) will be recognized by its customers as the provider of choice for organizational development products that are the best in the world.
- Business Express Airlines (BEA) will be recognized by customers as the premier air carrier in the United States for business travelers.
- Pendleton Manufacturing Company will be the leading producer in the United States of fireproof storage cabinets.

These vision statements illustrate the practical application of the criteria set forth in Figure 3–2. Are these statements easily understood? Yes. Any stakeholder could read the vision statements and understand the dreams of the organizations they represent. Are they briefly stated, yet clear and comprehensive in meaning? Yes. Each of the statements consists of one sentence, but the sentence in each case clearly and comprehensively conveys the intended message. Are these vision statements challenging, yet attainable? Yes.

Each vision presents its respective organization with the challenge of being the best in a clearly defined market and a clearly defined geographic area. Being the best in the United States or in the world is a difficult challenge in any field, but it is an attainable challenge. It can be done. Are these visions lofty, yet tangible? Yes. Trying to be the best is a lofty challenge, but still it is achievable and therefore tangible. Pick a field, and some organization is going to be the best in that field. It could be this organization. Are these visions capable of stirring excitement among stakeholders? Yes. Trying to be the best in any endeavor is an exciting undertaking, the kind in which people want to take part.

Are these visions capable of creating unity of purpose? Yes. All three give stakeholders a common rallying cry. This happens when a sports team sets its sights on the championship. The players, coaches, fans, and management all rally around the vision, pulling together as one in an attempt to achieve it. Do these statements concern themselves with numbers? No. Numbers are left for later in the strategic planning process. Do these visions set the tone for employees? Yes. Clearly, the organizations in question are going somewhere, and employees are expected to do their part to ensure that the organizations get there expeditiously.

DEVELOPING THE MISSION

We have just seen that the vision statement describes what an organization would like to be. It's a dream, but it's not "pie in the sky." The vision represents a dream that can come true. The mission takes the next step and describes *who* the organization is, *what* it does, and *where* it is going. Figure 3–3 contains the mission statements for the three organizations introduced in the previous section.

Assess these mission statements using the three *W's*—*who, what,* and *where*—as the criteria. In the first example, ICC describes *who* it is as follows: "a business-development company dedicated to helping organizations continually improve their ability to compete in the global marketplace." This description of who ICC is also describes who its customers are. Regardless of whether both "who's" can be explained in one sentence, both should be explained in the mission. *What* ICC does is described as follows: "provides high-quality, competitiveness-enhancing products and services." From this statement, an outsider with no knowledge of ICC could determine what the company does. *Where* ICC is going is described as reaching "an ever-increasing number of organizations in the United States." Clearly, ICC wants to grow as much as possible within the geographic boundaries of the United States.

In the second example, BEA describes *who* it is as a "domestic air carrier dedicated to providing business travelers with air transportation." This simple statement describes both who BEA is and who its customers are. BEA is a domestic air carrier, and its customers are business travelers. *What* BEA does is described as "providing business travelers with air transportation that exceeds their expectations." *Where* BEA is going can be seen in the following portion of the mission statement: "BEA provides air carrier service to and from a steadily increasing number of major hub airports in the United States." Like ICC, BEA wants to grow continually in the United States.

In the third example, Pendleton Manufacturing describes *who* it is as a "hazardous materials storage company dedicated to making your work environment safe

and healthy." From this statement, one can easily discern who Pendleton Manufacturing and its customers are. Any company that either produces hazardous waste or uses toxic materials is a potential customer. *What* Pendleton Manufacturing does is described as follows: "produces high-quality fireproof cabinets for safely storing toxic substances and hazardous materials." *Where* Pendleton Manufacturing is going can be seen in that part of the final sentence of the mission statement that says it wants to serve "an ever-broadening market in the United States."

All three of the companies in these examples want to grow continually but only in domestic markets. No interest is expressed in international markets. This is a major strategic decision that will determine the types of actions taken to achieve their respective missions.

In developing the mission statement for any organization, one should apply the following rules of thumb:

- Describe the *who, what,* and *where* of the organization, making sure the *who* component describes the organization and its customers.
- Be brief, yet comprehensive. Typically, one paragraph should be sufficient to describe an organization's mission.
- Choose wording that is simple, easy to understand, and descriptive.
- Avoid *how* statements. How the mission will be accomplished is described in the "Strategies" section of the strategic plan.

- The Institute for Corporate Competitiveness (ICC) is a business-development company dedicated to helping organizations continually improve their ability to compete in the global marketplace. To this end, ICC provides high-quality, competitiveness-enhancing products and services to an ever-increasing number of organizations in the United States.
- Business Express Airlines (BEA) is a domestic air carrier dedicated to providing business travelers with air transportation that exceeds their expectations in terms of cost, convenience, service, and dependability. To this end, BEA provides air carrier service to and from a steadily increasing number of major hub airports in the United States.
- Pendleton Manufacturing Company is a hazardous materials storage company dedicated to making your work environment safe and healthy. To this end, Pendleton produces high-quality fireproof cabinets for safely storing toxic substances and hazardous materials for an ever-broadening market in the United States.

FIGURE 3–3 Sample Mission Statements

DEVELOPING THE GUIDING PRINCIPLES

An organization's guiding principles establish the framework within which it will pursue its mission. Each guiding principle encompasses an important organizational value. Together, all of the guiding principles represent the organization's value system—the foundation of its corporate culture.

Freedom through control might be one such guiding principle. It is one of the cornerstones of total quality. It is a concept that applies at all levels, from line employees through executive managers. It means that once parameters have been established for a given job, level, or work unit, all employees to which the parameters apply are free to operate innovatively within them. In fact, they are encouraged to be innovative and creative within established parameters. This means that as long as they observe applicable controls, employees are free to apply their knowledge, experience, and judgment in finding ways to do the job better. Once a method is established that is better than the existing one, that new procedure should become the standard throughout the organization.

An organization's guiding principles establish the parameters within which it is free to pursue its mission. These principles might be written as follows:

- XYZ Company will uphold the highest ethical standards in all of its operations.
- At XYZ Company, customer satisfaction is the highest priority.
- XYZ Company will make every effort to deliver the highest quality products and services in the business.
- At XYZ Company, all stakeholders (customers, suppliers, and employees) will be treated as partners.
- At XYZ Company, employee input will be actively sought, carefully considered, and strategically used.
- At XYZ Company, continual improvement of products, processes, and people will be the norm.
- XYZ Company will provide employees with a safe and healthy work environment that is conducive to consistent peak performance.
- XYZ Company will be a good corporate neighbor in all communities where its facilities are located.
- XYZ Company will take all appropriate steps to protect the environment.

From this list of guiding principles, the corporate values of XYZ Company can be discerned. This company places a high priority on ethics, customer satisfaction, quality, stakeholder partnerships, employee input, continual improvement, a safe and healthy work environment, consistent peak performance, corporate citizenship, and environmental protection.

With these values clearly stated as the organization's guiding principles, employees know the parameters within which they must operate. When ethical dilemmas arise, as they inevitably will in business, employees know they are expected to do the right thing. If safety or health hazards are identified in the workplace, eliminating them will be a top priority. If employees spend their own time participating in community activities, they know it will reflect positively in their performance appraisals because XYZ Company values corporate citizenship.

Developing guiding principles is the responsibility of an organization's executive management team. However, the recommended approach in a total quality organization is for executive managers to solicit input from all levels before finalizing the guiding principles.

DEVELOPING BROAD STRATEGIC OBJECTIVES

Broad strategic objectives translate an organization's vision and mission into measurable terms. They represent actual targets the organization aims at and will expend energy and resources trying to achieve. Broad objectives are more specific than the mission, but they are still broad. They still fall into the realm of *what* rather than *how*. *What* must the organization do to achieve the vision? The *how* aspects of strategic planning come in the next step: developing specific tactics, projects, and activities for accomplishing broad objectives. As shown in Figure 3–4, well-written and broad organizational objectives

- Are stated broadly enough that they don't have to be continually rewritten
- Are stated specifically enough that they are measurable but not in terms of numbers
- Are each focused on a single issue or desired outcome
- Are tied directly to the organization's vision and mission
- Are all in accordance with the organization's guiding principles
- Clearly show what the organization wants to accomplish

In addition to having these characteristics, broad objectives apply to the overall organization, not to individual departments within the organization. In developing its broad objectives, an organization should begin with its vision and mission. A point to keep in mind is that broad strategic objectives should be written in such a way that their accomplishment will give the organization a sustainable competitive advantage in the marketplace. What follows is an organizational vision presented earlier as an example and its corresponding broad objectives:

The Institute for Corporate Competitiveness will be recognized by its customers as the provider of choice for organizational development products that are the best in the world.

Following are the broad objectives that translate this vision into measurable terms:

1. To produce organizational development products of world-class quality that are improved continually

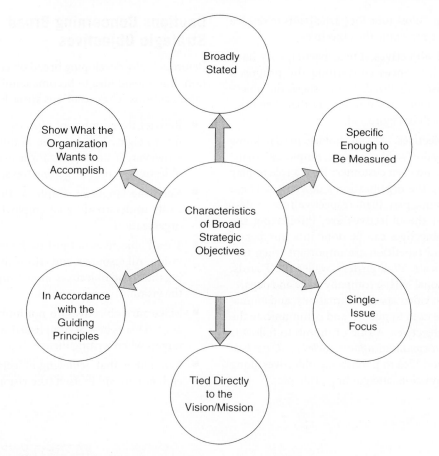

FIGURE 3–4 Characteristics of Well-Written Broad Strategic Objectives

2. To provide organizational development services of world-class quality that are improved continually

3. To establish and maintain a world-class workforce at all levels of the organization

4. To continually increase the organization's market share for its existing products and services

5. To continually introduce new products and services to meet emerging needs in the organizational development market

Five Steps for Writing Broad Strategic Objectives

In actually writing broad objectives for an organization, the following five steps should be observed (Figure 3–5):

1. **Assemble input.** Circulate the mission widely throughout the organization, and ask for input concerning objectives. Ask all stakeholders to answer the following question: "What do we have to accomplish as an organization in order to fulfill our mission?" Assemble all input received, summarize it, and prepare it for further review.

2. **Find the optimum input.** Analyze the assembled input, at the same time judging how well individuals' suggestions support the organization's vision and mission.

Discard those suggestions that are too narrow or that do not support the vision and mission.

3. **Resolve differences.** Proposed objectives that remain on the list after step 2 should be discussed in greater

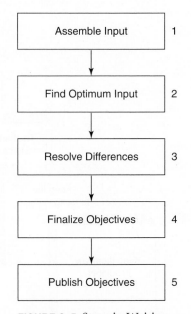

FIGURE 3–5 Steps in Writing Broad Strategic Objectives

depth in this step. Allow time for participants to resolve their differences concerning the objectives.

4. **Select the final objectives.** Once participants have resolved their differences concerning the proposed objectives, the list is finalized. In this stage, the objectives are rewritten and edited to ensure that they meet the criteria set forth in Figure 3–4.

5. **Publicize the objectives.** All stakeholders need to know what the organization's objectives are. Employees, managers, suppliers, and even customers have a role to play in accomplishing the organization's objectives. These stakeholders cannot play their respective roles unless they know what the objectives are. Publicizing the organization's objectives can be done in a number of ways. Variety and repetition are important when trying to communicate. Wall posters, wallet-sized cards, newsletters, personal letters, company-wide and departmental meetings, videotaped presentations, and annual reports can all be used to publish and communicate the organization's objectives. A rule of thumb to follow is *the more different communication vehicles used, the better.* It's also a good idea to publish the objectives along with the vision, mission, and guiding principles.

Cautions Concerning Broad Strategic Objectives

Before actually developing broad objectives for an organization, it is a good idea to become familiar with several applicable cautions. These cautions are as follows (Figure 3–6):

- Restrict the number of objectives to just a few—from five to eight. This is a rule of thumb, not an absolute. However, if an organization needs more than eight objectives, it may be getting too specific.

- Keep the language simple so that the objectives are easily understood by all employees at all levels of the organization.

- Tie all objectives not just to the mission but also to the vision. All resources and efforts directed toward achieving the broad objectives should support the mission and the vision.

- Make sure objectives do not limit or restrict performance. This is best accomplished by avoiding numerical targets when writing them.

- Remember that achieving objectives is a means to an end, not an end in itself (the vision is the end).

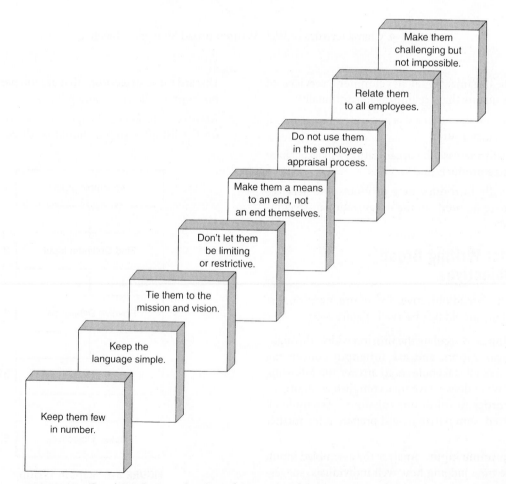

FIGURE 3–6 Cautions Concerning Broad Strategic Objectives

- Do not use broad objectives in the employee appraisal process. The only aspect of the overall strategic plan that might be used in the employee appraisal process is the specific-tactics component. This is because only the specific tactics in the strategic plan are assigned to specific teams or individuals and given specific time frames within which they should be completed. Broad objectives, on the other hand, are everyone's responsibility.

- Relate broad objectives to all employees. This means there should be objectives covering the entire organization. Employees should be able to see that their work supports one or more of the broad objectives.

- Make broad objectives challenging but not impossible. Good objectives will challenge an organization without being unrealistic.

DEVELOPING SPECIFIC TACTICS (ACTION PLAN)

The action plan consists of specific tactics that are well-defined, finite projects and activities undertaken for the purpose of accomplishing an organization's broad strategic objectives. Tactics have the following characteristics (Figure 3–7). They provide the "how" for achieving broad strategic objectives and

- Are specific in nature
- Are measurable
- Can be quantifiable
- Can be accomplished within a specified time frame
- Can be assigned to a specific individual or group
- Are tied directly to a broad objective

Drafting the Individual Tactics

In drafting tactics, an organization should begin with its broad strategic objectives. Each objective will have at least one, but typically three or four, tactics accompanying it. Figure 3–8 is a tool that can be used for drafting tactics. Notice that it contains the broad strategic objective to which the tactics relate. This is not necessarily a complete list of tactics for this objective; these are just examples of tactics that might be developed in support of the objective. The nature of tactics is such that they are accomplished and then replaced by new tactics relating to the relevant objective.

Evaluate the five tactics in Figure 3–8 by applying the criteria shown in Figure 3–7. Are these tactics specific in nature? Yes. They are finite and limited in scope. Are the tactics measurable? Yes. In each case, the organization can easily determine whether each activity was completed within the specified time frame. Are the tactics quantifiable? Only tangentially, in that the organization can determine whether *all* employees received the desired service within the specified time frame. It is desirable but not necessary for all tactics to be quantifiable. Can the tactics be accomplished within a specified time frame? Yes. A time frame is specified for the

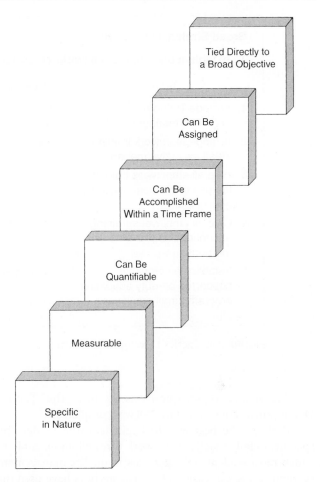

FIGURE 3–7 Characteristics of Specific Tactics

completion of each tactic. Can the tactics be assigned to a specific individual or group? Yes. In each case, a responsible party is named by position. Do the tactics tie directly to a specific broad objective? Yes. The related objective is shown on the form in the example. All of the tactics meet the applicable criteria.

Making Tactics Detailed and Specific

One of the most difficult aspects of developing the action plan component of a strategic plan is making tactics sufficiently detailed and specific. There is a tendency to stop short of the explicitness needed and write tactics that, although more detailed than the broad strategic objective to which they correspond, are still not as specific as they should be. Developing specific, detailed tactics is a process that takes practice. One of the best ways to learn how to develop well-written tactics is to ask the following three questions about the broad strategic objective to which the tactics relate:

1. What are the individual, specific activities that will have to be completed in order to achieve this broad strategic objective?

2. Who should be responsible for completing each individual activity identified?

3. By what date must each activity be completed?

Broad Strategic Objective

To establish and maintain a world-class workforce at all levels of the organization.

Tactic	Responsible Individual/Unit	Time Frame/Deadline
1. Arrange TQ training for all executive managers.	CEO	Completed by January 15
2. Arrange teamwork training for all executive managers.	CEO	Completed by January 30
3. Give all employees training in the use of problem-solving/ quality tools.	Department Managers	January 15–February 20
4. Give all employees training in continual improvement methods.	Department Managers	March 15–May 15
5. Establish a company-supported off-duty education program for all employees.	Human Resources Department	In place by February 28

FIGURE 3–8 Tactics Development Form

Answering these questions is how the Tactics Development Form in Figure 3–8 was completed.

Perhaps the best way to begin learning to develop specific, detailed tactics is to work through an example to which most students taking a class in quality management or engineering can easily relate. The authors have used the following example numerous times in college classes on quality management or engineering. First, suppose that you are a college student who wants to have a successful career in the field of quality. Assume that the vision for your career is as follows:

To have a long and successful career as a quality manager or engineer.

Now suppose that in support of this career vision you adopt the following mission statement pertaining to your college preparation:

I am an ambitious person who would like to begin a career in quality management or engineering and rise to the top of my profession. Consequently, my current mission is to complete a college degree in a field directly related to quality management or engineering.

You have both a vision and a mission. Now suppose that you develop your broad strategic objectives and that one of them reads as follows:

To successfully complete a course in quality management or engineering as part of my college studies.

Since you are already enrolled in college, we can skip the processes of admissions and academic advising. Let's assume you are at the point of wanting to enroll in the course referred to in your broad strategic objective (quality management or

QUALITY CASE ▼

The HON Company: Quality in the Manufacture of Office Furniture

The HON Company is based in Muscatine, Iowa, with manufacturing plants, dealers, and retailers located strategically throughout the United States. The company's products include workstations, desks, chairs, tables, and storage units—all for office environments. The HON Company was founded in 1944 as the Home-O-Nize Company. The original intent of its founders was to provide employment for veterans returning from service in the military during World War II.

The company originally manufactured kitchen cabinets but quickly transitioned into making aluminum gas bottle hoods. From aluminum gas bottles the company transitioned into a variety of products until it began manufacturing recipe file boxes. The file boxes led to the development of office furniture and that is where things have stood since 1967 when the office products division of Home-O-Nize Company became the HON Company.

The company's South Gate Plant in South Gate, California, was awarded the Shingo Prize for Excellence in Manufacturing for exemplifying the principles of total quality management. The Shingo award cited the following achievements by the HON Company's South Gate Plant: (1) lowest rate of customer complaints for manufacturing issues among all of the company's plants for 8 consecutive years, (2) a 99.6 on-time shipping rate while simultaneously reducing inventory, (3) emissions reduction of 79% (surpassing the high standards that apply to businesses in the Los Angeles area), and (4) a member/owner culture in which 1,935 employees' suggestions were implemented in just 1 year. The South Gate was also cited for being a good corporate neighbor. Its personnel contributed 2,800 hours of community service in a period of 3 years.

Source: www.reliableplant.com/Articles/Print/4697.

engineering). What are the specific and detailed activities you will have to complete? For the purpose of this exercise, assume that all of the activities will be your responsibility and that deciding on completion dates is not an issue. Focus all of your attention on identifying the specific activities that will be necessary in order to complete a course in quality management or engineering. What follows is a list developed by students in a class taught by one of the authors:

1. Go to the counseling and advising office and make sure that the course in question is part of your approved program of study.

2. Go to the registrar's office and register for the course.

3. Go to the business office and pay the tuition and fees for the course.

4. Go to the bookstore and purchase the required textbook and other related materials.

5. Begin attending classes and participate fully in all class discussions.

6. Complete all assignments for the course.

7. Prepare for all tests and examinations required for the course.

8. Complete all tests and examinations for the course with passing grades.

9. Create a permanent file of your course materials and text to use for reference once you begin your first job in quality management or engineering.

This is an adequately specific and detailed list. However, upon close scrutiny you will find that each of the activities could have been broken down even further and made even more specific. Deciding how specific to be when developing tactics requires practice and experience. Until you become well-versed in the art and science of developing action plans, it is better to err on the side of more specificity and more detail.

EXECUTING THE STRATEGIC PLAN

The old saying "The best-laid plans of mice and men often go astray" is, unfortunately, all too true. Many organizations devote time, energy, and money to developing comprehensive, thorough, detailed plans, only to see them come apart at the seams shortly after they begin to be executed. Execution is a critical component of strategic management, but for some reason, it rarely receives the attention it deserves. Even the best plan will do no good until it is effectively executed. Consequently, it is important to devote as much energy to execution as to developing the plan.

Picture the following scenario. A family plans a vacation to a national park. The parents envision a relaxing, fun-filled 2 weeks of camping, hiking, swimming, and biking. Their mission (that of the parents) is to get away together and share some quality time as a family. Certain guiding principles concerning behavior, spending, and work sharing are established by the parents. They also set up some broad objectives concerning the various activities the family wants to pursue. Wisely, the parents involve the children in this step. Also working with the children, the parents draft strategies for accomplishing their objectives.

The family had an excellent plan for an enjoyable vacation, but as soon as the plan went into execution, the problems began:

- Disagreements among the children concerning destinations and activities

- Problems when the children did not know how to perform some of their assigned duties (e.g., setting up the tent at the campsite, building a proper campfire, monitoring daily gas mileage while the parents drove)

- Attitude problems concerning various aspects of the trip, including what distance to cover daily, how many rest stops to make, and where to eat while driving to the eventual destination

As a result of these difficulties, the planned vacation of shared family fun and relaxation turned into an emotionally draining 2 weeks of stress, anger, and frustration. The family's problems were the results of faulty execution of the vacation plan. The parents in this example failed to apply the following steps, all of which are critical to successful execution:

- **Communicate.** Make sure all stakeholders understand the plan and where they fit into it.

- **Build capabilities.** Make sure all stakeholders have the skills needed to carry out their assignments and responsibilities in the plan.

- **Establish strategy-supportive stimuli.** People in the workplace respond to stimuli. When trying to execute a plan, it is important to ensure that strategy-supportive stimuli are in place. Typically, in a work setting the most effective stimuli are reward and recognition incentives. It is not uncommon to find that an organization's strategic plan expects people to move in one direction, while its incentives encourage them to move in another.

- **Eliminate administrative barriers.** Every organization establishes administrative procedures for accomplishing its day-to-day work. If executing a new strategy changes the intended direction of the organization, administrative procedures may need to be changed correspondingly. A mistake commonly made by organizations attempting to execute a plan is leaving outdated administrative procedures in place. Administrative procedures put in place when the organization was moving in one direction can become inhibitors when the organization decides to move in another direction.

- **Identify advocates and resisters.** In any organization, there will be advocates and resisters when it comes to executing the strategic plan. This is natural and should be expected. As the plan unfolds, if it is successful, resisters will become advocates. If it fails, advocates will try to distance themselves from the plan, and resisters will say, "I told you so." This is just human nature and should be expected. Consequently, it is important to give the plan the best possible chance of succeeding. One way to do this is to assign all initial activities to advocates. Giving initial assignments to resisters when executing a new strategic plan is likely to ensure failure of the plan. Eventually, all employees must play a role in executing the strategic plan, but in the critical early stages, stick with advocates and avoid resisters.

■ **Exercise strategic leadership.** It is important that managers at all levels set a positive example by (a) showing that they believe in the strategic plan, (b) ensuring that all decisions are based on the action that best supports the strategic plan, and (c) allocating resources based on priorities established in the strategic plan.

■ **Be flexible and improvise.** Plans, when they are developed, are based on assumptions that may not be accurate. They are also based on a presumed set of circumstances, circumstances that, even if they were accurate when the plan was developed, might change before the plan is executed. This is why strategic plans must be viewed as a set of flexible guidelines rather than a hard-and-fast road map from which it is impossible to deviate. Every traveler knows there will be detours on even the best planned trip. Managers who want to make their organizations competitive must be willing to improvise when necessary.

Teachers of grades K–12 used to learn how to develop lesson plans. They were taught by seminar leaders and college professors to plan their daily lessons right down to the minute, with each activity assigned a specific amount of time. Of course, the wiser, more experienced teachers were able to predict the outcome of this approach, but sometimes it is best to let reality make your point for you. As teachers attempted to hold rigidly to schedules built into their plans, they found themselves falling further and further behind as problems cropped up that they had not foreseen when developing their lesson plans.

Before long, lesson plans were scrapped and replaced by planned lessons. The difference between a lesson plan and a planned lesson can be summed up in one word: *flexibility*. Planned lessons give teachers a general direction, some expected outcomes, and loose guidelines on how to get where they are going. They contain no rigid time constraints but, more important, give teachers the flexibility to change directions and pursue a whole new set of activities if an opportunity for learning presents itself.

This example holds a lesson for managers who develop and execute strategic plans: be flexible. The assumptions on which the plan was built might not be accurate. The circumstances in which the plan was supposed to be implemented might change. Planning is necessary so that resources can be properly allocated and so that employees on whom the organization depends for progress can get a better picture of where the organization is trying to go. But if somebody moves the target, don't continue to shoot at the spot where it used to be.

Organizations should plan thoroughly and carefully, based on the most accurate assumptions possible at a given point in time. However, if upon implementing the plan it becomes obvious that the assumptions are not valid or that circumstances have changed, organizations should not rigidly adhere to steps that no longer make sense. If the plan, or any part of it, is no longer relevant, improvise and move on.

■ **Monitor and adjust as needed.** Developing and executing a strategic plan is an example of the *plan–do–check–adjust* cycle in action. The *plan* component of the cycle involves developing the strategic plan. The *do* component is the execution phase. The *check–adjust* components involve monitoring progress toward completion of specific strategies and making the necessary adjustments when roadblocks are encountered. Will it take longer than you thought to complete a project or activity? Adjust the time frame. Have unexpected barriers been encountered? Decide what needs to be done to overcome the barriers, and do it. Did you complete the project only to find it didn't yield the expected results? Develop a substitute tactic and try again.

STRATEGIC PLANNING IN ACTION: A "REAL-WORLD" CASE

This section guides the reader through the strategic planning process undertaken by a company that contracted with the authors to facilitate it. The process involved the company's executive management team and took place over a 3-day period at an off-site location away from the company's facility. The strategic planning process always varies from organization to organization in specific details. However, this particular company was selected as an example because the process it underwent is representative of what most companies go through in developing a comprehensive strategic plan. This case should help the reader see how the various components of the strategic plan fit together as well as how each respective component is actually developed.

Developing a Strategic Plan: Delcron Manufacturing Company

Delcron Manufacturing Company (DMC) started as a small, minority-owned Department of Defense contractor. When the company was classified as an "8A" firm, it became eligible for government set-asides. Set-asides under the government's 8A program are contracts awarded outside of the bidding process to minority-owned firms. The idea is to give such firms an opportunity to gain a foothold in business while learning how to compete without the set-asides. DMC entered this arena as a manufacturer of low-voltage power supplies for military aircraft. Its 8A status lasted for 5 years. During this time, DMC grew from a small shop in a garage to a company that employed almost 500 people.

When the company was just over a year from having to make the transition from 8A status to the competitive marketplace, its executive management team decided the company needed a strategic plan. For several years, these executives had been so busy establishing the company and helping it grow that they had given little thought to what would happen to DMC once it graduated from the 8A program. Would the company be able to compete successfully in the open marketplace? Should it attempt to diversify into other markets? Should the executives simply sell the company and move on to other endeavors? These questions had begun to weigh heavily on the minds of the DMC executives when the CEO suggested they hire a strategic planning consultant, go through the process, and see what transpires. The DMC executives hired the authors and went through the strategic planning process. The remainder of this section documents the process and its outcomes.

Overview of the Process

The authors set up the strategic planning process in the conference center of a resort about 75 miles from DMC's facility. The idea, as they explained it to the company's executives, was to conduct the strategic planning process at a location that would guarantee both privacy and focus. No cellular telephones or visits to the office or home were allowed. In addition, family members were not included. The authors explained that in order to come away with an acceptable draft of a strategic plan, the executives would need 3 entire days of uninterrupted, fully focused work. The group would be given a morning and afternoon break each day to make telephone calls and check e-mail messages. Beyond that, their administrative assistants and family members knew how to reach them in the event of an emergency.

The first hour of the first day was devoted to learning the process and how it works. The authors explained all of the various components of the strategic plan (the SWOT analysis, vision, mission, guiding principles, and broad strategic goals). This first 3-day session would conclude with the development of broad strategic goals. Another session would be scheduled during which the executives would develop the action plan component. The action plan session would involve a broader group that, in addition to the executive management team, would include other management and supervisory personnel. The session would be conducted

---

QUALITY TIP ▼

Importance of Executing Strategic Plans

Good strategic planning is essential if an organization is going to outperform the competition. But just having a good strategic plan is not enough. The plan must be effectively executed. Execution is what separates the winners from the also-rans in the global arena. The work is really just starting once the plan has been developed. Effective execution is the key to outperforming the competition.

---

by the authors after each member of the company's executive management team had solicited input from all these employees directly reporting to him or her.

The SWOT Analysis

Prior to beginning the SWOT analysis, the authors placed four large flipcharts in the room. The flipcharts were labeled *strengths*, *weaknesses*, *opportunities*, and *threats*. Beginning with strengths, the authors led participants through a brainstorming session. Each time a strength, weakness, opportunity, or threat was identified by a participant and agreed on by the group, the authors recorded it on the corresponding flipchart. Every time a flipchart page would fill up, the authors tore it off and taped it to the wall so that participants had a visible record of their work.

Discussion was intense at times, and there were disagreements among participants. One executive would identify a weakness in another executive's area of responsibility, and arguments would ensue. It took the authors a while to convince the executives to drop their defenses and to be open and frank without getting their feelings hurt or being territorial. Another dynamic was that what one executive saw as a strength was perceived by another as a weakness. Once the authors worked through these and other issues that inevitably occur during strategic planning sessions, a cohesive group emerged and began to cooperate well as a team. The results of the SWOT analysis follow.

Strengths Participants identified and reached consensus on the following strengths: strong manufacturing capability, solid business contacts in the Department of Defense industry, a proven track record of excellent performance in completing contracts on time, low turnover rate with regard to critical employees, comparatively low labor rates (most employees of DMC are retired military personnel who view their salary as a second income), and an up-to-date facility equipped with modern technology.

Weaknesses Participants identified and reached consensus on the following weaknesses: no experience outside of the Department of Defense market, no marketing component, no experience being the lead contractor on a major project (all of DMC's work up to this point had been subcontracted to it by larger Department of Defense contractors, such as Boeing and Lockheed-Martin), no experience in the international marketplace, no design component (DMC had been a build-to-print operation up to this point), and no research and development component.

Opportunities Participants identified and reached consensus on the following opportunities: expansion into commercial aircraft markets, expansion into international commercial markets, expansion into foreign military markets (military aircraft of America's allies), and availability of a strong international marketing team that can work both commercial and military markets (one of DMC's potential competitors in the commercial marketplace had just been purchased by a larger company and its entire marketing team had been eliminated as part of the buyout).

Threats   Participants identified and reached consensus on the following threats: DMC's pending loss of its 8A status, potential cutbacks in the development of new military aircraft in the United States, a tight labor market that could inflate labor costs, and the potential for ever-increasing levels of competition from foreign and domestic sources.

Developing the Vision

Before developing a vision for DMC, the company's executive management team had to decide if there would even be a DMC after graduation from the 8A program. Going ahead with the company would mean risking the investment of both their time and their money in DMC. On the other hand, these executives could probably sell their shares in the company, walk away with a handsome profit, and find high-level positions with other firms in their respective fields or even help start another 8A company. After a lively discussion, the executives decided they had invested too much of their money and themselves in DMC to walk away from the company now. Consequently, they turned to the task of developing a post–8A vision for DMC.

The authors led participants through a lengthy discussion that revolved around the following questions (which came from the SWOT analysis): Should DMC stick with just domestic military markets or expand into the commercial marketplace, too? Should DMC consider pursuing contracts with foreign militaries? Should DMC pursue international commercial contracts? Should DMC stick with low-voltage power supplies as its principal product or diversify into other product lines? Should DMC add a design function or continue as just a build-to-print company? Should DMC add a research and development function to develop new product lines?

Answering these questions was the most difficult part of the strategic planning process for DMC's executives. How they answered these questions would determine everything else about the future of the company and, correspondingly, about their professional futures. After an intense discussion, participants decided that DMC would need to expand into both commercial and foreign markets, while retaining its Department of Defense base. They also agreed that the company's expertise is in the production of low-voltage power supplies. Consequently, they ruled out adding a research and development function, but they did decide to expand into design. The rationale of DMC's executives was that the company would always be at the mercy of other, larger contractors unless it could design power supplies in addition to just manufacturing them.

With these questions answered, the authors were able to lead participants through the process of developing a vision statement that would encompass their dreams for DMC. The vision statement developed reads as follows:

> Delcron Manufacturing Company will be an international leader in the production of low-voltage power supplies for aircraft.

Developing the Mission

The executives at DMC found that developing a vision answers many important questions. With the vision in place, developing a mission statement was not overly difficult; it was just a matter of following the criteria set forth by the authors for well-written mission statements. Most of the discussion focused on wording as opposed to concepts. The mission statement the participants finally decided on reads as follows:

> Delcron Manufacturing Company (DMC) is a design and manufacturing firm dedicated to providing high-quality products for the aircraft industry. To this end, DMC designs and manufactures low-voltage power supplies for military and commercial aircraft in the United States and abroad.

Developing Guiding Principles

The authors described "guiding principles" to participants as written statements that convey DMC's corporate values. They encouraged the company's executives to mentally put the following sentence before the guiding principles in order to better understand what they represent: "While pursuing our vision and mission, we will apply the following guiding principles in everyday operations and in all decisions made."

The authors asked participants to brainstorm important corporate values without concern, for the moment, about wording. Participants were encouraged to simply offer up value-laden terms (e.g., *ethics, quality, customer satisfaction*) that the authors recorded on flipcharts. Once the terms had all been listed, the authors asked participants to select the six to ten that were most critical. With the most important corporate values identified, participants worked with the authors to develop more explicit wording for each one. The guiding principles developed are as follows:

1. **Ethics.** All of DMC's employees and management personnel are expected to exemplify the highest ethical standards in doing their jobs.
2. **Customer delight.** In dealing with customers, DMC will go beyond customer satisfaction to achieve customer delight.
3. **Continual improvement.** Continually improving its products, processes, and people is a high priority for DMC.
4. **Quality.** DMC is committed to delivering the highest quality products possible on time, every time.
5. **Employee empowerment.** DMC is committed to seeking, valuing, and using employee input and feedback.
6. **Partners.** DMC is committed to treating its customers, suppliers, and employees as partners.

Developing Broad Strategic Goals

The final component of the first strategic planning session involved developing broad strategic goals. These goals had to represent actions that, if accomplished, would move the company ever closer to the full realization of its corporate vision. Before beginning development of the goals, the authors gave participants typed copies of the results of the SWOT analysis. They explained to the executives that the broad goals developed should all satisfy one or more of the following criteria: (1) exploit one or more of the organization's strengths, (2) correct one or more of the organization's weaknesses, (3) take advantage of one or more of the opportunities available to the organization, or (4) respond to one or more of the threats facing the organization. With this guidance given, participants developed the following broad strategic goals for DMC:

1. Expand the company's business base to include both military and commercial markets in the United States and abroad.

2. Strengthen all functional units in the company in the area of commercial products and markets.

3. Expand the company's core capabilities to include both design and manufacturing.

4. Fully achieve a Six Sigma quality level in manufacturing low-voltage power supplies.

5. Develop and implement a supplier certification program to create a reliable group of dependable, high-quality supplier partners.

6. Establish a comprehensive training program to maximize the capabilities of all employees at all levels in the company.

With the broad strategic objectives established, the "strategic" portion of the plan was completed. Developing an action plan for carrying out the strategic portion of the plan would be scheduled later, after DMC's executive management team had communicated the vision, mission, guiding principles, and broad strategic goals to all employees. The action planning session took place 2 months later, and DMC began implementation of the new strategic plan immediately thereafter. Just 2 years after DMC graduated from the 8A program, it had expanded from under 500 employees to almost 700, and its business base was growing steadily. The company now is well-established in both commercial and military markets in the United States and abroad. The plan developed during a 3-day, off-site session is working.

SUMMARY

1. Strategies that organizations can adopt to gain a sustainable competitive advantage are cost leadership, differentiation, and market-niche strategies.

2. Core competencies are things an organization does so well they can be viewed as providing a competitive advantage.

3. Strategies are approaches adopted by organizations to ensure successful performance in the marketplace.

4. Strategic management is management that bases all actions, activities, and decisions on what is most likely to ensure successful performance in the marketplace. The two major components of strategic management are strategic planning and strategic execution.

5. Part of strategic planning is thinking creatively to eliminate "sacred cows" that work against competitiveness.

6. Strategic planning is the process whereby organizations develop their vision, mission, guiding principles, broad objectives, and tactics for accomplishing the broad objectives.

7. An organization's vision is its guiding force, the dream of what it wants to become, and its reason for being.

8. An organization's mission describes *who* an organization is, *what* it does, and *where* it is going.

9. An organization's guiding principles establish the framework within which it will pursue its mission. Together, the guiding principles summarize an organization's value system, the things it believes are most important.

10. An organization's broad strategic objectives translate its mission into more specific terms that represent actual targets at which the organization aims. The objectives are more specific than the mission, but they are still broad.

11. Tactics are well-defined, finite projects and activities undertaken for the purpose of specific desired outcomes in support of the broad objectives.

12. Even the best strategic plan will serve no purpose unless it is effectively executed. To promote successful execution of strategies, organizations should undertake the following activities: communicate, build capabilities, establish strategy-supportive stimuli, eliminate administrative barriers, identify advocates and resisters, exercise strategic leadership, and monitor results and adjust as needed.

KEY TERMS AND CONCEPTS

Advocates
Broad strategic objectives
Core competencies and competitive advantage
Cost leadership strategies
Differentiation strategies
Guiding principles
Market-niche strategies
Mission

Plan–do–check–adjust cycle

Resisters

Specific strategies

Strategic execution

Strategic management

Strategic planning

Vision

FACTUAL REVIEW QUESTIONS

1. What is strategic management?

2. List the steps in the strategic planning process.

3. What is a core competency?

4. Explain why creative thinking is important in strategic planning and how to encourage it.

5. What is SWOT analysis?

6. Write a sample vision statement for a hypothetical organization.

7. Write a mission statement for the hypothetical organization in question 6.

8. Draft a set of guiding principles for the hypothetical organization in question 6.

9. Establish two or three broad objectives for the hypothetical organization in question 6.

10. Describe the steps you would apply in executing your strategic plan developed in questions 6 to 9.

CRITICAL THINKING ACTIVITY

Locked Out of the Process

Alex Parker is the quality director at CompuTech Inc. His is a middle-management position. CompuTech's senior executives have announced that they intend to hire a strategic planning consultant to develop a plan for the company. Planning will begin in about 2 months. It will take place in the conference center of a local resort and will involve only executive-level managers and the consultant.

Parker has several ideas he would like to propose. In addition, he wants to make sure that quality is treated as a strategic issue during the planning process. Unfortunately, Parker and his fellow middle managers have not been invited to participate. They are locked out of the process.

What do you think of CompuTech's approach to strategic planning? Would you change the process in any way? If so, how? If the process remains as it is, how can Parker get his ideas included?

ENDNOTE

1. Robert Kriegel, speech presented at a conference of business leaders at Sandestin, Florida, October 15, 2007.

QUALITY MANAGEMENT, ETHICS, AND CORPORATE SOCIAL RESPONSIBILITY

It is easier to fight for one's principles than to live up to them. —*Alfred Adler*

MAJOR TOPICS

- Definition and Overview of Ethics
- Trust and Total Quality
- Values and Total Quality
- Integrity and Total Quality
- Responsibility and Total Quality
- Manager's Role in Ethics
- Organization's Role in Ethics
- Handling Ethical Dilemmas
- Ethics Training and Codes of Business Conduct
- Models for Making Ethical Decisions
- Beliefs Versus Behavior: Why the Disparity?
- Ethical Dilemmas: Cases
- Corporate Social Responsibility Defined

Engaging in insider trading, accepting a higher commission for selling an inferior product, accepting gifts from suppliers, and hiring a friend or relative instead of a more qualified applicant—these are all examples of ethics violations that are common in today's workplace. Yet, nearly universal agreement exists that business practices in the modern workplace should be above reproach with regard to ethical behavior. Few people are willing to defend unethical behavior, and for the most part, business and industry operate within the scope of acceptable legal and ethical standards. Ethical behavior is particularly important in a total quality setting in which trust, integrity, and values figure prominently in everyday human interactions.

DEFINITION AND OVERVIEW OF ETHICS

Ethics is about doing the right thing within a moral framework. In other words, it is the practical application of morality. What is ethical in a given situation is decided by applying the values that comprise the prevailing moral framework. The fundamental question that arises in any ethical dilemma

is this: *If I believe in a given standard of right and wrong, how should these beliefs guide my actions, behavior, attitude, and decisions?* The ever-present challenge, of course, is not just determining what is right but also following through and doing what is right.

Human Factors That Contribute to Unethical Behavior

Breaches of ethical conduct are, unfortunately, common in today's hectic, hypercompetitive global business environment. The most common impediment to ethical conduct is simply human nature. Human beings tend to behave according to the principle of *perceived personal interest*. An unfortunate fact of life is that it will often appear that a person's personal interests are best served—at least in the short run—by an unethical choice. Factors that contribute to this type of misguided perception include greed, impatience, ego, fear, expedience, ambition, and need.

Driven by greed, a CEO might decide to deliver a large lot of manufactured goods he knows are defective. Driven by impatience, a person might push her employees to perform a job in an unsafe manner that could lead to accidents and injuries. Driven by ego, a person might claim credit for superior work that was actually performed by someone else. Driven by fear of retribution, a person who knows his boss is lying to stockholders might simply ignore the fact and look the other way. Driven by expedience, a person might cut corners in ways that could lead to tragic results. Driven by misguided ambition, a person might lie on her resume, adding a degree she has not completed. Finally, driven by the need to pay the mounting hospital bills for his sick child, a person might use a company credit card for personal expenses.

In all of these cases, people made unethical choices based on misguided personal interest. Even though one might, understandably, feel sympathy for the individual who was struggling to pay mounting hospital bills, the choice he made to misuse a company credit card was still an unethical choice. Doing the wrong thing, even for the right reasons, is still wrong. Extenuating circumstances do not alter what is right or wrong, just as understanding why a person makes an unethical choice does not excuse her for doing so. This leads to an important point relating to human nature and ethics.

When deciding what is right and wrong in a given situation, it is often necessary to separate the choice from the extenuating circumstances that impinge on making it. These extenuating circumstances can create what is known as a *gray area* around a given choice. By "gray," the people involved in making the choice mean that what is right is neither black nor white. There is a gray area surrounding the decision that makes it difficult to see though the fog to find the right thing. There are cases when using the gray area argument is legitimate—for example, when doing what is right will help one person but hurt many. What is the right thing to do in such a case? Should the decision makers take a black-and-white approach or apply the principle of the greater good? This is a legitimate gray area in an ethical dilemma.

However, many times when decision makers say they are dealing with a gray area when facing an ethical dilemma, what is really happening is that they want to make a choice they know is unethical but for reasons of misguided personal interest are trying to find a way to justify it. In such cases, decision makers often use the extenuating circumstances as their justification. This is why it is so important to separate decisions concerning what is right and wrong from extenuating circumstances. The approach that is more likely to lead to an ethical choice is to decide what is right in a given situation and do it. Then find other ethical ways to deal with the extenuating circumstances.

For example, in the case above of the individual who misused a company credit card, there were a variety of ethical ways to deal with the extenuating circumstance (hospital bills for a sick child). He could have asked friends, family, colleagues, and charitable organizations for help. In every community, there are civic organizations that sponsor fund-raising events for just such situations. The individual involved was in a bind—of this there is no doubt—but he had options for dealing with his situation other than the unethical choice he made.

Organizational Factors That Contribute to Unethical Behavior

Human nature, coupled with the competitive pressure of the global marketplace, can make adhering to ethical principles a daily challenge. Organizations can either help relieve the pressure, thereby making it less difficult for their personnel to behave ethically, or create an environment that increases the pressure, thereby almost guaranteeing unethical behavior. Organizational factors that can contribute to unethical behavior include the following:

- *Failing to make ethics part of the organization's core values.* An important component of an organization's strategic plan is a statement of core values. Failing to make high ethical expectations a core value in the strategic plan is tantamount to approving unethical behav-

ior. Silence on ethics sends the wrong message from the top, and it is not sufficient to claim that "our organization takes ethical behavior for granted, so we don't need to make it part of our strategic plan."

- *Failing to set a consistent positive example.* Executives and managers in any organization set the tone for the organization. If management personnel expect ethical behavior, they have to set a consistent example of it. Employees will follow the actions of management personnel rather than their words. The words are important, but they must be consistently reinforced by ethical action, decisions, and behavior.

- *Putting personnel in ethical "corners."* Management personnel who box employees in by forcing them into ethical corners that offer no room to maneuver will almost surely produce unethical behavior. This can happen, for example, when the pressure to meet a deadline looms. A manager might say to his team, "I don't care how you do it, but I want you to meet the deadline." This manager has just told his direct reports that even if they have to take unethical shortcuts, they are to meet the deadline.

- *Failing to adopt, deploy, and enforce a corporate code of ethics.* If ethical behavior is a core value for an organization—as it must be—the organization should adopt, deploy, and enforce a corporate code of ethics that provides specific guidance for personnel. Even a code of ethics cannot cover every ethical exigency that might arise, but it can provide guidance that is specific enough to be meaningful but generic enough to allow for the application of good judgment.

- *Applying unrealistic pressure.* As the globalization of competition continues, organizations are under increasing pressure to perform at ever higher levels. This is why continual improvement is a foundational aspect of quality management. Competition creates pressure by shortening deadlines, demanding lower costs, expecting higher quality, and wanting better service. The pressure on the leaders of organizations that operate in a competitive environment is intense. When this pressure is passed down throughout the organization in a realistic manner, there is no problem. But when poor planning on the part of management causes pressure to be applied unrealistically, employees are forced to take unethical shortcuts.

- *Failing to reward ethical behavior.* There is an adage that "No good deed goes unpunished." Here is just one example of what this adage can mean in the workplace. An individual in an organization makes an ethical decision that results in a short-term loss of profits but that is clearly the right thing to do. Rather than being rewarded, she is punished—not overtly but in subtle ways. For example, a quality manager discovers that his company has just shipped a box of defective parts to a customer. He quickly contacts the customer, recalls the defective parts, and replaces them with parts that meet all quality standards.

This causes the manufacturing department's monthly report to show a major increase in waste; hence, the company suffers a temporary loss of profits. The company's CEO responds by giving the quality manager a bad performance review. This CEO actually punished his quality manager for doing the right thing instead of rewarding him. By failing to reward ethical behavior, the CEO actually encouraged unethical behavior—a fact that is sure to cost his company greater losses in the long run than the temporary losses incurred by doing the right thing.

Cost-Benefit Analysis and Ethics

Some argue that it costs too much to take the ethical high road in today's hypercompetitive global business environment. Those who make this argument mean that ethical behavior can cause their organization to lose contracts by tying up so much energy and so many resources in "doing good" that it becomes impossible to compete. This is the short-term perspective that overlooks the long-term benefits of ethical business practices.

The benefit of avoiding harm is the long-term maintenance of a good reputation. Unethical behavior that results in government investigations, lawsuits, and media-driven scandals can bankrupt even the largest, most powerful organizations. Those that are able to survive the investigations, lawsuits, and scandals often lose their reputation, a fact that causes their stock to plummet, their best employees to jump ship, and their customers to take their business elsewhere. How much is an organization's good reputation worth? Everything.

Affirmative benefits of ethical business practices include higher employee morale, a positive reputation in the marketplace, greater ability to attract and retain high-value personnel, higher ratings with creditors and investors, differentiation from the competition, and increased sales—especially to government organizations that insist on an excellent record in the area of ethics.

The so-called costs of ethical business practices are almost always short term in nature, while the benefits tend to be long term. This fact presents organizations with a major challenge. In order to enjoy the benefits of ethical business practices, they may have to occasionally make decisions that will cost them in the short run. However, making unethical decisions to serve some misguided short-term goal often means there will be no long-term future for an organization.

Guidelines for Determining Ethical Behavior

This section explains some guidelines that can be used in sorting out ethical and unethical behavior. However, before presenting the guidelines, we must distinguish between the concepts of *legal* and *ethical:* They are not the same thing. Just because a choice made is legal does not necessarily mean it is ethical. A person's behavior can be well within the prescribed limits of the law and still be unethical. Some tests for determining ethical behavior shown in Figure 4–1 assume the behavior in question is legal. By applying any one of these tests, a person should be able to see through the gray area surrounding an issue and determine the ethical route to take.

TRUST AND TOTAL QUALITY

The total quality approach cannot be successfully implemented in an organization that fails to subscribe to high standards of ethical behavior. This is because ethical behavior builds trust, and trust is an essential ingredient in total quality. Consider the various elements of total quality that depend on trust: communication, interpersonal relations, conflict management, problem solving, teamwork, employee involvement and empowerment, and customer focus (see Figure 4–2).

In human communication, receivers accept messages only from senders they trust. In interpersonal relations, trust is the most fundamental element. People who trust each other will be able to get along and work well together even in

Morning-After Test
How will you feel about this behavior tomorrow morning?

Front-Page Test
How would you like to see this behavior written up on the front page of your hometown newspaper?

Mirror Test
How will you feel about this behavior when you look in the mirror?

Role Reversal Test
How would you feel about being on the receiving end of this behavior?

Commonsense Test
What does everyday common sense say about this behavior?

FIGURE 4–1 Tests of Ethical Behavior
Source: Adapted with permission from David L. Goetsch, seminar titled "Business Ethics 101," April 2011.

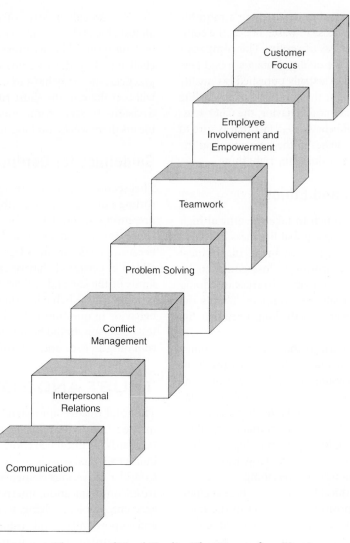

FIGURE 4–2 Elements of Total Quality That Depend on Trust

the worst of circumstances. On the other hand, people who do not trust each other will be unable to get along and work well together even in the best of circumstances. Trust is also a critical element in conflict management. A manager must be trusted by both sides in a human conflict to help resolve the conflict.

For people to put aside their personal agendas and work together as a team, they must trust each other. If even one team member is concerned that another team member is promoting his or her self-interests over those of the team, teamwork will not succeed. Managers will not involve and empower employees unless they trust them.

Ethics plays a critical role in the successful application of total quality. Ethical behavior on the part of the organization is just as important as the behavior of managers and employees. A company that fails to honor warranties, treats employees poorly, or pollutes its community cannot expect employees to disregard the example it sets and promote a trusting environment in the workplace.

If the trust that results from ethical behavior is so important to total quality, then it follows that modern managers need

to be good trust builders. Although it is important that managers be able to establish themselves as trustworthy, that by itself is not enough. Managers in a total quality setting must also be able to build trust in the organization and among its employees.

One of the best ways managers can help build trust is to protect the interests of those who are not present at the moment as if they are. When a manager speaks up for someone who is not present but is being questioned or attacked, employees get the following two simultaneous messages:

- Talking behind a colleague's back is not acceptable behavior.
- If this manager doesn't let me talk about fellow employees who are absent, he or she won't let others talk about me when I'm absent.

Knowing they will be included in any conversation that is about them or that affects them builds trust among employees. A sincere apology can also build trust. Managers sometimes make mistakes or do things that hurt employees. Making excuses, pointing the finger of blame at someone else, or ignoring the situation only exacerbates it. By simply and sincerely saying "This is my fault; I'm sorry," managers can build trust even when they have made mistakes.

Keeping promises is another way managers can build trust. Dependability builds trust. It is human nature to want to be able to depend on what others tell us. Promises in the workplace often take the form of deadlines. A deadline promised should be a deadline kept. Regardless of the type of promises made, managers and employees in a total quality setting should keep them and expect others to do the same. It is easier to trust people who are dependable, even when we don't agree with them, than it is to trust someone who is not dependable. "Be a person of your word" is a good rule of thumb to follow when trying to build trust.

In attempting to build trust in the workplace, managers should take the initiative, even though in a total quality setting trust building and other tasks necessary for success in the intensely competitive global marketplace are the responsibility of everyone. Managers should not sit back and expect trust building to just happen. Their role is to get things moving and to "stir the pot" as necessary to keep things moving.

Motivating employees and continually developing their job skills are important responsibilities of managers in a total quality setting. Managers who are not trusted will be ineffective at fulfilling these responsibilities. This is because employees must trust that they, as well as the organization, will benefit from new skills before they are willing to apply themselves to developing the skills.

VALUES AND TOTAL QUALITY

Values are those deeply held beliefs that form the very core of who we are. A person's conscience or internal barometer is based on his or her values. Our values guide our behavior. This statement also applies to organizations. An organization will not produce a quality product or provide a quality service unless the organization values quality. Knowledge and skills are important, but by themselves, they do not guarantee results. This is because individual employees and organizations as a whole will most willingly apply their knowledge and skills to what they value, what they believe in, and what they feel is important.

Ethical behavior begins with values. Values that lead to ethical behavior include fairness, dependability, integrity, honesty, and truthfulness. These values tend to encourage a work environment that involves, empowers, values, and nurtures people: one that not only holds employees responsible, but also gives them the support, leeway, and resources needed to fulfill their responsibilities.

INTEGRITY AND TOTAL QUALITY

Another aspect of ethical behavior is integrity. *Integrity*, as a personal and organizational characteristic, combines honesty and dependability. When an individual or an organization has integrity, ethical behavior automatically follows.

QUALITY TIP ▼

Corporate Values Are Not Just for Show—They Must Be Real

A mistake frequently made by organizations is adopting a set of corporate values that no one really intends to accept or follow. These values look impressive when displayed on the wall of an organization's lobby and on the organization's Web site, but when it comes to informing behavior or guiding decisions they are ignored. Adopting corporate values and then ignoring them is worse than not adopting them at all. Stakeholders will soon know if the organization's leadership is serious about its stated corporate values. A set of corporate values that is adopted and displayed but ignored soon becomes an indictment against the organization rather than a tool for lifting it up.

It is important for managers in a total quality setting to understand that although honesty is fundamental to it, integrity is more than just honesty. People with integrity can be counted on to do the right thing, do things correctly, accomplish tasks thoroughly and completely, finish work on time, and keep promises. The same is true of organizations.

Managers with integrity will keep the best interests of their organization and employees in mind when making decisions and in all other aspects of their jobs. Committing to not knowingly harming an employee, a customer, the organization, or the public at large forces managers to think about the consequences of their actions before taking them. This principle also applies to employees and the organization as a whole.

RESPONSIBILITY AND TOTAL QUALITY

Part of ethical behavior is accepting responsibility. This is critical in the modern workplace because employees are drawn from a society that, as a rule, shuns responsibility—which is why ours has become such a litigious society.

People want to blame others for their own shortcomings and failures. Students graduate from high school unable to read and immediately file lawsuits against the school board as if they had no part in their own failure. A burglar trips on a skateboard after robbing a house, sues the homeowner, and wins! Inmates upset over the quality of food take their guards hostage and burn down an entire wing of the prison, saying their rights have been violated. Modern society has evolved into one that focuses on rights but ignores the responsibilities that must accompany those rights.

Passing blame has become commonplace. Employees often refer to their employer as "they" rather than "we." Go to a fast-food restaurant or a retail store and complain to a salesclerk. Chances are good that the salesclerk will pass on the blame to an unseen "they." This is not ethical behavior. In a total quality setting, people are responsible for their actions and accountable for their performance. Accepting responsibility helps build trust, integrity, and all the other elements of ethics that are so important in a total quality environment.

MANAGER'S ROLE IN ETHICS

By applying the information set forth so far in this chapter, managers can make ethical decisions. Unfortunately, deciding what is ethical is much easier than actually doing what is ethical. In this regard, trying to practice ethics is like trying to lose weight. It is not so much a matter of knowing you should exercise and cut down on eating as it is a matter of following through and actually doing it.

This fact defines the manager's and the professional's role with regard to ethics in an organization. Managers and professionals in organizations are responsible for following through and actually exemplifying ethical behavior. They are responsible for establishing high ethical standards, setting a consistently positive example of exceeding those standards, and acting immediately when they observe unethical behavior. Figure 4–3 shows three approaches managers and professionals can use in carrying out these responsibilities.

Best-Ratio Approach

The best-ratio approach is a pragmatic approach based on the belief that people are basically good, that in the right circumstances they will behave ethically, and that under certain conditions they can be driven to unethical behavior. Therefore, managers should do everything possible to create conditions that promote ethical behavior and try to maintain the best possible ratio of good choices to bad choices and ethical behavior to unethical behavior. When hard decisions must be made, managers should make the choice that will do the most good for the most people. This approach is sometimes called *situational ethics.*

Black-and-White Approach

With the black-and-white approach, right is right, wrong is wrong, and conditions are irrelevant. The manager's job is to make ethical decisions and carry them out. It is also to help employees behave ethically regardless of circumstances. When difficult decisions must be made, managers should make fair and impartial choices regardless of the outcome and do the right thing without concern for short-term circumstances.

Full-Potential Approach

With the full-potential approach, decisions made are based on how they will affect the ability of those involved to achieve their full potential. The underlying philosophy is that people are responsible for realizing their full potential within the confines of morality. Choices that can achieve this goal without infringing on the rights of others are considered ethical.

The values of the organization and the manager will determine which approach is used. Which one is best is a philosophical question that could be debated at length without being resolved and can be discussed only within the context of a values system.

ORGANIZATION'S ROLE IN ETHICS

Organizations have a corporate responsibility for promoting and encouraging ethical behavior among their personnel. The organization's responsibilities are to: (1) create an ethical environment in which stakeholders know that they will be supported when making ethical choices and (2) ensure that all people in positions of authority in the organization set an example of living up to the highest ethical standards.

Creating an Ethical Environment

An organization creates an ethical environment by establishing policies and practices that ensure that all employees are treated ethically and then by enforcing those policies. Do employees have the right of due process? Do employees have access to an objective grievance procedure? Are appropriate health and safety measures in place to protect employees? Are employees protected from harassment based on race, gender, or other reasons? A company that establishes an

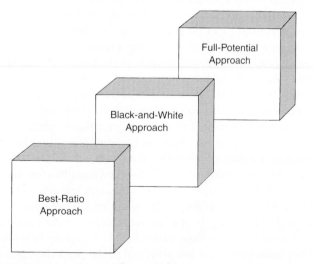

FIGURE 4–3 Approaches to Ethics

> **QUALITY TIP ▼**
>
> **An Organization's Reputation Can Be Destroyed Overnight**
>
> Organizations succeed in the long run by maintaining a reputation that makes them attractive to customers. Customers do not want to be associated with an organization that has a dark cloud hanging over it. Consequently, it is critical that executives, managers, and professionals understand that their organization's reputation can be destroyed overnight by unethical behavior. Financial irregularities, trashing the environment, personal indiscretions, inappropriate acts, irresponsible decisions, and mishandled responses to crises can quickly turn a market-leading organization into a mediocre or even failing organization.

environment that promotes, expects, and rewards ethical behavior can answer "yes" to all of these questions.

One effective way to create an ethical environment is to develop an ethics philosophy with specific guidelines for putting the philosophy into operation, to put it in writing, and to share it with all employees. What follows is a sample corporate ethics statement that could be used by any organization as a first step in creating an ethical environment.

At ABC Inc., all personnel are expected to uphold the highest ethical standards. As we interact with each other and with the customers, suppliers, and the general public, we will be guided by the following principles:

- We will be honest and tell the truth in all situations.
- We will fulfill all promises we make.
- We will be fair and impartial in dealing with others.
- We will be selfless in dealing with others, putting the team's needs before our own.
- We will accept responsibility and accountability for our actions, decisions, and behavior.
- We will endeavor to earn and maintain the trust of each other, customers, suppliers, and the general public.
- We will refuse to rationalize unethical behavior.
- We will obey all applicable laws, regulations, and rules—federal, state, local, and organizational.

A statement such as this sets the tone for all personnel in an organization. It lets them know that upper management not only supports ethical behavior, but also expects it. This approach makes it less difficult for managers when they find themselves caught in the middle between the pressures of business and the maintenance of ethical behavior in their departments.

Beliefs such as those in the preceding sample ethics statement tell employees that they have obligations that extend beyond the workplace and that how they perform their work can have an impact, negative or positive, on fellow employees and on their organization, customers, and country. Key concepts set forth in these statements are honesty, integrity, truth, and fairness. Managers who stress, promote, and model these concepts will make a major contribution to ethical behavior in the workplace.

Written philosophies and guidelines such as those developed by Wisconsin Public Service Corporation are the first step in creating an ethical environment in the workplace. Managers can play a key role in promoting ethical behavior on the job by encouraging upper management to develop written ethics philosophies, credos, or guidelines and then by modeling the behavior they encourage.

Setting an Example

Organizations that take the "Do as I say, not as I do" approach to ethics will not succeed. Employees must be able to trust their employers to conduct all external and internal dealings in an ethical manner. Companies that do not pay their bills on time, companies that pollute, companies that fail to live up to advertised quality standards or stand behind their guarantees, and companies that are not good neighbors in their communities fail to set a good ethical example. Such companies can expect employees to mimic their unethical behavior. Finally, in addition to creating an ethical internal environment and handling external dealings in an ethical manner, organizations must support managers who make ethically correct decisions—not just when such decisions are profitable but in all cases.

HANDLING ETHICAL DILEMMAS

Every manager will eventually confront an ethical dilemma. When this happens, the manager's response is very important. Figure 4–4 provides guidelines managers can use in such situations.

ETHICS TRAINING AND CODES OF BUSINESS CONDUCT

Ethical behavior and the rationale for it can be taught. In fact, almost 40% of the organizations in the United States with 100 or more employees provide ethics training. A survey by the Ethics Resource Center in Washington, DC, revealed that "28 percent of the 711 responding companies provide specific training on ethics."[1]

The Ethics Resource Center has identified the following as topics that are widely addressed in corporate-sponsored ethics training programs:[2]

- Drug and alcohol abuse
- Employee theft

Before taking any action in situations involving ethical dilemmas, answer the following questions:

- What solution is most likely to build trust among those involved?
- What solution fits best into the company's value system?
- What solution will pass the morning-after, front-page, mirror, role reversal, and commonsense tests?
- What solution is most likely to enhance the organization's integrity?
- What solution is the most responsible option?

FIGURE 4–4 Guidelines for Handling Ethical Dilemmas

- Conflicts of interest
- Quality control
- Misuse of proprietary information
- Abuse of expense accounts
- Plant closings and layoffs
- Misuse of company property
- Environmental pollution
- Methods of gathering competitors' information
- Inaccuracy of books and records
- Receiving excessive gifts and entertainment
- False or misleading advertising
- Giving excessive gifts and entertainment
- Kickbacks
- Insider trading
- Relations with local communities
- Antitrust issues
- Bribery
- Political contributions and activities
- Improper relations with local government representatives
- Improper relations with federal government representatives
- Inaccurate time charging to government
- Improper relations with foreign government officials
- Making exaggerated advertising claims

Codes of Business Conduct

Ethics training should not take place in a vacuum, nor should it be nothing more than a list of "thou shalt nots." Rather, organizations should develop codes of business conduct written from a positive perspective that encourage employees to do the right thing. Figure 4–5 is an example of one organization's code of business conduct.

Ethics training is becoming increasingly important as the pressures of succeeding in an intensely competitive global marketplace grow. Professionals operating in the hypercompetitive environment that is today's global marketplace will frequently face ethical dilemmas. This may be why such ethics-related problems as kickbacks, bribes, insider trading, tax evasion, fraud, environmental violations, sexual harassment, and discrimination seem to be so common in today's workplace. As a result, when providing ethics training, it is so important to observe the following rules of thumb:

- **Encourage two-way communication.** "Broadcasting" to people about rules, regulations, and policies is ineffective as a training strategy. Rather, it is important to encourage open, frank, informed discussion and give participants ample opportunities to state their views, ask questions, and propose solutions.
- **Make the training practical.** People need to see how the training applies specifically to them. An effective approach for ensuring that training is practical is to present real-life scenarios and ask participants to explain how they would handle each situation and why. It is also important to ask how the organization could help them do the right thing in each case.
- **Avoid dogmatic statements.** People are typically turned off by dogma. Rather, it is better to present and discuss ethical principles and then allow participants to decide how they apply. The trainer's role is to tactfully guide participants toward an ethical solution by helping them take their opinions to their logical conclusion. Rather than telling participants that an idea or opinion is wrong or right, it is better to lead them in such a way that they come to that conclusion themselves.

MODELS FOR MAKING ETHICAL DECISIONS

Ethics as a concept exists within a framework defined by organizational values. Just as the values of organizations can differ, so can the decision-making models used for determining the ethical course of action in a given situation. This section briefly describes several such models that can be used for making ethical decisions. The actual model chosen will depend on the values of the organization and of the larger community in which the organization does business.

Code of Business Conduct
INTERNATIONAL SERVICE CORPORATION

The owners and management of International Service Corporation (ISC) are committed to the highest ethical standards in the conduct of the company's business. All employees at all levels are expected to conduct their dealings with customers, suppliers, colleagues, and each other with honesty and integrity. At ISC, the ethical way is the right way. When making decisions, ISC personnel will endeavor to achieve fairness to all stakeholders. Our reputation is our most important strategic advantage in the global marketplace.

FIGURE 4–5 Example of a Company's Code of Business Conduct

In a total quality organization, all stakeholders—external and internal—have a say in establishing and judging the corporate values. Consequently, it is important to select a model that will withstand the scrutiny of all stakeholders. Having done so, an organization should stick with its model and apply it consistently. The most widely used models are as follows:

- *Categorical imperative model.* The categorical imperative model is also known as the *black-and-white model.* With this model, right is right, wrong is wrong, and there are no gray areas.

- *Full-disclosure model.* With this model, the functional criterion is a simple question: Could the organization explain its actions to the satisfaction of a broad cross-section of stakeholders? Only when this question can be answered in the affirmative is an action considered ethical. This model has the advantage of applying the values of stakeholders in deciding what is ethical.

- *Doctrine of the mean model.* In this model, the *mean* refers to the average or middle point between two extremes. Translated for practical application, this model suggests that in any situation, a moderate middle-ground option is likely to be an ethical option. Said another way, this model suggests that moderation is ethical.

- *Golden Rule model.* This model is based on the Golden Rule: "Do unto others as you would have them do unto you." It is one of the most popular models in Western society. Like the full-disclosure model, it takes the viewpoints of stakeholders into account in deciding what is ethical.

- *Market-ethic model.* This model is based on the belief that any legal action that promotes profitability is ethical. Proponents of this model profess that the purpose of a business is to make a profit. Consequently, what is ethical should be decided within a framework of profit and loss. They argue that in the long run the market will reject unethical corporate behavior, making it thereby unprofitable.

- *Organizational ethic model.* This model is based on loyalty to the organization. Its underlying premise is that the most ethical decision is the one that best serves the organization's interests. Unless an organization has adopted a set of guiding principles that ensure ethical behavior, the organizational ethic model is difficult to defend.

- *Equal freedom model.* The underlying principle of this model is that organizations have the freedom to behave as they wish unless their actions infringe on the rights of stakeholders. This is a more confining model than it might appear at first glance. For example, suppose an organization decides to use a new chemical that improves product quality and costs substantially less than the one it will replace. Before making a decision, the organization learns that the community's current water safety technology may not be able to screen out the chemical. The worst-case scenario is that it could contaminate the local water supply. Applying the equal freedom model, adopting the new chemical would be unethical because it might violate the rights of stakeholders (everyone who depends on the local water supply).

- *Proportionality ethic model.* This model is based on the assumption that the world is so complex that decisions are seldom clearly right or wrong. Consequently, the best an organization can do is to make sure that the good outweighs the bad when making decisions.

- *Professional ethic model.* This model is based on the principle of peer review. It states that a decision is ethical if it can be explained to the approval of a broad cross-section of professional peers. Professions that subscribe to this model typically adopt a professional code of ethics.

BELIEFS VERSUS BEHAVIOR: WHY THE DISPARITY?

Ethics in the workplace manifests itself through the application of such values as honesty, loyalty, fairness, caring, respect, tolerance, and duty. Most, but not all, people in the workplace subscribe to these values. Why, then, is there so often a gap between what people believe and what they do? In other words, if people believe in honesty, why are they sometimes dishonest? If people believe in fairness, why are they sometimes unfair? These are questions that could be debated at length in a broad philosophical context. However, several reasons explain the disparity, at least on a practical level.

Self-Interest and Self-Protection

People are, by their very nature, self-interested and, as a result, self-protective. The driving force behind such slogans as "Me First" and "Looking Out for Number One" is a self-centered attitude. Most people work against human nature to put someone else's needs ahead of their own. Yet, this is precisely what one must do to deal ethically with fellow employees and the public at large.

Being honest sometimes means putting yourself at a disadvantage or having to admit something you would rather not. In such situations, the natural instinct for self-protection takes over and the inclination is to evade the truth. Consider the example of John.

John had some minor repair work to do on his truck but didn't have a certain tool he needed. Consequently, at the end of his shift at Autoworld Inc., he borrowed the needed tool from the company's tool locker. That night he completed the work on his truck, but the next morning he forgot about the tool and left it at home. By the time he remembered the tool, it was too late to go back home without missing the beginning of his shift. John drove on to work hoping that the tool wouldn't be needed that day. If nobody needed it, the tool wouldn't be missed and he could return it the next day.

Everything went well until midmorning when a job came in requiring the missing tool. When it wasn't in its place in the tool locker, the shift supervisor began asking around to determine who was using it or who had used it last. Finally, when a thorough search of the shop failed to produce it, the supervisor asked if anyone had borrowed it.

John knew that Autoworld had a strict policy against just this sort of thing. He also knew that if he didn't speak up, the last person to have used the tool would be required to pay for it. That was the rule. Unfortunately, if he did admit having borrowed the tool, he would be reprimanded and fined, even if he returned it. John did not want to see a colleague forced to pay for his mistake. But, on the other hand, he had already been reprimanded and fined once this month. He certainly didn't want to go through that again. John faced a common dilemma: tell the truth and bear the consequences, or give in to his natural instinct for self-protection. Faced with such a dilemma, people will go one way or the other, depending on which factor—conscience or self-protection—has the strongest pull on them at the time.

It is not uncommon for self-interest or self-protection to win out under the pressure of the moment, only to have the conscience take over once there has been time for quiet reflection. This is why stories abound about thieves who later return the money or successful people who make a large financial contribution to assuage their guilt over an earlier transgression.

Conflicting Values

People who believe in ethical values (honesty, loyalty, fairness, etc.) sometimes find themselves in situations where these values seem to conflict. For example, consider the dilemma faced by Mary Ann, a sales representative for Construction Products Inc. (CPI).

CPI is having a bad year and desperately needs every contract it can get. Mary Ann has an opportunity to win a contract to supply all the kitchen cabinets for a 56-house subdivision that is going to be built in the near future. But there is a problem: CPI cannot deliver the cabinets by the required date. Failure to deliver on time will throw off the customer's entire production schedule. Mary Ann's boss is pressuring her to agree to the delivery date, even though they both know that the deadline cannot be met. Mary Ann wants to give an honest reply with a more realistic delivery date, but she is in a quandary over what to do.

This morning her boss took her aside and said, "You are so worried about honesty that you've forgotten about loyalty. What about loyalty to this company and your friends who work here? If we don't bring in some work soon, we are all going to be out looking for jobs!"

Honesty versus loyalty—what does one do when ethical values seem to conflict? People obviously choose one over the other based on their interpretation of the situation, the facts as they know them, and contributing personal influences. However, rather than asking what to do when ethical values seem to conflict, it might be better to ask whether the values do in fact truly conflict.

What kind of loyalty would require one to be dishonest, unfair, or disrespectful? Although ethical values sometimes appear to be in conflict, a closer look will usually reveal a different story. For example, the loyalty issue in Mary Ann's case was false loyalty. True loyalty would rarely, if ever, require dishonesty.

Tangible or Intangible, Immediate or Deferred

People frequently make decisions that run counter to their beliefs because the benefits of ethical decisions are often intangible or deferred. Put another way, the consequences of unethical behavior are often intangible or deferred, while the perceived benefits are usually both tangible and immediate.

Take the case of Mary Ann previously described. If she is willing to deceive the contractor by submitting a false delivery date, there will be a direct benefit that is both immediate and tangible. Her company will win a badly needed contract, and she will be the author of the victory. The downside is that at some point in the future the company will lose the trust and, as a likely result, the future business of the contractor she deceived. The benefit in this situation is immediate; the downside is deferred.

Making Ethics Tangible and Immediate

Because the benefits of ethical behavior can be perceived as being intangible and deferred, people will sometimes choose the unethical option—even people who believe in ethical values. The challenge to the management is to help employees see that the benefits of ethical behavior are tangible and that even when deferred they still accrue.

Periodic focus groups conducted by an outside facilitator in which employees discuss ethics-related issues can be an effective way to make ethics tangible. During these meetings, employees discuss very specific situations that include ethical dilemmas. The facilitator asks questions, such as "What would you do in this situation? Why? What is the right thing to do? What would keep you from doing the right thing? What are the consequences of choosing an unethical option?" Group members discuss the issue and respond to the facilitator's questions. The facilitator's job is to guide the discussion toward the tangible and immediate consequences of unethical behavior, or, put another way, the tangible and immediate benefits of ethical behavior.

Sometime during the meeting, the facilitator will ask the following types of questions and lead participants through discussion and debate:

- How does the management reward ethical behavior?
- How does the management unknowingly promote unethical behavior?
- Does the management unknowingly reward unethical behavior?

Discussing these questions will sometimes reveal that the management expects ethical behavior but does not reward it or, worse yet, unknowingly rewards unethical behavior. For example, is ethical behavior a part of the performance evaluation process? Does the management publish ethics guidelines and reward employees who follow them? Is the management's commitment to ethical values real or just lip service? For example, in the earlier case of Mary Ann, would the upper management have supported the supervisor or Mary Ann?

ETHICAL DILEMMAS: CASES

This section contains ethical dilemmas that are representative of those faced by managers every day in the world of business. While studying these dilemmas, the reader is encouraged to consider the various factors such as pressure from superiors or peers, personal interest, ambition, financial need, job security, and others that tend to promote unethical behavior on the part of the people who are normally honest and trustworthy. While reading these cases, ask yourself, "What would I do in the same situation if I were facing the same pressures?"

Let's consider some examples. Certain models of sport utility vehicles manufactured by Ford begin to show a pattern of high-speed accidents. The similarity in these accidents leads investigators to suspect tire defects. Ford quickly points to its supplier, Firestone. Firestone defends itself and points back at Ford. Union Carbide establishes a processing plant in Bhopal, India, where the laws protecting the safety of employees and the environment are less rigid than those in the United States. The processes at Union Carbide's Bhopal plant involve the use of extremely toxic chemicals and gases. When various emergency protection systems either are not working or fail, more than 40 tons of lethal gas are released into the atmosphere, killing more than 3,000 people.

Most of the discussion surrounding the Ford–Firestone and Union Carbide cases focused on litigation and who would eventually be held responsible for financial damages. However, very little attention was paid to the ethical questions involved. Did these multinational corporations behave in ways that were fair to all stakeholders? Should companies locate plants in developing nations to take advantage of less restrictive safety and environmental protection laws than those in the United States? Should the company that actually sells the product to the consumer pass along responsibility to its supplier or accept responsibility itself?

The Ford–Firestone and Union Carbide cases received a great deal of media attention worldwide. However, these "big name" cases represent just a few of the thousands of similar situations that arise in the corporate world every year. From small "mom-and-pop" operations to large multinationals, dealing with ethical dilemmas is an everyday part of doing business. In order to succeed in the long term, managers must know how to deal with these dilemmas, and they must understand that just knowing what is right is not enough. Most people who commit ethical violations know what is morally correct.

Typically, people intuitively know the difference between right and wrong. Since this is the case, why, then, do basically "good" people still sometimes behave unethically? This is a valid question and one that has been debated and discussed by philosophers for thousands of years. After all, if we know what is right, will we not do what is right? The answer to this question, unfortunately, is "not always." Even people who have a strong sense of right and wrong can be pressured to behave unethically. This is because an individual's sense of right and wrong can sometimes be overpowered by a stronger sense of ambition, need, fear of the consequences of making the ethical choice, peer pressure, pressure from superiors, and numerous other human factors.

Case 1: "I Need This Promotion"

Janice Carlson had always seen herself as an ethical person. She took pride in always telling the truth, even when doing so was uncomfortable. She also insisted that those she supervised at Comstock Engineering Company (CEC) do the same. Carlson frequently admonished her employees to be "straight" with her. She was fond of saying, "I can accept mistakes. They happen. I can even overlook an occasional bad day. But I will not put up with lying." Close friends knew that Carlson's distaste for lying grew out of an unhappy marriage she had endured for years with a husband who lied to her as a matter of course. When she could take her husband's dishonesty no more, Carlson had filed for divorce.

Her commitment to honesty is why Carlson now feels, as she quietly admits to herself, "lower than a snake in the grass." What makes things even worse is that this is a day on which Carlson should be overjoyed. After 15 years of loyal and effective service to CEC, several of which were spent as the only female engineer in the company, Carlson has just been promoted to director of the civil engineering department. Her promotion means a substantial salary increase, and Carlson needs it. Her daughter has just started college at a private institution. It is an excellent school, but the tuition rate is sky high, and her ex-husband, true to form, has refused to help. Why, then, on this day of all days does Carlson feel so bad? The answer is simple: She got the promotion because she lied.

The process for selecting CEC's new director of civil engineering had been difficult. The competition had been especially tough. One of Carlson's long-time colleagues and friends had also been a leading candidate. Since Carlson and her friend were equally qualified and equally experienced, the ultimate selection had come down to solving a complex engineering problem developed by the outgoing director, who was retiring.

A couple of days before the candidates were scheduled to take the promotion test, Carlson had gone to the director's office to return a file she had borrowed. The problem she would have to solve on the promotion test was on the director's desk. The director was out of the office for the day. Carlson saw the problem and knew immediately what it was. She started to turn away but felt herself drawn to it. Almost without realizing what she was doing, Carlson leaned over the director's desk and looked at the solution. It was a really tough problem.

When the two candidates had completed the test, Carlson's friend and colleague asked how she had done. "I think I solved it" was her response. "Not me," said her friend. "That was the trickiest engineering problem I've ever seen. I've heard that the director had this really complicated problem that no one has ever been able to solve, except him, of course. I don't suppose you had ever seen this problem before, had you?" Janice Carlson could not look her friend in the eye when she said, "No. I've heard about it, too. But that was the first time I had ever seen it. I guess I just got lucky." Her friend had smiled and held out his hand, saying, "Anyway, congratulations. It looks like you get the promotion."

Carlson is a person who prides herself on honesty, but in this case, her personal interest overcame her commitment to the truth. On the one hand, she needs the promotion in order to help pay her daughter's college costs. On the other hand, the way she received it was dishonest. Put yourself in Carlson's shoes. What would you have done?

Case 2: To Pay or Not to Pay? That Is the Question

John Hingas didn't know what to do, but he did know that he would have to make a recommendation, and soon. He had been the leading marketing representative for Government Products Inc. (GPI), for years. In fact, he was practically a legend in the company. That's why GPI's president had given him the current assignment to "break into the Mexican market." GPI produces various office products ranging from desks and chairs to filing cabinets and shelves. The company's major customers are local, state, and federal government organizations.

With the passage of the North American Free Trade Agreement (NAFTA), GPI's executives had decided to expand into Mexico. Unfortunately, they were getting nowhere. After 9 months of concerted effort, GPI had nothing to show for its attempts to gain a foothold in Mexican markets except a stack of invoices for airline tickets, motel rooms, and restaurants. Finally, GPI's executives decided to send in the "A Team." That is when John Hingas received the call. While meeting with GPI's executive management team, Hingas quickly showed why he had always been so effective. After analyzing the company's marketing plan for Mexico, Hingas told the executives, "I have just one question. How many of the marketing representatives we send to Mexico actually speak Spanish?" There was an embarrassed silence before Hingas said, "Why don't we step back from

the Mexico initiative for a while and give me a chance to look into it? I'll then come back with recommendations."

"How long do you need?" asked the company's CEO.

"Six months," said Hingas.

"Why so long?"

"Because before I go down to Mexico to look into things, I need to learn to speak the language."

Eight months and many trips to Mexico later, Hingas knew exactly what would be necessary to succeed in the Mexican markets. By learning to speak Spanish and by getting to know a number of key contact people, Hingas had learned precisely what GPI would have to do in order to compete in its targeted market in Mexico. In a word, the answer was "bribery." GPI could make the best products in the world at the most reasonable prices, but unless its marketing representatives became adept at playing the bribery game, the company would never sell one piece of furniture to a government organization in Mexico. GPI's competitors had already figured this out and were using it to their advantage.

Hingas knew GPI could "play the game" as well as or even better than its competitors, but should it? On the one hand, bribery is simply a way of life, a part of the culture in the markets GPI is trying to reach. The hard truth is clear to Hingas: no bribes, no contracts. However, with just a few well-placed bribes, GPI could increase its annual sales by more than 15% in less than 2 years. On the other hand, GPI enjoys a well-deserved reputation for integrity with its customers, and nobody in the company wants to damage that reputation. Hingas has a recommendation to make, and he will have to make it soon. Put yourself in his place. What would you recommend?

Case 3: The Product Is Inferior, but the Profits Are Good

The executive management team of Athletic Footwear Inc. (AFI), faces both a threat and an opportunity. The threat is that unless it can find a buyer for a large production run of soccer shoes, the company is going to lose a lot of money. The opportunity is that the vice president of marketing has found a buyer. The problem is that, although this batch of shoes is the company's best-selling, most popular model, the shoes are defective.

Several months earlier, AFI's management team had decided to save on production costs by using a different glue provided by a new supplier. The glue came highly recommended, and it was much less expensive than that previously used. Consequently, AFI's management team had jumped at the opportunity to save money without first running in-house tests on the glue. Much to their dismay, the new glue turned out to be inferior to that normally used when securing the sole of the shoe. Now, the company is stuck with a warehouse full of defective shoes.

Normally, the company would simply write off the defective shoes and absorb the loss. However, the company has just gone through a year-long battle to stave off a hostile takeover. As a result, its coffers are practically empty and its debt has nearly doubled. Nobody seated around the table in the executive conference room is in a mood to just absorb the potential loss they face. Legal action against the supplier has already been ruled out for fear of permanently damaging the company's image and credibility. Nobody wants the company's regular customers to know that a defective batch of shoes was produced. Management doesn't want customers thinking, "If AFI produces one large batch of defective shoes, maybe it will produce another."

The potential buyer is a distributor that has retail outlets throughout South America. This company is even willing to pay more than the market price for the shoes in order to be the first distributor in South America to carry the AFI brand. No sport in South America is more favored than soccer, and the AFI soccer shoe is very popular in the United States, Canada, and Europe. The shoe has a reputation for being comfortable and durable. It lasts a long time in even the most demanding conditions. But the defective batch in question won't; in fact, based on initial trial runs, the soles will probably begin to separate after less than 20 hours of use. What should AFI's executives do? Should they sell the shoes, knowing they are defective, or destroy them and find a way to take a loss they really don't need at this point in the company's history? If you were an AFI executive, what would you suggest?

CORPORATE SOCIAL RESPONSIBILITY DEFINED

The material presented so far in this chapter has dealt primarily with the behavior of individuals in organizations and the ethical ramifications of that behavior. This section deals with the issue of corporate behavior and its attendant ethical ramifications.

Business scandals tend to undermine the credibility of businesses in general by eroding public trust and confidence.

In an attempt to stem the tide of unethical behavior in business, the International Organization for Standardization (ISO)—the same organization that developed the international quality management guidelines known as ISO 9000 and the international environmental management guidelines known as ISO 14000—has taken on the issue of corporate social responsibility (CSR). The ISO defines CSR as follows:

[CSR is] a balanced approach for organizations to address economic, social and environmental issues in a way that aims to benefit people, communities and society.[3]

Key elements of CSR include the ethical aspects of the following business and workplace issues:

1. Human rights
2. Occupational safety and health
3. Business practices (fair or unfair)
4. Governance
5. Environmental management
6. Consumer relations
7. Marketplace activities
8. Community involvement
9. Social development

The CSR is critical because the credibility and, in turn, success of a free-market economic system rest on a foundation of trust. All the principles of total quality—continual improvement, competition, strategic management, and so on—are inextricably linked with free-market practices. Undermine that foundation of the free-market system and you undermine the entire system. When public trust is undermined, it is replaced by fear, suspicion, and protectionist attitudes. Businesses cannot survive and thrive in such an environment.

SUMMARY

1. *Ethics* is about doing the right thing within a moral framework. The most common impediment to ethical conduct is human nature, because people tend to behave according to perceived personal interest.

2. Trust is a critical element of ethics, which, in turn, makes ethics critical in total quality. Many of the fundamental elements of total quality, including communication, interpersonal relations, conflict management, problem solving, teamwork, employee involvement and empowerment, and customer focus, depend on trust and ethical behavior. Trust can be built by being loyal to those not present, keeping promises, and sincerely apologizing when necessary.

3. *Values* are those core beliefs that guide our behavior. Individuals and organizations apply their knowledge

and skills most willingly to efforts in which they believe. Managers should work to establish an environment in which values that lead to ethical behavior and values that lead to peak performance are the same.

4. Integrity requires honesty, but it is more than just honesty. *Integrity* is a combination of honesty and dependability. People with integrity can be counted on to do the right thing, do it correctly, and do it on time.

5. Accepting responsibility is part of ethical behavior. People who pass blame are not behaving ethically. In a total quality setting, people are responsible for their performance. When speaking of their organization, ethical people say "we" instead of "they."

6. Managers play a key role in ethics in an organization. They are responsible for setting an example of ethical behavior, helping employees make ethical choices, and helping employees follow through and behave ethically

after making an ethical choice. In carrying out these responsibilities, managers can use the best-ratio approach, black-and-white approach, or full-potential approach.

7. The organization's role in fostering ethical behavior includes creating an ethical environment and setting an ethical example. Key in creating an ethical environment is having a comprehensive ethics policy. Key in setting an example is following the policy, expecting all employees to follow the policy, and rewarding those who do.

8. In handling ethical dilemmas, managers should select the option that is most likely to build trust, integrity, and a sense of responsibility and that is most likely to pass the various ethics tests (i.e., front-page, morning-after, etc.).

9. People who believe in ethical values will sometimes make unethical decisions because of self-interest, self-protection, or conflicting values or because they see the benefits as being intangible or deferred.

10. Key elements of corporate social responsibility include the ethical aspects of the following issues: human rights, occupational safety and health, business practices, governance, environmental management, consumer relations, marketplace activities, community involvement, and social development.

KEY TERMS AND CONCEPTS

Best-ratio approach

Black-and-white approach

Conflicting values

Corporate social responsibility

Ethical dilemma

Ethics

Full-potential approach

Gray area

Integrity

Morality

Morning-after test

Perceived personal interest

Responsibility

Trust

Values

FACTUAL REVIEW QUESTIONS

1. Define the term *ethics*.

2. What is morality?

3. Explain how a certain behavior could be legal but not ethical.

4. What role does trust play in a total quality setting?

5. Describe how managers can build trust.

6. What role do values play in a total quality setting?

7. What role does integrity play in a total quality setting?

8. What role does responsibility play in a total quality setting?

9. Describe and differentiate among the following approaches to ethics: best-ratio approach, black-and-white approach, and full-potential approach.

10. What is the manager's role in ethics?

11. Explain the organization's role in promoting ethical behavior.

12. Why, in your own words, would an otherwise ethical person make an unethical decision?

13. Define the term *corporate social responsibility*.

CRITICAL THINKING ACTIVITY

An Ethical Dilemma

Image Products Inc. and Lovan Corporation are major producers of shampoos, conditioners, and other bath products for women. They are also intense competitors. Recently, Lovan has surged ahead in the marketplace on the strength of a new shampoo that is outselling the leading products of all competitors, including Image Products. This new product is based on a supersecret formula that produces a shampoo with a silky texture and a pleasant aroma. Consumers love it.

John Parker, supervisor of the research and development department for Image Products, is under intense pressure to replicate Lovan's formula. Unfortunately for Parker, all of his attempts to break the code have failed. As a result, Image Products has lost so much market share that company-wide layoffs are imminent. Parker's wife and their daughter, who is 3 months pregnant, both work at Image Products. Both will lose their jobs in the first round if layoffs are necessary. Because the firm is located in a rural one-company town, the chances of his wife and daughter finding other jobs are slim at best.

A potential solution has fallen into Parker's lap. A disgruntled chemist from Lovan has applied for a vacant position in Parker's department. He has made it clear to Parker that, if hired, he can bring Lovan's coveted formula with him. However, he will do so only if Parker brings him in at top dollar—a demand that is not justified by the chemist's credentials.

Assume that John Parker is a friend and that he asks your advice about how to handle this situation. What will you recommend to him, and why? What model would you apply in dealing with this dilemma if you were in Parker's position? Why?

DISCUSSION ASSIGNMENT 4–1

An Ethical Dilemma

Vanessa Jones is the manager of the phenolics department of PlastiTech, a manufacturer of industrial plastics and composite materials. She is facing a dilemma. There is an opening in her department, and her brother has applied for it.

Because her brother has been out of work for several months, he is having a great deal of trouble supporting his wife and two children. The family pressure on Vanessa to hire her brother is intense. But there is a problem: Although she has no doubt her brother could do the job well, two other applicants are better qualified. Further, Vanessa, her brother, and the two better-qualified applicants are all minorities, so her company's equal employment opportunity policies will not help her in making the decision, nor will the company's other employment policies, which allow the hiring of family members. Vanessa feels a strong sense of responsibility for the productivity of her department. She also loves her brother and wants to help him. This is the first real ethical dilemma she has ever faced.

If Vanessa doesn't hire her brother, she might be ostracized by her family, and her brother's already precarious financial condition might get even worse. On the other hand, she is responsible for hiring the best new team member she can identify. This type of ethical dilemma is not uncommon in the modern workplace.

DISCUSSION QUESTION

Discuss the following question in class or outside of class with your fellow students:

1. If you found yourself facing a similar dilemma, what would you do? Why?

ENDNOTES

1. Ethics Resource Center. Retrieved from www.ethics.org on January 6, 2011.

2. Ibid.

3. International Organization for Standardization Strategic Advisory Group on Corporate Responsibility. Retrieved from www.iisd.org/standards/ on March 11, 2011.

PARTNERING AND STRATEGIC ALLIANCES

A friendship founded on business is better than a business founded on friendship. —**John D. Rockefeller Jr.**

MAJOR TOPICS
- **Partnering or Strategic Alliances**
- **Innovative Alliances and Partnerships**
- **Internal Partnering**
- **Partnering with Suppliers**
- **Partnering with Customers**
- **Partnering with Potential Competitors**
- **Global Partnering**
- **Education and Business Partnerships**

Partnering for mutual benefit is fundamental to total quality. In an intensely competitive marketplace, where quality is defined by the customer, such practices as low-bid contracts, antagonistic internal relationships, and attempts to operate as an island are being replaced by *partnering*. Working together for mutual benefit sounds like a nice thing to do, and it is. However, being nice has little to do with this contemporary approach to doing business. On the contrary, the partnering philosophy is solidly grounded in the practical demands of the marketplace. This chapter provides the information needed to facilitate partnering relationships with suppliers, customers, internal units, and potential competitors.

PARTNERING OR STRATEGIC ALLIANCES

The simplest way to understand the concept of *partnering* or the strategic alliance is to think of it as working together for mutual benefit. Those who work together may be suppliers, fellow employees, customers, and even businesses that are potential competitors (see Figure 5–1).

The maximum benefits of partnering are realized when all parties in the chain of partners cooperate. In the traditional supplier–customer chain shown in Figure 5–2, each link in the chain operates independently. Invisible walls exist between each

one. The manufacturer in the middle of the chain produces a product used by the customers (end users). For this example, assume that the product is an upscale running shoe. The manufacturer receives leather, fabric, synthetic rubber, glue, and other materials from its suppliers. However, because there is no partnering among the three links in the chain, the manufacturer does not fully understand who buys its shoes and why, what the end users like and dislike about the shoes, or what changes end users think would improve the shoes. Because the manufacturer doesn't know its market and because it doesn't partner with suppliers, the suppliers can't help it better meet the needs of end users.

Now look at the contemporary supplier–customer chain (Figure 5–3). The walls are removed, and the overlapping portions represent partnering. In this model, the manufacturer knows who buys its shoes and why. Further, by involving its customers in the ongoing product development process, the manufacturer designs in the features important to end users and eliminates problems or undesirable characteristics.

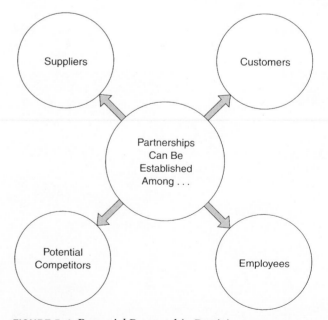

FIGURE 5–1 Potential Partnership Participants

FIGURE 5–2 Traditional Relationships: Supplier–Customer Chain

Because the manufacturer in the contemporary model knows its customers and their needs, it can work with its suppliers to enlist their help in meeting those needs.

Figures 5–2 and 5–3 depict relationships between external suppliers and customers. These same models are repeated numerous times within companies, in which employees are internal suppliers and internal customers to each other. The types of partnering relationships explained earlier must also occur within total quality companies. In traditional supplier–customer relationships, there are invisible walls that block out communication and cooperation (Figure 5–2). With contemporary supplier–customer relationships, these walls are broken down. There is communication, input, feedback, and cooperation (Figure 5–3).

Benefits of Partnering

Several benefits can be derived from partnering. Partnering can lead to continual improvements in such key areas as processes and products, relationships between customers and suppliers, and customer satisfaction. Internal partnering can improve relationships among employees and among departments within an organization. When taken as a whole, these individual benefits add up to enhanced competitiveness.

Partnering Model

Establishing partnering relationships with suppliers or customers is a process that should be undertaken in a systematic way. Haphazardly formed relationships based on halfhearted commitments are worse than having no partnerships at all. Figure 5–4 provides a model that can be used as a guide in the formation of partnering relationships with both external and internal suppliers and customers.

Develop a Partnering Briefing   Partnering is about creating cooperative alliances. Before trying to establish such an alliance, a partnering briefing must be developed to make sure everyone involved understands partnering as a concept.

Identify Potential Partners   Any external or internal supplier or customer is a potential partner. Choose partners in an order determined by how much value the partnership can have toward enhancing quality, productivity, and competitiveness. Internal partnerships between the design and manufacturing departments have considerable potential in this regard. Partnerships between the manufacturing department and major external suppliers also have excellent potential.

Identify Key Decision Makers   In every organization (unit, department, etc.), there are key people whose support is needed to make an initiative involving their organization work. Identify these key decision makers in any organization considered a potential partner. Their support must be won if a successful partnership is to be formed.

Conduct a Partnering Briefing   Call a meeting of the key decision makers in both the organizations—yours and the potential partner's. Present a briefing explaining the partnering concept, with time built in for discussion and questions. This briefing should answer such questions as the following:

- How can we mutually benefit from a partnership?
- What is expected of each partner?

Determine the Level of Commitment   After the key decision makers have been briefed, gauge their level of

FIGURE 5–3 Contemporary Relationships: Supplier–Customer Chain

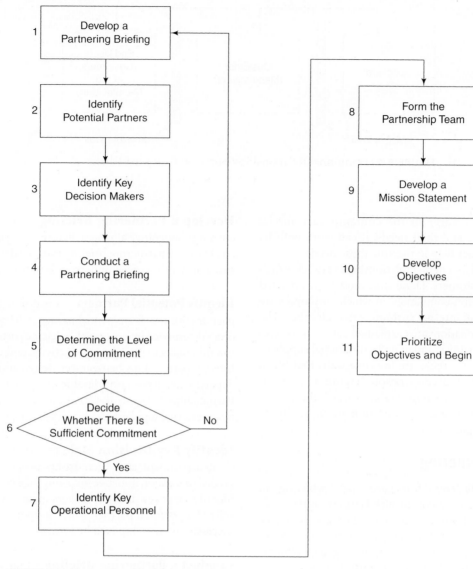

FIGURE 5–4 Partnering Model

commitment. Are they willing to commit to the partnership for the long term? Are they willing to make any and all procedural or philosophical changes that may be necessary for the partnership to work?

Decide Whether There Is Sufficient Commitment

If the key decision makers show noticeable reluctance, they are not likely to make a full commitment to the partnership. There is no need to proceed any further with potential partners who seem reluctant. The better course of action in such a case is to break off further involvement and begin the process again with another potential external partner. However, if the level of commitment is sufficient, proceed to the next step in the process.

Identify Key Operational Personnel

If the level of commitment is sufficient to proceed with the partnership, who are the key people from both organizations needed to put it into operation? Are personnel needed from marketing, purchasing, engineering, manufacturing, receiving, or

accounting? Identify the people who will be needed to put into action the commitment made by executive-level decision makers.

Form the Partnership Team The key people identified as necessary to putting the partnership into operation should be formed into a team. This means more than just naming them to the team. They must be given opportunities to get to know and trust each other. The success of the partnership will depend in great measure on the willingness and ability of these team members to work together in a mutually supportive and trusting manner.

Develop a Mission Statement The partnership team needs a clear and concise mission statement so that everyone involved understands what the team is supposed to do. The mission statement should be developed by executive-level decision makers from both organizations. Figure 5–5 is an example of a mission statement for a supplier–customer partnership.

This mission statement is the guiding vision of the customer–supplier partnership that exists between Keltron Electronics (the customer) and Precision Machining, Inc. (the supplier). The mission of this partnership is to promote a mutually supportive working relationship that will help maximize the quality, productivity, competitiveness, and profitability of both partners. In carrying out this mission, the following agreements apply:

- **Precision Machining, Inc.,** agrees to deliver quality discrete components to Keltron Electronics just in time and at the best possible price.
- **Keltron Electronics** agrees to purchase discrete machine components from Precision Machining, Inc., at a negotiated price as a sole source provider without requests for competitive bids.

FIGURE 5–5 Mission Statement: Keltron Electronics–Precision Machining, Inc., Customer–Supplier Partnership

Develop Objectives The mission statement is written in general terms. It is translated into more specific terms by objectives. These objectives should be developed by the partners and ratified by the executive-level decision makers of both partnership organizations. Well-written objectives are stated in measurable terms, such as the following:

- Each week 100 low-voltage power supplies will be delivered according to a just-in-time (JIT) schedule.
- All power supplies delivered will be free of defects.

These objectives are specific and measurable. In the first one, the expected quantity (100) and the delivery schedule can both be easily checked. In the second objective, if even one power supply is rejected, the objective has not been accomplished. All such objectives must be agreed to by both partners before being sent forward for ratification by executive-level personnel.

Prioritize Objectives and Begin It will typically take several objectives to completely translate the mission statement into measurable action. The importance of these objectives is relative. Although all are important, the objectives should be prioritized and listed in order from the most important to the least. After priorities have been established and confirmed by executive-level personnel, the work necessary to accomplish them begins. Results should be monitored and appropriate action taken when problems arise.

INNOVATIVE ALLIANCES AND PARTNERSHIPS

Partnering between and among companies can take many forms. A group of small- and medium-sized companies might form a partnership to save money through *consortium buying.* This is a concept wherein two or more companies get together to purchase common items in bulk: by doing so, they gain the cost benefits of size. Another innovative type of partnership involves suppliers and their customers. Major customers agree to welcome an *in-house supplier representative* who works with the customer's personnel to continually improve the supplier–customer relationship. Having an in-house supplier representative gives the customer an advocate who sees firsthand what is needed from the supplier, when, where, and why. In turn, it allows the supplier to gain firsthand knowledge of how to better serve the customer. Another innovative partnership takes the form of the *customer focus group.* The customer focus group is an example of a partnership between a supplier and the users of its products or services. Such a focus group consists of customers who are pulled together by a supplier to provide feedback concerning the quality of an existing product or service or input concerning a proposed product or service. There are many examples of innovative partnerships in today's highly competitive global marketplace.

Coca-Cola and Nestlé formed a research partnership to develop a line of ready-to-drink teas and coffees. Procter & Gamble and Walmart formed a partnership to better serve their shared customers through improved shipping and receiving procedures. IBM has a formal partnering program called the Business Partner Program in which IBM and more than 1,000 partners share information of mutual benefit and develop strategies to better serve mutual customers. Partnerships among automobile manufacturers are now common: Ford partners with Mazda, and General Motors with Suzuki.

QUALITY TIP ▼

Process Integration with Suppliers

Suppliers are among an organization's most important partners. But supplier partnerships can be high-maintenance in nature. Even the best supplier partnerships demand constant attention, nurturing, and improvement. One of the most difficult supply chain problems for organizations is process integration. The best supplier partnerships result when processes can be integrated to the point that the partners share forecasts, demand signals, inventory control, and transportation information.

There are no limits on the types of partnerships and alliances that businesses can form for mutual benefit, and there are no limits on the types of companies that might form partnerships; even competitors may do so. Anything that can be done better through cooperation represents a potential basis for a partnership.

INTERNAL PARTNERING

Partnering should begin at home. This means an organization should initiate its partnering efforts internally. Internal partnering occurs at the following three levels:

- Management-to-employee partnerships
- Team-to-team partnerships
- Employee-to-employee partnerships

The overall purpose of internal partnering is to harness the full potential of the workforce and focus it on the continuous improvement of quality.

Internal Partnering Defined

Internal partnering goes by a number of different names. It has been called *employee involvement*, *employee empowerment*, and various other terms. Regardless of what it is called, the concept can be defined as follows:

> Internal partnering is creating an environment and establishing mechanisms within it that bring managers and employees, teams, and individual employees together in mutually supportive alliances that maximize the human resources of an organization.

The key concepts in this definition are as follows:

- Environment
- Mechanisms
- Mutually supportive alliances
- Human resources

Does an organization have an environment that is conducive to internal partnerships? If it does, partnering is welcomed, encouraged, and rewarded. Providing a conducive environment is important, but by itself, it is not enough. Within the environment, mechanisms must exist through which employees are able to channel their ideas for improvement. Mutually supportive alliances among management and employees, teams, and individual employees are relationships in which each partner helps the other do better. Mutual support within an organization is a much more effective way to achieve continuous improvement than the traditional approach of internal competition among individuals and teams.

With internal competition, somebody within the organization loses. When this happens, the organization also loses. But with mutually supportive internal partnerships, all internal partners can win, and the organization's competitive energy is directed outward against other competing organizations. This is when the organization is truly victorious.

The definition speaks to the importance of human resources. Maximizing human resources is essential in a total quality setting. This is how the most significant workplace improvements are made and maintained. Employees and managers can work together as internal partners to continually improve quality and productivity in a variety of ways, including the following:

- Cross-functional problem-solving teams
- Quality circles
- Problem-specific ad hoc teams
- Brainstorming sessions

QUALITY CASE ▼

Robert Bosch Bursa Diesel Systems and Sustained Excellence

Robert Bosch Diesel Systems plant in Bursa, Turkey, produces diesel systems for other Bosch divisions as well as for automobile manufacturers. Specific products include highly complex nozzle-holder combination, common rail injectors, and unit injectors. Established in 1972, this plant has developed into a center of sustained excellence by consistently and effectively applying the principles of quality management. More than 95% of the plant's output is exported to more than 30 customers around the world. In order to satisfy its diverse group of demanding customers, the Bursa Plant has to maintain world-class quality. The plant is well-known for applying such total-quality principles as process management, process improvement, and effective partnerships. In fact, all three were cited as reasons for the plant's selection as a recipient of the prestigious EFQM Award for Excellence—Europe's highest award for quality.

Continual process improvement is deeply imbedded in all aspects of the plant's operations. One of the keys to successful process improvement at the Bursa Plant is the cross-functional customer team. The plant provides every customer it serves—more than 30—with its own dedicated cross-functional team that is available 24 hours a day 7 days a week. These customer teams are able to ensure that the plant responds to problems immediately while simultaneously using customer feedback to improve the process in question. Any time a process is improved on the basis of customer feedback, the problem and corresponding corrections are carefully documented and shared not just throughout the Bursa Plant but the entire Bosch organization.

One of the ways the Bursa plant holds down costs is by using a network of local suppliers. In fact, developing and maintaining effective supplier partnerships is a major part of the plant's success. The emphasis of the Bursa Plant's supplier partnerships is on partnership development—helping the local supplier meet the exacting quality standards required by the Bosch system and its customers. To help suppliers meet its world-class quality standards, the Bursa plant provides both training and audits. Frequent partnership meetings and supplier recognition are part of the plant's approach to build and maintain its network of dependable local suppliers. The EFQM Award citation referred to the Bursa Plant as having an "almost fanatical" approach to process improvement and partnership development.

Source: www.efqm.org

Involving both managers and employees as internal partners in these types of activities is an excellent way to maximize human resources and promote mutually supportive alliances. Such alliances will tap the creativity of all internal partners, allowing good ideas to be turned into improvements.

PARTNERING WITH SUPPLIERS

Relationships between an organization and its suppliers have traditionally been characterized by adversarial activities such as the low-bid process, in which at least one and often both parties lose. Rather than working together to find ways for both to win, buyers use their leverage to force suppliers to absorb costs to win the low bid, and suppliers look for ways to minimize their losses by barely meeting the buyer's specifications. Such relationships will not help either party succeed in the long run in a competitive marketplace.

To understand the rationale for partnering with suppliers, one must first understand the goal.

> The goal is to create and maintain a loyal, trusting, reliable relationship that will allow both partners to win, while promoting the continuous improvement of quality, productivity, and competitiveness.

The traditional adversarial relationship between suppliers and buyers is not likely to contribute much to the accomplishment of this goal.

Not all suppliers can participate in such relationships. In fact, suppliers should be required to qualify to participate. Qualifying a supplier shows that it can guarantee that its products will be delivered when and where they are needed in the specified quantities and without defects. Suppliers who can meet these criteria all of the time meet the technical requirements to qualify as a partner. Whether they will actually become a partner depends on their level of commitment and the synergism and trust that develop between buyer and supplier personnel.

Mandatory Requirements of Supplier Partnerships

Successful supplier partnerships require commitment and continual nurturing. The following points are mandatory requirements of supplier partnerships:[1]

- Supplier personnel should meet with buyer personnel beyond those in the purchasing office. It is particularly important for them to meet with personnel who actually use their products so that needed improvements can be identified and made.

- The price-only approach to buyer–supplier negotiations should be eliminated. Product features, quality, and delivery concerns should also be part of the negotiations. The goal of the negotiations should be to achieve the optimum deal when price, features, quality, and delivery issues are all factored in.

- The quality of supplier products should be guaranteed by the supplier's quality processes. The buyer should have no need to inspect the supplier's products.

- The supplier should fully understand and be able to practice JIT. Buyers should not need to maintain inventories.

- Both partners should be capable of sharing information electronically so that the relationship is not inhibited by paperwork. Electronic data exchange is particularly important for successful JIT.

Stages of Development in Supplier Partnerships

Successful supplier partnerships don't just happen overnight; they evolve over time. According to Poirier and Houser, this evolution occurs in the stages depicted in Figure 5–6 and detailed in the following sections:

Uncertainty and Tentativeness In the uncertainty and tentativeness stage, the buyer and seller are like two people on their first date. There is interest, but it is tentative and prefaced with uncertainty. Neither party knows exactly what to expect of the other. At this point, there is no trust between the partners.

Short-Term Pressures The typical short-term pressures that apply in a traditional business setting manifest themselves in this step. The buyer will be under the usual pressure to cut costs. The supplier will be under the usual pressure to increase sales volume. Both partners will be cautious, and initial attempts to begin putting some substance to the partnership will be probing and vague.

Need for New Approaches In the need for new approaches stage, traditional negotiations will inevitably occur. The buyer will press for price discounts, improved payment terms, freight allowances, and other concessions that save it money but cost the supplier. The supplier will press for higher volume to offset concessions made to the buyer. Then, if either partner has involved total quality-conscious personnel, it will dawn on them that quality is not being served by this traditional negotiating. Both will begin to realize that a new approach is needed. If this awareness does not occur, the partnership will fail.

Adoption of New Paradigms In the adoption of new paradigms stage, both partners explore ways to move toward the concept of *mutual benefit*. The key is for both partners to accept the principle that absorbing costs within the partnership (by either the supplier or the buyer) gives neither an advantage. The best way to promote competitiveness is for both partners to work together to lower costs. This new way of thinking (paradigm) will give the partnership a competitive advantage over other organizations that produce the same product.

Awareness of Potential In the awareness of potential stage, both partners become fully aware of the possible

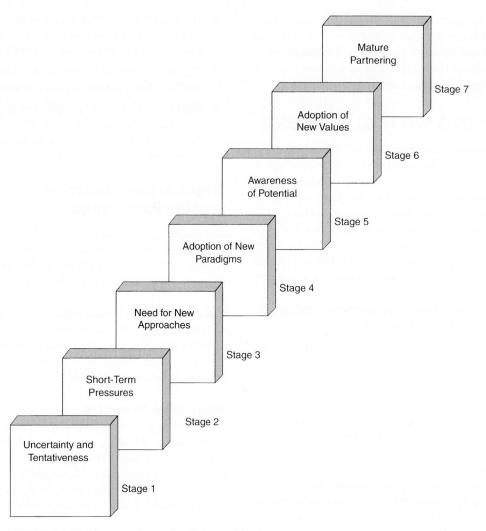

FIGURE 5–6 Evolution of Supplier Partnerships

benefits that can be realized from the partnership. The potential for a true win–win relationship can now be seen. Rather than negotiating price concessions and volume increases, both partners realize that by working together they can exceed any short-term advantages that might have been realized from these traditional negotiating strategies.

Adoption of New Values   In the adoption of new values stage, both partners adopt the new values inherent in a true supplier–buyer partnership. These values include trust, openness, and sharing. Each party trusts the other to protect the confidentiality of what they learn about one another. Both parties accept that the more information they share, including financial information, the better prepared they will be to help one another.

Mature Partnering   In the mature partnering stage, the partnership has solidified. A high level of trust and cooperation has been established between the partners. Continuous interfacing between pertinent employees at all levels of both organizations exists as fact. Each partner has a strong self-interest in the success of the other partner.

Emerging Issues in Supply-Chain Management

For years, the key issue in supply-chain management was increased speed—get the product produced and in the customer's hands as fast as possible. However, like most quality-related concepts, supply-chain management is still evolving and being improved on as organizations learn more about it and how best to apply the concept. Emerging issues in supply-chain management include the following:[2]

Security   With the rise of international terrorism, organizations are being forced to consider the issue of security when selecting suppliers. Companies that do business with the U.S. government are being forced to comply with new, more stringent security regulations throughout their supplier chain. This is especially the case for U.S. companies that do business overseas.

Adaptability and Responsiveness   Supply-chain management is an ever-changing concept. As an organization's competitors get better at using the concept and continually improve on its application, other organizations must adapt in order to stay competitive. Consequently, it is important to have suppliers in the chain that can adapt continually and respond quickly.

Globalization Globalization has changed the customer base for many organizations at the top of the supply chain. As a result, these companies are finding that their suppliers must also change accordingly. Large multinational companies that are accustomed to working with large suppliers are finding it necessary to work with much smaller suppliers in order to be responsive to markets in smaller countries throughout the world. The needs and capabilities of smaller suppliers are different than those of large suppliers. This is forcing large multinational companies at the top of the supply chain to reengineer their approach to supply-chain management.

Misalignment of Material Technologies and Product Life Cycles Companies that manufacture electromechanical systems, equipment, and devices that are designed with a product life expectancy of 10 to 15 years are finding that the materials and parts they purchase from suppliers for normal upgrades and maintenance are not available. This is especially the case with semiconductors. Parts suppliers might maintain a readily available inventory for just 18 to 36 months. This means that the system's manufacturer is forced to choose one of the following three alternatives, with all of them considered to be bad: (1) purchase at the outset a large enough inventory of spare parts to last 12 to 13 years; (2) divert the valuable time of engineers from product-development to reengineering of parts (which amounts to mortgaging the future); or (3) locate brokers who are willing to take the risk of maintaining an inventory of unique parts (which means paying extraordinarily high prices for the parts when they are needed). This is a major supply-chain management issue for many companies.

Transition and Crisis Management The ability to handle transitions and crises throughout the entire supply chain has become a critical issue for companies at the top of the chain. In fact, this ability can mean the difference between success and failure for companies that operate on a global level. What happens when a critical supplier in the chain suddenly closes its doors or when delivery of critical components is interrupted by a natural disaster or a terrorist act? The ability to quickly adjust to this type of crisis throughout the supply chain will be increasingly critical in the future.

PARTNERING WITH CUSTOMERS

The term *customer* as used in this section means the end user of the product in question and any buyer of a supplier's products. There are other uses of the term, of course. Internal customers exist in every organization. However, in this section, the term will be used to mean end users and customers of suppliers. In this context, for example, the customer of an automobile manufacturer might be a consumer who buys one of its models or a car rental agency that purchases its fleet from the manufacturer.

The rationale for forming partnerships with customers in this context is simple: It is the best way to ensure customer satisfaction, which is, in turn, the best way to be competitive. To understand this rationale, answer the following questions:

1. Who knows better what the customer wants, your organization or the customer?

2. What makes more sense, guessing what customers want or asking them?

3. Can a producer benefit from seeing how its product is used by customers?

4. What costs more, making design changes early in the product development cycle or recalling faulty products that have already been produced and purchased by customers?

The answers to these questions form the rationale for partnering with customers. No organization can possibly know better than its customers what the customers want. Customer-defined quality is a fundamental part of the total quality philosophy. Whether it is best to guess what a customer wants or to ask is obvious. No organization can afford to squander its resources and, in turn, its competitive edge guessing what customers want. Organizations should ask customers what they want. Any organization that produces a product can benefit from observing how it is used by customers.

By involving customers early in the product development cycle, a manufacturer can make changes inexpensively and with relative ease. The further along a product is in the development cycle, the more costly such changes become. If modifications are needed after the product is being used by customers, such as in the case of product recalls, the cost cannot be measured in just dollars and cents. Additional costs accrue in the form of lost consumer confidence, diminished trust, and a tarnished corporate image. Product defects can be corrected much more easily than consumer confidence or trust can be restored.

The customer feedback survey conducted by mail and telephone is a widely used strategy for measuring customer satisfaction. Such surveys have a place. However, their after-the-fact nature limits their usefulness. Unless they are just one part of a much broader set of strategies implemented a great deal earlier in the process, customer satisfaction surveys will have only a limited effect on an organization's ability to compete.

The key to success in partnering with customers is to get them involved early in the product development cycle. Let them preview the design. Allow them to observe and even try prototype models. Get their feedback at every stage in the product development cycle, and make any needed changes as soon as they are identified. When this approach is used, customer satisfaction surveys can solicit feedback from a broader audience to verify the input given earlier in the product development cycle. Discussion Assignment 5-1 illustrates this approach.

PARTNERING WITH POTENTIAL COMPETITORS

Partnering with potential competitors sounds like an odd strategy on the surface. Why would organizations that compete for business in the same markets want to form partnerships? The rationale for partnering with potential competitors is the same as that for partnering with suppliers and customers: competitiveness. This is a strategy that applies more frequently to small- and medium-sized firms, but it can also be used by even the largest organizations, and sometimes is. For example, the leading computer companies in the United States may form a partnership to develop the next technological breakthrough before a similar team in Japan, Germany, or some other country beats them to it.

Small- and Medium-sized enterprises (SMEs) don't typically develop major technological breakthroughs. However, there are many ways in which SMEs can work together to enhance their competitiveness in spite of being competitors in the same markets. The most widely practiced type of partnership among SMEs is the manufacturing network.

Manufacturing Networks of SMEs

A manufacturing network is a group of individual SMEs that cooperate in ways that increase their quality, productivity, and resultant competitiveness to levels beyond what the individual member companies could achieve by themselves. The concept originated in Europe after World War II. It is still practiced extensively in the Emilia-Romagna region of Italy and in Denmark.

These countries applied the concept to rebuild their manufacturing bases after the devastation of World War II, when resources were insufficient to allow manufacturers

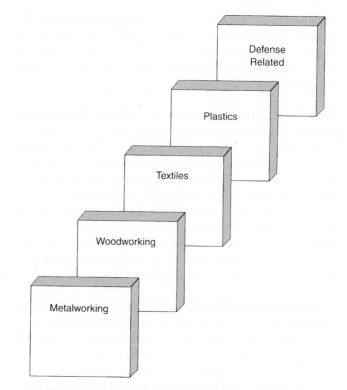

FIGURE 5–7 Industrial Clusters with Networks in the United States

to rebuild independent of one another. Consequently, rather than trying to completely retool and restaff independently, companies formed networks and shared both human and technological resources. Manufacturing networks were originally conceived as a way to rebuild. They have since evolved into a way to compete—particularly for SMEs.

Manufacturing networks began to appear in the United States in the 1980s. The earliest known network in the United States is the Garment Industry Development Center, established in New York City in 1984. Figure 5–7 shows the broad industrial clusters in which manufacturing networks can be found in the United States. Of these, the greatest number of networks can be found in the metalworking, woodworking, and textile industries.

Network Activities

The joint activities in which networks participate vary a great deal, depending on local objectives. Figure 5–8 shows some of the most widely practiced joint activities of manufacturing networks in the United States.

Production Networked SMEs are able to pursue production contracts larger than any individual member company could undertake alone. Through teaming arrangements, the work and the financing of it are divided among network members as appropriate.

The Technology Coast Manufacturing and Engineering Network (TeCMEN) in Fort Walton Beach, Florida, under-

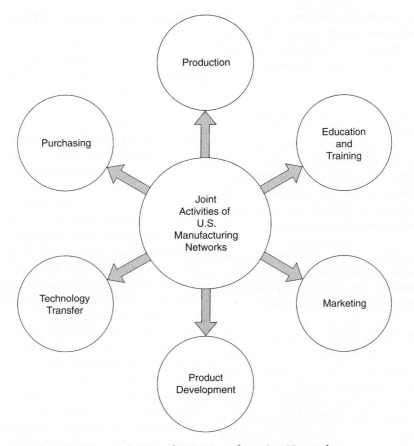

FIGURE 5–8 Joint Activities of U.S. Manufacturing Networks

takes joint projects and its members work together to meet joint needs such as training. The member organizations are Department of Defense Contractors that design and manufacture electromechanical military technologies. By participating in TeCMEN projects, individual members are able to pursue larger, more complex contracts than they could attempt alone.

Education and Training   Education and training are often a problem for SMEs. On the one hand, employees need ongoing education and training to continually improve quality, productivity, and competitiveness. On the other hand, they face the following problems because they have a limited employee base:

- Difficulty giving employees time off for education and training and still meeting production schedules

- Difficulty convincing educational institutions that typically need 15 to 20 students to form a class to bring courses on-site

- High expense for education because they do not get the substantial registration discounts large firms get when participating in training provided by private training firms

By partnering, SMEs can solve all three of these problems through economy of scale. Although giving employees time off for training will always be difficult, it can be made easier through the sharing of employees by network members on a reciprocal basis. By bringing together all employees from member companies who need a certain type of training, networks can produce classes large enough to attract educational institutions and to qualify for discounts from private training providers. The Garment Industry Development Corporation (GIDC) in New York City is an example of a network that provides joint training opportunities for its members (see Figure 5–9).

Marketing   Marketing is the most widely practiced joint activity among manufacturing networks of SMEs. Typically, the joint capabilities of the network are what is marketed. Member companies share the costs of producing marketing tools, such as brochures, videos, and promotional materials; of attending trade shows; and of marketing personnel and related expenses such as travel. The TeCMEN in Fort

- Sewing machine maintenance and repair
- Computer-assisted shop-floor management
- Manual working and grading operations
- Computerized working and grading operations
- Advanced training (whole-garment construction and quality control)

FIGURE 5–9 Joint Training Programs: Garment Industry Development Corporation (GIDC)

Walton Beach, Florida, conducts a joint marketing program. Members share the costs of participation in selected trade shows, production of a joint marketing brochure, and other miscellaneous related costs (e.g., telephone, travel, postage).

Product Development   Developing new products can be too expensive an undertaking for SMEs. It typically involves such activities as research, design, market analysis, competition analysis, prototype production, performance testing, and test marketing. The costs associated with these activities can be prohibitive for an individual SME. However, when the costs can be divided among network members, product development becomes a more feasible concept.

The True North Certified Forest Products Network Inc., in Bemidji, Minnesota, sponsors joint product development projects for its members. The products fall into three categories: craft items, furniture, and building materials.

Technology Transfer   Technology is the physical manifestation of knowledge. *Technology transfer* is the movement of technology from one arena to another. The form of technology transfer that is most readily and widely recognized is the transfer of a new technology from a research laboratory to a production setting. This is often referred to as *technology commercialization*. Another aspect of technology transfer is the movement of a commercialized technology into the hands of users. This aspect is often referred to as *technology diffusion*.

After it has been diffused, technology must be properly used to realize its potential benefits. Proper use of technology requires knowledge. Knowledge sharing is the approach networks use to promote effective technology transfer. An example of how knowledge sharing is applied is the Heat Treating Network Inc. (HTN), of Cleveland, Ohio. One of the partners in this network is the Edison Material Technology Center (EMTEC). The EMTEC provides a free hotline that HTN members can access for assistance in solving heat treatment problems. The hotline is the primary vehicle for information sharing.

When a technology-related problem is confronted, the member calls the EMTEC's hotline and explains it in detail. EMTEC personnel provide a solution within 72 hours or guide the company to another source that can help. The latter approach is known as *brokering*.

Purchasing   One of the most productive applications of the economy of scale gained from networking is in purchasing. SMEs working alone are not able to enjoy the cost savings that large firms achieve by purchasing bulk quantities of expendable materials and other necessities, such as insurance. However, by jointly purchasing necessities, networked SMEs can achieve similar cost savings. For example, members of The Metalworking Connection Inc., in Alabama jointly purchase casualty insurance, thereby saving between 20 and 30% of the cost of premiums.

GLOBAL PARTNERING

The partnering concept, like all contemporary business concepts, has a global aspect. Companies that market to customers worldwide should examine the possibility of partnering with suppliers worldwide. In some cases, the government of the host country will actually mandate supplier partnerships as an economic *quid pro quo*. This arrangement is often the case in nondemocratic countries. Government-mandated partnerships are not recommended here because they might be driven more by political than business considerations.

In countries where businesses are free to develop partnerships based on sound business principles rather than politics, the same rules apply as those set forth earlier for domestic partnerships. Modern transportation and telecommunication technologies make geographic separation a manageable issue. But the latter technologies do not take the place of on-site visits to the facilities of partners, nor do they replace face-to-face interaction with global customers.

A one-size-fits-all product will not suffice in the global marketplace. Local on-the-ground interaction with both suppliers and customers is critical in gearing up for product design. No designer, planner, or manufacturer in the United States can possibly understand all the cultural nuances or country-specific preferences of people from other nations. Put another way, product attributes that are popular in the United States may not be in another country. Consequently, access to suppliers and customers in these countries is critical. Partnering is the best way to gain the necessary access.

EDUCATION AND BUSINESS PARTNERSHIPS

Two of the most important factors in continually improving the performance of an organization are the quality of employees and the quality of human interaction with technology. To improve performance, organizations must first improve their people and the interaction of their people with process technologies. Individuals who lack fundamental work skills cannot perform at globally competitive levels, and people who lack process skills cannot get the most out of technologies available to them. For example, a person who cannot solve general algebraic equations will be unable to learn statistical process control, and a person who uses a word processing system as if it were a typewriter will not get the most out of this technology.

The need to continually improve employees' work skills is the primary force driving business and education partnerships. In such partnerships, educational institutions provide on-site customized training, technical assistance, and consulting services to help organizations continually improve their people and their processes. They also provide workshops and seminars and facilitate focus groups.

Partnering with business and industry has become a common practice for institutions of higher education. Discussion Assignment 5-2 contains two examples of the approaches educational institutions are taking to promote business and industry partnerships.

SUMMARY

1. *Partnering* means working together for mutual benefit. It involves pooling resources, sharing costs, and cooperating in ways that mutually benefit all parties involved in the partnership. Partnerships may be formed internally (among employees) and externally with suppliers, customers, and potential competitors. The purpose of partnering is to enhance competitiveness. The formation of partnerships should be a systematic process involving such steps as development of a partnering briefing, identification of potential partners, identification of key decision makers, presentation of the partnering briefing, determination of the level of commitment, identification of key personnel, formation of the partnering team, development of a mission statement, development of objectives, prioritization of the objectives, and implementation of the partnership.

2. Internal partnering operates on three levels: management-to-employee partnerships, team-to-team partnerships, and employee-to-employee partnerships. The purpose of internal partnering is to harness the full potential of the workforce and focus it on the continuous improvement of quality. Internal partnering is also called *employee involvement* and *employee empowerment*. Successful internal partnering requires a supportive environment, structured mechanisms, and mutually supportive alliances.

3. The goal of a supplier partnership is to create and maintain loyal, trusting relationships that will allow both partners to win, while promoting the continuous improvement of quality, productivity, and competitiveness. The requirements for success in supplier partnerships include the following: supplier personnel should interact with employees who actually use their products, the price-only criterion in the buyer–supplier relationship should be eliminated, the quality of products delivered should be guaranteed by the supplier, the supplier should be proficient in just-in-time (JIT), and both parties should be capable of sharing information electronically. Supplier partnerships typically develop in the following stages: uncertainty and tentativeness, short-term pressures, realization of the need for new approaches, adoption of new paradigms, awareness of potential, adoption of new values, and mature partnering.

4. The rationale for forming customer partnerships is customer satisfaction. The best way to ensure customer satisfaction is to involve customers as partners in the product development process. Doing so is, in turn, the best way to ensure competitiveness. Customer-defined quality is a fundamental aspect of total quality.

5. Small- and medium-sized enterprises, or SMEs, even those that compete in the same markets, can benefit from partnering. The most widely practiced form of partnership among SMEs is the manufacturing network. A manufacturing network is a group of SMEs that cooperate in ways that enhance their quality, productivity, and competitiveness. Mutual need and interdependence are the characteristics that make manufacturing networks succeed. Widely practiced network activities include joint production, education and training, marketing, product development, technology transfer, and purchasing.

6. Education and business partnerships are formed to help organizations continually improve their people and how well they interact with process technologies. Services provided include on-site customized training, workshops, seminars, technical assistance, and consulting.

KEY TERMS AND CONCEPTS

Brokering
Environment
Internal partnering
Level of commitment
Manufacturing network
Mature partnering
Mechanisms
Mutually supportive alliances
New paradigms
New values
Partnering
Partnering briefing
Partnering model
Partnership team
Partnering with customers
Partnering with potential competitors
Partnering with suppliers
Price-only approach
Short-term pressures
SME
Technology transfer
Uncertainty and tentativeness

FACTUAL REVIEW QUESTIONS

1. Define the term *partnering*
2. What are the benefits of partnering?
3. Describe each step in the partnering model.
4. Define the term *internal partnering*.
5. What is partnering with suppliers?
6. Explain the mandatory requirements of supplier partnerships.
7. List and explain the stages of development in supplier partnerships.

8. Explain the rationale for partnering with customers.

9. What is a manufacturing network?

10. What role does mutual need play in manufacturing networks?

11. List and explain the most widely practiced network activities.

12. What types of services do educational institutions typically provide to business and industry partners?

CRITICAL THINKING ACTIVITY

Does Training Cost or Pay?

John Andrews and Martha Stevens are supervisors in the production department of ATV Inc., a manufacturer of various types of all-terrain vehicles. ATV is beginning to feel the pressure of global competition. To continue the growth it has enjoyed over the last 5 years, ATV is going to have to improve quality, productivity, customer service, and supplier relationships.

One task force has been formed to investigate the feasibility of supplier partnerships. John and Martha have been appointed to another task force to determine whether a partnership with a local college is feasible as a way to improve employee performance. Representatives from the college have interviewed employees, supervisors, and managers to determine what types of assistance ATV needs.

The college's director of business services made a presentation to the Education Partnership Task Force this morning. He made the following recommendations: (a) all production employees should receive training in benchmarking, continuous process improvement, use of the quality tools, and problem solving; (b) the training should be provided on-site and on company time; and (c) the company should pay all costs associated with the training. John and Martha are discussing these recommendations.

"There is no way ATV is going to pay what the college wants to charge," said John. "And I guarantee there won't be any training conducted on company time. All of this is too expensive. Management will turn the college down flat."

"I don't think so," said Martha. "If the training improves our performance enough to keep us competitive, it will be worth every penny and more."

Join this debate. Does training for business and industry cost, or does it pay? What is your opinion?

DISCUSSION ASSIGNMENT 5-1

PARTNERING WITH CUSTOMERS PAYS OFF

Newspaper Concessions Corporation (NCC) manufactures vending machines for newspaper chains nationwide. The machines are placed in conspicuous locations and accessed using the appropriate combination of coins. A great deal of research has gone into continually improving this aspect of the vending machines. Even with this, NCC noticed a sharp drop-off in sales to newspapers serving large urban centers.

As part of its new customer partnership effort, NCC invited representatives from established customers in 10 large cities to spend time in its production facility and participate in all phases of the development of the latest model of its vending machine. Input from these representatives resulted in a major design change.

The NCC had put a great deal of effort into developing a stronger coin box that could stand up to vandals and thieves. As it turned out, theft of money was only part of the problem. More important to the newspaper representatives was theft of their newspapers. In their cities, people were putting in the correct combination of coins to pay for one newspaper but taking all of the newspapers in the box. The newspaper sellers speculated that drug users were selling the newspapers and keeping the money to support their habits.

What was needed was a vending machine that would drop just one newspaper at a time rather than opening its door to the entire supply. With the necessary design change made, NCC quickly regained its lost sales.

DISCUSSION QUESTION

Discuss the following question in class or outside of class with your fellow students:

1. Is there a store, restaurant, or other establishment with which you do business that could improve its service or products? If given the opportunity, what would you tell the owner or manager about improvements that are needed?

DISCUSSION ASSIGNMENT 5-2

BUSINESS AND EDUCATION PARTNERSHIPS

The Quality Institute

The Quality Institute (TQI) is a partnership of Northwest Florida State College, the University of West Florida, and the Economic Development Council of Okaloosa County. TQI is dedicated to the continual improvement of quality, productivity, and competitiveness in the private and public sectors. To this end, TQI offers education, training, consulting, and technical assistance in a wide range of areas, including quality management, supervision, manufacturing improvement, workplace health and safety, human resources and development, and management.

Institute for Professional Development

The Institute for Professional Development (IPD) of Northwest Florida State College was established to help business, industry, and government agencies as well as individuals continually improve their performance in the global marketplace. A knowledgeable and well-trained workforce can provide a formidable competitive advantage. The IPD provides seminars, short courses, workshops, and customized contract training to help continually improve the performance of people, processes, products, and organizations. The IPD's services are designed to help individuals and organizations not just survive in today's intensely competitive marketplace but also prevail.

DISCUSSION QUESTIONS

Discuss the following questions in class or outside of class with your fellow students:

1. Do you know of any companies that partner with educational institutions for training or technical assistance?

2. Does the institution you are attending partner with business and industry?

3. In both cases, what is the nature of the partnership (e.g., what kinds of courses, technical assistance)?

ENDNOTES

1. www.fao/org/ag/ags/publications/docs/AGSF_ OccasionalPapers/ags/op17.pdf. Retrieved on February 9, 2011.

2. *CSCMP Toolbox*, Council of Supply Chain Management Professionals. Retrieved from http:// cscmp.org/academics/educational.asp on January 12, 2011.

QUALITY CULTURE: CHANGING HEARTS, MINDS, AND ATTITUDES

On changing the culture: "Don't ever take a fence down until you know why it was put up." —**G. K. Chesterton**

MAJOR TOPICS
- **Understanding What a Quality Culture Is**
- **Quality Culture versus Traditional Cultures**
- **Activating Cultural Change**
- **Changing Leaders to Activate Change**
- **Laying the Foundation for a Quality Culture**
- **Learning What a Quality Culture Looks Like**
- **Countering Resistance to Cultural Change**
- **Establishing a Quality Culture**
- **Maintaining a Quality Culture**

One of the greatest obstacles faced by organizations attempting to implement total quality is the cultural barrier. Many organizations do an excellent job of committing to total quality, involving employees in all aspects of planning and implementation, and providing the training needed to ensure that employees have the necessary skills, only to have their efforts fall flat. The culprit in many of these cases is organizational inertia. No effort has been made to overcome the comfort employees at all levels feel in doing things the way they have always been done. In other words, no effort has been made to change the organization's culture. This chapter explains the concept of organizational culture as it relates to quality and how to go about changing it.

UNDERSTANDING WHAT A QUALITY CULTURE IS

To understand what a quality culture is, one must first understand the concept of *organizational culture*. Every organization has one. An organization's culture is the everyday manifestation of its underlying values and traditions. It shows up in how employees behave at work, what their expectations are of the organization and each other, and what is considered normal in terms of how employees approach their jobs. Have you ever shopped at a store or eaten in a restaurant in which the service was poor and the employees surly or disinterested? Such organizations have a cultural problem. Valuing the customer is not part of their culture. No matter what slogans or what advertising gimmicks they use, the behavior of their employees clearly says, "We don't care about customers."

An organization's culture has the following elements:

- Business environment
- Organizational values
- Cultural role models
- Organizational rites, rituals, and customs
- Cultural transmitters

The business environment in which an organization must operate is a critical determinant of its culture. Organizations that operate in a highly competitive business environment that changes rapidly and continually are likely to develop a *change-oriented* culture. Organizations that operate in a stable market in which competition is limited may develop a *don't-rock-the-boat* culture.

Organizational values describe what the organization thinks is important. Adherence to these values is synonymous with success. Consequently, an organization's values are the heart and soul of its culture.

Cultural role models are employees at any level who personify the organization's values. When cultural role models retire or die, they typically become legends in their organizations. While still active, they serve as living examples of what the organization wants its employees to be.

Organizational rites, rituals, and customs express the organization's unwritten rules about how things are done. How employees dress, interact with each other, and approach their work are all part of this element of an organization's culture. Rites, rituals, and customs are enforced most effectively by peer pressure.

Cultural transmitters are the vehicles by which an organization's culture is passed down through successive generations of employees. The grapevine in any organization is a cultural transmitter, as are an organization's symbols, slogans, and recognition ceremonies.

✓ Behavior matches slogans.

✓ Customer input is actively sought and used to continually improve quality.

✓ Employees are both involved and empowered.

✓ Work is done in teams.

✓ Executive-level managers are both committed and involved; responsibility for quality is *NOT* delegated.

✓ Sufficient resources are made available where and when they are needed to ensure the continuous improvement of quality.

✓ Education and training are provided to ensure that employees at all levels have the knowledge and skills needed to continuously improve quality.

✓ Reward and promotion systems are based on contributions to the continual improvement of quality.

✓ Fellow employees are viewed as internal customers.

✓ Suppliers are treated as partners.

✓ Peak performance of people, processes, and products is a top priority.

FIGURE 6–1 Characteristics Shared by Organizations with a Quality Culture

What an organization truly values will show up in the behavior of its employees, and no amount of lip service or advertising to the contrary will change this. If an organization's culture is its value system as manifested in organizational behavior, what is a quality culture?

A quality culture is an organizational value system that results in an environment that is conducive to the establishment and continual improvement of quality. It consists of values, traditions, procedures, and expectations that promote quality.

How do you recognize an organization with a quality culture? It is actually easier to recognize a quality culture than to define one. Organizations with a quality culture, regardless of the products or services they provide, share a number of common characteristics, presented in Figure 6–1.

How Are Organizational Cultures Created?

Many factors contribute to the creation of an organization's culture. The value systems of executive-level decision makers are often reflected in their organization's culture. How managers treat employees and how employees at all levels interact on a personal basis also contribute to the organizational culture. Expectations are important determinants of organizational culture. What management expects of employees and what employees, in turn, expect of management both contribute to an organization's culture. The stories passed along from employee to employee typically play a major role in the establishment and perpetuation of an organization's culture. All of these factors can either help or hurt an organization.

If managers treat employees with trust, dignity, and respect, employees will be more likely to treat each other in this way, and trust, dignity, and respect in everyday interaction will become part of the organization's culture. On the other hand, if management treats employees poorly, employees are likely to follow suit. Both situations, if not changed, will become ingrained as traditions. These traditions will be perpetuated both by the behavior of employees and by the stories they pass along to one another. This is why it is so important to establish a quality culture. If mistrust is part of the organizational culture, it will be difficult to build partnerships between internal and external customers. It will also be difficult to establish an environment of mutually supportive teamwork. Organizations that have these problems are not likely to be world-class competitors.

Commitment to quality cannot be faked. Employees know when management is just going through the motions. Changing an organization's culture requires a total commitment and a sustained effort at all levels of the organization.

QUALITY CULTURE VERSUS TRADITIONAL CULTURES

Organizations that develop and maintain a quality culture will differ significantly from those with a traditional culture. The differences will be most noticeable in the following areas:

- Operating philosophy
- Objectives
- Management approach
- Attitude toward customers
- Problem-solving approach
- Supplier relationships
- Performance-improvement approach

Operating Philosophy

In an organization with a traditional culture, the primary focus is return on investment and short-term profits. Often the methods used to maximize profits in the short term have a negative effect in the long run. In order to improve the organization's bottom line on the next quarter's profit-and-loss statement, executives might decide to "unload" a defective product on customers, put off critical technology upgrades, or eliminate training programs for employees. An organization might cut back on equipment maintenance, employee benefits, or performance-incentive programs. All of these shortsighted methods are common in organizations with traditional cultures, and while they might prop up the bottom line temporarily, they invariably lead to disaster in the long run. A short-term operating philosophy is the reason why traditional organizations often experience a large turnover at the top. The CEOs who apply this short-term operating philosophy are often "cut-and-run" managers who maximize short-term profits by eliminating essential functions, activities, and personnel. They then take their percentage of the resulting profits and leave, only to repeat the charade at another organization.

In an organization with a quality culture, the core of the operating philosophy is customer satisfaction. Quality organizations focus on doing what is necessary to exceed the reasonable expectations of customers. Such an approach can lower profits in the short run but is the key to long-term survival and prosperity. For example, making a major investment in an expensive technology upgrade can cause the next quarter's profit-and-loss statement to be flat. Over time, however, the benefits of the new technology will take hold and will be reflected in profit-and-loss statements for years to come. Organizations that adopt a quality culture typically have less turnover at the top. This is because such a philosophy encourages decision makers to stay in their positions long enough to either enjoy or suffer the consequences of their decisions.

Objectives

Organizations with traditional cultures typically adopt short-term objectives. The focus is on what the organization should accomplish over the next several weeks and months. Organizations that adopt a quality culture plan strategically. They develop both long- and short-term objectives, and they do so within the context of an organizational vision.

Management Approach

In organizations with traditional cultures, managers think and employees do. In fact, employees don't just do; they do what they are told. Managers are seen as "bosses" who give orders and enforce policies, procedures, and rules. In organizations with quality cultures, managers are seen as coaches of the team. They communicate the vision, mission, and goals; provide resources; remove barriers; seek employee input and feedback; build trust; provide training; and reward and recognize performance.

Attitude toward Customers

Organizations with traditional cultures tend to look inward. They are more concerned about their needs than those of customers. Customer relations might actually be adversarial. Organizations with a quality culture are customer-focused. Customer satisfaction is the highest priority and is the primary motivation driving continual improvement efforts.

Problem-Solving Approach

There is a lot of finger pointing in organizations with a traditional culture. When problems occur, decision makers and employees tend to expend more energy on deflecting or assigning blame than on identifying the root cause of the problem, which must occur before the problem can be solved. Traditional organizations suffer from the "most valuable player (MVP)" syndrome in which problem solving is viewed as an individual undertaking wherein independent "heroes" operating all alone jump into the breach to put things right just in the nick of time. At best, this approach is erratic.

Another phenomenon that occurs in traditional cultures is the "waiting game." With this strategy, decision makers hold back until someone appears to have the problem almost solved; then they jump on board and act as if the idea was theirs all along. Such an approach encourages manipulation and subterfuge rather than innovation and creative thinking.

When difficulties occur in organizations with a quality culture, the focus is on identifying and isolating the root cause so that the problem, and not just its symptoms, can be eliminated. Problem solving is typically a systematic process undertaken by teams, with input solicited from all stakeholders. The goal is to create solutions, not "heroes."

Supplier Relationships

In organizations with a traditional culture, suppliers are kept at arm's length in relationships that are often adversarial. The maximum possible pressure is exerted on suppliers to bring down prices and speed up delivery, even when such an approach is likely to drive the supplier out of business. In organizations with a quality culture, suppliers are viewed as partners. Supplier and customers work together cooperatively for the good of both. Each gets to know the other's processes, problems, strengths, and weaknesses, and they collaborate, using this information to continually improve the relationship and the performance of both.

Performance-Improvement Approach

In organizations with a traditional culture, performance improvement is an erratic, reactive undertaking that is typically triggered by problems. In organizations with a quality culture, continual improvement of processes, people, products, the working environment, and every other factor that affects performance is at the very core of the operating philosophy.

ACTIVATING CULTURAL CHANGE

To attempt the implementation of total quality without creating a quality culture is to invite failure. Organizations in which the prevailing culture is based on traditional management practices are not likely to succeed in the implementation of total quality. Successful total quality requires cultural change. Several primary reasons cultural change must either precede or at least parallel the implementation of total quality are described here.

1. **Change Cannot Occur in a Hostile Environment.** The total quality approach to doing business may be radically different from what management and employees are accustomed to. Managers who are used to sitting in their lonely towers at the top of the pecking order and issuing edicts from on high are likely to reject the concept of employee involvement and empowerment.

   Employees who are used to competing against their fellow employees for promotions and wage increases may not be open to mutually supportive internal partnerships and teamwork. Situations such as these can create an environment that is hostile toward change, no matter how desirable that change is. Change can be difficult, even when people want to do so. It can be impossible in a hostile environment.

2. **Moving to Total Quality Takes Time.** The nature of total quality is such that the organization may have to go down somewhat before it can turn things around and start to come up. In a conversion to total quality, positive results are rarely achieved in the short run. This characteristic gives nonbelievers and people who just don't want to change (and such people are often in the majority at first) the opportunity to promote the "I told you it wouldn't work" syndrome.

3. **It Can Be Difficult to Overcome the Past.** Employees who have worked in an organization for any period of time have probably seen a variety of management fads come and go. Promoting the latest management gimmick and then letting it die for lack of interest may be part of the existing organizational culture. If this is the case, it will be difficult to overcome the past. Employees will remember earlier fads and gimmicks and characterize total quality as being just the latest one; they may take a "This too shall pass" attitude toward it. The past is not just an important part of an organization's culture; it can also be the most difficult part to leave behind.

CHANGING LEADERS TO ACTIVATE CHANGE

Cultural change is one of the most difficult challenges an organization will ever face. It is hard to achieve under even the best of circumstances. Leadership from the top is essential. Consequently, sometimes an organization's culture simply cannot be changed without a change in leadership.

This possibility arises when the staunchest defenders of the status quo are the most senior managers. Senior managers are likely to be the individuals in an organization with the greatest investment in the past and, as a result, the greatest loyalty to orthodoxy. If the old adage holds true that "an organization is the lengthened shadow of one person," then the CEO must be the key player in changing an organization's culture.

How does one know or how can one tell when it will be necessary to change leaders to change the organization? What follows are several questions that can be used by senior executives for self-assessment or by the organization in making its own assessment of the need for new leadership:

1. Are the current leaders fully knowledgeable of the need to change and the ramifications of not changing?

2. Are the current leaders able to articulate a vision for the new organization?

3. Have the current leaders set the tone for change and established an organization-wide sense of urgency?

4. Are the current leaders willing to remove all obstacles to cultural change?

5. Do the current leaders have a history of following through on change initiatives?

6. Are the current leaders willing to empower employees at all levels of the organization to make cultural change?

In an organization that needs to make a major cultural change, the answer to all of these questions must be yes. Senior executives who fail to comprehend the need to change and the ramifications of a lack of change cannot lead an organization through a major cultural change. Senior executives who cannot envision the new organization or articulate what they see will be unable to lead an organization through the change. If they fail to set the tone for cultural change, they will inhibit rather than lead the organization.

Senior executives who fail to create a sense of urgency will see cultural change fall victim to complacency. Senior executives who are unwilling to remove obstacles that

---

QUALITY TIP ▼

Can There Really Be Shared Corporate Values in a Diverse Society?

America is one of the most diverse societies in the world, a fact that is reflected in the workplace. Since people who come from different backgrounds often have different values, one could reasonably ask if an organization can realistically adopt a set of shared corporate values. Surprisingly, the answer to this question is *yes*. Even in the most diverse settings, people still want to be treated with honesty, integrity, and dignity. Further, they understand the need to compete in order to survive. Consequently, self-interest promotes the sharing of values that in turn promotes competitiveness.

inhibit cultural change have the wrong set of priorities. This sometimes happens when the obstacles are perquisites, such as corporate aircraft or luxurious office suites to which executives have grown accustomed.

Senior executives who have a history of starting change initiatives but failing to follow through on them are poor candidates to lead an organization through a major cultural shift. With such executives in leadership roles, employees at all levels are likely to adopt an attitude of "This too shall pass." Finally, senior executives who are unwilling to empower employees at all levels to help lead change will actually ensure that the effort to bring change will fail. Cultural change requires support, ideas, and leadership from employees at all levels. Senior executives who are unwilling to empower employees to *think* and *do* will block cultural change.

LAYING THE FOUNDATION FOR A QUALITY CULTURE

Establishing a quality culture is a lot like constructing a building. The process begins with laying a solid foundation. Like a building, without a solid foundation an organization's corporate culture will quickly crumble. What follows a 10-step model that quality professional can use to establish a solid foundation for a quality culture in any organization.

1. **Understand.** Quality is at its heart a cultural concept. The tone for an organization's culture is set by the CEO and executive managers. Without the buy-in and commitment of executive management, there can be no quality culture. Consequently, the cornerstone of the cultural foundation must be an understanding on the part of executive managers of the concept of a quality culture and their role in establishing and maintaining such a culture. Brien Palmer recommends a three-pronged approach when attempting to sell higher management on the concept of quality culture: (1) align the concept with organizational goals, and get help to identify the financial benefits; (2) become the project manager of this challenge, and then measure and mitigate resistance, inertia, and opposition; and (3) prepare a brief but powerful presentation that can be made for executive managers.[1]

2. **Assess.** In this step, a comprehensive assessment of the existing corporate culture as it relates to quality is completed and the results are compiled. Figure 6–6, discussed later in the chapter, is a sample quality culture assessment instrument that can be used as a guide in developing a similar assessment instrument for any organization. The criteria in Figure 6–6 are suggested as examples of the kinds of items that should be contained in a quality culture assessment instrument. However, this example is not meant to be comprehensive. Most organizations will want to add other criteria and, perhaps, eliminate some of those shown. All employees should be allowed to complete the survey instrument without attribution, and the organization-wide average for each criterion should be compiled.

3. **Plan.** Based on the results of the survey in the previous step, develop a comprehensive plan for establishing

a quality culture. For example, if the first criterion in the checklist in Figure 6–6—All employees know the mission of the organization—receives an organization-wide average score that is unacceptably low (e.g., less than 3), specific actions should be planned for correcting this problem. The same is true of all criteria that receive low average ratings.

4. **Expect.** An organization's corporate culture is one of those phenomena in which you get what you expect. Consequently, it is important for executives, managers, and supervisors to make sure that all personnel know that quality-positive attitudes and behavior are expected. This can be achieved by (1) including a corporate value relating to quality in the organization's strategic plan, (2) including quality in the job descriptions of all personnel, (3) including quality in all of the organization's team charters, (4) including quality criteria in all of the organization's performance appraisal instruments, (5) talking about quality at all levels in the organization, (6) recognizing and rewarding quality-positive attitudes and behavior, (7) providing quality-related training for personnel at all levels, and (8) setting quality-related goals for all teams, units, departments, and divisions in the organization.

5. **Model.** Executives, managers, and supervisors must be consistently positive role models of the quality-related attitudes and behaviors expected of personnel. Employees are more likely to follow the behavior of management personnel than their words. Consequently, it is important to do more than talk a good game when it comes to quality. Management personnel must walk the talk.

6. **Orient.** New employee orientations should have a comprehensive quality component. A new employee's first exposure to the organization occurs during his or her initial orientation. Consequently, it is important to begin emphasizing the organization's quality-related expectations from the outset as part of the orientation process.

7. **Mentor.** Many organizations use mentors to help in the development of employees. Typically, mentors provide technically oriented assistance (e.g., helping new personnel learn the necessary job skills). By taking this concept one step further, organizations can help their new personnel develop quality-positive attitudes and behaviors.

8. **Train.** Providing quality training at all levels is not a new concept to competitive organizations. However, what might be new is the need to expand quality training beyond the typical technical topics to include attitudinal and behavioral topics. In other words, it is important to help personnel understand not just the "how" of quality but also the "why." The why can be summarized in just one word: *competition*. All personnel need to understand that the organization's survival depends on its ability to compete successfully every day over the long term and that they play a critical role in helping the organization do so.

9. **Monitor.** Attitudes and behaviors tend to be habitual. If people are allowed to continue inappropriate attitudes and behaviors relating to quality, those attitudes and behaviors

can become habitual. When this happens, such attitudes and behaviors can be almost impossible to change. Consequently, it is important that supervisors monitor the quality-related attitudes and behaviors of their direct reports continually. When quality-positive attitudes and behaviors are observed, they should be reinforced immediately. Correspondingly, when quality-negative attitudes and behaviors are observed, they should be corrected immediately.

10. Reinforce and maintain quality. In order to maintain a quality culture once it has been established, organizations must reinforce the quality-related attitudes and behaviors they expect of their personnel. This means that recognition and reward systems must factor in quality as a key criterion. Quality-related attitudes and behaviors should be factors in all decisions about raises, promotions, and recognition awards.

LEARNING WHAT A QUALITY CULTURE LOOKS LIKE

Part of laying the groundwork for a quality culture is understanding what one looks like. This is a lot like a person who wants to lose weight where an effective strategy is to tape a picture of a slender person to the mirror. The picture serves not only as a constant reminder of the destination, but also as a measurement device that indicates when a goal has been met. If a picture of a company with a strong quality culture could be taped to an organization's wall for all employees to see, it would have the following characteristics:[2]

- Widely shared philosophy of management
- Emphasis on the importance of human resources to the organization
- Ceremonies to celebrate organizational events
- Recognition and rewards for successful employees
- Effective internal network for communicating the culture
- Informal rules of behavior
- Strong value system
- High standards for performance
- Definite organizational character

Knowing the laws of organizational change and understanding the characteristics of organizations that have strong quality cultures are important to any executive team that hopes to change the culture of its organization. Before implementing any of the specific strategies for establishing a quality culture that are explained later in this chapter, every person who will be involved in the change or affected by it should be familiar with these laws and characteristics.

COUNTERING RESISTANCE TO CULTURAL CHANGE

Change is resisted in any organization. Resistance to change is normal organizational behavior. In this regard, an organization is similar to a biological organism. From the perspective of organizational culture, the alien is change, and the organism is the organization to be changed. Continual improvement means continual change. To ensure continual improvement, one must be able to facilitate continual change.

Why Change Is Difficult

Most people understand and accept that organizational change will be resisted. However, to be an effective agent of change, one must understand why it is resisted. Joseph Juran describes organizational change as a "clash between cultures."[3] As Figure 6–2 shows, any organization has two separate cultures relating to change: the advocates and the resisters.

Advocates focus on the anticipated benefits of the change. Resisters, on the other hand, focus on perceived threats to their status, beliefs, habits, and security. Often both advocates and resisters are wrong in how they initially approach change. Advocates are often guilty of focusing so intently on benefits that they fail to take into account the perceptions of employees who may feel threatened by the change. Resisters are often guilty of focusing so intently on threats to the status quo that they refuse to acknowledge the benefits. These approaches typically divide an organization into warring camps that waste energy and time instead of focusing resources on the facilitation of change. Table 6–1 shows how advocates and resisters can have different perceptions of the same proposed change.

FIGURE 6–2 Change Causes a Classic Confrontation: Irresistible Force versus Immovable Object

ADVOCATES OF CHANGE

- Desired Change
- Benefits of Change

RESISTERS OF CHANGE

- Desired Status Quo
- Potential Negative Consequences of Change

TABLE 6–1   Same Change, Different Perceptions

Proposed Change	Perception of Advocates	Perception of Resisters
Automate production processes	Improved productivity	Threat to job security
Initiate employee involvement and empowerment	More mental resources focused on continual improvement	Loss of authority
Establish a supplier partnership	Mutually beneficial business alliances	Disruption of established purchasing networks
Establish an employee education and training program	More knowledgeable, more highly skilled workforce	Too expensive
Join a manufacturing network	Enhanced competitiveness, shared costs, and shared resources	Competitors taking advantage of what they learn about us

How to Facilitate Change

The responsibility for facilitating change necessarily falls to its advocates. Figure 6–3 illustrates the broad steps in facilitating change.

Begin with a New Advocacy Paradigm   The first step in facilitating change is to adopt a facilitating paradigm. Juran summarizes the traditional paradigm of change advocates as follows:[4]

- Advocates of change tend to focus solely on expected results and benefits.
- Advocates are often unaware of how a proposed change will be perceived by potential resisters.
- Advocates are often impatient with the concerns of resisters.

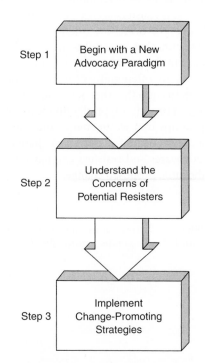

FIGURE 6–3 Steps in Facilitating Change

Step 1 — Begin with a New Advocacy Paradigm

Step 2 — Understand the Concerns of Potential Resisters

Step 3 — Implement Change-Promoting Strategies

If change is to happen, advocates must begin with a different paradigm. When a change is advocated, ask such questions as the following:

- Who will be affected by this change and how?
- How will the change be perceived by those it affects?
- How can the concerns of those affected be alleviated?

Understand the Concerns of Potential Resisters
The second step in facilitating change is to understand the concerns of potential resisters—to put yourself in their place.[5]

- **Fear.** Change brings with it the unwanted specter of the unknown, and people fear the unknown. Worst-case scenarios are assumed and compounded by rumors. In this way, fear tends to feed on itself, growing with time.
- **Loss of control.** People value having a sense of control over their lives. There is security in control. Change can threaten this sense of security and cause people to feel as if they are losing control of their lives, jobs, areas of responsibility, and so on.
- **Uncertainty.** It is difficult to deal with uncertainty. For better or worse, people like to know where they stand. Will I be able to handle this? What will happen to me if I can't? These are the types of questions people have when confronted with change.
- **More work.** Change sometimes means more work, at least at first. This concern includes work in the form of learning. To make the change, people may have to learn more information or develop new skills. For an undefined period, they may have to work longer hours.

Implement Change-Promoting Strategies   The third step in facilitating change is implementing change-promoting strategies. These are strategies that require an advocacy paradigm and take into account the concerns people typically have when confronted with change. Juran recommends the following strategies for handling and overcoming resistance to change:[6]

Involve Potential Resisters   At some point in the process, those affected by change (potential resisters) will have to take ownership of the change, or it will fail. By involving them from the outset in planning for the change, organizations can ensure that potential resisters understand it and have adequate opportunities to express their views and concerns about it. This type of involvement will help potential resisters develop a sense of ownership in the change that can, in turn, convert them to advocates.

Avoid Surprises   Predictability is important to people. This is one of the reasons they resist change. Change is unpredictable: it brings with it the specter of the unknown. For this reason, it is better to bring potential resisters into the process from the outset. Surprising potential resisters will turn them into committed resisters.

Move Slowly at First   To gain the support of potential resisters, it is necessary to let them evaluate the proposed change, express their concerns, weigh the expected benefits, and find ways to alleviate problems. This can take time. However, if advocates are perceived as rushing the change through, potential resisters will become distrustful and "dig in their heels."

Start Small and Be Flexible   Change will be more readily accepted if advocates start small and are flexible enough to revise strategies that are not working as planned. This approach offers several benefits, including the following:

1. Starting with a small pilot test or experiment is less threatening than a broad-based, all-encompassing implementation.
2. Conducting a small pilot test can help identify unanticipated problems with the change.
3. Using the results of a pilot test to revise the plans for change ensures that valuable resources are not wasted moving in the wrong direction.

Create a Positive Environment   The environment in which change takes place is determined by reward and recognition systems and examples set by managers. A reward and recognition system that does not reward risk taking or that punishes employees for ideas that don't work will undermine change. Managers that take "Do as I say, not as I do" attitudes will also undermine change. Well-thought-out, sincere attempts to make improvements should be recognized and rewarded even when they fail. Managers should "roll up their sleeves" and do their share of the work associated with change. This approach will create a positive environment that is conducive to change.

Incorporate the Change   Change will be more readily accepted if it can be incorporated into the existing organizational culture. Of course, this is not always possible. However, when it can be done, it should be done. An example might be using an established equipment maintenance schedule to make major new equipment adaptations (e.g., retrofitting manually controlled machine tools for numerical control).

Provide a Quid Pro Quo   This strategy could also be called *require something, give something*. If, for example, change will require intense extra effort on the part of selected employees for a given period of time, offer these employees some paid time off either before or immediately after the change is implemented. Using a *quid pro quo* can show employees that they are valued.

Respond Quickly and Positively   When potential resisters raise questions or express concerns, advocates should respond quickly and positively. Making employees wait for answers magnifies the intensity of their concerns. A quick response can often eliminate the concern before it becomes a problem, and it will show employees that their concerns are considered important. A quick response does not mean a surface-level or inaccurate response made before having all the facts. Rather, it means a response made as soon as one can be made thoroughly and accurately. It is also important to respond positively. Advocates should not be offended by or impatient with the questions of potential resisters. A negative attitude toward questions and concerns only magnifies them.

Work with Established Leaders   In any organization, some people are regarded as leaders. In some cases, those people are in leadership positions (supervisors, middle managers, team captains, etc.). In other cases, they are informal leaders (highly respected employees whose status is based on their experience or superior knowledge and skills). The support of such leaders is critical. Other employees will take cues from them. The best way to get their support is to involve them in planning for the change from the outset.

QUALITY TIP ▼

Can Organizations Instill Their Values or Must They Hire Only Those Who Already Have Them?

One of the issues that often comes up in discussions of corporate values is the *instill* versus *hire* question. This question is another form of the age-old *nature* versus *nurture* debate. The question is this: Can organizations instill their corporate values in the personnel they hire or must they hire only those personnel who already share their values? While it is wise to hire as many personnel as possible who already share the organization's corporate values, old dogs can learn new tricks when it comes to corporate values. In fact, the United States Marine Corps uses its boot camp for just that purpose. The primary goal of the Marine Corps boot camp is to instill the corps' values in the new recruits. Like the Marine Corps, organizations can instill their values in new personnel.

Treat People with Dignity and Respect This strategy is fundamental to all aspects of total quality. It requires behavior that acknowledges the human resource as the organization's most valuable asset. Without this strategy, the others won't matter.

Be Constructive Change is not made simply for the sake of change. It is made for the sake of continual improvement. Consequently, it should be broached constructively from the perspective of how it will bring about improvements.

ESTABLISHING A QUALITY CULTURE

Establishing a quality culture involves specific planning and activities for every business or department. This section identifies the steps involved, but first it outlines the emotional processes employees go through as the steps are being taken. Managers need to recognize and accommodate the emotional transition required not only of employees, but also of themselves while the steps toward making the conversion to quality take place.

Phases of Emotional Transition

A great deal of research has been done about how people undergo transitions from one state of being to another. Most of this research has focused on the stages of transition or recovery that people go through when they confront a major unexpected and unwanted change in their lives. The types of changes that have been studied most include divorce, the death of a loved one, a life-threatening illness, and the loss of a job. Figure 6–4 illustrates the transition process people go through when confronted by one of these major traumatic changes in their lives.

The first emotional response to any type of change is shock. A person is living from day to day, comfortable with the predictability of his or her life. Suddenly, an unexpected change intrudes. A typical response to the shock it produces is denial. The change is so unwanted that the natural human response is to simply deny that it has happened. This levels the state of mind somewhat from the low experienced during the shock phase. The length of the denial phase varies from person to person. Regardless of its length, the denial phase is temporary.

Events force the issue, and the realization of reality begins to set in. As this happens, the person's state of mind begins to fall. Depression is common during the realization phase. People need a lot of support during this phase. When realization bottoms out, acceptance occurs. Acceptance does not mean the person agrees with what has happened. Rather, it means that he or she is ready to say, "I have this problem; now what can I do about it?"

This attitude allows the rebuilding process to begin. During this phase, people need as much support as they did during the realization phase. As the rebuilding phase is accomplished, understanding sets in. In this phase, people have come to grips with the change, and they are dealing with it successfully. This phase blends into the final phase, recovery. In this phase, people are getting on with their lives.

Managers hoping to instill a quality culture should understand this transitional process. The change from a traditional organizational culture to a quality culture can be traumatic enough to trigger the process. Knowing this and understanding the process will help managers who are trying to instill a quality culture.

Steps in the Conversion to Quality

Figure 6–5 provides a checklist managers can use to guide their organizations through the conversion to a quality culture. The various strategies contained in the checklist are explained in the following subsections:

Identify the Changes Needed An organization's culture dictates how people in it behave, respond to problems,

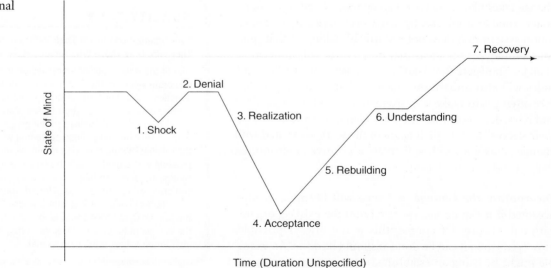

FIGURE 6–4 Emotional Transition

✓   Identify the attitudes, behaviors, processes, and procedures that are to be changed.

✓   Put the planned changes in writing.

✓   Develop a comprehensive plan for making the changes.

✓   Make sure all change advocates are familiar with the emotional transition people go through when confronted with change.

✓   Identify the key people in the organization who can either make the conversion work or make sure it doesn't work. Get the identified key people on the team (turn them into advocates).

✓   Take a hearts-and-minds approach when introducing the new culture.

✓   Apply courtship strategies to bring people along slowly but steadily.

✓   SUPPORT, SUPPORT, SUPPORT.

FIGURE 6–5 Quality Culture Conversion Checklist

and interact with each other. If the existing culture is a quality culture, it will have such characteristics as the following:

- Open, continual communication
- Mutually supportive internal partnerships
- Teamwork approach to problems and processes
- Obsession with continual improvement
- Broad-based employee involvement and empowerment
- Sincere desire for customer input and feedback

Does the organization's culture have these characteristics? The best way to answer this question is to involve the entire workforce from bottom to top in a systematic assessment that is stratified by level (i.e., executive management, middle management, first-line employee, etc.). Figure 6–6 is an example of an assessment instrument that can be used for collecting information on the perceptions of employees at all levels in an organization.

Put the Planned Changes in Writing A comprehensive assessment of an organization's existing culture will usually identify improvements that need to be made. These improvements will require changes in the status quo. These changes should be listed without annotation or explanation. For example, if the assessment reveals that customer input is not part of the product development cycle, the change list would contain an entry such as the following: *The product development cycle should be changed so that it includes the collection and use of customer input.*

Develop a Plan for Making the Changes The plan for effecting change is developed according to the who-what-when-where-how model. Each of these elements represents a major section of the plan, as follows:

- Who will be affected by the change? Who will have to be involved in order for the change to succeed? Who is likely to challenge the change?
- What tasks must be accomplished? What are the most likely barriers? What are the related processes and procedures that will be affected by the change?

- When should the change be implemented? When should progress be measured? When should the various tasks associated with the change be accomplished? When should implementation be completed?
- Where will the change be implemented? Where are the people and processes that will be affected?
- How should the change be made? How will it affect existing people and processes? How will it improve quality, productivity, and competitiveness?

The plan should contain all five elements, and each element should be dealt with comprehensively. However, the plan should be brief. Be comprehensive and thorough, but keep it as brief as possible.

Understand the Emotional Transition Process
Advocates of the change will play key roles in its implementation. The success of the implementation will depend to a large extent on how well advocates play their roles. It is essential that they understand the emotional transition people go through when forced to deal with change, particularly unwanted change (see Figure 6–4).

As noted above, the transition consists of seven steps: shock, denial, realization, acceptance, rebuilding, understanding, and recovery. People who confront a change they don't want to make may have to go through all seven steps in the transition. Advocates should understand this and proceed accordingly.

Identify Key People and Make Them Advocates
Key people are those who can facilitate and those who can inhibit implementation of the change. These people should be identified, brought together, and given the plan. Allow advocates and inhibitors opportunities to state their cases. Record all concerns and deal with them. This is the step in which a *quid pro quo* might be used to bring inhibitors around. Executive managers must use their judgment in applying the right amount of the "carrot," the "stick," and peer pressure (from advocates) to turn inhibitors into advocates.

Take a Hearts-and-Minds Approach Advocates should be conscious of human nature as they work to

Position (Type) _____

Date _____

Instructions

    The purpose of this survey is to assess the existing culture of our organization. The findings will be compared with what is known about a quality culture for the purpose of identifying the cultural changes needed in our organization to continually improve quality, productivity, and competitiveness. Respond to each of the criteria by circling the number you think best describes our organization as it is today. *Zero* (0) means that we do not meet this criterion at all. *Five* (5) means that we completely satisfy the criterion. Do not respond to items that don't apply or about which you are unsure.

1. All employees know the mission of the organization   0 1 2 3 4 5
2. All employees know their role in helping the organization accomplish its mission   0 1 2 3 4 5
3. Executive management is committed to the continual improvement of quality, productivity, and competitiveness   0 1 2 3 4 5
4. Management treats the workforce as a valuable asset   0 1 2 3 4 5
5. Open, continual communication exists at all levels of the organization   0 1 2 3 4 5
6. Mutually supportive internal partnerships exist between management and employees   0 1 2 3 4 5
7. Mutually supportive internal partnerships exist among employees   0 1 2 3 4 5
8. Quality is defined by customers, internal and external   0 1 2 3 4 5
9. Customers participate in the product development cycle   0 1 2 3 4 5
10. Employees are involved in the decision-making process   0 1 2 3 4 5
11. Employees are empowered to contribute their ideas for promoting continual improvement   0 1 2 3 4 5
12. Performance of processes is measured scientifically   0 1 2 3 4 5
13. Scientific data are used in the decision-making process   0 1 2 3 4 5
14. Employees receive the education and training they need to continually improve their performance   0 1 2 3 4 5
15. All employees at all levels are expected to maintain high ethical standards   0 1 2 3 4 5

FIGURE 6–6 Organizational Culture Employee Assessment Worksheet

implement change. On an intellectual level, people may understand and even agree with the reasons behind a change. But understanding intellectually is rarely enough. People tend to react to change more on an emotional (hearts) level than on an intellectual (minds) level, at least initially. Therefore, it is important to take the time to deal with the inevitable emotional response that occurs in the early stages of implementation.

Frequent, open communication—preferably face-to-face—is the best strategy. Advocates should allow even the most negative opponents to voice their concerns and objections in open forums. Then these concerns should be answered in an impartial, patient, nondefensive manner. When the majority of employees accept the change, critical mass will set in, and peer pressure will begin to work on the side of the advocates.

Apply Courtship Strategies Courtship is a phase in a relationship that moves slowly but deliberately toward a desired end. During the courtship, the partner hoping to move the relationship forward listens carefully to the other partner and patiently responds to any concerns expressed. This partner is on his or her best behavior. If advocates think of their relationship with potential resisters as a courtship, they will be better able to bring them along and eventually win them over.

Support, Support, Support This final strategy is critical. It means that the material, moral, and emotional support needed by people undergoing change should be provided. Undergoing change is a lot like walking a tightrope for the first time. It will go more smoothly if you have someone to help you get started, someone waiting at the other end to encourage progress, and a safety net underneath in case you fall. Planning is important. Communication is critical. But support is essential.

MAINTAINING A QUALITY CULTURE

Establishing a quality culture is a challenging undertaking for any organization. It is even more challenging to maintain a quality culture over time. The easiest thing in the world is to become complacent and let the organization's culture begin to slip back into its old mold. In order to maintain a quality culture, organizations must foster the following critical behaviors:[7]

1. Maintain an awareness of quality as a key cultural issue. This is accomplished through the regular dissemination of quality goals to all personnel and the corresponding results relating to these goals. Managers should "keep score" and let all stakeholders know what the score is.

2. Make sure that there is plenty of evidence of the management's leadership. Cheerleading is good, but it's not enough. Managers should provide leadership in strategic planning for quality, serve on quality councils, and be actively involved in the implementation of quality initiatives. Employees need to see managers "walking the walk" as well as "talking the talk."

3. Empower employees and encourage self-development and self-initiative among them. Managers should make sure that jobs are designed for as much self-control as possible, continually seek and use employee input, and encourage self-directed teamwork.

4. Keep employees involved. Do not just seek their involvement through empowerment: structure the organization and its processes in ways that ensure it. This means making employees fully empowered members of the quality council; maintaining a system that makes it easy, convenient, and nonthreatening for them to recommend improvements; and involving employees in areas, such as product or process design review.

5. Recognize and reward the behaviors that tend to nurture and maintain the quality culture. Recognition involves various forms of public acknowledgment. Rewards are tangible benefits, such as salary increases, bonuses, incentives, and promotions.

SUMMARY

1. A quality culture is an organizational value system that results in an environment that is conducive to the establishment and continual improvement of quality. It consists of values, traditions, procedures, and expectations that promote quality.

2. Implementing total quality necessitates cultural change in an organization, for the following reasons:
   - Change cannot occur in a hostile environment.
   - Moving to total quality takes time.
   - It can be difficult to overcome the past.

3. At times, it might be necessary to change an organization's leadership team to ensure needed cultural change. This situation arises when the organization's senior executives have a great deal invested in the status quo and, therefore, are staunch defenders of orthodoxy.

4. The steps in laying a foundation for a quality culture are these: understand, assess, plan, expect, model, orient, mentor, train, monitor, reinforce/maintain, and involve everyone affected by change in making it.

5. Change can be difficult because resisting change is natural human behavior. In any organization, there will be advocates of change and resisters. Sometimes, advocates focus so intently on the expected benefits of change that they fail to realize how the change will be perceived by potential resisters. People resist change for the following reasons: fear, loss of control, uncertainty, and more work. To overcome resistance to change, advocates can apply the following strategies:
   - Involve potential resisters.
   - Avoid surprises.
   - Move slowly at first.
   - Start small and be flexible.
   - Create a positive environment.
   - Incorporate the change.
   - Provide a *quid pro quo*.
   - Respond quickly and positively.
   - Work with established leaders.
   - Treat people with dignity and respect.
   - Be constructive.

6. Strategies for establishing a quality culture include the following:
   - Identify the changes needed.
   - Put the planned changes in writing.
   - Develop a plan for making the changes.
   - Understand the emotional transition process.
   - Identify key people and make them advocates.
   - Take a hearts-and-minds approach.
   - Apply courtship strategies.
   - Support.

KEY TERMS AND CONCEPTS

Advocates

Assess

Avoid surprises

Be constructive

Courtship strategies

Create a positive environment

Emotional transition process

Expect

Facilitating change

Fear

Hearts-and-minds approach

Hostile environment

Incorporate the change

Involve potential resisters

Loss of control

Mentor

Model

Monitor

More work

Move slowly at first

Organizational culture

Orient

Plan

Quality culture

Quid pro quo

Reinforce and maintain quality

Resisters

Respond quickly and positively

Start small and be flexible

Support

Treat people with dignity and respect

Uncertainty

Understand

Who-what-when-where-how model

Work with established leaders

FACTUAL REVIEW QUESTIONS

1. Define the expression *quality culture.*
2. Explain why the implementation of total quality requires cultural change.
3. List and describe the steps involved in laying the foundation for a quality culture.
4. What are the characteristics shared by companies that have a quality culture?
5. Why is change so difficult for people?
6. Describe the paradigm that should be adopted by advocates of change.
7. Explain four reasons why people resist change.
8. List and describe the strategies that can be used to overcome resistance to change.
9. What strategies would you use to establish a quality culture in organizations?
10. Explain which strategy from the two previous questions is the most important, and why.
11. Why is it sometimes necessary to change leaders to ensure cultural change?

CRITICAL THINKING ACTIVITY

Why Is Cultural Change So Hard?

Max Cutter is the envy of his fellow seniors at Stanfield Institute of Technology (SIT). He and his classmates all majored in business or technology disciplines that emphasized quality management. They all hope to begin careers soon as quality professionals, and Max just got a head start. In his very first interview, arranged by SIT's Career Center, Max was offered a job as quality manager for an old and well-established electric power company.

"I can't believe I got the job!" Max shouted to his classmates. "I spent 10 minutes trying to convince the personnel manager that I could do the job in spite of my lack of experience. When I finally stopped rambling on, he said, 'We want to hire you *because* you have no experience, not in spite of the fact. We need someone with fresh ideas, someone who is not wedded to the status quo. Frankly, we need to make major changes, and the sooner, the better. You will come in with no loyalties or biases.'"

"They are going to expect you to make major culture changes," said one of Max's classmates. "Do you think you're up to it? I remember studying the issue in class. Cultural change comes hard, if it comes at all."

"You've got a point there," said Max. "It does concern me. Why is cultural change so hard? I don't know why people can't just get with the program."

What about this question? Why is cultural change so hard? What is your opinion?

DISCUSSION ASSIGNMENT 6–1

The Indifferent Manager

The efforts of Public Communications Inc., to implement total quality had exceeded expectations at two of its three plants. However, the third plant just didn't seem to be able to get things off the ground. The plant manager, Merrill Stephens, was under a lot of pressure because his colleagues in the other two plants were succeeding and he was floundering. He didn't know what the problem was, and he didn't know how to find out.

Merrill decided to call together a group of line employees and ask for their input. Immediately, he sensed their reticence. Clearly, they had something to say but didn't want to say it. Finally, an employee who had been with the company for more than 20 years spoke up. "Mr. Stephens, we're just going through the motions to keep corporate off your back," he said. "We know you don't buy this total quality nonsense." Merrill had to admit that the employees were reading him like a book. Sure, he had followed the implementation guidelines to the letter. His executive team was the quality council. Policies had been developed and deployed. Employees were working in teams, and training in the use of quality tools was being provided. The problem was that Merrill himself was just going through the motions. He didn't really believe in total quality and had hoped it would turn out to be just one more corporate-mandated initiative that would fizzle and eventually go away.

He had only 4 more years until retirement and didn't need this in his life right now. His managers, middle managers, supervisors, and employees knew him and sensed his indifference and halfheartedness. Part of the organizational culture at this plant was that the employees took their lead from the plant manager. If Merrill was really behind an effort, they got behind it. If he wasn't, they didn't. When they accurately sensed his indifference to total quality, they responded accordingly.

DISCUSSION QUESTION

Discuss the following question in class or outside of class with your fellow students:

1. Have you ever been involved in an effort that was half-hearted because the leader of the effort didn't seem to be enthusiastic about it? If so, what happened? If not, discuss what it means for the person in charge in a given situation to set the tone.

ENDNOTES

1. Brien Palmer, "Selling Quality Ideas to Management," *Quality Progress* 39, no. 5. Retrieved from www.asq.org on February 15, 2011.

2. Joseph M. Juran and Joseph A. Defeo, *Juran's Quality Handbook,* 6th ed. (New York: McGraw-Hill, 2010), 267.

3. Ibid., 268.

4. Ibid., 269.

5. Rick Mauer, "The Resources You Need to Lead Change Without Resistance." Retrieved from www.beyondresistance.com on March 1, 2011.

6. Juran and Defeo, *Juran's Quality Handbook*, 312.

7. Frank M. Gryna, *Quality Planning and Analysis*, 4th ed. (New York: McGraw-Hill, 2001), 68–75.

CUSTOMER SATISFACTION, RETENTION, AND LOYALTY

The competitor to be feared is the one who never bothers about you at all but goes on making his own business better all the time. —*Henry Ford Sr.*

MAJOR TOPICS

- Understanding Who Is a Customer
- Understanding Customer-Defined Quality
- Identifying External Customer Needs
- Identifying Internal Customer Needs
- Communicating with Customers
- Using Customer Feedback to Make Design Improvements
- Customer Satisfaction Process
- Customer-Defined Value
- Customer Value Analysis
- Customer Retention
- Establishing a Customer Focus
- Recognizing the Customer-Driven Organization
- Value Perception and Customer Loyalty
- Customer Loyalty Model
- Customer Loyalty versus Customer Profitability
- Customers as Innovation Partners
- Product Innovation Model for Customer Retention

In a total quality setting, customers define quality and employees produce it. Historically, organizations have viewed customers as people who buy and use their products. These are external customers. There are also internal customers within any organization—the staff. With this background, an accurate recasting of the first sentence is as follows: In a total quality setting, external customers define quality and internal customers produce it. This chapter provides the information modern managers need to establish in their organizations a customer focus that encompasses both internal and external customers.

UNDERSTANDING WHO IS A CUSTOMER

Historically, the concept of suppliers and customers has been interpreted as shown in Figure 7–1. An organization uses certain processes by which it produces its products. People who interact with the company prior to these processes taking place have been considered suppliers. Those who interact with the company after these processes have produced the product have been viewed as customers. From this traditional perspective, customers and suppliers are both external entities. Figure 7–2 illustrates a more contemporary view of suppliers and customers.

In a total quality setting, customers and suppliers exist inside and outside the organization. Any employee whose work precedes that of another employee is a supplier for that employee. Correspondingly, any employee whose work follows that of another employee and is dependent on it in some way is a customer. For example, say Employee A attaches several components to a printed circuit board and then hands the board to Employee B to connect the components. In this relationship, Employee A is a supplier for Employee B, and Employee B is a customer

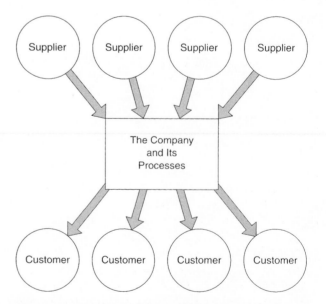

FIGURE 7–1 Traditional View of Suppliers and Customers Showing That Customers and Suppliers Are Strictly External Entities

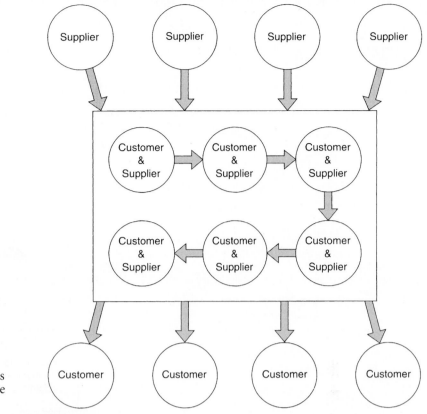

FIGURE 7–2 Contemporary View of Suppliers and Customers Showing That Employees Are Suppliers and Customers to Each Other

of Employee A. Employee B cannot do her job correctly unless Employee A has done his correctly. The quality of Employee A's work affects that of Employee B. This concept of *dependency* is critical in the supplier–customer relationship. A customer, whether internal or external, depends on suppliers to provide quality work and produce quality products.

UNDERSTANDING CUSTOMER-DEFINED QUALITY

In a total quality setting, quality is defined by the customer. When quality is defined by the customer, the following factors apply:[1]

- The customer must be the organization's top priority. The organization's survival depends on the customer.

- Reliable customers are the most important customers. A reliable customer is one who buys repeatedly from the same organization. Customers who are satisfied with the quality of their purchases from an organization become reliable customers. Therefore, customer satisfaction is essential.

- Customer satisfaction is ensured by producing high-quality products. It must be renewed with every new purchase. This cannot be accomplished if quality, even though it is high, is static. Satisfaction implies continual improvement. Continual improvement is the only way to keep customers satisfied and loyal.

If customer satisfaction is the highest priority of a total quality organization, then it follows that such an organization must have a customer focus. Traditional management practices that take the management-by-results approach are inward looking. An organization with a customer focus is outward looking.

The key to establishing a customer focus is putting employees in touch with customers and empowering those employees to act as necessary to satisfy the customers. There are a number of ways to put employees in touch with customers. Actual contact may be in person, by telephone, or through reviewing customer-provided data. Identifying customer needs and communicating with customers are covered later in this chapter. At this point, it is necessary to understand only that employee–customer interaction is a critical element in establishing a customer focus.

IDENTIFYING EXTERNAL CUSTOMER NEEDS

Historically, customers were excluded from the product development process. When this approach is used, the organization producing the product is taking a chance that it will satisfy the customer. In a competitive marketplace that is global in scope, such an approach can be disastrous. In a total quality setting, customer needs are identified clearly as a normal part of product development. Peter Scholtes, Barbara Streibel, and Brian Joiner recommend the six-step

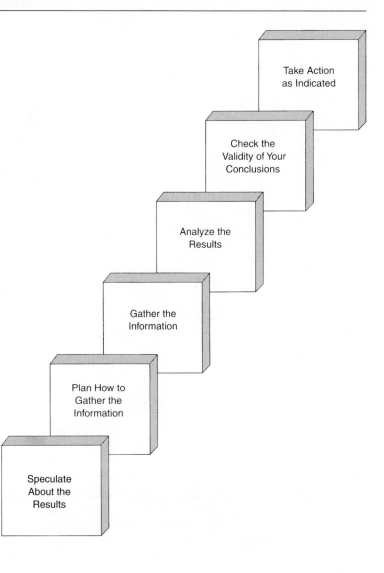

FIGURE 7–3 Six-Step Strategy for Identifying
Customer Needs

strategy for identifying customer needs that is illustrated in Figure 7–3 and described in the following subsections.[2] The authors of this text recommend a seventh step involving Internet research.

Speculate About Results

Before gathering information about customer needs, it is a good idea to spend some time speculating about what might be learned. Write down what you think customers will say so that you can compare your expectations with what is actually said. The purpose of this step is to help representatives of the organization determine whether they are in touch with customer needs.

Develop an Information-Gathering Plan

Information gathering should be systematically undertaken and well-organized. Before gathering information, develop a plan. Decide what types of information are needed and who will be asked to provide it. Whenever possible, structure the plan so that information is collected in face-to-face interviews. When personal visits are not possible, use the telephone. Written surveys sent out through the mail cannot produce a level of feedback equal to that gained from the nonverbal messages, impressions, and follow-up questions that are a part of person-to-person interviews.

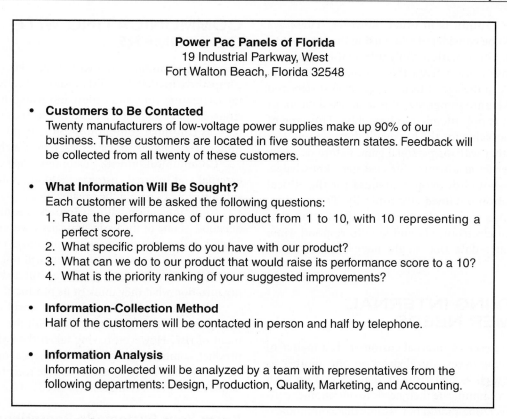

Power Pac Panels of Florida
19 Industrial Parkway, West
Fort Walton Beach, Florida 32548

- **Customers to Be Contacted**
  Twenty manufacturers of low-voltage power supplies make up 90% of our business. These customers are located in five southeastern states. Feedback will be collected from all twenty of these customers.

- **What Information Will Be Sought?**
  Each customer will be asked the following questions:
  1. Rate the performance of our product from 1 to 10, with 10 representing a perfect score.
  2. What specific problems do you have with our product?
  3. What can we do to our product that would raise its performance score to a 10?
  4. What is the priority ranking of your suggested improvements?

- **Information-Collection Method**
  Half of the customers will be contacted in person and half by telephone.

- **Information Analysis**
  Information collected will be analyzed by a team with representatives from the following departments: Design, Production, Quality, Marketing, and Accounting.

FIGURE 7–4 Information-Gathering Plan

Figure 7–4 is an example of an information-gathering plan. Notice that it is structured for collecting information either face to face or by telephone interviews.

Gather the Information

Before implementing the entire information-gathering plan, it is a good idea to conduct a smaller pilot study involving just a few customers. This will identify problems with the information-gathering methodology that should be corrected before you proceed on a larger scale. After the methodology has been appropriately refined, gather information in a timely manner.

Analyze the Results

Results should be analyzed carefully and objectively. Do they match the speculated results from the first step? How do they agree and disagree? What problems did customers identify? What strong points? Were there trends? How many customers complained of the same problem? What changes in the product or services relating to it were suggested?

Check the Validity of Conclusions

Having drawn conclusions based on the information gathered, the next step is to check the validity of those conclusions. Customers can be a valuable source of help. Select several customers and share the conclusions with them. Do they agree with the conclusions? Also share the conclusions

with other people in the organization and get their feedback. Adjust your conclusions as needed based on this external and internal feedback.

Take Action

Based on the final conclusions, what changes need to be made? Which of these changes are short term in nature, and which are long term? Which can be made immediately, and which will require a longer time? Take any corrective action that can be made immediately, and lay out a plan for completing any that is long term in nature. Meet with customers and let them know what is going to be done and when. Make sure that changes are made, to the extent possible, in the same order of priority as that dictated by customer needs.

Obtain Customer Information from the Internet

Obtaining customer information has become much easier with the advent of the World Wide Web. Most businesses now have extensive Web sites containing volumes of information about themselves. This information can be obtained by going online and accessing the Web site of the company in question. Careful scrutiny of a customer's Web site can reveal useful information about what is important to that customer. It can also reveal who the key players are, who is in charge of what, and who the best contact might be in a given situation.

A word of caution is in order, however. There are ethical issues to be considered when using the Internet to obtain customer information. Only information available for public consumption from the customer's Web site should be used. In the age of technology, Web surfers and computer hackers are sometimes able to access data about customers that is not intended to be public. This type of information has value for the hackers if they can sell it or use it in any other way for personal gain. Before deciding to use the Internet as a source for customer knowledge, organizations should develop guidelines for the ethical use of information obtained electronically. These guidelines should also specify the types of information that will be pursued electronically and how to respond when offered customer data that might have been obtained unethically.

IDENTIFYING INTERNAL CUSTOMER NEEDS

Identifying the needs of internal customers is a matter of ensuring that employees who depend on one another as individuals, as well as departments that depend on each other as units, communicate their needs to one another continually. However, one should not assume that communication will just happen. As important as it is, communication rarely just happens in any setting. Rather, it must be encouraged and facilitated.

Quality circles, self-managed teams, cross-departmental teams, and improvement teams are all examples of mechanisms for improving communication and, in turn, quality. These mechanisms facilitate communication among internal customers and suppliers. However, they are not the only mechanisms available. Communication that occurs over a cup of coffee in the break room or during lunch can be equally effective. Training that promotes communication and helps improve communication skills is also important (this is discussed in greater depth in Chapter 11). Teamwork and how it can improve communication is discussed in Chapter 10.

QUALITY TIP ▼

Employees Treat Customers as Management Treats Them

"It never ceases to amaze me. A company will have signs and banners promoting customer satisfaction. Management will lecture employees at length on the subject. But employees are perceptive. They watch managers. They know how the managers treat customers, and that is how they, the employees, will treat customers. Managers who want good customer service must set the example first and lecture second."

Source: David L. Goetsch, seminar entitled "Achieving Customer Delight," April 2011.

COMMUNICATING WITH CUSTOMERS

Continual communication with customers is essential in a competitive marketplace. Establishing effective mechanisms for facilitating communication and using them are critical strategies in establishing a customer focus. One of the main reasons continual communication is required is that customer needs change, and at times, they can change rapidly.

Communication with customers must extend to both external and internal customers. What applies on the outside also applies within the organization.

Communication with customers is sometimes misunderstood as one of the basic strategies used in a total quality setting. It does not mean asking customers what new products should be invented. Customers will not tell an organization what product to produce, but they will tell the organization what they think of its products.

All of the market research in the world won't spare the entrepreneur the anxiety of dealing with the inescapable element of risk. However, having taken the risk to produce a product, communicating with customers about that product can ensure that it gets the best possible reception in the marketplace and that it changes as the needs of customers change.

Know Your Customer's Operations

As a supplier to other companies (customers), it is important to know their operations. The more that is known about a customer's operations, the easier it will be to provide products that meet its needs.

What does the customer do with our product? How is it used? Is our product part of a larger assembly? Does the customer use our product in the way we expect or in some different way? Does the customer modify our product in any way? What processes does the customer use in working with our product? Knowing the answers to questions such as these can help a supplier improve customer satisfaction. The answers to these types of questions can lead to such benefits as the following:

- **Product enhancements.** By knowing a customer's operations, suppliers might be able to modify their products to fit in better with the customer's operations. They might also be able to add attributes that will make the product even more attractive to the customer.

- **Improved productivity.** By knowing a customer's operations, suppliers might be able to propose process modifications that will improve its productivity.

- **Internal improvements.** By knowing a customer's operations, suppliers might learn facts that lead to internal improvements in quality, productivity, and design in their own organizations.

Customers don't always use a product in the way a supplier assumes. By getting to know customers and their operations, suppliers have not just made process and product improvements; some have actually started new product lines. In any case, the better suppliers know their customers' operations, the better they can serve them. The better suppliers serve their customers, the greater the likelihood of satisfied, long-term customers.

USING CUSTOMER FEEDBACK TO MAKE DESIGN IMPROVEMENTS

It is important for organizations that compete in the global arena to collect customer input and feedback and use it to make continual improvements to the design of their products. Quality function deployment is an effective system for collecting customer input and factoring that input into the design process. Building affinity diagrams is an effective method for organizing customer feedback data so that it can be used to make ongoing design improvements.

Quality Function Deployment and Design Improvements

It is important to know that a product will meet the needs of customers before you put it into production. This is the main reason for conducting the research necessary to identify customer needs and for communicating with internal and external customers. Quality function deployment (QFD) was developed with this in mind.

QFD is an integrated approach to product development and quality in all preproduction activities. It was introduced in the United States by Professor Y. Akao of the University of Tamagawa as part of a paper he presented at a quality conference in Chicago. QFD is actually a model for incorporating customer input and feedback into product development. In effect, it establishes an operational structure for the concept of building in quality. The philosophy underlying QFD is that even a perfectly manufactured product may not satisfy the customer because it may be nothing more than a perfect example of what the customer doesn't want.

QFD allows for the systematic incorporation of customer needs, production capabilities and capacity, and all other relevant parameters into product development. QFD consists of the following basic activities:[3]

- Deployment of customer requirements (quality needs)
- Deployment of measurable quality characteristics
- Determination of the correlation between quality needs and characteristics
- Assignment of numerical values to each quality characteristic
- Integration of quality characteristics into the product
- Detailed design, production, and quality control of the product

QFD is discussed in greater detail in Chapter 17. It is introduced here only to show that it can have a positive role to play in making sure customer needs are satisfied or exceeded.

Affinity Diagrams and Design Improvements

Feedback from customers comes in many forms, and depending on the size of the organization, there can be vast amounts of it to deal with. However, if customer feedback can be collected, organized, and analyzed to identify patterns and trends, it can be an invaluable resource for making continual improvements in product design and the manufacturing process.

The affinity diagram is a useful tool for making sense out of large amounts of customer feedback that might come to an organization in any number of forms (e.g., customer complaints, surveys, feedback or comment cards, focus groups, and telephone discussions).[4] The steps in developing an affinity diagram are as follows:

1. Form a cross-functional team that includes representatives from all of the key functional areas in the organization (e.g., engineering, marketing, accounting, and customer service).

2. Ask the team to investigate the following question: What do our customers dislike the most about our product?

3. Study the data from all of the various customer feedback sources and identify categories of complaints, comments, concerns, and issues expressed by customers.

4. Write all of the feedback categories identified on a flipchart and post them on a wall where everyone on the team can easily view them.

5. Sort all of the categories into related groups so that there are no duplicate categories.

6. Develop header cards for each of the categories remaining on the wall charts. Each card is headed by a sentence that accurately and succinctly describes the type of problems for that category. Examples of possible headers are as follows:

   a. Product is too difficult to assemble.

   b. Product does not provide sufficient operating information.

   c. Product wears out too quickly.

7. Using the header cards, draw an affinity diagram. The affinity diagram is simply a table consisting of each header, with the corresponding frequently given customer feedback for that header listed under it. For example, assume the product is a piece of home exercise equipment. Using the first header from above, one part of the affinity diagram might look like this:

Product is too difficult to assemble:

   a. Assembly instructions are confusing.

   b. Fasteners require a special tool that is not provided.

   c. It takes at least three people to install the pulleys.

Under each header, the most frequently given feedback that corresponds with that header is listed. With the customer feedback data organized, patterns and trends become obvious. Given this information in this type of format, design personnel know specifically what they need to do to improve the design of the product. They can also see immediately if changes in the manufacturing process, packaging process, or other key processes are needed.

CUSTOMER SATISFACTION PROCESS

Customer focus is more than just sending out surveys. Customer focus is part of a process that leads to continual improvements in the organization that, in turn, result in customer satisfaction. Resources are limited; consequently, they must be applied where they will do the most to improve customer satisfaction and customer retention. The process described in the following list will help meet all these goals:[5]

- Determine who your customers are.
- Determine what attributes of your product or service are most important to your customers.
- Arrange these attributes in the order of importance indicated by your customers.
- Determine your customers' level of satisfaction with each of these attributes.
- Tie results of customer feedback to your processes.
- Develop a set of metrics (measurements) that tell how you are performing and which areas within the process are having the greatest impact on performance.
- Implement measurements at the lowest possible level in the organization.
- Work on those processes that relate to attributes that have high importance but low customer satisfaction ratings.
- Work on those areas within the process that offer the greatest opportunity to improve.
- Update customer input and feedback on a continual basis. Then, as process improvements correspondingly increase customer satisfaction, move on to the process improvements that are next in importance.
- Maintain open, continual communication with all stakeholders on what is being done and why and on what results are expected and when.
- Aggregate metrics organization-wide into a format for management review on a continual basis. Adjust as necessary.

CUSTOMER-DEFINED VALUE

It is important for organizations to understand how customers define value. The value of a product or service is the sum of a customer's perceptions of the following factors:

- Product or service quality
- Service provided by the organization
- The organization's personnel
- The organization's image
- Selling price of the product or service
- Overall cost of the product or service

All of these factors are important to customers. The product or service must have the attributes customers want, and those attributes must be of the quality expected. The customer's interaction with the organization and how this interaction is measured are important. Just making a good product or service available is not enough. Customer satisfaction will also be affected by how effectively, courteously, and promptly customers are served. The appearance, knowledge, and attitudes of an organization's personnel also affect the level of satisfaction that customers experience. Customers will build relationships with personnel in the organization who are knowledgeable, professional in appearance, and positive. Such relationships promote loyalty. On the other hand, no matter how satisfied customers are with a product or service, if they don't like an organization's people, they are likely to defect to the competition.

An organization's image is important to customers. Consequently, it is vital not just to have quality products, service, and personnel but also to project an image that is consistent with these quality characteristics. Think of the adage that one should "not just talk the talk but walk the walk." In establishing and nurturing an image, it is important to do both those things. The key is that organizations must be concerned with both substance and appearances. An organization's image is defined by what customers *believe* to be true about it.

Selling price is important to customers, of course. It is the easiest characteristic to compare. The point to understand here is that customers have become so sophisticated that they no longer confuse selling price and cost. In other words, they know the difference between *cheap* and *inexpensive*. A competitive selling price is a must in the modern workplace, but it should not be achieved by sacrificing quality or service.

Most customers know that the selling price is just the beginning of the actual cost of a product. Only when maintenance, upkeep, replacement parts, warranty issues, and service are factored in does one know the product's real cost. Customers who don't understand the difference between price and cost soon learn—the hard way. The organization that teaches this difficult lesson is not likely to retain its customers.

Whether customers are satisfied will depend on the sum of their perceptions relative to all of these factors. The issue of customer satisfaction is complicated even more by the fact that different customers place a different priority on these factors. That fact makes it even more critical that organizations maintain close, personal, and continual contact with their customers.

Customer-Defined Value at Federal Express

Federal Express is one of the most successful package delivery companies on the globe. Many businesspeople think Federal Express sets the worldwide standard in customer service. One of the keys to the success of this company is its commitment to customer-defined value. Part of the operating philosophy of Federal Express is that customers are the best judges of quality.

In order to capture customers' input in a meaningful and useful manner, Federal Express developed a system of Service Quality Indicators (SQIs). These indicators reflect the customers' views concerning their satisfaction with the performance of Federal Express. The list of SQIs is as follows:

1. Delivery on the right day but after the promised time
2. Delivery on the wrong day
3. Unsuccessful trace of a package
4. Customer complaints
5. Proof of performance is missing
6. Missed pickups from customers
7. Damaged packages
8. Lost packages
9. Unanswered calls from customers (not answered within 20 seconds)

Federal Express continually collects data for all of these criteria and uses the data to identify service problems and their root causes. Of course, identifying the problems is just the first step. Correcting them and eliminating the root causes follow quickly once a cause has been identified.

CUSTOMER VALUE ANALYSIS

What is it that customers want from our organization? What is it about our products or services that customers value? A total quality organization must know the answers to these questions. Organizations that don't know what their customers value run the risk of wasting valuable resources and, in turn, improve the wrong things. The process used to determine what is important to customers is called *customer value analysis (CVA)*. The CVA process consists of the following five steps:

1. Determine what attributes customers value most. Ask customers to describe the attributes of the product or service. At this point, no priority value is assigned to the attributes. This can be done using a written survey, a telephone survey, one-on-one interviews, or focus groups.

2. Rate the relative importance of the attributes. Ask customers to prioritize the list of attributes identified in the first step. The ranking should run from *most important* to *least important*.

3. Assess your organization's performance relative to the prioritized list of attributes. Is the most important attribute on the list the strongest attribute of the product or service in question? Ideally, the relative strength of the attributes of a given product or service will match the priorities established by customers.

4. Ask customers to rate all attributes of your product or service against the same attributes of a competitor's

product or service. To consistently beat the competition, an organization's product or service must have more value for customers on an attribute-by-attribute basis. By asking customers to rate attributes, the organization can determine how they perceive the value, on a relative basis, of its product or service attributes. This gives the organization the information it needs to improve the attributes of its products or services in accordance with customer preferences.

5. Repeat the process periodically. Over time, customer preferences might change, as might the attributes of competing products or services. Consequently, it is important to periodically repeat the CVA process.

QUALITY CASE ▼

Delivering Quality and Value at Cargill Corn Milling

Cargill Corn Milling (CCM) of North America began operations in 1967 as part of its parent firm Cargill Inc., a global provider of food, agriculture, and risk-management products. CCM manufactures corn and sugar-based foods, including whole-grain corn meal, corn oil, animal feed, ethanol, dextrose, and acidulants. CCM employs more than 2.300 personnel in nine manufacturing plants and eleven distribution centers throughout the United States. These personnel and facilities process more than 10,000 bushels of corn every day. CCM is one of three Cargill business units to receive the Baldrige National Quality Award.

By putting customers at the heart of all decisions and applying the other principles of total quality, CCM has been able to become a world-class organization able to compete successfully on the global stage. Examples of how CCM applies the principles of total quality include the following:

- Establishing and maintaining a team-based corporate culture that emphasizes effective communication, skill sharing, and leveraging of diverse ideas. This culture led to more than $15 million in cost savings from ideas generated by employees.

- Consistently maintaining an error-free delivery record of 99% or better.

- Committing to achieving the world-class benchmark of a 98% operational reliability effectiveness rate as established by the Society of Maintenance and Reliability Professionals (CCM has achieved a 95% record to date).

- Committing to maintaining steady "per bushel" costs even as such factors as energy and chemical costs have increased. CCM has achieved this goal by strictly applying such tactics as real-time and predictive monitoring of equipment health, careful energy use, and continual process improvement.

By applying the principles of total quality, CCM has become the partner of choice for its customers worldwide while maintaining its commitment to such corporate values as integrity, safety, customer focus, innovation, talent development, collaboration, and community involvement.

Source: www.nist.gov.

CUSTOMER RETENTION

Customer satisfaction is a fundamental cornerstone of total quality. An organization develops a customer focus to be better able to satisfy its customers. Consequently, forward-looking organizations use customer satisfaction data to measure success. But measuring customer satisfaction alone is not enough. Another important measure of success is customer retention.

It is a fact that even satisfied customers will sometimes migrate to a competitor. The customer whose feedback in a customer-satisfaction survey is very positive might, in reality, have migrated in spite of being satisfied. Consequently, it makes more sense to measure customer retention than just customer satisfaction. Customer retention is a more accurate indicator of customer loyalty than is customer satisfaction.

It is important to understand this point. No one is saying that customer satisfaction is not important. Customer satisfaction is critical, but it is a means to an end, not an end in itself. The desired end is customer retention. Organizations should measure success based on customer retention data rather than on customer satisfaction data. The issue is not whether customers are satisfied with the organization's products or services; it is whether they are satisfied enough to be retained. Satisfied customers will sometimes defect in spite of their satisfaction, if for no other reason than curiosity about a competitor or the everpresent lure of variety. How, then, can an organization go beyond just satisfying its customers to retaining them? The short answer to this question is as follows:

> To retain customers over the long term, organizations must turn them into partners and proactively seek their input rather than waiting for and reacting to feedback provided after a problem has occurred.

The following strategies can help organizations go beyond just satisfying customers to retaining them over the long term. These strategies will help organizations operationalize the philosophy of turning customers into partners.

Be Proactive—Get Out in Front of Customer Complaints

Many organizations make the mistake of relying solely on feedback from customers to identify problems; the most widely used mechanism in this area is the customer complaint process. Feedback-based processes, although necessary and useful, have three glaring weaknesses. First, they are activated by problems customers have already experienced. Even if these problems are solved quickly, the customer who complains has already had a negative experience with the organization. Such experiences are typically remembered—even if only subconsciously—no matter how well the organization responds.

Second, feedback-oriented processes are based on the often invalid assumption that dissatisfied customers will take the time to lodge a complaint. Some will, but many won't.

Some people are just too busy to take the time to complain. Others provide their feedback by simply going elsewhere. In a survey of retail customers conducted by the Institute for Continual Improvement (ICI), 72% of respondents said they would simply go elsewhere if dissatisfied rather than taking the time to complain.[6] Retail customers don't necessarily have the same characteristics as customers of service or production organizations. However, the ICI survey still points to a fundamental weakness with customer complaint processes, which rely on information collected *ex post facto*.

Third, the information that the customer complaint processes provide is often too sketchy to yield an accurate picture of the problem. This situation can result in an organization wasting valuable resources chasing after symptoms rather than solving root causes. The weaknesses associated with after-the-fact processes do not mean that organizations should stop collecting customer feedback. On the contrary, customer feedback can be important when used to supplement the data collected using input-based processes.

Customer input is customer information provided *before* a problem occurs. An effective vehicle for collecting customer input is the focus group. *Focus groups* consist of customers who agree to meet periodically with representatives of the organization for the purpose of pointing out issues before they become problems. Focus groups can provide a mechanism for overcoming all three of the weaknesses associated with feedback systems. Participants point out weaknesses or potential issues to the organization's representatives so that they can be dealt with preemptively. Focus group input does not depend on the willingness of customers to lodge complaints; participants agree to provide input at periodic meetings before becoming members of the group.

The focus group approach can also solve the problem of sketchy information. In a focus group, there is discussion, debate, and give and take. This type of interaction provides the organization's representatives with opportunities to dig deeper and deeper until they get beyond symptoms to root causes. Input provided by one participant will often trigger input from another.

To be effective, the focus group must consist of participants who understand what they are being asked to do. The organization is well-served by neither sycophants nor witch hunters. What is needed is information that is thoroughly thought out and objective, given in the form of open, honest, constructive criticism. Members of the focus group should change periodically to bring in new ideas and a broader cross-section of input.

A variation on the focus group concept is the input group. The purpose of both types of groups is to provide input the organization can use to improve its processes and its products and services. The difference between the two is that focus group participants meet together for group discussion. Input group participants provide their data individually, usually by mail, telephone, or facsimile machine. They do not meet together for group interaction.

Other methods for collecting customer input include hiring test customers and conducting periodic surveys of a representative sample of the customer base. *Test customers* are individuals who do business with the organization and report their perceptions to designated representatives of the organization. This method can backfire unless employees are fully informed that it is a method the organization employs. This does not mean that employees should know who the test customers are; they shouldn't, or this method will lose its value. However, they should know that any customer they interact with might be a test customer.

Customer surveys conducted periodically can help identify issues that may become problems. If this method is used, the survey instrument should be brief and to the point. One of the surest ways to "turn off" customers is to ask them to complete a lengthy survey instrument. Some type of reward should be associated with completing the survey that says, "Thank you for your valuable time and assistance." Each time a survey is conducted, care should be taken to select a different group of customers. Asking the same people to complete surveys over and over is sure to alienate even the most loyal customers.

Collect Both Registered and Unregistered Complaints

Many organizations make the mistake of acting solely on what customers say in complaints instead of going beyond what is said to include what is unspoken. Often, what is not said is more important than what is said. For this reason, it is important for organizations to collect both registered and unregistered complaints.

Focus groups—already discussed—are an excellent way to solicit unregistered complaints. Customer surveys and test customers can also serve this purpose. Another way to get at that part of the iceberg that floats beneath the surface is the *follow-up interview*. With this method, customers who have registered complaints are contacted either in person or by telephone to discuss their complaints in greater depth. This approach gives representatives of the organization the opportunity to ask clarifying questions and to request suggestions.

Another way to get at unregistered complaints is to use the organization's sales representatives as collectors of customer input. Sales representatives are the employees who have the most frequent face-to-face contact with customers. If properly trained concerning what to look for, what to ask, and how to respond, sales personnel can bring back invaluable information from every sales call. In addition to providing sales personnel with the necessary training, organizations should provide them with appropriate incentives for collecting customer input. Otherwise, they may fall into the trap of simply agreeing with the customer about complaints received, thereby undermining the customer relationship even further.

ESTABLISHING A CUSTOMER FOCUS

Companies that have successfully established a customer focus share a number of common characteristics that can be divided into the following clusters:[7]

- **Vision, commitment, and climate.** A company with these characteristics is totally committed to satisfying customer needs. This commitment shows up in everything the company does. Management demonstrates by deeds and words that the customer is important, that the organization is committed to customer satisfaction, and that customer needs take precedence over internal needs. One way such organizations show their commitment to customers and establish a climate in which customer satisfaction prevails is by making the goal of being customer focused a major factor in all promotions and pay increases.

- **Alignment with customers.** Customer-driven companies align themselves with their customers. Customers are included when anyone in the organization says, "we." Alignment with customers manifests itself in several ways, including the following: Customers play a consultative role in selling, customers are never promised more than can be delivered, employees understand what product attributes the customers value the most, and customer feedback and input are incorporated into the product development process.

- **Willingness to find and eliminate customers' problems.** Customer-driven companies work hard to continually identify and eliminate problems for customers. This willingness manifests itself in the following ways: Customer complaints are monitored and analyzed; customer feedback is sought continually; and internal processes, procedures, and systems that create no value for customers are identified and eliminated.

- **Use of customer information.** Customer-driven companies not only collect customer feedback but also use it and communicate it to those who need it to make improvements. The use of customer information manifests itself in the following ways: All employees know how the customer defines quality, employees at different levels are given opportunities to meet with customers, employees know who the "real" customer is, customers are given information that helps them develop realistic expectations, and employees and managers understand what customers want and expect.

- **Reaching out to customers.** Customer-driven companies reach out to their customers. In a total quality setting, it is never enough to sit back and wait for customers to give evaluative feedback. A competitive global marketplace demands a more assertive approach. Reaching out to customers means doing the following:

    Making it easy for customers to do business

    Encouraging employees to go beyond the normal call of duty to please customers

    Attempting to resolve all customer complaints

    Making it convenient and easy for customers to make their complaints known

- **Competence, capability, and empowerment of people.** Employees are treated as competent, capable professionals and are empowered to use their judgment in doing what is necessary to satisfy customer needs. This means that all employees have a thorough understanding of the products they provide and the customer's needs relating to those products. It also means that employees are given the resources and support required to meet the customer's needs.

■ **Continual improvement of products and processes.** Customer-driven companies do what is necessary to continually improve their products and the processes that produce them. This approach to doing business manifests itself in the following ways: Internal functional groups cooperate to reach shared goals, best practices in the business are studied (and implemented wherever they will result in improvements), research and development cycle time is continually reduced, problems are solved immediately, and investments are made in the development of innovative ideas.

These seven clusters of characteristics can be used as a guide in establishing a customer focus. The first step is a self-analysis in which it is determined which of these characteristics are present in the organization and which are missing. Characteristics that are missing form the basis for an organization-wide implementation effort.

RECOGNIZING THE CUSTOMER-DRIVEN ORGANIZATION

Is a given organization customer driven? In today's competitive business environment, the answer to this question must be yes. Since this is the case, it is important for quality professionals to be able to recognize a customer-driven organization and to be able to articulate its distinguishing characteristics.

A customer-driven organization can be recognized by the following characteristics: (1) promptly follows through on all promises, (2) can be trusted, (3) has credibility, (4) attends to even the smallest details, and (5) responsiveness.[8] In addition to these characteristics, customer-driven organizations exemplify the following management characteristics: (1) effective communication with customers and their personnel concerning customer needs, (2) use of customer-specific metrics, (3) systematic use of customer feedback, and (4) customer-focused organizational structure.[9]

By applying the characteristics and management factors set forth in this section, quality professionals can recognize customer-driven organizations. They can also quickly surmise where problems and shortcomings exist and develop a clearly focused plan of improvement.

VALUE PERCEPTION AND CUSTOMER LOYALTY

Companies work hard to build customer loyalty. Think of Coke and Pepsi, for example. The goal is to keep the customer on board for the long term. The theory is that a *loyal* customer is a customer forever. It is easy to see what drives the desire to create customer loyalty. Companies spend so much in marketing to attract customers that they must keep them for the long term to recoup their investments.

The best way to generate customer loyalty is to consistently provide customers with superior value. Superior value is a combination of superior quality, superior cost, and superior service. Think of a favorite restaurant. People are loyal customers to a given restaurant because it provides high-quality food and atmosphere at competitive costs and with excellent service. All three of these of these factors must be given the highest priority by organizations and continually improved in order to maintain the loyalty of customers.

CUSTOMER LOYALTY MODEL

Organizations attempt to consistently exceed customer expectations for the purpose of creating and maintaining customer loyalty.[10] Customers constantly evaluate—both formally and informally—the organizations they do business with. From these evaluations, they form perceptions of the performance of the organizations. These perceptions, if they are positive, can lead to customer loyalty. Customer loyalty, in turn, can lead to a higher level of competitiveness and better financial performance: in other words, success.

Steve Hoisington and Earl Nauman have transformed the process of creating customer loyalty into a four-phase model that has the following components: (1) business performance, (2) global perceptions, (3) loyalty behaviors, and (4) financial outcomes.[11] These four components are explained in the following paragraphs.

Business Performance

When evaluating the performance of an organization they do business with, customers consider a variety of factors, all of which fall into one of these categories:

■ Product quality (e.g., attributes, features, usability, compatibility, reliability)

■ Service quality (e.g., sales, after-purchase service, billing)

■ Relationship quality (e.g., communication, availability, responsiveness)

■ Image strength (e.g., when other performance indicators are equal, the organization's image can be an important consideration)

■ Price perceptions (e.g., initial purchase price, cost of maintenance and repairs, cost of upgrades)

Global Perceptions

Based on its evaluation of an organization, a customer will form global perceptions about that organization. There are many different types of perceptions that might be formed by a customer. For example, customers might form good or bad feelings about overall satisfaction, their willingness to recommend the organization to other potential customers, their willingness to do business with the organization again, their commitment to an ongoing relationship with the organization, the extent to which the organization met their needs, or the value they received for their money. If the perceptions formed by customers in these and other pertinent areas are positive, they can lead to loyalty behaviors on the part of those customers.

Loyalty Behaviors

Customer loyalty is a behavioral concept, but it can be measured. For example, an organization can measure the defection rate of its customers—especially those that do business on a regular basis. Another factor that can be measured is the business volume of individual customers. Is the volume of business for the customer going up or down? A customer that stays with an organization but significantly decreases his or her volume of business is not a loyal customer. Consequently, it is important to measure both the defection rate and the business-volume-by-customer rate. When customers exhibit loyalty behaviors, the organization benefits in the critical area of financial outcomes.

Financial Outcomes

Financial outcomes are affected by several key factors, including the following:

1. **Market share**—High customer loyalty leads to a larger market share, which, in turn, leads to better financial outcomes

2. **Reduced costs**—Repeat customers cost less to deal with than new customers, which means that customer loyalty decreases the cost of doing business

3. **Employee attitudes**—Positive employee attitudes promote positive customer relations

4. **Profit**—Increased market share can result in increased profits, provided the cost of doing business is held level or even decreased by customer loyalty

5. **Shareholder value**—Customer loyalty can result in higher profits, which, in turn, are a key driver of shareholder value

CUSTOMER LOYALTY VERSUS CUSTOMER PROFITABILITY

The common wisdom among quality professionals is that customer loyalty is a must for organizations that hope to survive and prosper in an intensely competitive global environment. Customer loyalty is, as a general rule, a desirable goal. However, the concept has become so ingrained in contemporary business thinking that some organizations are leaving out another critical factor in the success formula. That factor is profitability.[12]

The goal of organizations should be more than just earning the loyalty of customers; it should be earning the loyalty of customers who contribute to the organization's profitability. Loyal but unprofitable customers are still unprofitable. Organizations should never assume an automatic positive correlation between loyalty and profitability. Nor should they assume that because a customer is profitable initially he or she will remain profitable. "Just because a group of customers was profitable in the past, doesn't mean it will continue to be so in the future. Many nonloyal customers can be very profitable initially, causing companies to chase after them in vain for future profits."[13]

Werner Reinartz and V. Kumar make the critical point that "When customers are sorted according to their profitability and longevity, it becomes clear that the relationship between loyalty and profits is by no means assured."[14] Reinartz and Kumar document this point using a matrix in which study subjects of several different types of businesses were sorted into one of four quadrants:

- high profitability/short term
- high profitability/long term
- low profitability/short term
- low profitability/long term

Using the customers of a corporate service provider as a typical example, only 30% of the long-term (loyal) customers studied were found to be highly profitable for the service provider. More than 20% of the long-term customers were found to provide only low profitability. On the other hand, 20% of the corporate service provider's short-term (nonloyal) customers were found to be highly profitable, and only 29% of its short-term customers were found to provide low profitability.

The key point that Reinartz and Kumar make in this study is that "When profitability and loyalty are considered at the same time, it becomes clear that different customers need to be treated in different ways."[15] They go on to propose four strategies for dealing with customers based on an accurate segmentation of an organization's customers on the basis of their loyalty and profitability. They label customers according to where they fall in the customer loyalty/profitability matrix described above. High-profitability/short-term customers are called *butterflies*. High-profitability/long-term customers are called *true friends*. Low-profitability/short-term customers are called *strangers*. Low-profitability/long-term customers are called *barnacles*. The strategies recommended for each of these customer types follow.

Butterflies

Butterflies are highly profitable customers, but they don't stay around long. Consequently, the following strategies are recommended for dealing with butterflies: (1) aim to achieve transactional satisfaction rather than long-term loyalty; (2) work the accounts only as long as they are active—don't waste time chasing a rainbow; and (3) make wise decisions about the optimum time to break off the relationship.

True Friends

True friends are highly profitable, and they are loyal. Consequently, the following strategies are recommended for dealing with true friends: (1) communicate consistently, but don't overdo it; (2) build both attitudinal loyalty and behavioral loyalty; and (3) nurture, defend, and partner with them to create customer delight.

Strangers

Strangers provide only low profitability and are short-term customers. Consequently, the following strategies are recommended for dealing with strangers: (1) make the best profit possible on every individual transaction and (2) make no investment in the relationship.

Barnacles

Barnacles provide only low profitability but are long-term customers. Consequently, the following strategies are recommended for dealing with barnacles: (1) begin by measuring their buying potential and how much of it the organization gets; (2) if they have buying potential, try to increase the share of their business the organization gets by up-selling and cross-selling; and (3) if they don't have buying potential, impose strict cost controls on their account.

CUSTOMERS AS INNOVATION PARTNERS

Involving customers in the design, prototyping, and testing phases of product development is no longer considered an innovative strategy. The best companies in the global arena apply this strategy as a matter of course. However, a much smaller number of companies are taking the customer involvement strategy to the ultimate level by actually making them innovation partners—full partners in the development of new products and the modification of existing products.[16]

According to Stefan Thomke and Eric von Hippel,

> In the course of studying product innovation across many industries, we have discovered that a number of companies have adopted an intriguing approach, which at first seems counterintuitive. Essentially, these companies have abandoned their efforts to understand exactly what products their customers want and have instead equipped them with tools to design and develop their own products, ranging from minor modifications to major new innovations. The user-friendly tools, often integrated into a package we call a "tool kit for customer innovation," deploy new technologies like computer simulation and rapid prototyping to make product development faster and less expensive.[17]

The driver behind the move to partner with customers in the area of product innovation is what we refer to as the *customization revolution*. Customers have come a long way in their expectations since Henry Ford quipped that his customers could have any color Model T they wanted as long as it was black. Today's customers demand products that are customized to suit their individual needs. Unfortunately, determining what those needs are is an inexact and expensive science at best. This is why some forward-looking companies have stopped involving customers in only the product development process and have begun to actually give them a real voice in the process that produces the product.

According to Thomke and von Hippel,

> A variety of industries use this approach. Bush Boake Allen (BBA), a global supplier of specialty flavors to companies like Nestlé, has built a tool kit that enables its customers to develop their own flavors, which BBA then manufactures. In the materials field, GE provides customers with web-based tools for designing better plastic products. In software, a number of companies let people add custom-designed modules to their standard products and then commercialize the best of those components. Indeed the trend toward customers as innovators has the power to completely transform industries. In the semiconductor business, it has led to a custom-chip market that has grown to more than $15 billion.[18]

Traditional Product Development versus the Innovation Partnership Approach

The body of quality literature is replete with the concept of thinking outside the box and the need to adopt new paradigms, but few quality-related concepts emphasize these concepts more than making customers innovation partners. The relationship between customer and supplier is radically different when the customer is responsible for new product development.

With the traditional approach, the supplier was responsible for research and development, product design, and prototyping. Smart companies would involve customers at the testing phase to make sure the prototype developed actually satisfied their needs. Changes would then be made to the prototype design based on customer feedback. Once the design was revised, the product would go into production. With the innovation partnership approach, the supplier is still responsible for the research and development phase of product development. But the design, prototyping, and testing phases are turned over to the customer. This new approach tends to increase the pace of product change, which, in turn, requires manufacturers to be even more flexible, adaptable, and agile.

When the Innovation Partnership Approach Is Appropriate

Obviously, the innovation partnership approach is a concept with limitations. It is not appropriate or even advisable in every case. Thomke and von Hippel[19] identified the following signs that indicate when the innovation partnership approach makes sense:

1. An organization's market segments are shrinking, and customers are becoming more vocal in demanding customized products.

2. An organization and its customers need many iterations before coming to agreement on the right solution.

3. An organization and its competitors use high-quality computer-based simulation and rapid-prototyping tools internally to develop new products.

Implementing the Innovation Partnership Approach

Thomke and von Hippel recommend five steps for implementing the innovation partnership approach to product development:

1. Develop a tool kit for customers that is easy to use. The tool kit should (1) enable customers to run repeated trial-and-error experiments and tests quickly, easily, and efficiently; (2) use technology that allows customers to work in a familiar design language; (3) include a library of standard design modules to make it easier for customers to create complex designs quickly; and (4) use technologies that tie into manufacturing processes so that customer designs can be sent directly to manufacturing with little or no tailoring required.

2. Increase the flexibility of your production processes. Retool your manufacturing processes for flexible, lean, low-cost production of specialized products.

3. Carefully select the first customers to use your tool kit. The best prospects are customers that have a critical need for custom products that are developed quickly, have a skilled engineering and product development staff, and have limited experience with traditional customization services. This combination of experience and capabilities will cause these customers to stay the course as you work with them to identify and correct bugs in the innovation partnership processes.

4. Continually improve your tool kit and do so quickly to satisfy your best customers. Customers that are on the leading edge of technology will keep the pressure on you to continually improve your tool kit. Do it. Investments made in continually and quickly improving your tool kit will pay off with leading-edge customers.

5. Adapt your business practices to accommodate the innovation partnership. Don't outsource product development and then keep doing everything else in your business in the same old way. Change your business practices to match the new approach. Also, change your customers' communi-

cation practices to suit the new approach. For example, you might have more computer-to-computer interaction with customers that are innovation partners and less face-to-face interaction.

PRODUCT INNOVATION MODEL FOR CUSTOMER RETENTION

In order to retain customers over the long term in today's hyper-competitive global environment, organizations must innovate. If the key to customer loyalty is consistently providing superior value—superior quality, superior cost, and superior service—the key to providing superior value is innovation. Innovation is how organizations continually improve the quality and cost of their products as well as the quality of their services. It is also how they continually reduce the cost of doing business while increasing the volume of business they do. A well-known example of a business that lost customers by failing to innovate is Motorola's initial failure to upgrade its heretofore successful line of analog cellular telephones to digital. This failure allowed Nokia and several others to tap into Motorola's customer base.

Praveen Gupta has developed an innovation model that organizations can use to keep products up-to-date, attractive, and relevant for the customers. It contains the following five process steps:[20]

- **Target the Opportunity.** Focus on identifying customer needs and use them to guide innovations.

- **Explore the Idea.** Conduct a thorough research to ensure that the proposed innovation will be successful in the marketplace.

- **Develop Alternatives.** Develop a variety of alternatives for the innovation—prototypes—and test them thoroughly to determine which is the best.

- **Optimize the Solution.** Take the chosen alternative and optimize it for production and delivery.

- **Commercialize the innovation.** Develop and deploy an effective marketing program for the innovation. Never let an innovation fail for lack of effective marketing.

Gupta encourages creative thinking in applying his model, but makes the point that creativity by itself is not an innovation. According to Gupta, creativity is the idea and invention is the prototype of the new or improved product. But innovation has not occurred until the product is produced and marketed.[21]

SUMMARY

1. Historically, customers were considered outsiders who used a company's products, and suppliers were outsiders who provided the materials needed to produce the products. A more contemporary view is that every organization has both internal and external customers.

An *external customer* is the one referred to in the traditional definition. An *internal customer* is any employee whose work depends on that of employees whose work precedes his or hers.

2. In a total quality setting, customers define quality. Therefore, customer satisfaction must be the highest priority. Customer satisfaction is achieved by producing

high-quality products that meet or exceed expectations. It must be renewed with each purchase. The key to establishing a customer focus is to put employees in touch with customers so that customer needs are known and understood.

3. The six-step strategy proposed by Scholtes, Streibel, and Joiner for identifying customer needs is as follows: Speculate about results, develop an information-gathering plan, gather the information, analyze the results, check the validity of conclusions, and take action.

4. Customer needs are not static. Therefore, constant contact with customers is essential in a total quality setting. Whenever possible, this contact should be in person or by telephone. Written surveys can be used, but they will not produce the level of feedback that personal contact can generate.

5. Quality function deployment (QFD) is a mechanism for putting into operation the concept of building in quality. It makes customer feedback a normal part of the product development process, thereby improving customer satisfaction.

6. Measuring customer satisfaction alone is not enough. Many customers who defect are satisfied. Organizations should, in addition, measure customer retention.

7. Organizations should go beyond satisfying customers to creating value for them in every supplier–customer interaction.

8. The customer loyalty model consists of four components: (1) business performance, (2) global perceptions, (3) loyalty behaviors, and (4) financial outcomes.

9. The goal of organizations should be more than just earning customer loyalty; it should be earning the loyalty of profitable customers. Organizations should never assume a positive correlation between customer loyalty and profitability, nor should they assume that a customer who is initially profitable will always be profitable.

10. An innovative approach to product development that is gaining acceptance is turning customers into innovation partners. With this approach, the customer is given a technological tool kit for designing his or her own products and making product innovations. This approach is implemented using the following steps: (1) develop a tool kit for customers that is easy to use, (2) increase the flexibility of your own production processes, (3) carefully select the first customers to use your tool kit, (4) continually improve your tool kit, and (5) adapt your business practices to suit the innovation partnership approach.

11. The model for product innovation contains the following steps: target the opportunity, explain the idea, develop alternatives, optimize the solution, and commercialize the innovation.

KEY TERMS AND CONCEPTS

Business performance
Communicating with customers
Customer
Customer-defined quality
Customer focus
Customer loyalty model
Customer profitability
Customer satisfaction
Customer value analysis
External customers
Financial outcomes
Global perceptions
Information-gathering plan
Innovation partnership approach
Internal customers
Loyalty behaviors
Quality function deployment (QFD)
Registered complaints
Reliable customers
Supplier
Test customers
Unregistered complaints

FACTUAL REVIEW QUESTIONS

1. Explain the contemporary concepts of *customer* and *supplier*.
2. How does the contemporary view of customers and suppliers differ from the more traditional view?
3. Explain the role of the customer in a total quality setting.
4. What is a reliable customer?
5. What role does customer satisfaction play in the development of reliable customers?
6. How is customer satisfaction ensured?
7. Briefly describe what is meant by an organization that has customer focus.
8. How does an organization go about establishing a customer focus?
9. Explain the six-step strategy for identifying customer needs.
10. Describe how organizations should go about communicating with their customers.
11. Explain briefly the concept of QFD and how it relates to customer satisfaction.
12. Explain why it is important to measure customer retention.

13. Explain why just meeting customer specifications might not produce customer satisfaction.

14. Describe the customer loyalty model.

15. Explain the concept of customers as innovation partners and how to implement the concept.

CRITICAL THINKING ACTIVITY

Are Customers Really Loyal?

"I'll stick with you through thick and thin," or "What have you done for me lately?" Which best describes the attitude of customers in today's marketplace? Two quality managers are debating the concept of customer loyalty. One of them, Jack Hayes, claims that customer loyalty does exist, that it can be won, and that winning a customer's loyalty should be every organization's goal. According to Jack, "If you have a history of satisfying a customer, he will be loyal enough to overlook an occasional bad experience."

"No way," says Anna Cage. "It takes only one bad experience to lose a customer."

Join this debate. You are a customer. Are you loyal to any organizations? If so, how many bad experiences will it take to overcome your loyalty? Have you ever decided to withhold your business from a store, restaurant, or other service provider based on poor service? Do you usually give an organization more than one chance to win your business, or is one bad experience all it takes to turn you off?

DISCUSSION ASSIGNMENT 7–1

Federal Express Knows Customers Want It Now!

"You know you have hit the big time when the purple-and-orange-lettered Federal Express (FedEx) truck driven by a smiling courier pulls into your driveway or walks up your stairwell and hands you the purple-and-orange envelope. First off, it's always a blessed relief to get what's inside, because it absolutely, positively had to get there."

"Fred Smith, a 20-year-old sophomore at Yale University, understood this characteristic of American culture when he thought up his topic for his business class project. We all know the legend, how he wrote a term paper describing his idea for overnight delivery of documents anywhere in the country by means of a fleet of airplanes flying to a hub system converging on Memphis of all places. Fred got a C on the paper, and most of his buddies thought he was lucky.

But it took more than full faith in a sophomore's brainchild to make FedEx what it is today. The company serves one of the most important aspects of American culture and business: the need for a NOW response. And FedEx knows that the only thing it has to sell is NOW—without fail."

DISCUSSION QUESTIONS

Discuss the following questions in class or outside of class with your fellow students:

1. Americans have developed what has been called a "microwave mentality." We like quick service, instant food, and fast results. Does this describe you as a customer?

2. What American companies besides Federal Express base their success on NOW service?

DISCUSSION ASSIGNMENT 7–2

Winning Back Lost Customers Is a Costly Challenge

Perhaps the most famous case illustrating the enormous cost of winning back lost customers is that of the "Tylenol Murders." Seven people in the Chicago area died suddenly after taking Tylenol capsules. An investigation revealed that the capsules had been laced with cyanide, a deadly poison. When the story ran on the nightly news programs, a nationwide panic ensued that caused Tylenol's sales to plummet overnight. Many business analysts predicted that Tylenol's manufacturer, Johnson & Johnson, would not survive the tragedy. Johnson & Johnson surprised the analysts by undertaking one of the most successful campaigns in history to win back customers. It worked, but the cost was huge. This case led not just Johnson & Johnson but also all major drug manufacturers to develop the tamperproof bottle. Having done so, Johnson & Johnson undertook an intensive public relations campaign to win back the trust of its customers.

DISCUSSION QUESTIONS

Discuss the following questions in class or outside of class with your fellow students:
1. If the Tylenol incident were to happen today and you were a user of Tylenol, would Johnson & Johnson be able to win back your trust?

2. What would it take for Johnson & Johnson to win back your trust if one of the victims was a friend of yours?

ENDNOTES

1. Linda M. Doherty and James F. White, "Customer-Defined Quality in a Networked World." Retrieved from http://findarticles.com/p/articles/mi_M0HTO/is_1_29/ai_n25030928 on March 5, 2011.

2. Peter R. Scholtes, Barbara J. Streibel, and Brian L. Joiner, *The Team Handbook*, 3rd ed. (Madison, WI: Joiner Associates, 2003), 2–6.

3. Dorherty and White, "Customer-Defined Quality in a Networked World."

4. American Society for Quality, "Idea Creation Tools." Retrieved from www.asg.org/learn-about-quality/

idea-creation-tools/overview/affiuity.html on March 11, 2011.

5. Michael Butchko, Mike Butchko Consulting, "Customer Satisfaction Process," an unpublished white paper updated January 7, 2011. Used with permission.

6. "Customer Complaint Survey," Final Report, Institute for Continual Improvement, Report No. 2004–12 (Niceville, Florida, March 11, 2011).

7. Jef Menguin, "Characteristics of Customer-Centered Vision." Retrieved from http://jefmenguin.wordpress.com/2007/08/10/characteristics-of-customer-centered-vision/ on January 29, 2011.

8. Ibid.

9. American Society for Quality, "Manager of Quality/ Organizational Excellence Certification-Body of Knowledge." Retrieved from www.asq.org/certification/manager-of-quality/book.html on March 15, 2011.

10. "Customer Loyalty." Retrieved from http://knowledge.wharton.upenn.edu on February 12, 2011.

11. Ibid.

12. Werner Reinartz and V. Kumar, "The Mismanagement of Customer Loyalty," *Harvard Business Review* 80 (July 2002): 86–94.

13. Ibid., 91.

14. Ibid., 92.

15. Ibid., 93.

16. Stefan Thomke and Eric von Hippel, "Customers as Innovators," *Harvard Business Review* 80 (April 2002): 74–77.

17. Ibid., 74.

18. Ibid.

19. Ibid.

20. Jane Keathley et al., "Innovation-Driven Organizations: What, Why, and How," *The Quality Management Forum* 80, no. 1 (Spring 2010): 4.

21. Ibid.

EMPLOYEE EMPOWERMENT

*Light is the task where many share the toil. —**Homer***

MAJOR TOPICS
- **Employee Empowerment Defined**
- **Rationale for Empowerment**
- **Inhibitors of Empowerment**
- **Management's Role in Empowerment**
- **Implementing Empowerment**
- **How to Recognize Empowered Employees**
- **Empowerment Errors to Avoid**
- **Beyond Empowerment to Enlistment**

Involving people in decisions made relating to their work is a fundamental principle of good management. With total quality, this principle is taken even further. First, employees are involved not only in decision making, but also in the creative thought processes that precede decision making. Second, employees are not just involved; they are empowered. This chapter explains the concepts of involvement and empowerment, their relationship, and how they can be used to improve competitiveness.

EMPLOYEE EMPOWERMENT DEFINED

Employee involvement and empowerment are closely related concepts, but they are not the same. In a total quality setting, employees should be empowered:

> James Monroe, CEO of a midsized electronics manufacturing firm, decided more than a year ago to get his employees involved as a way to improve work and enhance his company's competitiveness. He called his managers and supervisors together, explained his idea, and had suggestion boxes placed in all departments. At first, the suggestion boxes filled to overflowing. Supervisors emptied them once a week, acted on any suggestions they thought had merit, and discarded the rest. After a couple of months, employee suggestions

dwindled down to one or two a month. Worse, recent suggestion forms have contained derisive remarks about the company and its suggestion system. Productivity has not improved, and morale is worse than before. Monroe is at a loss over what to do. Employee involvement was supposed to help, not hurt.

In this example, the CEO involved his employees by asking for their input in the form of suggestions but did not empower them. There are important differences between involvement and empowerment. Involved employees are asked for their input, but they are not given *ownership* of their jobs. Empowered employees are given ownership of the processes they are responsible for and the products or services generated by those processes. Empowered employees—employees with ownership—take pride in their work and the resulting products or services produced by it. Ownership creates a sense of urgency to continually improve processes, products, and services and to strive for customer delight because "my signature" is on the work. An empowered employee will care as much or even more about the quality of the work than the supervisor or the CEO.

How Employee Empowerment Is Achieved

In the old days, many managers had the following philosophy: *Managers think and employees work. Good employees just do what managers tell them.* This philosophy is so archaic and ineffective that few managers today would admit to ever subscribing to it. However, there are still many managers who, like the CEO cited in the example at the beginning of this chapter, have trouble bringing themselves to go all the way with empowering employees; they want to stop at just involvement—asking for employee input.

In order to have dedicated, motivated employees who feel a strong sense of ownership—employees who are physically, intellectually, and emotionally involved in their work—management must provide an open, nonthreatening, creative environment that encourages employee involvement; expects employees to think; recognizes employee value; and rewards employee ownership of processes, products, and services.

Facilitating empowerment is an important responsibility of management in a total quality environment. One of the authors personally experienced a powerful example of a top executive using empowerment as a tool for improvement. Years ago when the author was first selected to lead the manufacturing component of a large division of a well-known corporation, he was summoned to the office of the general manager—his new boss. The general manager wasted no words. Speaking to the author, he said words to the effect that "You can sit around and continue things as they are and fail, or you can try to make something of manufacturing. It's up to you."

The author immediately understood in deeply personal terms what is meant by the concept of empowerment. The company's manufacturing component was in his hands; he had ownership of its success or failure. In order to turn around the company's manufacturing component, the author would have to be physically, intellectually, and emotionally involved. He also understood immediately that in order to succeed, he would have to cascade the concept of empowerment down through the entire manufacturing organization—all 1,300 personnel. By applying the concept of employee empowerment and the other quality management concepts presented in this book, the author was able to transform his company's manufacturing component into the most profitable division in the corporation.

Management Tool or Cultural Change

The management strategies developed over the years to improve productivity, quality, cost, service, and response time would make a long list. Is empowerment just another of these management tools, another strategy to add to the list? This is an important question, and it should be dealt with in the earliest stages of implementing empowerment.

Employees who have been around long enough to see several management innovations come and go may be reluctant to accept empowerment if they see it as just another short-lived management strategy. This is known as the WOHCAO Syndrome (pronounced WO-KAY-O). WOHCAO is short for "Watch out, here comes another one."

Successful implementation of empowerment requires change in the corporate culture—a major new direction in how managers think and work. The division of labor between managers and workers changes with empowerment.

Empowerment Does Not Mean Abdication

It is not uncommon for traditional managers to view empowerment as an abdication of power. Such managers see involvement and empowerment as turning over control of the company to the employees. In reality, this is hardly the case. Empowerment involves actively soliciting input from those closest to the work and giving those individuals ownership of their jobs.

Pooling the collective minds of all people involved in a process, if done properly, will enhance rather than diminish managers' power. It increases the likelihood that the information on which decision makers base their decisions is comprehensive and accurate. Empowerment also lets managers focus more on the larger decisions because empowered employees don't have to bring them every little problem that comes up.

An example from medicine illustrates this point. Suppose that a child is gravely ill. Every established medical procedure known has been used without success. The only remaining option is a rarely used and unapproved procedure that has been performed by just 10 surgeons. There are variations of the procedure, each carrying its own specific risks as well as its own probability of success.

Because the procedure is not approved, the child's parents must decide which variation is to be applied. They may simply close their eyes, make a choice, and hope for the best, or they may take another approach in arriving at a decision. That other approach involves soliciting input from the 10 surgeons who have performed the operation in its several variations. The surgeons are willing and eager to give their advice.

Which approach is most likely to produce the best decision? Most people would want to pool the minds of the surgeons who have performed the operation. They are closest to the job and, therefore, likely to have valuable insight concerning how it should be done. Responsibility for ultimately making the decision still rests with the parents. However, these parents will probably solicit the input of the 10 surgeons in question and give it careful consideration. In other words, although they will ultimately make the decision, the parents in this example will involve and empower the surgeons.

The same concept applies in the workplace. Managers do not abdicate their responsibility by adopting empowerment. Rather, like the parents in this example, they increase the likelihood of making the best possible decisions and thereby more effectively carry out their responsibility.

RATIONALE FOR EMPOWERMENT

Traditionally, working hard was seen as the surest way to succeed. With the advent of global competition and the never-ending need to improve, the key to success became not just working hard but also working smart. In many cases, decision makers in business and industry interpreted working smart as adopting high-tech systems and automated processes. These smarter technologies have made a difference in many cases. However, improved technology is just one aspect of working smarter, and it's a part that can be quickly neutralized when the competition adopts a similar or even better technology.

An aspect of working smart that is often missing in the modern workplace is involving and empowering employees in ways that take advantage of their creativity and promote independent thinking and initiative on their part. In other words, what's missing is empowerment. Creative thinking and initiative from as many employees as possible will increase the likelihood of better ideas, better decisions, better quality, better productivity, and, therefore, better competitiveness. The rationale for empowerment is that it represents the best way to bring the creativity and initiative of the best employees to bear on improving the company's competitiveness.

Human beings are not robots or automatons. While working, they observe, think, sense, and ponder. It is natural for a person to continually ask such questions as the following:

- Why is it done this way?
- How could it be done better?
- Will the customer want the product like this?

Asking such questions is an important step in making improvements. As employees ask questions, they also generate ideas for solutions, particularly when given the opportunity to regularly discuss their ideas in a group setting that is positive, supportive, and mutually nurturing.

Empowerment and Motivation

One of the most motivating actions a manager can take is to ask the opinions of employees. Doing so says, "You matter."

Empowerment is sometimes seen by experienced managers as just another name for participatory management. However, there is an important distinction between the two. Participatory management is about managers and supervisors asking for their employees' help. Empowerment is about getting employees to help themselves, each other, and the company. This is why empowerment can be so effective in helping maintain a high level of motivation among employees. It helps employees develop a sense of ownership of their jobs and of the company. This, in turn, leads to a greater willingness on the part of employees to make decisions, take risks in an effort to make improvements, and speak out when they disagree.

INHIBITORS OF EMPOWERMENT

The primary inhibitor of empowerment, resistance to change, is an indigenous characteristic of human nature. Resistance can be magnified when suspicion replaces trust.

Resistance from Employees and Unions

Earlier in this chapter, the WOHCAO Syndrome was discussed. In this syndrome, employees have experienced enough flash-in-the-pan management strategies that either did not work out or were not followed through on that they have become skeptical.

In addition to skepticism, there is the problem of inertia. Resistance to change is natural. Even positive change can be uncomfortable for employees because it involves new and unfamiliar territory. However, when recognized for what they are, skepticism and inertia can be overcome. Strategies for doing so are discussed later in this chapter.

Unions can be another source of resistance when implementing empowerment. Because of the traditional adversarial relationship between organized labor and management, unions may be suspicious of management's motives in implementing empowerment. They might also resent an idea not originated by their own organization. However, unions' greatest concern is likely to be how empowerment will affect their future. If union leaders think it will diminish the need for their organization, they will throw up roadblocks.

Clear evidence exists that resistance to empowerment on the part of labor unions is becoming less and less an issue. Leaders of some of the largest unions in the United States—including the Communications Workers of America, International Chemical Workers Union, International Brotherhood of Electrical Workers, and Amalgamated Clothing and Textiles Workers Union—participated in a 2-year study as members of the government-sponsored Economic Policy Productivity Panel, which did much to mitigate the initial concerns of unions about the concept of empowerment.

Resistance from Management

Even if employees and labor unions support empowerment, it will not work unless management makes a full and wholehearted commitment to it. The importance of management commitment cannot be overemphasized. Employees take their cues from management concerning what is important, what the company is committed to, how to behave, and all other aspects of the job. Discussion Assignment 8-1 shows what can result when either a real or a perceived lack of commitment exists on the part of management. Because of a lack of management support, the company referred to in this assignment lost a program that had made substantial improvements in its ability to compete.

Some of the reasons behind management resistance to empowerment include insecurity, personal values, ego, insufficient and ineffective management training, personality characteristics of managers, and exclusion of managers.

Fear of Losing Control   An old adage states, "Knowledge is power." By controlling access to knowledge as well as the day-to-day flow of knowledge, managers can maintain power over employees. Managers who view the workplace from an "us-against-them" perspective tend to be insecure about any initiative they perceive as diminishing their power. Another source of management insecurity is accountability. Pooling the minds of employees for the purpose of making workplace improvements is a sure way to identify problems, roadblocks, and inhibitors. Some managers fear they will be revealed as the culprit in such a process. The natural reaction of an individual who feels threatened is to resist the source of the threat. Managers are no different in experiencing this feeling.

I'm-the-Boss Syndrome Many of today's managers have a dogmatic mindset when it comes to working with employees. This means they think employees should do what they are told, when they are told, and how they are told. Such a value system does not promote empowerment. Managers who feel this way will resist involvement and empowerment as being inappropriate. They are likely to think, "There can be only one boss around here, and that boss is me."

Status People who become managers may be understandably proud of their status and protective of the perquisites that accompany it. Status appeals to the human ego, and ego-focused managers may project an "I am the boss" attitude. Such managers may have difficulty reining in their egos enough to be effective participants in an approach they view as an encroachment on territory that should be exclusively theirs.

Outdated Management Training Many of today's managers were educated and trained by modern disciples of Frederick Taylor, the founder of "scientific management." Taylor's followers, whether university professors or management trainers, tend to focus on applying scientific principles to the improvement of processes and technology. Less attention is given to people-oriented improvements.

Such approaches are inappropriate in the modern workplace. Nevertheless, vestiges of Taylor's school of thought remain in college management programs throughout the United States. Actually, much of what Taylor professed about applying scientific principles in improving the workplace is valid and has gained new status with the advent of total quality. Function analysis, statistical process control (SPC), and just-in-time (JIT) manufacturing—all total quality tools—

are examples of science applied to workplace improvement. However, unlike Taylor's followers, proponents of total quality involve employees in the application of these scientific methods. Management schools that still cling, even subtly, to the management-as-thinkers and labor-as-doers philosophy produce graduates who are likely to resist empowerment. Experienced managers who were schooled in this philosophy in years past and have practiced it throughout their careers are also likely to resist empowerment.

Old-School Syndrome Old-school managers are often found to be more task oriented than people oriented. They tend to focus more on the task at hand and getting it done than on the people who actually perform the task.

Consider the case of a fictitious manager named Wanda Brown. Wanda is a task-oriented manager. Before her promotion, she did most of the work associated with task accomplishment herself. Her dependence on and interaction with other employees was minimal. As a result, Wanda's task-oriented personality served her and the company well. Now, as a manager, she is responsible for organizing work and getting it done by others.

In this new setting, Wanda has found that the quality and quantity of employees' work can be affected by problems they are having. She has found that, in spite of her well-earned reputation for getting the job done, other employees have ideas of their own about workplace improvements and that they want their ideas to be heard and given serious consideration. Finally, Wanda has learned that employees have feelings, egos, and personal agendas and that these things can affect their work. Managers such as Wanda who have a strong task orientation are not likely to support efforts such as empowerment that call for a balanced attitude in which the manager is concerned with both tasks and people (see Figure 8–1).

Fear of Exclusion Empowerment is about the total involvement of all personnel who will be affected by an idea or a decision. This includes the first level of management (supervisors), middle-level management, and executive management. Any manager or level of management excluded from the process can be expected to resist. Even with a full commitment from executives and enthusiastic support from employees, empowerment will not succeed if middle-level managers and supervisors are excluded. Those

FIGURE 8–1 Orientation of Managers

who are excluded, even if they agree conceptually, may resist simply because they feel left out.

Workforce Readiness

An inhibitor of employee empowerment that receives little attention in the literature is workforce readiness. Empowerment will fail quickly if employees are not ready to be empowered. In fact, empowering employees who are not prepared for the responsibilities involved can be worse than not empowering them at all. On the other hand, a lack of readiness—even though it may exist—should not be used as an excuse for failing to empower employees. The challenge to management is twofold: (a) determine whether the workforce is ready for empowerment and (b) if it is not ready, get it ready.

How, then, does one know whether the workforce is ready for empowerment? One rule of thumb is that the more highly educated the workforce, the more ready its members will be for empowerment. Because well-educated people are accustomed to critical thinking, they are experienced in decision making, and they tend to make a point of being well-informed concerning issues that affect their work. This does not mean, however, that less educated employees should be excluded. Rather, it means that they may need to be prepared before being included.

In determining whether employees are ready for empowerment, ask the following questions:

- Are the employees accustomed to critical thinking?
- Are the employees knowledgeable of the decision-making process and their role with regard to it?
- Are the employees fully informed of the "big picture" and where they fit into it?

Unless the answer to all three of these questions is yes, the workforce is not ready for empowerment. An empowered employee must be able to think critically. It should be second nature for an employee to ask such questions as these: Is there a better way to do this? Why do we do it this way? Could the goal be accomplished some other way? Is there another way to look at this problem? Is this problem really an opportunity to improve things?

These are the types of questions that lead to continual improvement of processes and effective solutions to problems. These are the sorts of questions that empowered employees should ask all the time about everything. Employees who are unaccustomed to asking questions such as these should be taught to do so before being empowered.

Employees should understand the decision-making process, both on a conceptual level and on a practical level (e.g., how decisions are made in their organization). Being empowered does not mean making decisions. Rather, it means being made a part of the decision-making process. Before empowering employees, it is important to show them what empowerment will mean on a practical level. How will they be empowered? Where will they fit into the decision-making process? They also need to be aware of the boundaries. What decisions will they be able to make themselves or within their work teams? Employees should know the answers to all of these questions before being empowered.

An employee who does not know where the organization is going will be unable to help it get there. Before empowering employees, it is wise to educate them concerning the organization's strategic plan and their role relative to it. When employees can see the goal, they are better able to help the organization reach it.

Organizational Structure and Management Practices

Most resistance to empowerment is attitudinal, as the inhibitors explained so far show. However, a company's organizational structure and its management practices can also mitigate against the successful implementation of empowerment. Before attempting to implement empowerment, ask these questions:

- How many layers of management are there between workers and decision makers?
- Does the employee performance-appraisal system encourage or discourage initiative and risk taking?
- Do management practices encourage employees to speak out against policies and procedures that inhibit quality and productivity?

Employees, like most people, will become frustrated if their ideas have to work their way through a bureaucratic maze before reaching a decision maker. Prompt feedback on suggestions for improvement is essential to the success of empowerment. Too many layers of managers who can say no between employees and decision makers who can say yes will inhibit and eventually kill risk taking and initiative on the part of employees.

Risk-taking employees will occasionally make mistakes or try ideas that don't work. If this reflects negatively in their performance appraisals, initiative will be replaced by a play-it-safe approach. This also applies to constructive criticism of company policies and management practices. Are employees who offer constructive criticism considered problem solvers or troublemakers? Managers' attitudes toward constructive criticism will determine whether they receive any. A positive, open attitude in such cases is essential. The free flow of constructive criticism is a fundamental element of empowerment.

MANAGEMENT'S ROLE IN EMPOWERMENT

Management's role in empowerment can be stated simply. It is to do everything necessary to ensure successful implementation and ongoing application of the concept. Everything management does to promote empowerment should have the goal of establishing a creative, open, nonthreatening environment

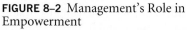

FIGURE 8–2 Management's Role in Empowerment

in which involved, motivated, dedicated employees can flourish. The three words that best describe management's role in empowerment are *commitment, leadership,* and *facilitation* (see Figure 8–2). All three functions are required to break down the barriers and overcome the inherent resistance often associated with implementation of empowerment or with any other major change in the corporate culture.

The manager's role in empowerment can be broken down into the following more specific behaviors by category:

- **Commitment.** Being consistently supportive of empowerment and reinforcing it in tangible ways.

- **Leadership.** Promoting empowerment by being a consistent role model, mentor, and trainer.

- **Facilitation.** Monitoring constantly to ensure that employees are being empowered and acting quickly on employee recommendations.

IMPLEMENTING EMPOWERMENT

Figure 8–3 shows the four broad steps in the implementation of empowerment. Creating a workplace environment that is positive toward and supportive of empowerment so that risk taking and individual initiative are encouraged is critical. Targeting and overcoming inhibitors of empowerment are also critical. These two steps were discussed earlier in this chapter. The third step is dealt with in this section. The fourth step is the standard management strategy of checking progress (assessing), making any adjustments that might be necessary, and continually improving.

Putting the Vehicles in Place

A number of different types of vehicles can be used for collecting input from empowered employees and getting it into decision-making channels. Such vehicles range from simply walking around the workplace and asking employees for their input, to holding periodic brainstorming sessions, to regularly scheduling quality circles. Widely used methods that are typically the most effective are explained in the following subsections:

Brainstorming With brainstorming, managers serve as catalysts in drawing out group members. Participants are encouraged to share any ideas that come to mind. All ideas are considered valid. Participants are not allowed to make judgmental comments or to evaluate the suggestions made. Typically, one member of the group is asked to serve as a recorder. All ideas suggested are recorded, preferably on a marker board, flipchart, or other medium that allows group members to review them continually.

After all ideas have been recorded, the evaluation process begins. Participants are asked to go through the list one item at a time, weighing the relative merits of each. This

FIGURE 8–3 Steps in Implementing Empowerment

process is repeated until the group narrows the choices to a specified number. For example, managers may ask the group to reduce the number of alternatives to three, reserving the selection of the best of the three to themselves.

Brainstorming can be an effective vehicle for collecting employee input and feedback, particularly if managers understand the weaknesses associated with it and how they can be overcome. Managers interested in soliciting employee input through brainstorming should be familiar with the concepts of groupthink and groupshift. These two concepts can undermine the effectiveness of brainstorming and other group techniques.

Groupthink is the phenomenon that exists when people in a group focus more on reaching a decision than on making a good decision. A number of factors can contribute to groupthink, including overly prescriptive group leadership, peer pressure for conformity, group isolation, and unskilled application of group decision-making techniques. The following strategies will help overcome groupthink:[1]

- Encourage criticism.
- Encourage the development of several alternatives. Do not allow the group to rush to a hasty decision.
- Assign a member or members to play the role of devil's advocate.
- Include people who are not familiar with the issue.
- Hold last-chance meetings. When a decision is reached, arrange a follow-up meeting a few days later. After group members have had time to think things over, they may have second thoughts. Last-chance meetings give employees an opportunity to voice their second thoughts.

Groupshift is the phenomenon that exists when group members exaggerate their initial position, hoping that the eventual decision will be what they really want.[2] If group members get together prior to a meeting and decide to take an overly risky or unduly conservative view, this can be difficult to surmount. Managers can help minimize the effects of groupshift by discouraging reinforcement of initial points of view and by assigning group members to serve as devil's advocates.

Nominal Group Technique The nominal group technique (NGT) is a sophisticated form of brainstorming involving five steps (see Figure 8–4). In the first step, the manager states the problem and provides clarification if necessary to make sure all group members understand. In the second step, each group member silently records his or her ideas. At this point, there is no discussion among group members. This strategy promotes free and open thinking unimpeded by judgmental comments or peer pressure.

In the third step, the ideas of individual members are made public by asking each member to share one idea with the group. The ideas are recorded on a marker board or flipchart. The process is repeated until all ideas have been recorded. Each idea is numbered. There is no discussion

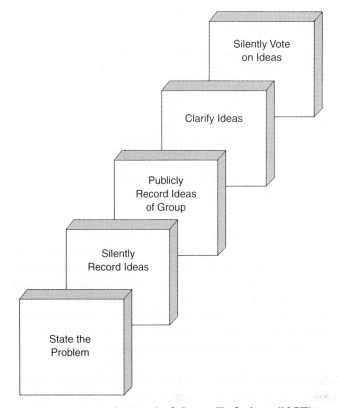

FIGURE 8–4 Steps in Nominal Group Technique (NGT)

among group members during this step. Taking the ideas one at a time from group members ensures a mix of recorded ideas, making it more difficult for members to recall what ideas belong to which individual.

In the fourth step, recorded ideas are clarified to ensure that group members understand what is meant by each. A group member may be asked to explain an idea, but no comments or judgmental gestures are allowed from other members. The member clarifying the ideas is not allowed to make justifications. The goal in this step is simply to ensure that all ideas are clearly understood.

In the final step, the ideas are voted on silently. There are a number of ways to accomplish this. One simple technique is to ask all group members to record the numbers of their five favorite ideas on five separate 3 × 5 cards. Each member then prioritizes his or her five cards by assigning them a number ranging from 1 (worst idea) to 5 (best idea). The cards are collected and the points assigned to ideas are recorded on the marker board or flipchart. After this process has been accomplished for all five cards of all group members, the points are tallied. The idea receiving the most points is selected as the best idea.

Quality Circles A *quality circle* is a group of employees that meets regularly for the purpose of identifying, recommending, and making workplace improvements. A key difference between quality circles and brainstorming is that quality circle members are volunteers who convene themselves and conduct their own meetings. Brainstorming sessions are typically convened and conducted by a manager. A quality circle has a team leader who acts as a facilitator, and the group may use brainstorming, NGT, or other group techniques; however, the team leader is typically not a manager and may, in fact, be a different group member at each meeting. Quality circles meet regularly before, during, or after a shift to discuss their work, anticipate problems, propose workplace improvements, set goals, and make plans.

Suggestion Boxes   This vehicle is perhaps the oldest method used for collecting employee input and feedback. It once consisted of placing receptacles in convenient locations into which employees may put written suggestions. In the age of computers, suggestion systems are now more likely to be online. Suggestions may be made by individuals or teams, and they require an explanation of the current situation, proposed improvements, and benefits expected from the improvements. The authors do not subscribe to suggestion systems, thinking they are the least effective approach to empowerment.

Walking and Talking   Simply walking around the workplace and talking with employees can be an effective way to solicit input. As mentioned earlier, this approach is sometimes referred to as management-by-walking-around (MBWA). An effective way to prompt employee input is to ask questions. This approach may be necessary to get the ball rolling, particularly when empowerment is still new and not yet fully accepted by employees. In such cases, it is important to ask the right questions and to use open-ended questions.

Regardless of the vehicles used for soliciting employee input, organizations need to continually improve the process.

HOW TO RECOGNIZE EMPOWERED EMPLOYEES

There will always be managers and supervisors who resist the concept of empowerment out of fear of losing control or losing their authority. Some will give lip service to empowerment while continuing to do things the same way they always have. How can an organization's leaders know that their empowerment efforts are working? In other words, how does one recognize an empowered employee? The following

comparisons will help leaders in an organization determine whether they have empowered employees. These will also help leaders to determine whether employees are required to do things as they have always been done by supervisors who talk about empowerment but do not really believe in it. The comparisons are as follows:

- **Waiting to be told versus taking the initiative.** Do employees wait to be told what to do or do they take the initiative in situations that are new, different, or ambiguous? Empowered employees will face ambiguous situations by taking the initiative to define the problem, consider alternative solutions, and move ahead with a solution.

- **Seeing only problems versus seeing opportunities.** When things go wrong do employees see only the problems or do they also see opportunities for improvement, learning, and professional growth? Rather than wringing their hands and fretting, empowered employees will turn problems into opportunities. Some of the best quality improvements come from approaching problems as opportunities.

- **Accepting input at face value versus thinking critically.** Do employees accept anything they are told at face value or do they think critically about the input they receive? Empowered employees apply logic, use reasoning, and call on their experience to challenge assumptions and question the status quo.

- **Pass decisions up the line versus building consensus for solutions.** Do employees pass the buck up the line when decisions must be made about solving problems or do they propose a solution and try to build consensus for it? Empowered employees do not let the fear of making a mistake prevent them from proposing solutions and seeking support for implementing them.

No matter what an organization's supervisors and leaders say about empowerment, and no matter how elaborate the systems put in place to promote empowerment are, employees are not empowered until they are willing and able to take the initiative when action is needed, identify opportunities for continual improvement in the problems that occur, build consensus for a given action or decision, and think critically when considering actions, decisions, and assumptions.

EMPOWERMENT ERRORS TO AVOID

Empowerment can be a powerful tool for continually improving quality, cost, service, productivity, performance, and competitiveness. Consequently, empowerment is an essential strategy for achieving total quality. It is also a concept that can quickly go awry unless the necessary foundation is in place to support it. Empowering an employee who has never been empowered is like giving a lot of money to an individual who has never had any. He is not likely to handle it well. Consequently, it is important for organizations that want to use empowerment as a total-quality strategy to prepare both managers and employees.

The following precautions will help organizations avoid the most common empowerment errors:

- **Clearly defining what empowerment means in the organization.** One of the authors once worked for a company that hoped to use empowerment to improve responsiveness to customer needs. The word was passed that all personnel at or above a certain level were empowered to do whatever was necessary to meet a customer's needs. The CEO assumed that personnel in these specified positions would apply common sense. Bad assumption. A project engineer received a call from a customer who was expecting one of our products to be delivered two hours earlier. The customer was upset and angry. He needed that part. This was before the days of overnight shipping. After some discussion, the engineer called a local airport and chartered a small airplane to deliver the part. When the bill showed up in the accounting department, the fur began to fly. The CEO was forced to step back and do a better job defining what empowerment meant on a practical level by establishing appropriate parameters.

- **Provide empowerment training for all personnel.** In order to gain the benefits of empowerment, organizations need their personnel to know more than just the parameters. They also need them to know how to be: (1) critical thinkers and (2) good decision makers. Never assume that anyone at any level is a critical thinker or a good decision maker. Instead, provide training for all personnel in these critical skills. Follow up the training with mentoring. Make sure the training includes hands-on simulations that reflect the types of situations personnel are likely to face and the types of decisions they may have to make when empowered.

- **Do not rush or become impatient.** Organizations that have never empowered their personnel cannot be expected to go and apply the traditional mode to empowerment overnight. The transition will take time—it is a growing process that should not be rushed. Do not become impatient. Give attitudes, perspectives, and skills time to develop. Further and perhaps most important, understand that the newly empowered personnel are going to make mistakes. Properly applying the concept of empowerment is like learning to roller skate. You are going to fall down a few times before you finally get the knack of it.

BEYOND EMPOWERMENT TO ENLISTMENT

Involvement and empowerment focus the experience, knowledge, creativity, and ideas of a broad cross-section of stakeholders on a problem. By involving and empowering stakeholders, organizations find better solutions

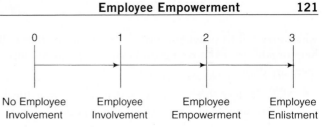

FIGURE 8–5 Involvement–Empowerment–Enlistment Continuum

to problems. Empowerment is now widely accepted and practiced in competitive organizations. What, then, is next? How can organizations go beyond involvement and empowerment?

To answer this question, it is necessary to view the issue as a continuum, as shown in Figure 8–5. The extreme left-hand position (zero) on the continuum represents the old management philosophy that *managers think and employees work.* Organizations that practice this philosophy neither seek nor allow employee input.

The next position (1) on the continuum is employee involvement. Organizations that practice employee involvement provide various mechanisms that allow employees to submit input concerning decisions that affect them. Involvement is a passive approach that *allows* employees to submit input.

The next position (2) on the continuum is employee empowerment. Organizations that practice employee empowerment don't just allow employee input—they actively seek it. Empowerment is an active approach in which employee input is sought and used. Empowered employees provide input concerning decisions that affect them and can apply their own ingenuity in seeking improvements themselves within specified limits. Like involvement, empowerment *allows* employees to be part of the decision-making process and to own their jobs.

The extreme right-hand position (3) on the continuum is employee *enlistment.* Enlistment goes beyond empowerment in that it not only allows employees to own their jobs and to innovate, but also *expects* them to do so. Mechanisms that allow employees to be a part of the decision-making process also let them not be a part. In other words, with involvement and empowerment, employees can choose not to participate; they can simply opt out. Employees who do this deny organizations the benefit of their knowledge, experience, point of view, and ingenuity.

Organizations trying to survive and thrive in a competitive environment need their employees to bring all of their intellectual tools to bear on continual improvement every day. To do this, they must go beyond empowerment to enlistment. Employee enlistment means not simply empowering employees to participate in the decision-making process but also expecting them to do so.

Every employee is a valuable resource. Consequently, organizations need to make full use of employees. This cannot be done if employees opt out of participating in the decision-making process, which is what employees do when they fail to provide input. Some strategies that will help organizations move beyond empowerment to enlistment are these:

- Make it clear to all employees that their ownership is not just wanted and needed but also expected.
- Make ownership a criterion in the performance appraisal process. However, make it clear that what

counts is well-thought-out input. Don't reward frivolous participation.

- In meetings, call on the wallflowers. Don't let employees just be present in the room; expect them to be engaged.
- Make enlistment a guiding principle in the organization's strategic plan and an organizational value that becomes part of the corporate structure.

SUMMARY

1. Empowerment means engaging employees in the thinking processes of an organization in ways that matter. *Involvement* means having input. *Empowerment* means having input that is heard and used, and it means giving employees ownership of their jobs. Empowerment requires a change in the organizational culture, but it does not mean that managers abdicate their responsibility or authority.

2. The rationale for empowerment is that it is the best way to increase creative thinking and initiative on the part of employees. This, in turn, is an excellent way to enhance an organization's competitiveness. Another aspect of the rationale for empowerment is that it can be an outstanding motivator.

3. The primary inhibitor of empowerment is resistance to change. Resistance might come from employees, unions, and management. Management-related inhibitors include insecurity, personal values, ego, management training, personality characteristics, exclusion, organizational structure, and management practices.

4. Management's role in empowerment is best described as commitment, leadership, and facilitation. The kinds of support managers can provide include having a supportive attitude, role modeling, training, facilitating, employing MBWA, taking quick action on recommendations, and recognizing the accomplishments of employees.

5. The implementation of empowerment has four broad steps: creating a supportive environment; targeting and overcoming inhibitors; putting the vehicles in place; and assessing, adjusting, and improving. Vehicles include brainstorming, nominal group technique (NGT), quality circles, suggestion boxes, and walking and talking.

6. A workforce that is ready for empowerment is accustomed to critical thinking, understands the decision-making process, and knows where it fits into the big picture.

7. Enlistment is empowerment is which ownership is not just allowed but also expected.

KEY TERMS AND CONCEPTS

Assessing

Brainstorming

Choose

Commitment

Empowerment

Enlistment

Facilitation

Groupshift

Groupthink

Initiative

Leadership

Nominal group technique (NGT)

Risk taking

FACTUAL REVIEW QUESTIONS

1. Define the term *empowerment*, being sure to distinguish between *involvement* and *empowerment*.
2. Explain the following statement: "Successful implementation of empowerment requires change in the corporate culture."
3. Give a brief rationale for empowerment.
4. What is the relationship between empowerment and motivation?
5. List three inhibitors of empowerment and how they can be overcome.
6. Explain the various root causes of management resistance to empowerment.
7. In what ways can an organization's structure and management practices inhibit empowerment?
8. Describe management's role in empowerment.
9. Describe how to use brainstorming to promote empowerment.
10. What is a quality circle?
11. Describe the concept of MBWA.
12. Explain the concept of workforce readiness as it relates to empowerment.
13. Distinguish between empowerment and enlistment.

CRITICAL THINKING ACTIVITY

Empowerment Can Be a Tough Sell

"We are the market leader in our field," said Mark Hansen, CEO of Gosport Shipbuilding Inc. (GSI). "I built this company from the ground up. I know more about constructing gambling ships than anybody in the business. That's why we are number one. My motto is 'I think and employees work.' This empowerment nonsense you're selling is just that—nonsense. If I want an employee's opinion, I'll give it to him!"

Luke O'Hara, GSI's new quality director, listened respectfully as his boss ranted on. But he had to admit that Hansen had a point. GSI's CEO could do every job in the yard better than the best employees on the payroll. He was also right about GSI's position of market leadership. He thought, "Employee empowerment is going to be a tough sell with Hansen. After all, strip away the bombast and what the CEO is saying is 'Why fix what isn't broken?'"

Put yourself in Luke O'Hara's place. You're the new quality director and want to convince your new boss of the benefits of employee empowerment. How would you persuade Mark Hansen to change his mind?

DISCUSSION ASSIGNMENT 8–1

A Lack of Management Commitment

The employees of a midsized printed circuit-board manufacturer had been excited about their empowerment program during its first several months of operation. A number of solid suggestions for improvement had been made, accepted, and implemented, saving the company substantial amounts of money by reducing throughput time by 19%. During this period, the management was very supportive. Because of its new employee-driven competitiveness, the company became a hot item and was sold at a sizable profit. The new management team voiced agreement with the empowerment program, but it soon became apparent that management support was hollow and half-hearted at best. Within 3 months of the sale, employee interest in the program had died, and the program had been dissolved.

DISCUSSION QUESTION

Discuss the following question in class or outside of class with your fellow students:

1. If you were the quality manager for this company and the employee empowerment effort had been your idea, how would you have gained a commitment to it from the new management team?

DISCUSSION ASSIGNMENT 8–2

The Task-Oriented Manager

Wanda Brown had worked hard to achieve her rapid advancement from shipping/receiving clerk to shipping/receiving manager. She had an uncanny ability to focus on a task, break it into its component parts, arrange the parts in a logical sequence, and tackle each part in order until the entire task has been accomplished—usually well-ahead of

schedule. She used this ability to quickly climb from the bottom of the ladder to the top in her department.

Now, as manager, things seem to be falling apart for Wanda. Rather than focusing exclusively on tasks, she is finding it necessary to deal with people. Often Wanda's subordinates don't agree with her concern over how best to do the job. They have ideas, problems, and feelings—none of which Wanda wants to hear about. Her attitude is "Forget your ideas, problems, and feelings; just focus on your work and do it my way."

DISCUSSION QUESTIONS

Discuss the following questions in class or outside of class with your fellow students:

1. Why might it be difficult for a manager who used to be a talented technician to let employees do their jobs?

2. What personal inhibitors will such an individual have to overcome to empower his or her employees?

DISCUSSION ASSIGNMENT 8–3

Patagonia's Opportunity for Improvement Program

Patagonia is a world-leading textile manufacturer that specializes in clothing for children and adults. Employees are the primary source of workplace improvements in this company, where empowerment is the norm and the suggestion system is called the Opportunity for Improvement Program. Patagonia employees submit written suggestions on a form that asks three questions: "What needs improvement?" "Why?" and "How should the improvements be implemented?" Employees keep a copy of their suggestion, send one to their supervisor, and send one to a central office where it is entered into a suggestions database and tracked. Rewards for suggestions that are implemented range from token gifts such as movie tickets to paid adventure holidays.

DISCUSSION QUESTIONS

Discuss the following questions in class or outside of class with your fellow students:

1. How does an organization know whether its suggestion system is worth the time and effort needed to make it work?

2. If a suggestion system is costing more to operate than it is generating in terms of improvements, how would you respond?

ENDNOTES

1. James Fraser, "Overcoming Groupthink to Improve Board Decision Making." Retrieved from www.rtc-nacd.org/PastProgramTopics/tabid/61/Default.aspx on March 2, 2011.

2. Ibid.

LEADERSHIP AND CHANGE

There is no way to make people like change. You can only make them feel less threatened by it. —**Frederick Hayes**

MAJOR TOPICS

- Leadership Defined
- Leadership for Quality
- Leadership Skills: Inherited or Learned?
- Leadership, Motivation, and Inspiration
- Leadership Styles
- Leadership Style in a Total Quality Setting
- Building and Maintaining a Following
- Leadership versus Management
- Leadership and Ethics
- Employees and Managers on Change
- Restructuring and Change
- How to Lead Change
- Lessons from Distinguished Leaders
- Servant Leadership and Stewardship
- Negative Influences on Leaders: How to Counter Them
- Leaders as Mentors

Leadership is an intangible concept that produces tangible results. It is referred to sometimes as an art and at other times as a science. In reality, leadership is both an art and a science.

The impact of good leadership can be readily seen in any organization where it exists. Well-led organizations, whether they are large companies or small departments within a company, share several easily identifiable characteristics:

- High levels of productivity
- Positive, can-do attitudes
- Commitment to accomplishing organizational goals
- Effective, efficient use of resources
- High levels of quality
- Mutually supportive teamwork approach to getting work done

Where good leadership exists, work is accomplished by teams. These teams are built deliberately, nurtured carefully, and improved continually. This chapter explains the concepts of leadership and leadership during times of change—and how they are applied in a total quality setting.

LEADERSHIP DEFINED

Leadership can be defined in many different ways, partly because it has been examined from the perspective of so many different fields of endeavor. Leadership has been defined as it applies to the military, athletics, education, business, industry, and many other fields. For the purpose of this book, *leadership* is defined as it relates specifically to total quality:

> Leadership is the ability to inspire people to make a total, willing, and voluntary commitment to accomplishing or exceeding organizational goals.

This definition contains a key concept that makes it particularly applicable in a total quality setting: the concept of inspiring people. Inspiring people is a higher order of human interaction than motivating them, which is a concept more frequently used in defining leadership. *Inspiration*, as used here, means motivation that has been internalized and, therefore, comes from within employees, as opposed to motivation that is simply a temporary response to external stimuli. Motivated employees commit to the organization's goals. Inspired employees make those goals their own. When employees are inspired, the total, willing, and voluntary commitment described in the definition follows naturally. Leaders must be able to apply positive influence, build consensus, overcome resistance, set a consistently positive example, endure criticism, persevere against doubt, communicate effectively, and convince followers to go where they may not yet be ready to go.

What Leaders Do   Leaders inspire others to commit to something bigger than themselves—the organization's vision, mission, and goals. They do so using the following leadership techniques:

- **Aligning personnel with the vision.** Leaders do more than just conveying the vision to their personnel. They help them see why it is a positive and commendable vision—one that is worthy of their commitment.

- **Provide a sense of direction.** Leaders make sure their personnel know where the organization is trying to go and what it is trying to do by helping them understand the organization's mission and goals.

- **Communicating effectively and often.** Leaders make sure their personnel have the information they need to achieve consistent peak performance. They keep them up-to-date and well-informed.

- **Empowering.** Leaders empower their personnel to do the jobs they were hired to do by (1) identifying the parameters within which they may make unilateral decisions, (2) seeking their input before making decisions that they will have to carry out, (3) encouraging them to think critically and creatively to find ways to continually improve quality, cost, and service, (4) encouraging them to take the initiative to solve problems, and (5) treating mistakes made, when taking the initiative, as learning opportunities.

- **Training and mentoring.** Leaders develop their personnel constantly through both mentoring and training. Every problem is approached as a learning activity and every weakness observed becomes a target for improvement.

What Is a Good Leader?

Good leaders come in all shapes, sizes, genders, ages, races, political persuasions, and national origins. They do not look alike, talk alike, or even work alike. However, good leaders do share several common characteristics. These are the characteristics necessary to inspire people to make a total, willing, and voluntary commitment. Regardless of their backgrounds, good leaders exhibit the characteristics shown in Figure 9–1.

Good leaders are committed to both the job to be done and the people who must do it, and they are able to strike the appropriate balance between the two. Good leaders project a positive example at all times. They are good role models.

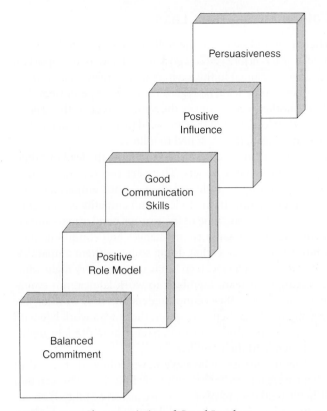

FIGURE 9–1 Characteristics of Good Leaders

Managers who project a "Do as I say, not as I do" attitude will not be effective leaders. To inspire employees, managers must be willing to do what they expect of workers, do it better, do it right, and do so consistently. If, for example, dependability is important, managers must set a consistent example of dependability. If punctuality is important, a manager must set a consistent example of punctuality. To be a good leader, a manager must set a consistent example of all characteristics that are important on the job.

Good leaders are good communicators. They are willing, patient, skilled listeners. They are also able to communicate their ideas clearly, succinctly, and in a nonthreatening manner. They use their communication skills to establish and nurture rapport with employees. Good leaders have influence with employees and use it in a positive manner. *Influence* is the art of using power to move people toward a certain end or point of view. The power of managers derives from the authority that goes with their jobs and the credibility they establish by being good leaders. Power is useless unless it is converted to influence. Power that is properly, appropriately, and effectively applied becomes positive influence.

Finally, good leaders are persuasive. Managers who expect people to simply do what they are ordered to do will have limited success. Those who are able to use their communication skills and influence to persuade people to their point of view and to help people make a total, willing, and voluntary commitment to that point of view can have unlimited success.

QUALITY TIP ▼

Organizational Leadership in India

"The leaders of India's biggest and fastest-growing companies take an internally focused, long-term view and put motivating and developing employees higher on the priority list than short-term shareholder interests."

Source: Peter Capelli, Harbir Singh, Jitendra V. Singh, and Michael Useem, "Leadership Lessons from India," *Harvard Business Review* (March 2010), 93.

Follow First—Then Lead

There is an old saying in the military: *You have to learn how to take orders before you can give them.* There is an important message contained in this saying that has relevance for those who hope to be leaders, regardless of the type of organization. Another way to convey the same message is this: *Follow first—then lead.* Part of the dues paid by leaders is that before they could lead, they first had to follow.

People who have never had to follow the lead of others typically make poor leaders. There are two reasons for this. First, having never followed they cannot empathize with those they are now trying to lead, and empathy is an important leadership trait. One of the reasons good leaders subject themselves to the same circumstances and conditions their followers must face is that doing so helps them empathize. For example, leaders who go home on time every night while expecting their team members to work late cannot empathize with them—they cannot understand how working late very night affects them. However, those who work late with their team members will understand how the late nights affect them and their families.

Second, leaders who have never followed the lead of others, have no credibility with their followers. This can be a difficult weakness to overcome because credibility is essential to leaders. People do not like to follow those who have never done what they ask their followers to do. One of the authors once served in the military under an officer who had flunked out of flight training and was, therefore, transferred to the infantry. When this officer would order his platoon to assault a particular objective, the response was lukewarm at best because having never assaulted an enemy position himself he had no credibility amongst his men.

The lesson in this for those who hope to become organizational leaders is simple: Pay your dues. Be a good team player before you try to become a team leader. Do not skip steps that are essential building blocks for the budding leader. Learn what it is like to carry out an order you disagree with or a decision that runs counter to what you would recommend. Develop a reputation as a good team player. Follow first—then lead.

Leaders versus Misleaders

In his book *Managing for the Future: The 1990s and Beyond*, Peter Drucker makes the point that leadership is not a function of charisma.[1] Too many managers have been led to believe that dressing for success and developing a charismatic personality are the keys to being a good leader. Although there is something to be said for personal appearance and charisma is certainly a positive quality, one should not make the mistake of confusing image with substance.

Some of the world's most effective leaders have had little or no charisma:

> Dwight Eisenhower, George Marshall, and Harry Truman were singularly effective leaders, yet none possessed any more charisma than a dead mackerel. No one had less

charisma than that of Lincoln of Illinois, the raw-boned, uncouth, backwoodsman of 1860. John F. Kennedy may have been the most charismatic person ever to occupy the White House, yet few presidents got as little done.[2]

Those who place image above substance and try to lead by charisma alone are misleaders, not leaders. What follows are several criteria Drucker uses to distinguish leaders from misleaders:[3]

- Leaders define and clearly articulate the organization's mission.
- Leaders set goals, priorities, and standards.
- Leaders see leadership as a responsibility rather than a privilege of rank.
- Leaders surround themselves with knowledgeable, strong people who can make a contribution.
- Leaders earn trust, respect, and integrity.

Myths about Leadership

Over the years, a number of myths have grown up about the subject of leadership. Managers in a total quality setting should be aware of these myths and be able to dispel them. Following are some common myths about leadership that are then dispelled by the authors:[4]

- **Leadership is a rare skill.** Although it is true that few great leaders of world renown exist, many good, effective leaders do. Renowned leaders such as Winston Churchill were simply good leaders given the opportunity to participate in monumental events (World War II in Churchill's case). Another example is General Norman Schwarzkopf. He had always been an effective military leader. That's how he became a general. But it took a monumental event—the first Gulf War—coupled with his leadership ability to make General Schwarzkopf a world-renowned leader. His leadership skills didn't appear suddenly; he had them all along. Circumstances allowed them to be displayed on the world stage.

  Most effective leaders spend their careers in virtual anonymity, but they exist in surprisingly large numbers, and there may be little or no correlation between their ability to lead and their relative positions in an organization. The best leader in a company may be the lowest paid wage earner, and the worst may be the CEO. In addition, a person may be a leader in one setting and not in another. For example, a person who shows no leadership ability at work may be an effective leader in his or her church. One of the keys to success in a total quality setting is to create an environment that brings out the leadership skills of all employees at all levels and focuses them on continually improving competitiveness.

- **Leaders are born, not made.** This myth will be addressed later in this chapter. Suffice it to say here that leadership, attitudes, and behaviors can be learned, even by those who do not appear to have inborn leadership potential.

- **Leaders are charismatic.** This myth was dispelled in the previous section. Some leaders have charisma and some don't. Some of history's most renowned leaders have had little or no charisma. Correspondingly, some of history's greatest misleaders have been highly charismatic. Generals Dwight Eisenhower and Omar Bradley are examples of great but uncharismatic leaders. Adolf Hitler and Benito Mussolini are examples of great misleaders who relied almost exclusively on charisma to build a following.

- **Leadership exists only at the top.** Total quality would not work if this myth were true. Total quality relies on building teams at all levels in an organization and teaching employees in these teams to be leaders. In reality, the opposite of this myth is often true. Top managers may be the least capable leaders in a company. Leadership is about producing results and generating continual improvement, not one's relative position within the organization.

- **Leaders control, direct, prod, and manipulate.** If practice is an indicator, this myth is the most widely believed. The "I'm the boss, so do what I say" syndrome is rampant in business and industry. It seems to be the automatic fallback position or default approach for managers who don't know better. Leadership in a total quality setting is about involving and empowering, not prodding and manipulating.

- **Leaders don't need to be learners.** Lifelong learning is a must for leaders. One cannot be a good leader without being a good learner. Leaders don't learn simply for the sake of learning (although to do so is a worthwhile undertaking). Rather, leaders continually learn in ways that help their organizations. A manager who is responsible for the metal fabrication department in a manufacturing firm might undertake to learn more about the classics of European literature. Although this would certainly make her a better educated person, studying European literature is not learning in an organizational context for the manager of a metal fabrication department. Examples of learning in an organizational context for such a manager include learning techniques to improve speed and feed rates, statistical process control (SPC), team-building strategies, computer numerical control programming, information about new composite materials, total productive maintenance, and anything else that will help improve the department's performance.

LEADERSHIP FOR QUALITY

Leadership for quality is leadership from the perspective of total quality. It is about applying the principles of leadership set forth in the preceding section in such a way as to continually improve the performance of people, processes, and products. Leadership for quality is based on the philosophy that continually improving people, processes, and products will, in turn, improve the following:

- Quality
- Value
- Productivity
- Service
- Market share
- Longevity
- Business expansion (more jobs and opportunities for advancement)
- Return on investment

Key Elements of Leadership for Quality

The key elements of leadership for quality include the following:

Customer Focus Leadership for quality requires a customer focus. This means the organization's primary goal is to meet or exceed customer expectations in a way that gives the customer lasting value. In a total quality setting, there are both internal and external customers. Internal customers are employees within the organization whose work depends on the work of other employees that precedes theirs. External customers are people who purchase or use the organization's products.

Obsession with Quality Obsession with quality is an attitude that must be instilled and continually nurtured by leaders in an organization. It means that every employee aggressively pursues quality in an attempt to exceed the expectations of customers, internal and external.

Recognizing the Structure of Work Leadership for quality requires that work processes be analyzed to determine their appropriate structural makeup (organization, order of steps, tools used, motion required, etc.). When the optimum structure is in place, work processes should be analyzed, evaluated, and studied continually in an attempt to improve them.

Freedom through Control Control in a total quality setting refers to human control of work methods and processes. All too often in the age of high technology, the "tail wags the dog" in that machines run people instead of people running machines. Leaders must ensure that managers and employees take control of work processes and methods by collaborating to standardize them. The goal is to reduce variations in output by eliminating variations in how work is done.

Unity of Purpose One of the most important responsibilities of a leader is to articulate the organization's mission clearly and accurately so that all employees understand it, believe in it, and commit to it. When there is unity of purpose, all employees pull together toward the same end.

Looking for Faults in Systems Quality pioneers W. Edwards Deming and Joseph M. Juran believed that 85%

of an organization's failures are failures of management-controlled systems. In their opinion, employees who do the work can control only 15% of what causes failures. Leadership for quality requires a change in focus from assessing blame for problems to assessing systems in an attempt to ferret out and correct systemic problems.

Teamwork   Rugged individualism has long been a fundamental element of the American character. The strong, silent stranger who rides into town and single-handedly runs out the bad guys (the character typified by Clint Eastwood over the years) has always had popular appeal in the United States. Individual performance has been encouraged and rewarded in the American workplace since the Industrial Revolution. Not until competition among companies became global in nature did it become necessary to apply a principle that has been known for years—that a team of people working together toward a common goal can outperform a group of individuals working toward their own ends. Leadership for quality requires team building and teamwork. These critical topics are covered in Chapter 10.

Continuing Education and Training   In the age of high technology, the most important machine in the workplace is the human mind. Continued learning at all levels is a fundamental element of total quality. Working hard no longer guarantees success. In the age of high technology, it is necessary to work hard and work smart.

Emphasis on Best Practices and Peak Performance
One of the goals of leaders is to ensure the absolute best possible performance from their personnel, processes, and products. Consequently, organizational leaders emphasize identifying and deploying best practices as one more way to ensure consistent peak performance.

The Juran Trilogy

Joseph M. Juran sets forth his trilogy on leadership for quality as follows: planning, control, and continual improvement.[5] The Juran Trilogy is composed of the following elements:[6]

- **Quality planning.** Quality planning consists of the following steps: identify customers, identify the needs of customers, develop products based on customer needs, develop work methods and processes that can produce products that meet or exceed customer expectations, and convert the results of planning into action.

- **Quality control.** Quality control consists of the following steps: evaluate actual performance, compare actual performance with performance goals, and take immediate steps to resolve differences between planned performance and actual performance.

- **Quality improvement.** Continual improvement of quality is a fundamental element of total quality. The steps involved are these: establish an infrastructure for accomplishing continual quality improvement; identify

specific processes or methods in need of improvement; set up teams responsible for specific improvement projects; and provide improvement teams with the resources and training needed to diagnose problems and identify causes, decide on a remedy, and standardize the improvements once they have been made.

Planning, control, and improvement of quality do not happen automatically in any organization. They happen as the result of leadership. Leaders in a total quality setting must ensure that these principles are applied daily at all levels of their organizations.

LEADERSHIP SKILLS: INHERITED OR LEARNED?

Perhaps the oldest debate about leadership revolves around this question: "Are leaders born or made?" Can leadership skills be learned, or must they be inherited? This debate has never been settled and probably never will be. There are proponents on both sides of the debate, and this polarity is not likely to change because, as is often the case in such controversies, both sides are partially right.

The point of view presented in this book is that leaders are like athletes: Some athletes are born with natural ability, whereas others develop their ability through determination and hard work. Inborn ability, or the lack of it, represents only the starting point. Success from that point forward depends on the individual's willingness and determination to develop and improve. Some athletes born with tremendous natural ability never live up to their potential. Other athletes with limited natural ability do, through hard work, determination, and continual improvement, perform beyond their apparent potential.

This phenomenon also applies to leadership. Some managers have more natural leadership ability than others. However, regardless of their individual starting points, managers can become good leaders through education, training, practice, determination, and effort.

LEADERSHIP, MOTIVATION, AND INSPIRATION

One of the characteristics shared by effective leaders is the ability to inspire and motivate others to make a commitment. The key to motivating people lies in the ability to relate their personal needs to the organization's goals. The key to inspiring people lies in the ability to relate what they believe to the organizational goals. Implicit in both cases is the leader's need to know and understand workers, including both their individual needs and their personal beliefs.

Understanding Individual Needs

Perhaps the best model for explaining individual human needs is that developed by psychologist Abraham H. Maslow. Maslow's Hierarchy of Needs (Figure 9–2) arrays the basic

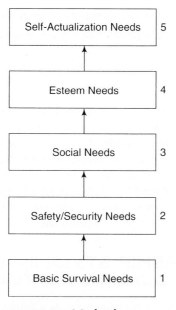

FIGURE 9–2 Maslow's Hierarchy of Needs

human needs on five successive levels. The lowest level in the hierarchy encompasses basic survival needs. All people need air to breathe, food to eat, water to drink, clothing to wear, and shelter in which to live. The second level encompasses safety/security needs. All people need to feel safe from harm and secure in their world. To this end, people enact laws, pay taxes to employ police and military personnel, buy insurance, try to save and invest money, and install security systems in their homes.

The third level encompasses social needs. People are social animals by nature. This fact manifests itself through families, friendships, social organizations, civic groups, special clubs, and even employment-based groups such as company softball and basketball teams. The fourth level of the hierarchy encompasses esteem needs. Self-esteem is a key ingredient in the personal happiness of individuals. All people need to feel self-worth, dignity, and respect. People need to feel that they matter. This fact manifests itself in a variety of ways. It can be seen in the clothes people wear, the cars people drive, and the behavior people exhibit in public.

The highest level of Maslow's hierarchy encompasses self-actualization needs. Complete self-fulfillment is a need that is rarely satisfied in people. The need for self-actualization manifests itself in a variety of ways. Some people seek to achieve it through their work; others through hobbies, human associations, or leisure activities.

Leaders need to understand how to apply Maslow's model if they hope to use it to motivate and inspire workers. Principles required for applying this model are as follows:

1. Needs must be satisfied in order from the bottom up.

2. People focus most intently on their lowest unmet need. For example, employees who have not met their basic security needs will not be motivated by factors relating to their social needs.

3. After a need has been satisfied, it no longer works as a motivating factor. For example, people who have satisfied their need for financial security will not be motivated by a pay raise.

Understanding Individual Beliefs

Each person has a basic set of beliefs that, together, form that individual's value system. If leaders know their fellow employees well-enough to understand those basic beliefs, they can use this knowledge to inspire them on the job. Developing this level of understanding of employees comes from observing, listening, asking, and taking the time to establish trust.

Leaders who develop this level of understanding of workers can use it to inspire employees to higher levels of performance. This is done by showing employees how the organization's goals relate to their beliefs. For example, if pride of workmanship is part of an employee's value system, a leader can inspire the person to help achieve the organization's quality goals by appealing to that value.

Inspiration, as a level of leadership, is on a higher plane than motivation. Managers who become good enough leaders to inspire their workers will achieve the best results.

LEADERSHIP STYLES

Leadership styles have to do with how people interact with those they seek to lead. Leadership styles go by many different names. However, most styles fall into the categories shown in Figure 9–3.

Autocratic Leadership

Autocratic leadership is also called *directive* or *dictatorial leadership*. People who take this approach make decisions without

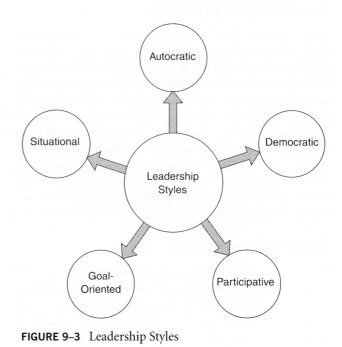

FIGURE 9–3 Leadership Styles

consulting the employees who will have to implement them or who will be affected by them. They tell others what to do and expect them to comply obediently. Critics of this approach say that although it can work in the short run or in isolated instances, in the long run it is not effective. Autocratic leadership is not appropriate in a total quality setting.

Democratic Leadership

Democratic leadership is also called *consultive* or *consensus leadership*. People who take this approach involve the employees who will have to implement decisions in making them. The leader actually makes the final decision but only after receiving the input and recommendations of team members. Critics of this approach say that the most popular decision is not always the best decision and that democratic leadership, by its nature, can result in the making of popular decisions, as opposed to right decisions. This style can also lead to compromises that ultimately fail to produce the desired result.

Participative Leadership

Participative leadership is also known as *open, free-rein,* or *nondirective leadership*. People who take this approach exert little control over the decision-making process. Rather, they provide information about the problem and allow team members to develop strategies and solutions. The leader's job is to move the team toward consensus. The underlying assumption of this style is that workers will more readily accept responsibility for solutions, goals, and strategies that they are empowered to help develop. Critics of this approach say consensus building is time consuming and works only if all people involved are committed to the best interests of the organization.

Goal-Oriented Leadership

Goal-oriented leadership is also called *results-based* or *objective-based leadership*. People who take this approach ask team members to focus solely on the goals at hand. Only strategies that make a definite and measurable contribution to accomplishing organizational goals are discussed. The influence of personalities and other factors unrelated to the specific goals of the organization is minimized. Critics of this approach say it can break down when team members focus so intently on specific goals that they overlook opportunities or potential problems that fall outside of their narrow focus. Advocates of total quality say that results-oriented leadership is too narrowly focused and often centered on the wrong concerns.

Situational Leadership

Situational leadership is also called *fluid* or *contingency leadership*. People who take this approach select the style that seems to be appropriate based on the circumstances that exist at a given time. In identifying these circumstances, leaders consider the following factors:

- Relationship of the manager and team members
- How precisely actions taken must comply with specific guidelines
- Amount of authority the leader actually has with team members

Depending on what is learned when these factors are considered, the manager decides whether to take the autocratic, democratic, participative, or goal-oriented approach. Under different circumstances, the same manager would apply a different leadership style. Advocates of total quality reject situational leadership as an attempt to apply an approach based on short-term concerns instead of focusing on the solution of long-term problems.

LEADERSHIP STYLE IN A TOTAL QUALITY SETTING

The appropriate leadership style in a total quality setting might be called participative leadership taken to a higher level. Whereas participative leadership in the traditional sense involves soliciting employee input, in a total quality setting it involves soliciting input from empowered employees, listening to that input, and acting on it. The key difference between traditional participative leadership and participative leadership from a total quality perspective is that, with the latter, employees providing input are empowered.

Collecting employee input is not new. However, collecting input, logging it, tracking it, acting on it in an appropriate manner, working with employees to improve weak suggestions rather than simply rejecting them, and rewarding employees for improvements that result from their input—all of which are normal in a total quality setting—extend beyond the traditional approach to participative leadership.

Discussion Assignment 9-2 illustrates the concept of participative leadership as applied in a total quality setting at a U.S.-based electronics company. This assignment illustrates how important freedom and respect for the individual are in today's intensely competitive world of business and industry.

BUILDING AND MAINTAINING A FOLLOWING

Managers can be good leaders only if the people they hope to lead will follow them willingly and steadfastly. Followership must be built and, having been built, maintained. This section is devoted to a discussion of how managers can build and maintain followership among the people they hope to lead.

Popularity and the Leader

Leadership and popularity are not the same thing. However, many managers confuse popularity with leadership and, in turn, followership. An important point to understand in leading people is the difference between popularity and respect. Long-term followership grows out of respect, not popularity. Good leaders *may* be popular, but they *must* be respected. Not all good leaders are popular, but they are all respected.

Managers occasionally have to make unpopular decisions. This is a fact of life for leaders, and it is why leadership positions are sometimes described as lonely ones. Making an unpopular decision does not necessarily cause a leader to lose followership, provided the leader is seen as having solicited a broad base of input and given serious, objective, and impartial consideration to that input. Correspondingly, leaders who make inappropriate decisions that are popular in the short run may actually lose followership in the long run. If the long-term consequences of a decision turn out to be detrimental to the team, team members will hold the leader responsible, particularly if the decision was made without first collecting and considering employee input.

Leadership Characteristics That Build and Maintain Followership

Leaders build and maintain followership by earning the respect of those they lead. Here are some characteristics of leaders that build respect, as shown in Figure 9–4:

- **Sense of purpose.** Successful leaders have a strong sense of purpose. They know who they are, where they fit in the overall organization, and the contributions their areas of responsibility make to the organization's success.
- **Self-discipline.** Successful leaders develop discipline and use it to set an example. Through self-discipline, leaders avoid negative self-indulgence, inappropriate displays of emotion such as anger, and counterproductive responses to the everyday pressures of the job. Through self-discipline, leaders set an example of handling problems and pressures with equilibrium and a positive attitude.
- **Honesty.** Successful leaders are trusted by their followers. This is because they are open, honest, and forthright with other members of the organization and with themselves. They can be depended on to make difficult decisions in unpleasant situations with steadfastness and consistency.
- **Credibility.** Successful leaders have credibility. Credibility is established by being knowledgeable, consistent, fair, and impartial in all human interaction; by setting a positive example; and by adhering to the same standards of performance and behavior expected of others.

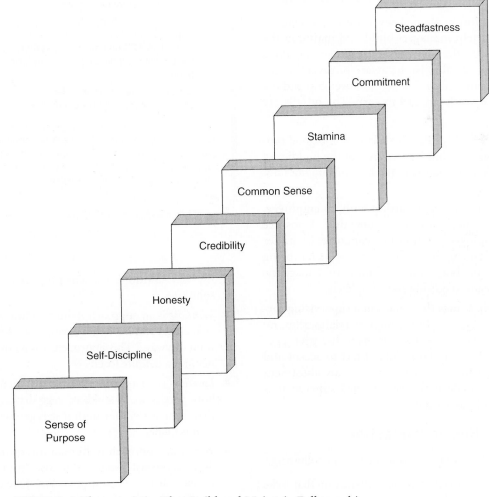

FIGURE 9–4 Characteristics That Build and Maintain Followership

- **Common sense.** Successful leaders have common sense. They know what is important in a given situation and what is not. They know that applying tact is important when dealing with people. They know when to be flexible and when to be firm.

- **Stamina.** Successful leaders must have stamina. Frequently, they need to be the first to arrive and the last to leave. Their hours are likely to be longer and the pressures they face more intense than those of others. Energy, endurance, and good health are important to those who lead.

- **Commitment.** Successful leaders are committed to the goals of the organization, the people they work with, and their own ongoing personal and professional development. They are willing to do everything within the limits of the law, professional ethics, and company policy to help their team succeed.

- **Steadfastness.** Successful leaders are steadfast and resolute. People do not follow a person they perceive to be wishy-washy and noncommittal. Nor do they follow a person whose resolve they question. Successful leaders must have the steadfastness to stay the course even when it becomes difficult.

Pitfalls That Can Undermine Followership

The previous section explained several positive characteristics that will help managers build and maintain the respect and, in turn, the followership of those they hope to lead. Managers should also be aware of several common pitfalls that can undermine that followership and the respect they must work so hard to earn. The pitfalls are listed as follows:

- **Trying to be a buddy.** Positive relations and good rapport are important, but leaders are not the buddies of those they lead. The nature of the relationship does not allow it.

- **Having an intimate relationship with an employee.** This practice is both unwise and unethical. A positive manager–employee relationship cannot exist under such circumstances. Few people can succeed at being the lover and the boss, and few things can damage the morale of a team so quickly and completely.

- **Trying to keep things the same when supervising former peers.** The supervisor–employee relationship, no matter how positive, is different from the peer–peer relationship. This can be a difficult fact to accept and a difficult adjustment to make. But it is an adjustment that must be made if the peer-turned-supervisor is going to succeed as a leader.

Paradigms of Human Interaction

The paradigms of human interaction include the following:[7]

- *Win/win* is an approach to human interaction that seeks mutual benefit. Rather than pursuing a your-way or

my-way solution, win/win proponents seek best-way solutions.

- *Win/lose* is an approach to human interaction that says, "Go ahead and have things your way. I never get what I want anyway." This approach results in a definite winner and a definite loser.

- *Lose/lose* is an approach to human interaction in which both parties are so stubborn, ego driven, and vindictive that, ultimately, they both lose regardless of what decision is made.

- *Win* is an approach to human interaction that says, "I don't necessarily want you to lose, but I definitely want to win." It is the result of a "You take care of yourself and I'll take care of myself" attitude.

Of the four paradigms just presented, the win/win approach is the one that will most help leaders build and maintain a following. Unlike the other paradigms, win/win places value on the opinions of both parties and requires them to work together to find solutions.

LEADERSHIP VERSUS MANAGEMENT

Although both leadership and management are needed in the modern workplace, they are not the same thing. To be a good leader and a good manager, one must know the difference between the two concepts. According to John P. Kotter, leadership and management "are two distinctive and complementary systems of action."[8] Kotter lists several differences between management and leadership which are as follows:[9]

- Management is about coping with complexity; leadership is about coping with change.
- Management is about planning and budgeting for complexity; leadership is about setting the direction for change through the creation of a vision.
- Management develops the capacity to carry out plans through organizing and staffing; leadership aligns people to work toward the vision.
- Management ensures the accomplishment of plans through controlling and problem solving; leadership motivates and inspires people to want to accomplish the plan.

Trust Building and Leadership

Trust is a necessary ingredient for success in the intensely competitive modern workplace. Building trust requires leadership on the part of managers. Trust-building strategies include the following:

- **Taking the blame but sharing the credit.** Managers who point the finger of blame at their employees, even when the employees are at fault, do not build trust. Leaders must be willing to accept responsibility for the performance of people they hope to lead. Correspondingly, when credit is due, leaders must be prepared to spread it around appropriately. Such unselfishness on the part of managers builds trust among employees.
- **Pitching in and helping.** Managers can show leadership and build trust by rolling up their sleeves and helping when a deadline is approaching. A willingness to "get their hands dirty" when circumstances warrant it helps managers build trust among employees.
- **Being consistent.** People trust consistency. It lets them know what to expect. Even when employees disagree with managers, they appreciate consistent behavior.
- **Being equitable.** Managers cannot play favorites and hope to build trust. Employees want to know that they

> **QUALITY TIP ▼**
>
> **Organizational Change Should Be Inclusive**
>
> It is often said that people in organizations do not like change. While it is true that people tend to become comfortable with the status quo, what they fear is not so much change but the unknown. People cling to the familiar because they fear the uncertainty of change. This is why the three most important rules of change leadership are *communicate, communicate,* and *communicate.*

are treated not just well but also as well as all other employees. Fair and equitable treatment of all employees will help build trust.

LEADERSHIP AND ETHICS

It is when making decisions that have high ethical content that the true character of a leader shows through—good or bad. Leaders have no more important responsibility than to set a positive example of maintaining high ethical standards. On issues large and small, leaders must be seen by those they hope to lead as not just living up to the ethical standards expected by the organization and society in general but also exceeding them and doing so consistently. There are two reasons for this: (1) people will not follow willingly and fully those they do not trust and (2) leaders set the tone when in comes to ethical behavior in organizations, and people are more likely to follow a leader's example than his or her words.

Ethical leaders have to take the long view. There will be times when unethical decisions or behavior might appear to serve the organization's short-term interests or even the self-interest of the leader. However, the truth has a way of outing itself in the long run, and expedients that once looked so attractive in the short term can come back to haunt a leader over time. An unethical leader is no leader. He or she is a misleader.

EMPLOYEES AND MANAGERS ON CHANGE

One of the difficulties organizations face when attempting to facilitate change is the differing perceptions of employees and managers concerning change. Employees often view change as something done to them. Managers often regard it as something done in spite of employees who just won't cooperate.

Managers who listen to employees can learn a valuable lesson. It's not that they dislike change so much. Rather, it's that they don't like how it's done. The key to winning the support of employees for change is *involvement*. Make them part of the process from the beginning. Give them a voice in how change is implemented. Make sure that change is something done *with* employees rather than *to* them.

From the perspective of employees, managers are often viewed as the "bad guys" when changes are made. This viewpoint is just as unfair and counterproductive as the one that sees employees as inhibitors of change.

To respond effectively to change, organizations must continually apply at least the following strategies:

- Promote a "we are in this together" attitude toward change.
- Make sure all employees understand that change is driven by market forces, not management.
- Involve everyone who will be affected by change in planning and implementing the response to it.

RESTRUCTURING AND CHANGE

Few words can strike as much fear into the hearts of employees at all levels as *restructuring*. The term at one time was synonymous with *reorganization*. However, as a result of the way so many organizations have used the word, it has become a euphemism for layoffs, terminations, plant closings, and workforce cuts.

Because of the ever-changing conditions of the global marketplace, few organizations will escape the necessity for restructuring, and few people will complete a career without experiencing one or more restructurings. Acquisitions, mergers, buyouts, and downsizing—common occurrences in today's marketplace—all typically involve corporate restructuring. This fact is market driven and can be controlled by neither individuals nor organizations. However, organizations and individuals can control how they respond to the changes brought by restructuring, and it is this response that will determine the effectiveness of the restructuring effort. The remainder of this section is devoted to explaining strategies for effectively handling the changes inherent in restructuring.

Understand the Employees' Point of View

Restructuring can be traumatic for employees. Managers should remember this point when planning and implementing the changes that go with restructuring. The following strategies can help maintain employee loyalty and calm employee fears during restructuring:

- Take time to show employees that management cares and is concerned about them on a personal level.
- Communicate with employees about why the changes are necessary. Focus on market factors. Use a variety of tools to ensure effective communication (e.g., face-to-face meetings, newsletters, videotaped messages, and posted notices).
- Provide formal outplacement assistance to all employees who will lose their jobs.
- Be fair, equitable, and honest with employees. Select employees to be laid off according to a definite set of criteria rather than as the result of a witch hunt.
- Remember to provide support to those individuals who will be the primary change agents.

Develop a Change Picture

One of the best ways to minimize the disruptive nature of change is to develop a clear picture of what the organization is going to look like after the change. A good question to ask is "What are we trying to become?" Managers should develop a change picture and be able to articulate it. This will give the organization a beacon in the distance to guide it through the emotional fog that can accompany change.

Use Incentives to Promote the Change

People respond to incentives, especially when those incentives are important to them on a personal level. Managers can promote the change that accompanies restructuring by establishing incentives for contributors to that change. Incentives can be monetary or nonmonetary, but they should motivate employees on a personal level.

An effective way to identify incentives that will work is to form an ad hoc task force of employees and discuss the issue of incentives. List as many monetary and nonmonetary incentives as the group can identify. Then give the members a week to discuss the list with their fellow employees. Once a broad base of employee input has been collected, the task force meets again and ranks the incentives in order of preference. The team then establishes a menu of incentives management can use to promote change. The menu concept allows employees to select incentives from among a list of options. This increases the likelihood that the incentives will motivate on a personal level.

Train, Train, Train

During times of intense change, the tendency of organizations is to put training on hold. The idea is "we'll get back to training again when things settle down." In reality, putting off training during restructuring is the last thing an organization should do.

One of the primary reasons employees oppose change is that it will require skills they don't have. Training should actually be increased during times of intense change to make sure that employees have the skills required during and after the transition period.

HOW TO LEAD CHANGE

Leading people in organizations through change initiatives require a concerted and systematic effort. The following change-implementation model is designed to help leaders systematically overcome the various factors that inhibit organizational change (Figure 9–5):

- Develop a compelling *change picture*
- Communicate the change picture to all stakeholders
- Conduct a comprehensive *roadblock analysis*
- Remove or mitigate all roadblocks identified
- Implement the change
- Monitor and adjust

Develop the
Change Picture
• Step 1

Communicate
the Change
Picture
• Step 2

Conduct the
Roadblock
Analysis
• Step 3

Remove or
Mitigate
Roadblocks
• Step 4

Implement
• Step 5

Monitor and
Adjust
• Step 6

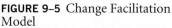

FIGURE 9–5 Change Facilitation
Model

Source: This model is adapted from
John P. Kotter, *Leading Change* (Boston:
Harvard Business School Press, 1996), 21.

Develop a Compelling Change Picture

One of the main reasons why people in organizations resist change is fear of the unknown. Once people become comfortable with the familiar, they tend to resist anything that threatens that comfort. Consequently, change, which represents the unknown and unfamiliar, is often viewed by people as a threat. To counteract fear of the unknown, organizational leaders can develop a compelling change picture.

A change picture is a brief but compelling written explanation of the *five Ws and one H* of change: what, where,

when, who, and why plus how. The change picture should be put in writing to ensure that all organizational leaders convey the same message. Mixed messages during a time of significant change can quickly undermine the success of the change initiative. The change picture explains what the change is going to be, where it is being made, when it is being made, who will be affected by it, why it is being made, and how stakeholders will be affected by it.

The change picture is made compelling by writing it from the perspective of the stakeholders it will be communicated to. This means that there may need to be more than one version of the change picture. Of course, the what, where, when, who, and why aspects must remain the same to avoid mixed messages. However, the how component should be tailored to the stakeholders in question. For example, with any major change a company's first-line employees will be affected differently than its investors and shareholders. The change picture shared with any constituent group should convey specifically how they will be affected by the change.

What follows is an example of a change picture that was developed by one of the authors for a family owned company that planned to go public and have its shares traded on the stock market (the company's name has been changed to protect privacy):

> For more than 60 years, ABC Inc. has been a family owned business. The company was founded by the current CEO's great grandfather. Many of our personnel have spent their entire careers at ABC. On January 1, ABC will become a publicly traded company with a board of directors. This change applies to all three of ABC's plants. The current management team will stay in place and continue to lead ABC as it has in the past. All personnel will be affected by this change in some way. However, we expect the effects to be positive. This change is being made to raise the investment capital needed to upgrade facilities, equipment, and personnel so that ABC can compete in the global arena. For first-line employees, the effects will include: (1) long-needed equipment upgrades, (2) the potential for promotions as ABC is able to expand using the capital raised by going public, and (3) better benefits. Expansion into new markets and stepping up to compete globally will mean that all personnel will need to focus on peak performance like never before. In order to operate new equipment and processes, first-line employees will need to undergo upgrading training that is likely to be ongoing and continual. In short, all personnel will be expected to do their part to ensure that ABC can develop into a world-class competitor.

This change picture explains the what (going public), where (at all of ABC's plants), when (January 1), who (all personnel), and why (upgrade to compete globally). The "how" component pertains specifically to first-line employees and answers their most important question: How will this change affect me? On the one hand, ABC's first-line personnel will enjoy new equipment, better benefits, and more potential for advancement. On the other hand, ABC is moving up to a higher level of competition where the performance expectations of first-line personnel will be correspondingly higher.

After receiving this change picture, most first-line personnel at this company welcomed both the opportunities and the challenges brought by the change. However, there were a few who did not. These few welcomed the opportunities, of course, but not the challenges. Predictably, these few unmotivated employees did not survive the transition from family business to publicly traded global competitor. However, they did have an opportunity to survive and succeed, something the overwhelming majority of first-line personnel did.

There is an important lesson in this example for other organizations planning major change initiatives. By developing a change picture that was comprehensive, forthright, and compelling, ABC lost a few employees. But those who left were marginal employees who did not want to give the level of effort necessary to step up to a higher level of competition. On the other hand, ABC retained its best employees. Organizations that fail to develop a comprehensive and compelling change picture run the risk of just the opposite result: losing their best employees who, frightened by rumors and misinformation, leave. It's important for organizational leaders to understand that while the well-explained certainties of change initiatives might frighten marginal employees into leaving, the ambiguities of unexplained change initiatives are more likely to cause the organization's better employees to leave.

Consequently, organizational leaders are well-advised to remember this unalterable fact of life about major change initiatives: Whether the news surrounding a major change is good or bad it should be conveyed completely and accurately to stakeholders and from their individual perspectives. No matter how bad or unwelcome certain news might be as the result of a change initiative, the rumor mill will make it appear worse. Even with bad news, a well-written change initiative allows organizational leaders to establish and control the context in which the change will be viewed by their personnel.

Communicate the Change Picture to Stakeholders

Once the change picture has been developed, it must be communicated to all stakeholders. The authors recommend a two-step approach: (1) give the change picture to stakeholders in writing and (2) explain the change picture verbally at the team or department level. Giving the change picture to stakeholders in writing will ensure that everyone gets the same message, thereby neutralizing the rumor mill. Explaining the change picture in face-to-face meetings will allow stakeholders to ask questions, seek clarification, state their concerns, and vent their feelings.

Giving personnel opportunities to ask questions, seek clarification, state concerns, and vent feelings is critical to the success of a major change initiative. Employees who are denied a chance to do these things might, at best, misunderstand the change initiative and at worst resent it. Employees who resent the change initiative are not likely to do anything to help it succeed. In fact, they are more likely to do just the opposite. This step in the model is designed to create allies for the change initiative, not enemies.

To ensure that this step in the model goes smoothly, higher management should conduct training sessions for department-level managers, supervisors, and team leaders, the organizational leaders who will conduct the face-to-face meetings with stakeholders. These sessions are used to anticipate the types of questions that might be asked and to formulate accurate responses. This will help ensure that all organizational leaders give the same responses to the same questions, a necessity to keep the rumor mill from resurfacing. The training for those who will leads of face-to-face meetings should also include a lesson on listening as employees vent without reacting. Leaders who become defensive when employees express anger or frustration will just make matters worse. Leaders who respond to venting with anger will just increase the resentment. During a time of significant organizational change, employees are like teapots: unless given a chance to vent they might explode.

Providing a written change picture and then following up with face-to-face meetings will sort out the personnel who are going to support the change initiative and those who are likely to fight it. This sorting out allows organizational leaders to enlist the help of supporters and take steps to either eliminate or, at least, mitigate the resistance of objectors. Supporters can now be brought together for the next step in the model: the roadblock analysis.

Conduct a Comprehensive Roadblock Analysis

The roadblock analysis is an essential step in the model, yet it is a step that very few organizations apply. The purpose of the roadblock analysis is to identify all potential roadblocks that might impede implementation of the change initiative. This step is accomplished by conducting face-to-face meetings with employees who are going to have to carry out the practical, day-to-day work of the implementation. It is important that the personnel involved in this step be supportive of the change initiative. Experience shows that objectors will use the roadblock to create roadblocks rather than eliminate them. The philosophy underlying the roadblock analysis is that the employees who are closest to the day-to-day work of the implementation are more likely than anyone else to see problems, glitches, or circumstances that could sidetrack the implementation.

One of the authors was once involved in leading a major change initiative at a large manufacturing and engineering firm: changing from a five-day to a four-day work week. This change meant that all employees would work from 7:00 a.m. to 6:00 p.m. with an hour off for lunch rather than 8:00 a.m. to 5:00 p.m. The change was initiated by the CEO of the company after he had read an article extolling the virtues of the four-day work week. Organizational leaders received more opposition than anticipated during the face-to-face meetings used to communicate the change picture. However, it was during the roadblock analysis that what was bothering the company's personnel was pinpointed.

Many of the company's personnel were either single parents or from families in which both the husband and wife worked. As a consequence of their family situations, these personnel operated on tight schedules when it came to getting their children to school or day care before getting themselves to work. The new schedule of four ten-hour days would just create havoc in their lives. Another group of personnel relied on getting off of work at 5:00 p.m. in order to attend night classes at the nearby university, classes they needed to complete degrees the company encouraged them to enroll in. Others had part-time jobs that began right after they got off of work. These were serious roadblocks, and many of the people with objections were key personnel. As a result of the roadblock analysis, higher management took stock and made the rational decision to drop the idea of the four-day work week.

Remove or Mitigate All Roadblocks Identified

In the previous section, the example of the company that attempted to adopt a four-day work week showed that, at times, the roadblock analysis will reveal that the proposed change initiative is a bad idea. However, more often it simply identifies roadblocks that must be removed or mitigated before they can impede implementation of the change initiative. For example, one of the authors once worked with an organization that decided to transition from what, at the time, was the leading office software package to a new package that was just emerging.

The organization planned to move forward with the transition quickly so as to take advantage of some breaks that were available for only a brief period of time. Sales personnel for the new software package had assured the organization's information technology director that employees who could operate the old software package could operate the new with no problem. However, during the roadblock analysis sessions, a theme quickly emerged in the feedback provided by employees: Training would be essential. The old program was menu-driven while the new program used the point-and-click system. A number of other operational issues were identified. Before long it became clear to higher management that unless training was provided the organization was going to have problems.

The organization's information technology director soon realized that his initial thoughts concerning transitioning the organization to the new software had been overly optimistic. To his credit, the director confronted the sales personnel he had been working with, explained that not only would training have to be part of the purchase price,

but also that he would not recommend the purchase unless the original cost savings still applied. The training, coupled with several organization-wide venting sessions, mitigated the roadblocks that not only would have impeded the transition process but might even have ensured failure.

Implement the Change

Once all roadblocks have been identified and either eliminated or mitigated, it is time to implement the change initiative. This is the step in which Murphy's Law comes into play more than in any other step. Murphy's Law suggests that anything that can go wrong will go wrong. This is a bit of an overstatement in most cases. However, the implementation—even after roadblocks have been removed—is not likely to go forward without problems. Consequently, it is important to have an implementation plan that turns the implementation into a systematic process.

The implementation plan contains a comprehensive list of all tasks that have to be completed, a schedule with deadlines for each task, and a responsible party assigned to each task. Nothing that has to be done in order for the implementation to succeed should be left to chance, and nothing should be assumed. There are no unimportant tasks when implementing a change initiative. Every task down to the most minor should be identified, put on a schedule, and assigned to an individual. Developing the implementation plan is similar to conducting the roadblock analysis in that it involves an ad hoc group of stakeholders who are familiar enough with the situation to know what must be done and to ensure nothing that must be done is overlooked.

Monitor and Adjust

Once the implementation plan has been developed, it becomes an invaluable tool for the organizational leaders who must monitor the progress of the implementation and make any necessary adjustments to keep it moving. Because every task in the overall process has been identified and assigned to a responsible individual, organizational leaders have a definite point of contact for monitoring. Because every task in the process has been put on a schedule, organizational leaders are able to tie their monitoring efforts to a schedule. By checking with responsible individuals well-ahead of deadlines, organizational leaders can determine when adjustments must be made. An adjustment might be a change to the schedule for a given task or solving a problem that has cropped up unexpectedly and is impeding progress.

In any case, even after developing a comprehensive and detailed implementation plan, organizational leaders should never assume that the process will simply take care of itself. Rather, they should monitor closely and quickly take any action necessary to remove impediments so that the momentum is not lost. The implementation is neither over nor is it successful until the change initiative represents the normal way of doing things.

LESSONS FROM DISTINGUISHED LEADERS

Some of the most distinguished leaders in America's history can be found in fields outside of business and industry. In many cases, their leadership philosophies and methods, though applied in other fields, have direct applications in the world of business. Three distinguished leaders from outside the field of business are profiled in this section. Those chosen for inclusion had to meet the following criteria: (1) recognized widely as a distinguished leader in a specific field, (2) deceased long enough for history to have formed an accurate perspective, and (3) advocated a leadership philosophy that has direct application in today's fast-paced, highly competitive business environment. The leaders chosen for inclusion here are Abraham Lincoln, Harry Truman, and Winston Churchill. Each of these individuals had a leadership style that distinguished him from his contemporaries and set him apart from competitors. No attempt is made to explain every aspect of each leader's philosophy; rather, key aspects have been gleaned from the many for their distinctive application to the contemporary world of global business.

Abraham Lincoln on Leadership

Abraham Lincoln has been called the man who "saved the Union," and deservedly so. He led the United States through four of the most bitter and difficult years in its history, those years when the North and South were embroiled in the American Civil War. In a horrific conflict that pitted brother against brother and friend against friend, Abraham Lincoln prevailed against the forces of secession by clinging steadfastly to his vision of one nation, undivided.

Lincoln was the 16th president of the United States. He gained a national reputation for opposing slavery, which led to his nomination for the presidency by the new Republican Party. He was elected in 1860 shortly before the onset of the Civil War. He led the northern states through the long and deadly years of a war most people expected to last only weeks. In 1863, seeking an issue to rally the North and save the Union, Lincoln issued the Emancipation Proclamation freeing the slaves in the areas under Confederate control. He was reelected in 1864. During its 1864 to 1865 session, Congress passed the Thirteenth Amendment abolishing slavery.

With slavery ended and the war over, Lincoln looked forward to healing the country's wounds and bringing the North and South back together "with charity for all and malice toward none." He never got the chance. In April 1865, shortly after the war ended, Lincoln was assassinated by John Wilkes Booth while attending a play at Ford's Theater in Washington, DC. With him died the hopes of a charitable reconciliation with the South. Instead, a period of "reconstruction" ensued that was punitive at best and, in many cases, brutal. In some ways, the country is still scarred by the Civil War and the reconstruction period that followed. But the nation survived, prevailed, and remains undivided, thanks to the steadfast determination of Abraham Lincoln to preserve the vision of America's founders.

Lincoln's vision for the United States grew out of the Declaration of Independence. To this self-educated country lawyer, the words of Thomas Jefferson represented what modern business leaders call the corporate vision. The Constitution represented the strategic plan for achieving the vision. Lincoln articulated this vision over and over to anyone who would listen and to many who wouldn't. So determined was Lincoln to preserve what the founding fathers had established that he was not above temporarily rescinding the very rights he was so committed to protecting (e.g., the writ of *habeas corpus*).

Lincoln exemplified many leadership strategies that have direct applications in today's global business environment. According to Donald T. Phillips, these were some of Lincoln's strongest beliefs about leading:[10]

- **Get out of the office and circulate among the troops.** Lincoln spent as much time as he could in the field with his commanders and troops. Apparently, Lincoln knew about management by walking around more than 100 years before Tom Peters made the concept part of the quality lexicon.

- **Persuade rather than coerce.** Lincoln used amusing stories and country-bumpkin humor to persuade people to his way of thinking. Building consensus rather than just dictating is fundamental to leadership in a quality management setting.

- **Honesty and integrity are the best policies.** Lincoln developed a reputation for telling the truth even when it hurt. Even people who disliked Lincoln, and these were many, usually trusted him. Trust is the cornerstone of quality leadership. People will follow only those they trust.

- **Have the courage to handle unjust criticism.** Lincoln was the most criticized president in our nation's history. Abolitionists criticized him for moving too slowly in freeing the slaves, while proslavery advocates criticized him for moving too fast. By its very nature, leadership involves promoting and facilitating change. Consequently, leaders are subject to the unjust criticism of those who oppose change.

- **Have a vision and continually reaffirm it.** Lincoln's vision for the country could be found in the words of the Declaration of Independence, and he took every opportunity to share his vision. Leaders must show those they would lead what is important, what they believe in, and where they want the organization to go. This is accomplished by articulating a clear, concise vision that is worthy of their commitment.

These are just a few of the leadership strategies exemplified by Abraham Lincoln in a life cut short by an assassin's bullet. There are many more, but it is the last strategy—*have a vision and continually reaffirm it*—that more than any of the others sets Lincoln apart as being worthy of emulation by today's business leaders.

It's well-known and documented that during the Civil War, Abraham Lincoln, through his speeches, writings, and conversations, "preached a vision" of America that has never been equaled in the course of American history. Lincoln provided exactly what the country needed at that precise moment in time: a clear, concise statement of the direction of the nation and justification for the Union's drastic action in forcing civil war.[11]

Many examples could be cited, but just two will adequately show how Lincoln continually articulated a clear and concise vision around which the North could rally. Speaking about the Civil War in a speech delivered to a special session of Congress on July 4, 1861, Lincoln said:

> This is essentially a people's contest. On the side of the Union, it is a struggle for maintaining in the world that form and substance of government whose leading object is to elevate the condition of men—to lift artificial weights from all shoulders—to clear the paths of laudable pursuit for all—to afford all an unfettered start, and a fair chance, in the race of life.[12]

Perhaps the best example of Lincoln articulating the national vision came during his address in November 1863, during ceremonies dedicating the national cemetery at Gettysburg, Pennsylvania. Standing on the site of a great and terrible battle that left more than 50,000 dead and wounded in its bloody aftermath, Lincoln said:

> Four score and seven years ago our fathers brought forth on this continent a new nation, conceived in Liberty, and dedicated to the proposition that all men are created equal. Now we are engaged in a great civil war; testing whether that nation, or any nation so conceived and so dedicated, can long endure. We are met on a great battlefield of that war. We have come to dedicate a portion of that field, as a final resting place for those who gave their lives that that nation might live. It is altogether fitting and proper that we do this. But in a larger sense, we cannot dedicate—we cannot consecrate—we cannot hallow—this ground. The brave men, living and dead, who struggled here have consecrated it, far above our poor power to add or detract. The world will little note, nor long remember what we say here, but it can never forget what they did here. It is for us the living, rather, to be dedicated here to the unfinished work which they who fought here have thus far so nobly advanced. It is rather for us to be here dedicated to the great task remaining before us—that from these honored dead we take increased devotion to that cause for which they gave the last full measure of devotion—that we here highly resolve that these dead shall not have died in vain—that this nation, under God, shall have a new birth of freedom—and that government of the people, by the people, and for the people, shall not perish from the earth.[13]

Lincoln's message was simple, yet inspiring, as any good vision must be. It told the people of the North, a people worn down and weary of war, that what they were fighting for was worthy of the terrible price being paid and that preserving the concepts of freedom and liberty for which the founding fathers had fought and died was the issue at stake. Business leaders struggling to keep their organizations focused on the difficult challenge of competing globally can profit from studying the lessons of Abraham Lincoln.

Harry Truman on Leadership

In his early years, Harry Truman was not a name that came to mind when the topic of conversation was leadership. Physically unimposing, he was small and nonathletic and wore thick glasses that magnified his eyes. As a boy, Harry Truman might have been called a "nerd," had the word existed at the time. He was inept at farming, had no profession, and showed little promise when World War I intervened. It was while serving in the army as a captain of artillery that Harry Truman first displayed evidence of the leadership ability for which he is now famous. Truman was put in charge of an artillery company made up of some tough characters who had already run off two previous commanders. But Harry Truman, they would soon find, was a different kind of leader. He quickly applied that leadership adage "When you are put in charge, take charge." Before long, Captain Truman had won both the respect and the admiration of his men, some of whom remained lifelong friends.

Truman was America's 33rd president, serving from 1945 to 1953. He succeeded to the office on the death of Franklin D. Roosevelt just as World War II was entering its final and most crucial phase. Later, he was the president who had to deal with the Korean War at a time when the last thing Americans wanted was another conflict. Although Harry Truman exemplified many important leadership strategies, he is best remembered for the following:

1. Making the hard decisions and sticking by them
2. Taking responsibility
3. Believing in yourself when no one else does

Making the Hard Decisions   As vice president, Harry Truman was not part of President Franklin D. Roosevelt's inner circle. In fact, he knew very little of what was going on as Roosevelt made the momentous decisions of a wartime president. Roosevelt died while resting at his "Little White House" in Warm Springs, Georgia, and Harry Truman was sworn in as president on April 12, 1945. Just hours after being sworn in, Truman was informed by Secretary of War Henry Stimson that the United States had successfully developed the most destructive bomb in the history of the world and that Truman would have to decide whether to drop it on Japan. After weighing the facts presented to him by his top military advisors, Truman decided to use the atomic bomb to bring the war to a speedy conclusion rather than risking the additional 1 million American casualties projected, should the United States have to invade the Japanese homeland. In making this decision, Harry Truman knew that he was sentencing thousands of Japanese people—military and civilian; men, women, and children—to a fiery death. Balancing this terrible knowledge against the almost certain 1 million American deaths, Truman made the tough decision to use the bomb. One could argue that no leader in history has had to make so monumental a choice and with so little time to consider it.

Another difficult decision Truman had to make involved the hugely popular military leader General Douglas MacArthur. By the time Truman became president, MacArthur was a living legend. One of the most charismatic and highly decorated military leaders in America's history, MacArthur had served with distinction in World War I and again in World War II, where he commanded all military forces in the southwest Pacific theater of war. MacArthur was awarded the Medal of Honor for leading the courageous but doomed garrison of American troops that held out against the Japanese army and navy at Bataan and Corregidor in the Philippines long enough to allow the United States to recover from the devastation of Pearl Harbor. When President Roosevelt ordered MacArthur to turn over his command to General Jonathan Wainwright and vacate the Philippines, MacArthur escaped by undertaking a perilous journey through Japanese-held waters to Australia. On arrival, he gave the famous speech in which he said, "I shall return," and return he did, freeing the Philippines from years of Japanese rule. In doing so, MacArthur garnered for himself a place not just in history but also in the hearts of the American people.

After the war, MacArthur served as military governor of Japan, helping rebuild the devastated country and draft its new constitution. He was serving in this capacity when the Communist North Korean Army crossed the 38th Parallel, caught South Korean forces off guard, and nearly overran the entire Korean peninsula. In a short time, the United States was at war again and General MacArthur was in charge. He added to an already brilliant military career by rallying the demoralized American and South Korean armies and pulling off an incredibly daring and risky invasion behind enemy lines at the port of Inchon, Korea. Soon he had the Communist North Korean Army on the run. In fact, his forces pushed them back across the 38th Parallel and kept pushing them almost to the border of China. This is where his problems with President Truman began.

MacArthur wanted permission to pursue the North Korean Army into China, which was giving the Koreans not just support but also sanctuary. Truman wanted to limit the war to Korea and prevent the tragedy of an all-out war with China. While MacArthur and Truman disagreed over the conduct of the war—sometimes publicly, much to the chagrin of Truman—the Chinese decided the matter of a broader war themselves by coming to the aid of the Communist North Korean Army. Soon the most advanced forces under MacArthur found themselves surrounded by 38 divisions of the army of the People's Republic of China. MacArthur advocated a strong response, including a nuclear attack against China, if necessary. Many Americans agreed with him. Truman refused, and his disagreements with

MacArthur became heated and public. Eventually, the feud reached the point where Truman thought MacArthur had crossed the line and become insubordinate. Consequently, Truman did the unthinkable: He fired one of the most popular, most highly decorated military heroes in America's history. The response of Americans was immediate and volatile. MacArthur returned home to a hero's welcome, complete with ticker-tape parades and the opportunity to address a joint session of Congress. Truman, on the other hand, found himself isolated and vilified. He quickly became one of the most unpopular presidents ever to hold office. He would later decide to forego running for reelection.

Firing MacArthur made Harry Truman a pariah for several years, but with the passing of time, people began to reassess the situation. Before he died, Harry Truman's firing of Douglas MacArthur had come to be viewed as not just the right thing to do but also one of the most politically courageous acts ever undertaken by an American president. It came to be seen for what it really was: the civilian commander in chief asserting his authority under the United States Constitution when a military leader presumed to challenge that authority. It could be said that Harry Truman sacrificed his political career to protect the integrity of the Constitution.

Taking Responsibility   A leader must be willing to share the credit and take the blame. Having the courage to take responsibility for one's decisions and behavior is an absolute necessity for a leader in any field. As president, Harry Truman became famous for his willingness to do what he thought was right and take responsibility for the consequences, a characteristic all too often missing in today's political leaders. He had a sign on his desk that read, "The buck stops here." In other words, everyone else might be able to take the politically expedient way out and "pass the buck" (meaning pass responsibility or blame to someone else), but as president, Truman would not.

He willingly accepted responsibility for the decision to drop the atomic bomb on Japan, and he took responsibility for firing General Douglas MacArthur, paying for the latter with his political career. This is an example that every business leader facing difficult decisions should seek to emulate.

Believing in Yourself   Every leader at one time or another will be faced with a "no confidence" situation. The leader has made a decision or outlined a course of action only to be met with opposition, dissension, and negativity. But leaders who have considered the dissent, weighed the facts, and still think they are right must have the strength of their own convictions to go forward, even if they are alone in believing in themselves.

Having to believe in himself when no one else would was a lifelong burden for Harry Truman. As a child, Truman was not one to garner the confidence of others. Nobody looked at Harry Truman and thought, "Here is a boy who might grow up to be president of the United States." Truman's bookish appearance and plain-spoken personality belied the fact that he was bright, well-read, had a will of iron, and possessed great depth of character. Because of this, even when no one else believed in Harry Truman, Harry Truman did. Never was this more apparent then when Truman ran for reelection to the presidency in 1948 against the Republican candidate, Thomas Dewey.

Dewey was everything that Truman wasn't: handsome, well-educated, and urbane. Political professionals and media figures gave Truman little or no chance of winning the election. Even Truman's own supporters did not think he could beat Dewey, but Truman did. Harry Truman believed he was the right man for the job, that his ideas for moving the country forward were the best ideas, and that the American people would support him if they heard the truth rather than the biased reporting of the media. In order to get around the media and directly to the American people, Truman undertook a nationwide "whistle-stop" campaign in which his train stopped at every little city, town, or community along the line and Truman spoke to the people from the back of the caboose (a car specially renovated for his use). The political professionals and the media gave Truman no chance. So sure were they of a Truman defeat that one newspaper printed its front-page headline proclaiming Dewey the victor even before the votes had been counted. When the votes were tallied, Truman shocked everyone but himself by winning convincingly. To this day, the most famous photograph of Harry Truman is one showing him holding up that newspaper and pointing to the erroneous headline. When the chips were down, Harry Truman believed in himself. This is an example that leaders in today's global world of business would do well to copy.

Winston Churchill on Leadership

Business leaders in need of a role model who exemplified perseverance in the face of adversity can learn much by studying the life of Sir Winston Churchill, especially his years as Great Britain's prime minister during World War II. Winston Churchill had already amassed a long record of public service to the British Crown when Adolph Hitler first came to power. Seeing the future more accurately than many of his fellow citizens, Churchill began urging the British government to rearm and prepare to defend itself against the rise of Nazism. Unfortunately, few paid Churchill any mind. Consequently, Great Britain was caught unprepared when, in September 1939, Hitler's troops quickly overran Poland, a British ally. Two days later, honoring its alliance with Poland, Britain declared war on Nazi Germany, and Churchill was elevated to the position of prime minister, a position he held from 1940 until the end of World War II in 1945. France joined Great Britain in declaring war on Germany.

In the early months of the war, nothing went right for Churchill's tiny island nation. Rather than joining Britain and France in an alliance against Hitler's Germany, the Soviet Union shocked the world by entering into a pact with the Nazis. In short order, Germany won a series of victories in Norway, Denmark, the Netherlands, Belgium, and Luxembourg. Then, on May 17, 1940, the German army and *Luftwaffe* (air force) swept into France, quickly brushing aside that nation's army

and simply bypassing the vaunted Maginot Line erected after World War I to prevent just such an invasion. British troops sent to help stop the Nazi *blitzkrieg* (lightning warfare) were quickly thrown back, along with their French counterparts. By May 26, 1940, more than 200,000 British and 100,000 French troops had been pushed all the way to the coast of France. They stood on the beaches of Dunkirk, their backs to the English Channel, surrounded by superior German forces. Only the incredible resourcefulness of the British people in organizing a cross-channel evacuation involving nearly every craft on the British coast that could float, coupled with bad weather that stymied the German Luftwaffe, saved the British army and the remnants of the French forces.

In June 1940, Italy declared war on Great Britain, and before the month was out, France had surrendered and agreed to German occupation. Every day brought more and more bad news for Churchill and his beleaguered compatriots. Then, when it seemed to the people of Great Britain that things could not possibly get any worse, they did. On July 10, 1940, Germany began a bombing assault on Great Britain that would continue into the summer of 1941. In addition, Germany declared a complete blockade of this tiny island nation. By the end of 1940, Britain stood practically alone in the world against the Nazi onslaught, cut off from help by German U-boats (submarines) that patrolled the Atlantic Ocean, sinking any ship that might carry much-needed supplies for the British.

Churchill's challenge was to hold his nation together—a nation surrounded by hostile forces, bombed mercilessly every night, and starved of badly needed provisions—until he could convince the United States to come to Britain's assistance. It was a challenge that Churchill accepted with courage, optimism, and unshakable resolve. In the words of Churchill associate and friend Maurice Hankey:

> We owed a good deal in those early days to the courage and inspiration of Winston Churchill who, undaunted by difficulties and losses, set an infectious example . . . . His stout attitude did something to hearten his colleagues.[14]

According to Steven Hayward,

> The key to Churchill's courage was his unbounded optimism. Only an optimist can be courageous, because courage depends on hopefulness that dangers and hazards can be overcome by bold and risky acts.[15]

Churchill combined an optimistic spirit and a bulldog tenacity into a "can do" attitude that was contagious. He convinced his beleaguered compatriots that if they would hang on and do their duty, the forces of good would overcome the forces of evil in due course. Churchill's favorite phrase was "All will come right." He repeated this phrase over and over again in speeches given during the darkest hours of World War II. Churchill never ended a speech on anything but an optimistic note, even during the worst of times. But his messages to the British people and to the world were not pie-in-the-sky cheerleading. He never flinched in telling the British people just how bad things were; after all, they knew. The bombs were falling on them every night. Their sons, husbands, and brothers were coming home from the war wounded or in coffins. The comforts of peacetime no longer existed. Churchill's message was not that "everything is fine." Rather, he told the people that things were bad and would probably get even worse, but in due course, the tide would turn. Britain would eventually prevail because it stood, even if at the time it stood alone, for what is right and good and decent in the world. His was a powerful message, and it worked.

Because of Churchill's steadfast courage, optimism, and perseverance in the face of adversity, Great Britain was able to hold on until the Japanese attack on Pearl Harbor (December 7, 1941) brought the United States into the war as an ally. With any less a leader than Sir Winston Churchill at the helm during those dark early years of the war, Great Britain might not have resisted. Had Britain fallen, one can only speculate as to how the world of today might look. Leaders of organizations going through difficult times, organizations that are barely holding on while trying to survive, can benefit from studying the life of Sir Winston Churchill.

SERVANT LEADERSHIP AND STEWARDSHIP

Leadership in business is about ensuring that organizations operate at peak performance levels on a consistent basis. It is about getting the best out of the organization in terms of efficiency and effectiveness. A concept that has this same goal at its core, but challenges the traditional approaches to leadership, is servant leadership and stewardship. Like the traditional approaches to leadership, servant leadership and stewardship must pass the tests of competitiveness in the global marketplace. Like any concept that seeks to ensure the optimum performance of an organization, servant leadership and stewardship seek to do a better job of serving both external and internal customers than do traditional approaches. In other words, the concept differs from conventional leadership ideas not so much in its overall goal as in its approach to achieving that goal.

Servant Leadership and Stewardship Defined

Advocates of servant leadership believe those who serve best lead best. According to Professor Sean Aland, servant leaders set an example of putting their employees, customers, organization, and community ahead of their own personal needs.[16] Being a servant leader is being a good steward in terms of the organization and its various stakeholders. Employees who see managers being good stewards are more likely to buy into the concept themselves. Advocates of this philosophy believe that employees at all levels should be committed to being good stewards; that is, they should, of their own volition and without coercion, do what is necessary to improve the organization because they feel an intense and personal responsibility for its performance. The servant leadership and stewardship philosophy is an approach to organization and management that seeks to go beyond employee empowerment to employee autonomy, while still meeting all the demands of a competitive marketplace.

Proponents of servant leadership and stewardship claim that this level of commitment cannot be achieved in a traditionally led organization. In an organization in which the philosophy of servant leadership and stewardship is fully accepted and practised, employees are given the autonomy to think and act for the greater good of the larger group (service and stewardship) rather than just themselves, a team, or some other individual unit. In order to do this, employees must feel that they are in control of their safety and security.

NEGATIVE INFLUENCES ON LEADERS: HOW TO COUNTER THEM

Leaders must be careful and think critically about the advice they receive from others. There are many reasons why followers sometimes give bad advice. The most negative of these occurs when followers have hidden agendas they are trying to advance and advising the leader to make a certain decision—although it might be bad for the organization—will be good for them personally.

Leaders fall prey to the negative influence of followers when they make such mistakes as letting the majority rule, being fooled by flattery, and relying too heavily on "knowledgeable" advisors. Offermann recommends the following strategies that leaders in any type of organization can use to counter the negative influences of followers:

1. **Keep the organization's vision and values uppermost in your mind.** How does the follower's recommendation square with where you are trying to take the organization? How does it square with the core values or guiding principles of the organization? How does it square with your personal core values? It's much easier to take the wrong road when you don't recognize the right road.

2. **Look for disagreement among your advisors.** People are too complex and opinionated to completely agree on most issues. If there is no disagreement, look for some.

3. **Encourage, promote, and reinforce truth telling.** Make sure you have advisors who will look you in the eye and tell you the truth, no matter what the issue is. You can encourage truth telling by making sure you don't shoot the messenger when what you hear runs counter to what you would like to hear. You can also encourage truth telling by reinforcing it in various ways. For example, publicly thank those who bring you facts that differ with the crowd during meetings.

4. **Set the right example.** The first rule of good leadership is to lead by example. Followers need to see you setting a good example when decisions are made. One of the best principles to follow is to let followers see you living out what you profess to believe. Never tell them to do what you say, not what you do.

5. **Follow your intuition.** If something feels wrong, it probably is. If you think you are being manipulated, you

probably are. Your intuition was developed over the course of many years, and you had to suffer through the consequences of many mistakes to gain intuition. Now that you have it, use it.

6. Delegate, don't abdicate. Watch a college or professional football game. When the best quarterbacks hand off the ball, they don't just sit back and say, "I gave you the ball—it's your problem now." Rather, they take some action—whether it be giving a fake or making a block—to help the runner succeed. Leaders should follow the example of the best quarterbacks. When you delegate, stay in touch—monitor. This does not mean you should micromanage. Rather, it means you should establish progress points and monitor to ensure that they are met. Leaders who delegate a task and then wash their hands of it are not delegating; they are abdicating.

LEADERS AS MENTORS

One of the most important responsibilities of organizational leaders is mentoring the next generation of leaders. Mentoring is an extension of stewardship. Leaders who are good stewards do everything they can to take care of the resources entrusted to them. The most important resource a leader has is the human resource—the people in his or her organization. The better the people in an organization perform, the better the organization performs. Consequently, helping people continually improve their performance is an important aspect of leadership. One of the best ways to help people improve is to mentor them.

Mentoring can provide a number of benefits for the individuals involved as well as for the organization as a whole. The potential benefits of mentoring include the following: [17]

- Facilitates relationship building which, in turn, improves teamwork.
- Gives personnel a stronger connection to the organization.
- Promotes communication.
- Helps personnel see the big picture and where they fit into it.
- Enhances performance.
- Improves the organization's retention rate.
- Develops the next generation of leaders.
- Enhances job knowledge and skills.

This list contains some of the more important potential benefits of mentoring. In order to translate potential into reality, organizational leaders need to know how to mentor. Mentoring is a leadership skill, and not all leaders have it. Fortunately, effective mentoring is a skill that can be learned.

Best Practices in Mentoring

In order for organizational leaders to become good mentors, they need to learn to apply best practices. Leaders who learn to apply the best practices explained in this section will become effective mentors. These best practices in mentoring are as follows:

- Set a positive example
- Establish definite learning goals
- Communicate effectively and often
- Think critically and innovate
- Empower protégés
- Inspire, support, and encourage

Set a Positive Example The mentor–protégé relationship is unique in the workplace. Everything a mentor does and says should be with the intention of helping the protégé learn, develop, and improve. The foundation of the relationship is the mentor's example. Mentors must be willing to consistently set a positive example of everything they expect of protégés. They must exemplify the best of what the organization expects of its personnel. Telling a protégé to "Do as I say not as I do" is the worst thing a mentor can do. Any person who is not willing and able to set a consistently positive example should not be allowed to serve as a mentor. Nor should an individual who will tell protégés to ignore what they were told during orientation and then show them the "real way we do things around here" be allowed to serve as a mentor. Leaders who serve as mentors must be committed to the organization's stated cultural values and developing protégés within the context of those corporate values.

Establish Definite Learning Goals Mentoring is a developmental process. Mentors attempt to help protégés develop their knowledge, skills, and attitudes in ways that will help them and help the organization. Consequently, the desired outcome of the mentor-protégé experience should never be left to chance. At the outset of the relationship, mentors and protégés should establish a specific set of learning goals. If the mentoring relationship is to help protégés get better, these goals should answer the question: Better at what?

The protégé might have some specific areas in which he or she wishes to improve. Correspondingly, the mentor might have observed areas in which the protégé needs improvement. Consequently, establishing learning goals is a two-way give-and-take exercise. The protégé might say, "I need help getting better at X, Y, and Z." The mentor might respond, "I can help you develop in those areas. In addition, let's work on developing your skills in A, B, and C." For example, the protégé might want to learn how to lead teams. That would be an appropriate learning goal. The mentor might want the protégé to learn how to conduct employee input meetings using such techniques as brainstorming and nominal group technique. This would also be an appropriate learning goal. Regardless of what learning needs to take place, the learning goals should be written down and agreed to by both parties.

Communicate Effectively and Often Effective communication between the mentor and protégé is critical. Protégés need to know how they are doing, if they are progressing satisfactorily, what they are doing well, and what they need to improve on. Correspondingly, mentors need to know what problems, difficulties, and challenges the protégés are facing. Communication between mentors and protégés should be confidential, but frank, tactful, and helpful. This is why building trust is so critical in developing a successful, productive mentor–protégé relationship. Without trust, communication will be limited and ineffective.

Constructive criticism—which is one of the core responsibilities of the mentor—will not be constructive unless it is delivered in a positive, nonthreatening, helpful way. If the protégé perceives the mentor's feedback as just criticism rather than constructive criticism, the value of the mentoring relationship will be lost. This is why it is important for mentors to be open with their protégés—to share some of their own fears, concerns, and challenges. Unless mentors are open with protégés, the protégés will not be open with them.

Think Critically and Innovate   Learning to think critically and innovate when facing problems should always be one of the learning goals in the mentor–protégé relationship. If protégés are going to advance in their careers and help achieve organizational excellence, they must become critical thinkers who know how to take the initiative and innovate when facing problems and making decisions. Even if they are already good at critical thinking and innovating, they should get even better as a result of the mentor–protégé relationship.

To help protégés develop their critical thinking and innovation skills, mentors should act as advisors and sounding boards rather than fixers when protégés confront problems they do not know how to solve. Mentors who step in and solve the problems for their protégés rob them of the opportunity to learn and grow, which is the purpose of the relationship in the first place. Mentors should not let protégés make serious or costly errors. However, on the other hand they should avoid jumping in and solving their problems for them. Guiding, advising, and gently steering protégés toward their own conclusions and solutions will allow them to develop their critical thinking and innovation skills.

Empower Protégés   Some mentors think they need to keep their protégés on a short reign. While it is certainly appropriate to communicate the parameters within which they are to operate, mentors should never create a situation in which protégés have to ask permission before attempting something new. Protégés making mistakes and what they learn from these mistakes are a part of the growth process. By establishing parameters, mentors can ensure that the mistakes are not major, costly, or harmful. However, a part of the mentoring process is helping protégés learn how to take the initiative, think for themselves, innovate, and confront new challenges. To satisfy this aspect of the relationship, it is necessary to empower protégés, give them the room needed to learn and grow, and support them when they make mistakes so that the mistakes can be turned into learning experiences.

Inspire, Support, and Encourage   Inspiring, supporting, and encouraging protégés may be the most important responsibility of mentors. Being a protégé, by its very nature, can create uncertainty and even fear. After all, in order to be a protégé, people must admit they need help—that they need to improve. Consequently, inspiring, supporting, and encouraging are critical responsibilities of the mentor. Protégés are going to make mistakes, they are going to fall short on performance targets, and they are going to make the wrong choices. If they feel supported and encouraged, these things can all be turned into learning experiences. If they do not feel supported and encouraged, they will not be willing to risk making a mistake, and the only people who never make mistakes are those who never do anything.

Leaders are people who inspire others to get better, do better, and be better. This is why the mentor's example is so important. To inspire protégés to get better, do better, and be better, mentors must be seen as always trying to perform in the same manner. Professional development is a journey not a destination. Even the best in the business need to strive to continually improve, and their protégés need to see them doing this. The best way to inspire a protégé is to exemplify what they are trying to become, what they would like to be. Mentors who do this while simultaneously supporting and encouraging protégés will serve their protégés and their organizations well.

SUMMARY

1. Leadership is the ability to inspire people to make a total, willing, and voluntary commitment to accomplishing or exceeding organizational goals. Good leaders overcome resistance to change, broker the needs of constituent groups inside and outside the organization, and establish an ethical framework. Good leaders are committed to both the job to be done and the people who must do it. They are good communicators, and they are persuasive.

2. Leadership for quality is based on the following principles: customer focus, obsession with quality, recognizing of the structure of work, freedom through control, unity of purpose, looking for faults in systems, teamwork, continuing education and training, emphasis on best practices and peak performance.

3. Common leadership styles include the following: autocratic, democratic, participative, goal-oriented, and situational. The appropriate leadership style in a total quality setting is participative taken to a higher level. Leadership characteristics that build and maintain followership are a sense of purpose, self-discipline, honesty, credibility, common sense, stamina, commitment, and steadfastness.

4. Leaders can build trust by applying the following strategies: taking the blame but sharing the credit, pitching in and helping, being consistent, and being equitable.

5. When restructuring, organizations should show that they care, let employees vent, communicate, provide outplacement services, be honest and fair, provide for change agents, have a clear vision, offer incentives, and train.

6. To lead change, leaders must develop a change picture, communicate, plan, assign, monitor, and adjust.

7. Servant leadership and stewardship go beyond employee empowerment to employee autonomy and seek to create an environment in which employees perform out of a spirit of ownership and commitment.

8. Leaders can counter the negative influence of followers by (a) keeping vision and values uppermost in their minds, (b) looking for disagreement among advisors, (c) encouraging truth telling, (d) setting the right example, (e) following their intuition, and (f) monitoring delegated work.

KEY TERMS AND CONCEPTS

Autocratic leadership
Common sense
Credibility
Customer focus
Democratic leadership
Juran Trilogy
Leadership
Leadership for quality
Lose/lose
Maslow's Hierarchy of Needs
Misleaders
Obsession with quality
Participative leadership
Restructuring
Self-discipline
Sense of purpose
Servant leadership
Situational leadership
Stamina
Steadfastness
Stewardship
Win/lose
Win/win

FACTUAL REVIEW QUESTIONS

1. Define the term *leadership*.
2. Explain the concept of a good leader.
3. How can one distinguish between leaders and misleaders?

4. Describe and debunk three common myths about leadership.
5. List and briefly explain the principles of leadership.
6. What is the Juran Trilogy?
7. Describe Maslow's Hierarchy of Needs and how it can be used in a total quality setting.
8. What leadership style is most appropriate in a total quality setting? Why?
9. Explain the leadership characteristics that build and maintain followership.
10. Explain the pitfalls that can undermine followership.
11. List the strategies leaders can use to play a positive role in facilitating change.
12. Explain what organizations must do to respond effectively to change.
13. What can organizations do to promote a positive response to restructuring?
14. Explain each step in change facilitation.
15. Explain the main leadership lessons that can be learned by studying the lives of Abraham Lincoln, Harry Truman, and Winston Churchill.
16. How do the concepts of servant leadership and stewardship differ from traditional leadership philosophies?
17. Explain the strategies for countering the negative influences of advisor and followers.

CRITICAL THINKING ACTIVITY

How Do You Change a Complacent Organization?

Mark Bolten, CEO of Trans-Tech Corporation, is frustrated. Trans-Tech is the market leader in the manufacture of avionics components for commercial airliners and has been for years. But looking to the future, Mark sees problems. Not now, but within 5 years Trans-Tech's situation could change drastically for the worse. Mark sees this and wants to get his company started right away making major but necessary changes.

The challenge he faces is organizational inertia based on complacency. Not even one member of his management team sees the need to change. The collective attitude of Trans-Tech's senior managers seems to be, "We are the market leaders—why rock the boat?"

What is especially frustrating for Mark is the fact that his senior managers are solid, talented professionals. Together with him, they built Trans-Tech into a leading company. He can't simply replace them with more future-minded managers. They need to be part of the solution.

Put yourself in Mark's place. What can he do to break through the inertia and get Trans-Tech started on making the necessary changes? How would you handle this dilemma?

DISCUSSION ASSIGNMENT 9–1

Leadership for Quality at Lincoln Electric

Lincoln Electric Company in Cleveland, Ohio, manufactures arc welding equipment. Lincoln has the highest paid workers in this extremely competitive market, and it is protected neither by patents nor by price supports. In spite of this, Lincoln Electric controls 40% of the arc welding market. How is this possible? Lincoln Electric outperforms its competitors in both quality and productivity. By way of comparison, Lincoln Electric has sales in excess of $167,000 per employee, while the industry average is $70,000 per employee.

This is accomplished by applying, in the age of high technology, the following leadership principles set forth by James F. Lincoln in 1895:

- Viewing people as the company's most valuable asset
- Practicing Christian ethics
- Making decisions based on principles
- Observing simplicity in all things
- Competing
- Focusing on the customer

DISCUSSION QUESTION

Discuss the following question in class or outside of class with your fellow students:

1. Compare these principles with the leadership principles explained in this chapter. How are they similar or different?

DISCUSSION ASSIGNMENT 9–2

Leadership for Quality at Kollmorgen Corporation

Kollmorgen Corporation is a diversified technology company that operates in the highly competitive electronics industry. Kollmorgen relies on its employees pulling together to outperform the competition worldwide in the areas of quality and productivity. The focus of leaders at Kollmorgen is on individuals and helping them want to achieve peak performance levels.

Kollmorgen achieves this by applying the following strategies:

- Managers make sure that employees can focus on their work rather than paperwork.
- The distance between people, both physical and psychological, is reduced to promote effective communication.
- Positive personal relationships are stressed.

DISCUSSION QUESTION

Discuss the following question in class or outside of class with your fellow students:

1. Compare these strategies with the leadership principles explained in this chapter. How are they similar or different?

ENDNOTES

1. William A. Cohen, *A Class with Drucker: The Last Lessons of the World's Greatest Management Teacher* (New York: AMACOM, 2007), 105–108.

2. Ibid., 106.

3. Ibid., 109.

4. Noel M. Tichy and Warren G. Bennis, *Judgment: How Winning Leaders Make Great Calls* (New York: Portfolio Hardcover, 2007), 142.

5. The Juran Trilogy® is a registered trademark of Juran Industries Inc.

6. Management for the Rest of Us, "Joseph Juran-The Quality Trilogy." Retrieved from www.mftrou.com/joseph-juran.html on February 2, 2011.

7. Businessballs, "Stephen Covey's Seven Habits of Highly Effective People®." Retrieved from www.businessballs.com/sevenhabitsstevencovey.htm on February 20, 2011.

8. John P. Kotter, "What Leaders Really Do," *Harvard Business Review* (December 1, 2001): 3 (Produ # R0111-PDF-ENG).

9. Ibid.

10. Donald T. Phillips, *Lincoln on Leadership* (New York: Warner Books, 1992), 13–137.

11. Ibid.

12. Ibid.

13. Ibid.

14. Steven F. Hayward, "Churchill's Personal Traits," *The CEO Advantage Journal*. Retrieved from www.tcajournal.com on February 15, 2011.

15. Ibid.

16. Sean Aland, Servant leadership seminar, updated January 2011.

17. Lois J. Zachary and Lory A. Fisher, "Those Who Lead, Mentor," (March 2010). Retrieved from www.astd.org/TD/TDpodcasts.htm on January 7, 2011

CHAPTER 10

TEAM BUILDING AND TEAMWORK

No member of a crew is praised for the rugged individuality of his rowing.
—*Ralph Waldo Emerson*

MAJOR TOPICS

- Overview of Team Building and Teamwork
- Building Teams and Making Them Work
- Four-Step Approach to Team Building
- Character Traits and Teamwork
- Teams Are Coached—Not Bossed
- Handling Conflict in Teams
- Structural Inhibitors of Teamwork
- Rewarding Team and Individual Performance
- Recognizing Teamwork and Team Players
- Leading Multicultural Teams

OVERVIEW OF TEAM BUILDING AND TEAMWORK

Teamwork is a fundamental element of total quality. The reason for this is simple and practical. It is organizations, not individuals, that produce products and provide services. Consequently, peak performance and continual improvement are group, not individual, endeavors.

What Is a Team?

A team is a group of people with a common, collective goal. The collective goal aspect of teams is critical. This point is evident in the performance of athletic teams. For example, a basketball team in which one player hogs the ball, plays the role of the prima donna, and pursues his or her own personal goals (a personal high point total, most valuable player or MVP status, publicity, or something else) will rarely win against a team whose players all pull together toward the collective goal of winning the game.

An example of teamwork succeeding over individualism is the No Name Defense of the Miami Dolphins of the National Football League (NFL) during the early years of the franchise. In a sport that promotes and spawns media stars, no member of the Dolphin defense stood out above the others. In fact, although it was arguably the best defense in the NFL at the time, individual members of the team were not well-known—hence the nickname No Name Defense.

Taken separately, the individual team members were not particularly impressive when compared with the league's best at their respective positions. Bigger defensive ends, stronger nose tackles, quicker linebackers, and swifter defensive backs played on competing teams. Where the Dolphins defense excelled was in working together as a team. Its members were a perfect example of the fact that a team's ability is more than just the sum of the abilities of the individual members.

Rationale for Teams

In the example of the No Name Defense, the team's ability was more than the sum of the abilities of individual members. This is one of the primary reasons for advocating teamwork. The following facts summarize the rationale for teamwork:

- Teams satisfy the human social need to belong.
- Two or more heads are better than one.
- The whole (the team) can be greater than the sum of its parts (individual members).
- People in teams get to know each other, build trust, and, as a result, want to help each other.
- Teamwork promotes better communication.
- Teamwork multiplies the potential of individual members.
- Teamwork produces positive peer pressure.

It is well-established that teams can outperform individuals, provided they are properly handled. A team is not just a group of people. A group of people becomes a team when the following conditions exist:

- Agreement exists as to the team's mission. For a group to be a team and a team to work effectively, all members must understand and agree on the mission.
- Members adhere to team ground rules. A team must have ground rules that establish the framework within which the team's mission is pursued. A group becomes a team when there is agreement as to mission and adherence to ground rules.
- Fair distribution of responsibility and authority exists. Teams do not eliminate structure and authority.

Football teams have quarterbacks, and baseball teams have captains. However, teams work best when responsibility and authority are shared and team members are treated as equals.

- People adapt to change. Change is not just inevitable in a total quality setting—it is also desirable. Unfortunately, people typically resist change. People in teams should help each other adapt to change in a positive way.

Learning to Work Together

A group of people does not make a team. People in a group do not automatically or magically find ways to work together.

One of the reasons teams don't always work as well as they might is certain built-in human factors that, unless understood and dealt with, can undermine success. These factors include:

- **Personal identity of team members.** It is natural for people to wonder where they fit into any organization. This tendency applies regardless of whether the organization is a company or a team within a company. People worry about being an outsider, getting along with other team members, having a voice, and developing mutual trust among team members. The work of the team cannot proceed effectively until team members feel as if they fit in.

- **Relationships among team members.** Before people in a group can work together, they have to get to know each other and form relationships. When people know each other and care about each other, they will go to great lengths to support one another. Time spent helping team members get acquainted and establish common ground among themselves is time invested well. This is especially important now that the modern workforce has become so diverse; common ground among team members can no longer be assumed.

- **Identity within the organization.** This factor has two aspects. The first has to do with how the team fits into the organization. Is its mission a high priority in the company? Does the team have support at the highest management levels? The second aspect of this factor relates to how membership on a given team will affect relationships with those who are not members. This concern is especially important in the case of task forces and project teams whose members will want to maintain relationships they have already established with fellow employees who are not on the team. They may be concerned that membership on the team might have a negative impact on their relationships with fellow workers who aren't included.

Team Excellence and Performance

Teamwork is not a magic cure-all. Poorly run teams can do more damage to an organization's performance and

corresponding competitiveness than having no teams at all. For this reason, it is critical that excellence in team performance be an overriding goal of the organization.

In order to ensure excellence in teamwork, team leaders should attempt to develop the following characteristics of effective teams:

- **Mutual support.** In teams, individual members depend on each other to get the job of the team done. They are *mutually dependent.* Since this is the case, they must also be mutually supportive: willing and able to assist each other as necessary in achieving peak performance for the team and continually improving performance.

- **Challenge.** Wise team leaders find that delicate balance between expecting too much and expecting too little. They set goals for the team that are challenging but not overwhelming.

- **Singleness of purpose.** A team has a purpose that should be clearly stated in its mission. That purpose must become the purpose of each individual team member as well as of the team.

- **Trust.** Wise team leaders work continually on building trust among their team members and between themselves and team members. People will not work well with others they do not trust, nor will they commit to a team leader they do not trust.

- **Participation.** Wise team leaders draw out reticent members who tend to hold back rather than contributing ideas, concerns, and recommendations during team discussions. Correspondingly, team leaders rein in members who tend to dominate team meetings. In the best teams, all members participate, but nobody dominates.

- **People skills.** The best teams consist of members who have developed the people skills necessary to prevent and resolve conflict and to work cooperatively to solve problems.

- **Accountability.** The best teams consist of members who know the teams' goals and expect to be held accountable for achieving them. Self-assessment of team performance is a constant, as is continual improvement.

- **Reinforcement.** The best teams reinforce success by celebrating it. Wise team leaders reinforce team-positive behaviors and attitudes by recognizing and rewarding them.

QUALITY TIP ▼

Teams Give Employees a Sense of Belonging

One of the most important functions of a team is providing its members with a sense of belonging. People have an inherent need to belong, to feel like they are part of something. Belonging to a team gives employees a sense of being *rooted*, of having a *home* within the larger organization.

BUILDING TEAMS AND MAKING THEM WORK

Some work teams are permanent (i.e., departments, sections, divisions, etc.). However, some are ad hoc—they are formed to complete a specific assignment or mission.

Part of building a successful team is choosing team members wisely. This section describes strategies for selecting team members, naming officers (or otherwise assigning responsibility), creating a mission statement, and developing collegial relations among team members.

Makeup and Size of Teams

Teams should be composed of those people who are most likely to be able to satisfy the team's mission efficiently and effectively. The appropriate makeup of a team depends in part on the type of team in question (whether it is departmental improvement, process improvement, or task force or project-oriented). Departmental improvement teams such as quality circles are made up of the employees of a given department. However, process improvement teams and task forces typically cross departmental lines.

The membership of such teams should be open to any level of employee—management, supervisors, and hourly wage earners. A good rule of thumb is that the greater the mix, the better.

Choosing Team Members

When putting together a team, the first step is to identify all potential team members. This is important because there will often be more potential team members than the number of members actually needed (maximum of 12 members). After the list has been compiled, volunteers can be solicited and actual team members selected from among those who volunteer. However, care should be taken to ensure a broad mix, as discussed in the previous section. This rule should be adhered to even if there are no volunteers and team members must be drafted. The more likely case is that there will be more volunteers than openings on most teams.

Responsibilities of Team Leaders

Most teams will have members who are managers, supervisors, and hourly employees. However, it should not be assumed that the highest level manager will automatically be the team leader. Correspondingly, it should not necessarily be assumed that the most junior hourly worker cannot be the team leader, at least in the case of ad hoc teams.

The first step in selecting a team leader is to develop an understanding of the role and responsibilities of this individual. Team leaders perform the following functions:

- Serve as the official contact between the team and the rest of the organization.
- Serve as the official record keeper for the team. Records include minutes, correspondence, agendas, and reports.

Typically, the team leader will appoint a recorder to take minutes during meetings. However, the team leader is still responsible for distributing and filing minutes.

- Serve as a full-fledged team member but exercise care to avoid dominating team discussions.
- Implement team recommendations that fall within the team leader's realm of authority and work with upper management to implement those that fall outside it.
- Motivate, monitor, and mentor other team members.

Other Team Members

In addition to the team leader, most teams will need a team recorder and a quality advisor. The *recorder* is responsible for taking minutes during team meetings and assisting the team leader with the various other types of correspondence generated by the team. The quality advisor is an important part of the team in a total quality environment and has the following responsibilities:

- Focus on team processes, as opposed to products, and on *how* decisions are made, as opposed to *what* decisions are made.
- Assist the team leader in breaking down tasks into component parts and assigning the parts to team members.
- Help the team leader plan and prepare for meetings.
- Help team members learn to use the scientific approach of collecting data, analyzing data statistically, and drawing conclusions based on the statistical analysis.
- Help team members convert their recommendations into presentations that can be made to upper management.
- Keep the team focused on peak performance of people, processes, and products and continual improvement of all the three.

Creating the Team's Charter

After a team has been formed, a team leader selected, a reporter appointed, and a quality advisor assigned, the team is ready to develop its charter. This is a critical step in the life of a team. The charter explains the team's reason for being and its operating ground rules. Hence, the two components of a team charter are the mission and the ground rules. A mission statement is written in terms that are broad enough to encompass all the team will be expected to do but specific enough that progress can be easily measured. This sample mission statement meets both of these criteria:

> The purpose of this team is to reduce the time between when an order is taken and when it is filled, while simultaneously improving the quality of products shipped.

This statement is broad enough to encompass a wide range of activities and to give team members room within which to operate. The statement does not specify by how much throughput time will be reduced or by how much quality will be improved. The level of specificity comes in the goals set by the team (e.g., reduce throughput time by 15% within 6 months; improve the customer satisfaction rate to 100% within 6 months). Goals follow the mission statement and explain it more fully in quantifiable terms.

This sample mission statement is written in broad terms, but it is specific enough that team members know they are expected to simultaneously improve both productivity and quality. It also meets one other important criterion: simplicity. Any employee could understand this mission statement. It is brief, to the point, and devoid of all esoteric nonessential verbiage.

When developing mission statements, team leaders should keep these criteria in mind: broadness, appropriate specificity, and simplicity. A good mission statement is a tool for communicating the team's purpose—within the team and throughout the organization—and not a device for confusing people or an opportunity to show off literary dexterity.

The second component of a team charter consists of the ground rules members agree to abide by as they work together to achieve the team's mission. Ground rules are typically based on such team-positive characteristics as honesty, trust, dependability, mutual support, responsibility, cooperation, patience, resourcefulness, punctuality, tolerance of and sensitivity to cultural differences, perseverance, and conflict management. A team's actual ground rules are developed by listing on a flipchart as many of these types of team-positive characteristics as the group can suggest and then asking each team member to select his or her top 10. The top 10 (or 8 to 12) are then converted into ground rules. For example, the conflict management characteristic—when converted into a ground rule—might read as follows:

> We are free to disagree on this team, but not to be disagreeable. We will endeavor to prevent counterproductive conflict or to quickly and positively resolve it when conflict occurs.

One final component that is sometimes included in a team charter consists of team goals. Ad hoc teams typically include goals and permanent work teams do not. Because ad hoc teams come together on a temporary basis to accomplish a finite set of goals, it is important to include those goals in the team charter. However, because the goals of permanent work teams are always evolving, it is better to make them a separate attachment to the team charter.

Developing Mutually Supportive Peer Relationships

A team works most effectively when individual team members form positive, mutually supportive peer relationships. These are sometimes called *collegial relationships*, and they can be the difference between a high-performing team and a mediocre one.

1. Help team members understand the importance of honesty, reliability, and trustworthiness. Team members must trust each other and know that they can count on each other.

2. Help team members develop mutual confidence in their work ability.

3. Help team members understand the pressures to which other team members are subjected. It is important for team members to be supportive of peers as they deal with the stresses of the job.

4. Help team members learn to be mutually supportive in doing their work.

5. Help team members think "we" rather than "me."

These are the basics. Competence, trust, communication, and mutual support are the foundation on which effective teamwork is built. Any resources devoted to improving these factors are an investment well-made.

Promoting Diversity in Teams

The American workplace has undergone an unprecedented transformation. Formerly dominated by young to middle-aged white males, the workplace now draws from a labor pool dominated by women and minorities. This means that today's employees come from a variety of different cultures and backgrounds. Consequently, they are likely to have different values and different outlooks. This situation can be good or bad, depending on how it is handled. Dealing with diversity in a way that makes it a strength has come to be known as *managing diversity*.

When diversity is properly managed, impediments to women and minorities that exist in some workplaces can be eliminated. By working together in well-supervised teams that include women and men, young and old, minorities and nonminorities, employees can learn how to realize the full potential of diversity. Diversity in teamwork can be promoted by applying the following strategies:

- **Continually assess circumstances.** Is communication among diverse team members positive? Do bias and stereotyping exist among team members? Do minorities and nonminorities with comparable jobs and qualifications earn comparable wages? Factors that might undermine harmonious teamwork should be anticipated, identified, and handled.

- **Give team members opportunities to learn.** Humans naturally tend to distrust people who are different, whether the differences are attributed to gender, culture, age, race, or any other factor. Just working with people who are different can help overcome this unfortunate but natural human tendency. However, it usually takes more than just working together to break down barriers and turn a diverse group of employees into a mutually supportive, complementary team in which the effectiveness of the whole is greater than the sum of its parts. Education and training aimed at promoting sensitivity to and appreciation of human differences should be provided. Such training should also help team members overcome the stereotypical assumptions that society in general seems to promote.

For metal to have optimum strength and resiliency characteristics, it must be alloyed with other metals. High-performance, space-age metals are all mixtures of several different component metals, each different from the others and each possessing its own desirable characteristics. In the modern workplace, this analogy can be applied to the team. Diverse employees, properly managed and trained, can make high-performance, world-class teams.

FOUR-STEP APPROACH TO TEAM BUILDING

Effective team building is a four-step process:

1. Assess
2. Plan
3. Execute
4. Evaluate

To be a little more specific, the team building process proceeds along the following lines: (a) assess the team's developmental needs (e.g., its strengths and weaknesses), (b) plan team-building activities based on the needs identified, (c) execute the planned team-building activities, and (d) evaluate results. The steps are spelled out further in the next sections.

Assessing Team Needs

If you were the coach of a baseball team about which you knew very little, what is the first thing you would want to do? Most coaches in such situations would begin by assessing the abilities of their new teams. Can we hit? Can we pitch? Can we field? What are our weaknesses? What are our strengths? With these questions answered, the coach will know how best to proceed with team-building activities.

This same approach can be used in the workplace. A mistake commonly made by organizations is beginning team-building activities without first assessing the team's developmental needs. Resources are often limited in organizations. Consequently, it is important to use them as efficiently and effectively as possible. Organizations that begin team-building activities without first assessing strengths and weaknesses run the risk of wasting resources in an attempt to strengthen characteristics that are already strong, while at the same time overlooking characteristics that are weak.

For workplace teams to be successful, they should have at least the following characteristics:

- Clear direction that is understood by all members
- "Team players" on the team
- Fully understood and accepted accountability measures

Figure 10–1 shows a tool that can be used for assessing the team-building needs of workplace teams. It consists of criteria arranged in three broad categories: *direction and understanding, characteristics of team members*, and *accountability*. Individual team members record their perceptions of the team's performance and abilities relative to the specific criteria in each category. The highest score possible for each criterion is 6; the lowest score possible is, 0. The team score for each criterion is found by adding the scores of individual members for that criterion and dividing by the number of team members. For example, a four-person team might produce the following score on a given criterion:

Team member 1:   4

Team member 2:   2

Team member 3:   2

Team member 4:   4

$$\overline{12}: 12 \div 4 = 3 \text{ (team average score)}$$

The lower the team score is for a criterion, the more work is needed on that criterion.

Team-building activities should be developed and executed based on what is revealed by this assessment. Activities should be undertaken in reverse order of the assessment scores (e.g., lower scores first, higher scores last). For example, if the team score for criterion 1 (clearly stated mission) is the lowest score for all the criteria, the first team-building activity would be to rewrite this mission statement so that it is clear and easily understood.

Planning Team-Building Activities

Team-building activities should be planned around the results of the needs assessment conducted in the previous step. Consider the example of a newly chartered team. The highest score for a given criterion in Figure 10–1 is 6. Consequently, any team average score less than 6 indicates a need for team building relating to the criterion in question. The lower the score, the greater is the need.

For example, say the team in question had an average score of 3 for criterion 2 ("All team members understand the mission"). Clearly, part of the process of building this team must be explaining the team's mission more clearly. A team average score of 3 on this issue indicates that some members understand the mission and some don't. This solution might be as simple as the responsible manager or team leader sitting down with the team, describing the mission, and responding to questions from team members.

On the other hand, if the assessment produces a low score for criterion 9 ("All team members are open and honest with each other at all times"), more extensive trust-building activities may be needed. In any case, what is important in this step is to (a) plan team-building activities based on what is learned from the needs assessment and (b) provide team-building activities in the priority indicated by the needs assessment, beginning with the lowest scores.

Executing Team-Building Activities

Team-building activities should be implemented on a just-in-time basis. A mistake made by many organizations that are interested in implementing total quality is rushing into team building. All employees are given teamwork training,

Instructions

To the left of each item is a blank for recording your perception regarding that item. For each item, record your perception of how well it describes your team. Is the statement *Completely True* (CT), *Somewhat True* (ST), *Somewhat False* (SF), or *Completely False* (CF)? Use the following numbers to record your perception.

CT = 6
ST = 4
SF = 2
CF = 0

Direction and Understanding

_____ 1. The team has a clearly stated mission.
_____ 2. All team members understand the mission.
_____ 3. All team members understand the scope and boundaries of the team's charter.
_____ 4. The team has a set of broad goals that support its mission.
_____ 5. All team members understand the team's goals.
_____ 6. The team has identified specific activities that must be completed in order to accomplish team goals.
_____ 7. All team members understand the specific activities that must be completed in order to accomplish team goals.
_____ 8. All team members understand projected time frames, schedules, and deadlines relating to specific activities.

Characteristics of Team Members

_____ 9. All team members are open and honest with each other at all times.
_____ 10. All team members trust each other.
_____ 11. All team members put the team's mission and goals ahead of their own personal agendas all of the time.
_____ 12. All team members are comfortable that they can depend on each other.
_____ 13. All team members are enthusiastic about accomplishing the team's mission and goals.
_____ 14. All team members are willing to take responsibility for the team's performance.

FIGURE 10–1 Team-Building Needs Assessment

even those who are not yet part of a chartered team. Like any kind of training, teamwork training will be forgotten unless it is put to immediate use. Consequently, the best time to provide teamwork training is after a team has been formed and given its charter. In this way, team members will have opportunities to apply what they are learning immediately.

Team building is an ongoing process. The idea is to make a team better and better as time goes by. Consequently, basic teamwork training is provided as soon as a team is chartered. All subsequent team-building activities are based on the results of the needs assessment and planning process.

Evaluating Team-Building Activities

If team-building activities have been effective, weaknesses pointed out by the needs assessment process should have been strengthened. A simple way to evaluate the effectiveness of team-building activities is to readminister the appropriate portion of the needs assessment document. The best

approach is to reconstitute the document so that it contains the relevant criteria only. This will focus the attention of team members on the specific targeted areas.

If the evaluation shows that sufficient progress has been made, nothing more is required. If not, additional team-building activities are needed. If a given team-building activity appears to have been ineffective, get the team together and discuss it. Use the feedback from team members to identify weaknesses and problems and to ensure that team-building activities become more effective.

CHARACTER TRAITS AND TEAMWORK

Organizations may be "missing the boat" unless character building is part of their team-building program.[1] This conclusion is based on the findings of Institute for Corporate Competitiveness' (ICC's) year-long study in which 10 focus groups were questioned at length concerning which factors contribute most to helping people work well in teams.

_____ 15. All team members are willing to cooperate in order to get the team's mission accomplished.

_____ 16. All team members will take the initiative in moving the team toward its final destination.

_____ 17. All team members are patient with each other.

_____ 18. All team members are resourceful in finding ways to accomplish the team's mission in spite of difficulties.

_____ 19. All team members are punctual when it comes to team meetings, other team activities, and meeting deadlines.

_____ 20. All team members are tolerant and sensitive to the individual differences of team members.

_____ 21. All team members are willing to persevere when team activities become difficult.

_____ 22. The team has a mutually supportive climate.

_____ 23. All team members are comfortable expressing opinions, pointing out problems, and offering constructive criticism.

_____ 24. All team members support team decisions once they are made.

_____ 25. All team members understand how the team fits into the overall organization/big picture.

Accountability

_____ 26. All team members know how team progress/performance will be measured.

_____ 27. All team members understand how team success is defined.

_____ 28. All team members understand how ineffective team members will be dealt with.

_____ 29. All team members understand how team decisions are made.

_____ 30. All team members know their respective responsibilities.

_____ 31. All team members know the responsibilities of all other team members.

_____ 32. All team members understand their authority within the team and that of all other team members.

_____ 33. All team goals have been prioritized.

_____ 34. All specific activities relating to team goals have been assigned appropriately and given projected completion dates.

_____ 35. All team members know what to do when unforeseen inhibitors impede progress.

FIGURE 10–1 (_Continued_)

Five of the focus groups consisted of participants who were members of successful teams. The other five groups consisted of participants who had been members of unsuccessful teams. Participants in each group were asked to discuss the factors that contributed most to their team's success or its failure, as applicable. ICC facilitators recorded the consensus responses of each group and summarized them in order of importance (as prioritized by the groups).

There was a strong correlation between the composite data of the successful groups and that of the unsuccessful groups. The factors that both types of groups identified as having the greatest impact on the success of teams in the workplace can best be described as character traits. These traits, in the order of importance established by the focus groups, are shown in Figure 10–2. Participants from successful teams identified the presence of selected character traits in team members as the most important determinant of team success. Participants from unsuccessful teams

identified the lack of these same character traits as the most important determinant of team failure.

Study subjects were vocal and clear on the contributions that the character traits shown in Figure 10–2 make to successful teamwork and, conversely, on the harmful impact

• Honesty/integrity	• Initiative
• Selflessness	• Patience
• Dependability	• Resourcefulness
• Enthusiasm	• Punctuality
• Responsibility	• Tolerance/sensitivity
• Cooperativeness	• Perseverance

FIGURE 10–2 Character Traits That Promote Successful Teamwork

Source: Institute for Corporate Competitiveness, _Final Report: Team Success Study_, 3rd ed. (Niceville, FL: Institute for Corporate Competitiveness, 2011), 3–4.

the lack of these traits can have. The input of study participants is summarized as follows:[2]

- **Honesty/integrity.** To build trust, team members must be honest with each other. Honesty is the cornerstone of trust, and trust is the cornerstone of teamwork. Team members depend on each other in ways that affect them every day on a personal level (e.g., job performance, job security, wages, and promotions). It is difficult at best for people to place their personal interests even partially in the hands of other people. To do so, there must be a high level of trust. Building that trust begins with honesty.

- **Selflessness.** This character trait means that people are willing to put the team's interests ahead of their own. A team can move only as fast as its slowest member. This means that there will always be team members who will get out in front of the pack unless they rein themselves in. Being willing to do this is critical to the success of a team. Rather than running ahead of the pack, faster team members should help slower team members improve so that the pace of the overall team is improved.

- **Dependability.** People who are dependable consistently do what they are supposed to do, when they are supposed to do it, and how they are supposed to do it. Because team members must depend on each other, this character trait is critical. The performance of the team depends on the performance of its members. Consequently, the team relies on its members and the members rely on each other.

- **Enthusiasm.** The concept of team spirit is real. People who are enthusiastic about their work typically do it better. The good news is that enthusiasm is contagious. The bad news is that despondency and negativism are also contagious. Every team will face roadblocks, unexpected barriers, and difficulties. Enthusiasm can help team members persevere when the road gets rocky. Despondency, on the other hand, promotes a defeatist attitude that says, "When times are tough, give up."

- **Responsibility.** This character trait means that people know what is expected of them and are willing to be held accountable for doing what is expected. Successful teams and team members take responsibility for their actions, decisions, and performance. Failing teams and team members tend to avoid responsibility. They are prone to blame others as well as each other when things go wrong. Taking responsibility holds teams together during difficult times. Pointing the finger of blame breaks up teams when things aren't going well.

- **Cooperativeness.** People who work together must cooperate with each other. Think of a team that runs relay races. Much of the success of the team depends on how well they cooperate in passing the baton. If the individual members of the team do not cooperate in this critical phase of the process, the team will lose no matter how fast each individual runs his or her portion of the race. The same concept applies to members of work teams. Moreover, in a work setting the race is run again every day, and the baton is passed more frequently.

- **Initiative.** Initiative means recognizing what needs to be done and doing it without waiting to be told. This character trait means that team members never say, "That's not my job." In a team setting, whatever is necessary to get the job done is everybody's job.

- **Patience.** The most difficult challenge facing members of teams is learning to work together. It is easier for people not to get along than it is to get along. In a sense, working in a team is contrary to human nature. People by nature tend to be individualistic. Consequently, there are going to be tensions and troubles as people make the difficult transition from individuals to group members. To stay together long enough to make this transition, team members must be patient with and supportive of each other.

- **Resourcefulness.** Resourceful people find ways to get the job done in spite of an apparent lack of resources. A resourceful person will make wise use of materials and ideas that others might overlook or even discard. Having such people on a team will make the team more effective.

- **Punctuality.** People who are punctual (on time, on schedule) show respect for their team members and their time. A team cannot function fully without all of its members present: Members who are tardy or absent impede the performance of their team. Team members who are punctual can be depended on to be where they are supposed to be when they are supposed to be there.

- **Tolerance/sensitivity.** The people in teams can be different in many ways. They might be different in terms of gender, race, or religion. They might have cultural differences and different political outlooks. The modern workplace is an increasingly diverse environment. Diversity can strengthen a team, provided that team members are sensitive to and tolerant of individual differences in people. Insensitive team members who can relate only to people like themselves don't make good team players.

- **Perseverance.** To persevere is to persist unrelentingly in trying to accomplish a task in spite of obstacles. People who persevere make valuable team members because they serve as beacons of encouragement when the team becomes engulfed in a fog of difficulty. The natural human tendency is to want to give up when problems arise. However, if just one or two team members are willing to persevere, the others will usually buckle down and keep trying.

TEAMS ARE COACHED—NOT BOSSED

If employees are going to be expected to work together as a team, managers and supervisors have to realize that teams are coached—they are not bossed. Team leaders, regardless of their respective titles (manager, supervisor, etc.), need to understand the difference between bossing and coaching. Bossing, in the traditional sense, involves planning work, giving orders, monitoring programs, and evaluating performance. Bosses approach the job from an "I'm in charge—do as you are told" perspective.

Coaches, on the other hand, are facilitators of team development and continually improved performance. They approach the job from the perspective of leading the team in such a way that it achieves peak performance levels on a consistent basis. This philosophy is translated into everyday behavior in several ways, which are as follows:

- Coaches give their teams a clearly defined charter.
- Coaches make team development and team building a constant activity.
- Coaches are mentors.
- Coaches promote mutual respect between themselves and team members and among team members.
- Coaches make human diversity within a team a plus.

Clearly Defined Charter

One can imagine a basketball, soccer, or track coach calling her team together and saying, "This year we have one overriding purpose—to win the championship." In one simple statement, this coach has clearly and succinctly defined the team's charter. All team members now know that everything they do this season should be directed at winning the championship. The coach didn't say the team would improve its record by 25 points, improve its standing in the league by two places, or make the playoffs, all of which would be worthy missions. This coach has a greater vision—this year the team is going for the championship. Coaches of work teams should be just as specific in explaining the team's mission to team members.

Team Development and Team Building

The most constant presence in an athlete's life is practice. Regardless of the sport, athletic teams practice constantly. During practice, coaches work on developing the skills of individual team members and the team as a whole. Team development and team building activities are ongoing forever. Coaches of work teams should follow the lead of their athletic counterparts. Developing the skills of individual team members and building the team as a whole should be a normal part of the job—a part that takes place regularly, forever.

Mentoring

Good coaches are mentors. This means they establish a helping, caring, nurturing relationship with team members. Developing the capabilities of team members, improving the contribution individuals make to the team, and helping team members advance their careers are all mentoring

activities. According to David Cottrell, effective mentors help team members by[3]

- Developing their job-related competence
- Building character
- Teaching them the corporate culture
- Teaching them how to get things done in the organization
- Helping them understand other people and their viewpoints
- Teaching them how to behave in unfamiliar settings or circumstances
- Giving them an insight into differences among people
- Helping them develop success-oriented values
- Helping them to establish themselves in the organization
- Giving them a better chance to succeed

Mutual Respect

It is important for team members to respect their coach, for the coach to respect his or her team members, and for team members to respect each other. In fact, it is more important to have mutual respect in teams than to have members who like each other. Respect is built on the following factors:

- **Trust made tangible.** Trust is built by (a) setting the example, (b) sharing information, (c) explaining personal motives, (d) avoiding both personal criticisms and personal favors, (e) handing out sincere rewards and recognition, and (f) being consistent in disciplining.
- **Appreciation of people as assets.** Appreciation for people is shown by (a) respecting their thoughts, feelings, values, and fears; (b) respecting their desire to lead and follow; (c) respecting their individual strengths and differences; (d) respecting their desire to be involved and to participate; (e) respecting their need to be winners; (f) respecting their need to learn, grow, and develop; (g) respecting their need for a safe and healthy workplace that is conducive to peak performance; and (h) respecting their personal and family lives.
- **Communication that is clear and candid.** Communication can be made clear and candid if coaches will do the following: (a) open their eyes and ears—observe and listen; (b) say what they want and say what they mean (be tactfully candid); (c) give feedback constantly and encourage team members to follow suit; and (d) face conflict within the team head-on; that is they don't let resentment among team members simmer until it boils over—they handle it now.
- **Ethics that are unequivocal.** Ethics can be made unequivocal by (a) working with the team to develop a code of ethics; (b) identifying ethical conflicts or potential conflicts as early as possible; (c) rewarding ethical behavior; (d) disciplining unethical behavior, and doing so consistently; and (e) before bringing in new team members, making them aware of the team's code of

ethics. In addition to these strategies, the coach should set a consistent example of unequivocal ethical behavior.

- **Team members are assets.** Professional athletes in the United States are provided the best medical, health, and fitness services in the world. In addition, they practice and perform in an environment that is as safe and healthy as it can be made. Their coaches insist on these conditions because they understand that the athletes are invaluable resources. Their performance determines the ultimate success or failure of the organization. Coaches of work teams should take a similar approach. To protect their assets (team members), coaches can apply the following strategies: (a) form a partnership between the larger organization and the team to promote healthy habits; (b) encourage monitoring and screening of high-risk conditions, such as high blood pressure, high cholesterol, and cancer; (c) promote nonsmoking; (d) encourage good nutrition and regular exercise; (e) organize classes, seminars, or workshops on such subjects as HIV/AIDS, prenatal care, stress management, stroke and heart attack prevention, workplace safety, nutrition, and ergonomics; (f) encourage upper management to establish an employee-assistance plan (EAP); and (g) stress important topics, such as accident prevention and safe work methods.

Human Diversity

Human diversity is a plus. Sports and the military have typically led American society in the drive for diversity, and both have benefited immensely as a result. To list the contributions to either sports or the military made by people of different genders, races, religions, and so on, would be a task of gargantuan proportions. Fortunately, leading organizations in the United States have followed the positive example set by sports and the military. The smart ones have learned that most of the growth in the workplace will be among women, minorities, and immigrants. These people will bring new ideas and varying perspectives, precisely what an organization needs to stay on the razor's edge of competitiveness. However, in spite of steps already taken toward making the American workplace both diverse and harmonious, wise coaches understand that people—consciously and unconsciously—tend to erect barriers between themselves and people who are different from them. This tendency can quickly undermine that trust and cohesiveness on which teamwork is built. To keep this from happening, coaches can do the following:

- **Conduct a cultural audit.** Identify the demographics, personal characteristics, cultural values, and individual differences among team members.
- **Identify the specific needs of different groups.** Ask women, ethnic minorities, and older workers to describe the unique inhibitors they face. Make sure all team members understand these barriers and then work together as a team to eliminate, overcome, or accommodate them.

- **Confront cultural clashes.** Wise coaches meet conflict among team members head-on and immediately. This approach is particularly important when the conflict is based on diversity issues. Conflicts that grow out of issues related to religion, culture, ethnicity, age, or gender are more potentially volatile than everyday disagreements over work-related concerns. Consequently, conflict that is based on or aggravated by human differences should be confronted promptly. Few things will polarize a team faster than diversity-related disagreements that are allowed to fester and grow.

- **Eliminate institutionalized bias.** A company in which the workforce had historically been predominantly male now has a workforce in which women are the majority. However, the physical facility still has 10 men's restrooms and only 2 for women. This imbalance is an example of institutionalized bias. Teams may find themselves unintentionally slighting members simply out of habit or tradition. This is the concept of *discrimination by inertia*. It happens when the demographics of a team change but its habits, traditions, procedures, and work environment do not.

An effective way to eliminate institutional bias is to circulate a blank notebook and ask team members to record—without attribution—instances and examples of institutional bias. After the initial circulation, repeat the process periodically. The coach can use the input collected to help eliminate institutionalized bias. By collecting input directly from team members and acting on it promptly, coaches can ensure that discrimination by inertia is not creating or perpetuating quiet but debilitating resentment.

HANDLING CONFLICT IN TEAMS

The following conversation took place in a meeting the authors once attended. A CEO had called together employees in his company to deal with issues that were disrupting work. Where the company wanted teamwork, it was getting conflict. Where it wanted mutual cooperation, it was getting bickering. The conversation started something like this:

CEO:	We all work for the same company, don't we?
EMPLOYEES:	[Nods of agreement.]
CEO:	We all understand that we cannot do well unless the company does well, don't we?
EMPLOYEES:	[Nods of agreement.]
CEO:	Then we want the company to do well, don't we?
EMPLOYEES:	[Nods of agreement.]
CEO:	Then we are all going to work together toward the same goal, aren't we?
EMPLOYEES:	[Silence. All employees stared uncomfortably at the floor.]

This CEO made a common mistake. He thought that employees would automatically work together as a team because this approach is so obviously the right thing to do. In other words, just give employees a chance and explain things to them and they'll work together. Some of the reasons that people might not work well in teams—reasons that, in turn, can lead to conflict—are as follows:

- Ambition to get ahead coupled with fear of being held back by the team.

- Rapid change can cause employees to conclude that they can trust no one but themselves.

- Employees who have a "me-centered" outlook can find it difficult to work with others.

- Employees steeped in the traditions of *rugged individualism* and *competition is king* can feel that cooperation is not fitting for a vigorous person or organization.

- Egos that do not like to share credit.

In addition to these personal inhibitors of teamwork and promoters of conflict, there is the *example* issue. Organizations that espouse teamwork among employees but clearly are not good team players themselves are setting an example that works against teamwork. Poor teamwork on the part of an organization will manifest itself in either or both of the following ways: (a) treating suppliers poorly, while advocating a partnership and (b) treating customers poorly, while advocating customer satisfaction.

If organizations want employees to be team players, they must set a positive example of teamwork. If organizations want employees to resolve team conflicts in a positive manner, they must set an example of resolving supplier and customer conflicts in a positive manner.

How People in Teams Respond to Conflict

People in teams respond to conflict in different ways depending on their psychological makeup, the quality of team leadership, the status of relationships within the team, and even seemingly unrelated outside factors such as financial or domestic problems. All the possible responses to conflict can be placed in one of the following categories: (1) personally negative, (2) team negative, or (3) positive. An important responsibility of team leaders is to ensure that team members respond to conflict in a positive way. A positive response to conflict is one that resolves the conflict in a way that builds team unity and supports the team's mission.

Personally Negative Responses Personally negative responses are those that are harmful to the individual in question but not necessarily to other team members. The negative results of such responses, even if they do not harm other individual team members, can harm the overall team, however. Personally negative responses are denial, retreat, and suicide. Each of these responses has its own harmful effects and its own set of recommended responses for team leaders.

Some people are so averse to human conflict that they respond by denying there is a conflict. All the while the conflict they claim does not exist and is causing them intense inner turmoil. Team members who are torn apart emotionally over a conflict, they deny the existence of, cannot focus on peak performance, continual improvement, or the team's mission. Team leaders who sense that this is happening should act immediately.

To be able to sense when a team member is responding to conflict by denial, team leaders have to get to know their team members well-enough to recognize changes in their behavior. Team leaders who think a team member is bottling up negative emotions caused by a conflict should immediately arrange a face-to-face session with the individual in question and discuss their observations. It is important to draw the employee out and help him or her confront the conflict in a positive way. An effective strategy is to draw the employee out and then allow him or her to vent. People who hold in their negative emotions are like a teapot—unless they can vent they will explode or implode. In either case, the end result is negative.

Another personally harmful response to conflict is retreat. People who retreat—physically or mentally—whenever there is a conflict hurt themselves in ways similar to those who deny the existence of a conflict. Physically retreating when there is a conflict means just what it says—walking away from the conflict without engaging. However, the more common version of the retreat response is mental retreat. Retreating mentally involves pulling back into oneself and refusing to engage. This response has an emotional effect on the individual in question which is similar to that of denial. Consequently, team leaders should deal with team members who retreat from the conflict in the same way they deal with those who deny it.

The most extreme version of the personally harmful response to conflict is suicide. This is also the rarest version of the response, but it does happen. Some people are so averse to conflict that if it persists over time with no apparent end in sight, they respond by killing themselves. In the rare cases when this happens, there are usually other emotional and psychological issues involved beyond just the ongoing stress of conflict. However, persistent and continual conflict can be the straw that finally breaks the camel's back if the individual in question is especially averse to conflict. This rare response to conflict illustrates once again why it is so important for team leaders to get to know their team members well, to observe their behavior regularly, and to act immediately if unexplained changes in behavior are seen.

Team Negative Responses Team negative responses to conflict are those in which the individuals involved attack each other. These attacks might take the form of covert backstabbing, grievances, lawsuits, physical assault, or even murder. When team members who are in conflict begin to attack each other, regardless of which attack mode they adopt, morale in the team will quickly fall followed shortly thereafter by productivity, quality, and all other performance measures. As it is with personally negative responses, it is important for team leaders to act quickly when they observe team negative responses because they have a tendency to be cumulative in nature. In other words, what starts out as covert backstabbing—if ignored by team leaders—can escalate to grievances, lawsuits, physical assault, or murder.

While it may be difficult to grasp that workplace conflict would ever escalate to the level of murder, it does happen. In fact, it happens more frequently. One of the authors had to deal with just such a situation in recent years when an individual who serviced snack machines at his campus murdered a coworker on campus. A workplace dispute escalated over time until the individual in question plotted to be on campus when his adversary was scheduled to perform routine maintenance on a soda machine. Hiding behind the machine, the angry team member waited until his colleague walked in to service the machine. Stepping quickly out of his hiding place, the angry individual fired several shots from a handgun, killing his colleague. A sad situation was made even sadder when the victim turned out to be the wrong person. The team member who was the murderer's target was tied up with other work so another team member made the fatal service call.

Instances of workplace violence such as this—although not everyday occurrences—are no longer uncommon. One needs to only watch the nightly news or read a newspaper to realize that harmful responses to conflict are becoming increasingly common. Consequently, it is important for team leaders to work closely with team members to expect and encourage positive responses to workplace conflict.

Positive Responses   A positive response to conflict in a team is one that resolves in the conflict in a way that promotes team unity and serves the team's mission. The most positive response is when team members in conflict work out their differences as responsible adults, putting aside personal issues for the good of the team. In fact, this should be the stated expectation of team leaders. This approach might involve both parties mutually agreeing to just forget it or it might involve them sitting down and negotiating with each other. In either case, what is important is that: (1) they settle their differences in a positive way and (2) they settle their differences without involving other team members or the supervisor.

When team members in a conflict either cannot or will not settle their differences by themselves, the next step on the ladder of positive responses is to take their conflict to the team leader. With this response, the team members in conflict are careful to not involve other members of the team. This is what makes this approach a positive response. Conflict between two team members can quickly spread and result in the other team members choosing sides. When this happens, the entire team will be focused on the conflict rather than peak performance and continual improvement.

When team members bring their conflict to the team leader, he or she can begin with mediation. With mediation, the team leaders are referees. They listen to both parties and

guide them to a positive reconciliation that is good for them and the team. If mediation does not work, the team leader moves to the next step: arbitration. With arbitration, team leaders act as judge rather than referee. They listen to both the sides and make a decision. Of course, it is better to reconcile team conflict through mediation than arbitration, but when team members will not cooperate they leave the team leader with no alternative.

Although mediation and arbitration are classified as positive responses to conflict, they do have a negative aspect that team members should understand. It is one thing to ask the team leader to intervene when two team members are in conflict because they are sincerely convinced that their recommendation or solution is the best one for the team, and it is the good of the team rather than ego or a personal agenda that has them digging in their heels. However, if team members must take their conflict to the team leader for resolution because their stubbornness, selfishness, or personal agendas get in the way of reconciliation, they are letting down the team.

If team leaders sense that team members in conflict are involving them for other than positive reasons, they should let them know that doing so will cost them. It will cost them in lost credibility in the eyes of the team leader, and it will cost them in terms of the conflict-resolution rating on their next performance appraisal. Bringing a conflict to the team leader is certainly better than the negative responses explained in this section, but it is the worst of the positive responses. Teams function best when their members can disagree without being disagreeable, when they can disagree over ideas and solutions without the conflict becoming personal, and when they can resolve the conflicts that inevitably arise between themselves without involving others.

Resolution Strategies for Team Conflicts

Conflict will occur in even the best teams. Even when all team members agree on a goal, they can still disagree on how best to accomplish it. Team leaders and members can apply the following strategies for preventing and resolving team conflict:[4]

- Plan and work to establish a culture where individuality and dissent are in balance with teamwork and cooperation.

- Establish clear criteria for deciding when decisions will be made by individuals and when they will be made by teams.

- Don't allow individuals to build personal empires or to use the organization to advance personal agendas.

- Encourage and recognize individual risk-taking behavior that breaks the organization out of unhelpful habits and negative mental frameworks.

- Encourage healthy, productive competition, and discourage unhealthy, counterproductive competition.

- Recognize how difficult it can be to ensure effective cooperation, and spend the energy necessary to get just the right amount of it.

- Value constructive dissent, and encourage it.
- Assign people of widely differing perspectives to every team or problem.
- Reward and recognize both dissent and teamwork when they solve problems.
- Reevaluate the project, problem, or idea when no dissent or doubt is expressed.
- Avoid hiring people who think they don't need help, who don't value cooperation, or who are driven by the desire to be accepted.
- Ingrain into new employees the need for balance between the concepts of cooperation and constructive dissent.
- Provide ways for employees to say what no one wants to hear.
- Realistically and regularly assess the ability and willingness of employees to cooperate effectively.
- Understand that some employees are going to clash, so determine where this is happening and remix rather than wasting precious organizational energy trying to get people to like each other.
- Ensure that the organization's value system and reward/ recognition systems are geared toward cooperation with constructive dissent rather than dog-eat-dog competition or cooperation at all costs.
- Teach employees how to manage both dissent (not let it get out of hand) and agreement.
- Quickly assess whether conflict is healthy or destructive, and take immediate steps to encourage the former and resolve or eliminate the latter.

STRUCTURAL INHIBITORS OF TEAMWORK

One of the primary and most common reasons that teamwork never gains a foothold in certain organizations is that those organizations fail to remove built-in structural inhibitors. A *structural inhibitor* is an administrative procedure, organizational principle, or cultural element that works against a given change—in this case, the change from individual work to teamwork. Organizations often make the mistake of espousing teamwork without first removing the structural inhibitors that will guarantee its failure.

Consider the following example of how a structural inhibitor can undermine the most well-intended plans. A college decided to implement distance learning as a delivery system for students whose personal circumstances made it difficult to attend in a traditional classroom setting. The college had no provision for paying professors extra for especially large classes. Because the physical size of classrooms limited traditional classes to 40 or fewer students, the issue had never come up. But distance learning students attend class at home. Consequently, an instructor might easily have more than 40 students. In fact, with distance learning, academic integrity was the only factor limiting class size.

When the new distance learning program was first established, the faculty showed no interest and the program fizzled. A survey of the faculty soon revealed several structural inhibitors that had guaranteed failure. The first was a salary schedule that would pay a faculty member the same for 15 students (the minimum class size) as for 100. The second was a decision-making process that gave professors no say in setting maximum enrollment limits. The final structural inhibitor was a policy that did not compensate professors for developing courses and the corresponding courseware.

These inhibitors virtually guaranteed that the college's faculty would turn its back on distance learning. However, when they were removed—with maximum input from faculty members—there was immediate buy-in and the program took off.

Structural inhibitors to effective teamwork that are commonly found in organizations:[5]

- **Unit structure.** Teams work best in a cross-functional environment as opposed to the traditional functional-unit environment. This allows teams to be process or product oriented. Failing to change the traditional unit structure can inhibit teamwork.
- **Accountability.** In a traditional organization, employees feel accountable to management. This perception can undermine teamwork. Teams work best when they feel accountable to customers. Managers in a team setting should view themselves as internal emissaries for customers.
- **Unit goals.** Traditional organizations are task oriented, and their unit goals reflect this orientation. A task orientation can undermine teamwork. Teams work best when they focus on overall process effectiveness rather than individual tasks.
- **Responsibility.** In a traditional organization, employees are responsible for their individual performance. This individual orientation can be a powerful inhibitor to teamwork. Teams work best when individual employees are held responsible for the performance of their team.
- **Compensation and recognition.** The two most common stumbling blocks to teamwork are compensation and recognition. Traditional organizations recognize individual achievements and compensate on the basis of either time or individual merit. Teams work best when both team and individual achievements are recognized and when both individual and team performances are compensated.
- **Planning and control.** In a traditional organization, managers and supervisors plan and control the work. Teams work best in a setting in which managers and teams work together to plan and control the work.

Organizations that are serious about teamwork and need the improved productivity that can result from it must begin by removing structural inhibitors. In addition to the inhibitors described earlier, managers should be diligent in rooting out others that exist in their organizations. An effective way to identify structural inhibitors in an organization is to form focus groups of employees and ask the following question: "*What existing administrative procedures, organizational principles, or cultural factors will keep us from working effectively in teams?*" Employees are closer to the most likely inhibitors on a daily basis and can, therefore, provide invaluable insight in identifying them.

REWARDING TEAM AND INDIVIDUAL PERFORMANCE

An organization's attempts to institutionalize teamwork will fail unless it includes implementation of an appropriate compensation system: in other words, if you want teamwork to work, make it pay. Employees are still compensated as individuals. The most successful compensation systems combine both individual and team pay.

This matter is important because few employees work exclusively in teams. A typical employee, even in the most team-oriented organization, spends a percentage of his or her time involved in team participation and a percentage involved in individual activities. Even those who work full-time in teams have individual responsibilities that are carried out on behalf of the team.

Consequently, the most successful compensation systems have the components shown in Figure 10–3. With such a system, all employees receive their traditional individual base pay. Then there are incentives that allow employees to increase their income by surpassing goals set for their individual performance. Finally, other incentives are based on team performance. In some cases, the amount of team compensation awarded to individual team members is based on their individual performance within the team or, in other words, on the contribution they made to the team's performance.

An example of this approach can be found in the world of professional sports. All baseball players in both the National and the American Leagues receive a base amount of individual compensation. Most also have a number of incentive clauses in their contracts to promote better individual performance. Team-based incentives are offered if the team wins the World Series or the league championship. When this happens, the players on the team divide

the incentive dollars into shares. Every member of the team receives a certain number of shares based on his perceived contribution to the team's success that year.

Figure 10–4 is a model that can be used for establishing a compensation system that reinforces both team and individual performance. The Step 1 in this model involves deciding what performance outcomes will be measured (individual and team outcomes). Step 2 involves how the outcomes will be measured. What types of data will tell the story? How can these data be collected? How frequently will the performance measurements be made? Step 3 involves deciding what types of rewards will be offered (monetary, nonmonetary, or a combination of the two). This is the step in which rewards are organized into levels that correspond to levels of performance so that the reward is in proportion to the performance.

The issue of proportionality is important when designing incentives. If just barely exceeding a performance goal results in the same reward given for substantially exceeding it, just barely is what the organization will get. If exceeding a goal by 10% results in a 10% bonus, then exceeding it by 20% should result in a 20% bonus, and so on. Proportionality and fairness are characteristics that employees scrutinize with care when examining an incentive formula. Any formula that is perceived as unfair or disproportionate will not have the desired result.

The final step in the model in Figure 10–4 involves integrating the compensation system with other performance-related processes. These systems include performance appraisal, the promotion process, and staffing. If teamwork is important, one or more criteria relating to teamwork should be included in the organization's performance appraisal process.

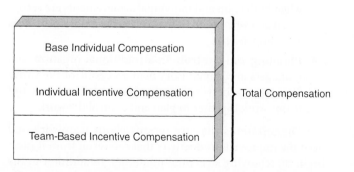

FIGURE 10–3 Typical Team Compensation Components

FIGURE 10–4 Model for Developing a Team and Individual Compensation System

Correspondingly, the employee's ratings on the teamwork criteria in a performance appraisal should be considered when making promotion decisions. An ineffective team player should not be promoted in an organization that values teamwork. Other employees will know, and teamwork will be undermined. Finally, during the selection process, applicants should be questioned concerning their views on teamwork. It is senseless for an organization that values teamwork to hire new employees who, during their interview, show no interest in or aptitude for teamwork.

Nonmonetary Rewards

A common mistake made when organizations first attempt to develop incentives is thinking that employees will respond only to dollars in a paycheck. However, nonmonetary rewards can be effective as incentives. Widely used nonmonetary rewards that have proven to be effective include the following: movie tickets, gift certificates, time off, event tickets, free attendance at seminars, getaway weekends for two, airline tickets, and prizes such as electronic or household products.

Different people respond to different incentives. Consequently, what will work can be difficult to predict. A good rule of thumb to apply when selecting nonmonetary incentives is "Don't assume—ask." Employees know what appeals to them. Before investing in nonmonetary incentives, organizations should survey their employees. List as many different potential nonmonetary rewards as possible and let employees rate them. In addition, set up the incentive system so that employees, to the extent possible, are able to select the reward that appeals to them. For example, employees who exceed performance goals (team or individual) by 10% should be allowed to select from among several equally valuable rewards on the "10% Menu." Where one employee might enjoy dinner tickets for two, another might be more motivated by tickets to a sporting event. The better an incentive program is able to respond to individual preferences, the better it will work.

RECOGNIZING TEAMWORK AND TEAM PLAYERS

One of the strongest human motivators is *recognition*. People don't just want to be recognized for their contributions; they *need* to be recognized. The military applies this fact very effectively. The entire system of military commendations and decorations (medals) is based on the positive human response to recognition. No amount of pay could compel a young soldier to perform the acts of bravery that are commonplace in the history of the United States military. But the recognition of a grateful nation continues to spur on men and women to incredible acts of valor every time our country is involved in an armed conflict. There is a lesson here for nonmilitary organizations.

The list of methods for recognizing employees goes on *ad infinitum*. There is no end to the ways that the intangible concept of employee appreciation can be expressed. What follows are just a few examples of recognition strategies:

- Write a letter to the employee's family members telling them about the excellent job the employee is doing.
- Arrange for a senior-level manager to have lunch with the employee.
- Have the CEO of the organization call the employee personally (or stop by in person) to say, "Thanks for a job well done."
- Find out what the employee's hobby is and publicly award him or her a gift relating to that hobby.
- Designate the best parking space in the lot for the "Employee of the Month."
- Create a "Wall of Fame" to honor outstanding performance.

These examples are provided to trigger ideas but are only a sampling of the many ways that employees can be recognized. Every individual organization should develop its own locally tailored recognition options. When doing so, the following rules of thumb will be helpful:

- Involve employees in identifying the types of recognition activities to be used. Employees are the best judge of what will motivate them.
- Change the list of recognition activities periodically. The same activities used over and over for too long will become stale.
- Have a variety of recognition options for each level of performance. This will allow employees to select the type of reward that appeals to them the most.

LEADING MULTICULTURAL TEAMS

Most industrialized countries are becoming more and more diverse in terms of their populations, but few can equal the level of diversity in the United States. The United States has become one of the most diverse countries in the world.

People from almost every other nation and culture in the world have immigrated and become American citizens. This means that work teams in American organizations are increasingly diverse. Leading multicultural work teams can pose several special challenges for managers, supervisors, and team leaders.

Culture-related challenges that often arise in work teams include differing (1) approaches to communicating, (2) attitudes toward work, (3) attitudes toward authority, and (4) approaches to decision making. For example, people from Western countries and particularly the United States tend to be direct and to the point when communicating ideas, recommendations, and opinions. People from Asian countries tend to be less so. This can cause miscommunication and frustration when people from the two cultures serve on the same team. In addition to the different approaches to communicating, problems can arise out of language fluency or a lack of it. People tend to think that someone who does not speak their language well is not intelligent. For example, a fluent English speaker might question the intelligence of a teammate from another country and culture whose English skills were not yet well-developed and vice versa.

Attitudes toward authority can cause problems in work teams. For example, people from Asian cultures tend to have a higher level of regard for hierarchical authority than do Westerners. In most high-performing Western organizations, all team members are expected to speak out, state opinions, make recommendations, and suggest solutions regardless of their relative rank outside of the team. However, people from Asian cultures tend to be more cognizant of challenging or disagreeing with others on the team who have more hierarchical authority outside of the team. An Asian team member would be reluctant to embarrass a person of higher authority and risk causing him or her to lose face, while people from the United States tend to view membership on a team in less hierarchical terms.

Cultural differences can also lead to differences in how decisions are made. For example, people from the United States tend to be as direct and to the point when making decisions as they are when communicating. But people from Asian and Latin countries tend to be more deliberate. In addition, once a decision is made, people from the United States like to move on to the next item. People from Asian and Latin cultures are likely to want to revisit items, even after they have been decided—at least in the minds of team members from the United States.

Strategies for Leading Multicultural Teams

People who lead multicultural teams can and should take steps to mitigate the problems that arise from the cultural differences of their team members. The following strategies can be used by those who face the challenge of leading multicultural teams:[6]

1. Adaptation. With this strategy, team members and leaders commit to adapting their attitudes and practices to accommodate cultural differences. The key to this strategy is willingness on the part of all involved to openly and objectively discuss and actually record cultural differences. Once the list of cultural differences has been developed, strategies for adapting practices and attitudes to accommodate the differences are developed. Adaptation is the most appropriate strategy for leading multicultural teams. It is particularly effective at preventing communication and decision-making conflicts because the types of cultural differences that are common in these areas are well-known. However, its underlying assumption—willingness of all involved to openly and objectively record cultural differences—will be a stretch for some teams.

2. Structural intervention. With this strategy, team members are reassigned or the team is reorganized to reduce problems growing out of interpersonal friction between and among team members or to remove a source of conflict. This strategy is particularly effective for solving problems relating to status and fluency issues. For example, if a given team member is the source of conflict within the team because he looks down on others who are not fluent English speakers, that member might need to be reassigned. If two or more team members are in conflict over perceived status issues—the team leader treats certain members better than others—the whole team might need to be reorganized.

3. Managerial guidance. With this strategy, higher management establishes ground rules—ideally before the team is constituted. This is the concept of the team charter explained earlier in this chapter. Either the team leader or a higher manager writes a mission statement for the team and then works with all team members to develop a comprehensive set of ground rules that govern how team members are expected to interact. Since the team charter has the authority of higher management but is developed with the involvement of team members, it can be an effective tool for preventing culture-related conflict in teams.

4. Exit. With this strategy, team members who are unhappy on the team and cannot be mollified by any of the other strategies are allowed to simply leave. This "opting out" strategy is the least desirable of the four presented. However, it is the most practical. There will be times when a given individual just cannot or will not fit into a team. This person might be a valuable asset to the organization but is not an effective member of the team in question. When this is the case, it is better to simply acknowledge the fact and replace him or her on the team.

SUMMARY

1. A team is a group of people with a common, collective goal. The rationale for the team approach to work is that "two heads are better than one." A group of people becomes a team when the following conditions exist: there is agreement as to the mission, members adhere to ground rules, there is a fair distribution of responsibility and authority, and people adapt to change.

2. Factors that can mitigate against the success of a team are personal identity of team members, relationships among team members, and the team's identity within the organization.

3. After a team has been formed, a mission statement should be drafted. A good mission statement summarizes the team's reason for being in existence. It should be broad enough to encompass all the team is expected to do but specific enough to allow for the measurement of progress. The mission statement should be accompanied by a set of ground rules.

4. Character traits that promote successful teamwork are honesty/integrity, selflessness, dependability, enthusiasm, responsibility, cooperativeness, initiative, patience, resourcefulness, punctuality, tolerance/sensitivity, and perseverance.

5. Teams are coached—they are not bossed. Coaches are facilitators and mentors. They promote mutual respect among team members and foster cultural diversity.

6. People in teams respond to a conflict in one of the following three ways: (1) personally negative, (2) team negative, or (3) positive.

7. Employees will not always work well together as a team just because it's the right thing to do. Employees might not be willing to trust their performance, in part, to other employees.

8. Common structural inhibitors in organizations are unit structure, accountability, unit goals, responsibility, compensation, recognition, planning, and control.

9. Team and individual compensation systems can be developed in four steps: (1) decide what performance to measure, (2) determine how to measure the performance, (3) identify the rewards to be offered, and (4) integrate related processes.

10. Challenges faced when leading multicultural teams include differing (1) approaches to decision making, (2) attitudes toward authority, (3) attitudes toward work, and (4) approaches to communication.

KEY TERMS AND CONCEPTS

Charter
Coaching
Collegial relationships
Conflict
Diversity
Ground rules
Mission statement
Needs assessment
Nonmonetary rewards
Proportionality
Structural inhibitors
Task force
Team building
Teamwork

FACTUAL REVIEW QUESTIONS

1. What is a team, and why are teams important?
2. When does a group of people become a team?
3. Explain the strategies for being an effective team leader.
4. What are the characteristics of a good team mission statement?
5. Define the concept of collegial relationships.
6. Describe how to promote diversity in teams.
7. Explain the concept of institutionalized bias.
8. Explain why some employees are not comfortable being team players.
9. List and describe four common structural inhibitors of teamwork in organizations.
10. Explain the concept of nonmonetary rewards.

CRITICAL THINKING ACTIVITY

Everybody Talks About Teamwork, but Nobody Does It

Teamwork is not working at Southeastern Electric Company (SEC). Juan Morales, quality director for SEC, is growing increasingly frustrated. The company's executive managers all advocate teamwork. A cross-functional team developed a promotional campaign with a teamwork motto, banners, bulletins, and a video. Everybody talks about teamwork, but nobody does it. Juan doesn't know what to do. If he asked for your advice, what would you tell him to do? How can he identify the problem, and what steps should he take to resolve it?

DISCUSSION ASSIGNMENT 10–1

It is important to learn how to develop a comprehensive, clearly articulated team charter. Assume that you and your fellow students are a team in an organization (you choose the kind and size of organization). The task is to develop a team charter.

DISCUSSION QUESTIONS

Discuss the following questions in class or outside of class with your fellow students:

1. Discuss with your class members how you would go about developing a team charter.

2. Following the discussion, each student should develop a comprehensive team charter. Once this assignment has been completed, exchange charters with your classmates and compare them. Discuss any differences and revise the individual charters to strengthen them, based on the discussion.

ENDNOTES

1. Institute for Corporate Competitiveness, *Final Report: Team Success Study*, 3rd ed. (Niceville, FL: Institute for Corporate Competitiveness, 2011), 3–4.

2. Ibid., 5, 10.

3. David Cottrell, *Monday Morning Mentoring: Ten Lessons to Guide You Up the Ladder* (New York: Harper Collins, 2006), 12.

4. "Resolving Conflict in Work Teams." Retrieved from www.innovativeteambuilding.co.uk/pages/articles/conflicts.htm on January 15, 2011.

5. Patrick M. Lencioni, "The Trouble with Teamwork." Retrieved from http://chapters.ewb.ca/pages/president/leadership-articles-and-links/The%20Trouble%20with%20Teamwork.pdf on March 4, 2011.

6. Jeanne Brett, Kristen Behfar, and Mary C. Kern, "Managing Multicultural Teams," *Harvard Business Review* 84 (November 2006): 88–91.

EFFECTIVE COMMUNICATION

Communicating is depositing a part of yourself in another person. —***Anonymous***

MAJOR TOPICS
- **Defining Communication**
- **Understanding the Role of Communication in Total Quality**
- **Understanding Communication as a Process**
- **Recognizing Inhibitors of Communication**
- **Establishing a Conducive Communication Climate**
- **Communicating by Listening**
- **Understanding Nonverbal Communication Factors**
- **Communicating Verbally**
- **Communicating in Writing**
- **Communicating Corrective Feedback**
- **Improving Communication**
- **How Interpersonal Skills Affect Communication**
- **Personality and Communication**

Of all the many skills needed by managers in a total quality setting, communication skills are the most important. All of the other total quality components and strategies presented in this book depend either directly or indirectly on effective communication. Communication is fundamental to leadership, decision making, problem solving, teamwork, training, employee involvement and empowerment, ethics, and all other areas of concern to modern managers. This chapter seeks to help practicing and prospective managers accomplish the following:

- Improve communication skills
- Improve interpersonal skills

These are critical skills in a total quality setting. Effective communication is essential to quality, productivity, and competitiveness.

DEFINING COMMUNICATION

Inexperienced managers sometimes confuse telling with communicating and hearing with listening. Then, when a problem arises, they blame everyone else but themselves. The following quotation illustrates the point that telling and hearing don't necessarily result in communication: "I know you believe you understand what you think I said, but I am not sure you realize that what you heard is not what I meant."

What you say is not necessarily what the other person hears, and what the other person hears is not necessarily what you intended to say. What is missing here is the understanding. Communication may involve telling, but it is much more than just telling. Communication may involve hearing, but it is much more than just hearing. For the purpose of this book, *communication* is defined as follows:

> Communication is the transfer of a message (information, idea, emotion, intent, feeling, or something else) that is both received and understood.

A message may be sent by one person and received by another, but until the message is understood by both, no communication has occurred (see Figure 11–1). This applies to all forms of communication, including verbal, nonverbal, and written.

Effective Communication in Total Quality

When the message received is understood, there is communication. However, communication by itself is not

FIGURE 11–1 Communication

necessarily effective communication. Effective communication means that the message is received, understood, and acted on in the desired manner. It is the sender's responsibility to ensure that there is effective communication.

For example, suppose a manager asks her team members to stay 15 minutes after quitting time for the next week to ensure that an important order goes out on schedule. Each team member receives the message and verifies that he or she understands it. However, two team members decide they are not going to comply. This is an example of ineffective communication. The two nonconforming employees understood the message but decided against complying with it. The manager in this case failed to achieve acceptance of the message.

Effective communication is a higher order of communication. It involves receiving, understanding, and acting on the message. This means that effective communication may require persuasion, motivation, monitoring, and leadership on the part of managers.

Communication Levels

Figure 11–2 shows the various levels at which communication can take place in a company. These levels are explained as follows:

- One-on-one–level communication involves one person communicating with one other person. This might involve a face-to-face conversation, a telephone call, or even a simple gesture or facial expression.
- Team- or unit-level communication is communication within a peer group. The primary difference between

one-on-one–level and team-level communication is that, with the latter, all team members are involved in the process at once. A team meeting called to solve a problem or to set goals would be an opportunity for team-level communication.

- Company-level communication is communication among groups. A meeting involving various different departments within a company is an opportunity for company-level communication.
- Community-level communication occurs among groups inside a company and groups outside the company. Perhaps the most common examples of community-level communication are a company's sales force communicating with clients and its purchasing department communicating with vendors.

UNDERSTANDING THE ROLE OF COMMUNICATION IN TOTAL QUALITY

If total quality is the engine, communication is the oil that keeps it running. Much of what total quality is all about depends on effective communication. Without it, total quality breaks down. Some of the key elements of the total quality concept are customer focus (internal and external), total employee involvement and empowerment, leadership, teamwork, decision making, problem prevention, problem solving, and conflict resolution. Each of these elements is dependent on effective communication.

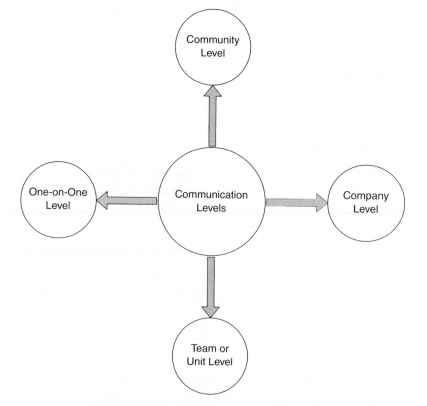

FIGURE 11–2 Communication Levels

QUALITY TIP ▼

Communicating the Importance of Quality

Organizations that want their personnel to commit to quality have to communicate the importance of quality. Communicating the importance of quality can be done in a number of ways that are as follows: (1) making quality a core value in the organization's strategic plan, (2) including quality expectations in all job descriptions, (3) including criteria about quality in all performance appraisal instruments, (4) posting quality benchmarks along with actual performance, (5) making decisions on the basis of how they will affect quality, and (6) talking about quality every time any group or team meets.

Customer focus means basing decisions and actions on the needs of customers. Determining the needs of customers involves listening, asking, observing, and probing, while simultaneously being mindful of not just what is said but also how it is said, and additionally what isn't said. Total employee involvement and empowerment require the establishment of a workplace environment that promotes open, frank communication.

Effective leadership by definition requires effective communication. Effective leaders are those who inspire others to make a full and willing commitment to the organization's goals. To accomplish this, managers must communicate with employees about the organization's goals and how accomplishing these goals will, in turn, help employees accomplish their own personal goals.

Teamwork, by its very nature, depends on communication. To succeed, a team must be comprised of employees who are informed concerning team goals, how they are to be accomplished, who is responsible for what, and how it all fits together. This means that team members must continually communicate among themselves, with managers, and with other teams, and their communication must be effective. This dependence on communication also applies in decision making, problem prevention, problem solving, and conflict resolution. Clearly, communication plays a critical role in total quality. The role it plays is *facilitation*.

UNDERSTANDING COMMUNICATION AS A PROCESS

Communication is a process with several components (see Figure 11–3). These components are the message, the sender, the receiver, and the medium. The *sender* is the originator or source of the message. The *receiver* is the person or group for whom the message is intended. The *message* is the information, idea, feeling, or intent that is to be conveyed, understood, accepted, and acted on. The *medium* is the vehicle used to convey the message.

There are four basic categories of media: verbal, nonverbal, written, and electronic. The *verbal* category includes face-to-face conversations, telephone conversations, speeches, public address announcements, press conferences, and other approaches for conveying the spoken word. The *nonverbal* category includes gestures, facial expressions, and body language. The *written* category includes letters, memorandums, billboards, bulletin boards, manuals, books, and any other method of conveying the written word. The *electronic* category includes the transmission of digital data as well as any other form of electronic transmission that can be converted into a message understood by humans (e.g., the dot and dash impulses of a telegraph).

Technological developments are having a major impact on our ability to convey information. These developments include word processing, satellite communication, computer modems, cordless telephones, cellular telephones, telephone answering machines, facsimile machines, pocket-sized dictation machines, and electronic mail. No matter how advanced these communication-enhancing devices have become, as many inhibitors of effective communication as there ever were still exist—maybe even more. Modern managers should be familiar with these inhibitors in order to be able to avoid or overcome them.

RECOGNIZING INHIBITORS OF COMMUNICATION

Managers should be familiar with the various factors that can inhibit effective communication in the workplace. If properly handled, these inhibitors can be overcome or avoided. The most common inhibitors of effective communication are as follows (see Figure 11–4):

- **Differences in meaning.** Differences in meaning can cause problems in communication. People have different backgrounds, levels of education, and cultures. As a result, words, gestures, and facial expressions can have altogether different meanings to different people. This is why managers should invest time getting to know employees.

- **Lack of trust.** A lack of trust can inhibit effective communication. If receivers do not trust senders, they may be overly sensitive and guarded. They might concentrate so hard on reading between the lines and looking for hidden agendas that they miss the message. This is

FIGURE 11–3 Communication as a Process

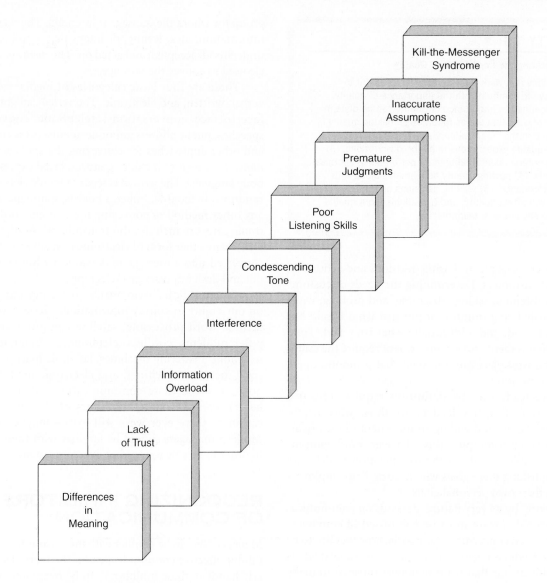

FIGURE 11–4 Inhibitors of Communication

why trust building between managers and employees is so important.

- **Information overload.** Information overload is more of an inhibitor than it has ever been. Computer modems, satellite communication, facsimile machines, e-mail, and the many other technological devices developed to promote and enhance communications can actually cause communication breakdown.

  Because of advances in communication technology and the rapid and continual proliferation of information, employees and managers often receive more information than they can deal with effectively. This is *information overload*. Managers can guard against information overload by screening, organizing, summarizing, and simplifying the information they convey to employees.

- **Interference.** Interference is any external distraction that inhibits effective communication. It might be something as simple as background noise or as complex

as atmospheric interference with satellite communications. Regardless of its source, interference distorts or completely blocks out the message. This is why managers must be attentive to the environment in which they plan to communicate.

- **Condescending tone.** A condescending tone when conveying information can inhibit effective communication. People do not like to be talked down to, and they typically respond to tone of voice as much as or more than the content of the message. It is a mistake to talk down to employees.

- **Poor listening skills.** Poor listening skills can seriously inhibit effective communication. Problems can result when the sender does not listen to the receiver and vice versa.

- **Premature judgments.** Premature judgments by either the sender or the receiver can inhibit effective communication. This is primarily because such judgments interfere with listening. When people make a judgment, they are prone to stop listening at that point. One cannot make premature judgments and maintain an open mind. Therefore, it is important for managers to listen nonjudgmentally when talking with employees.

- **Inaccurate assumptions.** Our perceptions are influenced by our assumptions. Consequently, inaccurate assumptions tend to shut down communication before it has a chance to get started.

- **Kill-the-messenger syndrome.** In the days when gladiators dueled in Rome's Coliseum, it was common practice to kill the bearer of bad news. A more civilized version of this practice is still very common, particularly in the workplace. Managers who "kill the messenger" when an employee tells the hard truth will eventually hear only what employees think management wants to hear. This dangerous situation quickly leads to uninformed, ill-advised managers.

ESTABLISHING A CONDUCIVE COMMUNICATION CLIMATE

Organizations that want effective communication must establish a climate that is conducive to communication. Such a climate is one in which people not only feel free to communicate, but also are expected to communicate. The information flow is two-way, continual, and intended to give people the information they need to achieve peak performance and continual improvement as they do their jobs. A bad communication climate is one in which information is pigeon-holed, people are afraid to ask questions, and organizational leaders consider knowledge as power—hence they keep it to themselves.

The following strategies will help organizational leaders establish and maintain a climate that is conducive to effective communication:

- Communicate often and openly. Avoid the *Knowledge-is-Power* Syndrome and communicate to empower.

- Condense the information to be communicated to a form that is easy for the recipient to absorb, understand, and remember. Avoid burying people in data rather than giving them information.

QUALITY TIP ▼

Verbal Communication and Stories

One of the highest levels of verbal communication occurs when speakers use stories to make their point. Using stories to illustrate the point one is trying to make is an excellent way to ensure that listeners understand what is being said and remember it. People listen to stories more attentively than to normal conversation. Notice how children will gather around and listen attentively when an adult tells a story. Adults are not different. They too will listen attentively to a story.

- Communicate with everyone who can benefit from the information in question. Avoid leaving people out of the loop.

- Encourage questions, comments, different perspectives, opposing opinions, and better ideas and take them seriously. Avoid one-way communication.

- Listen assertively and objectively. Avoid shooting the messenger when the news being communicated is bad or unwelcome.

These strategies will help organizational leaders create a climate in which effective communication is not just possible, it is the norm.

COMMUNICATING BY LISTENING

One of the most important communication skills is listening. It is also the skill people are least likely to have. Are you a good listener? Complete the listening skills assessment in Figure 11–5 to find out.

If you are a good listener, your answers to the questions in Figure 11–5 will be as follows: 1, no; 2, no; 3, no; 4, yes; 5, no; 6, no; 7, yes; 8, no; 9, no; and 10, no.

Good listeners typically listen more than they talk. It's one of the reasons they are good listeners. Interrupting people before they complete a statement is a sign of impatience and lack of interest in what is being said. This can have a doubly negative effect on communication. First, interrupting a speaker lessens the listener's chances of properly perceiving what is being said. Second, it can turn the speaker off because it sends the message, "I don't have time to listen to you."

People who tune out and think ahead to their response have more interest in their own message than that of the speaker. Accurate perception is difficult enough when tuned in. It is impossible when tuned out. A tuned-in listener should be able to digest a speaker's message, paraphrase it, and repeat it back. Paraphrasing does not mean parroting back the speaker's exact words: it means summarizing the message in your own words. This lets speakers know they have been heard and understood.

Stating an opinion before a speaker has finished his or her message and continuing to do other tasks while someone is speaking both send the same message: "I don't want to hear it." Managers who send this message will get what they ask for. The problem with this is that in a total quality setting, managers *need* to hear it.

Even the best listeners sometimes must ask questions for clarification. When the message isn't clear, managers should ask questions. Not only does questioning improve perception, but also it shows the speaker that the listener is tuned in and wants to understand. There are two ways to handle questions. The first is to wait until the speaker pauses or begins to move on to another train of thought. This is an appropriate time to raise a question; doing so at this point will not cause the speaker to lose his or her original train of thought. However, if it is critical that a point be clarified

QUESTION	RESPONSE	
	Yes	No
1. When in a group of people, do you talk more than you listen?		
2. When talking with someone, do you frequently interrupt before he or she completes a statement?		
3. In conversations, do you tune out and think ahead to your response?		
4. In a typical conversation, can you paraphrase what the speaker has said and repeat it?		
5. When talking, do you frequently state your opinion before the other parties have made their case?		
6. Do you continue doing other tasks when someone is talking with you?		
7. Do you ask for clarification when you don't understand what has been said?		
8. Do you frequently tune out and daydream during meetings?		
9. Do you fidget and sneak glances at your watch during conversations?		
10. Do you find yourself finishing statements for people who don't move the conversation along fast enough?		

FIGURE 11–5 Listening Skills Assessment

immediately, stopping the speaker by raising a hand in a gesture that says "Hold on a moment" is acceptable. If it is necessary to stop a speaker in this way, make a mental or written note of where he or she left off, in case a reminder is needed to get the conversation started again.

Daydreaming during meetings and sneaking glances at a watch both make the same statement: "I've got something better to be doing with my time." Time pressures and conflicting demands for a manager's time will always exist, but few things a manager does are as important as listening to employees. Managers who find themselves tuning out at meetings and stealing glances at their watches during conversations should give some thought to how they are organizing and managing their time.

Finishing sentences for people who don't move the conversation along fast enough sends the message, "I am in too big a hurry to listen to you." Of course, this might legitimately be the case. When it is, rather than finishing sentences for an employee, managers will get better results by saying, "I don't have time to give you the attention you deserve right now; let's compare schedules and find a time that works for both of us."

What Is Listening?

Hearing is a natural process, but listening is not. A person with highly sensitive hearing abilities can be a poor listener. Conversely, a person with impaired hearing can be an excellent listener. *Hearing* is the physiological decoding of sound waves, but *listening* involves perception. Listening can be defined in numerous different ways. In this book, we use the following definition:

Effective listening means receiving the message, correctly decoding it, and accurately perceiving what it means.

Inhibitors of Effective Listening

Effective listening occurs when the receiver accurately perceives the message. Unfortunately, several inhibitors can prevent this from happening. These inhibitors include the following (see Figure 11–6):

- Lack of concentration
- Interruptions
- Preconceived ideas

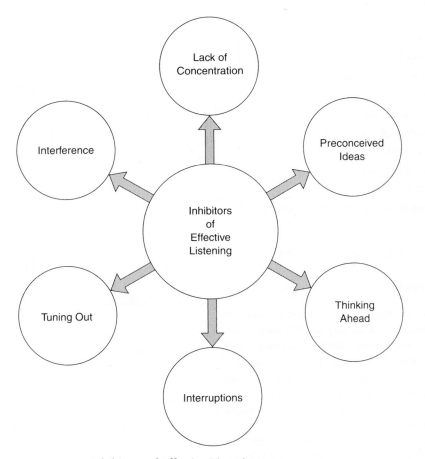

FIGURE 11-6 Inhibitors of Effective Listening

- Thinking ahead
- Interference
- Tuning out

To perceive a message accurately, listeners must concentrate on what is being said, how it is being said, and in what tone it is being said. Part of effective listening is properly reading nonverbal cues (discussed in the next section).

Concentration requires the listener to eliminate as many extraneous distractions as possible and to mentally shut out the rest. J. Lamar Roberts, chief executive officer and president of a successful and dynamic community bank, requires his managers to keep their desks clear of all projects except the one being worked on at the moment. In this way, when an employee enters the office, this project can be easily pushed aside, leaving a clean desk. Work left on the desk can distract the manager and make the employee feel like an intruder. Managers who jump to preconceived notions don't give themselves a chance to listen effectively. Preconceived ideas can cause them to make premature judgments that turn out to be wrong. Even the most experienced managers are better off waiting patiently and listening.

Managers who jump ahead to where they think the conversation is going often get there only to find they are alone. Thinking ahead is typically a response to being hurried, but managers will find that it takes less time to hear an employee out than it does to start over after jumping ahead to the wrong conclusion.

Interruptions not only inhibit effective listening, but also can frustrate and confuse the speaker. If clarification is needed during a conversation, it is best to make a mental note and wait for the speaker to reach an interim stopping point. Mental notes are always preferable to written notes. The act of writing notes may distract the speaker or cause the listener to miss a critical point. If managers find it necessary to make written notes, they should keep them short and to a minimum.

Tuning out inhibits effective listening. Some people become skilled at using body language to make it appear they are listening, while, in reality, their minds are focused on other areas of concern. Managers should avoid the temptation to engage in such ploys. Skilled speakers may ask the manager to repeat or paraphrase what they just said.

Interference is anything that distracts the listener, thereby impeding either hearing or perception, or both. Background noises, a telephone ringing, and people walking in and out of the office are all examples of interference. Such distractions should be eliminated before beginning a conversation. If they can't be, the conversation should be moved to another location. Figure 11-7 provides a checklist managers can use to improve their listening skills.

- ☑ Remove all distractions.
- ☑ Put the speaker at ease.
- ☑ Look directly at the speaker.
- ☑ Concentrate on what is being said.
- ☑ Watch for nonverbal cues.
- ☑ Make note of the speaker's tone.
- ☑ Be patient and wait.
- ☑ Ask clarifying questions.
- ☑ Paraphrase and repeat.
- ☑ No matter what is said, control your emotions.

FIGURE 11–7 Listening Improvement Checklist

Listening Assertively

It is important to properly perceive messages that are received from others in an organization. One way to improve perception is to learn to listen assertively. Effective listening is not a passive undertaking. Rather, to properly perceive what is being said in a conversation requires that people focus on what is being said, block out distractions, concentrate, watch for nonverbal cues, and apply both experience and intuition. In other words, people need to learn to listen assertively.

There is another aspect of assertive learning that deserves its own explanation. This aspect is empathy. When empathy is added to the mix, the chances of correctly perceiving what is being said increase markedly. Empathetic listening amounts to listeners putting themselves in the shoes of the speaker, trying to understand not just what is being said but the speaker's point of view and perspective—the *why* behind what is being said. Empathetic listening is the highest level of listening. It can move the listener from just perceiving what is said to understanding what the speaker felt when he or she said it. Empathetic listening can help listeners understand not just the message but the motivation behind the message. This level of understanding can be invaluable to organizational leaders as they strive to continually improve quality.

Listening Responsively

Responsive listening, like the other approaches explained in this chapter, is a way to ensure effective listening.[1] Responsive listening involves seeking to receive and affirm the messenger as well as the message. Figure 11–8 names descriptors associated with responsive listening. To listen responsively, managers and employees must learn to simultaneously use their ears, eyes, brains, and hearts.

Responsive listening can pay substantial dividends for managers in a total quality setting. Personal benefits to managers include these:

- Barriers are broken down.
- Valuable insights are gained.
- Communication is encouraged.

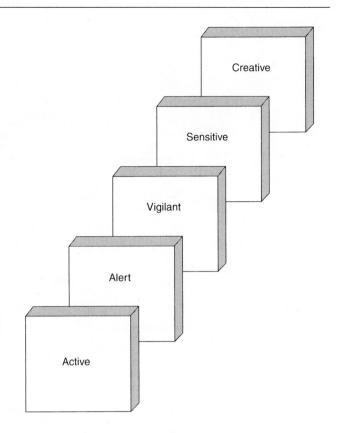

Creative

Sensitive

Vigilant

Alert

Active

FIGURE 11–8 Descriptors of Responsive Listening

- Misconceptions are cleared up.
- Learning takes place.

Some pointers that managers can use to become more responsive listeners and to help employees do the same include these:

- **Slow down.** Managers who respond, "OK, I can give you 2 minutes," when an employee needs to talk will not be responsive listeners. Hurrying an employee will only inhibit effective communication.
- **Allocate your listening time.** There will be times when managers do not have time to listen. This is to be expected. As important as listening is, there is more to management than listening. If an employee wants to talk at a bad time, rather than rushing him or begrudgingly stopping and listening halfheartedly, set up a time that is more conducive to responsive listening.
- **Concentrate fully.** Focus intently and simultaneously on both the verbal and the nonverbal aspects of the message. Remove all distractions, physical and mental.
- **Grant a fair hearing.** This means laying aside preconceived notions, biases, and prejudices. Managers should be especially attentive to avoiding the tendency to let an employee's lack of speaking ability bias them against the message. A message may have value, even if it isn't delivered well.
- **Make it easy for the person to talk.** A friendly smile, a warm handshake, a relaxed attitude, a comfortable

chair, and reassuring nonverbal cues will encourage the speaker. These efforts are especially important with employees who are reluctant or who find it difficult to communicate. This strategy applies regardless of the nature of the message. In other words, managers should make it easy for employees to talk even when they bring an unwelcome message.

- **Understand completely.** Practice paraphrasing and restating what has been said, and ask questions for clarification to ensure complete understanding. Never allow a conversation to end vaguely. Managers should make sure that they understand the message and that employees know they understand the message before concluding a conversation.

- **Clarify expectations.** Before ending a conversation, the wise manager asks, "What would you like me to do?" Even if the message is clear, it's a good idea to ask the question rather than making an assumption. A manager may or may not be able to fulfill the request. However, before concluding the conversation, the manager and employee should both know exactly what is going to happen, and when.

Improving Listening Skills

Most people have room for improvement in their listening skills. Fortunately, listening skills can be enhanced, particularly when there is an awareness of the need to improve. Managers can apply the following strategies for improving their listening skills:

- **Listen more and talk less.** Good management requires that managers listen more and talk less. For many managers, this will require a concerted and conscious effort to suppress the natural desire to talk. This is the verbal equivalent of sitting on your hands. Another strategy is to make a conscious effort to learn as much as possible from every conversation. This will force the issue of listening instead of talking.

- **Ask clarifying questions.** Two managers can hear the same words but receive different messages. Consequently, it is important to ask questions that will clarify the message. Three types of questions can be helpful in this regard. The first type of question is used to move the speaker on to his or her next point ("I understood your first concern; is there a second?"). The second type of question is used to gain an intermediate summary of the conversation before moving on to a new point ("Can you summarize this concern before we move to the next one?"). The third type of question is used to obtain a summary of the entire conversation ("Before leaving, can you summarize your major concerns for me?").

- **Listen intuitively.** This is a matter of listening to more than just words. It also involves observing nonverbal cues, rate of speech, tone of voice, intensity of the speaker, enthusiasm or a lack of it, and context clues. It involves going beyond what is said to *why* it is being said.

- **Concentrate.** Listening errors include failing to concentrate, tuning out, giving in to distractions, and interrupting. To eliminate these errors, keep tabs on how frequently you make each kind. After every conversation for a given week, jot down the listening errors you made during the conversation. This will help focus your efforts on correcting the listening errors you make most frequently.

UNDERSTANDING NONVERBAL COMMUNICATION FACTORS

Much of communication is nonverbal. Posture, gestures (body language), voice tone, and proximity speak as loudly as words. Table 11–1 lists the components of nonverbal communication.

Body Factors

Posture, body poses, facial expressions, gestures, and dress can convey a message. Even such extras as makeup or the lack of it, well-groomed or unkempt hair, and shined or scruffy shoes can convey a message. Managers should be attentive to these body factors and how they add to or distract from the verbal message.

One of the keys to understanding nonverbal cues lies in the concept of *congruence*. Are the spoken message and the nonverbal message congruent? They should be. *Incongruence* is when words say one thing but the nonverbal cues say another. When the verbal and nonverbal aspects of the message are not congruent, managers should take the time to dig a little deeper. An effective way to deal with incongruence is to confront it gently, with a simple statement such as "Mary, your words say one thing, but your nonverbal cues say something else."

Voice Factors

Voice factors are an important part of nonverbal communication. In addition to listening to the words, managers should listen for such factors as volume, tone, pitch of voice, and rate of speech. These factors can indicate anger, fear, impatience, unsureness, interest, acceptance, confidence, and a variety of other messages. As with body factors, it is

TABLE 11–1 Components of Nonverbal Communication

Body Factors	Voice Factors	Proximity Factors
Posture	Volume	Relative positions
Dress	Pitch	Physical arrangements
Gestures	Tone	Color of the room or environment
Facial expressions	Rate of speech	Fixtures
Body poses		

important to look for congruence. It is also advisable to look for groups of nonverbal cues.

Managers can mislead themselves by attaching too much meaning to isolated nonverbal cues. A single cue taken out of context might have little importance, but as part of a group of cues, it can take on significant meaning. For example, if you look through the office window and see a man leaning over a desk pounding his fist on it, it would be tempting to interpret this as a gesture of anger. But what kind of look does he have on his face? Is his facial expression congruent with desk-pounding anger? Or, could he simply be trying to knock loose a desk drawer that has become stuck? If he is pounding on the desk with a frown on his face and yelling in an agitated tone, your assumption of anger is probably correct. He might just be angry because his desk drawer is stuck, but he would still be angry.

Proximity Factors

Proximity involves factors ranging from where you position yourself when talking with an employee, to how your office is arranged, to the color of the walls, to the types of fixtures and decorations. A manager who sits next to an employee conveys a different message than one who sits across a desk from the employee. A manager who goes to the trouble to make his or her office a comfortable place to visit is sending a message that invites communication. A manager who maintains a stark, impersonal office sends the opposite message.

To send the nonverbal message that employees are welcome to stop and talk, try using the following strategies:

- Have comfortable chairs available for visitors.
- Arrange chairs so that you can sit beside visitors rather than behind your desk.
- Choose soft, soothing colors rather than harsh, stark, or overly bright or busy colors.
- If possible, have refreshments such as coffee, soda, and snacks available for visitors to your office.

COMMUNICATING VERBALLY

Verbal communication ranks close to listening in its importance in a total quality setting. Managers can improve their verbal communication skills by being attentive to the factors shown in Figure 11–9. These factors are explained in the following paragraphs.

- **Show interest.** When speaking with employees, show an interest in the topic of conversation. Show that you are sincerely interested in communicating your message to them. Also show interest in the receivers of the message. Look them in the eye, and when in a group, spread your eye contact evenly among all receivers.
- **Be friendly.** A positive, friendly attitude will enhance verbal communication. A caustic, superior, condescending, or disinterested attitude will shut off commu-

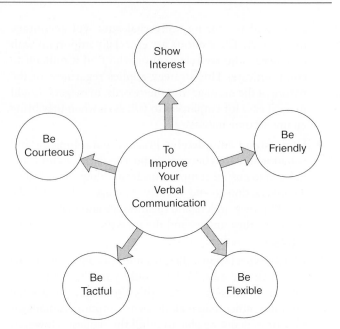

FIGURE 11–9 Improvement of Verbal Communication Skills

nication; so will an argumentative attitude. Be patient, be friendly, and *smile*.

- **Be flexible.** Flexibility can enhance verbal communication. For example, if a manager calls her team together to explain a new company policy but finds they are uniformly focused on a problem that is disrupting their work schedule, she must be flexible enough to put her message aside for the moment and deal with the problem. Until the employees work through what is on their minds, they will not be good listeners.
- **Be tactful.** Tact is an important ingredient in verbal communication, particularly when delivering a sensitive or potentially controversial message. Tact has been called the ability to "hammer in the nail without breaking the board." The key to tactful verbal communication lies in thinking before talking.
- **Be courteous.** Courtesy promotes effective verbal communication. Being courteous means showing appropriate concern for the receiver's needs. For example, calling a meeting 10 minutes before the quitting time is discourteous and will inhibit communication. Courtesy also means not monopolizing. When communicating verbally, give the receiver ample opportunities to ask questions, seek clarification, and state his or her point of view.

Asking Questions Effectively

In addition to applying the strategies just explained, managers should learn to be skilled questioners. Knowing how and when to question is an important verbal communication skill. It is how managers get at what employees really think and feel. Some general rules of questioning that professional counselors use to draw out their clients' feelings

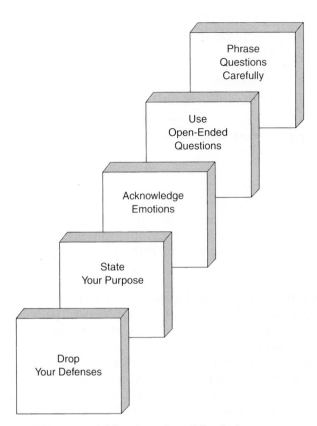

FIGURE 11–10 Asking Questions Effectively

and thoughts can be listed. Modern managers can apply these same rules to enhance their verbal communication with employees (Figure 11–10).

- **Drop your defenses.** Human interaction is emotional interaction. There is no such thing as fully objective discourse between people. All people have their public and private faces; rarely does what is said completely match what is felt. People learn early in life to build walls and put up defenses. To communicate effectively, it is necessary to get behind the walls and break through the defenses. A strategy counselors use for this is dropping their defenses first. When employees see you open up, they will be more likely to follow suit and respond more openly to your questions.

- **State your purpose.** The silent question people often ask themselves when asked a question is "Why is he asking that—what does he really want?" You will learn more from your questions by stating your purpose at the outset. This will allow the receiver to focus on your question rather than worrying about why you are asking it.

- **Acknowledge emotions.** Avoid what counselors call the "Elephant-in-the-Living Room" Syndrome when questioning employees. Human emotions can be difficult to deal with. As a result, some people respond by ignoring them. This is like walking around an elephant in the living room and pretending you don't see it. Ignoring the emotions of people you question may cause them to close up. If a person shows anger, you

might respond by saying, "I can see I've made you angry" or "You seem to feel strongly about this." Such nonjudgmental acknowledgments will often draw a person out.

- **Use open-ended questions and phrase questions carefully.** To learn the most from your questions, make them open ended. This allows the person being questioned to do most of the talking, and in turn, you to do most of the listening. Counselors feel they learn more when listening than when talking. Closed-ended questions force restricted or limited responses. For example, the question "Can we meet our deadline?" will probably elicit a yes-or-no response. However, the question "What do you think about this deadline?" gives the responder room to offer opinions and other potentially useful information.

Practice using these questioning techniques at home, at work, and even in social settings. It will take practice to internalize them to the point that they become natural. However, with effort managers can become skilled questioners and, as a result, more effective communicators.

QUALITY CASE ▼

AtlantiCare and the "Voice of the Customer"

Located in southeastern New Jersey, AtlantiCare is a nonprofit organization that provides acute and chronic health care services in the following areas: cancer, trauma, cardiac care, stroke, behavioral health, urgent care, hospice, home care, family medicine, occupational medicine, child care, early learning, and mission care for the homeless. Because of the nature of the services it provides quality is essential at AtlantiCare, and the organization delivers it. In fact, AtlantiCare applies the principles of total quality so comprehensively and consistently that the organization has received the prestigious Malcolm Baldrige National Quality Award.

At the core of AtlantiCare's quality program is a process the organization calls the "Voice of the Customer." This is a five-phase process used to make the organization's patients partners in its continual-improvement efforts. Voice of the Customer identifies patient requirements and then makes sure that AtlantiCare's services satisfy these requirements. The company's customer focus does not stop with external customers. It also includes internal customers—employees. AtlantiCare's employee loyalty index score from an Allegiance Technologies survey is at the top of the healthcare industry. Nursing has one of the highest turnover rates of any occupation. However, by focusing on the needs of its internal customers AtlantiCare has been able to maintain one of the lowest nurse turnover rates in the health care industry, a rate that continues to improve. In New Jersey, the average turnover rate for nurses is more than 12%. AtlantiCare's nurse turnover rate is approximately 6%.

By focusing on both external and internal customers and being responsive to their needs while applying the various other principles of total quality, AtlantiCare has become a world-class health care provider.

Source: www.nist.gov.

COMMUNICATING IN WRITING

The ability to communicate effectively in writing is important for managers in a total quality setting. The types of writing required of managers can be mastered, like any other skill, with the appropriate mix of coaching, practice, and genuine effort to improve. This section provides the coaching. Managers must provide the practice and effort for themselves.

Helpful Rules

Several rules of thumb that can enhance the effectiveness of your written communication are shown in Figure 11–11. These rules of thumb are explained in the following sections:

Plan Before You Write   One reason some people have trouble writing effectively is that they start writing before deciding what they want to say. This is like getting in a car and driving before deciding where to go. The route is sure to be confusing, as will the message, if you write without planning first.

Planning a memorandum or letter is a simple process. It is a matter of deciding to whom you are writing, why, and what you want to say. Figure 11–12 is a planning sheet that will help you plan before you write.

- Plan before you write.
- Be brief.
- Be direct.
- Be accurate.
- Practice self-editing.

FIGURE 11–11 Strategies for Improved Written Communication

Taking the time to complete such a planning sheet can ensure that the intended message is communicated. After you have used planning sheets for a while, you will be able to complete this step mentally without having to actually fill them out.

Be Brief   One of the negative aspects of modern technology is the potential for information overload. This compounds another negative aspect—the tendency toward shortened attention spans. Modern computer and telecommunication technology has conditioned us to expect instant information with little or no effort on our part.

Written documents can run counter to our expectation of instant information with no effort. Reading takes time

- I am writing to
- My purpose in writing is to
- I want to make the following points
  A.
  B.
  C.
  D.
  E.
- I want the recipient to do the following:

FIGURE 11–12 Planning Form for Letters and Memorandums

and work. Keep this in mind in writing. Be brief. In as few words as possible, explain your purpose, state your points, and tell recipients what you want them to do.

Be Direct   Directness is an extension of brevity. It means getting to the point without "beating around the bush." This is especially important when the message is one that readers will not particularly like. No purpose is served by obscuring the message. Come right to the point and state it completely and accurately.

Be Accurate   Accuracy is important in written communication. Be exact. Avoid vague phrases and terms, such as *some time ago*, *approximately*, and *as soon as possible*. Take the time to identify specific dates, numbers, quantities, and so on. Then double-check to make sure they are accurate.

Practice Self-Editing   A one-draft writer is rare. But people who send their first drafts are very common. Sending the first draft can cause you to overlook errors that are embarrassing and that obscure or confuse the message. In your first draft, concentrate on *what* you are saying. In the second draft, concentrate on *how* you say it. These are two different processes that should not be mixed. Even professional writers find it difficult to edit for content and to edit for grammar, sentence structure, and spelling simultaneously.

Writing Better Reports

Writing reports is an important task that goes with being a manager. To put it simply, managers must be able to write good reports. Robert Maidment recommends the following steps for writing better reports:[2]

1. **Define the problem.** Before beginning to write a report, managers should finish the following sentence:
"The purpose of this report is . . .." The problem statement for a report should be brief, to the point, descriptive, and accurate.

2. **Develop a workplan.** A workplan is a list of the tasks to be completed and a projected date of completion for each task. Having one will help keep the development of the report on schedule. An effective way to structure a workplan is to develop a table of contents for the report, list the tasks that must be accomplished under each major heading, and then assign a projected completion date to each task (see Figure 11–13).

3. **Gather relevant data.** This step involves collecting all data pertaining to the problem in question. This is the research step. It might involve searching through files, reading other reports, interviewing employees or customers, running tests, or taking any other action that will yield useful data.

4. **Process findings.** Information is simply data that have been converted into a useful form. Processing findings means converting the raw data collected in the previous step into information on which recommendations can be based. This involves both analysis and synthesis.

5. **Develop conclusions.** Having identified a problem, gathered all pertinent data relating to the problem, and analyzed and synthesized those data, you next draw conclusions. The conclusions explain what caused the problem. Conclusions should be based on hard facts, stated objectively, and free of personal opinions or editorializing.

6. **Make recommendations.** This section contains the writer's recommendations for solving the problem. They should logically grow out of the conclusions. Arrange recommendations sequentially in order of priority. Whenever possible and appropriate, give options.

Title of Report: Failure Rate of TP-10 Gear

Major Report Headings	Completion Date
• Problem Statement	
1. Collect a broad base of input	January 15
2. Write problem statement	January 15
• Background	
1. Research all pertinent files	January 17
2. Analyze and synthesize	January 18
3. Develop a background summary	January 18
• Conclusions	
1. Develop conclusions	January 20
2. Summarize conclusions	January 21
• Recommended Solution	
1. Select the best solution	January 22
2. Pilot-test the solution chosen	January 23
3. Summarize the results and the rationale for recommending the solution	January 24

FIGURE 11–13 Report Workplan

Recommendations should be specific and detailed, indicating time frames, the people responsible for carrying them out, costs, and any other pertinent information.

COMMUNICATING CORRECTIVE FEEDBACK

In dealing with employees, managers often must give corrective feedback. To be effective, corrective feedback must be communicated properly. The following guidelines can be used for enhancing the effectiveness of corrective feedback:[3]

- **Be positive.** For feedback to be corrective, the employee must accept and act on it. This is more likely to happen if it is delivered in a positive "can do" manner.

- **Be prepared.** Focus all feedback specifically on the behavior. Do not get into personality traits. Give specific examples of the behavior you would like to see corrected.

- **Be realistic.** Make sure the behaviors you want to change are controlled by the employee. Don't expect an employee to correct a behavior over which he or she has no control.

- **Don't be completely negative.** Find something positive to say. Give the employee the necessary corrective feedback, but don't focus wholly on the negative.

Two approaches managers can use when giving corrective feedback to employees are:

- **Talk–question–listen.** With this approach, the manager tells the employee about the behavior, asks for his or her input, and listens to that input. According to Luke, "The session will have been a success if the employee leaves feeling the issues are important, is appreciative of your input, and is committed to correcting the problem."[4]

- **Listen–question–talk.** With this approach, the manager listens first. It may be necessary to ask an open-ended, general question such as "How are things going with your job?" to get the ball rolling. When the employee starts talking, listen. If the employee talks adequately about the area in which corrective action is needed, reinforce his or her comments. Ask what he or she thinks can and should be done to improve. If the employee does not appear to be fully aware of the problem, move to the tell step.

IMPROVING COMMUNICATION

Kim McKinnon, manager of personnel development at the Santa Barbara Research Center, recommends the following strategies for improving communication skills:[5]

- **Keep up-to-date.** Managers should make an effort to stay up-to-date with new information relating to the workplace. You cannot communicate what you don't know. Accurate information is essential in a total quality setting.

- **Prioritize and determine time constraints.** Communicating does not mean simply passing on everything you learn to your employees. Such an approach might overload them and, as a result, inhibit communication. Analyze your information and decide what your employees need to have. Then prioritize it, from "urgent" to "when time permits," and share the information accordingly.

- **Decide whom to inform.** After you have prioritized your information, decide who needs to have it. Employees have enough to keep up with without receiving information they don't need. Employees need information that will help them do a better job or that will help them to help fellow employees do a better job.

- **Determine how to communicate.** There are a variety of different ways to communicate: orally, in writing, one on one, in groups, and others. A combination of methods will probably be more effective than any one method by itself. (The next section in this chapter deals with this issue in more depth.)

- **Communicate and follow up.** Don't just tell employees what you want them to know or write them a memorandum. Follow up. Ask questions to determine whether they have really gotten the message. Encourage employees to ask you questions for clarification. Agree on the next steps (what they should do with the information).

- **Check understanding and obtain feedback.** Check to see that your communication was understood. Are the employees undertaking the correct next steps? Obtain feedback from employees to ensure that their understanding has not changed and that progress is being made.

Selecting the Appropriate Communication Method

One of the steps to improved communication recommended in the previous section is "Determine how to communicate."

Written communication is typically more effective for communicating general information and information that requires action on the part of employees. For example, general information such as new company policies or announcements of activities that carry dates, times, places, or other specific data are appropriate for written communication. A message that says "Please bring your automobile registration to work no later than noon Friday if you want to have a parking sticker" is appropriately communicated in writing.

Verbal communication is appropriate when reprimanding employees or attempting to resolve conflict between or among employees. In these cases, verbal interaction in private is the best approach.

Written communication is less effective in the following situations:

- When immediate action is required. In such cases, a verbal message followed up in writing is the better approach.

- When recognizing personnel for jobs well done. In such cases, a publicly delivered "well-done" followed up in writing is the better approach.

- When reprimanding an employee. In such cases, a private conversation is best. For repeat offenders, the private conversation can be followed up in writing.
- When resolving conflict between and among the personnel. In such cases, the give and take of verbal communication is more effective.

Verbal communication is less effective in the following instances:

- When communicating a message requiring future action. In such cases, written communication that is given to the personnel in question and then explained verbally is the better approach.
- When communicating complicated information, such as organizational policies, personnel information, contractual information, directives, or orders.
- When communicating progress reports to a superior.
- When communicating safety information.

Pros and Cons of Electronic Communication

Electronic communication has brought a level of immediacy to the communication process unprecedented in history. In fact, electronic communication has done for written communication what the telephone did for verbal communication. Some benefits of electronic communication are that (1) it allows messages to be sent instantaneously, (2) it allows messages to be sent to any number of people simultaneously, (3) messages can be easily and permanently stored in electronic form, (4) messages can be acknowledged instantaneously, (5) messages can be forwarded to other parties, and (6) message can be prompted (i.e., recipients can be informed electronically that they have a message).

There are also some "cons" associated with electronic communication. These disadvantages include the following: (1) an inherent inability to convey the nonverbal aspects of verbal communication (this shortcoming can be partially overcome by the use of emoticons), (2) the tendency of some people to respond to electronic messages too quickly and say things they later regret, (3) the impersonal nature of the medium, and (4) the tendency of some to send too many messages or frivolous messages because the medium is so convenient and easy to use.

Regardless of the shortcomings associated with it, electronic communication is a powerful medium that is now second only to verbal communication as the most frequently used medium. As electronic communication technologies continue to develop and improve, its use will only increase. This means that organizational leaders must become proficient in the use of electronic communication and keep up with rapid changes in technology.

HOW INTERPERSONAL SKILLS AFFECT COMMUNICATION

Interpersonal skills are those needed for people to work together in a manner that is conducive to both personal and corporate success. For employees and managers to function effectively in a total quality setting, they must have good interpersonal skills. People who lack interpersonal skills typically do not communicate well, and effective communication is essential to total quality. Positive interpersonal relations among team members, between company representatives and customers, among internal customers, and between company officials and vendors are critical in a total quality setting.

Figure 11–14 summarizes the steps managers can take to ensure that members of the workforce have sufficient interpersonal relations to be effective communicators. These are as follows:

- **Recognition of the need.** To have employees with good interpersonal skills, managers must recognize the need for these skills. Historically, the focus of the staffing process has been technical skills and paper credentials. These are important considerations that should remain at the forefront in making staffing decisions. However, to these considerations must be added interpersonal skills.
- **Careful selection.** When interpersonal skills are made a part of the selection process, the process changes somewhat. The screening of written credentials and technical skills continues in the normal manner. After the candidates with the best credentials and technical skills have been identified, they are then carefully screened to determine whether they have such interpersonal skills as listening, patience, empathy, tact, open-mindedness, friendliness, and the ability not just to get along in a diverse workplace but also to be a positive agent in helping other employees get along with each other.
- **Training.** It is the uncommon individual who possesses inborn interpersonal skills. Some people are naturally good at dealing with others. However, most of us have

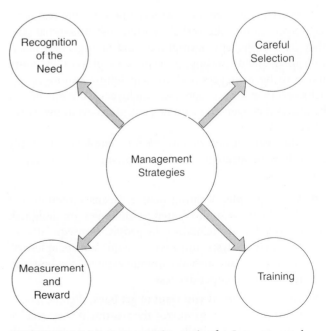

FIGURE 11–14 Management Strategies for Interpersonal Relationships

room for improvement in this key area of total quality. Fortunately, interpersonal skills can be acquired. People can learn to listen better, empathize with different types of people, be tactful, and facilitate positive interaction among fellow employees. (Training is the subject of Chapter 12.)

- **Measurement and reward.** If managers value interpersonal skills, these skills will be measured as part of the normal performance-appraisal process. Correspondingly, the results of such appraisals will be built into the reward system.

Making Human Connections in a World of Technology

In spite of the benefits of communication technologies, in some ways, technology has actually had a negative effect on communication because it has removed much of the need for face-to-face interaction. But the key to communication is perception. Receivers must be able to perceive feelings, emotions, intent, and other intangible, nonverbal aspects of the message that are missing in a facsimile transmittal, a computer message, or even a telephone conversation. For example, in certain situations, a simple human touch can communicate a powerful message, a message that cannot be transmitted by technology. Human connections have become more important than ever because technology has made it so easy to interact without really communicating.

In a total quality setting, managers should be especially attentive to human interrelationships, interdependence, and interaction and to the negative impact technology can have in each of these areas.

Promoting Perceptiveness among Employees

Perceptive people are those who can perceive the real message from among the verbal, written, and nonverbal cues they receive. Perceptive employees and managers are assets in a total quality setting: perceptive employees are more likely to be achievers and to help fellow employees be achievers than are unresponsive employees. Consequently, it behooves managers to promote perceptiveness in the workplace.

Managers can do this by teaching employees to apply the following strategies and by applying these strategies themselves:

- **Value people.** Valuing people means remembering that the most sophisticated technologies are designed, operated, and maintained by people. Consequently, in the final analysis, improving people and people-oriented processes such as communication is the best way to improve competitiveness.
- **Give people what you want to get back.** People have a natural tendency to mirror the treatment they receive from others. Typically, people who treat others with

decency and respect are, in turn, treated with decency and respect. People who are loyal to others are likely to be the beneficiaries of loyalty. Teaching employees to get by giving is a worthwhile task for managers in a total quality setting.

- **Make cooperation a habit.** World-class athletes practice the skills that make them great until these skills become automatic and habitual. Any habit is hard to break; just ask people who have tried to stop smoking or biting their nails. Consequently, employees who practice cooperation until it becomes habitual will practice cooperation for life.

  Cooperation in the workplace means learning to use the word *we* instead of *I* and *they*. It means chipping in to get the job done even when what needs to be done is not part of the job description. Cooperation means involving all employees who must do the work in decisions relating to that work.

  Cooperation does not mean always saying "yes." When the right answer to give is "no," that answer should be given, without sugarcoating it. Cooperation in such cases means showing employees they are valued by explaining why the answer must be "no."

PERSONALITY AND COMMUNICATION

Few factors affect communication so directly as the personalities of the individuals attempting to communicate. The term *personality* is used to describe a relatively stable pattern of behavior, thought, motives, emotions, and outlook that are distinctive to a given individual and that characterize that individual throughout life. Every person has a personality, and every individual's personality is different. However, there are certain identifiable central traits that people may share to varying degrees. Psychologists disagree over what these identifiable traits are and how many characteristics should be considered central personality traits. There is, though, something close to consensus among psychologists that the following group of characteristics is central to most people:[6]

Introversion versus extroversion. These traits describe the extent to which an individual is shy. An introvert is considered shy, while an extrovert is considered outgoing. There are, of course, varying degrees of introversion and extroversion. An extrovert is more likely to be talkative, sociable, adventurous, lively, cheerful, and enthusiastic. An introvert is more likely to be silent and reclusive. An extrovert is more likely to be a talker, whereas an introvert is more likely to be a listener. When trying to communicate with an extrovert, it might be difficult to get a word in, and you may have to ask the person to paraphrase what you have said and repeat it back. When trying to communicate with introverts, one must remember that they are not likely to volunteer much information; consequently, it can take an extra effort to draw them out.

Neuroticism versus emotional stability. These traits describe the extent to which an individual is emotionally stable. The more neurotic people are, the more anxiety they tend to feel, the less able they are to control their emotions, and the more likely they are to feel negative emotions, such as anger, resentment, and scorn. The more emotionally stable people are, the less likely they are to be worriers, complainers, and defeatists. Neurotic people tend to see the negative side of any situation, while emotionally stable people will generally have a more realistic perspective. When trying to communicate with neurotic people, it is necessary to be patient, understated, and calm. Disagreement should be conveyed gently and stated in the most positive light.

Agreeable versus stubborn. These traits describe the extent to which an individual is good natured or irritable, gentle or headstrong, cooperative or abrasive, and secure or suspicious. The communication style of agreeable people is typically characterized by friendliness; the communication style of stubborn people is typically characterized by hostility. When trying to communicate with stubborn people, it is wise to first invest some time earning their trust in order to overcome their inherent suspiciousness.

Conscientious versus undependable. These traits describe the extent to which an individual is responsible or irresponsible, persevering or fainthearted, and steadfast or fickle. When trying to communicate with undependable people, it is wise to summarize and repeat what was said. It is also important to be confident enough in what you are saying to offset the other person's tendency toward faintheartedness.

Open to experience versus preference for the familiar. These traits describe the extent to which an individual is original, creative, imagining, questioning, artistic, and capable of creative thinking or is conforming and predictable. When trying to communicate with "open" people, it is sometimes necessary to rein them in and keep them focused and on task. When trying to communicate with people who prefer the familiar, it is sometimes necessary to take the time to get them to think "outside the box."

One of the most popular tests used in business settings for identifying an individual's central personality traits is the Myers-Briggs Type Indicator. One CEO thought so much of the Myers-Briggs that he had all employees take the test and put these results (e.g., introvert or extrovert) on their desks like a name plate. The idea was that if his employees knew more about their respective personalities, they would be better able to communicate with each other. The authors do not recommend this approach, but it is wise to recognize personality traits when trying to communicate with people, particularly those with whom interaction is frequent and ongoing.

SUMMARY

1. Communication is the transfer of a message that is both received and understood. Effective communication is a higher order of communication. It means the message is received, understood, and being acted on in the desired manner.

2. Communication is the oil that keeps the total quality engine running. Without it, total quality breaks down. Communication plays the role of facilitation in a total quality setting.

3. Communication is a process that involves a message, sender, receiver, and medium. The message is what is being transmitted (information, emotion, intent, or something else). The sender is the originator of the message, and the receiver is the person to whom it goes. The medium is the vehicle used to transfer the message.

4. Various factors can inhibit communication. Prominent among these are differences in meaning, lack of trust, information overload, interference, premature judgments, "Kill-the-Messenger" Syndrome, condescending tone, inaccurate assumptions, and listening problems.

5. A climate conducive to communication gives people the information they need to do their jobs, builds morale, and promotes creativity. A bad communication climate creates conflict, confusion, and cynicism. A bad climate can be guaranteed by poor communication.

6. One of the most important communication skills is listening. Good listening means receiving the message correctly, decoding it, and accurately perceiving what it means. Inhibitors to good listening include the following: lack of concentration, preconceived ideas, thinking ahead, interruptions, tuning out, and interference. *Empathetic listening* means listening with the intent to understand. *Responsive listening* means seeking to receive and affirm both the messenger and the message.

7. Listening skills may be improved by upgrading the desire to listen, asking the right questions, judging what is really being said, and eliminating listening errors. Body factors and proximity must also be managed carefully to listen well.

8. Verbal communication can be improved by showing interest, being friendly, being flexible, being tactful, being courteous, dropping your defenses, stating your purpose, acknowledging emotions, and using carefully phrased open-ended questions.

9. Written communication can be improved by being brief, being direct, being accurate, and practicing self-editing. The following step-by-step strategy will help managers write better reports: (a) define the problem,

(b) develop a workplan, (c) gather relevant data, (d) process findings, (e) develop conclusions, and (f) make recommendations.

10. When it is necessary to communicate corrective feedback, be positive, be prepared, be realistic, and don't be completely negative. There are two approaches to use for communicating corrective feedback: tell–ask–listen and listen–ask–tell.

11. Adopting the following steps can help improve communication skills: (a) keep up-to-date, (b) prioritize and determine time constraints, (c) decide whom to inform, (d) determine how to communicate, (e) communicate and follow up, (f) check understanding, and (g) obtain feedback.

12. Electronic communication has advantages and disadvantages. The advantages include the following: messages can be transmitted rapidly, messages can be transmitted simultaneously to more than one person, messages can be printed if a hard copy is needed, and messages can be prompted and acknowledged electronically. Disadvantages are the inability to transmit nonverbal messages electronically and the potential for overuse.

13. Interpersonal skills are those needed for people to work together in a positive manner that is conducive to both personal and corporate success. To ensure that employees have good interpersonal skills, managers should recognize the need for them, select personnel carefully, provide training, measure skill, and reward improvement.

KEY TERMS AND CONCEPTS

Bad communication climate
Body factors
Communication
Company-level communication
Condescending tone
Corrective feedback
Effective communication
Effective listening
Empathetic listening
Inaccurate assumptions
Information overload
Interference
Interpersonal relations
Lack of concentration
Listen–ask–tell
Medium
Message
One-on-one–level communication

Open-ended questions
Preconceived ideas
Premature judgments
Proximity
Self-editing
Sender
Tact
Team-level communication
Tell–ask–listen
Thinking ahead
Tuning out
Verbal communication
Voice factors
Written communication

FACTUAL REVIEW QUESTIONS

1. Define the following terms relating to communication: *communication* and *effective communication*.
2. List and explain the four levels of communication.
3. Describe the role communication plays in a total quality setting.
4. Explain the process of communication.
5. List and briefly explain six inhibitors of communication.
6. Define *effective listening*.
7. List and briefly explain five inhibitors of effective listening.
8. What is empathetic listening?
9. What is responsive listening?
10. Explain how a person can become a responsive listener.
11. Explain four strategies for improving listening skills.
12. Define the following factors and explain how they affect listening: body factors, voice factors, proximity factors.
13. Describe how a person can improve his or her verbal communication skills.
14. List and explain five rules of thumb for improving written communication.
15. Explain the steps that can be used for improving written reports.
16. When it is necessary to communicate corrective feedback, what four guidelines should be applied?
17. Six guidelines to improved communication were set forth in this chapter. Explain all six.
18. Briefly describe the advantages and disadvantages of electronic communication.
19. Define *interpersonal relations*.
20. How can managers ensure that employees have good interpersonal skills?

21. How can a manager promote perceptiveness among employees?

22. List five personality traits and describe how they can affect communication.

CRITICAL THINKING ACTIVITY

Are You a Good Listener?

The purpose of this activity is to compare your self-perception with the perceptions of others concerning your listening skills. Figure 11–5 is a listening skills assessment instrument. Complete this instrument for yourself. Then ask at least two other people whom you trust to be open and honest to complete the instrument with *you as the subject*. Does their perception of your listening skills match your self-perception? If not, what are the differences? What do you need to do to improve your listening skills?

DISCUSSION ASSIGNMENT 11–1

The Busy Boss

John Gill is a busy man. No matter how fast he works, it seems he's always behind. Consequently, when an employee brings Gill a problem, he is not a good listener. He opens mail, answers the telephone, and constantly glances at his watch while the employee is talking. Because he does not listen well, John keeps being blindsided by new problems that seem to get more and more serious.

DISCUSSION QUESTIONS

Discuss the following questions in class or outside of class with your fellow students:

1. What can John do to become a better listener?

2. How might John's poor listening skills be adding to his growing list of problems?

ENDNOTES

1. Craig Borysowich, "What the heck is Responsive Listening?!?" Retrieved from http://ittoolbox.com on February 16, 2011.

2. The Roberts Group, "Writing Tips." Retrieved from www.editorialservice.com/11ways.html on January 7, 2011.

3. David Lee, "Constructive Feedback: How to Give It So Your Employees Want to Hear It and Use It." Retrieved from www.humannatureatwork.com/constructive-feedback-skills.htm on February 5, 2011.

4. Ibid.

5. Slideshare, "Seven Steps to Improve Your Communication." Retrieved from www.slideshare.net on February 11, 2011.

6. Robert R. McCrae and Paul T. Costa Jr., "Personality Trait Structure as a Human Universal," *American Psychologist* 52: 509–516.

EDUCATION AND TRAINING

Training is directly skills-related, but education is a people-building concept. —**David Hutchins**

MAJOR TOPICS

- Overview of Education, Training, and Learning
- Rationale for Training
- Training Needs Assessment
- Providing Training
- Evaluating Training
- Managers as Trainers and Trainees
- Workforce Literacy
- Improving Learning
- Why Training Sometimes Fails
- Quality Training Curriculum
- Orientation Training
- Customer Training
- Ethics Training
- Making E-Learning Work

One of the most fundamental elements of total quality is the ongoing development of personnel, which means education, training, and learning. This chapter provides readers with the information needed to justify, provide, and evaluate education, training, and learning.

OVERVIEW OF EDUCATION, TRAINING, AND LEARNING

It is common to hear the terms *education*, *training*, and *learning* used interchangeably in discussions of employee development. Although common practice is to use the term *training* for the sake of convenience, modern managers should be familiar with the distinctions among them. For purposes of this book, training is defined as follows:

Training is an organized, systematic series of activities designed to enhance an individual's work-related knowledge, skills, and understanding or motivation.

Training can be distinguished from *education* by its characteristics of practicality, specificity, and immediacy. Training should relate specifically to the job performed by

those being trained, and it should have immediate practical application on the job. *Education* is a broader term; training is a subset of education. Also, education tends to be more philosophical and theoretical and less practical than training.

The purpose of both education and training is learning. In an educational setting, the learning will tend to be more theoretical, whereas in a training setting, it will be more practical. However, with both, understanding is implicit in learning. Whether the point is to have the learner understand *why* or *how to*, the point is still to have the learner understand. Understanding is what allows an employee to become an innovator, initiative taker, and creative problem solver in addition to being an efficient and effective performer of his or her job.

Although education typically occurs in a classroom setting, while training typically occurs in a less formal environment, there is some overlap in the concepts. Education can certainly occur outside of a classroom, and training can certainly occur in one. For this reason and for the sake of simplicity, the term *training* will be used throughout the remainder of this chapter.

Corporate Training in the United States

Corporate America invests more than $55 billion per year in training.[1] However, there are serious questions about how wisely this money is spent. Is it being used in a way that will bring the best results, or is corporate America spending its training dollars on the wrong people? The following sections describe the status of training in the United States by job category, sources of training, instructional methods, and types of training in selected industry classifications.

Training Status by Job Category   Companies with more than 100 employees typically have personnel in several categories of employment:

- Executive managers
- Senior managers
- Middle managers
- Supervisors

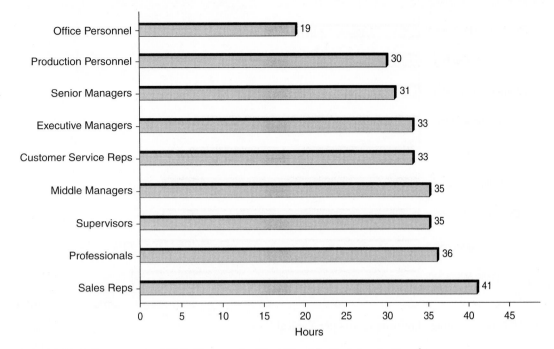

FIGURE 12-1 Percentage of U.S. Companies That Provide Training to Employees

- Professionals (engineers, scientists, technologists, and technicians)
- Sales representatives
- Customer service representatives
- Production personnel
- Office personnel

Training provided to personnel in these various categories can be compared in a number of different ways. Two of the most informative comparisons are the percentage of companies that provide training to employees in each category and the average number of hours of training received by employees in each category. Figure 12-1 compares the percentage of companies that provide training in each subject category of employment. The comparisons represent approximate figures for a typical year for companies with 100 or more employees.

Figure 12-1 shows that in the United States more companies provide training for managers than for any other category of employee. By comparison, only 33% of these companies provide training for production personnel. These figures raise serious questions about how effectively corporate America's training dollars are being spent.

In a total quality setting, training is a bottom-up enterprise in which the people who do the work receive top priority in the allocation of training dollars. The philosophy of the total quality approach concerning training can be summarized as spending the money where it will do the most good. In practice, this philosophy translates into giving training priority to those employees who are most actively involved in producing products or providing services. The further removed from these processes an employee is, the lower his or her training priority becomes. Followed to its logical conclusion, the total quality philosophy assigns the lowest training priority to managers, a reversal of the figures shown in Figure 12-1.

When training is compared using the average number of hours provided per year per employee, production workers, fare only slightly better. Figure 12-2 contains these comparisons for companies in the United States for a typical year. Again, the data are for companies with more than 100 employees. When average hours of training is the criterion, only office personnel receive less training than production personnel.

Figure 12-2 provides a stark illustration of what happened to many of the U.S. firms that managed themselves out of business over the past two decades. By putting more resources into training sales representatives than into training production personnel, they made a conscious decision to neglect quality. Such an attitude can be summarized by the statement "Forget quality, just sell harder." The total quality philosophy is the opposite and can be summarized by the statement "Improve quality and you won't have to sell so hard."

Sources of Training   Many sources of training are available to organizations that want to provide training for employees. This section discusses them in terms of broad categories; they are examined in greater detail later in this chapter. All of them fall into one of the following categories: in-house training, external training, or a combination of in-house and external. Figure 12-3 summarizes the percentages provided using each of these approaches.

Most training is provided through a combination of in-house training and external sources, with in-house training

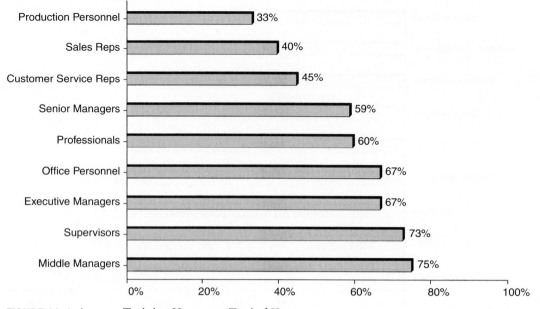

FIGURE 12–2 Average Training Hours per Typical Year

the second most widely used option. *In-house training* is a broad heading covering on-the-job training, in-house seminars and workshops, and on-site e-learning. *External training* is a broad category that includes college or university courses; workshops and seminars provided by colleges, universities, and private training organizations; correspondence courses; vendor-sponsored training; and training provided by technical, trade, and professional associations.

Instructional Methods   Numerous instructional methods are used to provide training for employees. Figure 12–4 displays a checklist of instructional methods that are widely employed for both internal and external training. Of the methods listed, the most commonly used are lectures and e-learning. The influence of technology on instruction is apparent from the checklist in Figure 12–4. Of the methods shown, several are technology depend-

ent. In addition, technology is often used with the other methods to enhance the quality and retention of instruction. For example, it is now common to supplement a lecture with PowerPoint slides. Simulation activities are often computerized, and self-study instruction is frequently centered around DVDs or CDs instruction or self-teaching computer software. Online classes are becoming more and more popular.

Types of Training by Industry   Four key industrial sectors in the United States are manufacturing, transportation, communication, and utilities. Figure 12–5 shows the types of training provided for employees in these key industrial sectors. Training topics that are especially important in a total quality setting are technical skills, supervision skills, communication, new work procedures, and customer relations (internal and external customers).

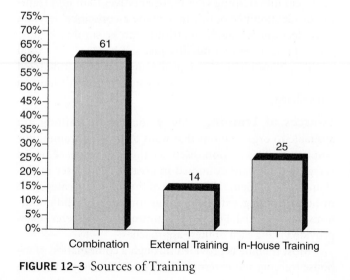

FIGURE 12–3 Sources of Training

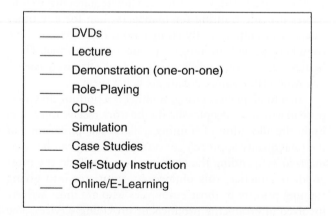

FIGURE 12–4 Instructional Methods Checklist

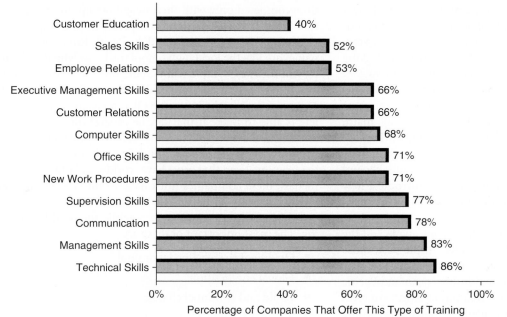

FIGURE 12–5 Types of Training (Manufacturing, Transportation, Communication, Utilities)

Technical skills training is provided by 86% of the manufacturing, transportation, communication, and utility companies in the United States. Supervision training is important in a total quality setting because supervisors need to learn to be facilitators, coaches, communicators, and leaders rather than bosses in the traditional sense. The need for supervision training is apparently felt in these four key industrial sectors, where 77% of the companies provide this type of training.

Communication skills are taught by 78% of the companies in the subject sectors. Nevertheless, a great many companies still show no understanding of the importance of communication in workplace improvement and competitiveness. Communication can have a direct influence on an organization's ability to compete.

Because continual process improvement is a fundamental element of total quality, work procedures change frequently in a total quality setting. This means that training in new work procedures should take place continually so that process improvements can be effectively and efficiently implemented. Figure 12–5 shows that 71% of the companies in the subject sectors offer this type of training.

QUALITY TIP ▼

E-Learning Continues to Grow

It is now rare to find a college or university that does not offer distance learning courses online. Traditional seminars and workshops augmented by various technologies such as PowerPoint presentations are still the leading approach to corporate training, but e-learning is the fastest growing approach. As the baby boomer generation continues to age and retire, each successive generation is likely to be increasingly computer savvy. As a result, e-learning will continue to grow as a viable option for corporate training.

Changing Role of Training   Although corporate training in the United States is more than 100 years old, it really got its start near the end of World War II. Establishment of the American Society for Training and Development (ASTD) was a milestone development that occurred at this time.

The mission of corporate training is becoming the maximization of competitiveness through continual improvements in all of the elements of value (i.e., quality, cost, and service). Since organizations win in the global marketplace by providing superior value for, customers, the role of corporate training now revolves around the concept of superior value in terms of quality, cost, and service.

Attitudes toward Training in the United States and Other Countries   The U.S. businesses place an alarmingly low priority on the skills of their employees as shown by the following facts:[2]

- Less than 10% of the companies planned to increase productivity by reorganizing work in ways that call for employees with broader skills.

- Only 15% expressed concern over the potential for a shortage of skilled workers.

- Less than 30% intended to offer special training programs for women and minorities, although these groups account for 85% of all new workers.

- More than 80% were more concerned about workers' attitudes than their skills.

American businesses are not taking a proactive role in demanding the improvements that are so badly needed in American education and training. Contrasting what is found in the United States with the situation in other industrialized countries, education and training for non-college-bound students is better in such countries as Germany, Japan, Sweden, and Denmark. Consequently, American students rank near the bottom in indicators of school performance when compared with students from these countries. The U.S. system for transitioning students from school to work is lacking when compared with other globally competitive nations.

Other industrialized countries are creating a high-performance workplace by reorganizing work in ways that call for multiple abilities and high levels of reading, math, science, and problem-solving skills. As a result, workers are better able continually to develop new skills as technology changes. The ability of such workers to adapt quickly and continually also allows their employers to introduce new products on shorter cycle times and make more frequent changes in production runs.

Traditionally, business and industry in Canada and the United States have had similar attitudes. In the past, those attitudes have been casual at best. However, although interest levels don't yet match those found in European and Pacific Rim countries, attitudes toward training in North America are changing for the better, particularly in Canada. According to the Canadian Labor and Business Center (CLBC):

- Both employers and unions should have a direct role in the training of workers, but the main responsibility for training and retraining—including funding—belongs to employers. Labor leaders strongly support the concept of a national training tax on corporations, commonly referred to in Canada as the 1% levy-grant proposal, to fund training programs. According to the CLBC, three-fourths of the business leaders oppose the idea of a training tax.

- Obstacles to improved training include inadequate facilities for workplace training, low interest in training by many employers, and the practice described by the survey report as interfirm poaching of trained workers.

- International competitiveness is generally regarded as vital to maintaining a high standard of living, but it is valued less by union leaders than by business leaders.

- One-third of the business leaders and one-half of the labor leaders described workers' reading, writing, and mathematical skills as inadequate. Respondents linked these shortcomings to low productivity, high training costs, poor quality control, and difficult recruitment.

- Universities, colleges, and vocational schools do a fair job of preparing people for the working world, according to most of the survey respondents. Elementary and secondary schools were deemed inadequate.

- Although respondents agreed that training was important, they were unhappy with current offerings. Forty percent of business leaders and 86% of labor leaders said workplace programs were inadequate.[3]

RATIONALE FOR TRAINING

The rationale for training can be found in the need to compete. To survive in the modern marketplace, organizations must be able to compete globally. Companies that at one time competed only with their neighbors up the street now find themselves vying against companies from Europe, Asia, Central and South America, and the Pacific Rim. These companies are like the local high school track star who decides to try out for the Olympic team. Suddenly, the competition is much more difficult, and it will be increasingly so at each successive level right up to the Olympic Games. If the athlete is able to make it that far, he or she will face the best athletes in the world. This is the situation in which modern business and industrial firms find themselves every day. Like the Olympic team that must have world-class athletes to win medals, these companies must have world-class employees to win the competition for market share.

Several factors combine to magnify the need for training. The most important of these are

- Quality of the existing labor pool
- Global competition
- Rapid and continual change
- Technology transfer problems
- Changing demographics

These factors and how they contribute to the rationale for training are explained in the following sections.

Quality of the Existing Labor Pool

The labor pool consists of the people who are available for and wish to have employment. New jobs are filled from the labor pool. For this reason, the quality of the labor pool is critical. Quality in this sense means both preparedness and potential. A high-quality labor pool is one in which its members are well-schooled in such fundamental intellectual skills as reading, writing, thinking, listening, speaking, and problem solving. Such people are well-prepared in terms of the basics and, as a result, have good potential to quickly learn and adapt when put in a job. The importance of basic knowledge and skills cannot be overstated.

How does the labor pool from which U.S. organizations draw their employees measure up with regard to quality? Consider the following, released by the Organization for Economic Cooperation and Development: When compared with their counterparts in Canada, Europe, and Asia, 23-year-old people in the United States consistently place lower in math and science.[4]

This deficiency does not result from the United States spending too little on public education. When comparing the percentage of gross national product (GNP) spent on education, the United States ranks among the highest. Of the most industrialized nations, only Canada (4.1%) devotes a larger percentage of its GNP to education than does the United States (3.5%). Japan and Germany spend less than 3%. These figures seem to indicate that the United States spends more on public education but gets less for its money than do most other industrialized nations. The implications of this situation in terms of the quality of the labor force are serious.

American companies must invest training dollars in teaching employees basics before they can begin to deal with higher level material that will more directly affect productivity and quality. Compare this situation with the Dutch labor force, which draws its members from high schools where 90% of the students take advanced math courses, or that of Japan, where 25% of the time elementary school children spend in school is devoted to math and science.[5] This puts U.S. employers in the position of having to spend more to get the same result.

Global Competition

American companies, even some of the smallest, find themselves competing in a global marketplace, and the competition is intense. A small manufacturer of automotive parts in Michigan might find itself competing with companies from Korea, Japan, Taiwan, Indonesia, and Europe as well as the United States. To win the contest, this small Michigan firm must make its products both better and less expensively than its competitors. Large companies face the same intense global competition.

Rapid and Continual Change

Change is a fact of life in the modern workplace. It happens fast and continually. Knowledge and skills that are on the cutting edge today may be obsolete tomorrow. In such an environment, it is critical that employees be updated constantly. The relative literacy of an organization's workforce will determine its ability to keep up. Figure 12–6 provides a checklist managers can use to get a feel for whether their organization has a literacy problem.

Rapid and continual change represents an insurmountable barrier to employees who are not functionally literate, meaning their academic performance is between grade levels 4.0 and 8.9. To understand the number of employees in the

United States who may not be able to keep pace, consider the following facts:

- Almost 30 million adults in the United States are functionally illiterate.

- Approximately 20% of the workforce in the United States has a reading comprehension level of eighth grade or lower, whereas 70% of the reading material in the modern workplace is at the ninth grade level or higher.

- Approximately 2.5 million people enter the workforce every year with only limited language skills. These include immigrants, high school dropouts, and high school graduates who are still functionally illiterate.

These facts from the U.S. Department of Education (www.ed.gov, retrieved March 11, 2011) are part of the rationale for workplace training. Organizations that do not provide it may find it difficult, if not impossible, to keep up with the rapid change that is sure to occur.

Technology Transfer Problems

Technology transfer is the movement of technology from one arena to another. The process has two steps. The first step is the commercialization of new technologies developed in research laboratories or by individual inventors. This is a business development issue and does not involve training.

The second step in the process is known as technology diffusion, and it is training dependent. *Technology diffusion* is the process of moving newly commercialized technologies into the workplace, where they can be used to enhance productivity, quality, and competitiveness.

This step breaks down unless the workers who will use the technology have been well-trained to use it efficiently and effectively. This is critical because new technologies by themselves do not enhance productivity. A word processing system given to an untrained traditional secretary will

	Yes	No
1. Do you notice employees having trouble reading and spelling at the level required by the job?		
2. Do you notice job applicants who have trouble completing application paperwork?		
3. Do you notice employees having trouble using fractions and decimals?		
4. Do you experience equipment problems because employees cannot read operating manuals?		
5. Do you notice problems in the workplace caused by employees with limited English proficiency?		
6. Do you notice employees who cannot keep up in workplace training programs?		

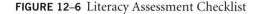

FIGURE 12–6 Literacy Assessment Checklist

be nothing more than an expensive typewriter with a screen. To take maximum advantage of the capabilities of new technologies, workers must know how to use them effectively. Knowledge comes from training. Two of the major inhibitors of effective technology transfer are fear of change and lack of know-how. Both of these inhibitors can be overcome by training.

Changing Demographics

Workplace demographics are changing in ways that make training even more important than it was in the past, Figure 12–7 summarizes some of the ways workplace demographics are changing in the United States. One word characterizes the modern workplace—*diversity*. Because teamwork is a fundamental element of total quality, training may be needed to teach employees from vastly different backgrounds how to work together in harmony.

Experienced employees may not adapt easily to an influx of women, minorities, and immigrants. They may even feel threatened and resentful. Women, minorities, and immigrants may not be comfortable in what may, at first, be an alien environment. Simply bringing diverse people together in the workplace does not guarantee that they will work together in harmony. Overcoming cultural, social, and gender differences requires training, commitment, and constant attention.

Benefits of Training

In spite of the fact that billions of dollars are spent on training every year, many employers still do not understand the role or benefits of training in the modern workplace. A study conducted by the National Center on Education and the Economy unfavorably compares the education and training of workers in the United States with those of workers in competing countries.[6]

This study concludes that less than 10% of U.S. companies use a flexible approach requiring better trained workers as a way to improve productivity. This approach is standard practice in Japan, Germany, Denmark, and Sweden. In addition, less than 30% of U.S. firms have special training programs for women, minorities, and immigrants, in spite of the fact that over 80% of all new workers come from these groups. It is critical to the competitiveness of U.S. industry that employers understand the need for training that results from such factors as intense international competition,

- More than 80 percent of all new entrants into the workforce are women, minorities, or immigrants.
- The average age of employed people is increasing.
- More than 20 percent of all new entrants into the workforce are immigrants with limited English language skills.

FIGURE 12–7 Changing Demographics in the Workplace
Source: Commission on Adult Basic Education, www.coabe.org.

____	Fewer Production Errors
____	Increased Productivity
____	Improved Quality
____	Decreased Turnover Rate
____	Lower Staffing Costs
____	Improved Safety and Health
____	Fewer Accidents
____	Minimized Insurance Costs
____	Increased Flexibility of Employees
____	Better Response to Change
____	Improved Communication
____	Better Teamwork
____	More Harmonious Employee Relations

FIGURE 12–8 Checklist of Training Benefits

rapid and continual change, technology transfer problems, and changing demographics.

According to the National Center on Education and the Economy, 69% of the companies in the United States with 50 or more employees provide training for middle managers, and 70% train executive-level personnel. However, only 30% train skilled personnel. Peters contrasts this with the Japanese and Germans, who outspend U.S. firms markedly in providing training for skilled personnel.[7]

Modern managers should understand the benefits of workforce training and be able to articulate these benefits to upper management. Figure 12–8 is a checklist that summarizes the most important of these. As can be seen from the checklist, the benefits of training build upon themselves. For example, reducing the turnover rate will also contribute to improving safety. Increased safety will, in turn, help minimize insurance costs.

Employers who are not familiar with the benefits of training but are beginning to take an interest in providing it often debate the applicability or job relatedness of training. The argument is often made that "We will provide only the training that relates directly to the job." According to total quality pioneer W. Edwards Deming, focusing too intently on direct applicability is a mistake. Any kind of learning can benefit employees and employers alike in ways that cannot be predicted.

TRAINING NEEDS ASSESSMENT
Identifying Training Needs

How do managers know what training is needed in their organizations? The answer is that many don't know. When compared with their competitors from other countries, U.S. companies appear to spend a great deal of money on the wrong kinds of training. It is a matter of emphasis: By placing the emphasis on management, employers are spending the bulk of their training dollars on those who organize and oversee the work rather than those who actually do it. This is akin to training the coaches instead of the players.

This is not to say that managers should forgo ongoing training. In a total quality setting, every employee needs continual training. However, the keys to maximizing the return on training dollars are to place the emphasis on training those who need it most and to ensure that the training provided is designed to promote the goals of the organization (quality, productivity, and competitiveness).

Satisfying the first criterion is simply a matter of reversing the emphasis so that it is bottom up in nature rather than top down. Satisfying the second involves assessing training needs. Begin by asking two broad questions:

- What knowledge, skills, and attitudes do our employees need to have to be world-class level?
- What knowledge, skills, and attitudes do our employees currently have?

The difference between the answers to these questions identifies an organization's training needs.

Managers may become involved in assessing training needs at two levels: the organizational level and the individual level. Managers who work closely enough with their team members can see firsthand on a daily basis their capabilities and those of the team as a whole. Observation is one method managers can use for assessing training needs. Are there specific problems that persist? Does an individual have difficulties performing certain tasks? Does work consistently back up at a given point in the process? These are indicators of a possible need for training that can be observed.

A more structured way to assess training needs is to ask employees to state their needs in terms of their job knowledge and skills. Employees know the tasks they must perform every day. They also know which tasks they do well, which they do not do well, and which they cannot do at all. A brainstorming session focusing on training needs is another method managers can use. Brainstorming is particularly effective in organizations where employees are comfortable speaking out as part of the continual improvement process.

The most structured approach managers can use to assess training needs is the *job task analysis survey*. With this method, a job is analyzed thoroughly and the knowledge, skills, and attitudes needed to perform it are recorded. Using this information, a survey instrument is developed and distributed among employees who do the job in question. They respond by indicating which skills they have and which they need.

Before preparing a survey instrument, step back and take in the big picture. A common mistake is to focus too intently on the finite tasks of a job to the exclusion of the broader, less tangible requirements. For example, while comprehensively breaking down technical process tasks, managers often overlook such criteria as teamwork skills, sensitivity to customer feedback (particularly internal customers), problem solving, and interpersonal skills. For this reason, it is a good idea to involve the employees who will be surveyed in the development of the survey instrument.

Another way to identify training needs is to ask employee groups to convene their own quality circles relating specifically to training. Employee-managed groups such as these that convene without managers and supervisors are often more open to admitting that there are training needs. They will also be less reluctant to identify the training needs they think supervisors and managers have. The organization's suggestion system should also be used to identify training needs.

Converting Training Needs to Training Objectives

Having identified training needs, the next step is to write training objectives. This responsibility will fall in whole or in part to the manager. Some organizations have training personnel who can assist; others do not. In either case, managers in a total quality setting should be proficient in writing training objectives. The key to writing good training objectives lies in learning to be specific and to state objectives in behavioral terms. For example, suppose a need for training in the area of mathematics has been identified. The manager might write the following training objective:

Employees will learn mathematics.

This training objective, as stated, lacks specificity and is stated in nonbehavioral terms. Mathematics is a broad concept. What is the need? What is the need for training in arithmetic? What is the need for training in algebra? What is the need for training in geometry? What is the need for training in trigonometry? What is the need for training in all of these? To gain specificity, this objective must be broken into several objectives and restated.

To be stated in behavioral terms, these more specific objectives must explain what the employee should be able to do after completing the training. Behavioral objectives contain action verbs. The more clearly training objectives are written, the easier it is to plan training to meet them. The sample training objectives in Figure 12–9 are stated in behavioral terms, they are specific, and they are measurable. Taking the time to write objectives in this way will make it easier to provide and evaluate training.

PROVIDING TRAINING

Many firms in the United States have learned the value of education and training and, as a result, are reaping their benefits. IBM, Nissan (in Tennessee), and Motorola are examples of such firms. At IBM, training immediately follows each promotion. All IBM employees must complete at least 40 hours of training each year. Today, as IBM faces intense pressure from foreign competitors, training is at the heart of its strategy for confronting the challenge. Before Nissan opened its plant in Smyrna, Tennessee, it spent $63 million training approximately 2,000 employees. This amounts to approximately $30,000 per employee, which is

1. Upon completion of this lesson, employees will be able to solve right triangles.
2. Upon completion of this lesson, employees will be able to apply the Law of Sines to the solution of triangles.
3. Upon completion of this lesson, employees will be able to apply the Law of Cosines to the solution of triangles.
4. Upon completion of this lesson, employees will be able to add, subtract, multiply, and divide decimal fractions.
5. Upon completion of this lesson, employees will be able to solve equations containing one unknown variable.

FIGURE 12–9 Sample Training Objectives

about average for a Japanese company. Motorola stays competitive in the semiconductor business by investing 2.5% of its annual payroll in education and training. In addition to its employees, Motorola trains its suppliers.

Several different methods for providing training are available to organizations. All fall into one of the following three broad categories: internal approaches, external approaches, and partnership approaches.

Internal Approaches

Internal approaches are those used to provide training on-site in the organization's facilities. These approaches include one-on-one training, on-the-job computer-based training, formal group instruction, and media-based instruction. *One-on-one training* involves placing a less skilled, less experienced employee under the instruction of a more skilled, more experienced employee. This approach is often used when a new employee is hired. It is also an effective way to prepare a replacement for a high-value employee who plans to leave or retire.

Computer-based training (CBT) has proven to be an effective internal approach. Over the years, it has continually improved so that now CBT is a widely used training method. It offers the advantages of being self-paced, individualized, and able to provide immediate and continual feedback to learners. Its best application is in developing general knowledge rather than company-specific job skills.

Formal *group instruction* in which a number of people who share a common training need are trained together is a widely used method. This approach might involve lectures, demonstrations, multimedia use, hands-on learning, question-and-answer sessions, role-playing, and simulation.

Media-based instruction has become a popular internal approach. Private training companies and major publishing houses produce an almost endless list of turnkey media-based training programs. The simplest of these might consist of a set of DVDs. A more comprehensive package might include DVDs and workbooks.

An example of an extensive internal training program is Motorola University, the in-house educational institution operated by Motorola Inc. Motorola University consists of institutes for manufacturing and engineering personnel, middle managers, and senior managers as well as an instruc-

tional design center. More than 60,000 employees have completed training in Motorola University. The company's goal is to have a minimum of 2% per year of an employee's time spent in training.

External Approaches

External approaches are those that involve enrolling employees in programs or activities provided by public institutions, private institutions, professional organizations, and private training companies. The two most widely used approaches are (a) enrolling employees in short-term training (a few hours to a few weeks) during work hours and (b) enrolling employees in long-term training such as a college course and paying all or part of the costs (i.e., tuition, books, fees). External approaches encompass training methods ranging from seminars to college courses. The external approach is typically used for developing broad, generic skills. However, some institutions will work with employers to develop customized courses.

Partnership Approaches

In recent years, universities, community colleges, and technical schools have begun to actively pursue partnerships with employers through which they provide customized training. These training partnerships combine some of the characteristics of the previous two approaches.

Customized on-site training provided cooperatively by colleges and private companies or associations has become very common. Many universities, community colleges, and technical schools have continuing education or corporate training divisions that specialize in providing training for business and industry. Managers should know the administrator responsible for continuing education at all colleges, universities, and technical schools in their communities.

Partnerships with institutions of higher education offer several advantages to organizations that want to arrange training for their employees. Representatives of these institutions are education and training professionals. They know how to transform training objectives into customized curricula, courses, and lessons. They know how to deliver instruction and have access to a wide range of instructional support systems (libraries, multimedia centers, and instructional design centers). They know how to design application activities that simulate real-world conditions. Finally, they know how to develop a valid and reliable system of evaluation and use the results produced to chart progress and prescribe remedial activities when necessary.

In addition to professional know-how, institutions of higher education have resources that can markedly reduce the cost of training for an organization. Tuition costs for continuing education activities are typically much less than those associated with traditional college courses. If these institutions do not have faculty members, on staff, who are qualified to provide instruction in a given area, they can usually hire a temporary or part-time instructor who is qualified. Other advantages institutions of higher education can offer are credibility, formalization, standardization, and flexibility in training locations. Associating with a community college, university, or technical school can formalize an organization's training program and give it credibility.

This is important because employers sometimes find their attempts at customized training hampered by a lack of credibility. Their employees have been conditioned to expect formal grade reports, transcripts, and certificates of completion. These things formalize training in the minds of employees and make it more real for them. Educational institutions can provide these credibility builders.

Another problem that the employers sometimes experience when providing their own customized training is lack of standardization. The same training provided in three different divisions might produce markedly different results. Professional educators can help standardize the curriculum and evaluation systems. They can also help standardize instruction to the extent possible by providing train-the-trainer workshops for employees who are serving as in-house instructors.

Regardless of the approach or approaches used in providing training, there is a widely accepted rule of thumb that should be observed and with which managers should be familiar:

> People learn best when the learning approach used involves them in seeing, hearing, speaking, and doing.

Education practitioners hold that the percentages in Figure 12–10 apply regarding what learners remember and retain. Clearly, for learning to be effective, it must involve activity on the part of learners, be interactive in nature, and comprise to the extent possible reading, hearing, seeing, talking, and doing.

- 10 percent of what is read
- 20 percent of what is heard
- 30 percent of what is seen
- 50 percent of what is seen and heard
- 70 percent of what is seen and spoken
- 90 percent of what is said while doing what is talked about

FIGURE 12–10 Learning Retention

Regardless of the approach used to provide training, there are several critical decisions that must be made. Quality pioneer Joseph M. Juran outlined these decisions in his landmark book *Juran on Leadership for Quality*. The book is dated but Juran's views on this subject are still valid today. Juran explains as follows:[8]

- **Should training be voluntary or required?** If training is an essential part of total quality and the organization is committed to total quality, training should be mandatory. According to Juran:

  Once it is determined that universal training in managing for quality is essential to meeting the company's quality goals, such training should not be put on a voluntary basis. Instead, training in managing for quality should be mandated by upper management.[9]

- **How should training be sequenced?** Although the emphasis in a total quality setting is typically bottom up in terms of how much training is provided, the sequence of training is top down. In other words, managers receive less training than employees, but they receive it first. According to Juran:

  Upper management should be the first to acquire the new training. The reasons are quite persuasive: (1) by being first, upper managers become better qualified to review proposals made for training for the rest of the organization and (2) by setting an example the upper managers change an element of the corporate culture, that is, for lower levels to take the new training is to do what has been done in respected circles.[10]

- **What subjects should be taught?** The subject matter of training is dictated by the organization's goals for quality, productivity, and competitiveness. As was discussed earlier in this chapter, training needs are determined by comparing the knowledge, skills, and attitudes needed to accomplish organizational goals to those that are present in the organization. Any gap between what is needed and what is present can be closed by providing appropriate training.

Because the training needs of personnel at different levels vary, it is important to have training tracks (non-management track, middle management track, executive management track). Training should be arranged so that it is upwardly mobile in nature. This means that training for first-line supervisors should build on that provided for employees. Training provided for middle managers should build on that provided for first-line supervisors, and so on up the line through executive management.

EVALUATING TRAINING

Did the training provided satisfy the training objectives? Are trainees using what they learned? Has the training brought results? Managers need to know the answers to these questions every time training is provided. However, these can be difficult questions to answer. Evaluating training begins with a clear statement of purpose. What is the purpose of the training? This broad purpose should not be confused with the more specific training objectives. The purpose of the training is a broader concept. The objectives translate this purpose into more specific, measurable terms.

The purpose of training is to improve the knowledge, skills, and attitudes of employees and, in turn, the overall quality and productivity of the organization so that it becomes more competitive. In other words, the purpose of training is to improve performance and, in turn, competitiveness. To know whether training has improved performance, managers need to know three things:

- Was the training provided valid?
- Did the employees learn?
- Has the learning made a difference?

Valid training is training that is consistent with the training objectives.

Evaluating training for validity is a two-step process. The first step involves comparing the written documentation for the training (course outline, lesson plans, curriculum framework, etc.) with the training objectives. If the training is valid in design and content, the written documentation will match the training objectives. The second step involves determining whether the actual training provided is consistent with the documentation. Training that strays from the approved plan will not be valid. Student evaluations of instruction conducted immediately after completion can provide information on consistency and the quality of instruction. Figure 12–11 is an example of an instrument that allows students to evaluate instruction.

Determining whether employees have learned is a matter of building evaluation into the training. Employees can be tested to determine whether they have learned, but be sure that tests are based on the training objectives. If the training is valid and employees have learned, the training should make a difference in their performance. Performance on the job should improve; this means quality and productivity should improve. Managers can make determinations about performance using the same indicators that told them training was needed in the first place. Can employees perform

tasks they could not perform before the training? Is waste reduced? Has quality improved? Is setup time down? Is in-process time down? Is the on-time rate up? Is the production rate up? Is throughput time down? These are the types of questions managers should ask to determine whether training has improved performance.

MANAGERS AS TRAINERS AND TRAINEES

To be good trainers, managers should have such characteristics as a thorough knowledge of the topics to be taught; a desire to teach; a positive, helpful, cooperative attitude; strong leadership abilities; a professional attitude and approach; and exemplary behavior that sets a positive example.[11]

In addition to having these characteristics, managers should be knowledgeable about the fundamental principles of learning and the four-step teaching method. The principles of learning summarize much of what is known about how people learn best. It is important to conduct training in accordance with these principles. The four-step teaching method is a basic approach to conducting training that has proven effective over many years of use.

Principles of Learning

The principles of learning summarize what is known and widely accepted about how people learn. Trainers can do a better job of facilitating learning if they understand the following principles:

- **People learn best when they are ready to learn.** You cannot make employees learn anything. You can only make them want to learn. Therefore, time spent motivating employees to want to learn is time well-spent. Before beginning instruction, explain why employees need to learn and how they and the organization will mutually benefit from their having done so.

- **People learn more easily when what they are learning can be related to something they already know.** Build today's learning on what was learned yesterday and tomorrow's learning on what was learned today. Begin each new learning activity with a brief review of the one that preceded it. Use examples to which all employees can relate.

- **People learn best in a step-by-step manner.** This is an extension of the preceding principle. Learning should be organized into logically sequenced steps that proceed from the concrete to the abstract, from the simple to the complex, and from the known to the unknown.

- **People learn by doing.** This is probably the most important principle for trainers to understand. Inexperienced trainers tend to confuse talking (lecturing or demonstrating) with teaching. These things can be part of the teaching process, but they do little good unless they are followed with application activities

Instructions
On a scale of 1 to 5 (5 = highest rating; 1 = lowest rating), rank your teacher on each item. Leave blank any item that does not apply.

Organization of Course   5 4 3 2 1
1. Objectives (Clear to Unclear) 1 2 3 4 5
2. Requirements (Challenging to Unchallenging) 1 2 3 4 5
3. Assignments (Useful to Not Useful) 1 2 3 4 5
4. Materials (Excellent to Poor) 1 2 3 4 5
5. Testing Procedures (Effective to Ineffective) 1 2 3 4 5
6. Grading Practice (Explained to Not Explained) 1 2 3 4 5
7. Student Work Returned (Promptly to Delayed) 1 2 3 4 5
8. Overall Organization (Outstanding to Poor) 1 2 3 4 5

Comments

Teaching Skills   5 4 3 2 1
9. Class Meetings (Productive to Nonproductive) 1 2 3 4 5
10. Lectures (Effective to Ineffective) 1 2 3 4 5
11. Discussions (Balanced to Unbalanced) 1 2 3 4 5
12. Class Proceedings (To-the-Point/Wandering) 1 2 3 4 5
13. Provides Feedback (Beneficial to Not Beneficial) 1 2 3 4 5
14. Responds to Students (Positively/Negatively) 1 2 3 4 5
15. Provides Assistance (Always to Never) 1 2 3 4 5
16. Overall Rating of Instructor's Teaching Skills
(Outstanding to Poor) 1 2 3 4 5

Comments

Substantive Value of Course   5 4 3 2 1
17. The course was (Intellectually Challenging to Elementary) 1 2 3 4 5
18. The instructor's command of the subject was
(Broad Accurate to Plainly Defective) 1 2 3 4 5
19. Overall substantive value of the course
(Outstanding to Poor) 1 2 3 4 5

Comments

FIGURE 12–11 Student Evaluation of Instruction

that require the learner to do something. Consider the example of teaching an employee how to ride a bicycle. You might present a thorough lecture on the principles of pedaling and steering and give a comprehensive demonstration on how to do it. However, until the employee gets on and begins pedaling, he or she will not learn how to ride a bicycle.

- **The more often people use what they are learning, the better they will remember and understand it.** How many things have you learned in your life that you can

no longer remember? People forget what they do not use. Trainers should keep this principle in mind. It means that repetition and application should be built into the learning process.

- **Success in learning tends to stimulate additional learning.** This principle is a restatement of a fundamental principle in management (success breeds success). Organize training into long enough segments to allow learners to see progress but not so long that they become bored.

- **People need immediate and continual feedback to know if they have learned.** Did you ever take a test and get the results back a week later? If so, that was probably a week later than you wanted them. People who are learning want to know immediately and continually how they are doing. Trainers should keep this principle in mind at all times. Feedback can be as simple as a nod, a pat on the back, or a comment such as "Good job!" It can also be more formal, such as a progress report or a graded activity. Regardless of the form it takes, trainers should concentrate on giving immediate and continual feedback.

Four-Step Teaching Method

Regardless of the setting, teaching is a matter of helping people learn. One of the most effective approaches for facilitating learning is not new, innovative, gimmicky, or high-tech in nature. It is known as the four-step teaching method, an effective approach to use for training. The four steps and a brief description of each follow:

- **Preparation** encompasses all tasks necessary to get participants prepared to learn, trainers prepared to teach, and facilities prepared to accommodate the process. Preparing participants means motivating them to want to learn. Personal preparation involves planning lessons and getting all of the necessary instructional materials ready. Preparing the facility involves arranging the room for both function and comfort, checking all equipment to ensure it works properly, and making sure that all tools and other training aids are in place.

- **Presentation** is a matter of presenting the material participants are to learn. It might involve giving a demonstration, presenting a lecture, conducting a question-and-answer session, helping participants interact with a computer or interactive videodisc system, or assisting those who are proceeding through self-paced materials.

- **Application** is a matter of giving learners opportunities to use what they are learning. Application might range from simulation activities in which learners role-play to actual hands-on activities in which learners use their new skills in a live format.

- **Evaluation** is a matter of determining the extent to which learning has taken place. In a training setting, evaluation does not need to be a complicated process. If the training objectives were written in measurable, observable terms, evaluation is simple. Employees were supposed to learn how to do X, Y, and Z well and safely. Have them do X, Y, and Z and observe the results. In other words, have employees demonstrate proficiency in performing a task and see how they do.

Preparing Instruction   Preparing instruction involves the following steps:

1. Preparing (planning) the instruction
2. Preparing the facility
3. Preparing the learners

It is important to accomplish all three steps before attempting to present instruction. The instruction delivered by managers will usually be part of a course, workshop, or seminar. In any case, a course outline must exist that summarizes the major topics covered by the instruction. The outline should state in broad terms the expected outcomes of the instruction or, in other words, what the learner is supposed to be able to do after completing the course, workshop, or seminar. The outline should also have a brief statement of purpose. More specific instructional objectives are developed later when preparing lesson plans. Figure 12–12 is a sample outline for a short course on W. Edwards Deming's Fourteen Points for quality improvement.

The course outline contains just two components: a statement of purpose and a list of intended outcomes. Some instructors prefer to add additional components such as a list of equipment or training aids needed, but the components shown in Figure 12–12 are sufficient. A good course outline is a broadly stated snapshot of the scope and sequence of the course. Specific details are typically shown in the lesson plans, which are developed next.

Lesson plans are an important part of the planning step. They are road maps or blueprints for the actual instruction that is to take place. In addition, they standardize instruction when more than one person might present the same lesson to different groups. Standardization is particularly important for quality training. If even one member of a work team receives less training than the others, the potential for quality problems is increased by his or her ignorance.

Lesson plans can vary in format according to the personal preferences of the trainer. However, all lesson plans should include the components discussed in the following paragraphs:

- **Lesson title and number.** The lesson title should be as descriptive as possible of the content of the lesson. The number shows where the lesson fits into the sequence of lessons that make up the course.

- **Statement of purpose.** Like the statement of purpose in the course outline, this component consists of a concise description of the lesson's contents, where it fits into the course, and why it is included.

- **Learning objectives.** Learning objectives are specific statements of what the learner should know or be able to do as a result of completing the lesson. Objectives should be written in behavioral terms that can be measured or easily observed.

- **Training aids list.** This component serves as a handy checklist to help trainers quickly and conveniently ensure that all the training aids they will need are present. The list should include every tool, handout, piece of equipment, video, chart, or other item needed to conduct the instruction for that lesson.

- **Instructional approach.** The instructional approach is a brief action plan for carrying out the instruction. It should begin with a short statement describing the instructional methodology to be used (lecture/discussion,

Statement of Purpose
The purpose of this seminar is to familiarize managers with the Fourteen Points set forth by W. Edwards Deming and how they might be used to improve quality in this organization.

Intended Outcomes
Upon completion of this seminar, managers should be able to explain the ramifications for our company of each of the following points:

1. Create constancy of purpose for improvement of product and service.
2. Adopt the new philosophy.
3. Depend less on mass inspection.
4. End the practice of awarding business on the price tag alone.
5. Improve constantly and forever the system of production and service.
6. Institute training.
7. Institute leadership.
8. Drive out fear.
9. Break down barriers between staff areas.
10. Eliminate slogans, exhortations, and targets for the workforce.
11. Eliminate numerical quotas.
12. Remove barriers of pride of workmanship.
13. Institute a vigorous program of education and retraining.
14. Take action to accomplish the transformation.

FIGURE 12–12 Course Outline: Deming's Fourteen Points for Quality Improvement

demonstration, computer-assisted instruction, or other method). This statement is followed by a step-by-step summary of the trainer's major activities: for example, deliver lecture on safety regulations or distribute safety regulations handout.

- **Application assignments.** The application assignments list details the tasks learners will be required to complete to apply what they are learning.

- **Evaluation methodology.** The evaluation methodology component explains how learning will be evaluated. Will there be a test? Will performance be observed? Will records be monitored for improvement? Such questions are answered in this section.

Presenting Instruction As shown earlier in Figure 12–10, educators hold that the following percentages apply regarding what learners retain from instruction they receive:

- 10% of what is read
- 20% of what is heard
- 30% of what is seen
- 50% of what is seen and heard
- 70% of what is seen and spoken
- 90% of what is said while doing what is talked about

Instruction can be presented in several different ways. The most widely used are the lecture/discussion, demonstration, conference, and multimedia methods. Regardless of the approach used, trainers should keep the percentages listed here in mind. What they indicate is that the trainers

should get the learners actively engaged in seeing, saying, listening, and, most important, doing.

The Lecture/Discussion Method The lecture/discussion method of teaching is the oldest, most familiar, most used, and probably most abused method. A lecture is a planned, structured, and sometimes illustrated (using slides, charts, or board) method of communicating information to a group of people. By itself, the lecture allows for only one-way communication. This serious deficiency is overcome by adding the discussion component. Discussion can be between the instructor and participants or among the participants. During discussion, the instructor's job is to keep the discussion on track and moving in the right direction.

The best justification for using the lecture/discussion method is that it is an effective way to communicate information to groups that are too large to allow for individual interaction between instructor and participants. Another reason for using this method is that it allows the instructor to generate enthusiasm among participants about a topic.

The lecture/discussion method, if used properly, can be an effective teaching technique. However, it does not work in every situation. Trainers need to know when to use it and when to use another method. Use the lecture/discussion method when any of the following things is true:

- The material to be presented deals strictly with data, theory, or information (no skills development).

- Participants need to be motivated before beginning a particular lesson.

- The material to be presented is not available in print.

- Sharing insight or experience in a particular area will enhance learning.

- It is necessary to communicate information to a large group in one session.

- Interaction among participants is desired.

Do not use the lecture/discussion method when any of these things is true:

- The subject matter deals with skills development or how-to information.

- The group of auditors is small enough to allow individual student–teacher interaction.

- There is no need for interaction among participants.

Participants must be thoroughly prepared prior to the session. If they are not, the session will be all lecture and no discussion. Require participants to approach a lecture/discussion session as if they were entering a debate. This will ensure that they are active, contributing participants rather than passive spectators.

Prepare participants for a lecture/discussion session as follows:

1. Give them a written outline or overview of the lecture.

2. Have participants use the outline as a study guide or a guide to research and reading.

3. Instruct your listeners to note anything that is unclear to them or about which they cannot locate information while reading and researching.

4. Have participants put their notes together in an annotated outline, leaving plenty of blank space for taking notes under each item during the lecture/discussion session.

There is a saying in teaching: "When giving a lecture, tell them what you are going to tell them, tell them, and then tell them what you told them." Although it is said with tongue in cheek, this is actually good advice. A well-planned, properly structured lecture contains three distinct components: the *opening*, in which you "tell them what you are going to tell them"; the *body*, in which you "tell them"; and the *closing*, in which you "tell them what you told them."

Discussion may be interspersed within the body or held until after the closing, depending on your preference. The recommended method is to allow discussion during the body of the lecture while questions and concerns are fresh in the participants' minds.

The opening, body, and closing of a lecture all contain specific tasks that should be accomplished in order:

1. Opening
   a. Greet the class.
   b. State the title of the lecture.
   c. Explain the purpose of the lecture.
   d. List the objectives so that participants know exactly what they should be learning.
   e. List and define any new terms that will be used during the session.
   f. Present a general overview of the content of the lecture/discussion.

2. Body
   a. Present the information in the order set forth on the participants' outline.
   b. Accomplish the purpose of the lecture.
   c. Make frequent reference to all visual aids and supportive materials.

3. Closing
   a. Restate the title, purpose, and objectives.
   b. Briefly summarize major points.
   c. State your conclusions.
   d. Answer remaining questions.
   e. Make follow-up assignments to reinforce and apply learning.

These elements are the fundamental or tangible tasks that should be performed in all lecture/discussion sessions. You should also keep in mind a number of intangibles when conducting lecture/discussion sessions:

- Make sure that the classroom is arranged to accommodate a lecture/discussion.

- Be enthusiastic. Enthusiasm is contagious.

- Call on participants by name. They will appreciate the recognition and feel more at ease.

- Spread your attention evenly. This will make all participants feel that they are part of the lecture/discussion.

- Maintain eye contact with all participants in the session.

- Speak clearly, evenly, and slowly enough to be understood but not in a monotone.

- Use facial expressions, body language, and movement to emphasize points.

- It is all right to use an outline or note cards to keep yourself on track, but never read a lecture to the participants.

- Use carefully prepared visual aids to reinforce major points.

- Do not dominate—facilitate. Participation is critical. Remember, this method is called *lecture/discussion*.

The Demonstration Method Demonstration is the process in which the instructor shows participants how to perform certain skills or tasks. While demonstrating, the instructor also explains all operations step-by-step. The key to giving a good demonstration is preparation. The following checklist contains specific tasks for preparing a demonstration:

1. Decide exactly what the purpose of the demonstration is, why it will be given, what participants should learn from it, what will be demonstrated and in what order, and how long the demonstration will last.

2. Gather all tools, equipment, and instructional aids, and make sure that everything is available and in working order. Never put yourself in the position of being forced to stop a demonstration in the middle because something does not work the way it should or because a necessary part of the demonstration is not on hand.

3. Set up the demonstration so that participants will be able to easily see what is going on and hear what you are saying.

4. Arrange all materials to be used in the demonstration so that they correspond with the order in which the various steps of the demonstration will be presented.

5. Practice the demonstration several times before giving it in order to work out any bugs.

Just as there are specific tasks to be performed in presenting a lecture, there are specific tasks to be performed in giving a demonstration. These are as follows:

1. Orient participants to the demonstration by explaining its purpose and objectives. Give them a brief overview of the content of the demonstration. Explain how the demonstration ties in with what the participants already know.

2. Present the demonstration in a slow, deliberate fashion so that participants can easily follow.

3. Pause between stages to determine whether participants are comprehending or have any questions that should be answered before continuing. Go back over any steps that they did not seem to grasp.

4. Conclude the demonstration with a brief summary and question-and-answer session.

Activity in skills development by class members is critical. Remember, no matter how well a demonstration is presented, it is really just showing. Showing is important, but participants learn best by doing, so it is vital to provide them with hands-on activities after a demonstration. An effective way to follow up demonstrations is to

- Select several participants and ask them to repeat the demonstration you have just given.

- Assign a number of practical application activities in which the participants are required to apply the skills demonstrated.

- Observe participants on an individual basis as they attempt to perform the practical application activities. Give individual attention and assistance where needed. Be sure to correct mistakes immediately so that the wrong way does not become a habit.

- Conduct performance evaluations so that skills development can be measured.

The Conference Method The conference method is particularly well-suited for corporate training settings. It is less formal than a traditional classroom setting and requires that the trainer serve as a facilitator rather than a teacher. It is best used as a problem-solving teaching method. For example, a manager might use the conference method to make all employees aware of a new quality problem, while simultaneously soliciting their input on how to solve the problem.

To be effective facilitators, managers must become adept at defining the problem, soliciting input from participants, drawing out all participants, summarizing and repeating information, and building consensus. The conference teaching method, when effectively used, should result in both well-informed participants and a plan for solving the problem.

Multimedia Methods In addition to the presentation methods already explained, several others can be employed. The most widely used are simulation, DVDs, and programmed instruction.

- **Simulation.** Simulation, as the name implies, involves structuring a training activity that simulates a live situation. For example, if a manager is teaching a group of workers how to respond when a fellow worker passes on faulty work, he or she might simulate that situation by having a worker role-play this situation. Simulation can also be technology based. Computer simulation activities and those based on interactive laser disc and video technology are becoming more commonly employed. The military has used technology-based simulation for many years to train pilots.

- **DVDs.** The use of DVDs for presenting instruction has become common in corporate training settings. In essence, the DVDs take the place of a lecture or demonstration. The pause or stop function on the DVD player can be used to allow for discussion, questions and answers, and group interaction. The playback feature can be used to review or replay portions of the material that are not fully understood by participants.

- **Programmed instruction.** Programmed instruction is a technique for individualizing instruction. Traditionally, the programmed medium has been a workbook or text that presents information in segments that proceed as follows:

  a. Information presentation
  b. Information review
  c. Questions, problems, or activities for the participant to complete based on the information presented
  d. A self-test

  Before proceeding to the next lesson, the learner must make a specified score on the self-test for the current lesson. Increasingly, programmed instruction is becoming computerized. This enhances the interactive nature of the instruction and, with good software, provides almost immediate feedback for the learner.

- **Online instruction.** Online training combines Internet and personal computer technologies to create an excellent high-tech approach to workplace training. Unlike many other media-based training methods, online training is not passive. Rather, it requires the learner to participate actively by making choices and participating in one-on-one simulations of workplace situations.

Applying Instruction   One of the fundamental principles of learning states that people learn by doing. To the trainer, this means that learners must be given opportunities to apply what they are learning. If the topic of a training session is how to apply statistics to quality, application should involve the learners in actually applying statistics. While the learners practice, the trainer observes, coaches, and corrects. Regardless of the nature of the material, learners should be given plenty of opportunities to apply what they are learning.

Evaluating Instruction   The final step in the four-step teaching method is evaluation, which was described in the list at the start of the "Four-Step Teaching Method" section.

Managers as Trainees

In a total quality setting, some managers will be trainers. However, all managers will be trainees. According to Juran, all managers in a total quality setting should complete training in the following areas:[12]

- **Quality basics,** including definitions, big Q and little Q, and the Juran Trilogy
- **Strategic quality management,** including developing a quality strategy and quality policies and establishing a quality council, goals, deployment, resources, measurement, and rewards
- **Quality planning,** including how to apply quality planning road maps
- **Quality improvement,** including infrastructure, cost of poor quality, return on investments in quality, and the project-by-project concept
- **Quality control,** including establishing quality measures, compiling quality report packages, and conducting quality audits

Several factors can undermine the process of providing training for managers. These include a lack of credibility on the part of trainers and discomfort with training that mixes managers and nonmanagers. Juran recommends that the following common behavior characteristics of managers be taken into account when providing training for them:[13]

- Managers prefer training sessions that enroll only managers.
- Managers are uncomfortable being trained by subordinates.
- Managers prefer to be trained by well-known outsiders.
- Managers enjoy learning of the experiences of other managers from well-managed companies.
- Managers prefer off-site training.
- Managers enjoy visiting companies that have reputations for excellence.

WORKFORCE LITERACY

In recent years, industry has been forced to face a tragic and potentially devastating problem: adult illiteracy, a problem that is having a major impact on the competitiveness of business and industry in the United States.[14] It is estimated that more than 60 million people, or approximately one-third of the adult population in this country, are marginally to functionally illiterate.[15]

Illiteracy has become a more compelling problem today because of technological advances and the need to compete in the international marketplace. The problem is compounded in the following ways:

- Basic skill requirements are being increased by technological advances and the need to compete in the international marketplace.
- Broader definitions of literacy go beyond just reading and writing to include speaking, listening, and mathematics.
- Old views of what constitutes literacy no longer apply.

Impact of Illiteracy on Industry

The basic skills necessary for a worker to be productive in the modern workplace are increasing steadily. At the same time, the national high school dropout rate continues to rise, as does the number of high school graduates who are functionally illiterate in spite of their diplomas. This means that while the number of high-skilled jobs in modern industry is increasing, the number of people able to fill them is on the decline. The impact this problem will have on industry in the United States can be summarized as follows:

- Difficulty in filling high-skill jobs
- Lower levels of productivity and, as a result, a lower level of competitiveness
- Higher levels of waste
- Higher potential for damage to sophisticated technological systems
- Greater number of dissatisfied employees in the workplace

What Industry Can Do

Global competition has made it necessary for organizations in the United States to confront the illiteracy problem head-on. Companies are doing this by providing remedial education for employees in the workplace. Some companies contract with private training firms, others provide the education themselves, and still others form partnerships with colleges, universities, or vocational schools.

The National Center for Research in Vocational Education conducts research into industry-based adult literacy training programs in the United States. It found that Texas Instruments requires math, verbal and written communication, and basic physics of its employees. Physics skills have not traditionally been viewed as being part of functional literacy. However, to succeed in this high-tech company, employees must have these skills. The approach used by Texas Instruments to provide literacy training can be one of the least expensive; by working in conjunction with public colleges or vocational schools, companies can provide literacy training at little and, in some cases, no cost. Managers should establish a close working relationship with the business and industry representatives in local colleges and vocational schools.

Rockwell International also defines literacy more stringently than has been typical in the past. To function effectively at Rockwell International, employees must be skilled in chemistry and physics. This is another example that is indicative of the need for higher skill levels to be functionally literate. To accomplish this goal for its employees, Rockwell hired its own certified teachers.

Of the companies studied, Polaroid takes the most aggressive approach in defining functional literacy. The skills taught in Polaroid's program are also indicative of the trend, especially in the areas of statistics, problem solving, and computer literacy. The need for these skills is technology driven. Knowledge of statistics is required to use statistical process control (SPC), which is widely employed in total quality settings. Few employees in a modern industrial firm get by without using a computer on the job—hence the need for computer literacy training. Problem-solving skills are critical to companies in a total quality setting. Programs that teach problem-solving skills involve employees in identifying and correcting problems that have a negative impact on quality or do not add value to the company's products. Polaroid considers problem solving part of functional literacy.

IMPROVING LEARNING

One of the difficulties with education and training is that many people don't know *how* to learn. Learning can be improved by teaching all employees good study skills before putting them in a training program and by using humor to improve teaching in company-sponsored training programs.

Time spent helping employees learn how to learn will be time invested well. The following strategies are widely recommended by education and training professionals:

- **Make a schedule and stick to it.** Allow 2 hours of study time for each hour of class time. Schedule time for review immediately before and immediately after the class. Take short breaks, at least one each hour. Reward yourself for sticking to your schedule.

- **Have a quiet place to study.** Designate a quiet place as your study site and equip it with everything you will need (reference books, paper, pens, and whatever else you need).

- **Listen carefully and take notes.** Concentrate on the presentation and take notes. Don't let your mind wander. In taking notes, don't try to write down everything that is said. Rather, write down key points only, leaving room to expand your notes afterward. Listening for key points will improve your listening ability and, in turn, your retention.

- **Outline.** Just reading course materials will not adequately prepare you for class activities. After reading such materials, go back and make an outline of major points and supportive points.

- **Study regularly—don't cram.** Don't cram for tests; instead, study regularly. When taking tests, skim over the entire document before answering individual items. Answer the questions you are sure of first. This will allow you to spend more time on those items about which you are less confident.

WHY TRAINING SOMETIMES FAILS

Training is an essential ingredient in total quality, but training is not automatically good. In fact, training often fails. Training fails for several reasons, such as poor teaching, inadequate curriculum materials, poor planning, insufficient funding, and a lack of commitment.

Some subtle and more serious reasons for training failures are explained by Juran as follows:[16]

- **Lack of participation in planning by management.** It is important to involve people at the line level in the planning of training. However, this does not mean management should be excluded; in fact, quite the opposite is true. Management must be involved, or the training may become task or technique oriented, as opposed to results oriented. It is critical that training be results oriented, or in the long run, it will fail.

- **Too narrow in scope.** Training that is to improve quality should proceed from the broad and general to the more specific. Often organizations jump right into the finite aspects of total quality such as statistical process control, just-in-time manufacturing, or teamwork before employees understand the big picture and where these finite aspects fit into it.

QUALITY TRAINING CURRICULUM

For managers to play a leadership role in a total quality setting, they must be well-trained in what Juran calls the Juran Trilogy: quality planning, quality control, and quality improvement.[17] A curriculum outline for each of these areas is provided in the following sections.

Quality Planning Training

Quality planning is the first component of the Juran Trilogy. According to Juran, quality planning should cover these topics:[18]

- Strategic management for quality
- Quality policies and their deployment
- Strategic quality goals and their deployment
- The Juran Trilogy

- Big Q and little Q
- The triple-role concept
- Quality planning road map
- Internal and external customers
- How to identify customers
- Planning macroprocesses
- Planning microprocesses
- Product design
- Planning for process control
- Transfer to operations
- Santayana review (lessons learned)
- Planning tools

Quality Control Training

Quality control is the second component of the Juran Trilogy. According to Juran, quality control training should cover the following topics:[19]

- Strategic management for quality
- The feedback loop in quality control
- Controllability (self-control)
- Planning for control
- Control subjects
- Responsibility for control
- How to evaluate performance
- Interpretation of statistical and economic data for significance
- Decision making
- Corrective action
- Quality assurance audits
- Control tools

Quality Improvement Training

Quality improvement is the third component of the Juran Trilogy. According to Juran, quality improvement training should cover the following topics:[20]

- Strategic management for quality
- The Juran Trilogy
- Quality Council and its responsibilities
- Cost of poor quality: how to estimate it
- Project-by-project concept
- Estimating return on investment
- Nominating, screening, and selecting projects
- Infrastructure for quality improvement
- Macroprocess improvement projects
- Diagnostic journey
- Remedial journey

- Progress review
- Using recognition and reward to motivate
- Quality improvement tools and techniques

By standardizing the curriculum as presented here and ensuring that all managers complete training in these three broad areas of quality, companies can come closer to achieving consistency of performance, and consistency of performance is critical in a total quality setting because it makes performance easier to measure and improve.

ORIENTATION TRAINING

New employees walk into a new job cold. They don't know the organization; its corporate culture; its rules, regulations, and expectations; or its employees. For this reason, orientation training is important. Although orientation is widely provided, too frequently it is haphazard and of poor quality.

Three recurring errors are associated with orientation training. These are as follows:[21]

- **Insufficient information.** People typically begin new jobs with some trepidation. They want to know where they fit in, what is expected of them, and with whom they will be working. A problem with some orientation programs is that they don't provide enough of the right information to give new employees a good start. The obvious difficulty in such cases is that employees take longer, through no fault of their own, to become productive.

- **Too much information.** Some organizations determined to give new employees a good start actually give them too much information too fast. The human mind can absorb and act on only so much data at a time. When it tries to take in too much too fast, information overload can occur. The net result is the same as when too little information is given.

- **Conflicting information.** A common problem with orientation programs is that new employees often receive conflicting information. The orientation provides new employees with the organization's approved approach to a given situation, only to have this information refuted by experienced employees who say, "Ignore that stuff; here is how we really do it."

These three problems can be prevented by applying the following strategies:[22]

- **Base orientation topics on a needs assessment.** Before developing an orientation program, assess the needs of both the organization and the new employees. Characteristics shared by good orientation programs are these: they afford new employees privacy as they proceed through the program; they provide new employees with ongoing access to information, people, and resources; and they reflect the culture (tone, feeling, spirit) of the organization.

■ **Establish an organizing framework.** Should information be organized chronologically, by major functions, or by mission? The first portion of the program might deal with people issues; the second, rules and regulations; the third, work processes; and so on. Regardless of the approach used to organize the training, it is important that the training be arranged logically and proceed in a step-by-step manner.

■ **Establish learner control.** This involves putting the learner in control of his or her learning. This can be accomplished only if instruction is self-paced and individualized. Fortunately, computers and instructional media such as videotapes have made the development and use of individualized instruction easier, which, in turn, puts learners in control, letting them pursue learning in their own order of priority.

■ **Make orientation a process, not just an event.** Typically, orientation programs are front loaded in the first day or so of employment and treated as a finite event. Such an approach can limit their value. Front-loading only the learning that must be accomplished before beginning work and then spreading the rest appropriately over a period of months can improve results. An important part of the extended orientation process should be regularly scheduled conferences with a supervisor or mentor who can observe progress, identify potential trouble spots, and help facilitate the continual growth of the new employees.

■ **Allow people and personalities to emerge.** Typically, new employees are keenly interested in the people who make up the human side of the organization. Consequently, information about key personnel should be included in orientation materials. This information should include a brief resume, a one-paragraph job description, and a recent photograph. Including personal information such as hobbies will help orientation trainees see their new colleagues as human beings.

■ **Reflect the organization's mission and culture.** New employees, regardless of their position in the organization, need to know its mission, goals, and priorities. They also need to know the values on which the organization's culture is based—new employees need to know what their employer thinks is important.

■ **Have a system for improving and updating.** Successful organizations are not static. They evolve as the circumstances in which they must compete, change. New people, processes, technologies, procedures, and priorities evolve and replace the old. As this happens, the orientation program must be updated accordingly. In addition, ongoing evaluations of the program will reveal weaknesses that should be converted quickly. This means that employees, new and old, and at all levels, should be involved in the continual improvement and updating of the orientation program.

CUSTOMER TRAINING

An old adage states, "The customer is always right." Although the message this saying conveys is a good one, in reality the customer is not always right. In fact, one of the main reasons for consumer product failure is improper use by the customer.

Customer training has several aspects, including shaping customer expectations, providing user support, and marketing. To be satisfied with a product, customers need to know what to expect from the product. This is important because in a total quality setting, quality is defined in terms of customer expectations. Customers with inaccurate or unrealistic expectations are less likely to be satisfied customers.

Customer expectations are shaped by the promotional literature used in marketing the product and by the user support materials provided with the product. For this reason, it is vital that promotional literature be accurate and that it not contain inflated claims about the product. Accurate customer expectations can also be promoted by the organization's customer service representatives. These employees should be adept at providing one-on-one training for customers in person or by telephone. Giving customers toll-free access to customer service trainers can be an effective way to promote accurate expectations.

User support might be provided in the form of user manuals, on-site technical assistance, or training provided at a central company facility. Regardless of the approach, providing user support gives a company an excellent opportunity to train customers in the proper use of its product. To take full advantage of this opportunity, an organization must make sure its user manuals are readable, train its technical representatives to be customer trainers, and give customers immediate access to additional help through a user support telephone number. People who provide user support are in an excellent position to turn a new customer into a satisfied, knowledgeable, loyal customer.

Customer training can also help market a product. The philosophy that joins customer training and marketing can be stated as follows: "You wouldn't buy a car if you did not know how to drive one." To get the full marketing value of customer training, it's a good idea to involve marketing personnel in the development of the training.

ETHICS TRAINING

Ethical behavior and the rationale for it can be taught. In fact, an increasing number of organizations in the United States provide ethics training.

Topics that are widely addressed in corporate-sponsored ethics training programs include the following:

■ Drug and alcohol abuse
■ Employee theft
■ Conflicts of interest
■ Sexual harassment
■ Corporate social responsibility

- Quality control
- Misuse of proprietary information
- Abuse of expense accounts
- Plant closings and layoffs
- Misuse of company property
- Environmental pollution
- Methods of gathering competitors' information
- Inaccuracy of books and records
- Receiving excessive gifts and entertainment
- False or misleading advertising
- Giving excessive gifts and entertainment
- Kickbacks
- Insider trading
- Antitrust issues
- Bribery
- Political contributions and activities
- Improper relations with local, state, and federal government officials
- Inaccurate time charging to government and private entities
- Improper relations with foreign government officials

Ethics training is becoming increasingly important as the pressures of succeeding in an intensely competitive global marketplace grow.

MAKING E-LEARNING WORK

Increasingly, e-learning is finding its way into the culture of corporate training. Computer and online resources can enhance both the quality and the availability of corporate training, provided they are used effectively. Several strategies will help make e-learning work effectively for providing corporate training:[23]

1. Understand that one of the strengths of e-learning is scalability. It is an excellent way to get information to many people quickly.

2. Don't try to provide e-learning opportunities without support. It works best when there are learning coaches and mentors provided. E-learning should not be viewed as a way to "economize by getting rid of instructors." It is another approach to training that works well under certain circumstances.

3. Blend e-learning and classroom instruction so that employees get the best of both methods.

4. Design student assessments of online learning in such a way that students cannot just copy answers to tests out of their reference books.

5. Don't force employees to make a quick switch from classroom instruction to online instruction. Give them time and assistance in getting comfortable with computer-based instruction.

6. Remember that e-learning is a tool, not a strategy.

SUMMARY

1. Training is an organized, systematic series of activities designed to enhance an individual's work-related knowledge, skills, understanding, and motivation. Training is distinguished from education by its characteristics of practicality, specificity, and immediacy. Education is a broader concept that is more philosophical and theoretical in nature than training. Corporate training in the United States has historically focused more on managers than on workers. However, with the advent of total quality, the focus is beginning to change.

2. Historically, corporate America has not placed as high a priority on training as have companies from such countries as Germany and Japan. However, with the increased pressure from global competition, this attitude is beginning to change.

3. The rationale for training can be found in the following factors: quality of the existing labor pool, global competition, rapid and continual change, technology transfer problems, and changing demographics.

4. It is important to place the emphasis of training on those who need it most and to ensure that training is designed to promote the organization's goals. These requirements are met by assessing training needs before providing training. Training needs can be assessed by observing, brainstorming, and surveying. Training needs should be converted to training objectives that are stated in behavioral terms.

5. Training can be provided in-house; through corporate-owned education and training facilities; in conjunction with colleges, universities, and professional organizations; or via satellite downlinks.

6. Evaluating training begins with a clear statement of purpose. With a statement of purpose drafted, the next step is to ask the following questions: Was the training provided valid? Did the employees learn? Has the training made a difference?

7. Managers who serve as trainers should understand the principles of learning and the four-step teaching method (preparation, presentation, application, and evaluation). In presenting instruction, trainers should remember that people learn by doing. Widely used instructional approaches are lecture/discussion; demonstration; conference; multimedia; and videotaped, programmed, and interactive video instruction.

8. Functional illiteracy affects business and industry as follows: difficulty in filling high-skill jobs, lower

productivity, higher levels of waste, higher potential for damage to sophisticated equipment, and more dissatisfied employees.

9. Before putting employees in training, it is a good idea to teach them study skills that will enhance their learning. They should learn to make a schedule and stick to it, have a quiet place to study, listen and take notes, outline, and study regularly instead of cramming.

10. When training fails, the reason is often a lack of participation by management or insufficient scope (focusing on the specifics before teaching the big picture).

11. Quality training should be divided into three broad categories of study: quality planning, quality control, and quality improvement.

12. Orientation training sometimes fails. When it does, the cause is usually one of the following factors: insufficient information, too much information, or conflicting information. To improve orientation training, organizations should base orientation topics on a needs assessment, establish an organizing framework, establish learner control, make orientation a process rather than an event, allow people and personalities to emerge, reflect the organization's mission and culture, and have a system for improving and updating.

13. Topics frequently dealt with in ethics training programs include drug and alcohol abuse, theft, conflicts of interest, abuse of expense accounts, misuse of company property, kickbacks, bribery, improper relations with government officials, and false advertising.

14. E-learning works best when learning coaches and mentors are provided.

KEY TERMS AND CONCEPTS

Application
Body
Changing demographics
Closing
Conference method
Customer training
Demonstration method
Education
Ethics training
Evaluation
External approaches
Four-step teaching method
Global competition
Immediate and continual feedback
In-house training
Internal approaches
Lecture/discussion method

Lesson plans
Opening
Orientation training
Partnership approaches
Preparation
Presentation
Principles of learning
Programmed instruction
Quality control training
Quality improvement training
Quality of the existing labor pool
Quality planning training
Rapid and continual change
Simulation
Study skills
Technology transfer problems
Training
Training aids list
Training objectives
Valid training

FACTUAL REVIEW QUESTIONS

1. Define *training*, and explain how it differs from *education*.

2. Explain the total quality philosophy of training.

3. Name 10 widely used instructional methods.

4. Describe the traditional attitude of corporate America toward training. How does this view compare with that of other industrialized countries?

5. List the five factors that magnify the need for training.

6. What is technology transfer? What effect can it have on an organization's competitiveness?

7. Explain the potential benefits of training.

8. If asked to assess a department's training needs, how would you go about it?

9. What is a training objective? Write a sample training objective in behavioral terms.

10. List and explain five strategies for maximizing training resources.

11. What does a manager need to know to be sure that training provided satisfied the training objectives? How can these things be determined?

12. Describe how to evaluate a training program before purchasing it.

13. List and explain the principles of learning.

14. Describe the four-step teaching method.

15. What are the minimum recommended contents of a lesson plan?

16. As an instructor, what can you do to help participants retain what they are learning?

17. List and explain the three components of a lecture.

18. Describe the following presentation methods:
    ■ Simulation
    ■ Programmed instruction
    ■ Conference

19. Summarize the status of literacy in the United States and the impact it has on the competitiveness of U.S. companies.

20. What can an industry do to deal with workforce illiteracy?

21. Describe what managers in a total quality setting should know about literacy training.

22. List and describe the study skills that employees should learn before beginning a training program.

23. Why does training sometimes fail?

24. What are the three major components in quality training recommended by Juran?

25. List 10 widely taught ethics topics.

26. Explain the strategies for making e-learning programs work.

CRITICAL THINKING ACTIVITY

A Training Problem

Amanda Carr is a quality management troubleshooter who has been brought in as a consultant by The Werner Corporation (TWC). TWC is applying the principles of quality management in an attempt to continually improve every aspect of the company's performance—something it must do to compete globally.

TWC's top executive has done everything right as far as he can tell. The company has a good strategic plan, employees are involved and empowered, executive-level commitment is in place, and there is a unity of purpose from top to bottom in the organization. Employees and executives alike want the company's performance to improve, and they all want to do their part. Unfortunately, things are just not improving. Something is wrong, but TWC's management team has been unable to determine what it is. Hence, the contract with Amanda Carr.

Amanda thinks she has found the problem. TWC's managers and employees have plenty of *want-to* but very little *know-how*. Training is needed from top to bottom in the company. How should Amanda proceed? What types of training are needed? How should it be provided? What obstacles will have to be overcome? How can they be overcome?

DISCUSSION ASSIGNMENT 12–1

Corporate Training at Rockwell International

The Rocky Flats Plant of Rockwell International is committed to hiring hard-core unemployed people for entry-level positions with the intention of migrating them upward. However, many new employees have serious deficiencies in basic education skills. Technological changes compound the problem. As a result, Rockwell has established an in-house training program to help new employees develop basic skills and the more advanced skills needed to migrate upward.

A heavy emphasis is placed on algebra, chemistry, and safety. Rockwell pays all training costs, including the costs of college courses taken off-site. Required courses are taken on company time. Courses for promotion are taken on the employee's time. Self-paced and computer-aided instruction methods are used for teaching basic skills.

DISCUSSION QUESTIONS

Discuss the following questions in class or outside of class with your fellow students:

1. What is your opinion of Rockwell's commitment to hiring the hard-core unemployed and training them?

2. How do you think this commitment affects Rockwell's ability to compete?

DISCUSSION ASSIGNMENT 12–2

CEO Who Does Not Support Training

The CEO of ABC Inc. is dynamic and visionary in every area but one. He does not believe in providing corporate training to his personnel. In fact, he is fond of saying, "I hire personnel and pay them well. They should have the skills we need when they walk in the door. If they don't, it's their responsibility to get training. We are a technology firm not a college or public school." The company's top managers, including the quality manager, have tried but failed to convince the CEO that the company will not be able to remain competitive unless it commits to corporate training as a normal part of doing business.

DISCUSSION QUESTIONS

Discuss the following questions in class or outside of class with your fellow students:

1. What do you think about the CEO's attitude toward training? Why do you think he is right or wrong?

2. If you worked at this organization as the quality manager and the CEO asked you to explain why he should approve making a commitment to corporate training, what would you tell him?

ENDNOTES

1. "Training Today's Professionals." Retrieved from www.zenofbrand.com/education_marketing/corpEd1d4web.htm on February 21, 2011.

2. Prentice Hall, "Training Industry Report for 2010," in *Training and Development Yearbook 2009* (Paramus, NJ: Prentice Hall, 2010), 32–36.

3. Retrieved from www.cLbc.ca/Research_and_Reports/Archive in March 2011.

4. Organization for Economic Cooperation and Development, "OECD Statistical Profile of the United States 2010," 9–12.

5. Ibid.

6. "Tough Choices Education Coalition." Retrieved from www.skillscommission.org/?p=614 on August 29, 2011.

7. Ibid.

8. Joseph M. Juran, *Juran on Leadership for Quality: An Executive Handbook* (New York: Free Press, 1989), 323–327.

9. Ibid., 323–324.

10. Ibid., 324.

11. This section is based on David L. Goetsch, *Occupational Safety and Health*, 7th ed. (Upper Saddle River, NJ: Prentice Hall, 2011), 391–402.

12. Juran, *Juran on Leadership*, 331–332.

13. Ibid., 334.

14. This section is based on Juran, *Juran on Leadership*, 332.

15. Goetsch, *Occupational Safety and Health*, 413–415.

16. Juran, *Juran on Leadership*, 342.

17. Ibid., 337.

18. Ibid., 325.

19. Ibid., 336.

20. Ibid., 337.

21. "New Employee Departmental Orientation." Retrieved from www.indiana.edu/~uhrs/training/dep_obj.html on February 12, 2011.

22. Ibid.

23. SIMPEL, "SIMPEL-IMPROVING eLEARNING PRACTICES IN SMEs." Retrieved from www.simpel-net.eu on February 19, 2011.

CHAPTER 13

OVERCOMING POLITICS, NEGATIVITY, AND CONFLICT IN THE WORKPLACE

A time-conscious manager can grind genius into gruel. —**Thomas A. Stewart**

MAJOR TOPICS
- Internal Politics Defined
- Power and Politics
- Organizational Structure and Internal Politics
- Internal Politics in Action
- Internal Politicians and Their Methods
- Impact of Internal Politics on Quality
- Controlling Internal Politics in Organizations
- Overcoming Negativity in Organizations
- Overcoming Territorial Behavior in Organizations
- Managing Conflict in Organizations

Internal politics is the game everybody plays, but nobody talks about. It is one of the most underemphasized but overpractised barriers to organizational performance that exists. In fact, there are actually books on the market that have the expressed purpose of making people better internal politicians—that is, better practitioners of the art and science of organizational manipulation. The root causes of internal politics are personal insecurity, self-interest, a hunger for power, ambition, and the need for acceptance. In other words, the root cause of internal politics is human nature. Consequently, some people think that internal politics in organizations is inevitable and should be accepted as an unavoidable fact of life. Although it is true that internal politics is an organizational disease that has no known cure, it is equally true that the disease can be controlled, and it should be. Internal politics has no place in a total quality organization. Quality is about *we*. Internal politics is about *me*.

The success of total quality depends, in part, on organization-wide collaboration. One of the fundamental cornerstones of total quality is *unity of purpose*. This means that all employees at all levels understand the vision and are united in their efforts to accomplish it. Consequently, all decisions are based on the same criterion: What option best supports the vision? This requires putting the interests of the overall organization ahead of the interests of individual divisions, departments, units, teams, and employees. Because human beings tend to be self-serving by nature, establishing unity of purpose and collaboration is a challenging undertaking that requires constant attention.

In an organization with unity of purpose, collaboration is the norm. In an organization infected with internal politics, the promotion of self-interest is the norm. Internal politics drains the competitive energy of thousands of organizations every day. To derive the full benefit of total quality, organizations must rid themselves of the debilitating scourge of internal politics.

INTERNAL POLITICS DEFINED

A historic example of internal politics at its worst occurred during World War II. Pearl Harbor and the Philippines had fallen before the Japanese onslaught in the Pacific, and it looked as if New Guinea and Australia would be next. The Allied forces were in a real bind. On the one hand, they couldn't allow these two countries to fall into enemy hands. But on the other hand, they couldn't pull enough troops away from the European and Atlantic theaters of operation to stop Japan.

In desperation, General Douglas MacArthur was ordered by President Franklin D. Roosevelt to leave Bataan, the tiny sliver of land in the Philippines to which MacArthur and his American and Filipino troops had clung tenaciously for several months. MacArthur and his beleaguered troops were holding out against great odds to give the United States time to recover from the devastating blow suffered at Pearl Harbor. This was a monumental decision because if Bataan fell—which it surely would without MacArthur's presence—the Japanese would add the Philippines to their list of conquests. Reluctantly, MacArthur and a small staff slipped away under cover of darkness aboard patrol torpedo (PT) boats of the American navy. Slipping through the Japanese blockade, they eventually reached Australia.

In short order, MacArthur rallied the dangerously understaffed and underequipped military units available to him. Relying on innovative strategy, raw courage, and stubborn determination, MacArthur and his troops made their stand and stopped the Japanese juggernaut on the Owen Stanley mountain range in New Guinea. From that point on, MacArthur conducted one of the most brilliant military campaigns in the annals of war, eventually pushing a stronger, healthier, better fed, better equipped Japanese military out of the Southwest Pacific.

The Japanese army and navy were well-trained, well-led, and fanatically determined, but they weren't MacArthur's most difficult foe. Also working against him was the insidious scourge of internal politics. To conduct the type of island-hopping warfare that was necessary in the Southwest Pacific, MacArthur needed the U.S. Army, Navy, Marines, and Air Corps, as well as military units from both Australia and New Zealand, to work together in a closely coordinated, collaborative effort. As it turns out, trying to achieve coordination and collaboration among the disparate groups under his command was General MacArthur's greatest challenge and most persistent frustration.

Rivalries among different branches of the U.S. military, as well as within individual branches of the military, were legendary at the time Japan attacked Pearl Harbor. The personal ambitions of military leaders, service loyalties, disagreements over the allocation of resources, and jealousy relating to who was in command of what were all ongoing sources of problems that created almost as much trouble for MacArthur as did the Japanese. In the European theater, General Eisenhower faced the same frustrations daily as he tried to coordinate the military forces of the various Allied nations.

This same kind of situation can be found in almost any organization. Internal politics is a natural, if unfortunate, outgrowth of human nature.

Politics, in general, is the art and science of wielding influence in such a way as to gain advantage. We generally think of politics in relation to influencing government. However, politics as a means of influencing outcomes is not limited to government enterprises. In fact, one will find politics practised with great skill in virtually every type of organization. Internal politics, as practised in organizations, is defined as follows:

> Internal politics consists of activities undertaken to gain advantage or influence organizational decision making in ways intended to serve a purpose other than the best interests of the overall organization. Internal politics consists of the games people play to promote decisions that are based on criteria other than merit.

Internal politics manifests itself in a number of different behaviors, all of which amount to individuals or groups within an organization putting their interests ahead of those of the overall organization. Internal politics is not necessarily an inherently bad concept. For example, internal politics practised for the purpose of furthering the interests of

the overall organization would be acceptable. The problem with the concept is that it is rarely practised in a positive way. Even though most invariably claim they are acting in the best interests of the organization, internal politicians typically have their own interests at heart in every action they take.

In a worst-case scenario, internal politicians are people who put self-interest ahead of organizational interests. In a scenario that is better but not good, internal politicians are people who put not self-interest but the interests of their divisions, departments, or teams ahead of those of the overall organization. It is this—the self-serving nature of the concept as it is typically practised—that makes internal politics such a negative phenomenon in organizations. It undermines collaboration, trust, and unity of purpose—all fundamental elements of total quality.

POWER AND POLITICS

Power is the ability to exert influence. Power is neither inherently positive nor inherently negative. It is a concept that can cut either way, depending on how it is used. Power, properly applied in an organization, is used to move the organization closer to the realization of its vision. Power, improperly applied in an organization, is used to advance an agenda other than that of the overall organization. This is the way in which internal politicians use power. The five different sources of power in an organization are personal, position, capability, reward, and coercive power. Internal politicians may use any or all of these sources of power to advance their personal agendas.

Personal Power

Personal power is the power of an individual's personality. Individuals with personal power are generally persuasive or charismatic. They tend to have strong beliefs, an aura of confidence, and an air of determination. In the military, such people are said to have the intangible attribute of *command presence.* Their personalities appeal to certain people—their followers—on an emotional level.

Position Power

Position power is that bestowed officially by higher authority. People with the authority to hire and fire, allocate resources, evaluate performance, and make decisions that affect the jobs of others have position power. People with position power may or may not be adept at using their power to influence others. Weak leaders in positions of authority often find that their position alone is not enough to ensure their influence in an organization. An important aspect of power is knowing how to use it and being willing to do so. For example, if a supervisor is unwilling to confront nonproductive employees, he or she will not be able to influence their behavior for the better, in spite of having position power.

Capability Power

Capability power comes from having special knowledge, skills, or talents that are important to an organization and in short supply. In any organization, there are critical tasks that are fundamental to the organization's success. People who can perform these tasks often gain power. In some instances, their power will extend well beyond that which might be expected of a person in their position. Since automation in the workplace became the norm, people who are knowledgeable about computers have been afforded capability power.

Reward Power

Reward power comes from the authority to control, administer, or withhold something of value to others. Often the something in question is money; people in positions to give or withhold money from others in organizations have reward power. In addition to money and resources, rewards that might be granted or withheld include recognition, promotion, positive feedback, and inclusion in a group. The reward of inclusion is one of the favorite tools of the internal politician. People have a natural desire to be part of a group. Consequently, the ability to exclude others gives an individual power over those who want to be associated with a given group.

Coercive Power

People who have the ability to punish others or subject them to unpleasant circumstances have coercive power. Coercive power is founded in fear, and its application is based on threats. The threat—whether implicit or explicit—is to punish those who don't respond as expected.

In a workplace setting, the coercive threat usually has to do with the victim's job security, work schedule, or pay. The threat can also be one of physical abuse, although this is less common in the workplace than are threats to job security. The threat of ostracism is also a commonly used coercive tactic. It involves threatening to remove or exclude an individual from a group with which he or she wants to be associated.

ORGANIZATIONAL STRUCTURE AND INTERNAL POLITICS

Internal politics can exist, and usually does, in every type of organization regardless of organizational structure. In other words, internal politics is not caused by organizational structure; consequently, it cannot be eliminated by simply changing the structure. This point can be illustrated easily enough by considering the most widely used organizational structures: the functional, geographic, decentralized line-of-business, strategic business-unit, and matrix structures.

Each of these structures has its own set of advantages and disadvantages, but they are all susceptible to internal politics. In considering organizational structures, keep in mind this rule of thumb: Factors that promote internal competition—whether intentionally or unintentionally—also promote internal politics. This is because internal politics is just one more tool (or weapon) to be used anytime people within an organization compete among themselves. The competition might be about questions of who reports to whom, who gets the lion's share of limited resources, who will fill key positions, what department will be reorganized and how, what are the lines of authority, and any number of other issues in which people have vested interests.

The next few figures exemplify the five most widely used organizational structures. Even a cursory examination of these various structures will reveal built-in characteristics that tend to promote competition and, in turn, internal politics. In the functional structure represented in Figure 13–1, the CEO would want to be sensitive to political machinations among the functional vice presidents. These could grow out of competition for limited resources, personality clashes, competition among the vice presidents for a future promotion to the CEO position, or misguided loyalty to the respective functional areas on the part of employees at all levels within the organization.

The geographic structure (Figure 13–2) is particularly susceptible to internal politics. The Achilles' heel of this structure is distance. Distance has a tendency to promote an "us against them" mentality that can lead to counterproductive internal competition and other forms of negative behavior. The reason for this is simple: it is only natural to be suspicious of people you seldom or never see but with whom you compete for resources. In addition, it is difficult to establish trust, unity of purpose, and collaboration across distance. For this reason, executives in companies that are organized geographically should be especially sensitive to the issue of internal politics.

The decentralized line-of-business structure, as shown in Figure 13–3, tends to promote competition among the various business enterprises as well as between functional

FIGURE 13–1 Functional Structure

FIGURE 13–2 Geographic Structure

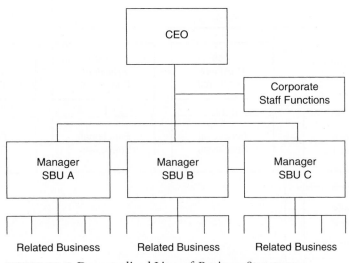

FIGURE 13–3 Decentralized Line-of-Business Structure

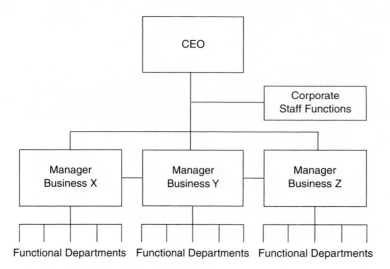

FIGURE 13–4 Strategic Business-Unit Structure

departments within these separate enterprises. This is also true of the strategic business-unit structure (Figure 13–4).

The matrix structure is the least used of the five common organizational structures. With this structure, functional specialists—human resources, accounting, marketing, and so on—are organized under functional areas, with each area having its own manager. Business ventures undertaken by the overall organization then draw on these functional areas as needed. For example, in Figure 13–5 the company is currently pursuing three business ventures. Business Ventures 1 through 3 all draw the functional expertise they need (e.g., marketing, accounting, engineering) from the respective functional areas.

This structure tends to promote internal competition and, in turn, internal politics both vertically and horizontally within the matrix. Vertically, there is competition for resources among the various business ventures. For example, say that all business ventures in Figure 13–5 want to draw engineering services at the same time, and the functional vice president of engineering has an insufficient number of engineers. How will available engineers be allocated? Another spin on this same situation occurs when two or more business ventures want the services of the same engineer, a particularly talented individual.

Horizontally, there is competition among the functional areas, certainly over resources, and possibly over personalities

FIGURE 13–5 Matrix Structure

and misguided loyalties. For example, say the marketing vice president wants to increase the size of his staff. At the same time, the accounting vice president wants to upgrade her computer system. Resources are limited. Who gets the lion's share?

These few examples, without even considering such other drivers as the need to fit in or personal insecurity, show that regardless of structure, the potential for internal politics exists in any organization. This section is not intended to be an exhaustive description of how organizational structures contribute to the potential for internal politics. Rather, it simply makes the point that regardless of organizational structure, the potential for internal politics exists. Consequently, managers in organizations trying to implement total quality should be sensitive to symptoms of internal politics regardless of how their organizations are structured.

INTERNAL POLITICS IN ACTION

Several motivations—personal insecurity, self-interest, a hunger for power, ambition, ego, and the need for acceptance—are the primary drivers of internal politics. The examples of internal politics provided in this section illustrate these drivers in action. All cases presented are real. The names of people and organizations have been changed, but the facts of the cases have not.

Politics in Reorganization

The two department chairs actually agree with the college administration that a reorganization is in order. Under pressure to cut administrative costs, the college's president has begun merging smaller departments. For example, the history, political science, sociology, and psychology departments have all been merged to form a new social science department. The chair of the old history department is now the chair of the new social science department, and the other three chairs—political science, sociology, and psychology—have returned to the faculty as professors.

A similar scenario has been enacted by combining the art, literature, drama, and music departments to form a new humanities department. Speech and English were combined to form the new communications department. In every case, the savings in administrative overhead have been substantial.

The college president is finally down to the last planned merger on her list: the mathematics and statistics departments. These two separate departments are to be merged to form a new mathematics and statistics department with one department chair.

The other mergers have been accomplished with a minimum of discord. In each case, the individual best qualified to become the surviving administrator was obvious and had the support of his or her colleagues. However, this is not the case with the mathematics and statistics departments. For years, the chairs of these two departments have been at war with each other. Their ongoing feud began when both were upstart professors struggling to impress their respective supervisors and gain a foothold in the academic world. Since that time, their disagreements have become legendary. Now,

they are competing to see which will emerge as chair of the new mathematics and statistics department and which will become the other's subordinate.

Both are lobbying their dean and the college president persistently—so persistently, in fact, that they are beginning to interfere with the duties of these two administrators. Both are building coalitions, electioneering among the faculty, calling in favors, and even making threats to nontenured faculty members in an attempt to win their support.

In the meantime, their normal duties are being neglected, the faculty is becoming polarized, and the atmosphere on campus has become tense and stressful. These two department chairs have become so intent on satisfying their own personal interests that they are harming the overall organization. Their self-serving political machinations are interfering with the mission of the college: teaching and learning.

The postscript to this case is as follows: Fed up with the self-serving internal politics of her mathematics and statistics chairs, the college president returned them both to the classroom and appointed a less senior professor as chair of the new mathematics and statistics department.

Politics in Resource Allocation

There is constant tension at Noonan Computer Center Inc. (NCCI) between the sales and service departments. John Gates is the manager of the sales department. Amanda Blakely manages the service department. Gates can make a convincing case for hiring additional sales and marketing personnel, and he does so frequently. Blakely can make an equally convincing case for hiring additional service technicians, and she doesn't hesitate to do so.

The two managers are always at odds with each other, feuding over which department should receive the bulk of NCCI's limited resources. They both think their respective departments hold the key to the struggling new company's survival and eventual prosperity. Gates generally states his case as follows: "We need more sales personnel out there knocking on doors, or we will never achieve the volume needed to get over the start-up hump." Blakely typically counters this argument by saying, "Good service is the key. It's how we will gain a reputation that will give us a competitive edge. If we don't service what we sell, we will never be able to sell enough computers to overcome the bad reputation that will result, no matter how many sales reps we hire."

The problem confounding NCCI's owner and CEO, Debbie Parks, is that both Gates and Blakely are right. The company needs more sales reps and more service technicians; there is no question about it. NCCI is still in its infancy. Parks is reinvesting every dollar she earns in the company as fast as she earns it. But it will be some time, even if things continue to go as well as they are now, before NCCI will be able to meet the types of demands Gates and Blakely are making.

Parks needs the cooperation of these two key managers badly. Their constant bickering is dividing the workforce into battling coalitions. Hostility between Gates and Blakely is subtle, but it is always there. Parks is convinced that they covertly undermine each other, even to the point of circulating unfounded rumors, recruiting spies in each other's departments, and promoting vicious gossip about each other.

Parks faces a dilemma. Gates and Blakely are the best there is at what they do, but their internal political maneuvering is distracting employees and draining them of the physical, emotional, and intellectual energy they need to constantly perform at peak levels. Parks needs peak performance from all her employees if she is going to gain a foothold in an intensely competitive marketplace.

There is a postscript to this case: NCCI never gained the foothold it needed. After just 18 months in business, the company folded, a victim of internal politics.

Politics in Status

On the company's organizational chart, all departmental directors at Payton Temporary Employees Inc. (PTE) are equal. However, in the minds of the individuals filling these positions, equality among directors at PTE is a concept that looks good on paper but doesn't exist in reality. The more equal among equals are those directors whose offices are located in closest proximity to that of the company's CEO, John Davis. The real winners, according to company folklore, are the directors whose offices are located on the same floor as Davis's office.

If one is to believe company gossip, the directors with offices on the third floor with Davis gain a tangible advantage in that they are more likely to bump into him in the hall, at the water cooler, or, if they are male, even in the restroom. This gives them enhanced access and opportunities for sharing their ideas and proposals. Other directors, without this proximity advantage, must wait for scheduled meetings or make appointments for one-on-one time with the CEO. Right or wrong, at PTE there is a perception of proximity advantage, and this perception creates counterproductive competition, political maneuvering, and ill will among the company's department directors.

The political machinations of the directors take several different forms. Prominent among these are building coalitions, undermining, electioneering when special committees and task forces are established, and spreading gossip. As a result, the company is a balkanized organization of warring factions with an ever-shifting set of loyalties. What it isn't, is a company in which there is a unity of purpose and a concerted effort to have all managers and employees pulling on the same end of the rope toward a common vision.

The postscript to this case is as follows: John Davis's failure to deal with the issue of internal politics at PTE eventually led to his termination. His replacement immediately set about establishing a collaborative culture at PTE; as a result, the company survived and is currently prospering.

Politics and Promotion

Karin Newhouse and Ronald Gorman have a lot in common. Both are plant managers for Northwest Manufacturing Company (NMC), an electronics manufacturer with plants in 10 different locations. Newhouse and Gorman were both gifted college athletes. Newhouse was the best player on a tennis team that won the national championship in her senior year, and Gorman was an Olympic-caliber track star. Both majored in electrical engineering and began their careers with NMC just 15 years ago. Both have been on the fast track to the upper ranks of the company, and both were named managers of their respective plants within a month of each other. There is something else these two fast movers have in common: They both know that NMC's president, Marvin Stanley, plans to retire in 18 months. Newhouse and Gorman both want his job.

Over the years, Newhouse and Gorman have maintained the competitive spirit they developed as champion athletes. Both have used their competitive drive in positive ways to advance their careers. But the moment Marvin Stanley announced his impending retirement, the competition between Newhouse and Gorman intensified. Before long, it began to get out of hand. Eventually, it became so bad that both managers, instead of being promoted, were fired, and Marvin Stanley was forced to postpone his retirement to pick up the pieces and get NMC moving forward again.

Here is what happened. Both managers knew they were on the short list to replace Stanley. In fact, they *were* the short list. None of NMC's other eight plant managers was in the running. Newhouse and Gorman decided—independently—that the decision would be made based on whose plant performed best during Stanley's last 18 months on the job. Consequently, both undertook aggressive cost-cutting campaigns. Some of their initial cost-cutting decisions were popular and well-received by the company's board of directors. But soon one-upmanship set in. Before long, Newhouse and Gorman were making decisions that—although they paid off in the short run—would actually hurt the company in the long run. And so they did.

Two months before Stanley was scheduled to retire, the employees of Newhouse's plant revolted. All 610 nonmanagement employees took either sick leave or vacation and simply did not show up for work, all on the same day. A spokesperson for the employees said, "We're just trying to get the attention of corporate management. This is a good plant, and we are proud of what we do here, but Newhouse is driving this company into the ground. As a result of her unilateral cost-cutting decisions, we can no longer maintain the quality we are known for, nor can we fill orders on time, which has always been one of our hallmarks. We don't know what has been driving the behavior of our plant manager for the last several months, but somebody from corporate needs to find out before it's too late."

At first, Gorman delighted in the news from Newhouse's plant. "This," he thought, "should clinch the job for me." But what he didn't know was that several of NMC's most important customers had contacted Marvin Stanley complaining about problems with Gorman's plant. The gist of their complaints was that quality had slipped markedly over the past several months and that on-time deliveries were off by 60%.

Unable to believe what was happening, Stanley got his two star plant managers together in his office for a conference. His intentions had been to find out where things had gone awry and get them straightened out. The reports he was hearing from their plants were so out of character for these two go-getters—both of whom he considered proteges—that Stanley simply could not believe them. The meeting had barely gotten started, however, before Newhouse and Gorman were attacking each other with accusations and recriminations. They even made threats.

Stanley was heartbroken. These two were his stars, the two managers he had nurtured and groomed to ensure that NMC would have the leadership it needed to survive and thrive after his retirement. After an hour of unrelenting bitterness between Newhouse and Gorman, Stanley—with reluctance—admitted the obvious to himself. His two stars were so intent on advancing their personal agendas that they had lost sight of what was best for NMC. In his mind, Stanley had just one option: Terminate Newhouse and Gorman, and find someone else to take over the reins at NMC.

Stanley undertook a national search for his replacement and was able to find a dynamic leader who not only knew NMC's business, but also was well-versed in controlling internal politics. The postscript to this case: Under the new CEO's leadership, NMC won back both its employees and its customers and was once again a thriving company.

INTERNAL POLITICIANS AND THEIR METHODS

Internal politicians have many of the characteristics of special interest groups. Special interest groups consist of people who share narrowly focused common goals. Internal politicians are individuals with narrowly focused interests—namely, their own. Special interest groups seek to gain advantage so as to influence governmental decision making. Internal politicians seek to gain advantage so as to influence organizational decision making. With such strong similarities, it should come as no surprise that internal politicians and spe-

✓	Lobbying
✓	Building coalitions
✓	Applying pressure
✓	Electioneering
✓	Spreading rumors and gossip

FIGURE 13–6 Methods Checklist: Internal Politicians

cial interest groups use many of the same methods. The most widely used of these methods are as shown in Figure 13–6.

Lobbying

Lobbying is trying to influence the decision makers. Legend has it that the term *lobbying* is based on the fact that many of the earliest attempts to influence members of Congress occurred in the lobby of the Willard Hotel and other hotels in Washington, DC.

Governmental lobbyists use favors, financial contributions, and information to influence government officials. Internal politicians, when lobbying, use similar tactics. By doing favors for people in positions to help them, internal politicians hope to curry favor. Ideally, they will establish a *quid pro quo* relationship with someone in a position of influence. Although they don't make financial contributions, internal politicians do have their version of this concept. They might contribute to easing the workload of, or solving a problem for, someone with whom they hope to gain favor.

Sharing of information is another widely practiced lobbying tactic. There is an old saying that knowledge is power. By providing information to carefully selected people, internal politicians attempt to endear themselves. Figure 13–7 contains a list of lobbying tactics commonly used by internal politicians.

Doing favors, making contributions, and providing information are not inherently negative activities; quite the contrary. What transforms these otherwise positive activities into negative endeavors is their misuse. If these things

- Contacting people formally (by appointment) to present a personal point of view
- Engaging people in informal discussions (over lunch, on the golf course, in the hall, etc.) and presenting a personal point of view
- Providing carefully screened information on a selective basis
- Doing favors to establish *quid pro quo* relationships
- Helping lighten the workload of selected people
- Applying pressure directly to individuals
- Applying pressure through third parties
- Exploiting personal relationships

FIGURE 13–7 Lobbying Tactics of Internal Politicians

are done with the best interests of the organization in mind, they are admirable activities. However, when done for the purpose of advancing a personal agenda at the expense of or without sufficient consideration for the organization's needs, they become negative.

The information-sharing aspect of lobbying is frequently the most misused of the various lobbying tactics. Information provided for lobbying purposes is carefully shaded in favor of the information provider. An internal politician is not going to volunteer information that fails to serve his or her purpose. This does not mean that internal politicians necessarily lie, or that they even need to do so. Rather, it means that they carefully control the information they provide, and to whom it is provided, to gain the greatest possible benefit. What follows are some examples of how internal politicians can shade information in their favor when lobbying in support of their own personal agendas:

- Myron Conley's boss, John Upfield, is a proud graduate and active alumnus of Centerbury College. Conley has his eye on a promotion. Consequently, he has been looking for an opportunity to mention in casual conversation with Upfield that he, too, attended Centerbury College. When the opportunity finally presented itself, Conley was delighted to see that the association seemed to have a positive effect. What Conley didn't tell Upfield was that he completed less than a year at Centerbury before being expelled for disciplinary reasons and had to finish his degree at another college.

- Myra Gladstone couldn't believe her luck. At the annual corporate banquet, she was seated next to her company's corporate vice president, the very person who would decide which unit would get the huge new Johnson account. Gladstone knew that if she got the Johnson account, and if her unit performed well, it would mean a promotion for her. She also knew that corporate would be wiser to give the account to Amanda Perry's unit. Gladstone's unit was good, but for this particular type of account, Perry's unit was better, much better. No matter, Gladstone wanted the account and intended to get it. Taking advantage of her good luck with seating arrangements, Gladstone told the corporate vice president exactly how her unit would handle the Johnson account. Emphasizing strengths and carefully avoiding weaknesses, Gladstone made a convincing case for her unit. The capabilities of Amanda Perry's unit were not mentioned.

- Mack Parmentier knew his division needed more business. In fact, if he didn't increase sales soon, his division would be merged with another larger division, and he would be demoted from division vice president back to his old job of product manager in somebody else's division. But what to do? He was struggling with this very question when opportunity knocked—literally. The person knocking on his office door turned out to be Mary Washington, corporate head of marketing. Washington had a new contract, a big multiyear contract, and she was talking with all division vice presidents before recommending which division should get it. Her message was clear: The company had to perform beyond expectations on this contract. If this happened, there would be much more work in the future. If not, the current contract would be the first and last the company would receive from a very important client. Washington told Parmentier she had narrowed down the list of divisions to two: his and the company's eastern division. What appealed to her about Parmentier's division was its strength in the area of precision machining. The contract would involve a great deal of this type of work. Washington told Parmentier, "The eastern division has a strong precision machining unit, but you've got Mike Bates. He is a genius." Seizing on the opportunity, Parmentier pressed his case. "You're right. With Mike and his team, we can outperform anyone on this contract." What Parmentier didn't tell Washington was that Mike Bates and his two best team members had given notice of their intention to resign within 15 days. Parmentier did everything he could to convince Mike Bates and his team to stay. However, their reasons for leaving went beyond just money, and he was unable to hold on to them. As a result, his division did not perform up to par on the contract. Despite assistance provided belatedly by the eastern division, the company did not satisfy expectations and, therefore, lost an important client.

Building Coalitions

A coalition is a group of diverse people brought together by a common interest. In governmental politics, coalitions are formed for the purpose of electing individuals to office, keeping other individuals from being elected, securing budget appropriations, and passing legislation. Organizational coalitions are formed for various reasons, such as getting selected individuals promoted, ensuring that others are not promoted, securing resources, guaranteeing the adoption of favorable policies or procedures, and fostering a favorable organizational structure. The individuals or individual groups that make up a coalition may have nothing in common except the simple cause that brought them together. This fact gave rise to the old adage that "politics makes strange bedfellows." Consequently, once a cause has been satisfied, the coalition typically dissolves. In its place, others will form as interests, conditions, and circumstances change.

Perhaps the classic example of a coalition of radically disparate groups working together toward a common goal is the anticrime coalition in the United States. This coalition consists of groups and individuals from both ends of the political spectrum as well as points in between. The fact that they believe that crime has gotten out of hand in the United States may be the only issue on which these groups agree. However, on this particular issue, they do concur. Consequently, a strong anticrime coalition exists and is having a major impact on legislation at the state and federal levels.

For the sake of illustration, suppose that the marketing and accounting departments of a hypothetical organization have never gotten along. Marketing personnel in this organization think that their colleagues from accounting are shortsighted and tightfisted and don't understand that the organization must spend money to make money. Accounting personnel think that their colleagues from marketing are a bunch of high-rolling big spenders who can't work within a budget no matter how large it is. Then, one day, the organization's management team announced its plan to purchase a building across the street from the organization's existing facility. By retaining its existing facility and relocating some of its personnel to the new building across the street, the company will gain badly needed work space. The only downside is that at least one department is going to have to move to the new building.

After analyzing space requirements, the executive team decides that either the engineering department alone or the marketing and accounting departments together must move. It is not a good time for engineering to be disrupted by a relocation because the company has just received a large contract that is engineering intensive and has a "short fuse." There is no problem with marketing and accounting moving except that they are comfortable where they are and don't want to move. The current building that houses their offices has some amenities the new building won't have (e.g., covered parking, a cafeteria). Occupants of the new building will have to park their cars in a lot that is exposed to the weather and walk across the street to the old building to use the cafeteria.

Sensing that they are about to lose some of their valued perquisites, the accounting and marketing vice presidents, along with their respective staffs, form a coalition to lobby against moving. While engineering personnel are busy working on the organization's new contract, the accounting and marketing departments mount an effective lobbying campaign to have engineering relocated to the new building. Their lobbying efforts pay off, and the engineering department is moved across the street. Unfortunately, the disruption causes the department to fall behind in its work, and the organization's new contract goes over schedule. Late fees are assessed, and the relationship with a valuable new customer gets off to a bad start.

Applying Pressure and Harassment

In governmental politics, when pressure is applied there is an implicit threat from voters: "Do what I ask or I won't vote for you." From lobbyists, the threat is more along the lines of "Vote as we ask or lose our financial support." From colleagues in Congress, the unspoken message is "Support my bill or else I won't support yours." In organizations, pressure is applied differently, but the implicit threat is still there. Here are examples of messages and tactics used by internal politicians to apply pressure:

- Help me out, or you will be socially ostracized by your peers; or the opposite, help me out, and you will be part of the crowd.

- Help me out, or something you don't want known will be revealed.

- If you help me out, I'll help you when I win. If you don't, you'll be left out when I win.

- Help me out, or something undesirable will happen to someone you care about; or the opposite, help me out, and something good will happen to someone you care about.

- Ongoing harassment that ranges from distracting to threatening behavior.

The following scenario illustrates how internal politicians use pressure to serve their self-interests.

John Brown is the purchasing agent for Orlando A & M University. Because he has a master's degree in accounting, Brown is able to earn extra income teaching night classes in first-year accounting. With twins on the way, Brown and his wife need the extra income.

In addition to his job as a purchasing agent, Brown chairs the university's staff development committee. This is the committee that allocates the funds used by faculty and staff members to attend professional conferences and to participate in professional development activities. There are always more requests for funds than there are funds available. Consequently, Brown and his committee have established some ironclad rules about the number of activities that will be funded for a given individual within a specified time frame. These rules ensure that the largest possible number of employees of the university gets an opportunity to participate in professional development activities.

As chair of the development committee, Brown is accustomed to being in the "hot seat" when someone wants an activity funded and the committee cannot comply. But Brown has never been pressured so hard as he is currently being pressured by Amos Andrews, chair of the department of business and accounting. The committee, sticking to the rules, has turned down a request from Andrews. After Andrews exhausted the list of tactics typically used by people trying to influence the committee, he began to get desperate.

That's when Brown really began to feel the pressure. Working through other faculty members in the business and accounting department, Andrews made sure Brown knew that the extra income he earned by teaching night classes in accounting was in jeopardy. The message given to Brown was clear: If Andrews's request for a waiver of the committee's rules is not approved, Brown has taught his last accounting course. Brown needs the extra income from teaching, but he cannot approve Andrews's request without bumping Maxine Denny from a conference that is very important to the social science department. Brown is in a bind, and he is feeling the pressure.

This is just one example of the many ways that pressure can be applied in the workplace by internal politicians. There are many other ways that internal politicians can and do use personal pressure to advance their individual agendas.

Electioneering

In governmental politics, electioneering means participating in the election process. Participation can take many different forms, including raising money for candidates, making contributions, and getting out the vote. Of course, the purpose of electioneering is to ensure that a certain candidate is elected. Electioneering in an organization is a similar process.

Internal politicians use electioneering tactics to ensure that selected individuals are promoted, that the *right* people are appointed to prestigious committees, and that selected people are chosen to chair important committees and task forces. The following example illustrates electioneering as it might be used in an organizational setting.

Tim Jones is in a bind. In just 6 months, he will be promoted to a planning position at the corporate office—unless, that is, someone at corporate learns the truth about his division. Brierfield Products Inc. (BPI) is undergoing a corporation-wide implementation of total quality. As a division director, Jones is a key player. However, he hasn't played the leadership role the company needs him and its other directors to play.

It is not that Jones is opposed to total quality. It's just that he had hoped to be off to his new position before having to bother with implementing it. "After all," he thought, "why go through all the trouble when I won't be around to enjoy the benefits?" This type of thinking has led Jones to procrastinate. As a result, his division is lagging behind the company's other divisions. Jones has belatedly decided to get started, but he has a long way to go to catch up, and the TQ monitoring visit is scheduled to occur in just 1 week.

When he made the decision to skate through his last 6 months, leaving the work of the implementation to his successor, Jones had not known that corporate would conduct monitoring visits. Now a monitoring visit was right around the corner. If he didn't do something soon, not only would his promotion be lost, but also he'd be lucky to keep his current job. But Jones isn't finished yet. He hadn't gotten to be one of the company's youngest division directors by accident. He possesses considerable skills as an internal politician, and it will be his political skills that will save him.

It was while scanning the list of personnel appointed by corporate to serve as implementation monitors that

---

QUALITY TIP ▼

Eliminate Counterproductive Internal Competition

Organizations can devote their time and energy to the battle of the marketplace. Or they can devote it to internal battles, but not to both. Resources are finite. Time and energy wasted on internal squabbling are resources that could have been used to improve performance.

Source: David L. Goetsch.

Jones saw his chance for salvation. The third person on the list was Jake Burns. Jones couldn't believe his luck. He and Burns went way back, and, better yet, Burns owed him. Now, all he had to do was make sure that Jake Burns was selected as the monitor for his division. Jones began electioneering in earnest, pulling out all the stops. He made telephone calls, got other people to make telephone calls, applied pressure, made promises, made threats, and called in favors. By the time he was done, Jake Burns had been chosen as the TQ monitor for the upcoming visit. Jones could finally relax. Jake Burns would write an appropriately worded, appropriately positive—albeit misleading—monitoring report.

Gossiping and Spreading Rumors

One of the most pernicious weapons in the arsenal of the internal politician is the creation of doubt. Doubt can be created effectively by using gossip to spread rumors about a targeted individual or group. When used by internal politicians, rumors and gossip are not of the harmless chit-chat variety. Rather, they are intentional, coldly calculated attempts to advance the agenda of one individual or group at the expense of another.

Rumors and gossip have the greatest impact when they cast doubt on an individual relative to high-priority organizational values. The following scenario demonstrates how gossip can be used by internal politicians to gain an advantage.

Patricia Chitwood is both ambitious and smart. She knows that her company, Drake Services Inc. places a high priority on ethics, and she plans to use this fact to her advantage. Chitwood and her colleague Pamela McGraw have both applied for the soon-to-be-vacant position of regional sales manager at Drake Services. Like Chitwood, McGraw is good. In terms of both credentials and performance, the two sales reps could be twins. As things stand now, the race for the promotion is dead even—it could go either way. But Chitwood has a plan. At lunch today, she will start a rumor that is sure to sow seeds of doubt about McGraw's ethics. Nothing major—just a few whispered comments and well-placed winks concerning McGraw's expense account. Within an hour, the office grapevine will be buzzing. Within a day, the CEO of Drake Services will be wondering about the ethics of one of his best sales reps. Within a week, Chitwood should be the new regional sales manager.

There is no question that Patricia Chitwood is a resourceful internal politician. However, her shortsighted methods may cost her in the long run. The rumor Chitwood started about her rival is likely to make Pamela McGraw's position with Drake Services tenuous at best. Even if McGraw isn't fired, she will probably leave; and with her record, landing a position with a competitor won't be difficult. As regional sales manager, the last thing Chitwood will need is to have her best sales rep, Pamela McGraw, joining forces with the competition.

IMPACT OF INTERNAL POLITICS ON QUALITY

The approach that is the opposite of internal politics is *collaboration*. The rationale for collaboration can be found in the negative impact internal politics can have on an organization. To appreciate just how powerfully negative this impact can be, consider the following scenario:

> The U.S. Marine Corps has an outstanding rifle team that competes in tournaments worldwide. Members of the team are the best marksmen in a branch of the military that places a high priority on marksmanship. The Marine Corps Rifle Team performs well in competition, typically taking top honors. But how well would the team do if its members shot at each other instead of their respective targets?

Is it a far-fetched scenario? Perhaps. But it illustrates exactly what happens in organizations suffering from the scourge of internal politics. Individuals in organizations—frequently the organizations' key decision makers—sometimes become so intent on fulfilling their personal ambitions, satisfying their individual needs, or feeding their own egos that they lose sight of what is best for the organizations that employ them.

Internal politics can affect an organization in the same way that cancer affects an individual. Both start covertly inside the victim, often remaining invisible until the damage done is serious, and both can spread quickly. Organizations stricken with the disease of internal politics ultimately suffer the effects shown in Figure 13–8.

An organization's morale suffers when infighting, buck passing, and rumormongering—all of which invariably result from the practice of internal politics—are allowed to become part of the dominant corporate culture. Decisions that are questionable at best and even potentially unsound are not uncommon in organizations that condone internal politics. Any time decisions are made based on criteria other than what is best for the organization, the organization suffers.

Internal politics invariably leads to counterproductive internal competition. Ideally, the only competition in which an organization would engage is market competition. Internal cooperation in the pursuit of a common purpose serves an organization better in the long run than internal competition among its own departments and employees. Organizations can devote their time and energy to the battle of the marketplace, or they can devote it to internal battles, but not to both. Resources are finite; time and energy wasted on internal squabbling are resources that could have been used to improve performance.

Organizations that are suffering the ill effects of internal politics often lose the best and brightest employees. If a work group is low performing and does not want to do better, its members may actually drive out anyone who tries to improve. Their methods range from peer pressure to harassment to outright ostracism. As they become increasingly frustrated by decisions based on politics rather than merit, employees with the most marketable credentials often show their dissatisfaction by leaving. Those who stay tend to be employees that fall into one of two categories. The first category consists of employees who stay because weak credentials make it difficult for them to find a better job. The second category consists of employees who give in to reality, and become internal politicians themselves.

Internal politics tends to perpetuate outdated processes, procedures, and technologies. This is because the tactics of the internal politician are ideally suited for opposing change. Change comes hard for most people. Psychological comfort with the status quo is inherent in the human condition. When internal politics becomes part of the corporate culture, organizations find it even more difficult than usual to make the changes necessary to stay competitive. With a little lobbying, some electioneering, and just the right amount of pressure wisely applied, the natural resistance of people to change can be magnified exponentially by internal politicians opposed to change. When this happens, the employees of an organization gain the psychological comfort associated with the status quo, but the organization loses the competitive edge associated with change.

- *Loss of morale* due to infighting, buck passing, and rumormongering
- *Questionable decisions* made for reasons other than what is best for the organization
- *Counterproductive internal competition* that saps the organization of its competitive energy
- *Loss of the best and brightest employees* as they make a statement about their dissatisfaction by leaving
- *Perpetuation of outdated processes, procedures, and technologies* as internal politics is used to promote organizational inertia by those opposed to change
- *Constant conflict* as the political machinations of one group are countered by those of others
- *Loss of quality, competitiveness, and customers* as the organization's focus is diverted from what really matters

FIGURE 13–8 Effects of Internal Politics on an Organization

Partnership Development at Bursagas

Bursagas is a natural gas distribution company that serves business, industrial, and residential customers in the Bursa Province of Turkey. Bursagas received the prestigious EFQM Excellence Award—the highest European award for quality—for exemplifying the principles of total quality. In selecting Bursagas for this award, the EFQM panel of experts made special note of several factors including the following:

- Seamless integration of the organization's strategy and process management and the positive results that have resulted from this seamlessness.

- Deploying a leadership style that engages people throughout the organization and has led to high levels of employee and customer satisfaction.

- Establishing and maintaining collaborative partnerships that continually enhance service, quality, and performance.

It is this final factor—collaborative partnerships—that most impressed the panel of experts at EFQM. The panel found that Bursagas's collaboration with partners was so fully integrated that it was difficult to distinguish between Bursagas employees and the employees of partner organizations. This is important because partners are not just important to Bursagas's success, they are essential. Bursagas is responsible for establishing and maintaining the infrastructure necessary for efficiently delivering natural gas to customers after receiving it from importers and wholesalers at specified ports of entry.

At the core of Bursagas's collaboration model is the "out-task" approach to partnerships. With the out-task approach, partners provide the management of the employees and processes that form the necessary distribution infrastructure. Bursagas recruits the staff for partner companies, provides training for their personnel, maintains the performance-management system, and provides all human resources related services. Bursagas personnel work constantly with personnel from the partner organizations to continually improve all aspects of their collaborative performance. The collaboration between Bursagas and its various partners proves the point that quality is everybody's job.

Source: www.efqm.org. 2011

Internal politics invariably multiplies both the frequency and the intensity of conflict in an organization. Infighting, backbiting, and ill will are antithetical to quality and competitiveness. Total quality requires unity of purpose and a trusting, mutually supportive work environment. Such environments cannot be maintained in the face of constant conflict that occurs on a personal rather than a professional level. All of the individual deleterious effects of internal politics, when taken together, have the cumulative effect of diverting an organization's attention from what really matters. This can occur to such an extent that the organization's quality suffers. When this happens, the organization loses its ability to satisfy and retain customers and, in turn, its ability to survive in a competitive marketplace.

CONTROLLING INTERNAL POLITICS IN ORGANIZATIONS

How does one go about convincing people in organizations—all of whom have their own interests, ambitions, and egos—to put aside the natural inclination to practice internal politics and, instead, practice collaboration? Interestingly, trying to control internal politics in organizations is a lot like trying to prevent overeating in individuals. Both involve finding ways to subdue human nature, both require persistent effort, and both demand constant vigilance. Controlling internal politics in an organization requires a comprehensive effort involving all employees. Such an effort should have at least the components listed in Figure 13–9 and elaborated on in the following sections.

Strategic Planning Component

Controlling internal politics begins with the organization's strategic plan. One of the keys to controlling internal politics over the long term is creating a cultural expectation that all decisions will be based on what is best from the perspective of the organization's strategic plan. If employees are to make all decisions based on this criterion, they have to know the organization's vision, mission, guiding principles, and broad objectives. In other words, if their behavior and decisions are supposed to support the strategic plan, employees have to know the plan. The strategic planning components of an organization's effort to control internal politics should have at least these two elements:

- Explaining to all employees the content of the strategic plan and how it is to be used in guiding all decisions and actions in the organization

- Building a guiding principle into the strategic plan that conveys the message that collaboration is the expected approach in the organization

Explaining the Strategic Plan All employees should have a copy of the strategic plan, the plan should be thoroughly explained, and employees should be given ample opportunity to ask questions and seek clarification about the plan. In other words, it's not enough for employees to have a plan—they need to understand it.

In explaining the strategic plan to employees, managers should make sure that they convey the following message:

Everything we do in this organization is to be guided by one criterion: support of the strategic plan. A good decision is one that supports accomplishing what is set forth in the strategic plan. A decision that does not meet this criterion is a bad decision. Good policy, good procedures, and good work practices are those that support the strategic plan. Others are unacceptable. Consequently, there is no room in the organization for the advancing of personal agendas or the promotion of self-interest to the detriment of organizational interests. In short, internal politics has no place in this organization.

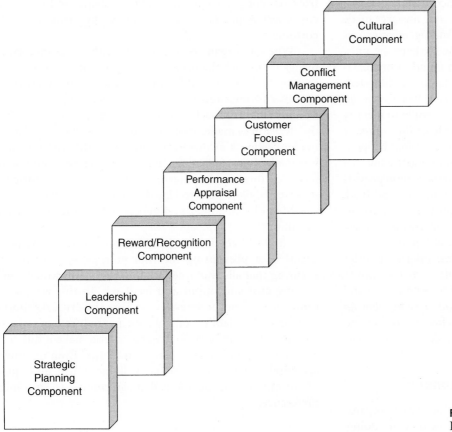

FIGURE 13–9 Main Components of an Internal Politics Prevention Program

Conveying this message to all employees, in conjunction with an explanation of the strategic plan, sets the proper tone, establishes the proper expectations, and brings the issue of internal politics into the open. Setting the proper tone and establishing expectations are essential to developing an organizational culture that does not promote or condone internal politics. Bringing the issue into the open removes the shroud of secrecy on which internal politicians thrive.

Using Collaboration as a Guiding Principle   One of the most important components of a strategic plan is the one that contains the organization's guiding principles. The organization's core values are described in its guiding principles. These principles explain in writing what is most important to the organization and how it intends to do business. Consequently, one of the guiding principles of every organization should be *collaboration*. Here is an example of such a guiding principle:

> ABC Company places a high priority on collaboration among all employees at all levels. We base all policies, procedures, practices, and decisions on what is best for the organization, rather than what serves the personal interests, agendas, or ambitions of individuals or individual units within the company.

If employees, from the CEO to line workers, know that collaboration is a high priority, it becomes more difficult for them to play the games collectively known as internal politics. This principle, coupled with the remaining strategies in this section, can go a long way toward controlling the practice of internal politics in the organization.

Leadership Component

A fundamental premise of leadership is setting a positive example. Managers must be consistent role models of the behavior they expect of employees. If a manager practices internal politics, employees will respond in kind. Consequently, it is important that managers be seen using the organization's strategic plan as the basis for all actions and that they insist on all employees following suit.

Setting an example goes beyond just adopting policies and making decisions based on what best supports the organization's strategic plan. It also involves refusing to condone—explicitly or implicitly—counterproductive behavior on the part of employees (e.g., gossiping). In fact, counterproductive behavior such as gossiping gives managers excellent opportunities for demonstrating the point that internal politics is not condoned. By openly and consistently refusing to gossip, spread rumors, or respond to either, managers can help take away two of the most potent weapons of internal politicians.

Reward/Recognition Component

If you want to promote a certain type of approach—for example, collaboration—reward it, and recognize employees who practice it. This is a simple but effective management principle.

Unfortunately, it's a principle that is preached more than it is practised. One of the most frequent systemic mistakes made in organizations is failing to match up management expectations with reward/recognition systems. Perhaps the most common example of this failing can be found in organizations that expect teamwork but still maintain a reward system that is based on individual performance. Managers should examine their organization's incentives carefully to identify ways in which internal politics is rewarded, either directly or indirectly. The most obvious question is "What happens to employees at any level who are found to practice internal politics?" Another question is "Does the organization provide incentives that promote employee collaboration, and if so, what are those incentives?" A well-designed reward/recognition system will simultaneously provide disincentives to internal politics and incentives that promote collaboration.

Disincentives that can work against internal politics include negative performance appraisals, verbal warnings, and written reprimands. Incentives can be both formal and informal, and there are hundreds of both varieties. For an excellent source of help in identifying effective formal and informal incentives, refer to *1,001 Ways to Reward Employees* by Bob Nelson (Workman 2005).

Performance Appraisal Component

The periodic performance appraisal is how most organizations formally let employees know how they are doing. Consequently, one or more of the criteria in an organization's performance-appraisal instrument should relate to collaboration. Examples of this type of criteria include the following:

> This employee bases all actions on what is best for the organization.

- Always
- Sometimes
- Usually
- Never

> What is this employee's collaboration rating?

- Excellent
- Above average
- Average
- Poor

Making collaboration an issue in performance appraisals ties it directly to pay and promotions. This is critical. Remember that internal politics is driven by self-interest. Tying pay and promotion to an employee's willingness to practice collaboration means that internal politics no longer serves his or her self-interest.

Customer Focus Component

Customer focus is a fundamental cornerstone of total quality. In organizations with a customer focus, quality is defined by customers, and the organization's strategic plan is written from the perspective of attracting, satisfying, and retaining customers. A customer focus is achieved by partnering with customers.

When an organization partners with its customers, it brings them into the decision-making process by actively seeking their input and feedback. Input, remember, consists of customer recommendations made *before* the decision is made. Feedback is customer information given *after* the decision is made. Input influences the decision that is made. Feedback evaluates the quality of the decision that was made. In organizations that factor customer input and feedback into the decision-making process, it is difficult for internal politicians to play their games. When decisions are driven by customer preference, they cannot be driven by politics.

The full benefit of a customer focus—from the perspective of preventing internal politics—is gained by ensuring that all employees are thoroughly informed concerning customer input and feedback. In this way, customer needs and preferences become the critical criteria by which the viability of policies, procedures, practices, and decisions can be judged. Such criteria make it difficult for internal politicians to play their games. Even the most accomplished internal politician will find it difficult to justify recommending decisions that run counter to customer preferences.

Conflict Management Component

Internal politics tends to generate counterproductive conflict. This is one of the reasons that managers in organizations should do what is necessary to prevent internal politics. However, it is important to distinguish between conflict and counterproductive conflict. Not all conflict is bad. In fact, properly managed conflict that has the improvement of products, processes, people, or the work environment as its source is positive conflict.

Counterproductive conflict—the type associated with internal politics—occurs when people in organizations behave in ways that work against the interests of the overall organization. This type of conflict is often characterized by deceitfulness, vindictiveness, and personal rancor. Productive conflict occurs when right-minded, well-meaning people disagree, without being disagreeable, concerning the best way to support the organization's strategic plan.

Positive conflict leads to discussion, debate, and give-and-take interaction among people whose only goal is to find the best solution or make the best decision. This type of interaction exposes the viewpoints of all participants to careful scrutiny and judges the merits of all arguments by applying criteria that are accepted by all stakeholders. By putting every point of view under the microscope of group scrutiny, weaknesses in arguments are identified, the issue is viewed from all possible angles, and, ultimately, the best solution can be identified. Contrast this approach with that of internal politicians whose only goal is to promote self-interest. Internal politicians reveal only that information that serves their interests, while concealing any information that might weaken their case. They lobby, practice electioneering, and apply pressure to influence people to make decisions based on criteria other than merit.

By practicing conflict management, managers in an organization can make it difficult for internal politicians to play their games. Conflict management has the following components:

- Establishing conflict guidelines
- Helping all employees develop conflict prevention and resolution skills
- Helping all employees develop anger management skills
- Stimulating and facilitating productive conflict

Establishing Conflict Guidelines   Conflict guidelines establish ground rules for discussing and debating differing points of view, varying ideas, and an array of opinions concerning how best to accomplish the organization's vision, mission, and broad objectives. Figure 13–10 shows an example of an organization's conflict guidelines. Guidelines such as these should be developed with a broad base of employee involvement from all levels in the organization.

Developing Conflict Prevention and Resolution Skills   If managers are going to expect employees to disagree without being disagreeable, they are going to have to ensure that all employees are skilled in the art and science of conflict resolution. The second guideline in Figure 13–10 is an acknowledgment of human nature. It takes advanced human relation skills and constant effort to disagree without being disagreeable. Few people are born with this ability, but

fortunately it can be learned. The following strategies will help prevent and resolve conflict:[1]

Explore the Other Person's Viewpoint   A good start on preventing conflict can be made by acknowledging the importance of the other person's point of view. Begin the discussion by giving the other party an opportunity to present his or her point of view and, listening carefully, say, "Your viewpoint is important to me, and I'm going to hear you out." These strategies will help make this phase of the discussion more positive and productive:

1. Establish that your goal at this point in the discussion is mutual understanding.
2. Elicit the other person's complete point of view.
3. Listen nonjudgmentally and do not interrupt.
4. Ask for clarification if necessary.
5. Paraphrase the other person's point of view and restate it to show that you understand.
6. Ask the other person to correct your understanding if it appears to be off-base or incomplete.

Explain Your Viewpoint   After you accurately and fully understand the other person's point of view, present your own. The following strategies will help make this phase of the discussion more positive and productive:

1. Ask for the same type of fair hearing for your point of view that you gave the other party.
2. Describe how the other person's point of view affects you. Don't point the finger of blame or be defensive. Explain your reactions objectively, keeping the discussion on a professional level.

Jones Engineering Company encourages discussion and debate among employees at all levels concerning better ways to continually improve the quality of our products, processes, people, and work environment. This type of intellectual interaction, if properly handled, will result in better ideas, policies, procedures, practices, and decisions. However, human nature is such that conflict can easily get out of hand, take on personal connotations, and become counterproductive. Consequently, in order to promote productive conflict, Jones Engineering Company has adopted the following guidelines. These guidelines are to be followed by all employees at all levels:

- The criterion to be applied when discussing/debating any point of contention is as follows: Which recommendation is most likely to move our company closer to realizing the strategic vision?
- Disagree, but don't be disagreeable. If the debate becomes too hot, stop and give all parties an opportunity to cool down before continuing. Apply your conflict-resolution skills and anger management skills. Remember, even when we disagree about how to get there, we are all trying to reach the same destination.
- Justify your point of view by tying it to either the strategic plan or customer input/feedback and require others to follow suit.
- In any discussion of differing points of view, ask yourself the following question: *Am I just trying to win the debate for the sake of winning (ego), or is my point of view really the most valid?*

FIGURE 13–10 Jones Engineering Company: Conflict Guidelines

3. Explain your point of view accurately and completely.

4. Ask the other party to paraphrase and restate what you have said.

5. Correct the other party's understanding, if necessary.

6. Review and compare the two positions (yours and that of the other party). Describe the fundamental differences between the two points of view, and ask the other party to do the same.

Agree on a Resolution Once both viewpoints have been explained and are understood, it is time to move to the resolution phase. This is the phase in which both parties attempt to come to an agreement. It is also the phase in which both parties may discover that they cannot agree. Agreeing to disagree—in an agreeable manner—is an acceptable solution. Three strategies will help make this phase of the discussion more positive and productive:

1. Reaffirm the mutual understanding of the situation.

2. Confirm that both parties are ready and willing to consider options for coming to an acceptable resolution.

3. If it appears that differences cannot be resolved to the satisfaction of both parties, try one or more of these techniques:

   ■ Take time out to reflect and then try again.

   ■ Agree to third-party arbitration or neutral mediation.

   ■ Agree to a compromise solution.

   ■ Take turns suggesting alternative solutions.

   ■ Yield (this time) once your position has been thoroughly stated and is understood. The eventual result may vindicate your position.

   ■ Agree to disagree, while still respecting each other.

Developing Anger Management Skills It is difficult, if not impossible, to keep conflict positive when anger enters the picture. If individuals in an organization are going to be encouraged to question, discuss, debate, and even disagree, they must know how to manage their anger. *Anger is an intense emotional reaction to conflict in which self-control may be lost.* Anger occurs when people feel that one or more of their fundamental needs are being threatened. These needs include

1. Need for approval

2. Need to be valued

3. Need to be appreciated

4. Need to be in control

5. Need for self-esteem

When one or more of these needs are threatened, a normal human response is to become angry. An angry person can respond in one of four ways:

1. **Attacking.** With this response, the source of the threat is attacked, usually verbally. For example, when someone disagrees with you (threatens your need for approval), you might attack by questioning his or her veracity or credentials.

2. **Retaliating.** With this response, you fight fire with fire, so to speak. Whatever is given, you give back. For example, if someone calls your suggestion ridiculous (threatens your need to be valued), you might retaliate by calling his or her suggestion dumb.

3. **Isolating.** This response is the opposite of venting. With the isolation response, you internalize your anger, find a place where you can be alone, and simmer. The childhood version of this response was to go to your room and pout. For example, when someone fails to even acknowledge your suggestion (threatens your need to be appreciated), you might swallow your anger, return to your office, and boil over in private.

4. **Coping.** This is the only positive response to anger. Coping does not mean that you fail to become angry. Rather, it means that even when you do, you control your emotions instead of letting them control you. A person who copes well with anger is a person who, in spite of his or her anger, stays in control. All employees at all levels of a total quality organization need to be able to cope with their anger. The following strategies will help employees manage their anger by becoming better at coping:

   ■ Avoid the use of anger-inducing words and phrases, including *but, you should, you made me, always, never, I can't,* and *you can't.*

   ■ Admit that others don't make you angry but that you allow yourself to become angry. You are responsible for your emotions and your responses to them.

   ■ Don't let pride get in the way of progress. You don't have to be right every time.

   ■ Drop your defenses when dealing with people. Be open and honest.

   ■ Relate to other people as equals. Regardless of position or rank, you are no better than they and they are no better than you.

   ■ Avoid the human tendency to rationalize your angry responses. You are responsible and accountable for your behavior.

Stimulating or Facilitating Productive Conflict
Sycophantic agreement with the boss has no place in the total quality organization. Ideas, suggestions, and proposals should be subjected to careful, even intense scrutiny. Consequently, productive conflict is not only allowed in a total quality organization, but also promoted. Productive conflict consists of genuine, harmonious disagreement over the best way to solve a problem.

Productive conflict is productive because the only agenda being advanced is the good of the organization. With productive conflict, no hidden agendas or political machinations are at work. All parties are attempting to reach the same destination; the disagreement has to do with how best to get there. Because there are no hidden agendas, all parties are open to questions, challenges, and constructive criticism. In addition, all parties agree on the criteria by which their ideas will be judged.

In a total quality organization, managers actually stimulate discussion and debate (productive conflict) if they think a proposal is moving down the track too fast unimpeded by careful scrutiny. Productive conflict is stimulated using methods, such as

- Openly communicating the message "We want ideas and constructive criticism of ideas. We believe discussion and debate sharpen our ideas."
- Playing devil's advocate and teaching employees to play this role.
- Requiring employees to identify the downside when making suggestions.

Cultural Component

There are many different definitions for the term *culture*. As applied to an organization, the concept means the way things are done in the organization. In other words, an organization's culture is the everyday manifestation of its actual beliefs. It is important to note that the concept grows out of *actual* beliefs, as opposed to *written* beliefs. An organization's culture *should be* the everyday manifestation of the guiding principles found in its strategic plan.

However, some organizations are guilty of practicing a set of beliefs that differ from those written down as guiding principles. Culture cannot be mandated. Rather, it develops over time based on actions, not words. This is why it is so important to live out the organization's professed beliefs on a daily basis.

If collaboration is a high priority, it should be promoted, modeled, rewarded, and reinforced on a daily basis at all levels in the organization. Correspondingly, internal politics must be seen to be ineffective and detrimental. For every incentive to collaborate, there should also be a disincentive to play political games. The ultimate disincentive is social pressure. This is why establishing a collaborative culture is so important and beneficial. It ensures that social pressure, which is the most effective enforcer of culture, works *for* collaboration instead of against it.

By applying the various strategies described in this section on a daily basis, organizations can make collaboration a fundamental part of their culture. When this happens, social pressure within the organization will keep the practice of internal politics under control.

OVERCOMING NEGATIVITY IN ORGANIZATIONS

Negativity is any behavior on the part of any employee at any level that works against the optimum performance of the organization. The motivations behind negativity can be as different and varied as the employees who manifest it.

However, negative behavior can be categorized. The most common categories of negative behavior are

- Control disputes
- Territorial disputes (boundaries)
- Dependence and independence issues
- Need for attention and responsibility
- Authority
- Loyalty issues

Recognizing Negativity in the Organization

Managers should be constantly alert to signs of negativity in the workplace because negativity is contagious. It can spread throughout an organization quickly, dampening morale and inhibiting performance. What follows are symptoms of the Negativity Syndrome that managers should watch for:

- **"I can't" attitudes.** Employees in an organization that is committed to continual improvement have "can-do" attitudes. If "I can't" is being heard regularly, negativity has crept into the organization.
- **"They" mentality.** In high-performance organizations, employees say "we" when talking about their employer. If employees refer to the organization as "they," negativity has gained a foothold.
- **Critical conversation.** In high-performance organizations, coffee-break conversation is about positive work-related topics or topics of personal interest. When conversation is typically critical, negative, and judgmental, negativity has set in. Some managers subscribe to the philosophy that employees are not happy unless they are complaining. This is a dangerous attitude. Positive, improvement-oriented employees will complain to their supervisor about conditions that inhibit performance, but they don't sit around criticizing and whining during coffee breaks.
- **Blame fixing.** In a high-performance organization, employees fix problems, not blame. If blame fixing and finger-pointing are common in an organization, negativity is at work.

Overcoming Negativity   Managers who identify negativity in their organizations should take the appropriate steps to eliminate it. The following strategies can be used to overcome negativity in organizations:

- **Communicate.** Frequent, ongoing, effective communication is the best defense against negativity in organizations, and it is the best tool for overcoming negativity that has already set in. Organizational communication can be made more effective using the following strategies: acknowledge innovation, suggestions, and concerns; share information so that all employees are informed; encourage open, frank discussion during meetings; celebrate milestones; give employees ownership of their jobs; and promote teamwork.

- **Establish clear expectations.** Make sure all employees know what is expected of them as individuals and as members of the team. People need to know what is expected of them and how and to whom they are accountable for what is expected.

- **Provide for anxiety venting.** The workplace can be stressful in even the best organizations. Deadlines, performance standards, budget pressures, and competition can all produce anxiety in employees. Consequently, managers need to give their direct reports opportunities to vent in a nonthreatening, affirming environment. This means listening supportively. This means letting the employee know that you will not shoot the messenger and then listening without interrupting, thinking ahead, focusing on preconceived ideas, or tuning out.

- **Build trust.** Negativity cannot flourish in an atmosphere of trust. Managers can build trust between themselves and employees and among employees by applying the following strategies: always delivering what is promised; remaining open-minded to suggestions; taking an interest in the development and welfare of employees; being tactfully honest with employees at all times; lending a hand when necessary; accepting blame but sharing credit; maintaining a steady, pleasant temperament even when under stress; and making sure that criticism is constructive and delivered in an affirming way.

- **Involve employees.** It's hard to criticize the way things are done when you are a part of how they are done. Involving employees by asking their opinions, soliciting their feedback, and making them part of the solution are some of the most effective deterrents to and cures for negativity in organizations.

OVERCOMING TERRITORIAL BEHAVIOR IN ORGANIZATIONS

Territory in the workplace tends to be more a function of psychological boundaries than of physical boundaries. Territorial behavior can manifest itself in a variety of ways.

Manifestations of Territoriality

The territorial instinct shows up in a variety of ways in an organization. The following are manifestations of territoriality in an organization:[2]

- **Occupation.** These games include actually marking territory as *mine*; playing the *gatekeeper* game with information; and monopolizing resources, information, access, and relationships.

- **Information manipulation.** People who play territorial games with information subscribe to the philosophy that information is power. To exercise power, they withhold information, bias information to suit their individual agendas (spin), cover up information, and actually give out false information.

- **Intimidation.** One of the most common manifestations of territoriality is intimidation—a tactic used to frighten others away from certain turf. Intimidation can take many different forms, from subtle threats to blatant aggression (physical or verbal).

- **Alliances.** Forming alliances with powerful individuals in an organization is a commonly practiced territorial game. The idea is to say without actually having to speak the words that "you had better keep off my turf, or I'll get my powerful friend to cause trouble."

- **Invisible wall.** Putting up an invisible wall involves creating hidden barriers to ensure that a decision, although already made, cannot be implemented. There are hundreds of strategies for building an invisible wall, including stalling, losing paperwork, and forgetting to place an order.

- **Strategic noncompliance.** Agreeing to a decision up front but with no intention of carrying the decision out is called *strategic noncompliance*. This tactic is often used to buy enough time to find a way to reverse the decision.

- **Discrediting.** Discrediting an individual as a way to cast doubt on his or her recommendation is a common turf protection tactic. Such an approach is called an *ad hominem* argument, which means that if you cannot discredit the recommendation, try to discredit the person making it.

- **Shunning.** Shunning, or excluding, an individual who threatens your turf is a common territorial protection tactic. The point of shunning is to use peer pressure against the individual being shunned.

- **Camouflage.** Other terms that are sometimes used to describe this tactic are *throwing up a smoke screen* and *creating fog*. This tactic involves confusing the issue by raising other distracting controversies, especially those that will produce anxiety such as encroaching on turf.

- **Filibuster.** *Filibustering* means talking a recommended action to death. The tactic involves talking at length about concerns—usually inconsequential—until the other side gives in just to stop any further discussion or until time to make the decision runs out.

Overcoming Territorial Behavior

Overcoming territorial behavior requires a two-pronged approach: (a) recognizing the manifestations described earlier and admitting that they exist and (b) creating an environment in which survival is equated with cooperation rather than territoriality. The following strategies can be used for creating a cooperative environment:[3]

- **Avoid jumping to conclusions.** Talk to employees about territoriality versus cooperation. Ask to hear their views, and listen to what they say.

- **Attribute territorial behavior to instinct rather than people.** Blaming people for following their natural instincts is like blaming them for eating. The better approach is to show them that their survival instinct is tied to cooperation, not turf. This is done by rewarding cooperation and applying negative reinforcement to territorial behavior.

- **Ensure that no employee feels attacked.** Remember that the survival instinct is the motivation behind territorial behavior. Attacking employees, or even letting them feel as if they are being attacked, will only trigger their survival instinct. To change territorial behavior, it is necessary to put employees at ease.

- **Avoid generalizations.** When employees exhibit territorial behavior, deal with it in specifics as opposed to generalizations. It is a mistake to witness territorial behavior on the part of one employee and respond by calling a group of employees together and talking about the issue in general terms. Deal with the individual who exhibits the behavior and focus on specifics.

- **Understand "irrational" fears.** The survival instinct is a powerful motivator. It can lead employees to cling irrationally to their fears. Managers should consider this point when dealing with employees who find it difficult to let go of survival behaviors. Be firm but patient, and never deal with an employee's fears in a denigrating or condescending manner.

- **Respect each individual's perspective.** In a way, an individual's perspective or opinion is part of his or her psychological territory. Failure to respect people's perspectives is the same as threatening their territory. When challenging territorial behavior, let employees explain their perspectives and show respect for them, even if you do not agree.

- **Consider the employee's point of view.** In addition to giving an appropriate level of respect to employees' perspectives, managers should try to "step into their shoes." How would you, the manager, feel if you were the employee? Sensitivity to the employee's point of view and patience with that point of view are critical when trying to overcome territorial behavior.

MANAGING CONFLICT IN ORGANIZATIONS

Human conflict is a normal and unavoidable aspect of the highly competitive modern workplace, even in a total quality setting. One of the human relations skills needed by people in such a setting is the ability to disagree with fellow workers without being disagreeable. However, even if most members of an organization have this skill, conflicts still may arise among workers. When people work together, no matter how committed they are to a common goal, human conflict is going to occur. Consequently, managers in a total quality setting must be proficient in resolving conflict. This section contains information managers need to know to be catalysts in resolving human conflict in the workplace.

Causes of Workplace Conflict

The most common causes of workplace conflict are predictable. They include those shown in Figure 13–11.

Limited resources often lead to conflict in the workplace. It is not uncommon for an organization to have fewer resources (funds, supplies, personnel, time, equipment, etc.) than might be needed to complete a job. When this happens, who gets the resources and in what amounts? *Incompatible goals* often lead to conflict, and incompatibility of goals is inherent in the workplace. For example, conflicts between engineering and manufacturing are common in modern industry. The goal of engineering is to design a product that meets the customers' needs. The goal of manufacturing is to produce a high-quality product as inexpensively as possible. In an attempt to satisfy the customer, engineering might create a design that is difficult to manufacture economically. What is the result? A conflict.

Role ambiguity can also lead to conflict by blurring "turf lines." This makes it difficult to know who is responsible and who has authority. *Different values* can lead to conflict. For example, if one group values job security and another values maximum profits, the potential for conflict exists. *Different perspectives* can lead to conflict. How people perceive a given situation depends on their background, values, beliefs, and individual circumstances. Because these factors are sure to differ among both individuals and groups, particularly in an increasingly diverse workplace, perception problems are not uncommon.

The final predictable cause of conflict is *communication problems*. Effective communication is difficult at best. Improving the communication skills of employees at all levels is an ongoing goal of management. Knowing that communication will never be perfect, communication-based conflict should be expected.

How People React to Conflict

To deal with conflict effectively, managers need to understand how people react to conflict. The ways in which people react to conflict can be summarized as competing, accommodating, compromising, collaborating, and avoiding.[4]

A typical reaction to conflict is *competition* in which one party attempts to win, while making the other lose. The opposite reaction to conflict is *accommodation*. In this reaction, one person puts the needs of the other first. *Compromise* is a reaction in which the two opposing sides attempt to work out a solution that helps both to the extent possible. *Collaboration* involves both sides working together to find an acceptable solution for both. *Avoidance* involves shrinking away from conflict. This reaction is seen in people who are not comfortable facing conflict and dealing with it.

In some situations, a particular reaction to conflict is more appropriate than another. Managers who are responsible for resolving conflict need to understand what is and what is not an appropriate reaction to conflict. The various

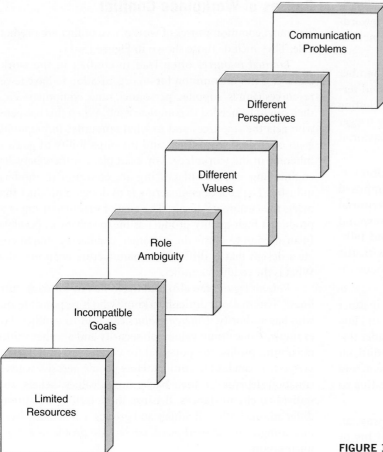

Communication
Problems

Different
Perspectives

Different
Values

Role
Ambiguity

Incompatible
Goals

Limited
Resources

FIGURE 13–11 Causes of Workplace Conflict

situations in which specific reactions to conflict are appropriate are summarized as follows:[5]

- Competing is appropriate when quick action is vital or when important but potentially unpopular actions must be taken.

- Collaborating is appropriate when the objective is to learn or to work through feelings that are interfering with interpersonal relationships.

- Avoiding is appropriate when you perceive no chance of satisfying your concerns or when you desire to let people cool down and have time to regain a positive perspective.

- Accommodating is appropriate when you are outmatched and losing anyway or when harmony and stability are important enough to work out a compromise.

How Conflict Should Be Handled

Managers focus most of their attention on preventing and resolving conflict, but occasionally they might have to stimulate conflict when team members agree too easily with new ideas or when the organization has become stagnant, it might be necessary to stimulate conflict. Conflict resolution and stimulation, taken together, are known as *conflict management*.

The following guidelines can be used by managers for resolving a conflict:[6]

- Determine how important the issue is to all people involved.

- Determine whether all people involved are willing and able to discuss the issue in a positive manner.

- Select a private place where the issue can be discussed confidentially by everyone involved.

- Make sure that both sides understand that they are responsible for both the problem and the solution.

- Solicit opening comments from both sides. Let them express their concerns, feelings, ideas, and thoughts, but in a nonaccusatory manner.

- Guide participants toward a clear and specific definition of the problem.

- Encourage participants to propose solutions. Examine the problem from a variety of different perspectives and discuss any and all solutions proposed.

- Evaluate the costs versus the gains (cost-benefit analysis) of all proposed solutions and discuss them openly. Choose the best solution.

- Reflect on the issue and discuss the conflict resolution process. Encourage participants to express their opinions as to how the process might be improved.

How and When Conflict Should Be Stimulated

Occasionally, an organization will have too little conflict. Such organizations tend to be those in which employees have become overly comfortable and management has effectively suppressed free thinking, innovation, and creativity. When this occurs, stagnation generally results. Stagnant organizations need to be shaken up before they die. Managers can do this by stimulating positive conflict or conflict that is aimed at revitalizing the organization. The need for conflict stimulation exists when:[7]

- You are surrounded by employees who always agree with you and tell you only what you want to hear.
- Your employees are afraid to admit they need help or that they've made mistakes.
- Decision makers focus more on reaching agreement than on arriving at the best decision.
- Managers focus more on getting along with others than on accomplishing objectives.
- Managers place more emphasis on not hurting feelings than on making quality decisions.
- Managers place more emphasis on being popular than on high job performance and competitiveness.
- Employees are highly resistant to change.
- The turnover rate is unusually low.
- Employees, supervisors, and managers avoid proposing new ideas.

Each of these situations is an indication that conflict may need to be stimulated. It may be possible to have a vital, energetic, developing, improving organization without conflict, but this isn't likely to happen. Innovation, creativity, and the change inherent in continual improvement typically breed conflict. Therefore, the absence of conflict can also be an indication of the absence of vitality. Because this is the case, managers need to know how to stimulate positive conflict.

The techniques for stimulating conflict fall into three categories: improving communication, altering organizational structure, and changing behavior.[8]

- Improving communication will ensure a free flow of ideas at all levels. Open communication will introduce a daily agitation factor that will ensure against stagnation, while at the same time providing a mechanism for effectively dealing with the resultant conflict.
- Altering organizational structure in ways that involve employees in making decisions that affect them and that empower them will help prevent stagnation. Employees in organizations that are structured to give them a voice will use that voice. The result will be positive conflict.
- Changing behavior may be necessary, particularly in organizations that have traditionally suppressed and discouraged conflict rather than dealing with it. Managers who find themselves in such situations may find the following procedure helpful: (a) identify the types of behaviors you want employees to exhibit, (b) communicate with employees so that they understand what is expected, (c) reinforce the desired behavior, and (d) handle conflict as it emerges using the procedures described in the previous section.

Communication in Conflict Situations

The point was made in the previous section that human conflict in the workplace is normal, to be expected, and, in certain instances, to be promoted. In managing conflict—which in essence means resolving conflict when it is having negative effects and promoting conflict when doing so might help avoid stagnation—communication is critical.

The following guidelines for using communication in managing conflict will be helpful:[9]

- **The initial attitude of those involved in the conflict can predetermine the outcome.** This means that if a person enters into a situation spoiling for a fight, he or she will probably get one. Communication prior to such a situation aimed at convincing either or both parties to view it as an opportunity to cooperatively solve a problem can help predetermine a positive outcome.
- **When possible, conflict guidelines should be in place before conflicts occur.** It is not uncommon for conflict to be exacerbated by disagreements over how it should be resolved. Before entering into a situation in which conflict might occur, make sure all parties understand how decisions will be made, who has the right to give input, and what issues are irrelevant.
- **Assessing blame should not be allowed.** It is predictable that two people in a conflict situation will blame each other. If human interaction is allowed to get hung up on the rocks and shoals of blame, it will never move forward. The approach that says "We have a problem. How can we work together to solve it?" is more likely to result in a positive solution than arguing over who is to blame.
- **"More of the same" solutions should be eliminated.** When a particular strategy for resolving conflict is tried but proves to be ineffective, don't continue using it. Some managers get stuck on a particular approach and stay with it even when the approach clearly doesn't work. Try something new instead of using "more of the same" solutions.
- **Maintain trust by keeping promises.** Trust is fundamental to all aspects of total quality. It is especially important in managing conflict. Trust is difficult to win but easy to lose. Conflict cannot be effectively managed by someone who is untrustworthy. Consequently, managers in a total quality setting must keep their promises and, in so doing, build trust among employees.

Each of the strategies set forth in this section depends on communication. Communication that is open, frank, tactful, continuous, and inclusive can do more than anything else to ensure that conflict is properly managed in the workplace.

SUMMARY

1. Internal politics consists of activities undertaken to gain advantage or influence organizational decision making in ways intended to serve a purpose other than the best interests of the overall organization. It is the games people play to promote decisions that are based on criteria other than merit.

2. Organizational structure is not the cause of internal politics. All of the widely used organizational structures are susceptible to internal politics.

3. Several concepts—personal insecurity, self-interest, a hunger for power, ambition, ego, and the need for acceptance—are the primary drivers of internal politics.

4. The most commonly used methods of internal politicians are lobbying, building coalitions, applying harassment and pressure, electioneering, gossiping, and spreading rumors.

5. The rationale for collaboration is found in the debilitating effect internal politics can have on an organization. Internal politics can drain an organization of its intellectual and physical energy and in the process take away its ability to compete.

6. An organization's effort to control internal politics should have at least the following components: strategic planning, leadership, reward/recognition, performance appraisal, customer focus, conflict management, and culture.

7. The most common categories of negative behavior are control disputes, territorial (boundary) disputes, dependence and independence issues, need for attention and responsibility, authority issues, and loyalty issues.

8. The following symptoms are indicators of negativity in the workplace: "I can't" attitudes, a "they" mentality, critical conversation, and blame fixing among employees.

9. To overcome negativity, organizations should communicate, establish clear expectations, provide opportunities for anxiety venting, build trust, and involve employees.

10. Territorial behavior in organizations manifests itself in occupation, information manipulation, intimidation, alliances, invisible walls, strategic noncompliance, discrediting, shunning, camouflage, and filibuster.

11. The following strategies will help when trying to overcome territorial behavior: Avoid jumping to conclusions, attribute the behavior to instinct rather than people, ensure that employees don't feel attacked, avoid generalizations, understand irrational fears, respect each individual's perspective, and consider the employee's point of view.

12. Causes of workplace conflict include limited resources, incompatible goals, role ambiguity, different perspectives, and poor communication.

13. Managers have two responsibilities regarding conflict in the workplace: conflict resolution and conflict stimulation. Conflict should be stimulated to overcome excessive compliance and complacency.

KEY TERMS AND CONCEPTS

Alliances
Ambition
Anxiety venting
Blame fixing
Building coalitions
Camouflage
Conflict management
Critical conversation
Culture
Customer focus
Ego
Electioneering
Gossiping and spreading rumors
Harassment and pressure
Hunger for power
"I can't" attitudes
Information manipulation
Internal politics
Intimidation
Invisible wall
Leadership
Lobbying
Need for acceptance
Occupation
Performance appraisal
Personal insecurity
Reward/recognition
Self-interest
Shunning
Strategic noncompliance
Strategic planning
"They" mentality

FACTUAL REVIEW QUESTIONS

1. Define *internal politics*.

2. Explain the role organizational structure can play in promoting internal politics.

3. Give an example of internal politics in action in an organization.

4. List and briefly describe the most commonly used methods of internal politicians.

5. Describe the impact internal politics can have on the implementation of total quality.

6. Describe how managers can control internal politics in an organization.

7. What are the categories of negativity in the workplace?

8. Explain the strategies for overcoming territorial behavior.

9. When should conflict be encouraged in an organization?

CRITICAL THINKING ACTIVITY

A Toxic Work Environment

When Maggie Lance took over Air-Tech's packaging and shipping (P & S) department, it was notorious within the company as a dead-end, high-stress, uncomfortable place to work. Internal politics, territoriality, negativity, and conflict were the rule rather than the exception in the P & S department. Other employees joked that "P & S" stands for "push and shove." The best word Maggie could find to describe the work environment in her new department was *toxic*.

Turnover is high, morale is low, productivity is substandard, and quality is a joke. Clearly, Maggie has her work cut out for her. Put yourself in her place. Where should she start? How should she proceed? What should be the key elements in her turn-around plan?

DISCUSSION ASSIGNMENT 13–1

Conflict over Conflict

"We have too much conflict in this organization," said Larry Parette. "Nobody agrees on anything. It's beginning to get to me."

"Nonsense, Larry," said Mack Porter. "We need conflict. Our best ideas come when smart people disagree, not when everyone goes along just to get along." Parette and Porter are the founders and managing partners of P&P Design, a firm they have grown from just the two of them to more than 300 employees.

"Well, this conflict you like so much has cost us two good employees this month," said Parette. "Both of them told me that working here had become too stressful because of the constant arguing and bickering."

"All right, we lost two good designers," said Porter. "But just last week we saved $250,000 on the Morgandale project because one of our junior designers refused to go along with the crowd and practically forced us to consider his ideas. His ideas caused a lot of grief in several meetings, and some of our senior designers even went after his job. But now that his ideas have worked so well, suddenly everyone claims they agreed with him from the beginning. We need this kind of conflict."

DISCUSSION QUESTIONS

Discuss the following questions in class or outside of class with your fellow students:

1. Who is right in this case? Is it Parette, Porter, neither, or both?

2. What, if anything, should be done about the conflict at P&P Design?

DISCUSSION ASSIGNMENT 13–2

Keep Off My Turf!

The best way to describe the relationship between the design and manufacturing departments at Waverly Prestressed Concrete (WPC) is *warfare*. A typical conversation between the vice president for design and the vice president for manufacturing goes like this: "If you knew anything about manufacturing, you might design a product we can actually make every once in a while," says the vice president for manufacturing.

"If you knew my job better, you could manufacture anything we design," responds the vice president for design.

They are actually both right. The design and manufacturing departments need to work together closely and cooperatively as partners. The designers need to apply the principles of design for manufacturing (DFM) so that the product is not just functional but also can be produced economically. Manufacturing personnel need to be a part of the design team so that their input is part of the process from the outset. Unfortunately, both departments have built invisible walls around their domains and adopted attitudes toward each other that clearly say "Keep off my turf!"

DISCUSSION QUESTIONS

Discuss the following questions in class or outside of class with your fellow students:

1. What, if anything, should be done to improve relations at WPC?

2. How can the invisible walls be pulled down?

ENDNOTES

1. Rachel Levy Sarfin, "Conflict Resolution Strategies in the Workplace." Retrieved from www.ehow.com/about_7303532_conflict-resolution-strategies-workplace-teams.html on February 20, 2011.

2. Annette Simmons, "Territorial Games: Understanding and Ending Turf Wars at Work." Retrieved from http://groupprocessconsulting.com/flow/territorialchapone%20doc.pdf on January 15, 2011.

3. K. W. Thomas, *Introduction to Conflict and Teams* (Mountain View, CA: CPP, 2004), 27–29.

4. Ibid.

5. Ibid.

6. "Conflict Resolution." Retrieved from www.mindtools.com/pages/article/newLDR_81.htm on January 18, 2011.

7. Mary Coulter and Steven P. Robbins, *Foundation of Organizational Behavior and Administration* (Englewood Cliffs, NJ: Pearson Custom Publishing, 2008), 37–39.

8. Ibid.

9. Elizabeth Scott, "Conflict Resolution Mistakes to Avoid." Retrieved from http://stress.about.com/od/relationships/tp/conflictres.htm on February 7, 2011.

ISO 9000 AND TOTAL QUALITY: THE RELATIONSHIP

There can be no improvements where there are no standards. —**Masaaki Imai**

MAJOR TOPICS

- ISO 9000: The International Standard for Quality Management Systems
- ISO 9000's Objective
- How ISO 9000 Is Applied to Organizations
- The ISO 9000 Quality Management System: A Definition
- Authority for Certification/Registration
- ISO 9001 and Industry-Specific Applications
- Organizational Registration to ISO 9001
- The Benefits of ISO 9000
- The Origin of ISO 9000
- Comparative Scope of ISO 9000 and Total Quality Management
- Management Motivation for Registration to ISO 9001
- ISO 9000 and Total Quality Management Working Together
- The Future of ISO 9000
- ISO 9000: Versions/Updates

ISO 9000: THE INTERNATIONAL STANDARD FOR QUALITY MANAGEMENT SYSTEMS

The ISO 9000 is a family of standards and guidelines related to the quality management system (QMS). It sets the requirements for the assurance of quality and for management's involvement. The thrust of ISO 9000 is for organizations to implement a QMS conforming to the standard's requirements and, through the consistent, rigorous employment of the QMS, to

- Improve customer satisfaction by fulfilling customer requirements;
- Achieve continual improvement of organizational performance and competitiveness;
- Continually improve its processes, products, and services; and
- Comply with regulatory requirements.

It is important to note that ISO 9000 does not specify a level of quality or performance for any product or service provided by an organization. That is left to the organization to determine with its customers. The ISO 9000 is about standardizing the approach organizations everywhere use to manage and improve the processes that ultimately result in their products and services. The ISO 9000 is applicable to any organization, whether in the private or the public sector, whether large or small, and applies to those components of the organization that can have an impact on product or service quality. These typically include the departments responsible for engineering/design, purchasing, manufacturing, quality assurance, and delivery of the organization's products and services.

When an organization demonstrates conformity to ISO 9001 to an independent (3rd party) registrar firm, the registrar can certify (or register) the organization. Registration provides assurance to customers worldwide that products or services from the organization can be expected to consistently meet customer requirements. To maintain its registration, the organization must constantly strive to ensure that the QMS continues to function effectively and that it is continually improved. That is done through consistent and rigorous application of the QMS and a system of formal, documented internal audits in interaction with the organization's top management, interspersed with periodic independent audits by the registrar firm. Registration may be lost if the registrar's audits determine that the organization is not conforming to the requirements of its registered QMS.

The Eight Principles: ISO 9000's Basis

The ISO 9000 QMS is based on eight principles from total quality management (TQM):

1. **Customer Focus.** Understand the customer's needs, meet the customer's requirements, and strive to exceed the customer's expectations.
2. **Leadership.** Establish unity of purpose and organizational direction and provide an environment that promotes employee involvement and achievement of objectives.
3. **Involvement of People.** Take advantage of fully involved employees, using all their abilities for the benefit of the organization.

FIGURE 14–1 Plan–Do–Check–Act Cycle

4. **Process Approach.** Recognize that things accomplished are the results of processes and that processes along with related activities and resources must be managed.

5. **System Approach to Management.** The multiple interrelated processes that contribute to the organization's effectiveness are a system and should be managed as a system.

6. **Continual Improvement.** Continual improvement should be a permanent objective applied to the organization and to its people, processes, systems, and products.

7. **Factual Approach to Decision Making.** Decisions must be based on the analysis of accurate, relevant, and reliable data and information.

8. **Mutually Beneficial Supplier Relationships.** Both the organization and the supplier benefiting from one another's resources and knowledge results in value for all.

These eight principles will be recognized from your study of TQM and from Dr. Deming's Fourteen Points. They represent the total quality philosophy to which the organization must adhere in order to develop the cultural environment necessary for an effective, conforming QMS.

Plan–Do–Check–Act: ISO 9000's Operating Principle

Plan–Do–Check–Act is now the *operating principle* of ISO's management system standards. Its function is to operate in a never-ending loop, as described in the following steps and shown in Figure 14–1, resulting in continual improvement for products/services, processes, and systems of processes.

1. **Plan.** Establish objectives and develop the plans to achieve them.

2. **Do.** Put the plans into action.

3. **Check.** Measure the results of the action; that is, is the planned action working, or were the objectives met?

4. **Act (or Adjust).** Learn from the results of the third (Check) step, make any necessary changes to the plans, and repeat the cycle.

ISO 9000'S OBJECTIVE

Aims of ISO 9000

The original aim of ISO 9000 was to ensure that the products or services provided by registered organizations were consistently fit for their intended purpose. The ISO 9000 raised the standard's aim to a new level. Customer focus and continual improvement, along with the other six quality management principles that have been incorporated into the standard, are intended to make registered organizations more competitive. This is essentially the same objective as that of total quality management.

HOW ISO 9000 IS APPLIED TO ORGANIZATIONS

No organization is required by any government to use ISO 9000. Some government and corporate customers may well require their suppliers to be ISO 9000 registered (or at least conforming), but usually whether to adopt the ISO 9000 QMS is strictly up to the organization's management. Once management decides to go with ISO 9000, then it is faced with the task of developing its QMS to conform to the requirements of ISO 9001. The ISO 9001 lays down the requirements for *what* an organization's QMS must do but does not dictate *how* the QMS should do it in any particular organization. The organization determines that for itself and, if seeking registration, employs an accredited registrar firm to verify its conformance to ISO 9001. Without getting into details beyond the scope of this chapter, the organization, once registered, must

- Apply its QMS to its operations according to the standard and exactly as the QMS states.
- Continually assess the effectiveness of the QMS and make changes to improve it.
- Conduct periodic internal QMS audits.
- Submit to external (3rd party) surveillance audits at least annually by its registrar.
- Submit to a new registration audit every third year by a registrar.

As mentioned earlier, customer requirements for their suppliers to be registered to ISO 9001:2000 have become widespread in several industrial sectors. The U.S. government routinely requires ISO 9001 in its contracts to the defense industry, replacing military requirements (for example, MIL-Q-9858A, Quality Program Requirements) having the same or similar objectives. Several global business sectors have adopted ISO 9001 as the basis for quality management systems mandated throughout their supply chains. Each sector has adapted the standard to its unique requirements and renamed the standard accordingly. Organizations in the concerned industrial sectors are required to operate under these tailored standards. For example, an organization supplying products to the automotive industry should be registered to QS 9000, the auto industry's version of ISO 9001. Similarly, organizations within the aerospace sector would be registered to AS 9100, the tooling and equipment sector to TE 9000, and the telecommunications sector to TL 9000. The ISO 9001 is embedded in each of these standards, along with additional requirements to satisfy the sector's unique needs.

THE ISO 9000 QUALITY MANAGEMENT SYSTEM: A DEFINITION

To secure registration, organizations must develop and use quality management systems conforming to the requirements of ISO 9001. The first question asked by someone unfamiliar with ISO 9000 is "What is a quality management system?"

We provide the following definition:

The quality management system is composed of all the organization's policies, procedures, plans, resources, processes, and delineation of responsibility and authority, all deliberately aimed at achieving product or service quality levels consistent with customer satisfaction and the organization's objectives. When these policies, procedures, plans, and so forth are taken together, they define how the organization works and how quality is managed.

QUALITY TIP ▼

ISO 9000 Is Not Prescriptive

Some organizational leaders fear that ISO 9000 registration will be such a prescriptive process that their company will be locked into a book full of rules that will undermine creativity and innovation. In reality, just the opposite is true. The ISO compliance is about the organization stating what it is going to comply and then following through and doing it. The ISO auditors do not tell organizations how to conduct business. Rather, they check to ensure that the organization is actually doing what it says it does to comply with the standard.

The quality management system will include this documentation:

1. **A quality policy.** This statement describes how the organization approaches quality.

2. **The quality manual.** This must address each clause of the ISO 9001 standard. It will also typically include an organization chart, or some such device, illustrating management responsibility for operating the quality system. Quality procedures may be part of this manual, or they may be referenced.

3. **Quality objectives.** These are the goals related to quality and must be in harmony with the quality policy. Quality objectives are assigned to the relevant organizational functions and levels and are tracked by top management.

4. **Quality procedures.** These describe step by step what the company does to meet the quality policy. As a minimum, there will be a procedure for each of the ISO 9001 clauses outlining requirements. There may also be procedures for any processes that can impact quality.

5. **Forms, records, and so on.** These provide proof of activities for the firm and for the auditors.

This documentation is used to ensure the necessary consistency in the firm's operations and processes. Auditors use it to verify conformance.

AUTHORITY FOR CERTIFICATION/REGISTRATION

When an organization says it is certified or registered to ISO 9001, one may ask, "By what authority?" You understand by now that registration (or certification—they are synonymous, with registration more commonly used in the United States) is awarded by a registrar firm. These firms, sometimes referred to as certification bodies, are almost always private companies that have auditing expertise. Well, then, who gives them the authority to grant ISO 9000 registration certificates? How do we know that they are competent to determine which organizations get registered and which do not? The answer is that all certification bodies for ISO 9000 must themselves be accredited by a higher level group called—you guessed it—an accreditation body. There are lots of certification bodies (the registrars) but far fewer accreditation bodies. Now one would think that the authority of the accreditation bodies must emanate from the International Organization for Standardization (ISO), but that is not the case. There is another level of oversight connected with ISO conformity assessment: the International Accreditation Forum (IAF), made up of accreditation bodies, industry representatives, and other stakeholders. Members of the IAF are required to give assurance that they will comply with the international standards and IAF guidance. The IAF takes its authority from Article 6 of the World Trade Organization's Agreement on Technical Barriers to Trade, which stated the need for bodies involved

International Accreditation Forum

(Assesses Accreditation Bodies)

↓

Accreditation Body

(Accredits Certification Bodies)

↓

Certification Body

(Registers Organizations)

↓

Organization Seeking Registration

FIGURE 14–2 Authority Flow for ISO 9001 Registration

in conformity assessments (i.e., the registrars) to be proven technically competent through a process of accreditation.[1] The flow of certification authority from the IAF to the registrar is shown in Figure 14–2.

ISO 9001 AND INDUSTRY-SPECIFIC APPLICATIONS

The ISO 9001 standard is intentionally generic so that it can be applied to any given organization, public or private. However, selected industries have found it helpful to tailor the ISO 9001 standard specifically for their use. The benefits of developing industry-specific versions of the ISO 9001 standard are that it encourages: (1) the training and deployment of auditors with industry-specific knowledge rather than ISO 9000 generalists and (2) a more accurate interpretation of the standard for a given industry. The most widely used industry-specific applications of ISO 9001 are as follows:

- **TickIT.** Developed by the United Kingdom's Board of Trade specifically for the information technology industry.
- **AS 9000.** Developed specifically for the aerospace industry.
- **PS 9000.** Developed specifically for the pharmaceutical packaging materials industry.

- **ISO/TS 16949.** Developed specifically for the automotive industry (replaced QS 9000, an earlier version).
- **TL 9000.** Developed specifically for the telecommunications industry.
- **ISO 13485.** Developed specifically for the medical industry.
- **ISO/TS 29001.** Developed specifically for the petroleum, petrochemical, and natural gas industries.

ORGANIZATIONAL REGISTRATION TO ISO 9001

Whether an organization manufactures a product or provides a service, whether it is a company or a governmental agency, whether it is large or small, ISO 9000 can apply and be used to advantage. There is nothing to prevent an organization from implementing and using a conforming QMS without going through the rigors and expense of actually registering. However, without being registered, credibility becomes an issue. The results could conceivably be the same, whether registered or not—except for a couple of factors. The organization that is registered by a recognized certification body will have more credibility in the world's marketplace, something that may be crucially important. In addition, the registered organization must conform to ISO 9001 and have an independent third party (the registrar) continually observe its conformance in order to maintain its ISO 9001 certificate. Without that impetus, the unregistered organization may not always feel the pressure to maintain conformance and may overlook issues that need attention or correction. We recommend that any organization going to an ISO 9000 QMS take the extra step of registration. Either way, the organization that wants a conforming ISO 9000 QMS must go through a process that includes the following steps (steps 5 and 7 are omitted for nonregistering organizations):

1. Develop (or upgrade) a quality manual that describes how the organization will assure the quality of its products or services.

2. Document procedures (or upgrade existing documentation) that describe how the various processes for design, production, continual improvement, and so on, will be operated. This must include procedures for management reviews and audits.

3. The organization must secure (and provide evidence of, if registering) top management's commitment to the QMS and continual improvement.

4. The organization's top management must ensure that customer requirements are determined and met.

5. If registering, the organization must hire an accredited registrar company to examine its systems, processes, procedures, quality manual, records, and related items. If everything is in order and if the registrar is satisfied that the organization is effectively using the QMS, reg-

istration will be granted. Otherwise, the registrar will inform the organization of the areas requiring work (but will not tell the company specifically what must be done), and another audit will be scheduled.

6. Whether registered or not, the organization must conduct its own internal audits to ensure that the systems, processes, and procedures are working effectively.

7. Once registered, the outside registrar will make periodic audits for the same purpose. These audits must be passed to retain registration.

An important point to remember about ISO 9000 is that the organization has to respond to all ISO 9001 requirements and tell the registrar specifically *what it is going to do and how it is to be done*. The ISO does not tell the organization what it must do or how to do it. To retain registration, the organization *must do what it said it would do*.

THE BENEFITS OF ISO 9000

Organizational Benefits

The ISO claims that beyond customer satisfaction, cost and risk-management benefits will also accrue to the organization. These benefits translate to improved competitiveness—the same as TQM's objective. The ISO claims these benefits result from emphasizing the eight quality management principles on which the standard is based.

Customer Benefits

Customers want products or services that meet their requirements, and they want them at a competitive price. Like TQM, ISO 9001 can help the organization in both areas. Customer requirements will be met if the organization listens to customers and designs and manufactures its products accordingly. Prices can be more competitive because waste is minimized as improved processes become more efficient, benefiting both the organization and its customers. Customers have increased confidence in the products and services of ISO 9000-registered organizations because they know that appropriate quality management processes are employed and that an independent registrar ensures that this continues to occur.

THE ORIGIN OF ISO 9000

The ISO 9000 and total quality management originated independently of each other, for different reasons, in different parts of the world, and at different times. From earlier chapters, you are already familiar with the post–World War II origins in Japan of the total quality movement. The ISO 9000 series of standards was originally developed in response to the need to harmonize dozens of national and international quality standards that then existed throughout the world. To that end, the ISO, a worldwide federation of national standards organizations from more than 158 nations, formed Technical Committee 176 to develop ISO 9000.

The ISO 9000 was developed by this international team that includes the American National Standards Institute (ANSI), the U.S. member of ISO. The ANSI was represented by the American Society for Quality (ASQ), its affiliate responsible for quality management and related standards. The first version of ISO 9000 was released in 1987. By that time, the total quality management movement was more than 35 years old. As a result of this standard, suppliers of products and services are able to develop and employ a QMS that is recognized by all their customers regardless of where on the planet those customers might be.

COMPARATIVE SCOPE OF ISO 9000 AND TOTAL QUALITY MANAGEMENT

There are two principal quality initiatives at work in the world today: ISO 9000 and Total Quality Management. Consequently, it is helpful to explain the relationship between the two. The following statements outline the relationship. Each statement is explained in the sections that follow in this chapter.

- ISO 9000 and TQM are not interchangeable.
- ISO 9000 is compatible with, and can be viewed as a subset of, TQM.
- ISO 9000 is frequently implemented in a non-TQM environment.
- ISO 9000 can improve operations in a traditional environment.
- ISO 9000 may be redundant in a mature TQM environment.
- ISO 9000 and TQM are not in competition.

ISO 9000 and TQM are Related but Not Interchangeable

Although ISO 9000 made a great leap toward TQM with the 2000 release, they are not yet the same, and probably never will be. By definition, ISO 9000 is concerned only with quality management systems for the *design, development, purchasing, production, installation,* and *servicing* of products and services.

On the other hand, total quality management, by definition, encompasses every aspect of the business or organization, not just the systems used to design, produce, and deploy its products and services. This includes all support systems such as human resources, finance, and marketing. Total quality management involves every function and level of the organization, from top to bottom.

Total quality management also means that management is responsible for developing the organization's vision (what it hopes to be at a point in the future), establishing guiding principles (a code of conduct for the organization and all of its employees), and setting the strategy and tactics

Characteristics	ISO 9000	TQM
Customer focus (internal and external)	✓	✓
Obsession with quality		✓
Scientific approach to problem solving	✓	✓
Long-term commitment	partial	✓
Teamwork		✓
Continual process and product improvement	✓	✓
Education and training intensive	✓	✓
Freedom through control		✓
Unity of purpose	✓	✓
Employee involvement and empowerment	partial	✓

FIGURE 14–3 Total Quality Management Characteristics Compared with Those of ISO 9000

for achieving the vision within the constraints of the guiding principles. In a TQM organization, the vision is pursued with input from an empowered workforce that cooperates and collaborates with management.

Total quality management, based on the teachings of Deming, Juran, Ishikawa, and others, with criteria defined by Deming's Fourteen Points, Juran's Ten Steps to Quality Improvement, and the Malcolm Baldrige National Quality Award, is more pervasive and demanding—literally requiring the transformation of the organization.

The primary difference between ISO 9000 and TQM is in the degree to which the total organization is involved. Whereas TQM requires the involvement of all functions and levels of the organization, ISO 9000 does not require the QMS to include functions and levels that play only indirect roles in the management and execution of the product or service realization processes. Functions that typically are not involved under the QMS include human resources, finance (accounting), sales, and marketing.

Figure 14–3 illustrates how close ISO 9000's evolution has brought it to TQM.

TQM is defined as an approach to doing business that attempts to maximize the competitiveness of an organization through the continual improvement of the quality of its processes, products, services, people, and environments by emphasizing the characteristics listed in Figure 14–3.

ISO 9000 is Compatible with, and Can Be Viewed as a Subset of, TQM

Clearly, TQM and ISO 9000 are not quite the same thing. However, there is nothing inherent in ISO 9000 that would prevent it from becoming part of a larger total quality management environment. There are many examples today of companies that have successfully included ISO 9000 as part

of a larger total quality effort. Organizations that are already at some level of TQM maturity typically have found it easy to implement ISO 9000. This is because a TQM environment, with its infrastructure of top-management commitment, documented processes and procedures, continuous improvement, obsession with quality, and so on, easily supports the requirements of ISO 9000.

ISO 9000 is Frequently Implemented in a Non-TQM Environment

Although total quality is compatible with and may well facilitate an ISO 9000 implementation, it is by no means a prerequisite for ISO 9000. In fact, it is safe to say that the majority of ISO 9001–registered organizations have not fully adopted total quality—at least, not yet.

ISO 9000 Can Improve Operations in a Traditional Environment

By "traditional environment," we mean an organizational environment that has persisted in companies for decades, until the total quality management movement began to change things. A traditional organizational environment is one that still operates according to the "old way of doing things" rather than according to the principles of TQM.

When ISO 9000 is implemented by a traditional organization, the company should be the better for it. We will not go so far as to say it *will* be the better for it because much depends on the organization's reasons for adopting ISO 9000 and the degree of executive-level commitment to it. Put another way, if ISO 9000 is approached inappropriately and for the wrong reasons, it can become nothing more than a marketing ploy, and the organization's functional departments might develop even more problems than they had before ISO 9000.

ISO 9000 May Be Redundant in a Mature TQM Environment

Just as ISO 9000 should help traditional organizations, it should also benefit TQM organizations. However, in an organization that has achieved a high level of maturity in its total quality journey—say, in the 400–600 range on the Baldrige scale of 1,000 points—all ISO 9000 criteria may already be in place. In such a case, the only compelling reason for registration under ISO 9001 would be for marketing purposes. What would a company such as Toyota gain from ISO 9000 registration? Probably nothing. It already does everything required by ISO 9000. Its products and processes are recognized as world class. Consequently, it wouldn't gain even a marketing advantage. However, there are many fine TQM organizations that are not as well-known as Toyota. Such organizations, even though they may already meet or exceed the requirements of ISO 9000, may find it necessary to register in order to let potential customers know that their products or services satisfy the international standard.

ISO 9000 and TQM are Not in Competition

This is not a case of one or the other. Organizations can adopt TQM or ISO 9000, or both. While there may be those who advocate one to the exclusion of the other, in the larger scheme of things the two concepts fit well with each other. Both have worthwhile and similar aims. Our view is that not only are TQM and ISO 9000 compatible but they also actually support each other and are complementary. There are good reasons for using both in a single management system.

MANAGEMENT MOTIVATION FOR REGISTRATION TO ISO 9001

Management motivation for adopting either ISO 9000 or TQM can vary widely. There are both appropriate and inappropriate motives. For example, if a company seeks ISO 9001 registration merely to obtain a marketing advantage, its motive is inappropriate. As a result, the organization will likely give little more than lip service to adopting the standard. Appropriate motives for adopting ISO 9000 include the following:

- To improve operations by implementing a QMS that satisfies the ISO 9000 requirements for management responsibility; resource management; product realization; and measurement, analysis, and continual improvement
- To create or improve a QMS that will be recognized by customers worldwide
- To improve product or service quality or the consistency of quality
- To improve customer satisfaction
- To improve competitive posture

- To conform to the requirements of one or more major customers (although adoption would be better motivated by internal considerations, such as the preceding five)

What we are saying here is that, ideally, management will adopt ISO 9000 as a way to make real improvements in the company's operations, serve its customers in a more responsible way, and, as a result, be more successful. This approach is more likely to ensure commitment and participation by top management. Approaching ISO 9000 from a strictly marketing perspective may result in a negative reaction to the amount of work required by the functional departments and in only enough management commitment to do the bare minimum for registration. In other words, if ISO 9000 is viewed as a necessary evil that one must adopt to compete in certain markets, every dollar and every hour spent on ISO 9000 will be seen as a burden to be endured rather than an investment in the organization's future. By definition, a burden is a load that is difficult to bear; the connotation is negative. When negative feelings abound among employees, commitment to ISO 9000 will suffer. It may be possible to fool the ISO 9000 registrar's auditor, but we guarantee that customers will not be fooled for long. Newfound markets will soon wither and disappear. If ISO 9000 is to have a real and permanent effect, it must be approached with a positive attitude and the unwavering commitment of top management.

ISO 9000 AND TOTAL QUALITY MANAGEMENT WORKING TOGETHER

We have discussed the fact that ISO 9000 and TQM are different in scope and were developed from different perspectives but now have similar requirements and objectives. Today, more than ever, the two concepts are compatible. With the exception of certification and audits, TQM requires everything required by ISO 9000 registration. However, even a mature TQM organization, one that does everything it would do under ISO 9000 and more, may not have the worldwide recognition afforded by ISO 9000 registration. There is no corresponding international certification for TQM. For this reason, even the mature TQM organization may find it necessary to seek ISO 9000 registration as a way to satisfy the demands of its customers. On the other hand, a traditional organization that is registered under ISO 9001 may find that it needs the larger TQM implementation to become or stay competitive. The ISO 9001 registration can be a good first step into TQM.

In fact, people who understand both ISO 9000 and total quality have concluded that the two are compatible and that ISO is properly seen as a subset of total quality.

Movement from ISO 9000 to TQM and Vice Versa

An organization that has its processes documented and under control, such as a company involved in total quality management, should find it relatively easy to prepare for

ISO 9000. Correspondingly, a traditional organization that has successfully registered under ISO 9001 will have a head start, should it decide to implement total quality. The major issues with ISO 9000 are securing top-management commitment, focusing on customer requirements and satisfaction, and documenting processes and procedures. Total quality management requires the same.

ISO 9000 as an Entry into Total Quality Management

How to get started is always an issue for organizations just beginning their total quality journey. Organizations beginning the process may find that a good strategy is registration to the ISO 9001 standard. The ISO 9000 preparation projects can be pursued as the entry projects for implementing total quality management.

We have already discussed the fact that ISO 9000 and total quality are compatible, making many of the same demands on the organization, and also that ISO 9000 is, for all practical purposes, a subset of total quality. For an organization that is attempting to adopt total quality and that would also benefit from ISO 9000, our 20-step implementation process should be considered. At the planning phase, steps 12 through 15, the initial implementation approach should be designed to include the steps necessary for ISO 9001 registration. By adopting this strategy, the organization will be engaged in both a total quality management implementation and an ISO 9000 preparation. The ISO 9000 effort will benefit from the total quality preparation phase by having the following components: an executive-level steering committee, a vision with the attendant guiding principles, a set of broad objectives, baselines on employee and customer satisfaction, an objective view of the organization's strengths and weaknesses, and an indication of which employees at all levels can be counted on for support during the implementation. In addition, the organization will have a well-thought-out means of communicating with employees and all other stakeholders to keep them apprised of the changes taking place, why they are happening, and what they will mean to everyone.

The recommendations in the preceding paragraph apply to organizations that have not yet implemented total quality or ISO 9001 but that are thinking about it. However, what about the organization that has already started working on ISO 9000 or has already achieved registration? How should such an organization approach the larger task of implementing total quality? The effort expended on ISO 9001 clearly should be seen as a head start, assuming ISO 9001 registration is approached as a way to improve the organization and not simply as a marketing gimmick. To the degree that the organization has already accomplished the early steps of the 20-step implementation process for total quality management, count it as progress toward the eventual complete implementation of TQM.

This organization should go back and execute any steps that have not already been completed before moving on. For example, there is no requirement in ISO 9001 for forming a steering committee (Step 2) composed of the top managers, so it is doubtful one has been established. Similarly, steps 3 (team building for the steering committee) and 4 (total quality training for the steering committee) are not required by ISO 9000 and will not have been done. The same may be said for steps 5, 8, 9, 10, and 11. The ISO 9001 does not require registered organizations to have a vision statement or a set of guiding principles under which the organization will operate.

Nothing in ISO 9001 would require an examination of organizational strengths and weaknesses or the baselining of employee and customer satisfaction. All of these should be done for TQM, and all will benefit ISO 9000. Having gone back to complete steps 1 through 11, the steering committee should start its planning phase by incorporating its ISO 9001 activities into the total quality initiative, using steps 12 through 17, and then expand beyond ISO 9000 from there.

In summary, the organization that is already involved in ISO 9000 should see itself as having a head start on the larger TQM implementation. One that has started neither, although seeing TQM and ISO 9000 as beneficial, might approach ISO 9001 as a logical part of the initial total quality journey.

THE FUTURE OF ISO 9000
Credibility of the Standard

Consider for a moment the importance of credibility as related to ISO 9000 registrations. The ISO 9000 is viable as a standard only as long as its registrations are honestly and competently issued. If that cannot be assured, then ISO 9000 will die. Many, including the authors, believe that the credibility of ISO certification has become diluted because there has been insufficient oversight of the registrars. Some are excellent, but others have been less than stellar in their assessments and awarding of certificates. To correct this problem, ISO, together with the International Electrotechnical Commission (IEC), has issued a new standard ISO/IEC 17021:2006, which is designed to restore the confidence in management system registration. It places rigorous requirements for competence and impartiality on the certifying bodies. Registrar conformity will be verified by the accrediting bodies, both by reviewing the registrar's organization, personnel, and procedures and by observing actual audits performed by the registrar. With this step, ISO has implemented a critical safeguard for the credibility of ISO 9000.

Updating ISO 9000

The ISO 9000 has been revised three times since its original release. The 2000 version incorporated major changes in the standard as it was being developed and improved through the incorporation of features from total quality management. The 2008 version has few significant changes.

ISO 9000: VERSIONS/UPDATES

Since the development of the first ISO standard in 1987, the standard has been updated periodically to reflect lessons learned and changes in the international business arena. The various updates to ISO 9000 are summarized as follows:

- **ISO 9000:1987.** This initial version of the ISO 9000 standard contained three models for quality management systems. It was structured like the United Kingdom's BS 5750 Standard. The three models for quality management systems were: (1) ISO 9001:1987—Quality Assurance in Design, Development, Production, and Installation Services; (2) ISO 9002:1987—Quality Assurance in Production, Installation, and Servicing (did not cover the development of new products); and (3) Quality Assurance in Final Inspection and Test. This version required mountains of paperwork as evidence of compliance with documented procedures. Many organizations thought the "cure" was worse than the "disease" when applying this version of the standard.

- **ISO 9000:1994.** This version continued to require comprehensive evidence of compliance with properly documented procedures, but it did begin to move toward process improvement by emphasizing preventive actions rather than just checking the final product. However, it was a burdensomely bureaucratic standard in which the "cure" was still worse than the "disease."

- **ISO 9001:2000.** This version combined ISO 9001, 9002, and 9003 into one document that is ISO 9001. The distinguishing feature of this version is that it was brought more closely in line with the basic tenets of quality management. For example, the most significant change is that this version of the standard makes process management its centerpiece. It also requires active involvement of an organization's executives. In other words, it does not allow responsibility for ISO registration to simply to be delegated to mid-ranking personnel and forgotten about. A final significant change in this version is its goal of improving organizational effectiveness through the application of performance metrics.

- **ISO 9001:2008.** This version is not substantively different from ISO 9001:2000, but there are several additional requirements that are important. These are as follows:

(1) The quality policy must be a formal statement from upper management that is linked to the organization's business and management plan, (2) The quality policy must be understood and used by all personnel at all levels, (3) All personnel must have measureable work objectives, (4) The quality system is audited regularly for conformance and effectiveness, (5) Decisions about the quality system are based on recorded data, (6) Records allow problems to be traced to their source by including where and how raw materials were processed, (7) The organization must have a comprehensive system for communicating with customers about any and all aspects of the relationship, (8) Product development must have planned stages with testing at every stage, and test results must be documented to indicate whether the product meets all applicable requirements, (9) Organizational performance must be regularly reviewed, and (10) The organization must have documented procedures for dealing with non-conformances.

ISO 9001: The Contents

When the original three ISO standards—9001, 9002, 9003—were combined to create ISO 9001:2000, the contents of the new document were also standardized. The contents of ISO 9001 are now as follows:

- Foreword
- Introduction
- Requirements

    Section 1: Scope

    Section 2: Normative Reference

    Section 3: Terms and Definitions

    Section 4: Quality Management System

    Section 5: Management Responsibility

    Section 6: Resource Management

    Section 7: Product Realization

    Section 8: Measurement, Analysis, and Improvement

Organizations seeking ISO 9000 registration are required to address all eight sections of the standard, but only sections 4 through 8 require implementation within the QMS.

SUMMARY

1. The following statements describe the relationship between ISO 9000 and TQM: ISO 9000 and TQM are not completely interchangeable; ISO 9000 is compatible with, and can be a subset of, TQM; ISO 9000 is frequently implemented in a non-TQM environment; ISO 9000 can improve operations in a traditional environment; ISO 9000 may be redundant in a mature TQM environment; and ISO 9000 and TQM are not in competition.

2. The origins of ISO 9000 and total quality management are vastly different. The ISO 9000 was developed in response to the need to harmonize dozens of national and international standards relating to quality. Total quality got its start in Japan around 1950 as a way to help that nation compete in the international marketplace.

3. The aim of ISO 9000 is to enable organizations to better serve their customers and to be more competitive through adherence to the standard's eight quality management principles.

4. Appropriate motivations for implementing ISO 9000 are as follows: to improve operations, to improve or create a quality management system, to improve the consistency of quality, to improve customer satisfaction, to improve competitive posture, and to conform to the requirements of customers.

5. The ISO 9000 and TQM are compatible in that ISO 9000 can be a complementary subset of TQM. The ISO 9000 can give an organization a head start in implementing TQM.

KEY TERMS AND CONCEPTS

Accreditation

Accredited registrar

Aims of ISO 9000

American National Standards Institute (ANSI)

American Society for Quality (ASQ)

Authority for certification/registration

Benefits of ISO 9000

Credibility of the standard

International Organization for Standardization (ISO)

ISO 9000

ISO 9000 and TQM are not interchangeable

ISO 9000's eight quality management principles

ISO 9001

Management motivation for registration

Origin of ISO 9000

Plan–do–check–act cycle

QMS audits

Quality management system (QMS)

Quality objectives

Quality policy

Tailored standards

Technical Committee 176

Traditional organizational environment

FACTUAL REVIEW QUESTIONS

1. List six statements that summarize the comparative scope of ISO 9000 and TQM.

2. Explain the origins of ISO 9000 and TQM. How are they different?

3. Contrast the aims of ISO 9000 and TQM.

4. List three appropriate reasons for implementing ISO 9000.

5. What is the most appropriate rationale for implementing TQM?

6. What are the industry-specific standards for the automotive, aerospace, and telecommunication industries?

7. Describe how you would use ISO 9000 as an entry into TQM.

CRITICAL THINKING ACTIVITY

Implementing Total Quality

Create a matrix that shows how ISO 9000 registration fits into a broader total quality implementation.

DISCUSSION ASSIGNMENT 14-1

ISO 9000 or TQM: Which Will It Be?

Reliance Control Systems is a large manufacturer of control systems for the electrical power generation and distribution industry. Over the past few years, Reliance has watched overseas competitors take away market share with products that are priced lower and that, at the same time, have developed a reputation for better reliability. The company is not in a dangerous position yet, but the Board of Directors wants to see a concerted effort to improve the company's competitive posture. Among the senior management, two factions have developed. One, led by the vice president of operations, is pressing the CEO to implement total quality management. After all, the aim of TQM is improved competitiveness, and that is just what is needed. On the other hand, the manufacturing vice president (VP) and the director of quality assurance are making the case for ISO 9000:2000.

DISCUSSION QUESTIONS

Discuss the following questions in class or outside of class with your fellow students:

1. Assume that you are siding with the VP of operations, and list the arguments for implementing TQM.

2. Now assume that you are with the heads of manufacturing and quality assurance. List the arguments for ISO 9000.

3. You have heard both sets of arguments, and you believe there might be a third approach that could satisfy both factions. What would you propose?

ENDNOTE

1. World Trade Organization, "Technical Barriers to Trade." Retrieved from www.wto.org/english/tratop_e/tbt_e.htm on March 1, 2011.

PART
TWO

TOOLS AND TECHNIQUES

OVERVIEW OF TOTAL QUALITY TOOLS

The significant problems we face cannot be solved at the same level of thinking we were at when we created them. —Albert Einstein

MAJOR TOPICS
- Total Quality Tools Defined
- Pareto Charts
- Cause-and-Effect Diagrams
- Check Sheets
- Histograms
- Scatter Diagrams
- Run Charts and Control Charts
- Stratification
- Some Other Important Tools Introduced
- Management's Role in Tool Deployment
- Selecting the Right Tool for the Job

One of the basic tenets of total quality is *management by facts*. This is not in harmony with the capability so revered in North America and the West in general: the ability to make snap decisions and come up with quick solutions to problems in the absence of input beyond intuition, gut feel, and experience. Management by facts requires that each decision, each solution to a problem, is based on relevant data and appropriate analysis. Once we get beyond the very small business (in which the data are always resident in the few heads involved, anyway), most decision points and problems will have many impacting factors, and the problem's root cause or the best-course decision will remain obscure until valid data are studied and analyzed. Collecting and analyzing data can be difficult. The total quality tools presented in this chapter make that task easy enough for anyone. Their use will ensure better decision making, better solutions to problems, and even improvement of productivity and products and services.

Writing about the use of statistical methods in Japan, Dr. Kaoru Ishikawa said:

The above are the so-called seven indispensable tools . . . that are being used by everyone: company presidents, company directors, middle management, foremen, and line workers. These tools are also used in a variety of [departments], not only in the manufacturing [department], but also in the [departments] of planning, design, marketing, purchasing, and technology.[1]

No matter where you fit into your organization today, you can use some or all of these tools to advantage, and they will serve you well for your future prospects.

This chapter explains the most widely used total quality tools and their applications, provides some insights on the involvement of management and the cross-functional nature of the tools, and issues some cautions.

TOTAL QUALITY TOOLS DEFINED

Carpenters use a kit of tools designed for very specific functions. Their hammers, for example, are used for the driving of nails and their saws for the cutting of wood. These and others enable a carpenter to build houses. They are *physical* tools. Total quality tools also enable today's employees, whether engineers, technologists, production workers, managers, or office staff, to do their jobs. Virtually no one can function in an organization that has embraced total quality without some or all of these tools. Unlike those in the carpenter's kit, these are *intellectual* tools. They are not wood and steel to be used with muscle; they are tools for collecting and displaying information in ways to help the human brain grasp thoughts and ideas. When thoughts and ideas are applied to physical processes, the processes yield better results. When they are applied to problem solving or decision making, better solutions and decisions are developed.

The seven tools discussed in the following seven sections of this chapter represent those generally accepted as the basic total quality tools. Some authors would include others, and we discuss some of the others briefly later in this chapter. A case can be made that *just-in-time (JIT), statistical process control,* and *quality function deployment* are total quality tools. But these are more than tools: They are complete systems under the total quality umbrella. This book devotes an entire chapter to each of these systems.

A tool, like a hammer, exists to help do a job. If the job includes *continual improvement*, problem solving, or decision making, then these seven tools fit the definition. Each of these tools is some form of chart for the collection and display of specific kinds of data. Through the collection and display facility, the data become useful information—information that can be used to solve problems, enhance decision making, keep track of work being done, and even predict future performance and problems. The beauty of the charts is that they organize data so that we can immediately comprehend the message. This would be all but impossible without the charts, given the mountains of data flooding today's workplace.

PARETO CHARTS

The *Pareto* (pah-ray-toe) *chart* (see Figure 15–1) is a very useful tool wherever one needs to separate the important from the trivial. The chart, first promoted by Dr. Joseph Juran, is named after Italian economist and sociologist Vilfredo Pareto (1848–1923). He had the insight to recognize that in the real world a minority of causes lead to the majority of problems. This is known as the Pareto Principle. Pick a category, and the Pareto Principle will usually hold. For example, in a factory you will find that of all the kinds of problems you can name, only about 20% of them will produce 80% of the product defects: Eighty percent of the cost associated with the defects will be assignable to only about 20% of the total number of defect types occurring.[2] Examining the elements of this cost will reveal that once again 80% of the total defect cost will spring from only about 20% of the cost elements.

Charts have shown that approximately 20% of the professionals on the tennis tour reap 80% of the prize money and that 80% of the money supporting churches in the United States comes from 20% of the church membership.

All of us have limited resources. That point applies to you and to me, and to all enterprises—even to giant corporations and to the government. This means that our resources (time, energy, and money) need to be applied where they will do the most good. The purpose of the Pareto chart is to show you where to apply your resources by distinguishing the significant few from the trivial many. It helps us establish priorities.

The Pareto chart in Figure 15–1 labels a company's customers A, B, C, D, E, and all others. The bars represent the percentages of the company's sales going to the respective customers. Seventy-five percent of this company's sales are the result of just two customers. If one adds customer C, 90% of its sales are accounted for. All the other customers together account for only 10% of the company's sales. Bear in mind that "all others" may include a very large number of small customers. Which customers are the ones who should be kept happy? Obviously, A, B, and perhaps C are the most critical. This would suggest that customers A, B, and C are the company's core market and all the other customers represent a marginal business. Decisions on where to allocate resources should be made accordingly.

The Pareto chart in Figure 15–2 shows bars representing the sales of a particular model of automobile by age group of the buyers. The curve represents the cumulative percentage of sales and is keyed to the *y*-axis scale on the right. The manufacturer has limited resources in its advertising budget, and the chart reveals which age groups are the most logical choice to target. Concentrating on the 26 to 45 age bracket will result in the best return on investment because 76% of the Swift V-12 buyers come from the combination of the 36 to 45 and 26 to 35 age groups. The significant few referred to in the Pareto Principle are in the 26 to 45 age group. The insignificant many are all those under 26 and over 45.

Cascading Pareto Charts

You can cascade Pareto charts by determining the most significant category in the first chart, making a second chart related only to that category, and then repeating this as far as possible, to three, four, or even five or more charts. If the cascading is done properly, root causes of problems may be determined rather easily.

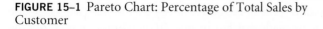

FIGURE 15–1 Pareto Chart: Percentage of Total Sales by Customer

FIGURE 15–2 Swift V-12 Sales by Age Group

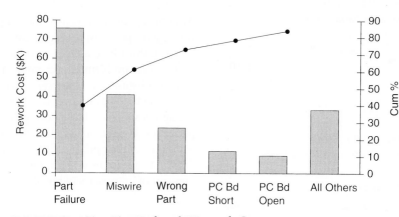

FIGURE 15–3 Top Five Defects by Rework Cost

Consider the following example. A company produces complex electronic assemblies, and the test department is concerned about the cost of rework resulting from test failures. It is costing more than $190,000 per year, and that amount is coming directly out of profit. The department formed a special project team to find the cause of the problem and reduce the cost of rework. The Pareto chart in Figure 15–3 showed them that about 80% of the cost was related to just five defect causes. All the others, and there were about 30 more, were insignificant—*at least at that time.*

The longest bar alone accounted for nearly 40% of the cost. If the problem it represents could be solved, the result would be an immediate reduction of almost $75,000 in rework cost. The team sorted the data again to develop a level 2 Pareto chart, Figure 15–4, to focus on any part types that might be a major contributor to the failures.

Figure 15–4 clearly showed that one type of relay accounted for about 60% of the failures. No other part failures came close. In this case and at this time, the relay was the significant one, and all the other parts were the insignificant many. At this point, another team was formed to analyze the failure modes of the relay in order to determine a course of action for eliminating the relay problem. It was determined that there were a number of failure modes in the

relay. They were plotted on the Pareto chart shown in Figure 15–5, which immediately revealed that 66% of all the failures were associated with one failure mode. The second longest bar in Figure 15–5 represented another manifestation of the same root cause. The relay contacts were not switching on *at all* (longest bar) or were not switching on *completely* (next longest bar). With this information known, the relay contacts were carefully examined, and it was determined that the relays were being damaged at incoming inspection where they were tested with a voltage that was high enough to damage the gold plating on the contacts. Changing the incoming test procedure and working with the relay vendor to improve its plating process eliminated the problem.

Earlier in this chapter, we implied that although a particular problem might be insignificant at one point in time, it might not stay that way. Consider what happens to the bars on the cascaded charts when the relay contact problem is solved. The second longest bar on the chart in Figure 15–3 clearly becomes the longest (assuming it was not being solved simultaneously with the relay problem). At this point, more than $100,000 a year is still being spent from profit to rework product rather than making it properly in the first place. The cycle must continue to be repeated until perfection is approached.

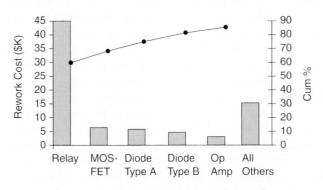

FIGURE 15–4 Rework Cost by Top Five Part Failure Categories

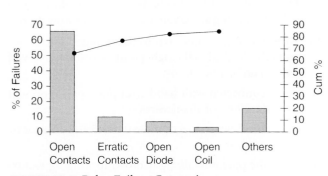

FIGURE 15–5 Relay Failure Categories

FIGURE 15–6 Second Cascading of Pareto Charts

Note: The tallest bar becomes the subject of the next Pareto chart.

The next cycle of Pareto charts might look like those in Figure 15–6. Starting at the top, we see the following points:

1. Miswires (wires connected to the wrong point or not properly attached to the right point) account for 40% of the remaining rework cost.

2. Wires connected with hand-wrapping tools represent more than 70% of all miswires.

3. Of the hand-wrap defects, more than 65% are caused by operator error.

4. Of all the operators doing hand-wrap work, operators 33 and 28 contribute more than 80% of the defects.

Attention must be given to those operators in the form of training or, perhaps, reassignment.

The third Pareto chart cascading would break down the Wrong Part problem. For example, perhaps Part abc is mistakenly substituted for Part xyz on a printed circuit board. The cycle may be repeated over and over, each time dealing with the significant few, while ignoring the trivial many. Eventually, perfection is approached. A few companies are getting close with some of their products, but most have ample opportunity for significant improvement. One need not worry about running out of improvement possibilities.

CAUSE-AND-EFFECT DIAGRAMS

A team typically uses a *cause-and-effect diagram* (see Figure 15–8) to identify and isolate causes of a problem. The technique was developed by the late Dr. Ishikawa, a noted Japanese quality expert, so sometimes the diagram is called an *Ishikawa diagram*. It is also often called a fishbone diagram because that is what it looks like.

In his book *Guide to Quality Control*, Ishikawa explains the benefits of using cause-and-effect diagrams as follows:[3]

Creating the diagram itself is an enlightening, instructive process.

Such diagrams focus a group, thereby reducing irrelevant discussion.

Such diagrams separate causes from symptoms and force the issue of data collection.

Such diagrams can be used with any problem.

The cause-and-effect diagram is the only tool of the seven tools that is not based on statistics. This chart is simply a means of visualizing how the various factors associated with a process affect the process's output. The same data could be tabulated in a list, but the human mind would have a much more difficult time trying to associate the factors with each other and with the total outcome of the process under investigation. The cause-and-effect diagram provides a graphic view of the entire process that is easily interpreted by the brain.

Suppose an electronics plant is experiencing soldering rejects on printed circuit (PC) boards. People at the plant decide to analyze the process to see what can be done; they begin by calling together a group of people to get their thoughts. The group is made up of engineers, solder machine operators, inspectors, buyers of materials, production control specialists, and others. All the groups in the plant who have anything at all to do with PC boards are represented, which is necessary to get the broadest possible view of the factors that might affect the process output.

The group is told that the issue to be discussed is the solder defect rate and that the objective is to list all the factors in the process that could possibly have an impact on the defect rate. The group uses brainstorming to generate the list of possible *causes*. The list might look like Figure 15–7.

The group developed a fairly comprehensive list of factors in the PC board manufacturing process—factors that

machine	solderability	operator
solder	conveyer speed	temperature
preheat	materials	parts
operator attitude	operator attention	flux
conveyer angle	wave height	cleanliness
age of parts	age of boards	part preparation
parts vendors	board vendors	type of flux
specific gravity	machine maintenance	training
skill	vibration	storage
instruments	lighting	calibration
handling	wait-time	contamination
air quality	humidity	

FIGURE 15–7 Brainstormed List of Possible Causes for Solder Defects

could *cause* the *effect* of solder defects. Unfortunately, the list does nothing in terms of suggesting which of the 35 factors might be major causes, which might be minor causes, and how they might relate to each other. This is where the cause-and-effect diagram comes into play. Ishikawa's genius was to develop a means by which these random ideas might be organized to show relationships and to help people make intelligent choices.

Figure 15–8 is a basic cause-and-effect diagram. The spine points to the *effect*. The effect is the "problem" we are interested in—in this case, machine soldering defects. Each of the ribs represents a cause leading to the effect. The ribs are normally assigned to the causes considered to be *major factors*. The lower level factors affecting the major factors branch off the ribs. Examine Figure 15–7 to see whether the major causes can be identified. These causes are assigned to the ribs.

Six major groupings of causes are discernible listed as follows:

1. The solder machine itself is a major factor in the process.

2. The operators who prepare the boards and run the solder machine are also major factors.

3. The list includes many items such as parts, solder, flux, boards, and so on, and these can be collected under the word *materials*, which also appears on the list. Materials is a major factor.

4. Temperature within the machine, conveyor speed and angle, solder wave height, and so on are really the *methods*

(usually published procedures and instructions) used in the process. Methods is a major factor.

5. Many of these same items are subject to the plant's methods (how-to-do-it) and measurement (accuracy of control), so measurement is a major factor, even though it did not appear on the list.

6. The cleanliness, lighting, temperature and humidity, and quality of the air we breathe can significantly affect our performance and thus the quality of output of processes with which we work. We will call this major factor *environment*.

The designated six major factors, or causes, are those that the group thinks might have an impact on the quality of output of the machine soldering process: machine, operator, materials, methods, measurement, and environment. The cause-and-effect fishbone diagram developed from this information has six ribs, as shown in Figure 15–9.

Having assigned the major causes, the next step is to assign all the other causes to the ribs they affect. For example, *machine maintenance* should be assigned to the Machine rib because machine performance is obviously affected by how well or how poorly the machine is maintained. *Training* will be attached to the Operator rib because the degree to which operators have been trained certainly affects their expertise in running the machine. In some cases, a possible cause noted on the list may appropriately branch not from the rib (major cause) but from one of the branches (contributing cause). For example, *solderability* (the relative ease—or difficulty—with which materials

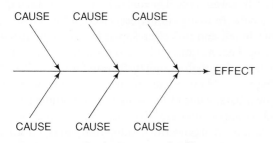

FIGURE 15–8 Basic Cause-and-Effect or Fishbone Diagram

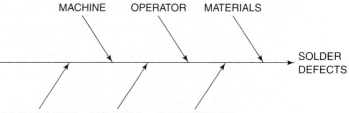

FIGURE 15–9 Cause-and-Effect Diagram with Major Causes and Effect Assigned

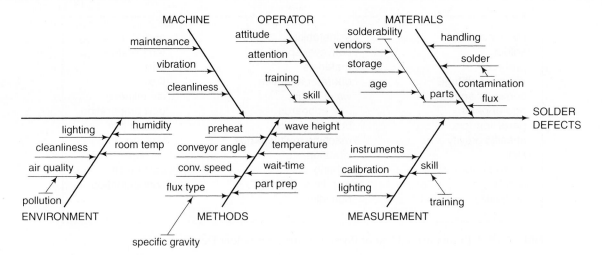

FIGURE 15–10 Completed Cause-and-Effect Diagram

can be soldered) will branch from the Materials rib because it is a contributor to the materials' cause of solder defects. An important cause of poor solderability is age of parts. So *age of parts* will branch not from Materials but from solderability. Study Figure 15–10 to get a graphic sense of the relationships described in this paragraph.

Figure 15–10 is the completed fishbone diagram. It presents a picture of the major factors that can cause solder defects and, in turn, the smaller factors that affect the major factors. Examination of the Materials rib shows that there are four factors directly affecting materials in regard to solder defects: the parts themselves, the handling of the materials, and the solder and flux used in the process. The chart points out that contamination can affect the solder's performance and also that the big issue affecting the parts is solderability. In this case, the branches go to three levels from the rib, noting that solderability can be affected by the vendor supplying the parts, storage of the parts before use, and age of the parts.

Now you may say, "The diagram didn't configure itself in this way. Someone had to know the relationships before the diagram was drawn, so why is the diagram needed?" First, picture these relationships in your mind—no diagram, just a mental image. If you are not familiar with the process used in the example, pick any process involving more than two or three people and some equipment, such as the process of an athletic event. If you try this, you will probably find it virtually impossible to be conscious of all the factors coming into play, to say nothing of how they relate and interact. Certainly, the necessary knowledge and information already existed before the 35 factors were arranged in the cause-and-effect diagram. The key to the diagram's usefulness is that it is very possible that no *one* individual had all that knowledge and information. That is why cause-and-effect diagrams are normally created by teams of people widely divergent in their expertise.

The initial effort by the team is developing the list of possible factors. This is usually done using brainstorming techniques. Such a list can be made in a surprisingly short time—usually no more than an hour. It is not necessary that the list be complete or even that all the factors listed be truly germane. Missing elements will usually be obvious as the diagram is developed, and superfluous elements will be recognized and discarded. After the list has been compiled, all the team members contribute from their personal knowledge and expertise to assemble the cause-and-effect diagram.

The completed diagram reveals factors or relationships that had previously not been obvious. The causes most likely responsible for the problem (solder defects) will normally be isolated. Further, the diagram may suggest possibilities for action. It is conceivable in the example that the team, because it is familiar with the plant's operation, could say with some assurance that solderability was suspected because the parts were stored for long periods of time. They might recommend that, by switching to a JIT system, both storage and aging could be eliminated as factors affecting solderability.

The cause-and-effect diagram serves as an excellent reminder that the items noted on it are the things the company needs to pay attention to if the process is to continually improve. Even in processes that are working well, continual improvement is the most important job any employee or team can have. In today's competitive global marketplace, it is truly the key to survival.

CHECK SHEETS

The *check sheet* (see Figure 15–12) is introduced here as the third of the seven tools. The fuel that powers the total quality tools is data. In many companies, elaborate systems of people, machines, and procedures exist for the sole purpose of collecting data. At times, this quest for data has become zealous to the point of obscuring the reason for data collection in the first place. Many organizations are literally drowning in their own data, while at the same time not knowing what is actually going on; they are "data rich and information poor." With the advent of powerful desktop computers, information collection has become an end unto itself in many instances.

Having access to data is essential. However, problems arise when trivial data cannot be winnowed from the important and when there is so much of it that it cannot be easily translated into useful information. Check sheets help deal with this problem.

The check sheet can be a valuable tool in a wide variety of applications. Its utility is restricted only by the imagination of the person seeking information. The check sheet can take any form. The only rules are that data collection must be the equivalent of entering a check mark and that the displayed data must be easily translated into useful information. For example, it may take the form of a drawing of a product with the check marks entered at appropriate places on the drawing to illustrate the location and type of defect. An accounts receivable department might set up a check sheet to record the types and numbers of mistakes on invoices prepared. Check sheets apply to any work environment—not just to the factory floor.

The purpose of the check sheet is to make it easy to collect data for specific purposes and to present it in a way that facilitates conversion from data to useful information. For example, suppose we are manufacturing parts that have a specified dimensional tolerance of 1.120 to 1.130 inches (in.). During the week, each part is measured and the data are recorded. Figure 15–11 is a summary of the week's results.

This figure contains all the data on shaft length for the week of July 11. Without a lot of additional work, it will be difficult to glean much useful information from this list of data. Imagine how much more difficult it would be if, instead of a table, you were presented with a stack of computer runs several inches thick. That is frequently the case in the information age. (The information age should be called the *data age*, in our opinion, reflecting the abundance of raw, often meaningless data and the real paucity of *useful* information.)

The computer could be programmed to do something with the data to make them more useful, and in some situations, that would be appropriate. After all, computers are good at digesting raw data and formatting the result for human consumption. But before the computer can do that, some human must tell it exactly what it must do, how to format the information, what to discard, what to use, and so on. If we can't first figure out what to do with the data, no amount of computer power will help. On the supposition that we do know what to do with the data, it is possible that we could *preformat* the data so that it will be instantly useful *as it is being collected*. This is one of the powerful capabilities of the check sheet.

The importance of the data in Figure 15–11 rests in reporting how the shafts being produced relate to the shaft length specification. The machine has been set up to produce shafts in the center of the range so that normal variation would not spill outside the specified limits of 1.120 and 1.130 in. and thereby create waste. If the raw data could give us a feel for this as it is being collected, that would be very helpful. We would also like to know when the limits are exceeded. The check sheet in Figure 15–12 has been designed to facilitate both data collection and conversion to information.

The check sheet of Figure 15–12 is set up to accept the data very easily and at the same time display useful information. The check sheet actually produces a histogram as the data are entered. (See the following section for information

Shaft length: Week of	7/11	(Spec: 1.120–1.130")				
Date	Length	Date	Length	Date	Length	Rem
11	1.124	11	1.128	11	1.123	
11	1.126	11	1.128	11	1.125	
11	1.119	11	1.123	11	1.122	
11	1.120	11	1.122	11	1.123	
12	1.124	12	1.126	12	1.125	
12	1.125	12	1.127	12	1.125	
12	1.121	12	1.124	12	1.125	
12	1.126	12	1.124	12	1.127	
13	1.123	13	1.125	13	1.121	
13	1.120	13	1.122	13	1.118	
13	1.124	13	1.123	13	1.125	
13	1.126	13	1.123	13	1.124	
14	1.125	14	1.127	14	1.124	
14	1.126	14	1.129	14	1.125	
14	1.126	14	1.123	14	1.124	
14	1.122	14	1.124	14	1.122	
15	1.124	15	1.121	15	1.123	
15	1.124	15	1.127	15	1.123	
15	1.124	15	1.122	15	1.122	
15	1.123	15	1.122	15	1.121	

FIGURE 15–11 Weekly Summary of Shaft Dimensional Tolerance Results

Note: This is *not* a check sheet.

Check Sheet

Shaft length: Week of _____7/11_____ (Spec: 1.120–1.130")

- -

1.118**	13	
1.119**	11	** Out of Limits
1.120	11 13	
1.121	12 13 15 15	
1.122	11 11 13 14 14 15 15 15	
1.123	11 11 11 13 13 13 14 15 15 15	
1.124	11 12 12 12 13 13 14 14 14 15 15 15	
1.125	11 12 12 12 12 13 13 14 14	
1.126	11 12 12 13 14 14	
1.127	12 12 14 15	
1.128	11 11	
1.129	14	Enter day of month for data point.
1.130		
1.131**		
1.132**		

- -

FIGURE 15–12 Check Sheet of Shaft Dimensional Tolerance Results about histograms.) Data are taken by measuring the shafts, just as was done for Figure 15–11. But rather than logging the measured data by date, as in Figure 15–11, the check sheet in Figure 15–12 only requires noting the date (day of month) opposite the appropriate shaft dimension. The day-of-month notation serves as a check mark, while at the same time keeping track of the day the reading was taken.

This check sheet should be set up on an easel on the shop floor, with entries handwritten. That will make the performance of the machine continually visible to all—operators, supervisors, engineers, or anyone else in the work area.

The data in Figure 15–11 are the same as the data in Figure 15–12. Figure 15–11 shows columns of sterile data that, before meaning can be extracted, must be subjected to hard work at someone's desk. Assuming it does get translated into meaningful information, it will probably still remain invisible to the people who could make the best use of it—the operators. That can, of course, be overcome by more hard work, but in most cases, the data will languish. On the other hand, Figure 15–12 provides a simple check sheet into which the data are entered more easily and, once entered, provide a graphic presentation of performance. If the check sheet reveals that the machine is creeping away from the center of the range or if the histogram shape distorts, the operator can react immediately. No additional work is required to translate the data to useful information, and no additional work is required to broadcast the information to all who can use it.

To set up a check sheet, you must think about your objective. In this example, we were making shafts to a specification. We wanted data indicating how well the machine was performing, a graphic warning whenever the machine started to deviate, and information about defects. Setting up the check sheet as a histogram provided all the information needed. This is called a *Process Distribution Check Sheet* because it is concerned with the variability of a process. Other commonly used check sheets include Defective Item Check Sheets (detailing the variety of defects), Defect Location Check Sheets (showing where on the subject product defects occur), and Defect Factor Check Sheets (illustrating the factors—time, temperature, machine, operator—possibly influencing defect generation).

If we wanted to better understand what factors might be contributing to excessive defects on the shop floor, we could set up a Defect Factors Check Sheet. As an example, go back to the section on Pareto charts and look at Figure 15–6. The top

chart there revealed that miswires were the most significant defect in terms of cost. To collect some data about the factors that might be contributing to the miswire defects, a reasonable approach would be to set up a Defect Factors Check Sheet and collect data for a week. We are primarily concerned with the operators themselves and the factors that may influence their performance. The check sheet will list each operator's number and bench location within the factory. To determine whether the day of the week or the time of day has anything to do with performance, the data will be recorded by day and by morning or afternoon. We could have included tool numbers as well, but using a tool that produces faulty connections is something the operator must guard against. In other words, we will not consider a tool to be at fault—only the operator if he or she continues to use a defective tool.

In the check sheet shown in Figure 15–13, five types of miswire defects, covering all types experienced, are coded by symbols, and these symbols are the only raw data entered on the chart. Sums of all defect categories are shown at the bottom of each column, and the weekly total for each operator is shown at the end of each row. A quick glance at the check sheet points to operators 28 and 33 as the sources of the problem. We don't know the *cause* at this point, but we know where to start looking.

In past times, these two people might very well have been summarily fired. In a total quality setting, that decision would be considered the last resort. Most employees want to do a good job and will if they are provided with the necessary resources and training. In a case like this, it is not unusual to find that the fault lies with management. The employees were not adequately trained for the job, or some environmental factor (noise, temperature, lighting, or something else) is at fault, or the operators may simply not be equipped for the task (because of vision impairment, impaired motor skills, or some other problem). In any of those scenarios, management is at fault and, therefore, should do the morally right thing to correct the problem.

Check sheets can be valuable tools for converting data into useful and easy-to-use information. The key is teaching operators how to employ them and empowering them to do so.

Operator No.	Bench No.	11/2 AM	11/2 PM	11/3 AM	11/3 PM	11/4 AM	11/4 PM	11/5 AM	11/5 PM	11/6 AM	11/6 PM	Week Totals
8	A3					●				o □		o - 1 ● - 1 3 □ - 1
10	A2			● ●			□					● - 2 □ - 1 3
11	B1	o						o				o - 2 2
13	A1		o				△				□ □	o - 1 △ - 1 4 □ - 2
28	C2	o ● o	o △	o o o	△ o o	o	o o	o △	□ o	o o	o ● o	o - 17 ● - 2 △ - 3 23 □ - 1
33	C3	o o o △ o	● o o o	o △ o o	o o □	o ●	□ o o	△ o o	o o	o o o o △ o	o o o o	o - 28 ● - 2 △ - 4 36 □ - 2
40	B2	+						o ●				o - 1 ● - 1 3 + - 1

Half-day totals		10	7	9	6	4	7	6	6	10	9	39 35
Full-day totals		17		15		11		12		19		74

LEGEND: o = Hand wrap
● = Solder point to point
△ = Harness
+ = Ribbon
□ = Other

FIGURE 15–13 Check Sheet: Defect Factors—Miswires

HISTOGRAMS

Histograms are used to chart frequency of occurrence. How often does something happen? Any discussion of histograms must begin with an understanding of the two kinds of data commonly associated with processes: *attributes* and *variables* data. Although they were not introduced as such, both kinds of data have been used in the illustrations of this chapter. An *attribute* is something that the output product of the process either has or does not have. From one of the examples (Figure 15–6), either an electronic assembly had wiring errors or it did not. Another example (Figure 15–30) shows that either an assembly had broken screws or it did not. These are attributes. The example of making shafts of a specified length (Figures 15–11 and 15–12) was concerned with

measured data. That example used shaft length measured in thousandths of an inch, but any scale of measurement can be used, as appropriate for the process under scrutiny. A process used in making electrical resistors would use the scale of electrical resistance in ohms, another process might use a weight scale, and so on. *Variables data* are something that results from measurement.

Using the shaft example again, an all-too-common scenario in manufacturing plants would have been to place a Go–No Go screen at the end of the process, accepting all shafts between the specification limits of 1.120 and 1.130 in. and discarding the rest. Data might have been recorded to keep track of the number of shafts that had to be scrapped. Such a record might have looked like Figure 15–14, based on the original data.

Shaft Acceptance: Week of 7/11 (Spec: 1.120–1.130")		
Date	Accepted	Rejected
11.	11	1
12.	12	0
13.	11	1
14.	12	0
15.	12	0
Totals:	58	2

FIGURE 15–14 Summary Data: Weekly Shaft Acceptance

An Important Distinction to Remember

Attributes Data

- Has or has not
- Good or bad
- Pass or fail
- Accept or reject
- Conforming or nonconforming

Variables Data

- Measured values (dimension, weight, voltage, surface, etc.)

Figure 15–14 would tell us what we wanted to know if we were interested only in the number of shafts accepted versus the number rejected. Looking at the shaft process in this way, we are using *attributes data*: either they passed or they failed the screening. This reveals only that we are scrapping between 3 and 4% of all the shafts made. It does not tell us anything about the process adjustment that may be contributing to the scrap rate. Nor does it tell us anything about how robust the process is—might some slight change push the process over the edge? For that kind of insight, we need *variables data*.

One can gain much more information about a process when variables data are available. The check sheet of Figure 15–12 shows that both of the rejects (out-of-limits shafts) were on the low side of the specified tolerance. The peak of the histogram seems to occur between 1.123 and 1.124 in. If the machine were adjusted to bring the peak up to 1.125 in., some of the low-end rejects might be eliminated without causing any new rejects at the top end. The frequency distribution also suggests that the process as it stands now will always have occasional rejects—probably in the 2 to 3% range at best.

Potential Trap with Histograms

Be aware of a potential trap when using histograms. The histogram is nothing more than a measurement scale across one axis (usually the *x*-axis) and frequency of like measurements on the other. (Histograms are also called *frequency distribution diagrams*.) The trap occurs when measurements are taken over a long period of time. Too many things can affect processes over time: wear, maintenance, adjustment, material differences, operator influence, and environmental influence. The histogram makes no allowance for any of these factors. It may be helpful to consider a histogram to be the equivalent of a snapshot of the process performance. If the subject of a photograph is moving, the photographer must use a fast shutter speed to prevent a blurred image. If the histogram data are not collected over a suitably short period of time, the result will be blurred, just as if the camera's shutter is too slow

for the action taking place, because it is possible that the process's performance changes over time. Blurred photographs and blurred histograms are both useless. A good histogram will show a crisp snapshot of process performance as it was at the time the data were taken, not before and not after. This leads some people to claim that histograms should be used only on processes that are known to be *in control*. (See the section on control charts later in this chapter.)

That limitation is not necessary as long as you understand that histograms have this inherent flaw. Be careful that any interpretation you make has accounted for time and its effect on the process you are studying. For example, we do not know enough about the results of the shaft-making process from Figure 15–12 to predict with any certainty that it will do as well next week. We don't know that a machine operator didn't tweak the machine two or three times during the week, trying to find the center of the range. What happens if that operator is on vacation next week? Would we dare predict that performance will be the same? We can make these predictions only if we know the process is statistically in control; thus, the warnings. Taking this into consideration, the histogram in Figure 15–12 provides valuable information.

Histograms and Statistics

Understanding a few basic facts is fundamental to the use of statistical techniques for quality and process applications. We have said that all processes are subject to variability, or variation. There are many examples of this. One of the oldest and most graphically convincing is the Red Bead experiment.[4] This involves a container with a large number of beads. The beads are identical except for the color. Suppose there are 900 white beads and 100 red beads, making a total of 1,000. The beads are mixed thoroughly (Step 1). Then 50 beads are drawn at random as a sample (Step 2). The red beads in the sample are counted. A check mark is entered in a histogram column for that number. All the beads are put back into the container, and they are mixed again (Step 3). When you repeat these steps a second time, the odds are that a different number of red beads will be drawn. When a third sample is taken, it will probably contain yet another number of red beads. The process (steps 1, 2, and 3) has not changed, yet the output of the process does change. This is *process variation* or *variability*. If these steps are repeated over and over until a valid statistical sampling has been taken, the resulting histogram will invariably take on the characteristic bell shape common to process variability (see Figure 15–15).

It is possible to calculate the process variability from the data. The histogram in Figure 15–15 was created from 100 samples of 50 beads each. The data were as shown in Figure 15–16.

The flatter and wider the frequency distribution curve, the greater the process variability. The taller and narrower the curve, the lesser the process variability.

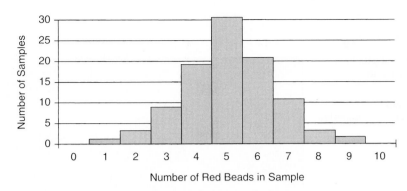

FIGURE 15–15 Frequency Distribution of Red Beads in Samples

Even though the variability may change from process to process, it would be helpful to have a common means of measuring, discussing, or understanding variability. Fortunately, we do. To express the process's variability, we need to know only two things, both of which can be derived from the process's own distribution data: *standard deviation* and *mean*. Standard deviation is represented by the lowercase Greek letter sigma (σ) and indicates a deviation from the average, or *mean*, value of the samples in the data set. The mean is represented by the Greek letter mu (μ). In a normal histogram, μ is seen as a vertical line from the peak of the bell curve to the base, and it is the line from which deviation is measured, minus to the left of μ and plus to the right. Standard deviation (σ) is normally plotted at -3σ, -2σ, and -1σ (left of μ) and $+1\sigma$, $+2\sigma$, and $+3\sigma$ (right of μ); refer to Figure 15–18. Because mean and standard deviation are always derived from data from the process in question, standard deviation has a constant meaning from process to process. From this, we can tell what the process can do in terms of its statistical variability (assuming that it remains stable and no changes are introduced):

- 68.26% of all sample values will be found between $+1\sigma$ and -1σ.

- 95.46% of all sample values will be found between $+2\sigma$ and -2σ.

- 99.73% of all sample values will be found between $+3\sigma$ and -3σ.

- 99.9999998% of all sample values will be found between $+6\sigma$ and -6σ.

Note: As we discussed in Chapter 1, Six Sigma practitioners use 99.99966% rather than the actual statistical value.

This information has a profound practical value, as we shall see as we develop the discussion.

In order to calculate the process mean value (μ) and standard deviation (μ), we must first use the raw process data from Figure 15–16 to develop the information required for those calculations. As we develop the information, we will post it in the appropriate columns of Figures 15–17a, b, and c.

Columns 1 and 2 of Figures 15–17a, b, and c contain the measured raw data from the colored bead process from Figure 15–16. Column 1 lists the number of red beads possible to be counted (from 0 to 10) in the various samples. Column 2 lists the number of samples that contained the corresponding number of red beads. The number of samples in column 2 is totaled, yielding $n = 100$.

Samples with 0 red beads	0
Samples with 1 red bead	1
Samples with 2 red beads	3
Samples with 3 red beads	9
Samples with 4 red beads	19
Samples with 5 red beads	31
Samples with 6 red beads	21
Samples with 7 red beads	11
Samples with 8 red beads	3
Samples with 9 red beads	2
Samples with 10 red beads	0
Total samples taken	100

FIGURE 15–16 Data on Red Beads in Samples

Calculating the Mean

For a histogram representing a truly normal distribution between $\pm$ infinity, the mean value would be a vertical line to the peak of the bell curve. Our curve is slightly off normal because we are using a relatively small sample, so the mean (μ) must be calculated. The equation for μ is

$$\mu = \sum X \div n$$

where X is the product of the number of red beads in a sample times the number of samples containing that number of red beads, or for Figure 15–17a, the product of columns 1 and 2. We calculate column 3 of Figure 15–17b.

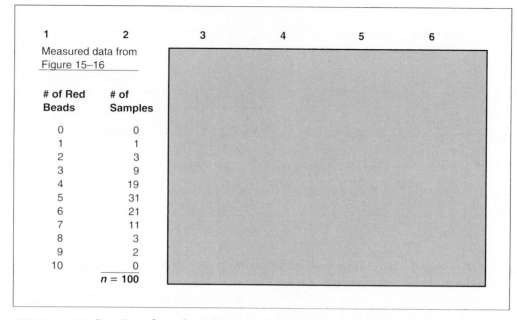

FIGURE 15–17a Raw Data from the Colored Bead Experiment (see Figure 15–16)

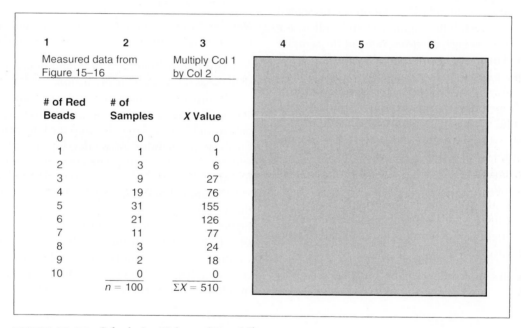

FIGURE 15–17b Calculating Values of X and ΣX

Now that we have the X values, we simply add them up to give us the sum of the X values (ΣX). The figure tells us that $n = 100$ and $\Sigma X = 510$. Using the equation for μ,

$$\mu = \sum X \div n$$

$$\mu = 510 \div 100$$

$$\mu = 5.1$$

The mean (μ) is placed at 5.1 on the histogram's x-axis, and all deviations are measured relative to that. (See Figure 15–18.)

Calculating Standard Deviation (σ)

To understand the process's variability, we must know its standard deviation. The formula for standard deviation is

$$\sigma = \sqrt{\sum d^2/(n - 1)}$$

where

d = the deviation of any unit from the mean
n = the number of units sampled

1	2	3	4	5	6
Measured data from Figure 15–16		Multiply Col 1 by Col 2	Deviation from μ (Col 1 − μ)	Deviation squared (Col 4)^2	Sum of deviations squared (Col 2 × Col 5)
# of Red Beads	# of Samples	*X* Value	*d*	d^2	
0	0	0	−5.1	26.01	0
1	1	1	−4.1	16.81	16.81
2	3	6	−3.1	9.61	28.83
3	9	27	−2.1	4.41	39.69
4	19	76	−1.1	1.21	22.99
5	31	155	−0.1	0.01	0.31
6	21	126	0.9	0.81	17.01
7	11	77	1.9	3.61	39.71
8	3	24	2.9	8.41	25.23
9	2	18	3.9	15.21	30.42
10	0	0	4.9	24.01	0
	$n = 100$	$\Sigma X = 510$			$\Sigma d^2 = 221$

FIGURE 15–17c Completed Deviation Data Table

We already have the value of *n* (100), but we have not calculated the values of *d*, d^2, or Σd^2. We will perform these calculations and post the information in the remaining three columns of Figure 15–17c. The values of the deviations (*d*) are determined by subtracting μ (5.1) from each of the red bead values (0 through 10) of column 1. The first entry in column 4 (deviation from μ) is determined by subtracting μ from the value in column 1, that is, 0 − 5.1 = −5.1. Similarly, the second entry in column 4 is the value of column 1 at the 1-bead row minus μ, or 1 − 5.1 = −4.1. Repeating this process through the 10-bead row completes the deviation column.

Column 5 of Figure 15–17c is simply a list of the column 4 deviation values squared. For example, in the 0-bead row, column 4 shows *d* = −5.1. Column 5 lists the square of −5.1, or 26.01. The 1-bead row has *d* = −4.1. Column 5 lists its square, 16.81. This process is continued through the 10-bead row to complete column 5 of the figure.

Column 6 of Figure 15–17c lists the results of the squared deviations (column 5) multiplied by the number of samples at the corresponding deviation value (column 2). For the column 6 entry at the 0-bead row, we multiply 0 (from column 2) by 26.01 (from column 5); since, 0 × 26.01 = 0, 0 is entered in column 6. For the 1-bead row, we multiply 1 by 16.81; 16.81 is the second entry in column 6. At the 2-bead row, we multiply 3 by 9.61 and enter 28.83 in column 6. This process is repeated through the remaining rows of the figure.

Next we add column 6's entries to obtain the sum of the squared deviations, $\Sigma d^2 \cdot \Sigma d^2$ for our bead process experiment is 221.

Now we have all the information we need to calculate the standard deviation (σ) for our process.

$$\sigma = \sqrt{\sum d^2/(n - 1)}$$
$$\sigma = \sqrt{221 \div 99}$$
$$\sigma = \sqrt{2.23} \text{ (2.23 is called the } \textit{mean squared deviation.)}$$
$$\sigma = 1.49 \text{ (1.49 is called the } \textit{root mean squared deviation.)}$$

Note: Calculations are to two decimal places.

Next calculate the positions of, $\mu \pm 1\sigma$, 2σ, and 3σ.

$$\sigma = 1.49 \quad 2\sigma = 2.99 \quad 3\sigma = 4.47$$

These values are entered in Figure 15–15 to create Figure 15–18:

$$\mu - 1\sigma = 5.1 - 1.49 = 3.61$$
$$\mu + 1\sigma = 5.1 + 1.49 = 6.59$$
$$\mu - 2\sigma = 5.1 - 2.99 = 2.11$$
$$\mu + 2\sigma = 5.1 + 2.99 = 8.09$$
$$\mu - 3\sigma = 5.1 - 4.47 = 0.63$$
$$\mu + 3\sigma = 5.1 + 4.47 = 9.57$$

Suppose we have a process that is operating like the curve in Figure 15–18. We have specifications for the product output that require us to reject any part below 3.6 and above 6.6. It turns out that these limits are approximately ±1σ. We know immediately that about one-third of the process output will be rejected. (Refer to the first bullet in the list on page 255.) If this is not acceptable, which is highly probable, we will have to improve the process or change to a completely

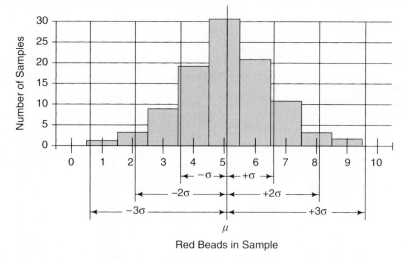

FIGURE 15–18 Application of Standard Deviation Calculations to Red Bead Histogram

different process. Even if more variation could be tolerated in the product and we took the specification limits out to 2 and 8, about 5 of every 100 pieces flowing out of the process would still be rejected. In a competitive world, this is poor performance indeed. Many companies no longer consider 2,700 parts per million defective (±3σ) to be good enough. A growing number of organizations are seeking the Motorola version of Six Sigma quality performance. These companies target a defect rate of 3.4 nonconformances per million opportunities (NPMO) for nonconformance. Technically speaking, 3.4 NPMO is not very close to the statistically pure 6-sigma rate of 0.002 per million opportunities, or 1 nonconformance in 500 million. (We explain this difference in the Six Sigma section of Chapter 19.) Although the popular Six Sigma does not match the true 6-sigma, 3.4 NPMO is a remarkable achievement. Whatever the situation, with this statistical sampling tool properly applied, there is no question about what can be achieved with any process because you will be able to predict the results.

Shapes of Histograms

Consider the shape of some histograms and their position relative to specification limits. Figure 15–19 is a collection of histograms. Histogram A represents a normal distribution. So does B, except it is shallower. The difference between the process characteristics of these two histograms is that process A is much tighter, whereas the looser process B will have greater variances. Process A is usually preferred. Processes C and D are skewed left and right, respectively. Although the curves are normal, product will be lost because the processes are not centered. Process E is bimodal. This can result from two batches of input material, for example. One batch produces the left bell curve, and the second batch the curve on the right. The two curves may be separated for a better view

of what is going on by stratifying the data by batch. (See the "Stratification" section later in this chapter.)

Histogram F suggests that someone is discarding the samples below and above a set of limits. This typically happens when there is a 100% inspection and only data that are within limits are recorded. The strange Histogram G might have used data from incoming inspection. The message here is that the vendor is screening the parts and someone else is getting the best ones. A typical case might be electrical resistors that are graded as 1%, 5%, and 10% tolerance. The resistors that met 1% and 5% criteria were screened out and sold at a higher price. You got what was left.

Histogram H shows a normal distribution properly centered between a set of upper and lower control limits. Histograms I and J illustrate what happens when the same normal curve is allowed to shift left or right, respectively. There will be a significant loss of product as a control limit intercepts the curve higher up its slope.

Histograms K through P show a normal, centered curve that went out of control and drifted. Remember that histograms do not account for time and you must, therefore, be careful about making judgments. If all the data that produced Histograms K through P were averaged, or even if all the data were combined to make a single histogram, you could be misled. You would not know that the process was drifting. Plotting a series of histograms over time, such as K through P, clearly illustrates any drift right or left, shallowing of the bell, and the like.

The number of samples or data points has a bearing on the accuracy of the histogram, just as with other tools. But with the histogram, there is another consideration: How does one determine the proper number of intervals for the chart? (The intervals are, in effect, the data columns of the histogram.) For example, Figure 15–15 is set up for 11 intervals: 0, 1, 2, and so on. The two outside intervals are not

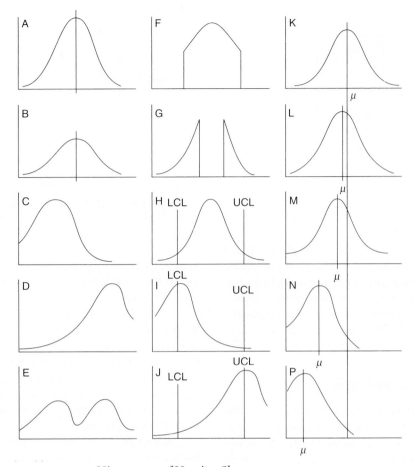

FIGURE 15–19 Histograms of Varying Shapes

used, however, so the histogram plots data in nine intervals. The rule of thumb is as follows:

Number of Observations (N)	Number of Intervals (k)
<75	5–7
75–300	6–10
>300	10–20

Or, you may use the formula

$$k = \sqrt{N}$$

It is not necessary to be very precise with this. These methods are used to get close and adjust one way or the other for a fit with your data.

Suppose we are using steel balls in one of our products and the weight of the ball is critical. The specification is 5 ± 0.2 grams. The balls are purchased from a vendor, and because our tolerance is tighter than the vendor's, we weigh the balls and use only those that meet our specification. The vendor is trying to tighten its tolerance and has asked for assistance in the form of data. Today 60 balls were received and weighed. The data were plotted on a histogram. To give the vendor the complete information, a histogram with intervals every 0.02 gram is established.

Figure 15–20 does not look much like a bell curve because we have tried to stretch a limited amount of data (60 observations) too far. There are 23 active or skipped

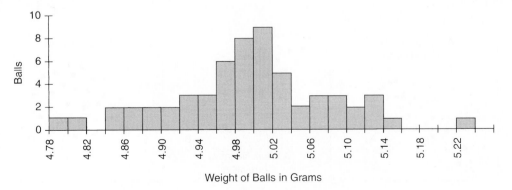

FIGURE 15–20 Histogram with Limited Amount of Data Stretched

FIGURE 15–21 Histogram with Appropriate Intervals for the Amount of Data

FIGURE 15–22 Scatter Diagram: Speed Versus Fuel Consumption for Four Automobiles

intervals. Our rule of thumb suggests 5 to 7 intervals for less than 75 observations. If the same data were plotted into a histogram of 6 intervals (excluding the blank), it would look like Figure 15–21. At least in this version, it looks like a histogram. With more data—say, 100 or more observations—one could narrow the intervals and get more granularity. Don't try to stretch data too thin because the conversion to real information can become difficult and risky.

SCATTER DIAGRAMS

The fifth of the seven tools is the *scatter diagram*. It is the simplest of the seven and one of the most useful. The scatter diagram is used to determine the correlation (relationship) between two characteristics (variables). Suppose you have an idea that there is a relationship between automobile fuel consumption and the rate of speed at which people drive. To prove, or disprove, such an assumption, you could record data on a scatter diagram that has miles per gallon (mpg) on the *y*-axis and miles per hour (mph) on the *x*-axis; mpg and mph are the two characteristics.

Examination of the scatter diagram of Figure 15–22 shows that the aggregate of data points contains a slope down and to the right. This is correlation, and it supports the thesis that the faster cars travel, the more fuel they use. Had the slope been upward to the right, as it actually appears to be (for three of the four cars) between 20 and 30 mph, the correlation would have suggested that the faster you travel, the better the fuel mileage. Suppose, however, that the data points did not form any recognizable linear or elliptical pat-

tern but were simply in a disorganized configuration. This would suggest that there is no correlation between speed and fuel consumption.

Figure 15–23 is a collection of scatter diagrams illustrating strong *positive correlation* (Diagram A), weak *negative correlation* (Diagram B), and *no correlation* (Diagram C). To be classified as a strong correlation, the data points must be tightly grouped in a linear pattern. The more loosely grouped, the less correlation, and, therefore, the term *weak correlation*. When a pattern has no discernible linear component, it is said to show no correlation.

Scatter diagrams are useful in testing the correlation between process factors and characteristics of product flowing out of the process. Suppose you want to know whether conveyor speed has an effect on solder quality in a machine soldering process. You could set up a scatter diagram with conveyor speed on the *x*-axis and solder rejects or nonconformities on the *y*-axis. By plotting sample data as the conveyor speed is adjusted, you can construct a scatter diagram to tell whether a correlation exists.

In this case, Figure 15–24 suggests that the correlation is a curve, with rejects dropping off as speed is initially raised but then increasing again as the conveyor speed continues to increase. This is not atypical of process factors that have optimum operating points. In the case of the conveyor, moving too slowly allows excess heat to build up, causing defects. So increasing speed naturally produces better results, until the speed increases to the point where insufficient preheat-

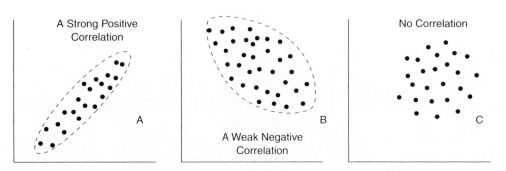

FIGURE 15–23 Scatter Diagrams of Various Correlations

QUALITY TIP ▼

Six Sigma Process Capability

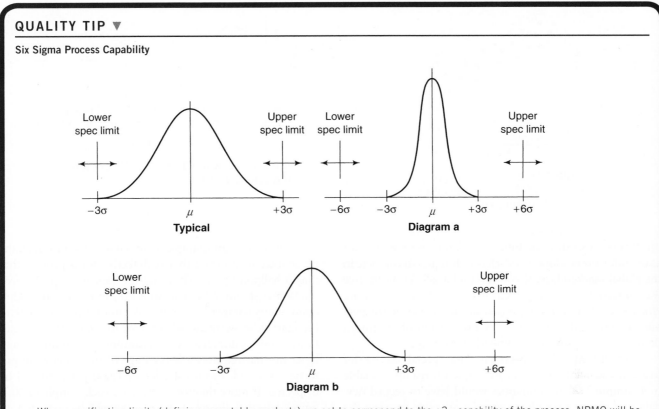

- When specification limits (defining acceptable products) are set to correspond to the ±3σ capability of the process, NPMO will be 2,700. This may mean that out of every 1 million parts produced, 2,700 are unacceptable; that out of 1 million operations, 2,700 mistakes will be made; and so on.

- When specification limits correspond to the ±6σ process capability, a vanishingly small 0.002 NPMO will be achieved. See Diagrams a and b. (Note that at ±6σ the Motorola Six Sigma method will yield a still small 3.4 NPMO.)

- One method used in striving for statistical 6σ (or Motorola's Six Sigma) performance involves narrowing the bell curve through the development of superior processes. Compare the Typical 3σ diagram above with Diagram a. Note that the specification limits have remained constant, but the process variation has been reduced, moving the process's ±6σ points inward to the specification limits.

- Another method for working toward Six Sigma performance involves designing products that can tolerate wider physical or functional variation in their component parts, while still performing to product specifications. Compare the Typical 3σ diagram above with Diagram b. This technique is usually referred to as *robust design*.

ing increases the number of defects. Figure 15–24, then, not only reveals a correlation, but also suggests that there is an optimum conveyor speed, operation above or below which will result in increased product defects.

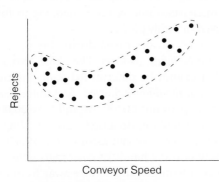

FIGURE 15–24 Scatter Diagram: Conveyor Speed versus Rejects

It is also possible to determine a correlation between two process factors. If your manufacturing process includes the washing of parts in a cleaning agent and you are interested in reducing the time the parts are in the cleaning tank, you might want to know whether the temperature of the solution is correlated with the time it takes to get the parts thoroughly clean. The scatter diagram could have temperature of the cleaning agent on one axis and time to clean on the other. By adjusting the temperature of the solution and plotting the cleaning time, a scatter diagram will reveal any existing correlation.

Assume that the scatter diagram shows a discernible slope downward to the right, as in Figure 15–25. This shows that over the temperature range tested, there *is* a correlation between cleaning solution temperature and cleaning time. With this information, you might be able to reduce the cycle time of the product. *Cycle time* in manufacturing is basically elapsed time from the start of your build process until the

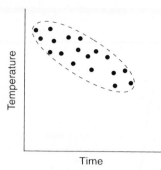

FIGURE 15–25 Scatter Diagram: Cleaning Solution Temperature versus Cleaning Time

FIGURE 15–26 Run Chart: Pen Defect Rate for 21 Working Days

product is finished. Cycle time is becoming more important as manufacturers adopt world-class techniques to compete in the global marketplace. If you can find a safe, cost-effective way to raise the cleaning agent temperature to some more efficient level, and in the process shorten the cycle (or perhaps maintain the cycle and do a better job of cleaning), doing so might provide a competitive advantage.

Not all scatter diagrams require that special tests be run to acquire raw data. The data are frequently readily available in a computer. Few companies would have to record new data to determine whether a correlation exists between the day of the week and employee performance. Such data are often available from the day-to-day inspection reports. In fact, where people are involved, it is advisable to use existing data rather than collecting new data to be sure that the data were not influenced by the test itself. Imagine people being told they were to be part of a test to determine whether their performance was as good on Friday or Monday as the rest of the week. This knowledge would undoubtedly affect their performance.

RUN CHARTS AND CONTROL CHARTS

The run chart is straightforward, and the control chart is a much more sophisticated outgrowth of it. Therefore, the two are usually thought of together as a single tool. Both can be very powerful and effective for the tracking and control of processes, and they are fundamental to the improvement of processes.

Run Charts

The *run chart* records the output results of a process over time. The concept is strikingly simple, and, indeed, it has been used throughout modern times to track performance of everything from AAA membership to zwieback production. Because one axis (usually the *x*-axis) represents time, the run chart can provide an easily understood picture of what is happening in a process as time goes by. That is, it will cause trends to "jump" out at you. For this reason, the run chart is also referred to as a *trend chart*.

Consider as an example a run chart set up to track the percentage of product that is defective for a process that makes ballpoint pens. These are inexpensive pens, so production costs must be held to a minimum. On the other hand, many competitors would like to capture our share of the market, so we must deliver pens that meet the expectations of our customers—as a minimum. A sampling system is set up that requires a percentage of the process output to be inspected. From each lot of 1,000 pens, 50 will be inspected. If more than one pen from each sample of 50 is found defective, the whole lot of 1,000 will be inspected. In addition to scrapping the defective pens, we will attempt to discover why the defects were there in the first place and to eliminate the cause. Data from the sample will be plotted on a run chart. Because we anticipate improvements to the process as a result of this effort, the run chart will be ideal to show whether we are succeeding.

The run chart of Figure 15–26 is the result of sample data for 21 working days. The graph clearly shows that significant improvement in pen quality was made during the 21 working days of the month. The trend across the month was toward better quality (fewer defects). The most significant improvements came at the 12th day and the 17th day as causes for defects were found and corrected.

The chart can be continued indefinitely to keep us aware of performance. Is it improving, staying the same, or losing ground? Scales may have to change for clarity. For example, if we consistently found all samples with defects below 2%, it would make sense to change the *y*-axis scale to 0 to 2%. Longer term charts would require changing from daily to weekly or even monthly plots.

Performance was improved during the first month of the pen manufacturing process. The chart shows positive results. What cannot be determined from the run chart, however, is what *should* be achieved. Assuming we can hold at two defective pens out of 100, we still have 20,000 defective pens out of a million. Because we are sampling only 5% of the pens produced, we can assume that 19,000 of these find their way into the hands of customers—the very customers our competition wants to take away from us. So it is important to improve further. The run chart will help, but a more powerful tool is needed.

FIGURE 15–27 Basic Control Chart

Control Charts

The problem with the run chart and, in fact, many of the other tools is that it does not help us understand whether the variation is the result of *special causes*—things such as changes in the materials used, machine problems, lack of employee training—or *common causes* that are purely random. Not until Dr. Walter Shewhart made that distinction in the 1920s was there a real chance of improving processes through the use of statistical techniques. Shewhart, then an employee of Bell Laboratories, developed the control chart to separate the special causes from the common causes.[5]

In evaluating problems and finding solutions for them, it is important to distinguish between special causes and common causes. Figure 15–27 shows a typical control chart. Data are plotted over time, just as with a run chart; the difference is that the data stay between the upper control limit (UCL) and the lower control limit (LCL) while varying about the centerline or average *only so long as the variation is the result of common causes (i.e., statistical variation)*. Whenever a special cause (nonstatistical cause) impacts the process, one of two things will happen: Either a plot point will penetrate UCL or LCL, or there will be a "run" of several points in a row above or below the average line. When a penetration or a lengthy run appears, this is the control chart's signal that something is wrong that requires immediate attention.

As long as the plots stay between the limits and don't congregate on one side or the other of the process average line, the process is in statistical control. If either of these conditions is not met, then we can say that the process is not in statistical control or simply is "out of control"—hence the name of the chart.

If you understand that it is the UCL, LCL, and process average lines added to the run chart that make the difference, you may wonder how those lines are set. The positioning of the lines cannot be arbitrary. Nor can they merely reflect what you want out of the process, for example, based on a specification. Such an approach won't help separate common causes from special causes, and it will only complicate attempts at process improvement. UCL, LCL, and process average must be determined by valid statistical means. Determination of UCL, LCL, and process average is fully covered in Chapter 18, which is dedicated to the use of control charts in statistical process control.

All processes have built-in variability. A process that is in statistical control will still be affected by its natural random variability. Such a process will exhibit the normal distribution of the bell curve. The more finely tuned the process, the less deviation from the process average and the narrower the bell curve. (Refer to Figure 15–19, Histogram A and Histogram B.) This is at the heart of the control chart and is what makes it possible to define the limits and process average.

Control charts are the appropriate tool to monitor processes. The properly used control chart will immediately alert the operator to any change in the process. The appropriate response to that alert is to stop the process at once, preventing the production of defective product. Only after the special cause of the problem has been identified and corrected should the process be restarted. Having eliminated a problem's root cause, that problem should never recur. (Anything less, however, and it is sure to return eventually.) Control charts also enable continual improvement of processes. When a change is introduced to a process that is operated under statistical process control charts, the effect of the change will be immediately seen. You know when you have made an improvement. You also know when the change is ineffective or even detrimental. This validates effective improvements, which you will retain. This is enormously difficult when the process is not in statistical control because the process instability masks the results, good or bad, of any changes deliberately made.

To learn more about statistical process control and control charts, study Chapter 18.

STRATIFICATION

Stratification is a simple tool in spite of its name. It involves investigating the cause of a problem by grouping data into categories. This grouping is called *stratification*. The groups might include data relative to the environment, the people involved, the machine(s) used in the process, materials, and so on. Grouping data by common element or characteristic makes it easier to understand the data and to pull insights from them.

Consider an example from a factory floor. One of the factory's products requires five assemblers, all doing the same thing at the same rate. Their output flows together for inspection. Inspection has found an unacceptably high rate of defects in the products. Management forms a team to investigate the problem with the objective of finding the cause and correcting it. They plot the data taken over the last month (see Figure 15–28).

The chart in Figure 15–28 plots all operator-induced defects for the month. The team believes that for this product, zero defects can be approached. If you were going to react to this chart alone, how would you deal with the problem? You have five assemblers. Do they all contribute defects equally? This is hardly ever the case. The data can be stratified by the operator to determine each individual's defect performance. The charts in Figure 15–29 do this.

FIGURE 15–28 Chart of Operator Defects for November

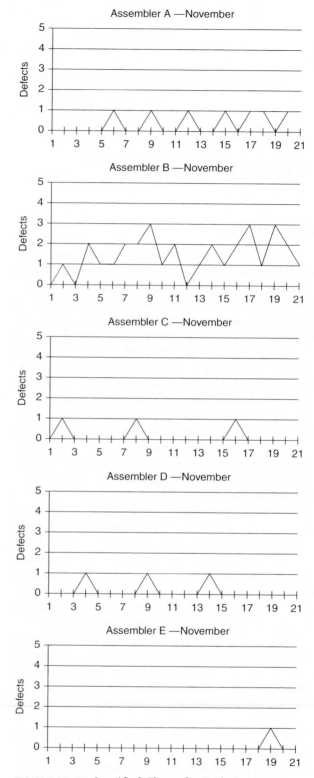

FIGURE 15–29 Stratified Charts for Each Operator

The five stratified charts in Figure 15–29 indicate that one operator, Assembler B, is responsible for more defects than the other four combined. Assembler A also makes more than twice as many errors as Assembler C or Assembler D and eight times as many as Assembler E, the best performer of the group.

The performance of Assembler A and Assembler B must be brought up to the level of the others. Possible causes of the operator-induced defects could be inherent skill, training, vision, attitude, attentiveness, and environmental factors, such as noise, lighting, and temperature in the operator's workstation area. The charts provide an indication of the place to start making changes.

The Pareto charts of Figure 15–6 also represent stratification. Figure 15–6 started with a series of defect types that were the most costly (the first chart). Then it took the worst case, Miswires, and divided it into the *kinds* of miswires (the second chart). Then the worst kind, Hand Wrap, was split into several categories (the third chart). The dominant Hand-Wrap defect category was operator induced. Finally, the Operator category was stratified by individual operator (the fourth chart).

The power of stratification lies in the fact that if you stratify far enough, you will arrive at a *root cause* of the problem. Only when root causes are corrected will the problem be solved. Any other kind of solution is a *work-around* fix. Work-arounds are often used in the real world, but when they are, the underlying problem remains and will eventually cause disruption again.

In the present example, we probably did not go all the way to the root cause, unless Assembler B has serious mental, vision, or motor problems that could not be corrected. The most likely root cause is that Assembler B has not been adequately trained for the job; something readily ascertained when the focus is on that individual. One or two more charts looking at the time of day when the mistakes are being made might yield some information, but once the problem is isolated to a person, discussion will usually take you quickly to the root cause. If, on the other hand, Assembler B is a robot and not a human (which is entirely possible in today's automated environment), the stratification should go to at least one more level. We would have to determine the kinds of defects that Assembler B (the robot) is making. That may lead to adjustment or repair of the machine.

Figure 15–30 shows that the defects induced by this machine are almost all concerned with screws. The robot is either damaging the screws or breaking them off. Show this chart to the robot maintenance technician, and that person will immediately recognize that the robot needs an adjustment or replacement of its torque controller. The root cause

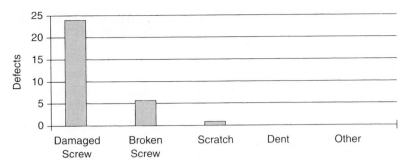

FIGURE 15–30 Robot B Defect Category for November

of the problem is either misadjustment or a defective controller. The technician can confirm the diagnosis by running tests on the robot before certifying it for return to service.

Data collected for Pareto charts and run charts (Figure 15–28) can be stratified. Virtually any data can be subjected to stratification. This includes the data collected for control charts, check sheets, histograms, and scatter diagrams. Consider an example of a stratified scatter diagram.

Scatter diagrams, which show the relationship between the x- and y-axes, lend themselves well to stratification. In this example, parts are being finished on two identical machines. A scatter diagram is plotted to correlate surface flatness and machine speed.

Figure 15–31 suggests that there is a correlation between machine speed (revolutions per minute, or rpm) and surface flatness between 500 and 1,000 rpm but no correlation at higher revolutions per minute. When the same data are stratified in the charts of Figure 15–32, the picture becomes clearer.

In Figure 15–32, the charts reveal that the two machines react similarly to speed increase, but Machine 1 is better than Machine 2 by about 0.00010 in its ability to produce a flat surface. The Machine 1 chart also suggests that increases beyond 1,000 rpm do not produce much improvement. A finish of 0.000950 is about as good as the machine will produce. On the other hand, the Machine 2 chart does show some improvement (two data points) past 1,300 rpm. Given the difference between the two machines, one message coming from the charts is that Machine 2 should be examined to determine the cause of its poorer performance. (More than likely it will be found that bearing wear is the factor in question, and that can be corrected easily.) After the machine has been repaired, new data should be taken to verify that 1,000 to 1,100 rpm is the best practical machine speed.

The charts in Figure 15–32 indicate another message. Both machines had data points better than normal at 550 and 1,100 rpm. It appears that the machines have a natural resonance that affects performance. The clue here is that both machines show it at 550 rpm and at double that speed

FIGURE 15–31 Scatter Diagram: Surface Flatness versus Revolutions per Minute

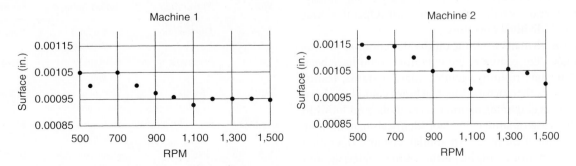

FIGURE 15–32 Stratified Scatter Diagrams: Surface Flatness versus Revolutions per Minute

Delphi Packard Chihuahua and Lean Manufacturing

The Delphi Packard plant in Chihuahua, Mexico, produces power and signal distribution systems (wire harnesses) for the automotive industry. Competition in the production of wire harnesses is intense and global. Consequently, Delphi Packard must produce world-class quality and its personnel must commit to continual improvement. One of the most effective continual-improvement strategies for the company has been lean manufacturing.

By effectively deploying the concept of lean manufacturing, Delphi Packard has been able to achieve the following results:

- Inventory reduction of 34% over a 12-month period
- Improvement in uptime to a level of 93.5% of a 12 month period
- Savings of $750,000 in one year from continual-improvement projects undertaken by salaried personnel
- Made the manufacturing system sufficiently flexible to serve 86 different customers and produce 1,100 different parts or products

In recognition of its effective application of the principles of total quality, Delphi Packard-Chihuahua was awarded the prestigious Shingo Prize for excellence in manufacturing.

Source: www.reliableplant.com/Articles/Print/4697

(1,100 rpm). This should be checked out because it could be adversely affecting performance across the range. If vibration and resonance could be "quieted" across the operating range as it apparently is at 550 and 1,100 rpm, the performance might be significantly improved in both machines. The data that gave us this signal are in the scatter diagram of Figure 15–31, but they don't jump out at you the way they do in the stratified charts of Figure 15–32.

In these examples, we have stratified assembly defects by operator, machine-induced defects by type of defect, and machine performance by machine. It was also pointed out that the earlier Pareto chart discussion involved stratification in which defects were stratified to types of defects, the worst of which was, in turn, stratified to the processes producing those defects. The process (Hand Wrap) producing the most defects was stratified to process factors, and, finally, the factor revealed as the most significant (Operator) was stratified to individual operators.

There is virtually no limit on the directions stratification can take. For example, the operators could have been stratified by age, training, gender, marital status, teams, experience, or other factors. The machines could have been stratified by age, date of maintenance, tools, and location (and in the case of similar but not identical machines, by make and model number). In similar fashion, operating procedures, environment, inspection, time, materials, and so on, can be introduced.

SOME OTHER IMPORTANT TOOLS INTRODUCED

The preceding sections have discussed the statistical tools that have come to be known as "the seven tools." One should not conclude, however, that these seven are the only tools needed for pursuing world-class performance. These seven are the ones that have been found most useful for the broadest spectrum of users. Ishikawa referred to them as the "seven indispensable tools for quality control."[6] He went on to say that they are useful to everyone from company presidents to line workers and across all kinds of work—not just manufacturing. These seven probably represent the seven basic methods most useful to all the people in the workplace. We recommend five more as necessary to complete the tool kit of any business enterprise, if not each of the players within the business:

Five-S

Flowcharts

Surveys

Failure mode and effects analysis (FMEA)

Design of experiments (DOE)

Five-S

Five-S is considered as essential to continual improvement. Its most significant proponent is Hiroyuki Hirano, author of *5 Pillars of the Visual Workplace*, who claims that an organization that cannot implement five-S successfully will be unable to integrate any large-scale change. Hirano holds that Total Quality Management (TQM), Just-in-time/Lean (JIT/Lean), and Kaizen are supported by the five pillars represented by the five S's and are probably unattainable without five-S. The authors heretofore have considered these five S's to be an integral part of TQM and JIT/Lean, but we have come to believe that they should be recognized as a tool that is separable from TQM but that may serve as an entry point for TQM in many organizations.

The five S's were originally conceived in Japanese, as represented by five words beginning with the letter s. Translated to English, the words did not, as you might expect, begin with s, so five-S required some "adjustment" in order to make sense in English. The table below shows the evolution from Japanese to English.

Japanese Word	Translation	Action Implied	English Word for Five-S
Seiri	Organization	Sort useful from useless	Sort
Seiton	Neatness	Everything in its place	Store
Seiso	Cleaning	Workplace and equipment clean	Shine
Seiketsu	Standardization	Select the best practice	Standardize
Shitsuke	Discipline	Make sure rules are followed	Sustain

Five-S is a way of doing things that eliminates waste and reduces errors, defects, and injuries. A recurring comment from executives returning from visits to Japanese industrial plants in the seventies and eighties was that the Japanese plants were spotlessly clean and orderly and seemed far less chaotic than corresponding plants in the West. Much of that was the result of Hiroyuki Hirano's five-S philosophy. Five things must happen under five-S, which are as follows:

1. *Sort:* First, one has to *sort* through items in the workplace to determine which are useful and which are not. Those that are not are discarded. That might include tools, equipment, inventory of stock, spare parts, documentation—everything in the area. If it is not useful, dispose of it, or at least get it out of the work area. The objectives are the elimination of unnecessary items from the workplace and the elimination of time wasted in continually having to search through or work around clutter in order to do the job.

2. *Store:* The things remaining, the useful items, must be *stored* in such a manner that they are visible and immediately available to the workforce. An example is a shadow board with the silhouettes of the tools assigned to a workstation. The silhouette shows where the tool is to be stored when not in use. There has to be an assigned place for everything, and everything should always be kept in its place. The objective is elimination of time wasted looking for tools, parts, and so on by having it easily at hand and visible every time it is needed.

3. *Shine:* The work area and everything in it must *shine*; that is, it must be kept clean at all times. An important consideration here is that this cleaning is not left to a "cleaning crew" but is the responsibility of the employees assigned to the work area. Once cleaned, it is kept that way at all times, not just after the workday. While cleanliness is a good thing in its own right, the act of keeping everything clean becomes a form of inspection of machines, tools, and environmental conditions. The objective is reduced errors and defects that result from defective tools and equipment and from contamination.

4. *Standardize:* Next we must develop the rules and procedures for the work area, *standardizing* on the best practices (the best known way of doing something). When a best practice for accomplishing a task is adopted, everyone doing that task must do it the same way—until a better way is found through continual improvement. The objective is reduced errors and improved consistency and reliability of work, while being alert to discovering or inventing process improvements.

5. *Sustain:* Then we must establish the discipline necessary to follow the rules and practices, improve upon them, and thereby sustain the gains made through five-S. Sort, Store, Shine, and Standardize are all tangible functions. Sustain, however, is intangible from the standpoint of being able to touch it or see it. Sustain, or keeping the five-S philosophy alive and functioning in

an organization, is undoubtedly the most difficult of the S's and requires the full support and leadership of the top management team and managers all the way down through the organization. Slipping back into old (pre-five-S) habits must not be allowed, and the expectation for continual improvement must always be understood. The objective of Sustain is to keep five-S alive, functioning, and improving.

Flowcharts

Both W. Edwards Deming[7] and Joseph Juran[8] promote the use of flowcharts. A *flowchart* is a graphic representation of a process. A necessary step in improving a process is to flowchart it. In this way, all parties involved can begin with the same understanding of the process. It may be revealing to start the flowcharting process by asking several different team members who know the process to flowchart it independently. If their charts are not the same, one significant problem is revealed at the outset; there is not a common understanding of the way the process works. Another strategy is to ask team members to chart how the process *actually* works and then chart how they think it *should* work. Comparing the two versions can be an effective way to identify causes of problems and to suggest improvement possibilities. The most commonly used flowcharting method is to have the team, which is made up of the people who work within the process and those who provide input to or take output from the process, develop the chart. It is important to note that to be effective, the completed flowchart must accurately reflect the *way the process actually works*, not how it should work. After a process has been flowcharted, it can be studied to determine what aspects of it are problematic and where improvements can be made.

You may already be familiar with the flowchart, at least to the point of recognizing one when you see it. It has been in use for many years and in many ways. The application we have in mind here is for flowcharting the inputs, steps, functions, and outflows of a process to more fully understand how the process works, who or what has input to and influence on the process, what its inputs and outputs are, and even what its timing is.

A set of standard flowcharting symbols for communicating various actions, inputs, outflows, and so on, is used internationally. These symbols may be universally applied to any process. The most commonly used symbols are shown in Table 15–1. To illustrate their use, a simple flowchart using the most common symbol elements is given in Figure 15–33. Flowcharts may be as simple or as complex as you may need. For example, in Figure 15–33 the rectangle labeled "Troubleshoot" represents an entire subprocess that itself can be expanded into a complex flowchart. If an intent of the flowchart had been to provide information on the troubleshooting process, then each troubleshooting step would have to be included. Our purpose for Figure 15–33 was merely to chart the *major* process steps for receiving and repairing a defective unit from a customer, so we did not

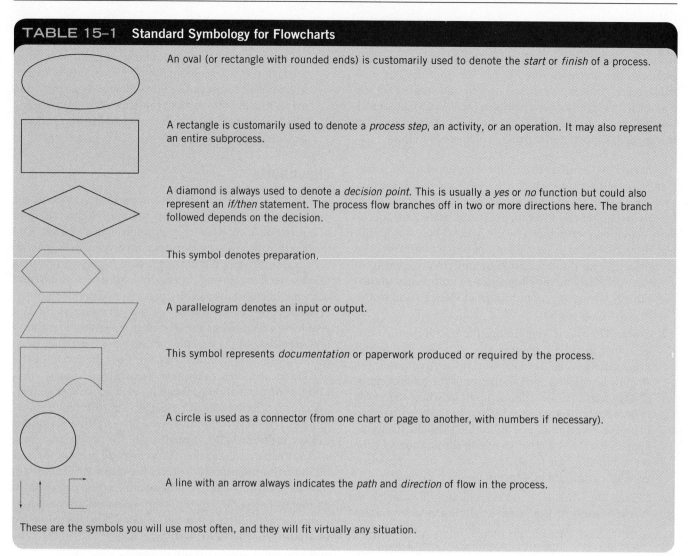

TABLE 15-1 Standard Symbology for Flowcharts

An oval (or rectangle with rounded ends) is customarily used to denote the *start* or *finish* of a process.

A rectangle is customarily used to denote a *process step*, an activity, or an operation. It may also represent an entire subprocess.

A diamond is always used to denote a *decision point*. This is usually a *yes* or *no* function but could also represent an *if/then* statement. The process flow branches off in two or more directions here. The branch followed depends on the decision.

This symbol denotes preparation.

A parallelogram denotes an input or output.

This symbol represents *documentation* or paperwork produced or required by the process.

A circle is used as a connector (from one chart or page to another, with numbers if necessary).

A line with an arrow always indicates the *path* and *direction* of flow in the process.

These are the symbols you will use most often, and they will fit virtually any situation.

require subprocess detail. This is a common starting point. From this high-level flowchart, it may be observed that (a) the customer's defective unit is received, (b) the problem is located and corrected, and (c) and the repaired unit is tested. (d) If the unit fails the test, it is recycled through the repair process until it does pass. (e) Upon passing the test, paperwork is completed. (f) Following that, the customer is notified, and (g) the unit is returned to the customer along with a bill for services. With this high-level flowchart as a guide, your next step will be to develop detailed flowcharts of the subprocesses you want to improve. Only then can you understand what is really happening inside the process, see which steps add value and which do not, find out where the time is being consumed, identify redundancies, and so on. Once you have a process flowcharted, it is almost always easy to see potential for improvement and streamlining. Without the flowchart, it may be impossible.

More often than not, people who work directly with a process are amazed to find out how little understanding of their process they had before it had been flowcharted. Working with any process day in and day out tends to breed a false sense of familiarity.

We once took over a large manufacturing operation that was having major problems with on-time delivery of systems worth $500,000 to $2 million apiece. Several reasons accounted for the difficulty, but a fundamental problem was that we were not getting the input materials on time—even with a 24-month lead time for delivery. One of the first things we did was flowchart the entire material system. We started the chart at the signing of our customer's order and completed it at the point where the material was delivered to the stockroom. The chart showed dozens of people involved, endless loops for approval and checking, and flawed subprocesses that consumed time in unbelievable dimensions.

When the flowchart was finished, it was clear that the best case from the start of the order cycle until material could be expected in our hands required 55 weeks. The worst case could easily double that. With this knowledge, we attacked the material process and quickly whittled it down to 16 weeks and from there to 12 weeks. The point is this: Here was a process that had grown over the years to the point that it was no longer tolerable, much less efficient. But the individual players in the process didn't see the problem. They were all working very hard, doing what

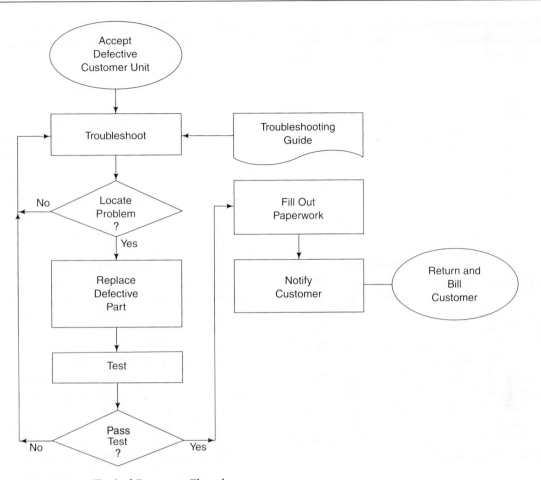

FIGURE 15–33 Typical Processes Flowchart

the process demanded, and fighting the fires that constantly erupted when needed material was not available. The flowchart illuminated the process problems and showed what needed to be done.

If you set out to control or improve any process, it is essential that you fully understand the process and why it is what it is. Don't make the assumption that you already know, or that the people working in the process know, because chances are good that you don't, and they don't. Work with the people who are directly involved, and flowchart the process as a first step in the journey to world-class performance. Not only will you better understand how the processes work, but also you will spot unnecessary functions or weaknesses and be able to establish logical points in the process for control chart application. Use of the other tools will be suggested by the flowchart as well.

Surveys

At first glance, the survey may not seem to be indispensable. When you think about it, though, all of the tools are designed to present information—information that is pertinent, easily understood by all, and valuable for anyone attempting to improve a process or enhance the performance of some work function. The purpose of a survey is to

obtain relevant information from sources that otherwise would not be heard from—at least not in the context of providing helpful data. Because you design your own survey, you can tailor it to your needs. We believe that the survey meets the test of being a total quality tool. Experience has shown that the survey can be very useful.

Surveys can be conducted internally as a kind of employee feedback on problem areas or as *internal customer* feedback on products or services. They can also be conducted with *external customers*, your business customers, to gain information about how your products or services rate in the customers' eyes. The customer (internal or external) orientation of the survey is important because the customer, after all is said and done, is the only authority on the quality of your goods and services. Some companies conduct annual customer satisfaction surveys. These firms use the input from customers to focus their improvement efforts.

Surveys are increasingly being used with suppliers as well. We have finally come to the realization that having a huge supplier base is not the good thing we used to think it was. The tendency today is to cut back drastically on the number of suppliers utilized, retaining those that offer the best *value* (not best price, which is meaningless) and that are willing to enter into partnership arrangements. If a company goes this route, it had better know how satisfied the suppliers are with the past and present working relationship and what they think of future prospects. The survey is one tool for determining this. It is possibly the best initial method for starting a supplier reduction/supplier partnership program.

Even if you are not planning to eliminate suppliers, it is vital to know what your suppliers are doing. It would make little sense for you to go to the trouble of implementing total quality if your suppliers continue to do business as usual. As you improve your processes and your services and products, you cannot afford to be hamstrung by poor quality from your suppliers. Surveys are the least expensive way of determining where suppliers stand on total quality and what their plans are for the future. The survey can also be a not-too-subtle message to the suppliers that they had better "get on the bandwagon."

A typical department in any organization has both internal suppliers and internal customers. Using the same customer-oriented point of view in a survey has proven to be a powerful tool for opening communications among departments and getting them to work together for the common goal rather than for department glory—usually at the expense of the overall company.

The downside of surveys is that the right questions have to be asked, and asked in ways that are unambiguous and designed for short answers. A survey questionnaire should be thoroughly thought out and tested before it is put into use. Remember that you will be imposing on the respondents' time, so make it easy and keep it simple.

Failure Mode and Effects Analysis

Failure mode and effects analysis (FMEA) tries to identify all possible potential failures of a product or process, prioritize them according to their risk, and set in motion action to eliminate or reduce the probability of their occurrence. FMEA cannot by itself bring about this happy ending, since it is an analytical tool, not a problem solver. But it will point to the problems that must be solved through the use of the other tools.

Failure mode and effects analysis—the name itself is enough to scare off the unfamiliar. So you don't give up on FMEA before we get into it, let's simplify the concept. FMEA just tries to identify all the possible types (modes) of failures that could happen to a product or a process before they happen. Once the possible "failure modes" have been identified, the "effects analysis" kicks in and studies the potential consequences of those failures. Next, the consequences of each potential failure are ranked by

Seriousness/Criticality to the customer

Probability of the fault's occurrence

Probability of the fault's detection by the systems responsible for defect prevention or detection

Seriousness of consequence, likelihood of occurrence, and difficulty of detection all work together to determine the criticality of any specific failure mode. Comparing the criticality of all the identified potential failure modes establishes the priority for corrective action. That is the objective of FMEA. FMEA tells the organization where its resources should be applied, and this is very important because all possible failures are not equal and the organization should always deploy its resources to correct the problems that are most critical. Without the benefit of FMEA, it is doubtful that an organization could identify its most critical failure modes very accurately. Remember, usually FMEA addresses problems that have not yet happened. Next time you are cruising at 600 miles per hour at 35,000 feet, consider whether the designers of your airliner should have used FMEA—or the next time you really, really need your brakes to work (Am I going to go over the cliff?)—or when you buy that new $2,000 high-definition TV (So much technology—is it going to be reliable?). We might also consider it if we have to go to a hospital—or when we ship our original, no-copy-available manuscript to our publisher by overnight express. Looking at it from another viewpoint, had FMEA been available, could it have prevented the *Titanic*'s disaster? Given what we now know about the ship's collision with the iceberg, we are convinced that had FMEA been employed, the *Titanic* might have plied the seas through most of the twentieth century. Of course, FMEA did not come along until four decades later.

There are several kinds of FMEA. Design FMEA is employed during the design phase of a product or service, hopefully starting at the very beginning of the project. In this way, the designers will be able to develop a design that has fewer potential failures, and those that cannot be avoided can be made less severe. Also, by using FMEA concurrently with the design activity, it is more likely that test and inspection methods will be able to catch the problems before they get to the customer.

A second version is process FMEA. In this case, FMEA is looking at the potential failures (errors, miscues) of a process. The process might be that of an accounting firm, a hospital, a factory, a governmental agency, or any other entity. One can imagine that in a hospital there are many processes that can have lots of failure modes, some probably not too important, but some as severe as they come. One would hope that FMEA is in every hospital's tool kit.

Ford Motor Company uses FMEA even before it gets to the design stage of a vehicle. As the concept for a new vehicle is being developed, FMEA is employed to make sure that the vehicle will not bring problems related to the concept into the design and production stages.

FMEA can also be used after the fact (as in the case of a product repeatedly failing in the hands of the customer). This may lead to a retrofit or recall of the product if the problem is severe or simply to a design change for future production if the problem is not critical. The procedure is essentially the same for every kind of FMEA.

FMEA is not new, although until recently its use was mainly associated with military and aerospace programs. It was developed by the U.S. military in 1949 and has seen increasing use in industry, especially since the 1980s, its importance being driven by the worldwide quality movement under TQM and ISO 9000 and by litigation in the United States against companies whose products are involved in customer injuries or deaths. FMEA is now considered an invaluable quality tool.

The Language of FMEA

FMEA has its own unique set of terms. We have captured most of them in the following list:

Failure mode. The way in which something might fail. For example, a race car's tire might fail by puncture from a sharp object. It might also fail from a blowout resulting from wear. Puncture and blowout are two (of many) tire failure modes.

Failure effect. The failure's consequence in terms of operation, function, or status of the item.

Effects analysis. Studying the consequences of the various failure modes to determine their severity to the customer. Of the two tire failure modes mentioned earlier, the blowout is likely to have the most serious consequence, since when a tire suddenly explodes, the speeding race car usually goes out of control, often with dire consequences. On the other hand, a puncture usually allows the tire pressure to decrease gradually, allowing the driver time to sense the problem before he or she loses control. Neither failure mode is something the driver wants, but of the two, the puncture is preferred.

Failure mode analysis (FMA). An analytical technique used to evaluate failure modes with the intent to eliminate the failure mode in future operations.

Design FMEA. FMEA applied during the design phase of a product or service to ensure that potential failure modes of the new product or service have been addressed.

Process FMEA. FMEA applied to a process (as in a factory or office) to ensure that potential failure modes of the process have been addressed.

Risk assessment factors.

- *Severity (S):* A number from 1 to 10, depending on the severity of the potential failure mode's effect: 1 = no effect, 10 = maximum severity.

- *Probability of occurrence (O):* A number from 1 to 10, depending on the likelihood of the failure mode's occurrence: 1 = very unlikely to occur, 10 = almost certain to occur.

- *Probability of detection (D):* A number from 1 to 10, depending on how unlikely it is that the fault will be detected by the system responsible (design control process, quality testing, etc.): 1 = nearly certain detection, 10 = impossible to detect.

- *Risk Priority Number (RPN):* The failure mode's risk is found by the formula $RPN = S \times O \times D$. Said another way, RPN = Severity × Probability of Occurrence × Probability of Detection. RPN will be a number between 1 (virtually no risk) and 1,000

(extreme risk). The auto industry considers an RPN of 75 to be acceptable, although in light of some recent manufacturer recalls for safety related failures, we anticipate that may change.

FMEA Illustration

Let's consider a simplified FMEA to illustrate how the process works. We will assume we manufacture bicycles and we are designing a new bike that will be made largely of composite materials. Since this is a new technology for our company, we are using design FMEA to make sure we've considered all the possible problem areas of the design before we go into production. The FMEA team has listed several potential failure modes, one involving sudden, unwarned breakage of the front fork. It is obvious that should the fork fail, the effect on the customer could be severe. Since the rider will probably have no warning before the fork breaks, we rate the severity a 10 (S = 10).

We then identify possible causes of the fork failure and conclude that the probability of the most likely cause occurring is moderate, with five occurrences per thousand bikes. We rate the probability of occurrence a 6 (O = 6). Of course, it is our intention to detect the defective forks and discard them before they are attached to the bicycle frame. After we examine our fork testing methods, we conclude that the probability of detecting the failure mode flaw in the fork is low. We assign it a 6 (D = 6).

Plugging these numbers into our equation, $RPN = S \times O \times D$, we have

$$RPN = 10 \times 6 \times 6$$
$$= 360$$

All other failure modes result in RPNs in the range of 40 to 70, so our focus should be on eliminating, or drastically reducing, this potential fork failure mode. We could redesign the fork so that it is more robust, thereby lowering the occurrence value (O), or change the test process so that it is much more likely to detect a fork that might fail, thereby lowering the detection value (D).

Notice that if our fork testing process gave us complete assurance of detecting the fault—say, at the D = 1 level—RPN would be 60, and we probably wouldn't need to put a lot of resources on this fault mode. The same could be said if D remained at 6, but the probability of occurrence of the fault mode turned out to be remote (O = 1).

When to Use FMEA

FMEA should be employed at the following points:

During the design or redesign of a process, product, or service

When improvements are needed or planned for existing processes, products, or services

When existing processes, products, or services are to be used in a new way

During after-the-fact failure analysis

When safety or health is an issue

This is intended to be a brief introduction to FMEA. Going into it more thoroughly is beyond the scope of this text. Should you find that you need more, the Internet is a good source of information, and there are many books dedicated to the subject.

Design of Experiments

Design of experiments (DOE) is a very sophisticated method for experimenting with processes with the objective of optimizing them. If you deal with complicated processes that have multiple factors affecting them, DOE may be the only practical way of bringing about improvement. For example, such a process might be found in a wave soldering machine. Wave solder process factors include the following:

Solder type	Conveyor speed
Flux specific gravity	Solder temperature
Conveyor angle	Wave height
Preheat temperature	PC board layer count
Flux type	PC board groundplane mass

These 10 factors influence the process, often interacting with one another. The traditional way to determine the proper selection or setting was to vary one factor while holding all others fixed. That kind of experimentation led to making hundreds of individual runs for even the simplest processes. With that approach, it is unusual to arrive at the optimum setup because a change in one factor frequently requires adjustment of one or more of the other factors for best results.

The DOE method reduces the number of runs from hundreds to tens as a rule, or by an order of magnitude. This means of process experimentation allows multiple factor adjustment simultaneously, shortening the total process, but equally as important, revealing complex interaction among the factors. A well-designed experiment can be concluded on a process such as wave soldering in 30 to 40 runs and will establish the optimum setting for each of the adjustable parameters for each of the selected factors. For example, optimal settings for conveyor speed, conveyor angle, wave height, preheat temperature, solder temperature, and flux specific gravity will be established for each PC board type, solder alloy, and so on.

DOE also shows which factors are critical and which are not. This information enables you to set up control charts for those factors that matter, while saving the effort that might have been expended on the ones that don't. While design of experiments is beyond the scope and intent of this book, the DOE work of Deming, Taguchi, and others may be of help to you. Remember that DOE is available as a tool when you start trying to improve a complex process.

MANAGEMENT'S ROLE IN TOOL DEPLOYMENT

Management's role is changing from one of directing to one of facilitating. Since the Industrial Revolution, management has supplied the place of work, the machinery and tools, and the work instructions. The concept has been that management knows what the job is and needs only to hire the muscle power to get it accomplished. The workers were there only because management could not get the job done without their labor. Workers were not expected to think about doing things differently but simply to follow the boss's orders. Work was typically divided into small tasks that required minimal training, with little or no understanding on the part of laborers as to how their contribution fit into the mosaic of the whole.

During much of the twentieth century, and certainly since World War II, changes have been creeping into the management–labor relationship. Some people think that the labor unions were responsible for these changes, and they did help obtain better pay, shorter hours, workplace improvements, and other benefits for workers. However, the relationship changes between management and labor have happened largely in spite of the unions. Unions have had at least as difficult a time as management has had in dealing with employee involvement. Nor has management at large been responsible for the changes sweeping across the industrial world today. Certainly, there are champions representing management, but the changes are coming about for one reason and one reason only: They are necessary in order for businesses to survive in an increasingly competitive marketplace.

After World War II, when Deming went to Japan to teach industrialists about quality and the use of statistics for achieving it, Japan had just lost the war. Its industrial base was a shambles. The Japanese needed to resurrect their factories and put people to work quickly. That meant they had to be able to sell their products abroad—to the same people who had defeated them. To do that, it was essential that their products be of high quality. Their survival depended on it. You know the rest of the story.

Not only did the Japanese listen to Deming and Juran, but also they embraced them and their philosophy (whereas in the United States we were abandoning their teaching amid a seemingly insatiable market for manufactured goods). Japan developed its own quality gurus (Ishikawa, Taguchi, Shingo, and others) who expanded the work of Deming and Juran. For 30 years, into the 1980s, Japanese manufacturers perfected their quality and production methods. The 1980s found Japan ahead of the rest of the world, not just the United States, in product quality and value. During that decade, companies in the United States began to wake up to the fact that Japan's products were the best in the world and that they were running roughshod over U.S. companies not only in the world markets, but also right here at home. Whole markets were conceded to Japan as U.S. companies found they could not compete.

The survival mentality finally surfaced. We woke up to the fact that not only our industrial survival but perhaps even our national survival was at stake. Either we became competitive in the global marketplace, or we lost the first war fought without bullets since the invention of gunpowder.

Now that the wake-up call has been received, many people have come to realize that we have been managing poorly for a very long time—say, since 1945. We (those of us who have heard the alarm) have come to understand that management's proper role is to facilitate, not to direct. Management provides the place of work and the machines and tools as before, but in addition, we do everything we can to *help* our employees do the job. That means training. It means listening to their thoughts and ideas—more than that, it means *seeking* their thoughts and ideas. It means acting on them. It means giving them the power to do their jobs without management interference. It means giving them time to think and discuss and suggest and experiment. It means communicating—fully and honestly. No secrets, no smoke screens. It means accepting every employee as a valued member of the corporate team.

This approach does not mean that management abdicates its responsibility to set the direction for the enterprise, to establish the corporate vision, to steer the course. But with the enlistment of all the brain power that had formerly gone untapped, even this job becomes easier than it was before.

It is management's responsibility to train employees to use not only physical tools (and that is very important) but also intellectual tools. The tools discussed in this chapter should eventually be used by most employees—*eventually* because it is a mistake to schedule all employees for training on the tools if they will not be using them very soon. You would not train a person on a new machine a year before the machine arrives because without putting the training to practice, its effect will be lost. So it is with the total quality tools. When a group of people is ready to put some of the tools into practice, that is when the group should be trained. As the total quality concept takes root, it will be only a matter of time until everyone has the need. Train them as required.

Management must also provide the internal experts, often called *facilitators*, to help the new teams get started and to develop their expertise. Facilitation is probably a never-ending function because the total quality envelope is constantly being expanded and there will always be the need for a few to be on the leading edge and to bring the others along.

It is management's responsibility to ensure that the people who are solving the problems have the proper training and facilitation. It is also management's responsibility to make sure the problems being attacked are of interest to the enterprise and not trivial. Management must populate the problem-solving team with the cross-functional expertise the problem requires. The team must be given the power and support necessary to see the effort brought to its conclusion.

Management must be vigilant that data used in problem solving are valid, which is a function that usually falls to the facilitator. Especially when teams are immature in total quality, they have a tendency to grab at the first set of data that comes along. Management must ensure that the data and the statistical techniques employed are appropriate for the problem at hand.

Finally, management must ensure that there are results. Too many problem-solving, process improvement, and related efforts take on a life of their own and go on forever.

This cannot be allowed. People are watching. Especially in the early stages, some people will hold the view that "This too shall pass." If results do not come rather quickly, the detractors will be given the ammunition they need to subvert the whole total quality effort. For this reason, it is important that the first projects attempted have a high probability of success, and management must monitor them closely, even to the point of being involved in the activity. As the process matures and successes are tallied, an occasional failure will not be an issue. In fact, people must be given the chance to fail, and failure must be free of repercussions for the team or its members.

Precautions

Implementing the use of statistical tools and the whole concept of process improvement, problem solving by the rank and file, and empowerment—in short, the total quality culture—represents a profound change from the way things have been done in the past. People generally resist change until they see that it will benefit them. For that reason, management must champion change and convince everyone that the effort will benefit all. Those who would undermine the effort must rapidly be converted or removed from the operation. People will be looking to management for evidence that management really believes in total quality. If for no other reason than that, it must be obvious to all that management is using the same techniques the other employees are being taught. Above all, management must support and facilitate the employees as they use the techniques of total quality to solve problems and improve processes.

> *Communicate.* Let everyone know what is going on and what the results are. Help them understand why it is good for them, for the whole enterprise, and, yes, even for the nation.
>
> *Never assume that you know it all.* The people who live with the processes day in and day out know far more about what is wrong with them and how to improve them than any manager. Never delude yourself that you have learned all you need to know about total quality. It will never happen because total quality is a dynamic and ever-expanding concept.
>
> *Start slowly.* Don't try to organize an entire factory or office complex into improvement teams and train everyone in sight on day one. Take it one or two steps at a time, training as you go. Be careful to pick early projects that have high prospects for success.
>
> *But start.* The worst choice a manager could make today is to decide that total quality is not for his or her business. It is for every conceivable kind of business, whether large or small, whether public, private, military, civilian, mass production, job shop, classroom, or office. It would be a tragedy to decide not to start this journey when so much is at stake.

Although results should be evident quickly, do not expect the necessary cultural change to occur overnight.

TABLE 15–2 Functionality Matrix: Quality Tools

	Cause & Effect Diagram	Check Sheet	Control Chart	Design of Experiments	Five-S	FMEA	Histogram	Pareto Chart	Run Chart	Scatter Diagram	Stratification	Survey	Flowchart
Alert operator to change in process			X						X				
Alert operator to special cause			X										
Analyze by sorting into categories											X		
Analyze potential causes	X							X		X	X		X
Collect data from targeted groups												X	
Determine relationships between variables (correlation)				X						X			
Experiment with a process				X									X
Find patterns in data									X		X		
Frequency distribution (frequency of values to occur)							X						
Identify possible causes	X							X			X		X
Improve/sustain work efficiency					X								
Investigate causes	X							X		X	X		X
Monitor a process (continuing)		X	X						X				
Observe results over time			X						X				
Present information while collecting data		X						X	X				
Process analysis	X	X	X	X		X		X	X	X	X		X
Process capability		X					X						
Process optimization				X			X			X			X
Rank potential product/process failures for elimination						X							
Separate significant from trivial								X					
Study a process	X	X			X	X							X
View process over time			X						X				

This is a long process, requiring several years to get to the point where total quality is considered "just the way we do things" and not some special "project." Even so, during all that time, problems are being solved, improvements are being made, and efficiency, productivity, and competitiveness are all increased.

SELECTING THE RIGHT TOOL FOR THE JOB

In this chapter, we have discussed 13 quality tools, some in great detail and a few on an introductory basis. Your challenge will be selecting the appropriate tool (or tools) for the task at hand. This can be confusing, especially at first. For that reason, we have included Table 15–2, a functionality matrix for the tools. It is by no means complete in terms of the possible uses of the tools or tasks that may be required, but it illustrates the common functionality of our tools. For example, if your task is to obtain data from a group of customers, the matrix will point you to the *Survey*. If you are looking for something that will provide useable information in graphic form even as the data are being collected, then the matrix suggests a *Check Sheet*, *Pareto Chart*, or *Run Chart*. Your selection will be determined by which tool you think will best satisfy your requirement. Note that most of the tools are useful in more than one situation. Your knowledge of the task will often make the selection clear, although there may also be some trial and error involved initially. The matrix is intended to illustrate the kinds of functions that may be appropriate for the tools. Once you start using them, you will find the selection to be virtually automatic.

SUMMARY

1. Pareto charts are useful for separating the important from the trivial. They are named after Italian economist and sociologist Vilfredo Pareto, who developed the theory that a majority of problems are caused by a minority of causes. Pareto charts are important because they can help an organization decide where to focus limited resources. On a Pareto chart, data are arrayed along an x-axis and a y-axis.

2. The cause-and-effect diagram was developed by the late Dr. Kaoru Ishikawa, a noted Japanese quality expert; others have thus called it the Ishikawa diagram as well as the fishbone diagram. Its purpose is to help identify and isolate the causes of problems. It is the only one of the seven basic quality tools that is not based on statistics.

3. The check sheet is a tool that facilitates collection of relevant data, displaying it in a visual form easily understood by the brain. Check sheets make it easy to collect data for specific purposes and to present them in a way that automatically converts them into useful information.

4. Histograms have to do with variability. Two kinds of data are commonly associated with processes: attributes data and variables data. An *attribute* is something that the output product of the process either has or does not have. *Variables data* are data that result when something is measured. A *histogram* is a measurement scale across one axis and a frequency of like measurements on the other.

5. The scatter diagram is arguably the simplest of the seven basic quality tools. It is used to determine the correlation between two variables. It can show a positive correlation, a negative correlation, or no correlation.

6. In the context of the seven total quality tools, run charts and control charts are typically thought of as being one tool together. The *control chart* is a more sophisticated version of the run chart. The *run chart* records the output results of a process over time. For this reason, the run chart is sometimes called a *trend chart*. The weakness of the run chart is that it does not tell whether the variation is the result of special causes or common causes. This weakness gave rise to the control chart. On such a chart, data are plotted just as they are on a run chart, but a lower control limit (LCL), an upper control limit (UCL), and a process average are added. The plotted data stay between the UCL and LCL, while varying about the centerline or average, only so long as the variation is the result of common causes such as statistical variation.

7. Stratification is a tool used to investigate the cause of a problem by grouping data into categories. Grouping of data by common elements or characteristics makes it easier to understand the data and to draw insights from them.

8. Other useful quality tools are five-S, flowcharts, surveys, failure mode and effects analysis (FMEA), and design of experiments (DOE). Five-S is used to eliminate waste and reduce errors, defects, and injuries. Flowcharts are used in a total quality setting for charting the inputs, steps, functions, and outflows of a process to understand more fully how the function works and who or what has input into and influence on the process, its inputs and outputs, and even its timing. The survey is used to obtain relevant information from sources that otherwise would not be heard from in the context of providing helpful data. FMEA tries to identify all possible product or process failures and prioritize them for elimination according to their risk. DOE is a sophisticated method for experimenting with complex processes for the purpose of optimizing them.

KEY TERMS AND CONCEPTS

Attributes data

Cause-and-effect diagram

Check sheet

Common causes

Control chart

Correlation

Design of experiments (DOE)

Effects analysis

Failure mode

Five-S

Flowchart

FMEA

Frequency distribution

Histogram

In statistical control

Lower control limit (LCL)

NPMO

Pareto chart

Pareto Principle

Process average

Process variability

Risk

Risk assessment

Run chart

Scatter diagram

Seriousness of consequence

Shine

Six Sigma

Special causes

Specification limits

Standard deviation

Standardize

Stratification

Survey

Sustain

Total quality tools

Trend chart

Upper control limit (UCL)

Variables data

Variation

FACTUAL REVIEW QUESTIONS

1. Explain the purpose of a Pareto chart. Give an example of when one would be used.

2. Describe the origin and use of cause-and-effect diagrams.

3. How would a check sheet be used in a modern production facility?

4. What is a histogram, and how is one used?

5. What accounts for the disparity in NPMO between the statistical 6 and the popular Six Sigma approach?

6. Describe two methods for improving the yield of a process (i.e., taking it to a higher sigma value).

7. Explain the purpose of the scatter diagram. Give an example of how one would be used.

8. Contrast and compare run charts and control charts.

9. What is the most common use of stratification?

10. What purpose is served by flowcharts?

11. Give an example of how a survey might be used in a modern production setting.

12. What is the purpose of design of experiments?

13. In the context of the five-S philosophy, what is the intent of the word *Standardize*?

14. Explain the difference between design FMEA and process FMEA.

15. What are FMEA's three risk assessment factors?

CRITICAL THINKING ACTIVITIES

Which Tool to Use

As the manager of a department that is beginning to use the total quality tools, Marion thinks a wall chart in the team meeting room would be helpful when the teams decide on which tools to apply to their problem-solving or decision-making efforts. She has listed the most commonly used tools

and wants a simple one-line "purpose statement" for each tool, similar to the one she developed for the flowchart. Your task: Develop the rest of the purpose statements for the wall chart here.

Total Quality Tools: What They Are Used For	
Tool	**Purpose Statement**
Flowchart	Helps us understand our processes; facilitates thinking about improving them.
Pareto chart	
Cause-and-effect diagram	
Histogram	
Stratification	
Run chart	
Control chart	
Scatter diagram	
Check sheet	
Survey	

Constructing a Flowchart: Scheduling a Meeting

Marion read that even the most routine tasks can be flowcharted and that when they are, the diagram may reveal complexity that is both surprising and unnecessary. She thought she would test this by flowcharting a process that seemed to be the most used in her organization, scheduling a meeting. She convened a meeting of her direct subordinates, and together they have listed the steps involved in scheduling a meeting. Now they are ready to develop the chart. You are the facilitator. Lead them through the diagramming process. (Draw the flowchart.)

Steps in Scheduling a Meeting	The Flowchart
• Select a topic.	
• Select participants.	
• Select date.	
• Select time.	
• Select place (accommodate any conflicts in the earlier steps).	
• Prepare draft agenda.	
• Distribute draft for comments.	
• Review comments (accommodate as appropriate).	
• Prepare meeting room.	
• Hold meeting.	

Selecting Improvement Subjects Using Pareto Charts and Stratification

Starlight Homes Inc. is a building contractor specializing in upscale homes in the Southwest. Before each new home is sold, Starlight conducts a final inspection of the home and repairs any defects. In addition, Starlight receives a "punch list" of defects (to be corrected) compiled by the buyers following the sale. Ricardo Alvarez, Starlight's lead supervisor, has concluded that even if it should cost more to do the work right in the first place, it will be a lot cheaper than going back later to fix the defects. In an effort to reduce costs, improve the quality of Starlight's homes, and reduce the number of complaints after the sale, Ricardo has assembled data from his final inspections and the punch lists for the last 20 homes sold. These data are listed in the following chart:

Defect Type	Occurrences	Defect Type	Occurrences
Damaged walls	13	Doors	14
Exterior paint	5	HVAC	11
Plumbing	33	Roof	3
Caulking	28	Masonry	2
Electrical	25	Interior paint	61
Cabinetry	12	Landscaping	16
Woodwork	46	Fixtures	7

Construct a Pareto chart to illustrate the defect types by number of defects. Which two defect types appear to be the most significant? Should Ricardo focus his attention on these two categories of defects? Ricardo decided to stratify the Pareto chart by cost before making any decision. His bookkeeper developed the average cost per repair event per category. The data are shown here:

Average Cost per Repair Event			
Defect Type	Average Cost	Defect Type	Average Cost
Damaged walls	$126	Doors	$11
Exterior paint	25	HVAC	110
Plumbing	78	Roof	72
Caulking	7	Masonry	290
Electrical	74	Interior paint	4
Cabinetry	88	Landscaping	34
Woodwork	5	Fixtures	31

The second-level chart developed from these numbers should show Ricardo which two or three defect types are the most significant in terms of cost, enabling him to put his efforts where they will do the most good. What are they? Was Ricardo justified in going to the second level (of stratification) before making a decision on where to focus his efforts? Why?

Constructing a Cause-and-Effect Diagram

Your team has been given the charter to make recommendations for improving the cleanliness of the company's restrooms. The team has finished compiling a list that it considers to be the possible contributors to less than desirable restroom cleanliness:

Janitor service	Use of paper towels	Lack of paper towels
Slobs	User carelessness	User attitude
Janitor attitude	Paper dispensers	Poor lighting
Too small	Unreliable plumbing	Type of floor material
Janitor pay	Management inattention	Janitor supervision
Air conditioning	Insufficient exhaust	In-house plumbers
Cleaning materials	Cleaning equipment	Paper receptacles
Maintenance	Cleaning schedule	Leaking faucets
Janitor procedures		

Construct a cause-and-effect diagram incorporating all these ideas.

Translating Your Histogram

Your process has a normal histogram with μ located at 10 millimeters, 1s points at 9.9 and 10.1 millimeters, 2s points at 9.8 and 10.2 millimeters, and 3s points at 9.7 and 10.3 millimeters.

-3σ	-2σ	$-\sigma$	μ	$+\sigma$	$+2\sigma$	$+3\sigma$
9.7 mm	9.8 mm	9.9 mm	10.0 mm	10.1 mm	10.2 mm	10.3 mm

If your customer will accept parts measuring between 9.7 and 10.3 millimeters, how many parts of every 1,000 produced would you expect to scrap? If your customer notified you that henceforth it would accept only parts between 9.9 and 10.1 millimeters, what would you anticipate your scrap rate to be? What would have to be done to bring the scrap rate at this new customer requirement back down to what it had been at the former customer specification? Compared with the bell curve above, what would the new histogram have to look like?

DISCUSSION ASSIGNMENT 15–1

Reacting to a Process Gone Wrong

Cignet Plastics Corporation is a contract plastics die-casting house serving a wide range of clients. Over the years, Cignet has been a favored supplier of precision die castings for a major producer of model airplane kits. In recent days the defect rate of these parts has increased. (Acceptance is based on a visual inspection of the parts for appearance.) After a thorough audit of the process, Quality Assurance has concluded that there has been no change to the process. It claims that the increase in defects must be variation that is related to some assignable cause. The president of Cignet Plastics does not have a clue as to what that means, and he has called you in for an explanation.

DISCUSSION QUESTIONS

Discuss the following questions in class or outside of class with your fellow students:

1. What will you tell the president?

2. He wants you to change the process to reduce the number of defects, but you know that is the wrong approach. How do you talk him out of it?

3. What approach would you use to get the operation back to normal?

ENDNOTES

1. Kaoru Ishikawa, *Guide to Quality Control* (Tokyo: Asian Productivity Organization, 1976).

2. The 80–20 rule is an approximation, and one should not expect the numbers to land exactly at 80% or 20%.

3. Ishikawa, *Guide to Quality Control*, 24–26.

4. W. Edwards Deming, *Red Bead Experiment*. Retrieved from www.redbead.com on July 7, 2010.

5. W. W. Scherkenbach, *The Deming Route to Quality and Productivity* (Rockville, MD: Mercury, 1991), 100.

6. Kaoru Ishikawa, *What Is Total Quality Control?* (Upper Saddle River, NJ: Prentice Hall, 1985), 198.

7. Scherkenbach, *The Deming Route*, 104.

8. Joseph M. Juran, *Juran on Planning for Quality* (New York: Free Press, 1988), 18.

PROBLEM SOLVING AND DECISION MAKING

It is a capital mistake to theorize before you have all the evidence. It biases the judgment. —*Sir Arthur Conan Doyle*

MAJOR TOPICS
- Problem Solving for Total Quality
- Two Models for Solving and Preventing Problems
- Problem-Solving and Decision-Making Tools
- Decision Making for Total Quality
- The Decision-Making Process
- Objective versus Subjective Decision Making
- Scientific Decision Making and Problem Solving
- Employee Involvement in Problem Solving and Decision Making
- Role of Information in Decision Making
- Using Management Information Systems
- Creativity in Decision Making

Problem solving and decision making are fundamental to total quality. On the one hand, good decisions and problem solutions will decrease the number of problems that occur. On the other hand, the workplace will never be completely problem free. The purpose of this chapter is threefold:

- To help readers learn how to solve problems effectively, positively, permanently, and in ways that don't create additional problems

- To help readers become better decision makers

- To help readers learn to make decisions and handle problems in ways that promote quality

Our lives seem full of problems requiring solutions and situations in need of decisions. Some are trivial, but others may be of extreme importance. The same is true in our business or professional lives. Our organizations develop problems that must be solved and situations that demand decisions. This chapter is designed to provide the knowledge needed by the employee at any level to contribute to problem solving and decision making in the workplace. It is common practice to treat problem solving and decision making as a single subject, since the mechanics of solving problems and making decisions are the same, or at least very closely related. It will be helpful, however, to maintain a mental distinction between the two.

For our purposes here, problem solving will be concerned with problems that can impact the organization or its customers in some way—usually negatively. Problems, if not solved, may adversely affect the organization's products or processes, leading to higher costs, safety issues, customer dissatisfaction, lowered competitiveness, and so on—and ultimately may even result in failure of the organization.

For decision making, we will be concerned with decisions that impact the organization in some significant, tangible way: for example, those that can affect the future path of the organization; its mission, staffing, culture, environment, equipment, or training; and the like. Decisions of this type can lead the organization to success or, if not the correct ones, to destruction.

Problem solving is most often (though not always) a reaction to the problem presenting itself (i.e., something that has happened). Decision making is frequently aimed at the future rather than at an event that has taken place. As such, it is akin to, and an integral part of, planning. As we move into our discussion of problem solving and decision making, remember that all problem solutions also require decisions. Similarly, all good decisions require the same kind of mental activity as problem solving.

PROBLEM SOLVING FOR TOTAL QUALITY

If you ask the typical manager to describe his or her biggest problem in today's workplace, the response will probably include one or more of the following:

- We spend all our time in meetings trying to resolve problems.
- We are constantly fighting problems and that doesn't leave us time to do our real jobs, such as planning, leading, and so on.
- As soon as we "put out one fire," another pops up.
- We've got more problems than we can handle, and it bogs us down.

The actual words may vary, but the message is the same. The workplace can be so burdened with problems that managers and others spend much of their time trying to fix them and nothing gets done right. Leadership suffers—there is just no time to lead. Performance suffers, from the standpoint of both the individual and the organization. Quality of product or service deteriorates. Competitiveness is negatively impacted. Failure of the organization becomes a real probability, especially if its competitors have turned to total quality and its philosophy for solving problems—once and for all. Why is it that with all the effort we put into it, consuming so much time in the process, we cannot solve our problems and get on with the jobs we are paid to do? The answer is simply that most of our problem solving is anything but that.

Consider this scenario from the authors' past. One night while driving home from a meeting, our Chrysler's engine suddenly quit. It would start when the key was turned but immediately quit when the key was released. The car's wiring diagram showed a resistor (an electrical component) that was switched into the engine's running circuit only after the engine was started. We suspected it might be the problem. Sure enough, by putting a plain piece of wire between the two terminals of the resistor, effectively replacing the resistor with the wire having no resistance, the engine ran fine, and we got home with no further difficulty. Was the problem solved? Of course not. On the way to work the next morning, the ignition coil, normally protected by the resistor but now subjected to too much electrical current by our piece of wire, burned up. That necessitated replacing not only the resistor but also the ignition coil, which cost six times as much as the resistor. After replacing the two components, everything was once again in working order. But was the problem solved? At this point, most people would say so.

This is the level of problem solving in many (if not most) organizations. When something breaks, fix it or replace it. Job done, problem solved. The most we should claim for this kind of problem solving is that we are back where we started (i.e., before the problem came up). But remember, if it happened once, it can happen again.

The Chrysler's resistor failed twice more while we owned the car. Over the next 25 years, we owned two more

Chrysler vehicles, both of which also had multiple failures of the same resistor. Clearly, replacing the resistor did not solve the problem. For the problem to be truly solved so that the failure rate of that part would be sufficiently reduced so as to be satisfactory would have required Chrysler to gather all the electrical, physical, and reliability data relating to the resistor, and the circuit it operated in, and then redesign the circuit or make use of a more robust resistor or some other change, as the data required. Had that been done, we could justifiably call it a solved problem. We could also call such a solution a product *improvement* because the probability of failure would be greatly reduced.

The point is that in total quality jargon, a problem is solved only when its recurrence has become impossible or significantly less probable. That will always be the objective of total quality problem solving. Any problem that is merely fixed by restoring the situation to what it was before the problem was manifested will return again. That is why managers spend so much time with problem issues. The problems are not being solved—just put into a recycle loop. In those organizations that have adopted total quality, problems are solved once and for all. The same problems do not return time and time again. That means that there will be fewer problems tomorrow than there were today, fewer next month than this month, fewer next year than this year. Managers will have more time to manage, leaders to lead. When problem solutions lead to process or products or services improvement,

- product or service quality improves,
- costs decrease (through less waste and warranty action),
- customer satisfaction improves,
- competitiveness improves, and
- the probability for success improves.

Clearly, all of these outcomes are desirable. They are all achievable by applying the total quality principles to problem solving.

TWO MODELS FOR SOLVING AND PREVENTING PROBLEMS

Even the best-managed organizations have problems. A problem is any situation in which what exists does not match what is desired, or put another way, there is a discrepancy between the current state of affairs and the one desired. The greater the disparity between the two, the greater the problem. Problem solving in a total quality setting is not just "putting out fires" as they occur. Rather, it is one more way to make continual improvements in the workplace and its products or services. This section contains two models for solving problems in ways that simultaneously lead to workplace or product improvements: the PDCA cycle and Toyota's Practical Problem-Solving Process.

For this discussion, we will separate problems into two categories: *existent* and *latent*. Existent problems are the ones that have manifested themselves as processes that have gone wrong, as defective products, as errors in work, and through other symptoms of trouble. These are the problems that demand our immediate attention. Organizations face and react to existent problems every day. On the other hand, latent problems lie waiting in the wings for the right combination of circumstances to bring them to life. Because they have yet to occur, they are not obvious until we go searching for them. Like existent problems, latent problems also exist in all organizations.

World-class organizations find ways of dealing with both existent problems and latent problems. Although many of the tools and techniques are the same, the initial approach is different. In the case of the existent problem, the approach to a solution is reactive: a problem has occurred, and it must be solved before we can move on. For the latent problem, the initial approach is proactive; if conditions are right, this problem could occur, and we need to prevent it. Notice that the existent problem always announces itself. We know that a problem has occurred. The latent problem is silent; it hasn't occurred yet. We must seek it out. The objective of the solution to both problem types should always be to eliminate the potential for the problem to occur (latent) or repeat (existent).

The best organizations pay a lot of attention to both existent and latent problems. It is not enough just to fix existent problems as they come up because all of those latent problems out there are just waiting to happen. The organization should place a heavy emphasis on preventing future problems as well as solving those that are already obvious. All problem solving should be seen as a continual improvement activity. If, for example, a problem "solution" merely returns a process to the state that existed before the problem occurred, then we suggest that it has not been solved at all. Certainly, no improvement has been achieved. The problem will return. On the other hand, if a problem is solved in a manner that renders the same problem unable to recur, then process improvement has taken place. By following this philosophy for every problem, over time processes, products, and services will become better and more robust, and the organization will face fewer and fewer problems. That should be the objective of all problem-solving activity.

The Plan–Do–Check–Adjust Cycle

This continual improvement model goes by several names. The Japanese call it the *Deming Cycle* after Dr. W. Edwards Deming, who introduced it to them. In the West, it is commonly called simply the *PDCA cycle*, standing for plan–do–check–act. In this book, we have taken the liberty to suggest that the letter *A* more correctly means *adjust*.

The PDCA cycle has evolved from that which Deming presented to his Japanese audience in the summer of 1950. The cycle started with *design the product*, followed in order by *production, sales*, and *market research*. His emphasis was on developing products that would be accepted in the world's markets, and that was precisely the requirement of the moment in Japan. In the design phase, he stressed finding out

what is needed by potential customers, designing a product to meet the need, and planning sufficient production to validate the product's viability. That has become the Plan part of the cycle. The production plan was to be executed in the second quadrant of the cycle. That has become the Do phase. After producing the product, the firm was to sell it. Whether it sold well or poorly provided information on whether the firm had correctly chosen a product type. This has become the Check phase. Having sold the product, the firm was urged to find out from its customers whether the product met their expectations and how the product could be changed to better serve the customer. That has become the Act or Adjust phase. The concept was that a second cycle would commence immediately, taking into consideration everything that was learned from the first cycle; then there would be a third, a fourth, and so on, continually applying information learned to redesign the product and find ways to make production more efficient, always with customer requirements as a very important input to the process.

The PDCA cycle consists of four major components (see Figure 16–1), each of which can be subdivided into the necessary step-by-step problem-solving activities:

1. **Plan.** Before any corrective action is taken on the problem at hand, a number of activities should be undertaken. The problem must be defined, relevant information gathered, the root cause of the problem identified, possible solutions developed and considered, and the best alternative selected for implementation. All of this needs to be done by people carefully selected on the basis of their association with the process involved and their special relevant knowledge, skills, experience, and so on.

2. **Do.** Implement the solution chosen as best. (Note that in the real world "best" often means "most likely" to produce the desired result.)

3. **Check.** Monitor the implemented solution and gather data relevant to the original problem and any other areas of concern—for example, concerns about unintended consequences of the solution. Analyze the data to determine whether the implemented solution eliminated the problem (or made it much less likely to recur).

4. **Adjust.** If the Check step confirmed that the problem has been eliminated and that it is not likely to recur, then the job is done. If, however, it was found that the solution has not accomplish the intended result or that there is still a possibility of recurrence, then it will be necessary to "adjust" the implemented solution. Adjust can also mean discard the implemented solution and try a different approach. Whether the implemented solution has failed completely or does not quite measure up to expectation, the conceptual adjustment will be carried forward to the Plan step of another PDCA cycle.

This cycle can be repeated as many times as is necessary to eliminate the problem successfully. If progress is not evident after several cycles, however, it would be a good idea to stop,

FIGURE 16–1 Plan–Do–Check–Adjust Cycle

stand back, and take another look at the original problem, perhaps aided by some new viewpoints (i.e., from new people added to the problem-solving team). Never let a team become bogged down.

The PDCA problem-solving technique is equally useful whether you are reacting to an existent failure event or proactively seeking a means to head off a latent problem that has not yet happened but that can happen. The PDCA cycle is a kind of generic, basic format for bringing order and logic to the problem-solving process. As you can see from Figure 16–1, it is not detailed in terms of the specific steps of problem solving but is intended to put all the steps into a logical sequence and then to start a simple cycle that is allowed to continue until a solution's results match the planned outcome.

General Procedure for Problem Solving: The Toyota Model

Whether you are reacting to an existent problem that has just come up or working to prevent future problems, it will be helpful to follow a procedure that defines the methodology of problem solving and establishes an order of execution of the critical steps. Figure 16–2 shows a flowchart of the problem-solving process employed by one of the great manufacturers. Toyota's "Practical Problem-Solving Process"[1] is said to have seven main steps, although the number of steps may depend on one's definition of "step." Note that Step 2, for example, is broken into several subprocesses. Regardless of how the process steps are counted, the excellent Toyota process

is appropriate for almost all situations, including both latent and existent problem categories. The following step-by-step discussion explains the Toyota problem-solving model. You may want to refer to the flowchart in Figure 16–2 and to Figure 16–3, which presents a textual overview of the process.

Step 1: Perceive the Initial Problem The action in Step 1 simply perceives that a problem (latent or existent) exists. One may be brought to that perception by an alarm, a failed inspection, a limit being breached, a search for potential future failure modes (as with FMEA), or many other events. Existent problems will usually be obvious and must be dealt with expeditiously. Latent problems are often discovered by improvement teams searching processes and product or service designs for vulnerability. Their method is typically an examination of key processes and designs, looking for potential weaknesses, trouble spots, areas of too little or too much control, illogical operations, or steps that add no value. Most of the total quality tools may be used, but especially useful are FMEA and flowcharts constructed to illustrate how the processes actually work (as opposed to how they should work). If the team perceives that a process or a product design contains a latent problem, the "unborn" problem is listed for possible problem-solving action and continual improvement.

Step 2: Clarify the Problem Toyota rightly holds that before action can be taken, problem solvers must "grasp the situation." Experience has shown Toyota that grasping the situation thoroughly *before* proceeding with the problem

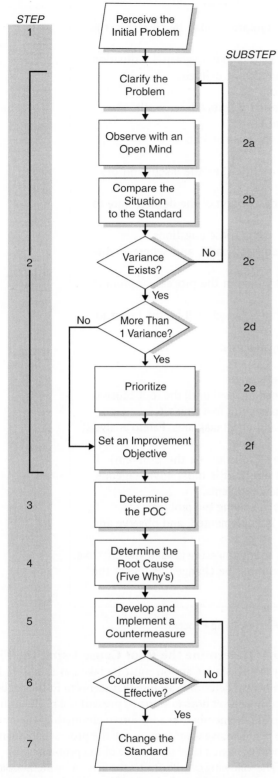

FIGURE 16–2 Toyota's Practical Problem-Solving Process

Substep 2a Observe with an open mind. This is a reminder to refrain from assuming anything relative to the problem at this point. Rather, be an unbiased observer of the facts surrounding the problem.

Substep 2b Compare the actual situation to the standard. This requires the problem solver to compare the actual data from the process or product with that specified in the relevant standard. The word *standard* is used to denote the *recognized, approved* procedure, specification, or other document. Process operators are expected to adhere to the instructions contained in the standard that applies to the process. The engineer is expected to design a product that conforms to the established product requirements and specifications. If there is a problem, the comparison of the actual process or product to the standard will reveal a variance.

Substep 2c Does a variance exist? If there is no variance, then either the situation is problem free or the problem is not what it seemed to be. In either case, it is necessary to take another look at what the problem really is. The *No* output of substep 2c takes us back to the beginning of Step 2 for a new attempt at identifying or describing the problem. On the other hand, if a variance is found, we proceed to substep 2d.

Substep 2d Is there more than one variance? If only a single variance is indicated, the *No* output of this diamond takes us directly to the last element of Step 2, substep 2f, bypassing the need to prioritize. However, if upon examination more than one variance exists, then the *Yes* output of the diamond takes us to substep 2e.

Substep 2e Prioritize. When improvement teams analyze processes, it is not uncommon to find multiple possibilities for variances. Usually, some will be more important than others. Since it is impossible to solve them all at once, it is important to rank them so that the most significant is solved first. Pareto analysis, probably Toyota's most used statistical tool,[2] is employed to establish priority. As we saw in Chapter 15, Pareto analysis is very simple, yet extremely powerful. The FMEA techniques are also useful.

Substep 2f Set an improvement objective. We arrive at this block with a single problem in mind, either because there was only one problem or because we deliberately selected the most important of a set of problems. At this point, you will notice that we do not have a solution in mind, nor do we necessarily have a handle on what is causing the problem. Knowing only that we have a problem, what do we want the eventual problem solution to accomplish? If we simply want the production line to start moving again, then our objective might be to find a quick fix and go back to work. However, notice that Toyota does not say "set a *repair* objective" or even "set a *solution* objective." Instead, Toyota consciously uses the phrase "set an *improvement* objective." In the Toyota culture, a solution to a problem that is merely a fix or repair to the previous state or that is anything less than an improvement is unthinkable.

solving is vitally important, but it is a very difficult concept to teach. Most of us are too eager to jump to conclusions and get on with it. That approach is not allowed at Toyota—even if a production line is stopped. Before a solution can be offered, the problem must be defined and objectives for improvement set. To do that, Step 2 takes us through substeps 2a through 2f.

1. Perceive the initial problem. At this point, symptoms may be clear, but the problem may not be well defined.
2. Clarify the problem. It is critical for problem solvers to fully grasp the situation before proceeding. From this analysis, the problem is defined.
   a. Observe the situation with an open mind.
   b. Compare the actual situation to the standard (procedure, work instruction, flowchart, specifications, etc.).
   c. Determine if variance exists. If not, then try again at step 2.
   d. Determine if multiple variances exist.
   e. If multiple variances exist, prioritize by severity. (See the discussion of FMEA in Chapter 15.)
   f. Set an improvement objective. This is a description of the desired state to be achieved by the problem's solution.
3. Determine the actual point of cause (POC), using these questions:
   a. Where do we observe the problem geographically, and where in the process or product function?
   b. Where is the cause geographically, and where in the process or product function?
   Questions lead upstream toward the root cause, which will be the target for improvement.
4. Determine the root cause. Use the Five-Why analysis:
   a. Ask why the observed variance exists.
   b. Ask why the answer to that question is as stated.
   c. Repeat the "why" question at each succeeding level until the root cause is determined. (*Note:* It is permissible to go beyond five why's.)
   d. Use other total quality tools (e.g., cause-and-effect diagrams, Pareto analysis) as appropriate.
5. Develop and implement a countermeasure (solution to the problem). If multiple solutions are possible, select the one that is most advantageous, being careful to avoid introduction of any new problems.
6. Evaluate the countermeasure's effectiveness in solving the problem.
   a. Evaluate by analysis before the solution is implemented, and observe and monitor after implementation.
   b. Achieve consensus that the implemented countermeasure is valid and effective.
7. Change the standard. The original standard must be changed to reflect the countermeasure.

FIGURE 16–3 Overview of the Toyota Practical Problem-Solving Process

Depending on the kind of problem being worked, the objective might be to make the relevant process step foolproof (in Japanese, *poka-yoke*) so it is impossible for the problem to recur or to make a product more reliable.

Step 3: Determine the Point of Cause (POC) Armed with a problem definition and an improvement objective from Step 2, we now have to determine the location, geographically and within the process or product, of the problem's cause. Where did the problem manifest itself? Was it in a production process? Was it in the test department? Was it in a review of a process or design? The intent of this step is to move our attention upstream to where the problem's cause took life. That could be far removed from where the problem was first detected.

Answers to these questions lead to the next step.

Step 4: Determine the Root Cause Using the Five-Why Analysis Caution must be taken at this step. It is often easy to determine a cause that seems to fit the problem perfectly and yet does nothing to prevent the problem from recurring. Remember, in addition to eliminating the immediate problem, we want to improve the process in a manner that will prevent a later recurrence of the problem.

The following case illustrates the Five-Why methodology:

A firm discovers that it has been purchasing materials that are not actually required. In addition to the cost of purchasing, these unneeded materials represent an expensive inventory that requires warehousing, handling, and tracking. All of those costs translate directly to the firm's bottom line as loss of profit. A team is established to determine what is causing the problem and to develop a solution.

We pick up at Step 4 of the Toyota Practical Problem-Solving Process, as the team is beginning to employ Five-Why analysis to determine the real cause of the problem.

First Why By asking "Why are we buying materials that we do not need?" the team quickly determines that the unneeded purchases are the result of purchasing department purchase orders. These purchase orders are being issued in response to material requests from the company's 2-year-old enterprise resource planning (ERP) system. The team's collective reaction is "Aha!" The team has heard many horror stories of flawed implementation of ERP (and MRP II, ERP's predecessor) at other companies and is leaning toward the conclusion that their new ERP is yet another automated system run amok. But is a faulty ERP system really the cause?

Second Why To understand the problem more fully, the team members have to understand how ERP works, so they ask, "Why does the ERP system issue requests for material?" The answer takes them a layer deeper. An ERP system plans material purchases by comparing *anticipated demand* to *on-hand inventory*. If the comparison shows a demand that cannot be satisfied by materials on hand, ERP generates material requests to the purchasing department to fill that shortage. For example, if the ERP knows that the factory is to produce 100 widgets next month and it knows that in order to do that manufacturing will require 100 X assemblies and 300 Y assemblies, ERP will check inventory to see how many X and Y assemblies are in stock beyond current demand. ("Current demand" refers to assemblies already set aside for another purpose.) If the inventory shows 116 X assemblies and 240 Y assemblies in stock beyond current demand, then ERP will recognize that the stockroom has 16 more X assemblies than needed but has a shortage of 60 Y assemblies. ERP will then generate a material request to notify the purchasing department that 60 additional Y assemblies must be purchased. ERP is doing exactly what is intended: it is making certain that when a production schedule is activated in the factory, the necessary materials are on hand to support it. Still, a large percentage of its material requests are subsequently found to be invalid, and the stockroom is becoming bloated with material for which there is no known future demand. The team agrees that it does not yet know the cause of the problem.

Third Why The team members need to determine the cause of the erroneous material requests. They ask, "Why are many of the ERP material requests invalid?" The ERP system is a computer program with access to various relevant data and information relative to the enterprise. As is almost always the case, the computer has to assume that its information and data are valid, accurate, and up-to-date. As we have already seen, only two sets of data come into play when the system checks to see what material should be ordered: material demand and inventory. Either of those being incorrect will result in (1) invalid material requests, (2) the absence of needed material requests, or, more likely, (3) both. The ERP determines material demand based on production require-

ments that are entered by the various product lines. The team finds those data accurate. Inventory data are fed by the stockroom directly to the ERP database. The team's physical spot-checks of inventory associated with several of the invalid material requests reveal inventory errors. The team is now satisfied that the ERP system is not the cause of the problem. The cause instead seems related to inventory accuracy. Is inventory accuracy the root cause? No. Something else had to cause the inventory to be inaccurate.

Fourth Why Having determined that the inventory data contain errors, the team asks, "Why are the inventory data inaccurate?" The team is told that for the last decade, the stockroom of over 5,000 line items has maintained an inventory accuracy of 95 to 97%. The accuracy level yielded by the inventory control system is a real point of pride among those in the stockroom responsible for charting the inventory data. Indeed, an inventory accuracy of 95 to 97% was probably adequate before the company implemented the ERP system. But with the implementation of ERP's automation, there is now little human intervention or double-checking of purchase transaction validity. What is more, the people who used to do that have been shifted to other jobs or are no longer with the company. It is all left to the computer. With an inventory accuracy of 95 to 97%, it is guaranteed that many, if not most, of ERP's material requests will be invalid in one way or another. The team concludes that inventory accuracy that had been satisfactory under the old manual system is no longer good enough. When the ERP system was implemented, no corresponding upgrading of the inventory system had taken place. Is this the root cause?

Fifth Why The team members are beginning to think they are almost there, but they decide to probe at least one layer deeper. They ask, "Why wasn't the inventory system upgraded in concert with the ERP implementation?" The evidence is that when management decided to replace the company's long-standing manual planning system with ERP, the organization did not understand that a virtually error-free, real-time inventory would be required. Inventory accuracy had not been a problem over the years; hence, no effort was made to change inventory equipment, procedures, or methods. Management had been in the dark. Is that the root cause? The team doesn't think so. After all, no one—not even experienced, well-paid managers—knows everything. The root cause, as determined by the team, is that *the organization has no effective internal planning process in place to ensure that when new systems are implemented, the relevant infrastructure is capable of supporting it.* Had such a process been in place, the right people would have found that the existing inventory system was incapable of supporting ERP.

Beyond the Fifth Why Five Why's will usually lead to a root cause, but occasionally a sixth or seventh may be useful. In this case, we could have asked "Why?" once or twice more to find out why the cited procedure didn't exist, but that would not seem to be very productive.

Step 5: Develop and Implement a Countermeasure
Continuing, the team found it easy to articulate their solution (countermeasure). It has four components:

To correct the immediate problem,

1. The team must acquaint the management with ERP requirements for inventory accuracy.

2. Management must commit to, and support, the upgrading of the inventory system.

3. Until virtually 100% inventory database accuracy is achieved, the organization must restore manual checks on the system to prevent unnecessary material orders.

To prevent similar problems in the future,

4. A procedure must be implemented to ensure

   a. Understanding of the needs of prospective new systems before committing to them.

   b. Concurrent availability of suitable infrastructure support for any new systems that are implemented.

Step 6: Determine the Effectiveness of the Countermeasure The team now has to determine whether the improvement objective developed in substep 2f is being satisfied by the implementation of the countermeasure. This may be done by testing and monitoring until the accumulation of data can determine a statistically valid "yes" or "no" answer. Should the answer be "no," then the team must come up with a different countermeasure. Once the answer is "yes," the team can proceed to the final step.

Step 7: Change the Standard Whether the "standard" in question is a product specification, a manufacturing process, or a work instruction, the team must update it to reflect any change(s) made through the countermeasure. This documents the improvement made and becomes the new standard for the process or product, to which all relevant employees will adhere.

PROBLEM-SOLVING AND DECISION-MAKING TOOLS

The models presented in the previous section can help organizations determine better solutions and make better decisions, provided that they are based on facts. Decisions and solutions based on information that is inaccurate or tainted by personal opinions, exaggeration, or personal agendas are not likely to be optimal, regardless of the problem-solving model used. The information collection step can be made more effective through the use of the total quality tools introduced in Chapter 15.

In today's competitive environment, organizational decisions and problem responses can no longer be made the way we have been making them for the last 100 years. Today's business decisions and problem solutions cannot be made without sufficient knowledge of all the relevant factors, which often means that the collective knowledge of the organization must be tapped. At the least, we must be smart in our decision making and problem solving, or we may find ourselves on the path to ruin.

DECISION MAKING FOR TOTAL QUALITY

All people make decisions. Some are minor. (What should I wear to work today? What should I have for breakfast?) Some are major. (Should I accept a job offer in another city? Should I buy a new house?) Regardless of the nature of the decision, decision making can be defined as follows:

> Decision making is the process of selecting one course of action from among two or more alternatives.

Decision making is a critical task in a total quality setting. Decisions play the same role in an organization that fuel plays in an automobile engine: They keep it running. The work of an organization cannot proceed until decisions are made.

Consider the following example. Because a machine is down, the production department at DataTech Inc. has fallen behind schedule. With this machine down, DataTech cannot complete an important contract on time without scheduling at least 75 hours of overtime. The production manager faces a dilemma. On the one hand, no overtime was budgeted for the project. On the other hand, there is substantial pressure to complete this contract on time because future contracts with this client may depend on it. The manager must make a decision.

QUALITY TIP ▼

Decision Making in Today's Business Environment

"Today's business environment:

- Demands more large-scale change via new strategies, reengineering, restructuring, mergers, acquisitions, downsizing, new product or market development, and so on.

Decisions made inside the firm:

- Are based on bigger, more complex, more emotionally charged issues and are made more quickly.

- Are made in a less certain environment.

- Require more sacrifice from those implementing the decisions.

A new decision-making process:

- Is required because no one individual has the information needed to make all major decisions or the time and credibility needed to convince lots of people to implement the decisions.

- Must be guided by a powerful coalition that can act as a team."

Source: "Implementing Change Powerfully and Successfully." Retrieved from www.mindtools.com/pages/article/newPPM_82.htm.

In this case, as in all such situations, it is important to make the right decision. But how do managers know when they have made the right decision? In most cases, there is no single right choice. If there were, decision making would be easy. Typically, several alternatives exist, each with its own advantages and disadvantages.

For example, in the case of DataTech Inc. the manager had two alternatives: authorize 75 hours of unbudgeted overtime or risk losing future contracts. If the manager authorizes the overtime, his or her company's profit for the project in question will suffer, but its relationship with a client may be protected. If the manager refuses to authorize the overtime, the company's profit on this project will be protected, but the relationship with this client may be damaged. These and other types of decisions must be made all the time in the modern workplace.

Managers should be prepared to have their decisions evaluated and even criticized after the fact. Although it may seem unfair to conduct a retrospective critique of decisions that were made during the "heat of battle," having one's decisions evaluated is part of accountability, and it can be an effective way to improve a manager's decision-making skills.

Evaluating Decisions

There are two ways to evaluate decisions. The first is to examine the results. In every case when a decision must be made, there is a corresponding result. That result should advance an organization toward the accomplishment of its goals. To the extent that it does, the decision is usually considered a good decision. Managers have traditionally had their decisions evaluated based on results. However, this is not the only way that decisions should be evaluated. Regardless of results, it is wise also to evaluate the process used in making a decision. Positive results can cause a manager to overlook the fact that a faulty process was used, and in the long run, a faulty process will lead to negative results more frequently than to positive ones.

For example, suppose a manager must choose from among five alternatives. Rather than collecting as much information as possible about each, weighing the advantages and disadvantages of each, and soliciting informed input, the manager chooses randomly. He or she has one chance in five of choosing the best alternative. Such odds occasionally produce a positive result, but typically they don't. This is why it is important to examine the process as well as the result, not just when the result is negative but also when it is positive.

THE DECISION-MAKING PROCESS

Decision making is a process. For the purpose of this textbook, the decision-making process is defined as follows:

> The decision-making process is a logically sequenced series of activities through which decisions are made.

Numerous decision-making models exist. Although they appear to have major differences, all involve the various steps shown in Figure 16–4 and discussed next.

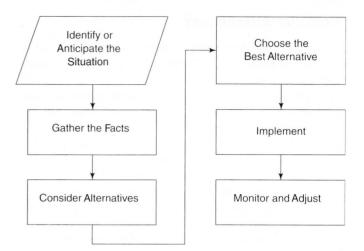

FIGURE 16–4 Decision-Making Model

Identify or Anticipate the Situation

Anticipating the situation is like driving defensively; never assume anything. Look, listen, ask, and sense. For example, if you hear through the grapevine that a team member's child has been severely injured and hospitalized, you can anticipate the consequences that may occur. She is likely to be absent, or if she does come to work, her pace may be slowed. The better managers know their employees, technological systems, products, and processes, the better able they will be to anticipate troublesome situations.

Gather the Facts

Even the most perceptive managers will be unable to anticipate all situations or to understand intuitively what is behind them. For example, suppose a manager notices a "who cares?" attitude among team members. This manager might identify the problem as poor morale and begin trying to improve it. However, he or she would do well to gather the facts first to be certain of what is behind the negative attitudes. The underlying cause(s) could come from a wide range of possibilities: an unpopular management policy, dissatisfaction with the team leader, a process that is ineffective, problems at home, and so on. Using the methods and tools described earlier in this chapter and in Chapter 15, the manager should separate causes from symptoms and determine the root cause of the poor attitude. Only by doing so will the situation be permanently resolved. The inclusion of this step makes possible *management by facts*—a cornerstone of the total quality philosophy.

It should be noted that the factors that might be at the heart of a bad situation include not only those for which a manager is responsible (policies, processes, tools, training, personnel assignment, etc.) but possibly also the ones beyond the manager's control (personal matters, regulatory requirements, market and economic influences, etc.). For those falling within the manager's domain of authority, he or she must make sound, informed decisions based on fact. For the others, the organization has to adapt.

Consider Alternatives

Considering the alternatives involves two steps: (1) list all of the various alternatives available and (2) evaluate each alternative in light of the facts. The number of alternatives identified in the first step will be limited by several factors. Practical considerations, the manager's range of authority, and the cause of the situation will all limit a manager's list of alternatives. After the list has been developed, each entry on it is evaluated. The main criterion against which alternatives are evaluated is the desired outcome. Will the alternative being considered produce the desired result? If so, at what cost?

Cost is another criterion used in evaluating alternatives. Alternatives always come with costs, which might be expressed in financial terms, in terms of employee morale, in terms of the organization's image, or in terms of a customer's goodwill. Such costs should be considered when evaluating alternatives. In addition to applying objective criteria and factual data, managers will need to apply their judgment and experience when considering alternatives.

Choose the Best Alternative, Implement, Monitor, and Adjust

After all alternatives have been considered, one must be selected and implemented, and after an alternative has been implemented, managers must monitor progress and adjust appropriately. Is the alternative having the desired effect? If not, what adjustments should be made? Selecting the best alternative is never a completely objective process. It requires study, logic, reason, experience, and even intuition. Occasionally, the alternative chosen for implementation will not produce the desired results. When this happens and adjustments are not sufficient, it is important for managers to cut their losses and move on to another alternative.

Managers should avoid falling into the ownership trap. This happens when they invest so much ownership in a given alternative that they refuse to change even when it becomes clear the idea is not working. This can happen at any time but is more likely when a manager selects an alternative that runs counter to the advice he or she has received, is unconventional, or is unpopular. The manager's job is to optimize the situation. Showing too much ownership in a given alternative can impede the ability to do so.

OBJECTIVE VERSUS SUBJECTIVE DECISION MAKING

All approaches to decision making fall into one of two categories: objective or subjective. Although the approach used by managers in a total quality setting may have characteristics of both, the goal is to minimize subjectivity and maximize objectivity. The approach most likely to result in a quality decision is the objective approach.

Objective Decision Making

The objective approach is logical and orderly. It proceeds in a step-by-step manner and assumes that managers have the

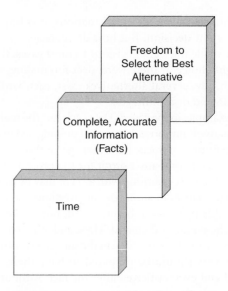

FIGURE 16–5 Factors That Contribute to Objective Decision Making

time to systematically pursue all steps in the decision-making process (see Figure 16–5). It also assumes that complete and accurate information is available and that managers are free to select what they feel is the best alternative.

Measured against these assumptions, it can be difficult to be completely objective when making decisions. Managers don't always have the luxury of time and complete information. This does not mean that objectivity in decision making should be considered impossible. Managers should be as objective as possible. However, it is important to understand that the day-to-day realities of the workplace may limit the amount of time and information available. When this is the case, objectivity can be affected.

Subjective Decision Making

Whereas objective decision making is based on logic and complete, accurate information, subjective decision making is based on intuition, experience, and incomplete information. This approach assumes decision makers will be under pressure, short on time, and operating with only limited information. The goal of subjective decision making is to make the best decision possible under the circumstances. In using this approach, the danger always exists that managers might make quick, knee-jerk decisions based on no information and no input from other sources. The subjective approach does not give managers license to make sloppy decisions. If time is short, they should use the little time available to list and evaluate alternatives. If information is incomplete, they should use as much information as is available. Subjective decision making is an anathema in the total quality context, and it should be avoided whenever possible.

SCIENTIFIC DECISION MAKING AND PROBLEM SOLVING

As explained in the previous section, sometimes decisions must be made subjectively. However, through good man-

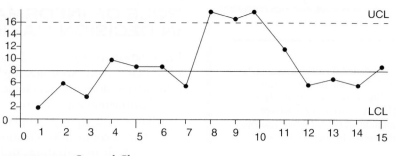

FIGURE 16–6 Control Chart

agement and leadership, such instances should and can be held to a minimum. One of the keys to success in a total quality setting is using a scientific approach in making decisions and solving problems. One method is to use Joseph M. Juran's 85/15 rule. Decision makers in a total quality setting should understand this rule. It is one of the fundamental premises underlying the need for scientific decision making.

Complexity and the Scientific Approach

In the language of scientific decision making, complexity is introduced when improvements are not based on the scientific approach. Several different types of complexity exist, including the following: errors and defects, breakdowns and delays, inefficiency, and variation. The Pareto Principle, explained in Chapter 15, should be kept in mind when attempting to apply the scientific approach.

Errors and Defects Errors cause defects and defects reduce competitiveness. When a defect occurs, one of two things must happen: the part or product must be scrapped altogether, or extra work must be done to correct the defect. Waste or extra work that results from errors and defects adds cost to the product without adding value.

Breakdowns and Delays Equipment breakdowns delay work, causing production personnel either to work overtime or to work faster to catch up. Overtime adds cost to the product without adding value. When this happens, the

organization's competitors gain an unearned competitive advantage. When attempts are made to run a process faster than its optimum rate, an increase in errors is inevitable.

Inefficiency *Inefficiency* means using more resources (time, material, movement, or something else) than necessary to accomplish a task. Inefficiency often occurs because organizations fall into the habit of doing things the way they have always been done without ever asking why.

Variation In a total quality setting, consistency and predictability are important. When a process runs consistently, efforts can begin to improve it by reducing process variations, of which there are two kinds:

- **Common-cause variation** is the result of the sum of numerous small sources of natural variation that are always part of the process.
- **Special-cause variation** is the result of factors that are not part of the process and that occur only in special circumstances, as when a shipment of faulty raw material is used or a new, untrained operator is involved.

The performance of a process that operates consistently can be recorded and plotted on a control chart such as the one in Figure 16–6. The data points in this figure that fall within the control limits (i.e., between the upper control limit [UCL] and the lower control limit [LCL]) are likely to be related to common causes. The data points in this figure that fall outside the control limits are likely to be the results of a special cause of variation. In making decisions about the process in question, it is important to separate common and special causes of variation.

The concept of using control charts and statistical data in problem solving and decision making is discussed in greater depth in Chapter 18.

EMPLOYEE INVOLVEMENT IN PROBLEM SOLVING AND DECISION MAKING

Chapter 8 showed how employee involvement and empowerment can improve decision making and problem solving. Employees are more likely to show ownership in a decision or solution they had a part in reaching. Correspondingly, they are more likely to support a decision or solution for which they feel ownership. There are many advantages to

QUALITY TIP ▼

Juran's 85/15 Rule

"There is a widely held belief that an organization would have few, if any, problems if only workers would do their jobs correctly. As Dr. Joseph M. Juran pointed out years ago, this belief is incorrect. In fact, the potential to eliminate mistakes and errors lies mostly in improving the 'systems' through which work is done, not in changing the workers. This observation has evolved into the rule of thumb that at least 85% of problems can only be corrected by changing systems (which are largely determined by management) and less than 15% are under a worker's control—and the split may lean even more toward the system."

Source: "Tool #2 The Pareto Principle." Retrieved from www.managementthroughleadership.com.

be gained from involving employees in decision making and problem solving, as was shown in Chapter 8. There are also factors that, if not understood and properly handled, can lead to problems.

Advantages of Employee Involvement

Involving employees in decision making and problem solving can have a number of advantages. It can result in a more accurate picture of what the problem really is and a more comprehensive list of potential solution and decision alternatives. It can help managers do a better job of evaluating alternatives and selecting the best one to implement.

Perhaps the most important advantages are gained after the decision is made. Employees who participate in the decision-making or problem-solving process are more likely to understand and accept the decision or solution and have a personal stake in making sure the alternative selected succeeds.

Potential Problems with Employee Involvement

Involving employees in decision making and problem solving can lead to problems. The major potential problem is that it takes time, and managers do not always have time. Other potential difficulties are that it takes employees away from their jobs and that it can result in conflict among team members. Next to time, the most significant potential problem is that employee involvement can lead to democratic compromises that do not necessarily represent the best decision. In addition, disharmony can result when a decision maker rejects the advice of the group.

Nevertheless, if care is taken, managers can gain all of the advantages, while avoiding the potential disadvantages associated with employee involvement in decision making or problem solving. Several techniques are available to help increase the effectiveness of group involvement. Prominent among these are brainstorming, the nominal group technique (NGT), and the use of teams. Be particularly wary of the dangers of *groupthink* and *groupshift* in group decision making, as outlined in Chapter 8.

ROLE OF INFORMATION IN DECISION MAKING

Information is a critical element in decision making. Although having accurate, up-to-date, comprehensive information does not guarantee a good decision, lacking such information can guarantee a bad one. The old saying that "knowledge is power" applies in decision making—particularly in a competitive situation. To make decisions that will help their organizations to be competitive, managers need timely, accurate information.

> Information can be defined as data that are relevant to the decision-making process that have been converted into a useable format.

Data that are relevant to decision making are those that might have an impact on the decision. Communication is a process that requires a sender, a medium, and a receiver. In this process, information is what is provided by the sender, transmitted by the medium, and received by the receiver. For the purpose of this chapter, decision makers are receivers of information who base decisions at least in part on what they receive.

Advances in technology have ensured that the modern manager can have instant access to information. Computers and telecommunications technology give decision makers a mechanism for collecting, storing, processing, and communicating information quickly and easily. The quality of the information depends on people (or machines) receiving accurate data, entering them into technological systems, and updating them continually. This dependence on accurate information gave rise to the expression "garbage in/garbage out" that is now associated with computer-based information systems. The saying means that information provided by a computer-based system can be no better than the data put into the system.

Data versus Information

Data for one person may be information for another. The difference lies in the needs of the individual. Managers' needs are dictated by the types of decisions they make. For example, a computer printout listing speed and feed rates for a company's machine tools would contain valuable information for the production manager; the same printout would be just data to the warehouse manager. In deciding on the type of information they need, decision makers should ask themselves these questions:

- What are my responsibilities?
- What are my organizational goals?
- What types of decisions do I have to make relative to these responsibilities and goals?

Value of Information

Information is a useful commodity. As such, it has value. Its value is determined by the needs of the people who will use it and the extent to which the information will help them meet their needs. Information also has a cost. Because it must be

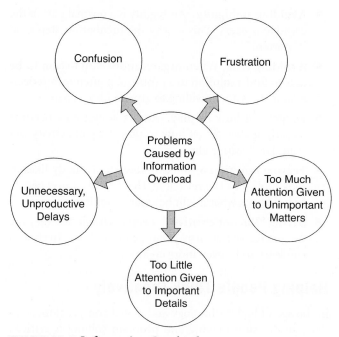

FIGURE 16–7 Information Overload

collected, stored, processed, continually updated, and presented in a useable format when needed, information can be expensive. This fact requires managers to weigh the value of information against its cost when deciding what information they need to make decisions. It makes no sense to spend $100 collecting the information to make a $10 decision.

Amount of Information

An old saying holds that a manager can't have too much information. This is no longer true. With advances in information technologies, not only can managers have too much information, but also they frequently do. This phenomenon has come to be known as *information overload*, the condition that exists when people receive more information than they can process in a timely manner. The phrase "in a timely manner" means in time to be useful in decision making (see Figure 16–7).

To avoid information overload, apply a few simple strategies. First, examine all regular reports received. Are they really necessary? Do you receive daily or weekly reports that would meet your needs just as well if provided on a monthly basis? Do you receive regular reports that would meet your needs better as exception reports? In other words, would you rather receive reports every day that say everything is all right or occasional reports when there is a problem? The latter approach is *reporting by exception* and can cut down significantly on the amount of information that managers must absorb.

Another strategy for avoiding information overload is formatting for efficiency. This involves working with personnel who provide information. If your organization has a management information systems (MIS) department or an information technology (IT) department, ensure that reports are formatted for your convenience rather than theirs (MIS will be discussed in the next section). Decision makers should not have to wade through reams of computer

printouts to locate the information they need. Nor should they have to become bleary-eyed reading rows and columns of tiny figures. Work with MIS personnel to develop an efficient report form that meets your needs. Also, have that information presented graphically whenever possible.

Finally, make use of online, on-demand information retrieval. In the modern workplace, most reports are computer generated. Rather than relying on periodic printed reports, learn to retrieve information from the MIS database when you need it (on demand) using a computer terminal or a networked personal computer (online).

USING MANAGEMENT INFORMATION SYSTEMS

The previous section contained references to management information systems (MIS) and MIS personnel. *Note:* For our purposes, consider MIS and IT to be interchangeable.

A management information system (MIS) is a system used to collect, store, process, and present information used by managers in decision making.

In the modern workplace, a management information system is typically a computer-based system. A management information system has three major components; hardware, software, and people. *Hardware* consists of the computer (be it a mainframe, mini-, or microcomputer), all of the peripheral devices for interaction with the computer, and output devices such as printers and display screens.

Software is the component that allows the computer to perform specific operations and process data. It consists primarily of computer programs but also includes the database, files, and manuals that explain operating procedures. *Systems software* controls the basic operation of the system. *Applications software* controls the processing of data for specific computer applications (word processing, databases, computer-assisted planning, spreadsheets, etc.).

A *database* is a broad collection of data from which specific information can be drawn. For example, a company might have a personnel database in which many different items of information about its employees are stored. From this database can be drawn a variety of different reports—such as printouts of all employees in order of employment date, by job classification, or by ZIP code. Data are kept in electronic files stored under specific groupings or file names.

The most important component is the people component. It consists of the people who manage, operate, maintain, and use the system. Managers who depend on a management information system for part of the information needed to make decisions are *users*.

Managers should not view a management information system as the final word in information. Such systems can do an outstanding job of providing information about predictable matters that are routine in nature. However, many of the decisions managers have to make concern problems that are unpredictable (or that simply have not been predicted) and for which data are not tracked. For this reason, it is important to have sources other than the management information system from which to draw information.

CREATIVITY IN DECISION MAKING

The pressures of a competitive marketplace are making it increasingly important for organizations to be flexible, innovative, and creative in decision making. To survive in an unsure, rapidly changing marketplace, organizations must be able to adjust rapidly and change directions quickly. To do so requires creativity at all levels of the organization.

Creativity Defined

Like leadership, creativity has many definitions, and viewpoints vary about whether creative people are born or made. In modern organizations, creativity can be viewed as an approach to problem solving and decision making that is imaginative, original, and innovative. Developing such perspectives requires that decision makers have knowledge and experience regarding the issue in question.

Creative Process

The creative process proceeds in stages: preparation, incubation, insight, and verification.[3] What takes place in each of these stages is summarized as follows:

- **Preparation** involves learning, gaining experience, and collecting or storing information in a given area. Creative decision making requires that the people involved be prepared.

- **Incubation** involves giving ideas time to develop, change, grow, and solidify. Ideas incubate while decision makers get away from the issue in question and give the mind time to sort things out. Incubation is often a function of the subconscious mind.

- **Insight** follows incubation. It is the point in time when a potential solution falls in place and becomes clear to decision makers. This point is sometimes seen as a moment of inspiration. However, inspiration rarely occurs without having been preceded by perspiration, preparation, and incubation.

- **Verification** involves reviewing the decision to determine whether it will actually work. At this point, traditional processes such as feasibility studies and cost-benefit analysis are used.

Factors That Inhibit Creativity

A number of factors can inhibit creativity. Some of the more prominent of these follow:[4]

- **Looking for just one right answer.** Seldom is there just one right solution to a problem.

- **Focusing too intently on being logical.** Creative solutions sometimes defy logic and conventional wisdom.

- **Avoiding ambiguity.** Ambiguity is a normal part of the creative process. This is why the incubation step is so important.

- **Avoiding risk.** When organizations don't seem to be able to find a solution to a problem, it often means decision makers are unwilling to give an idea a chance.

- **Forgetting how to play.** Adults sometimes become so serious they forget how to play. Playful activity can stimulate creative ideas.

- **Fearing rejection or looking foolish.** Nobody likes to look foolish or feel rejection. This fear can cause people to hold back what might be creative solutions.

- **Saying "I'm not creative."** People who decide they are uncreative will be. Any person can think creatively and can learn to be even more creative.

Helping People Think Creatively

In the age of high technology and global competition, creativity in decision making and problem solving is critical. Although it is true that some people are naturally more creative than others, it is also true that any person can learn to think creatively. In the modern workplace, the more people who think creatively, the better. The following strategies will help employees think creatively:[5]

- **Idea vending.** This is a facilitation strategy. It involves reviewing literature in the field in question and compiling files of ideas contained in the literature. Periodically, circulate these ideas among employees as a way to get people thinking. This will facilitate the development of new ideas by the employees. Such an approach is sometimes called *stirring the pot*.

- **Listening.** One of the factors that causes good ideas to fall by the wayside is poor listening. Managers who are perpetually too hurried to listen to employees' ideas do not promote creative thinking. On the contrary, such managers stifle creativity. In addition to listening to the ideas, good and bad, of employees, managers should listen to the problems employees discuss in the workplace. Each problem is grist for the creativity mill.

- **Idea attribution.** A manager can promote creative thinking by subtly feeding pieces of ideas to employees and encouraging them to develop the idea fully. When an employee develops a creative idea, he or she gets full attribution and recognition for the idea. Time may be required before this strategy pays off, but with patience and persistence it can help employees become creative thinkers.

How does a football team that is no better than its opponent beat that opponent? Often the key is more creative game planning, play calling, and defense. This phenomenon also occurs in the workplace every day. The organization that wins the competition in the marketplace is often the one that is the most creative in decision making and problem solving.

SUMMARY

1. *Decision making* is the process of selecting one course of action from among two or more alternatives. Decisions should be evaluated not just by results but also by the process used to make them.

2. A *problem* is a situation in which what exists does not match what is desired, or put another way, there is a discrepancy between the current state of affairs and the one desired. Problem solving in a total quality setting is not about putting out fires. It is about continual improvement. Two effective problem-solving models are the PDCA cycle and the Toyota Practical Problem-Solving Process.

3. Securing reliable information is an important part of problem solving and decision making. W. Edwards Deming recommends the use of the following tools: cause-and-effect diagrams, flowcharts, Pareto charts, run charts, histograms, control charts, and scatter diagrams.

4. The decision-making process is a logically sequenced series of activities through which decisions are made. These activities include identifying or anticipating the problem; gathering relevant facts; considering alternative solutions; choosing the best alternative; and implementing, monitoring, and adjusting. All approaches to decision making are objective, subjective, or a combination of the two.

5. Scientific decision making means making decisions based on data rather than on hunches. Complexity in scientific decision making means nonproductive, unnecessary work that results when organizations try to improve processes in a haphazard, nonscientific way. The different types of complexity include errors and defects, breakdowns and delays, inefficiency, and variation.

6. There are advantages and disadvantages to employee involvement. Techniques to enhance group decision making are brainstorming, NGT, and the use of teams. Managers should be prepared to counteract groupshift and groupthink.

7. *Information* is data that are relevant to the decision-making process and that have been converted into a useable format. Decision makers are receivers of information who base decisions in whole or in part on what they receive. Technological developments have introduced the potential for information overload, the condition that exists when people receive more information than they can process in a timely manner.

8. A management information system (MIS) is a system used to collect, store, process, and present information. Such a system has three components: hardware, software, and people. A management information system can do an outstanding job of providing information about predictable and routine matters. However, many decisions that managers have to make concern problems that are not predictable (or simply have not been predicted) and for which no data are tracked.

9. *Creativity* is an approach to problem solving and decision making that is imaginative, original, and innovative. The creative process proceeds in four stages: preparation, incubation, insight, and verification. Factors that inhibit creativity include looking for just one right answer, being too logical, avoiding ambiguity, avoiding risk, forgetting how to play, fearing rejection, and saying "I'm not creative." Three strategies for helping people think creatively are idea vending, listening, and idea attribution.

KEY TERMS AND CONCEPTS

Brainstorming

Cause-and-effect diagrams

Complexity

Control chart

Creativity

Decision making

Decision-making process

Deming Cycle

Existent problem

Five Why's

Flowchart

Groupshift

Groupthink

Histograms

Idea attribution

Idea vending

Incubation

Insight

Juran's 85/15 rule

Latent problem

Management by facts

Management information systems (MIS)

Nominal group technique (NGT)

Objective decision making

Pareto charts

PDCA cycle

Preparation

Preventing problems

Problem-solving team

Root cause

Run charts

Scatter diagrams

Subjective decision making

Toyota's Practical Problem-Solving Process

Variation

Verification

FACTUAL REVIEW QUESTIONS

1. Contrast decision making with problem solving.
2. Define *decision making* as it relates to total quality.
3. Explain how to evaluate decisions in a total quality environment.
4. Describe the PDCA cycle.
5. Describe the Toyota method for problem solving.
6. Name and describe three problem-solving tools.
7. Define the decision-making process and explain each step in it.
8. Contrast and compare objective and subjective decision making.
9. What is Juran's 85/15 rule? State the rule.
10. Describe the scientific approach to decision making and problem solving.
11. Explain four types of complexity in the scientific approach.
12. What are the advantages and disadvantages of employee involvement in decision making?
13. Explain three techniques for increasing the effectiveness of group involvement.
14. What is the role of information in decision making?
15. Explain *creativity* as a concept and the role it can play in decision making.

CRITICAL THINKING ACTIVITY

Using Data for Problem Solving

Rod Simmons is a civil service employee, managing a state Department of Motor Vehicles (DMV) office. The DMV office issues annual auto registrations, renews driver's licenses, and conducts driver examinations. The office is organized into departments, each with a supervisor reporting to Rod. The Vehicle Registration Department has eight clerks. The Motor Vehicle Operator License Department is staffed with four clerks and four examiners.

Rod has become increasingly concerned because documented taxpayer complaints directed at his office have been increasing over the past year. This has recently come to the attention of his superiors at the state capitol, who have begun putting pressure on him to stop the complaints—somehow. Rod is not sure at this point how to go about it. He knows that it would be better to look at the available data to try to find the cause, or causes, rather than just giving a "pep talk" to his employees. He starts by assembling the following:

- The office handles about 35,000 license or registration transactions annually.
- Workforce history:

Nine of the 12 clerks have been with the office for 5 years or more. Three were added during the last year.

Two of the examiners have over 5 years' tenure, while the other two have less than 1 year.

- Office work schedule and hours available:

Office hours are 8:00 a.m. until 5:00 p.m. with one hour for lunch, Monday through Friday.

Lunch hours are staggered for clerks and examiners, half from 11:00 a.m. until noon, and the other half from noon until 1:00 p.m. (By doing this, the office is open for business 9 hours per day.)

Clerk hours available/year: 23,000

Examiner hours available/year: 7,800

Supervisor hours available/year: 3,800

- Procedures:

A driver's license must be renewed every 3 years during the driver's birth month.

Vehicle registration must be renewed annually within the 12th month of the current registration.

- Total complaints last 2 years:

Month	Complaints This Year	Complaints Last Year
January	14	6
February	10	7
March	14	5
April	20	10
May	19	9
June	21	10
July	27	13
August	31	16
September	36	19
October	24	13
November	28	14
December	30	12
Totals	274	134

- Total taxpayer complaints by category for the current year:

Berating by examiners	21
Clerks ignoring customers (taxpayers)	35
Incompetence	33
Long waits in line	75
Rudeness	60
All others	50

If you were Rod, how would you use the problem-solving methods and tools covered in this chapter and Chapter 15 to highlight trends, determine how to proceed, and attempt to find root cause(s)?

DISCUSSION ASSIGNMENT 16–1

Why It is Important to Ask Why

The plant managers of ABC Corporation's five plants have met at a common location at 8:00 am every Monday morning for 20 years. The people serving as plant managers have changed several times during this period, but the meeting has not. Every Monday morning all five plant managers are seated around a conference table in the home office. It is not uncommon for the managers to have no pressing business to discuss and the meeting amounts to nothing more than a Monday morning coffee session. Not only is the meeting inconvenient, but it is also costly, time-consuming, and occasionally interferes with the work of the plant managers. Finally, one of the plant managers had had enough. He decided to conduct a cost-benefit analysis of the meeting. When he presented it at a meeting of the plant managers, ABC's CEO and the other plant managers were shocked to learn that the company could save $50,000 if the managers met only when there was pressing business to discuss.

DISCUSSION QUESTION

Discuss the following question in class or outside of class with your fellow students:
1. How does this case illustrate the need to constantly review the status quo and ask "Why?"?

DISCUSSION ASSIGNMENT 16–2

Defective Steel in a New Aircraft

New Piper, an aircraft manufacturer, issued a Mandatory Service Bulletin grounding 76 new aircraft manufactured during the first 5 months of 2004. Thirty-nine of the airplanes were in customers' hands, and the rest were at dealers or at the New Piper factory. The bulletin was issued after a production-line worker noted a bent seatbelt bracket in a new airplane. The defective bracket had been fabricated of high-strength steel that should have been very difficult to bend. Investigation revealed that the steel was insufficiently strong. New Piper traced the steel to a particular order and determined that a large number of other aircraft parts requiring the use of high-strength steel were manufactured from the same batch of steel. This signaled a flight-safety issue resulting in the grounding order and meant that New Piper must locate, remove, and replace all the affected parts in all the airplanes.

Grounding a fleet of airplanes is a costly move. New Piper had to absorb the cost of repairs, many of which were very difficult and, therefore, expensive. In addition, with half the airplanes scattered all over the globe, the manufacturer endured significant travel costs just getting to the planes. On the other hand, owners of the airplanes had to bear the cost of lost productive flight time while their planes remained grounded. The extent of damage to New Piper's reputation, along with customer loyalty and satisfaction, is unknown but could pose a blow to the company's future bottom line—all from a single order of high-strength steel.

It would be in the interest of all parties to find and eliminate the root cause of the problem. This information was known at the start of the investigation:

- New Piper purchased this batch of high-strength steel from its supplier, Wilco Inc. of Wichita, Kansas.
- Wilco sent the raw (untreated) sheet steel to Certified Steel Treating, a Los Angeles company, to be "normalized" in a process that heats the steel to specified temperatures and then cools it at a controlled rate to increase its strength.
- Then, as required for all normalized steel, it was sent to an independent lab for testing.
- The steel and its certifying paperwork (which was all in order) subsequently went to New Piper in Florida where it was used in the manufacture of critical aircraft parts.

DISCUSSION QUESTIONS

Using the information available here, apply the seven steps of Toyota's Practical Problem-Solving Process.
1. Describe the initial problem perception.
2. Clarify the problem and set an improvement objective.
3. Determine the most likely point of cause (POC).
4. Suggest a root cause.
5. Develop a plausible countermeasure.

ENDNOTES

1. "The Toyota Way." Retrieved from www.thetoyotaway.org/services/problem_solving.html on February 13, 2011.
2. Ibid., 255.
3. "Von Oech and the Creative Process." Retrieved from www.bemorecreative.com on February 20, 2011.
4. Ibid.
5. Min Basadur, "Leading Others to Think Innovatively Together: Creative Leadership." Retrieved from .www.train4creativity.en/B998534D.en.aspx on September 14, 2011.

QUALITY FUNCTION DEPLOYMENT

Because it is the customers who must buy the product and who must be satisfied with it, the product must be developed with their needs and wants as the principal inputs to the new product development project. When that is not the case, the new product is often disappointing.—**Ronald G. Day**

MAJOR TOPICS

- **What Is Quality Function Deployment?**
- **Introducing Quality Function Deployment's House of Quality**
- **Developing the Set of Customer Needs (WHATs): House of Quality Matrix Number 1**
- **Planning the Improvement Strategy: House of Quality Matrix Number 2**
- **Selecting the Technical Requirements (HOWs): House of Quality Matrix Number 3**
- **Evaluating Interrelationships between WHATs and HOWs: House of Quality Matrix Number 4**
- **Evaluating the Direction of Correlation between HOWs: House of Quality Matrix Number 5**
- **Selecting the Design Targets (Values) of the HOWs: House of Quality Matrix Number 6**

A consistent theme throughout this book and a fundamental element of total quality is customer-defined quality. Chapter 7 dealt with how organizations can establish a customer focus. Chapter 19 explains several different approaches for achieving continual improvement. A key element in each approach is customer involvement. Customer involvement is the fuel that powers Quality Function Deployment.

WHAT IS QUALITY FUNCTION DEPLOYMENT?

Quality function deployment (QFD) is a specialized method for making customer needs/wants important components of the design and production of the product or service. We advise you not to get hung up on the name of the process. There has been both a loss of meaning in the translation from Japanese to English, and an evolution in the QFD process which has morphed into something rather different

from that to which the name was first attached. However, the original English name, Quality Function Deployment, and its abbreviation QFD are apparently with us to stay, and we should have no difficulty with that.

Since QFD was first introduced in the West in the 1980s its history has been spotty. Should you search the internet for success stories you may find more detractors than proponents. The primary complaints seem to be:

- The Matrices are difficult to use and too time consuming for our new lean organizations.
- The math used to establish priorities lacks the precision necessary for a Six Sigma company.
- Questions regarding the validity of the math.
- Difficulty in obtaining a clear understanding of customer wants.

That being said, there are many organizations around the world that successfully use QFD, often in a tailored form that best fits their specific needs. The motivation to use it is logical—everyone would agree that it is preferable to design and manufacture a product that satisfactorily addresses the needs of prospective customers than one that doesn't. Further, in going through the QFD process, all the functional departments of the organization are involved from day one, and this is a primary objective of TQM. So we think there is a place for QFD in Total Quality, and this chapter is intended to acquaint you with the concepts and the basics of its process. Just be aware, should you decide to use QFD at some point, that it may not be appropriate for all cases, and that your particular application may have to be tailored to your specific circumstances. Quality Function Deployment is still evolving, and software is now available to make the process easier and more reliable.

One of the keys to achieving customer satisfaction and continual improvement is understanding your customer's needs and wants, and using them to guide the design and follow-on processes that create a product your customer will purchase and use. This was, and remains, the main focus of QFD. Developed by Japanese quality expert Dr. Yoji Akao

FIGURE 17–1 QFD's House of Quality

in 1966, QFD combined quality strategies with "function deployment" from the field of *Value Engineering*. In a sense, with QFD the customer—the potential user of the product—becomes part of the team that designs the product. It is a system that guides designers and planners to focus on the attributes of a product which are the most important to the customer. It involves:

1. Identifying customer needs known in QFD-speak as the "Voice of the Customer" (VOC).

2. Identifying the product attributes that will most satisfy the VOC.

3. Establishing product development and testing targets and priorities that will result in a product or service that satisfies the VOC.

One might think that all of this is rather obvious. Of course, any product should be designed to do something that customers want done. So, naturally, any company that develops a product or service must do all of these things already, right? It may seem to be common sense. Unfortunately, the list of new products coming into the market has a surprising rate of failure. Customers quickly reject products that do not satisfy their wants. The road to market is strewn with the likes of the Edsel automobile (1958), New Coke (1985), the smokeless cigarette (1988). These are some of the more noteworthy and costly (all over $1 billion) market flops, but countless other less-infamous offerings have crashed and burned because they were products that no one had asked for. This must mean that companies do not always ask for their customers' input, or they do not understand what their customers tell them, or that they simply don't do a good job of translating customer wants into product functions and attributes that will satisfy them. Over half a century General Motors went from the largest

corporation to bankruptcy by making it a virtual religion to ignore customer wants. Many others, large and small, have followed similar paths. The QFD requires that you obtain customer-want input and translate it into the set of product attributes most likely to satisfy the VOC, and can even follow through the processes of production and testing that best satisfies the customer wants. The QFD process involves the development and analysis of the set of matrices known as the "House of Quality" (HOQ) explained in this chapter.

INTRODUCING QUALITY FUNCTION DEPLOYMENT'S HOUSE OF QUALITY

The heart of QFD is the set of interrelated matrices known as the House of Quality (HOQ), so named because the complete matrix takes on the appearance of a house. Examining Figure 17–1 you will see that the HOQ is made up of six submatrices. The HOQ is utilized by a multifunctional QFD team (1) to take input requirements from the customers, and translate them into a set of customer needs, known in the QFD world as the "voice of the customer" (VOC) and (2) from the VOC, and some benchmarking with competing products, determine the prioritized features of a new (or improved) product or service that will best respond to the VOC.

The component matrices making up the HOQ are utilized in formal sequence from 1 through 6. In this chapter we will take you through the process using a relatively simple and fictitious project of improving a publishing company's marketing position for its textbooks.

DEVELOPING THE SET OF CUSTOMER NEEDS (WHATs): HOUSE OF QUALITY MATRIX NUMBER 1

Gathering Customer Needs Input

Our hypothetical company publishes a series of textbooks for the college market. The company is not happy with its current position in the market, and intends to rework its offerings with the objective of improving its market share. The company realizes that to do that, they must produce textbooks that potential customers will want. They plan to apply QFD to the publishing world.

The premise of QFD is that before any product or service is designed, the producer should have a good understanding of his potential customers' needs in order to improve the likelihood that the product or service will be a market success. That the producer should be aware of customer needs seems logical, but it sounds far easier than it is. Before the textbook rework is started, the QFD team must work diligently to determine what potential customers would like to see in terms of attributes and features of the product—and perhaps—what they don't like about our current product. How do we get that customer input? For any product category there are a number of ways, including focus groups, user groups, polling customers of existing similar products, surveys, questionnaires, customer service inputs, warranty activity, and in any other way the organization can think of. Any of these methods can take several weeks, and some will cost a lot of money.

Refining the Customer Needs Inputs

Once the cross-functional QFD team has assembled sufficient information on what characteristics, attributes and features customers say they need, the information must be distilled into something useful. Typically the problem is that the inputs invariably cover the spectrum from some really good ideas and nuggets of information to some that are trivial or frivolous, and the volume of information so great that the designers are unable to cope with it. The data must be sorted into a prioritized set of the most important customer needs. At this point we will call on some QFD Tools, the first of which is the *Affinity Diagram*. Refining a large collection of data into something that represents the essence of the VOC is done through the analysis techniques of the affinity diagram, and QFD team discussion.

Using the Affinity Diagram

Affinity diagrams are used to promote creative thinking. They can be very helpful in breaking down barriers created by past failures and in getting people to give up ingrained paradigms

---

---

that impede our ability to find new and different approaches. This is a critical element in achieving continual improvement. Affinity diagrams give structure to the creative process by organizing ideas in a way that allows them to be discussed, improved, and interacted with by all the participants. Affinity diagrams are used most appropriately when the following conditions exist:

- When the issue in question is so complex and/or the known facts so disorganized that people can't quite "get their arms around" the situation

- When it is necessary to shake up the thought processes, get past ingrained paradigms, and get rid of mental baggage relating to past solutions that failed

- When it is important to build a consensus for a proposed solution

Figure 17–2 is an affinity diagram developed by the publisher's QFD team. With it, the goal was to organize the

Issues Resulting in Poor Sales of Textbooks

Artwork Issues	Pedagogical Issues	Production Issues	Writing & Editing Issues
• Implausible examples • Color would help • Must be accurate • Simplistic figures	• No chapter objectives • No chapter summaries • Accuracy • Poor pedagogy	• Too expensive • Substandard binding strength • Choice of fonts for easier reading	• Writing style among co-authors inconsistent • Writing often difficult to understand • Paragraphs too long

FIGURE 17–2 Affinity Diagram: Issues Resulting in Poor Sales of Textbooks

customer input (both what they want that the publisher didn't offer, and what they did not like about the current books) to clarify the reasons the books were not selling well. The result will be a categorized list of the customers' issues which can then be reviewed and analyzed. Such affinity diagrams are developed through these steps:

1. A cross-functional team of employees is used. It may be the QFD team or another one specifically charged with developing the affinity diagram. Either way, teams typically have membership from all relevant functional departments (e.g., sales/marketing, design/engineering, production/manufacturing, quality, finance, materials/procurement, warehousing). Our team has participants from sales, marketing, production, editorial, and finance.

2. The issue to be discussed is stated without detailed explanation. Too much detail can inhibit creative thinking and throw up barriers that prejudice participants. In our case, the issue was stated as follows: "Why are our textbooks not selling better?"

3. Responses of participants, armed with customer input, are stated verbally and recorded on 3 × 5 cards—one idea per card. Care must be taken to use the actual words of the customers to avoid any inadvertent translation of ideas. Also, at this point there should be no judgmental comments about the ideas proposed. The goal is to solicit and record as many ideas as possible. Judgmental comments will inhibit the process.

4. The cards are spread on a large table, and participants are asked to group them. Cards with related ideas are grouped together. Cards that don't fit with any particular group are put together as a miscellaneous group.

5. Participants examine the cards in each group and try to find a descriptive word that contains the essence of the various cards in that group. This word or brief phrase is written on a card that is placed at the top of the group and becomes the heading for that group of ideas.

6. The information on the cards is replicated on paper with boxes around each group of ideas. Copies of the draft

affinity diagram are distributed to all participants for corrections, revisions, additions, or deletions. The finished diagram should resemble the one in Figure 17–2.

Using the Tree Diagram

The next tool to be used is the Tree Diagram. Tree diagrams can be used for countless purposes. It will be used here simply to refine the affinity diagram results to make the list the customer needs, or WHATs that will be placed in the HOQ. Although a tree diagram could go all the way down into the nuts and bolts of a new design, remember that the objective here is not to design the new product, but to list the items to be addressed by the design team once the entire HOQ is completed. Follow these steps:

1. Clearly identify the issue/problem to be solved. It can be taken from the affinity diagram, or it can be a problem that was identified through discussion of the affinity diagram. Write it on a card and place the card at the top of a large table.

2. Have the team conduct a brainstorming session in which participants record on 3 × 5 cards all possible tasks, methods, solutions, and activities relating to the affinity diagram issues. Continually repeat the following question: "To achieve this, what must happen first?" Continue this until all ideas have been exhausted.

3. Lay all the "what-must-happen" cards on the table below problem card. Put them in order based on what must happen first, working from top to bottom. As this task progresses, it may be necessary to add task cards that were overlooked during the brainstorming session.

4. Duplicate the table's layout of cards on a sheet of paper and distribute copies to all participants. Allow participants to revise and correct the document.

5. Figure 17–3 is a partial tree diagram that was developed to address the issues identified in Figure 17–2. We have deliberately oversimplified our tree diagram to keep the HOQ construction easier to follow. Notice that the

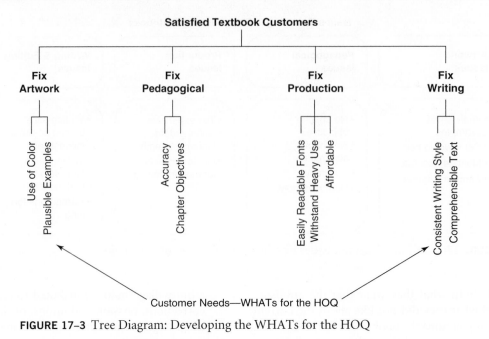

FIGURE 17–3 Tree Diagram: Developing the WHATs for the HOQ

team's choice of things that must happen to make our textbook artwork acceptable to customers includes the use of color in the artwork, and ensuring that examples are plausible. These two items represent the abbreviated customer needs with respect to our artwork issues.

In practice, the team reduces the total list of needs to those considered by the team to be the most significant. The final list of customer needs covering the complete set of issues may be as many as twenty or thirty, or a few as eight to ten, depending on the situation. These needs are *what* the customers would like to see in (or have corrected in) the product. They are *what* the company must address in order to produce a product that will find favor with customers. This list representing the VOC, is entered into the first HOQ matrix called *Customer Needs*, or *WHATs*. We illustrate this in Figure 17–4.

Note: The final customer needs should be nonlimiting and nonspecific in terms of solution and measurement to allow the team to consider without bias all possible approaches to meet the needs.

Customer Importance

Also coming out of the analysis is the team's best estimate of the relative importance of each listed customer need. Customer importance is usually based on a scale of 1 to 5 with 5 being the highest priority. This information is solicited from customer sources, but unanimity in ranking by the customers is unlikely, so the team has to do its best to evaluate and assign priorities as they believe the aggregate of customers would. These importance rankings are entered

FIGURE 17–4 Customer Needs (WHATs) and Customer Importance Applied to the HOQ

in the *Customer Importance* column to the right of the *Needs* entries, as shown in Figure 17–4.

PLANNING THE IMPROVEMENT STRATEGY: HOUSE OF QUALITY MATRIX NUMBER 2

Competitive Benchmarking

Next we must gather and analyze customer satisfaction data relative to our product and competing products, develop a planned satisfaction rating target for our forthcoming product, and calculate improvement factors and sales points.

First we are going to engage in some competitive benchmarking between our existing product and its competition. We are interested in customer satisfaction ratings of competing products because they will come into play in determining what we have to do to make our products more appealing than those of our competitors. In order to obtain that information, we might use a focus group to compare our product against its competition. We could also send questionnaires to customers who use competing products and to those who use ours. In both situations, participants will be asked to rate the products on each of the characteristics listed in the customer needs matrix, using the familiar 1 to 5 scale (5 being most favorable).

Our publisher collects this information for its own existing books, and for competing books of two prime competitors. The information is plotted on the planning matrix as shown in Figure 17–5.

Planned Customer Satisfaction Performance

Also plotted on the planning matrix will be the team's desired customer satisfaction performance for the new product for each of the customer needs. The same 1 to 5 scale is used. One might ask, why wouldn't the team desire the best rating (5) for every need? The reason the company has to back off perfection is money. The practical objective is to produce a textbook that will satisfy customers while not pricing itself out of the market. That is not to say that improvements should not be made if they can be done without putting the book out of reach of its prospective customers or making the book uncompetitive for cost reasons in the market. The publisher would like to be the competitive leader, but not necessarily the most expensive producer.

The team works out a target customer satisfaction goal for each of the customer needs. These are also plotted on Figure 17–5.

Improvement Factor

The team next calculates the improvement factor for each need for the new product. The equation for Improvement Factor with a 1 to 5 scale is:

$$\text{Improvement factor} = \{(\text{Planned CS Rating} - \text{Existing CS Rating})0.2\} + 1$$

where *CS* is *Customer Satisfaction*

For example, if a planned CS rating is a "4" and our CS rating for our existing product is a "3," then the Improvement

Customer Needs		CS Rating Our Textbooks	CS Rating Competitor A	CS Rating Competitor B	Our Planned CS Rating	Improvement Factor	Sales Point	Overall Weighting	% of Total Weight
Comprehensible text	5	4	5	4	5	1.2	1.1	6.6	13
Easily readable fonts	3	3	5	5	5	1.4	1.0	4.2	8
Accuracy	5	4	4	5	5	1.2	1.5	9.0	18
Plausible examples	3	2	3	4	4	1.4	1.2	5.0	10
Chapter objectives	3	2	4	2	4	1.4	1.3	5.5	11
Consistent writing style	2	4	3	4	4	1.0	1.0	2.0	4
Withstand heavy use	3	3	5	3	4	1.2	1.3	4.7	9
Affordable	4	1	2	2	3	1.4	1.5	8.4	16
Use of color	3	1	3	4	3	1.4	1.4	5.9	12

Customer Needs   Interrelationships   **Planning Matrix**

Customer Importance

(Note: CS is Customer Satisfaction)

FIGURE 17–5 Competitive Benchmark Data Applied to the HOQ

Factor is:

$$\{(4-3)\times 0.2\}+1=1.2$$

These data are also plotted in the Planning Matrix, as shown in Figure 17–5.

Sales Point   A strategic marketing factor, sometimes called a *Sales Point*, may also be placed in the Planning Matrix. Sales point is a number from 1 to 1.5 that is used to place emphasis on the customer needs. It is an estimate of the marketing importance of the need in the promotion of the new product, and is therefore used, along with customer importance and improvement factor, in the calculation for overall weighting of the customer needs. A sales point of 1 results in no change in the overall weighting, whereas a 1.5 sales point increases the overall weighting half again beyond that indicated by the customer importance of the need and its improvement factor. The team develops the sales point data, and places it in the planning matrix.

Overall Weighting   The team next calculates the overall weighting for the individual needs using the formula:

Overall Weighting = Customer Importance × Improvement Factor × Sales Point

For example, the Comprehensible Text need has a Customer Importance rating of 5, an Improvement Factor of 1.2, and a Sales Point of 1.1. Therefore, the overall weighting is:

$$5\times 1.2\times 1.6=9.6$$

The calculated overall weightings are entered into the planning matrix as shown on Figure 17–5.

Percentage of Total Weighting   Next, we convert the overall weightings to percentages in order to better understand how much of the design or improvement effort should be placed on each of the customer needs. The percentage of total weighting is calculated by the following equation:

% of Total Weighting = (Overall Weighting ÷ Sum of Overall Weightings) × 100

For example, the sum of the overall weightings in Figure 17–5 is 51.3. The Comprehensible Text need has an overall weighting of 6.6. Therefore, the percentage of overall weighting for the Comprehensible Text need is:

$$(6.6\div 51.3)\times 100=13$$

Percent data are entered in the final column of the planning matrix. See Figure 17–5.

From the planning matrix then, you can see that considering together *customer importance* (how critical is this need to the customer), *improvement factor* (how much of an improvement do we have to make in our product for this need), and *sales point* (importance of this need from the marketing point of view) leads to an *overall weighting* for the need. That in turn tells us through the *percent of total weighting* roughly how our resources need to be allocated across the total design or improvement project. For example, the need for *accuracy* has the highest overall weighting and percent of total weight. It is very important that the publisher achieves its *planned rating* of 5 for accuracy. Affordability comes in a close second, with comprehensibility of text third.

Before we move on to the next matrix, we want to leave you with a caution. We do not recommend that the company allocate the work of improving the product or service strictly or solely by these numbers. They are, after all is said and done, the result of a lot of opinion and estimating all the way from the customer, through the team's deliberations and discussions. The math is going to produce numbers accurately reflecting the various ratings and factors—but the source data for those numbers should not be considered to be absolutely accurate. Remember, it evolved from opinion and estimates. Our best advice is to consider it to be guidance rather than absolute. It seems to work well in most situations, but if the *customer needs* input is faulty, the organization can do the HOQ matrix work perfectly, deploy its resources in accordance with the matrices, and end up designing the wrong product that no one wants. Keep your sensors wide open for information that may warn you of problems.

SELECTING THE TECHNICAL REQUIREMENTS (HOWs): HOUSE OF QUALITY MATRIX NUMBER 3

The Technical Requirements room of the HOQ states *how* the company intends to respond to each of the *Customer Needs*. It is sometimes referred to as the *voice of the company*. We must state at the outset that the technical requirements are *not* the design specifications of the product or service. Rather, they are characteristics and features of a product that is perceived as meeting the customer needs. They are measurable in terms of satisfactory achievement. Some may be measured by weight, strength, speed, and so on. Others by a simple yes or no, for example a desired feature, appearance, test, or material is or is not incorporated. The other side of the coin is that the technical requirements must not be limiting, but must be flexible enough to allow the company to consider every creative possibility in its attempts to satisfy the need.

The technical requirements are generated by the QFD team through discussion and consultation with the *Customer Needs* and *Planning* matrices used as guidance. The team may use affinity or tree diagrams to develop, sort, and rank the requirements, similar to the Customer Needs development process. The difference here is that the input is from within the company rather than from external customers.

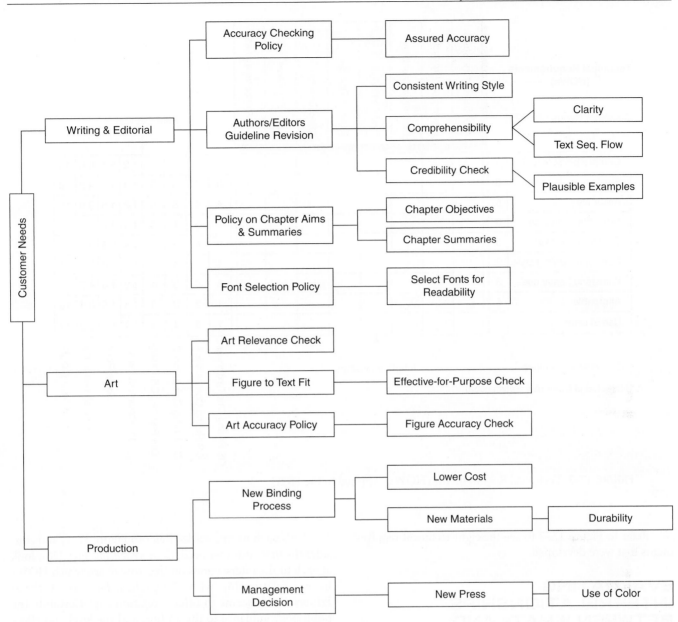

FIGURE 17–6 Tree Diagram for Developing Technical Requirements

The use of an affinity diagram or tree diagram will help the team focus on the textbook characteristics and features, procedures, and production processes likely to achieve the planned improvement. Our publisher's team developed the tree diagram of Figure 17–6. They categorized the diagram in three elements, listing the points considered most likely to produce customer acceptance. For example, under the first category, *Writing and Editorial,* cards for four issues are displayed:

- Accuracy checking policy
- Revision to the *Authors/Editors Guideline* manual
- Policy on Chapter Aims and Summaries
- Font Selection Policy

This is carried down through successive tree diagram nodes until the technical requirements are developed. For example, the *Authors/Editors Guideline Revision* node branches into a triple node consisting of relevant items to be addressed in the revised Guidelines:

- Consistent Writing Style
- Comprehensibility
- Credibility Check

This general tree development pattern is repeated for the remaining categories to form the list of items from which the Technical Requirements to be placed in the HOWs room of the HOQ are finally selected by the QFD team.

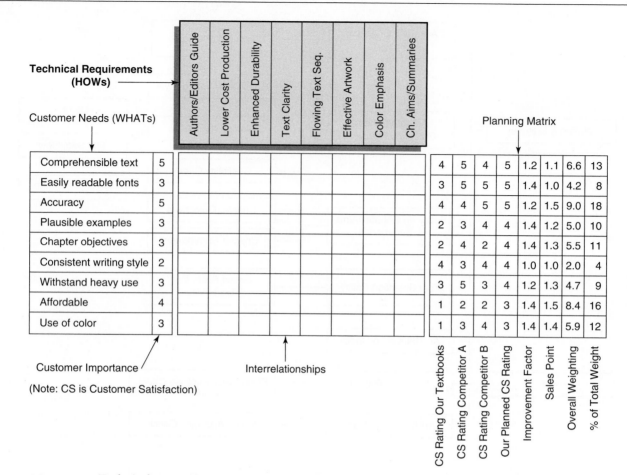

Technical Requirements (HOWs)

Customer Needs (WHATs)

Planning Matrix

Customer Needs (WHATs)	Customer Importance	Authors/Editors Guide	Lower Cost Production	Enhanced Durability	Text Clarity	Flowing Text Seq.	Effective Artwork	Color Emphasis	Ch. Aims/Summaries	CS Rating Our Textbooks	CS Rating Competitor A	CS Rating Competitor B	Our Planned CS Rating	Improvement Factor	Sales Point	Overall Weighting	% of Total Weight
Comprehensible text	5									4	5	4	5	1.2	1.1	6.6	13
Easily readable fonts	3									3	5	5	5	1.4	1.0	4.2	8
Accuracy	5									4	4	5	5	1.2	1.5	9.0	18
Plausible examples	3									2	3	4	4	1.4	1.2	5.0	10
Chapter objectives	3									2	4	2	4	1.4	1.3	5.5	11
Consistent writing style	2									4	3	4	4	1.0	1.0	2.0	4
Withstand heavy use	3									3	5	3	4	1.2	1.3	4.7	9
Affordable	4									1	2	2	3	1.4	1.5	8.4	16
Use of color	3									1	3	4	3	1.4	1.4	5.9	12

Customer Importance

Interrelationships

(Note: CS is Customer Satisfaction)

FIGURE 17–7 Technical Requirements (HOWs) Applied to the HOQ

Refer to Figure 17–7 to see the eight technical requirements that were developed.

EVALUATING INTERRELATIONSHIPS BETWEEN WHATs AND HOWs: HOUSE OF QUALITY MATRIX NUMBER 4

Now that we have the QFD team's technical requirements (HOWs) in the HOQ, the next step is to examine how they relate to the WHATs of the Customer Needs. The results will be shown in the *Interrelationships* matrix, which links the HOWs and the WHATs. At each intersection cell of the inter-relationship matrix the team must assess the degree of relationship between the WHAT and the corresponding HOW. This is usually done using scales of significance of 1 to 5 or 1 to 9, with the higher number indicating a stronger relationship. Sometimes these numbers are entered, but often symbols are used. For our example we will use symbols as follows:

◎ = 9 (strongest relationship)

○ = 3 (medium relationship)

△ = 1 (weak relationship)

Blank cell indicates No relationship

Let's see how this works. Refer to Figure 17–7, and consider the first customer need, *Comprehensible text*. Now look at each of the intersections on that row to see which HOWs have a relationship with *Comprehensible text*. *Authors/Editors Guide* seems to offer a relationship. Certainly the publisher's guidance to the author, and the level and effectiveness of the editing process will impact the quality and comprehensibility of the text. We have identified an inter-relationship, but how strong is it? The team has to decide, and the result may not be very exact, but rather is a well-discussed estimate. Let's say that the strength is *high*. We should enter either a "9" or the double-circle symbol in that cell. The next *Comprehensible Text* relationship cell appears to be under *Text Clarity*. The interrelationship between this WHAT and HOW is strong, so a 9 or the double-circle symbol is entered. All cells must be checked for interrelationships, and when such exists, the strength of the relationship must be evaluated.

As we have mentioned, either numbers or symbols may be used. If you use numbers, use only 1, 3, and 5 or 1, 3, and 9 rather than 1, 2, 3, 4, 5, and so on. Remember, we are only estimating the interrelationship's strength: Is it strong, medium, weak, or nonexistent? There is little to be gained by trying to be precise in an area where the result is a best guess or an estimate.

FIGURE 17–8 Interrelationships between WHATs and HOWs

There is a rule of thumb in QFD that only about 15% of the interrelationship cells will show a relationship between WHATs and HOWs. So don't be concerned when your matrix appears a bit empty. There is, however, one firm rule with the interrelationship matrix—*every row and every column must have at least one entry.* An empty *column* means that the HOW (a technical requirement) is not delivering value to the customer-needs. For example, if Figure 17–8 had a technical requirement to make the books smaller we would find that it does not relate to any of the figure's customer needs, and the column would be empty. To expend any effort to reduce the book's size would be a waste of resources since the customers will not find value in a smaller book. On the other hand, a horizontal *row* with all cells blank indicates that the WHAT (a customer need) is not being addressed. For example, if Figure 17–8 showed a customer need for an e-book version for an electronic book reader, that row would have no cell entry because that need is not addressed by any of the technical requirements. Just remember that all the listed customer needs must be addressed in the technical requirements, and any technical requirement that does not address a customer need probably shouldn't be there. Figure 17–8 shows the Interrelationship matrix completed.

EVALUATING THE DIRECTION OF CORRELATION BETWEEN HOWs: HOUSE OF QUALITY MATRIX NUMBER 5

As a product or service is being designed there will inevitably be some technical requirements that tend to benefit one another and some that tend to work against one another. Those that benefit each other are said to have a supportive or positive correlation. Those working against each other have an impeding, or negative correlation. It is always helpful to know what kind of correlation exists in order to take advantage of the supportive correlations, and to contrive trade-offs for those that impede. Failure to know this may result in a product that does not meet requirements, or one that requires expensive redesign in order to conform to customer requirements. Getting it right the first time is the purpose of the Correlation Matrix or Roof of the HOQ. One might say that getting it right the first time is the purpose of the entire QFD process.

The correlation matrix is constructed by drawing a triangle (looking like a roof) over the Technical Requirements section of the HOQ. Refer to Figure 17–9. Intersecting diagonal columns are drawn within the triangle from the top of each technical requirement column. Next the correlation

**Correlation Matrix
HOQ's Roof**

**Type of Correlation
+ = Supportive
− = Impeding**

Technical Requirements
(HOWs)

Customer Needs

Planning Matrix

Customer Needs		Authors/Editors Guide	Lower Cost Production	Enhanced Durability	Text Clarity	Flowing Text Seq.	Effective Artwork	Color Emphasis	Ch. Aims/Summaries		CS Rating Our Textbooks	CS Rating Competitor A	CS Rating Competitor B	Our Planned CS Rating	Improvement Factor	Sales Point	Overall Weighting	% of Total Weight
Comprehensible text	5	◎			◎	○					4	5	4	5	1.2	1.1	6.6	13
Easily readable fonts	3				△						3	5	5	5	1.4	1.0	4.2	8
Accuracy	5	◎					△				4	4	5	5	1.2	1.5	9.0	18
Plausible examples	3	◎									2	3	4	4	1.4	1.2	5.0	10
Chapter objectives	3								◎		2	4	2	4	1.4	1.3	5.5	11
Consistent writing style	2	○									4	3	4	4	1.0	1.0	2.0	4
Withstand heavy use	3			◎							3	5	3	4	1.2	1.3	4.7	9
Affordable	4		◎								1	2	2	3	1.4	1.5	8.4	16
Use of color	3							◎			1	3	4	3	1.4	1.4	5.9	12

Customer Importance

Interrelationships

Note: CS is Customer Satisfaction

◎ = 9 (high)
○ = 3 (medium)
△ = 1 (weak)

FIGURE 17–9 HOQ's Roof

type, whether *supportive, impeding,* or having *no correlation* is determined for each of the technical requirements against all other technical requirements. A supportive correlation is indicated by a plus sign (+) at the intersecting columns of the two technical requirements under consideration. A negative correlation is indicated by the use of the minus sign (−). If there appears to be no significant correlation, that intersection cell is left blank. Should it be beneficial, the *Supportive* and *Impeding* classifications may be expanded to *Strongly Supportive, Supportive, Impeding* and *Strongly Impeding.*

In practice, the QFD team asks some variation of this question, "Does improving this technical requirement result in the other's improvement, or does it result in degradation of the other?" If neither improvement nor degradation is indicated, there is apparently no correlation between the two.

In our example, the QFD team will first ask the question, "Will employing a better *Authors/Editors Guide* support or impede *Lower Cost Production*?" It might impede lower cost production if the new-and-improved Guide significantly increased the work for the authors and editors, but the team doesn't think that will be so, so the intersection cell for those two columns is left blank. Next, the team will look for correlation between *Authors/Editors Guide* and the technical requirement for *Enhanced Durability.* Clearly there is no correlation there. The next correlation check is between *Authors/Editors Guide* and the technical requirement for *Text Clarity.* The better the guide, the better the text clarity should be, so this represents a supportive correlation. A plus sign will be placed in the intersecting cell of the technical requirements of *Authors/Editors Guide* and *Text Clarity.* There are four more correlation checks for the *Authors/Editors Guide* technical requirement, and all turn out to be supportive. Next, we will examine the possible remaining correlations for the *Low Cost Production* requirement. The first will be with *Enhanced Durability*. In this case the correlation is impeding, because making the product more durable would be expected to directly increase the cost of production, not lower it. The intersecting cell will get a minus sign. This means that during the design process, either some tradeoffs must be made between the needs for *lower cost* and *enhanced durability*, or better yet, that some process must be discovered to improve the book's durability while holding or reducing cost. This examination is repeated for all remaining correlation cells, and the correlation matrix you see in Figure 17–9 is complete.

For an HOQ with eight technical requirements such as our example, there are 28 possible correlations. Adding one more technical requirement expands that number to 36, adding two more results in 45, and so on. Real world HOQ diagrams are often much larger than ours, suggesting that a lot of time and effort must be expended before the team has it completed. The bigger and more complex they become, however, the greater the need for the power of the HOQ. The HOQ's information presentation makes it easier to work through complex situations with assurance that all important factors have been considered and evaluated. That should make it much more likely that our new product will be successful with our customers.

SELECTING THE DESIGN TARGETS (VALUES) OF THE HOWS: HOUSE OF QUALITY MATRIX NUMBER 6

The HOQ is almost complete, needing only a final section called *Design Targets*. If the *customer requirements* describe WHAT the customer needs, and the *design requirements* tell HOW the company is going provide the product characteristics necessary to address those needs, then the *design targets* specify HOW MUCH of the characteristic needs to be provided. For example, in our HOQ the customer has said he wants our books to withstand heavy use without having the binding fall apart. In our design requirements we said we needed to enhance the binding's durability. Now in the *Design Targets* matrix we need to determine HOW MUCH more durable the binding must be. That will be determined by the data that we have already entered into the HOQ, along with data from benchmarking and testing as required. This section summarizes the conclusions of the QFD process and translates them into product specifications.

The Design Targets section is completed in three sections:

- Technical Priorities (from data already in the HOQ)
- Technical Benchmarking (newly developed data)
- Design Target Values (developed from the previous two)

Technical Priorities

To determine the relative importance, or priorities, of each of the stated *Technical Requirements* (HOWs) in meeting the *Customer Needs* (WANTs), the QFD team simply multiplies each of the interrelationship ratings of the technical requirement (0, 1, 3, or 9) from the *Interrelationship* matrix, times the corresponding customer need's *Overall Weighting* value in the *Planning* matrix; and then sums the columns. All of the data for these calculations are already in the HOQ of Figure 17–9. Starting with the technical requirement for a new and responsive set of *Authoring/Editing Guidelines*, we find that its relationship to the customer need for a *Comprehensible Text* was indicated in the *Interrelationship* matrix as a 9. Looking across the row to the *Overall Weighting* column of the *Planning* matrix we find a value of 6.6. Multiplying them gives us a value of 59.4

There are three more Interrelationship values for the *Authors/Editors Guide* technical requirement, so a total of four multiplications must be done and then summed.

For the *Comprehensible Text* need	$9 \times 6.6 = 59.4$
For the *Accuracy need*,	$9 \times 9 = 81.0$
For the *Plausible Examples* need,	$9 \times 5 = 45.0$
For the *Consistent Writing Style* need,	$3 \times 2 = 6.0$
Authors/Editors Guide Technical Priority	$= 191.4$

The value of 191.4 is entered in the *Technical Priorities* row of the *Technical Targets* matrix under the column for the *Authors/Editors Guide*. See Figure 17–10. The technical priorities row is completed by repeating the process for each of the other *Technical Requirements*.

The meaning of the resulting technical priorities numbers like 191.4 and 42.3 does not jump out at you like a percentage does. For that reason, some QFD users translate the priority values into a percentage scale. This is done, of course, by dividing the individual technical priority values by the sum of all the priority values, and multiplying by 100.

$$\% \text{ total priority} = (\text{Technical Requirement Priority} \div \Sigma \text{ Technical Priorities}) \times 100$$

In the case of the Authors/Editors Guide technical requirement,

$$\% \text{ of total priority} = [191.4 \div (191.4 + 75.6 + 42.3 + 63.6 + 19.8 + 9 + 53.1 + 49.5)] \times 100$$
$$= (191.4 \div 504.3) \times 100$$
$$= 38$$

The rest of the *% of Total Priority* values are calculated, and placed in a row just below the Technical Priorities. See Figure 17–10. Except for small errors for rounding, the row's sum should equal 100.

With 38% of the total priorities, and with the next highest at 15%, and decreasing from there, that means that in meeting the customer's needs, the new *Authors/Editors Guide* is by far the most important technical requirement. That this technical requirement has a much higher percent

Technical Requirements (HOWs)

Interrelationships

Customer Importance

Customer Needs (WHATs)

Legend:
- ◎ = 9 (high)
- ○ = 3 (medium)
- △ = 1 (weak)

Planning Matrix

Customer Needs (WHATs)	Imp.	Authors/Editors Guide	Lower Cost Production	Enhanced Durability	Text Clarity	Flowing Text Seq.	Effective Artwork	Color Emphasis	Ch. Aims/Summaries	CS Rating Our Textbooks	CS Rating Competitor A	CS Rating Competitor B	Our Planned CS Rating	Improvement Factor	Sales Point	Overall Weighting	% of Total Weight
Comprehensible text	5	◎			◎	○				4	5	4	5	1.2	1.1	6.6	13
Easily readable fonts	3				△					3	5	5	5	1.4	1.0	4.2	8
Accuracy	5	◎					△			4	4	5	5	1.2	1.5	9.0	18
Plausible examples	3	◎								2	3	4	4	1.4	1.2	5.0	10
Chapter objectives	3								◎	2	4	2	4	1.4	1.3	5.5	11
Consistent writing style	2	○								4	3	4	4	1.0	1.0	2.0	4
Withstand heavy use	3			◎						3	5	3	4	1.2	1.3	4.7	9
Affordable	4		◎							1	2	2	3	1.4	1.5	8.4	16
Use of color	3							◎		1	3	4	3	1.4	1.4	5.9	12
Technical Priorities		191.4	75.6	42.3	63.6	19.8	9	53.1	49.5								
% of Total Priorities		38	15	8	13	4	2	11	10								
Technical Benchmark: Our Product		5	$40	1.1	7	No	7	0%	No								
Technical Benchmark: Competitor A		6	$34	1.5	10	Yes	7	15%	Yes								
Technical Benchmark: Competitor B		7	$34	1.2	9	No	9	25%	No								
Design Targets		8	$30	1.4	10	Yes	9	15%	Yes								

Design Targets Matrix

(Note: CS is Customer Satisfaction)

FIGURE 17–10 HOQ's Adding the Design Targets Matrix

of total priorities than the others seems reasonable since it impacts four customer needs while the others only relate directly to one or two. This information is used by the organization as guidance for the appropriate deployment of limited resources for the project.

Technical Benchmarking

The next section of the Design Targets matrix involves comparing the organization's *intended* product with competing products, in our case from same competitors A and B that we used in the *Planning* Matrix. In *HOQ Matrix 3* the team identified the technical requirements—how they plan to meet the customer needs. The *Technical Benchmarking* section is intended to provide specific information on where the organization's current product (assuming there is one) stands relative to competing products, with respect to each of the *technical requirements*. The source of information for the competing products may come from customers, focus groups, the press, by actual testing and measurement of those products, and so on. Usually it is dredged from a combination of all possible sources. The team starts by gathering the data on its own existing product for each of the technical requirements.

Authoring/Editing Guidelines. This proposed new set of guidelines is intended to respond to several elements where the publisher's books are a bit weak: namely comprehensibility of text, accuracy, plausible examples, and consistent writing style. The team grades those elements for the publisher's current books, and sets the overall score at 5 on a 1 to 10 scale, with 10 being best.

Lower Cost Production. This one is easy. What does the book cost to produce? The answer on average for the current books is $40, so that is the score.

Enhanced Durability. The publisher's books have had a tendency to come apart more often than its competitors do. Testing suggests that the binding process and the materials used could be better. Destructive testing yields a relative strength (the ratio of pull strength to binding stress) of 1.1 for current products.

Text Clarity. This is related to two customer needs: comprehensible text and easily readable fonts. Upon evaluation the team assigned a 1 to 10 based score of 7 for the current books.

Flowing Text Sequence. In this case, rather than trying to determine a score, the team used a YES-NO system. If the text seemed to flow in a logical, orderly sequence it was graded YES. If the flow jumped back and forth from subject to subject, it was given a NO. The publisher's books tended toward the latter, and got the NO.

Effective Artwork. The purpose of artwork, that is the figures, drawings, and illustrations, is to clarify and illuminate the text. The team used a 1 to 10 scale to grade how effectively the books' artwork accomplished those goals. They gave the current versions a 7.

Color Emphasis. Color can be used not only in the artwork, but also in the text to make something more interesting, eye-catching, and hopefully more memorable. The team concluded that a telling rating would be the percentage of pages having color. It was easy to grade the publisher's current books because no color was used except on the covers. Score 0%.

Chapter Aims and Summaries. This is another YES-NO category. A book either uses them or it does not. The current books mostly did not, so they got a NO score.

These scores were entered in the *Our Product* row of the *Technical Benchmark* section. See Figure 17–10.

Next, the same data were developed by the team for the books of competitors A and B. You will find that data in the next two rows of Figure 17–10's Technical Benchmark section. The data shows that this publisher's books come off second or third-best of the three. Good reason for low market share, the issue that prompted the company to get involved with QFD in the first place.

If you compare these ratings with those of the planning matrix, you should notice that the rankings of this publisher's books versus those of its competitors are very much in agreement. If that does not turn out to be the case, then something is wrong, and should be discovered before proceeding. Was the customer understood correctly? Was the data reliable? Have we put our emphasis on the wrong thing?

Design Targets

The objective of the design targets is to establish specific objectives for the design team. For example, the QFD team determined that through the application of, and adherence to an improved set of guidelines for all the people involved in authoring and editing the books, increasing the score to an eight would better the competition, and should be possible. Similarly, setting a target of $30 per book (on average) for production cost will beat the competition by $4 per book. However, that represents a 25% reduction from the present situation, and the publisher is also asking to markedly improve the durability of its books. This is the kind of situation where one must consider a radical change that can

achieve both goals, and that is what the QFD team is counting on. They expect a complete change in the materials and processes used in binding the books.

A measurement of book durability is relative strength. That is the ratio of pull strength divided by binding stress. The publisher's current products have a relative strength of 1.1, while the competitors A and B score 1.5 (much better) and 1.2 (somewhat better). By investing enough, the publisher can equal Competitor A's 1.5, but is that necessary? Competitor B's books have a relative strength of 1.2, and the books seem quite durable. This becomes a tradeoff. The publisher can switch its current binding process to new modern processes and materials making the bindings more robust than most customers would ever need, or the company can scale the improvement back a bit in the interest of economy, and still have adequate durability while simultaneously achieving lower production costs. The QFD team sets the target at 1.4.

Our books scored 7 out of a possible 10 for clarity of text, against the competitors' scores of 10 and 9. The QFD team sets the design target value at 10—there is no reason to publish anything lacking clarity, and the competition proves it.

In similar fashion, the team sets *YES* for the design objective for text sequence flow. If the authors can't manage it, the editors must.

The design goal for having artwork that is effective in clarifying and illuminating the text was elevated from the current level of 7 to a 9, the same as leading Competitor B. The target for color emphasis was set at having 15% of the pages with some use of color. That is much less than Competitor B, but in line with the customer's needs. And finally, the team determined that the publisher must include chapter aims or objectives and chapter summaries in its books. This is indicated as a *YES*. See Figure 17–10 for all the inputs to the Design Targets matrix.

At this point the HOQ is complete. See Figure 17–11. What happens next? That depends on the situation. HOQ is often used at this level to guide all departments in their efforts to design and produce the product. The HOQ will help the organization ensure that all aspects of the product's design adheres to the customer's needs, that extraneous bells and whistles are prevented, and that all relevant activities of the company are involved and participating.

In some cases, depending on the application, an HOQ like the one we have just developed will be just the starting point, with lower level HOQs being developed for the various organizational functions. For example, subordinate HOQs may be utilized for the actual design of the product, procurement of parts and materials, gearing up to manufacture the product, and so on. It is important to understand that QFD is appropriate for services as well as for tangible products. Our development of an HOQ involved a tangible product, but we could as easily have addressed the improvement or development of a service instead. Our objective here has been to acquaint you with the purpose of QFD, and its language, layout, processes, and functions.

**Correlation Matrix
HOQ's Roof**

**Type of Correlation
+ = Supportive
− = Impeding**

Technical Requirements
(HOWs)

◎ = 9 (high)
○ = 3 (medium)
△ = 1 (weak)

Interrelationships

Customer Importance

Customer Needs

Planning Matrix

Customer Needs		Authors/Editors Guide	Lower Cost Production	Enhanced Durability	Text Clarity	Flowing Text Sequence	Effective Artwork	Color Emphasis	Ch. Aims/Summaries		CS Rating Our Textbooks	CS Rating Competitor A	CS Rating Competitor B	Our Planned CS Rating	Improvement Factor	Sales Point	Overall Weighting	% of Total Weight
Comprehensible text	5	◎			◎	○					4	5	4	5	1.2	1.1	6.6	13
Easily readable fonts	3				△						3	5	5	5	1.4	1.0	4.2	8
Accuracy	5	◎					△				4	4	5	5	1.2	1.5	9.0	18
Plausible examples	3	◎									2	3	4	4	1.4	1.2	5.0	10
Chapter objectives	3								◎		2	4	2	4	1.4	1.3	5.5	11
Consistent writing style	2	○									4	3	4	4	1.0	1.0	2.0	4
Withstand heavy use	3			◎							3	5	3	4	1.2	1.3	4.7	9
Affordable	4		◎								1	2	2	3	1.4	1.5	8.4	16
Use of color	3							◎			1	3	4	3	1.4	1.4	5.9	12

Technical Priorities		191.4	75.6	42.3	63.6	19.8	9	53.1	49.5
% of Total Priorities		38	15	8	13	4	2	11	10
Technical Benchmark	Our Product	5	$40	1.1	7	No	7	0%	No
	Competitor A	6	$34	1.5	10	Yes	7	15%	Yes
	Competitor B	7	$34	1.2	9	No	9	25%	No
Design Targets		8	$30	1.4	10	Yes	9	15%	Yes

Design Targets Matrix

(Note: CS is Customer Satisfaction)

FIGURE 17–11 The Completed HOQ

SUMMARY

1. Quality Function Deployment (QFD) is an approach to product/service design and continual improvement that brings customers into the design process. It is used to translate what the customer wants into what the organization produces.

2. QFD was originally developed by Dr. Yoji Akao in 1966, combining quality strategies with features of value engineering.

3. QFD requires the involvement of all functional departments of the organization at the start of, and throughout the project. This is also a primary objective of TQM.

4. There are many examples of products being brought to market only to be rejected because they did not satisfy customer wants/needs. An objective of QFD is to avoid that fiasco.

5. The House of Quality (HOQ) employs six attached submatrices.

6. QFD requires the organization to collect and analyze inputs from customers regarding attributes they would like in a product.

7. Some tools used in QFD include affinity diagrams and tree diagrams.

8. QFD requires competitive benchmarking to compare customer satisfaction with the company's *current* prod-

uct versus competing products, and technical benchmarking comparing how the *intended* product will rate against that competition.

9. A QFD rule of thumb is that only about 15% of the Interrelationship matrix cells will be filled.

10. A QFD rule requires that all interrelationship rows and columns must have at least one entry.

11. The Correlation Matrix (roof) indicates which technical requirements support another, which impede another, and which do neither.

12. *Customer Needs* define *what* the customers want, *Technical Requirements* define *how* the organization plans to provide the product characteristics the customers need, and *Design Targets* define *how much* of the characteristics must be provided.

KEY TERMS AND CONCEPTS

Affinity Diagram

Competitive Benchmarking

Correlation Matrix

Cross-Functional QFD Team

Customer Importance

Customer Needs (WHATs)

Design Targets

House of Quality (HOQ)

Impeding Correlation

Improvement Factor

Interrelationships

Planning Matrix

Quality Function Deployment (QFD)

Sales Point

Supportive Correlation

Technical Benchmarking

Technical Priorities

Technical Requirements (HOWs)

Tree Diagram

Value Engineering

Voice of the Customer (VOC)

FACTUAL REVIEW QUESTIONS

1. Define Quality Function Deployment.

2. Describe the basic structure of the QFD House of Quality.

3. Explain the rationale for QFD.

4. List the principle benefits of QFD.

5. Explain the need for the QFD team to be cross-functional.

6. Describe the function of an affinity diagram as used in QFD.

7. Describe the function of the Sales Point.

8. Explain why it is not advantageous to use more precise rating/ranking scales.

9. Describe the function of the HOQ's roof.

10. Describe the fundamental purpose of the Design Targets.

CRITICAL THINKING ACTIVITY

Customer Demands versus Organizational Capabilities

"I don't know why we keep collecting all this customer input and feedback. It's clear they want a better product than our processes can produce," said Derrick Kramer, CEO of Ronkel Inc.

"That's true," said Linda Carver, Ronkel's director of quality. "But we are going to lose our customers if we don't improve our processes. We need to do more than collect customer feedback. We need to use it to keep our processes up-to-date."

Clearly, Ronkel needs to translate customer demands into process improvements. Explain how QFD could be used to help this company. How should Kramer and Carver proceed if they choose to apply QFD?

OPTIMIZING AND CONTROLLING PROCESSES THROUGH STATISTICAL PROCESS CONTROL

In the middle of difficulty lies opportunity.—**Albert Einstein**

MAJOR TOPICS

- Statistical Process Control Defined
- Rationale for SPC
- Control Chart Development
- Management's Role in SPC
- Role of the Total Quality Tools
- Authority over Processes and Production
- Implementation and Deployment of SPC
- Inhibitors of SPC

The origin of what is now called statistical process control (SPC) dates back to 1931 and Dr. Walter Shewhart's book *The Economic Control of Quality of Manufactured Product.* Shewhart, a Bell Laboratories statistician, was the first to recognize that industrial processes themselves could yield data, which, through the use of statistical methods, could signal that the process was in control or was being affected by special causes (causes beyond the natural, predictable variation). The control charts used today are based on Shewhart's work. These control charts are the very heart of SPC. What may not be as obvious is that Shewhart's work became the catalyst for the quality revolution in Japan[1] and the entire movement now called total quality. We tend to look at SPC as one piece of the whole total quality picture, and it is, but it is also the genesis of total quality.

Since the first edition of this book was written in 1993, two very significant things have occurred in the SPC field. First, many organizations have adopted SPC as a preferred way of controlling manufacturing processes. Much of this has come about as a result of the quality quest by first-tier companies, making it necessary to require that their second-tier suppliers practice SPC.

We have seen this ripple down to at least the fourth tier. Nowhere is this more evident than in the auto industry. But even beyond the mandate by corporate customers, more and more small companies are using SPC as part of their quality and competitiveness initiatives.

The second big change we have seen is that SPC users have backed away from the shotgun approach, where every process, no matter how trivial or foolproof, had to have SPC charts. Several years ago we visited a North American semiconductor plant and were overwhelmed by the sheer numbers of SPC charts. Everywhere you looked you saw control charts. The plant proudly admitted to having over 900 processes under control charts. When we visited the same plant a couple of years later, the picture was very different. You could still find control charts, but only where they offered real benefit. The company had discovered that about 800 of its original charts had not been worthwhile. Control charts were being used with those processes that needed them, and no more. It is evident that this is the current thinking in industry. Don't waste time, energy, and money with more control charts than you need. In those process applications where you do need them, the control chart is invaluable. For all the rest, it is just window dressing. The important thing is to know the difference.

STATISTICAL PROCESS CONTROL DEFINED

Although SPC is normally thought of in industrial applications, it can be applied to virtually any process. Everything done in the workplace is a process. All processes are affected by multiple factors. For example, in the workplace a process can be affected by the environment and the machines employed, the materials used, the methods (work instructions) provided, the measurements taken, and the manpower (people) who operate the process—the Five M's. If these are the only factors that can affect the process output, and if all of these are perfect—meaning the work environment facilitates quality work; there are no misadjustments in the machines; there are no flaws in the materials; and there are totally accurate and precisely followed work instructions, accurate and repeatable measurements, and people who work with extreme care, following the work instructions perfectly and concentrating fully on their work—and if all of these factors come into congruence, then the process will be in statistical control. This means that there are no special causes adversely affecting the process's output. Special causes are (for the time being, anyway) eliminated. Does that mean that 100% of the output will be perfect? No, it does not. Natural variation is inherent in any process, and it will affect the output. Natural variation is expected to account for roughly 2,700 out-of-limits parts in every 1 million produced by a 3-sigma process ($\pm 3\sigma$ variation), 63 out-of-limits parts in every 1 million produced by a 4-sigma process, and so on. Natural variation, if all else remains stable, will account for 2 out-of-limits parts per billion produced by a true 6-sigma process.

SPC does not eliminate all variation in the processes, but it does something that is absolutely essential if the process is to be consistent and if the process is to be improved. SPC allows workers to separate the special causes of variation (e.g., environment and the Five M's) from the natural variation found in all processes. After the special causes have been identified and eliminated, leaving only natural variation, the process is said to be in statistical control (or simply in control). When that state is achieved, the process is stable, and in a 3-sigma process, 99.73% of the output can be counted on to be within the statistical control limits. More important, improvement can begin. From this, we can develop a definition of statistical process control:

> Statistical process control (SPC) is a statistical method of separating variation resulting from special causes from variation resulting from natural causes in order to eliminate the special causes and to establish and maintain consistency in the process, enabling process improvement.

Note: As explained in Chapter 1, the 6-sigma numbers given in this section differ from the Motorola Six Sigma numbers (2 parts per billion vs. 3.4 parts per million).

RATIONALE FOR SPC

The rationale for SPC is much the same as that for total quality. It should not be surprising that the parallel exists because it was Walter Shewhart's work that inspired the Japanese to invite W. Edwards Deming to help them get started in their quality program in 1949 to 1950. SPC was the seed from which the Japanese grew total quality.

The rationale for the Japanese to embrace SPC in 1950 was simple: a nation trying to recover from the loss of a costly war needed to export manufactured goods so that it could import food for its people. The Asian markets once enjoyed by Japan had also been rendered extinct by the war. The remaining markets, principally North America, were unreceptive to Japanese products because of poor quality. If the only viable markets rejected Japanese products on the basis of quality, then Japanese manufacturers had to do something about their quality problem. This is why Shewhart's work interested them. This also is why they called on Deming, and later Joseph Juran, to help them. That the effort was successful is well-documented and manifestly evident all over the world. Deming told the Japanese industrialists in 1950 that if they would follow his teaching, they could become active players in the world markets within 5 years. They actually made it in 4 years.

The Western world may not be in the same crisis Japan experienced following World War II, but the imperative for SPC is no less crucial. When one thinks of quality products today, Japan still comes to mind first. Many of the finest consumer products in the world come from Japan. That includes everything from electronics and optical equipment to automobiles, although U.S., European, and Korean car manufacturers have effectively eliminated the quality gap as of 2010.[2] They have done this by adopting such total quality strategies as SPC.

As we approached the twenty-first century, the Japanese were the quality leaders in every level of the automobile market. Cars made by Toyota, Nissan, Honda, and Mazda (including those produced in their North American factories) were of consistently excellent quality. But manufacturers outside of Japan adopted SPC and other total quality strategies, and the outcome of the race for quality leadership can no longer be predicted for each new product year. For example, in J. D. Power and Associates *2010 Initial Quality Study*, the top-rated cars in its ten car-type segments were: four from Japan, three from the United States, two from Europe, and one from Korea.

Automakers know that consumers pay close attention to these and other quality ratings and that there is an impact, positive or negative, on sales. Thus, the rationale for automakers to embrace SPC has not only been to improve product quality and simultaneously reduce costs, but also to improve product image in order to compete successfully in the world's markets. The same is true for virtually all industries.

To comprehend how SPC can help accomplish this, it is necessary to examine five key points and understand how SPC comes into play in each one: control of variation, continual improvement, predictability of processes, elimination of waste, and product inspection. These points are discussed in the next five sections.

Rationale: Control of Variation

The output of a process that is operating properly can be graphed as a bell-shaped curve, as in Figure 18–1. The horizontal *x*-axis represents some measurement, such as weight or dimension, and the vertical *y*-axis represents the frequency count of the measurements, that is, the number of

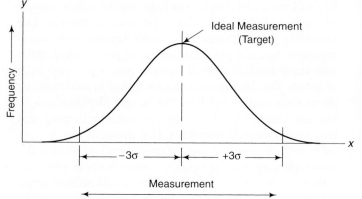

FIGURE 18–1 Frequency Distribution Curve: Normal Curve

times that particular measurement value is repeated. The desired measurement value is at the center of the curve, and any variation from the desired value results in displacement to the left or right of the center of the bell. With no special causes acting on the process, 99.73% of the process output will be between the $\pm 3\sigma$ limits. (This is not a specification limit, which may be tighter or looser.) This degree of variation about the center is the result of natural causes. The

process will be consistent at this performance level as long as it is free of special causes of variation.

When a special cause is introduced, the curve will take a new shape, and variation can be expected to increase, lowering output quality. Figure 18–2 shows the result of a machine no longer capable of holding the required tolerance, or an improper work instruction. The bell is flatter, meaning that fewer parts produced by the process are at, or close to, the target, and more fall outside the original 3σ limits. The result is more scrap, higher cost, and inconsistent product quality.

The curve of Figure 18–3 could be the result of input material from different vendors (or different batches) that is not at optimal specification. Again, a greater percentage of the process output will be displaced from the ideal, and more will be outside the original 3σ limits. The goal should be to eliminate the special causes so the process operates in accordance with the curve shown in Figure 18–1 and then to improve the process, thereby narrowing the curve (see Figure 18–4).

When the curve is narrowed, more of the process output is in the ideal range, and less falls outside the original 3σ limits. Actually, each new curve will have its own 3σ limits. In the case of Figure 18–1, they will be much narrower than the original ones. If the original limits resulted in 2,700

FIGURE 18–2 Frequency Distribution Curve: Process Not as Precise as Figure 18–1

FIGURE 18–3 Bimodal Frequency Distribution Curve

FIGURE 18–4 Frequency Distribution Curve: Narrowed (Less Variation) Relative to Figure 18–1

pieces out of 1 million being scrapped, the improved process illustrated by Figure 18–4 might reduce that to 270 pieces, or even less, scrapped. Viewed from another perspective, the final product will be more consistently of high quality, and the chance of a defective product going to a customer is reduced by an order of magnitude.

Variation in any process is the enemy of quality. As we have already discovered, variation results from two kinds of causes: special causes and natural causes. Both kinds can be treated, but they must be separated so that the special causes—those associated with environment and the Five M's—can be identified and eliminated. After that is done, the processes can be improved, never eliminating the natural variation but continually narrowing its range and approaching perfection. It is important to understand why the special causes must first be eliminated. Until that happens, the process will not be stable, and the output will include too much product that is unuseable, therefore wasted. The process will not be dependable in terms of quantity or quality. In addition, it will be pointless to attempt improvement of the process because one can never tell whether the improvement is successful—the results will be masked by the effect of any special causes that remain.

In this context, elimination of special causes is not considered to be process improvement, a point frequently lost on enthusiastic improvement teams. Elimination of special causes simply lets the process be whatever it will be in keeping with its natural variation. It may be good or bad or anything in between.

When thinking of SPC, most people think of control charts. If we wish to include the elimination of special causes as a part of SPC, as we should, then it is necessary to include more than the control chart in our set of SPC tools because the control chart has limited value until the process is purged of special causes. If one takes a broad view of SPC, all of the statistical tools discussed in Chapter 15 should be included. Pareto charts, cause-and-effect diagrams, stratification, check sheets, histograms, scatter diagrams, and run charts are all SPC tools. Although the flowchart is not a statistical device, it is useful in SPC. The SPC uses of these

techniques are highlighted later in this chapter. Suffice it to say that the flowchart is used to understand the process better, the cause-and-effect diagram is used to examine special causes and how they impact the process, and the others are used to determine what special causes are at play and how important they are. The use of such tools and techniques makes possible the control of variation in any process to a degree unheard of before the introduction of SPC.

Rationale: Continual Improvement

Continual improvement is a key element of total quality. One talks about improvement of products, whatever they may be. In most cases, it would be more accurate to talk about continual improvement in terms of processes than in terms of products and services. It is usually the improvement of processes that yields improved products and services. Those processes can reside in the engineering department, where the design process may be improved by adding concurrent engineering and design-for-manufacture techniques, or in the public sector, where customer satisfaction becomes a primary consideration. All people use processes, and all people are customers of processes. A process that cannot be improved is rare. We have not paid sufficient attention to our processes. Most people have only a general idea of what processes are, how they work, what external forces affect them, and how capable they are of doing what is expected of them. Indeed, outside the manufacturing industry, many people don't realize that their work is made up of processes.

Before a process can be improved, it is necessary to understand it, identify the external factors that may generate special causes of variation, and eliminate any special causes that are in play. Then, and only then, can we observe the process in operation and determine its natural variation. Once a process is in this state of statistical control, it can be tracked, using control charts, for any trends or newly introduced special causes. Process improvements can be implemented and monitored. Without SPC, process improvement takes on a hit-or-miss methodology, the results of which are often obscured by variation stemming from undetected factors (special causes). SPC lets improvements be applied in a controlled environment, measuring results scientifically and with assurance.

Rationale: Predictability of Processes

A customer asks whether a manufacturer can produce 300 widgets within a month. If it can, the manufacturer will receive a contract to do so. The parts must meet a set of specifications supplied by the customer. The manufacturer examines the specifications and concludes that it can comply but without much margin for error. The manufacturer also notes that in a good month it has produced more than 300. So the order is accepted. Soon, however, the manufacturer begins having trouble with both the specifications and the production rate. By the end of the month, only 200 acceptable parts have been produced. What happened? The same units with the same specification have been made before, and at a higher production rate. The problem is unpredictable processes. If the same customer had approached a firm that was versed in SPC, the results would have been different. The managers would have known with certainty their capability, and it would have been clear whether the customer's requirements could, or could not, be met. They would know because their processes are under control, repeatable, and predictable.

Few things in the world of manufacturing are worse than an undependable process. Manufacturing management spends half its time making commitments and the other half living up to them. If the commitments are made based on unpredictable processes, living up to them will be a problem. The only chance manufacturing managers have when their processes are not predictable is to be especially conservative when making commitments. Instead of keying on the best past performance, they look at the worst production month and base their commitments on that. This approach can relieve a lot of stress but can also lose a lot of business. In today's highly competitive marketplace (whether for a manufactured product or a service), organizations must have predictable, stable, consistent processes. This can be achieved and maintained through SPC.

Rationale: Elimination of Waste

Only in recent years, many manufacturers have come to realize that production waste costs money. Scrap bins are still prominent in many factories. In the electronics industry, for example, it is not unusual to find that 25% of the total assembly labor cost in a product is expended correcting errors from preceding processes. This represents waste. Parts that are scrapped because they do not fit properly or are blemished represent waste. Parts that do not meet specifications are waste. To prevent defective products from going to customers, more is spent on inspection and reinspection. This, too, is waste. All of these situations are the result of some process not producing what was expected. In most cases, waste results from processes being out of control; processes are adversely influenced by special causes of variation. Occasionally, even processes that have no special causes acting on them are simply not capable of producing the expected result.

Two interesting things happen when waste is eliminated. The most obvious is that the cost of goods produced (or services rendered) is reduced—a distinct competitive advantage. At the same time, the quality of the product is enhanced.

Even when all manufactured parts are inspected, it is impossible to catch all the bad ones. When sampling is used, even more of the defective parts get through. When the final product contains defective parts, its quality has to be lower. By eliminating waste, a company reduces cost and increases quality. This suggests that Philip Crosby was too conservative when he said quality is free: quality is not just free;[3] it pays dividends. This is the answer to the question of what happened to the Western industries that once led but then lost significant market share since the 1970s; total quality manufacturers simply built better products at competitive prices. These competitive prices are the result of the elimination of waste, not (as is often presumed) cheap labor. This was accomplished in Japan by applying techniques that were developed in the United States in the 1930s but ignored in the West after World War II. Specifically, through application of SPC and later the expansion of SPC to the broader concept of total quality, Japan went from a beaten nation to an economic superpower in just 30 years.

By concentrating on their production processes, eliminating the special causes as Shewhart and Deming taught, and bringing the processes into statistical control, Japanese manufacturers could see what the processes were doing and what had to be done to improve them. Once in control, a relentless process improvement movement was started, one that is still ongoing more than half a century later—indeed, it is never finished. Tightening the bell curves brought ever-increasing product quality and ever-diminishing waste (nonconforming parts). For example, while U.S. automakers were convinced that to manufacture a more perfect transmission would be prohibitively expensive, the Japanese not only did it but also reduced its cost. In the early 1980s, the demand for a particular Ford transmission was such that Ford second-sourced a percentage of them from Mazda. Ford soon found that the transmissions manufactured by Mazda (to the same Ford blueprints) were quieter, smoother, and more reliable than those produced in North America. Ford customers with Mazda transmissions were a lot happier than the others, as well. Ford examined the transmissions, and while it found that both versions were assembled properly with parts that met all specifications, the component parts of the Mazda units had significantly less variation piece to piece. Mazda employed SPC, and the domestic supplier did not. This demonstrated to Ford that the same design, when held to closer tolerances, resulted in a noticeably superior transmission that did not cost more. Shortly thereafter, Ford initiated an SPC program. To Ford's credit, its effort paid off. In 1993, the roles were reversed, and Ford began producing transmissions for Mazda, and in 2010 only Porsche, Acura, Mercedes Benz, and Lexus automobiles were ranked higher than Ford for initial quality. Twenty-eight nameplates ranked below Ford's.[4]

Statistical process control is the key to eliminating waste in production processes. It can do the same in virtually any kind of process. The inherent nature of process improvement is such that as waste is eliminated, the quality of the process output is correspondingly increased.

Rationale: Product Inspection

It is normal practice to inspect products as they are being manufactured (in-process inspection) and as finished goods (final inspection). Inspection requires the employment of highly skilled engineers and technicians, equipment that can be very expensive, factory space, and time. If it were possible to reduce the amount of inspection required, while maintaining or even improving the quality of products, money could be saved and competitiveness enhanced.

Inspection can be done on every piece (100% inspection) or on a sampling basis. The supposed advantage of 100% inspection is, of course, that any defective or nonconforming product will be detected before it gets into the hands of a customer (external or internal). The term *supposed advantage* is used because even with 100% inspection, only 80% of the defects are found.[5] Part of the problem with 100% inspection is that human inspectors can become bored and, as a result, careless. Machine inspection systems do not suffer from boredom, but they are very expensive, and for many applications, they are not a practical replacement for human eyes. It would be faster and less costly if it were possible to achieve the same level of confidence by inspecting only 1 piece out of 10 (10% sampling) or 5 out of 100 (5% sampling) or even less.

Such sampling schemes are not only possible but accepted by such critical customers as the U.S. government (see the U.S. government military standard, MIL-STD-1916) and the automobile industry, but there is a condition: for sampling to be accepted, processes must be under control. Only then will the processes have the consistency and predictability necessary to support sampling. This is a powerful argument for SPC.

After supplier processes are under control and being tracked with control charts, manufacturers can back off the customary incoming inspection of materials, resorting instead to the far less costly procedure of periodically auditing the supplier's processes. SPC must first be in place, and the supplier's processes must be shown to be capable of meeting the customer's specifications.

This also applies internally. When a company's processes are determined to be capable of producing acceptable products, and after they are in control using SPC, the internal quality assurance organization can reduce its inspection

QUALITY TIP ▼

SPC Software Availability

The SPC software is widely available. The least expensive may manage your SPC data as it is processed and charted in Microsoft Excel. More costly packages automatically collect the raw data from the process, manipulate it, and produce the charts. Some may even assume control of the process. Some level of SPC software is appropriate for many SPC applications, but before you get to that point, you need to know how SPC works, why it works, and what you have to do before you can think about using SPC. This is what we are going to learn through the rest of the chapter. Having gained that knowledge, you will be in a position to intelligently determine whether you should use a manual SPC system, or automate SPC through software, and the degree of automation that is appropriate.

and process surveillance efforts, relying to a greater degree on a planned program of process audits. This reduces quality assurance costs and, with it, the cost of quality.

CONTROL CHART DEVELOPMENT

Just as there must be many different processes, so must there be many types of control charts. Figure 18–19 lists the seven most commonly used control chart types. You will note that the first three are associated with measured values or variables data. The other four are used with counted values or attributes data. It is important, as the first step in developing your control chart, to select the chart type that is appropriate for your data. The specific steps in developing control charts are different for variables data than for attributes data.

Control Chart Development for Variables Data (Measured Values)

Consider an example using $\bar{x}$-charts and R-charts. These charts are individual, directly related graphs plotting the mean (average) of samples ($\bar{x}$) over time and the variation in each sample (R) over time. The basic steps for developing a control chart for data with measured values are these:

1. Determine sampling procedure. Sample size may depend on the kind of product, production rate, measurement expense, and likely ability to reveal changes in the process. Sample measurements are taken in subgroups of a specific size (n), typically from 3 to 10. Sampling frequency should be often enough that changes in the process are not missed but not so often as to mask slow drifts. If the object is to set up control charts for a new process, the number of subgroups for the initial calculations should be 25 or more. For existing processes that appear stable, that number can be reduced to 10 or so, and sample size (n) can be smaller, say, 3 to 5.

2. Collect initial data of 100 or so individual data points in k subgroups of n measurements.

   ■ The process must not be tinkered with during this time—let it run.

   ■ Don't use old data—they may be irrelevant to the current process.

   ■ Take notes on anything that may have significance.

   ■ Log data on a data sheet designed for control chart use.

3. Calculate the mean (average) values of the data in each subgroup $\bar{x}$.

4. Calculate the data range for each subgroup (R).

5. Calculate the average of the subgroup averages $\bar{\bar{x}}$. This is the *process average* and will be the centerline for the $\bar{x}$-chart.

6. Calculate the average of the subgroup ranges $\bar{R}$. This will be the centerline for the R-chart.

7. Calculate the process upper and lower control limits, UCL and LCL respectively (using a table of factors, such as the one shown in Figure 18–6). UCL and LCL represent the $\pm 3\sigma$ limits *of the process averages* and are drawn as dashed lines on the control charts.

8. Draw the control chart to fit the calculated values.

9. Plot the data on the chart.

The following is a step-by-step example of control chart construction. First, we have to collect sufficient data with which to make statistically valid calculations. This means we will usually have to take at least 100 data measurements in at least 10 subgroups, depending on the process, rate of flow, and so on. The measurements should be made on samples close together in the process to minimize variation between the data points within the subgroups. However, the sub-

groups should be spread out in time to make visible the variation that exists between the subgroups.

The process for this example makes precision spacers that are nominally 100 millimeters thick. The process operates on a two-shift basis and appears to be quite stable. Fifty spacers per hour are produced. To develop a control chart for the process, we will measure the first 10 spacers produced after 9:00 a.m., 1:00 p.m., 5:00 p.m., and 9:00 p.m. We will do this for 3 days, for a total of 120 data points in 12 subgroups.

At the end of the 3 days, the data chart is as shown in Figure 18–5. The raw data are recorded in columns x_1 through x_{10}.

Next, we calculate the mean (average) values for each subgroup. This is done by dividing the sum of x_1 through x_{10} by the number of data points in the subgroup.

$$\bar{x} = \Sigma x \div n$$

where n = the number of data points in the subgroup. The $\bar{x}$ values are listed in the Mean Value column.

The average $\bar{\bar{x}}$ of the subgroup average $\bar{x}$ is calculated by summing the values of $\bar{x}$ and dividing by the number of subgroups (k):

$$\bar{\bar{x}} = \Sigma \bar{x} \div k$$

In this case,

$$\bar{\bar{x}} = 1{,}200.8 \div 12$$
$$= 100.067$$

The range (R) for each subgroup is calculated by subtracting the smallest value of x from the largest value of x in the subgroup.

$$R = (\text{maximum value of } x) - (\text{minimum value of } x)$$

Subgroup range values are listed in the final column of Figure 18–5.

Date	Subgroup #	x_1	x_2	x_3	x_4	x_5	x_6	x_7	x_8	x_9	x_{10}	Sum Σx	Mean Value $\bar{x}$	Rng. R
7/6	1	101	98	102	101	99	100	98	101	100	102	1002	100.2	4
7/6	2	103	100	101	98	100	104	102	99	101	98	1006	100.6	6
7/6	3	103	101	99	102	100	99	102	98	103	100	1007	100.7	5
7/6	4	96	99	102	99	101	102	98	100	99	97	993	99.3	6
7/7	5	99	102	100	99	103	101	102	98	100	100	1004	100.4	5
7/7	6	101	103	99	100	99	98	100	100	99	100	999	99.9	5
7/7	7	100	103	101	98	99	100	99	102	100	98	1000	100.0	5
7/7	8	97	101	102	100	99	96	99	100	103	98	995	99.5	7
7/8	9	102	97	100	101	103	98	100	102	99	101	1003	100.3	6
7/8	10	100	105	99	100	98	102	97	97	99	101	998	99.8	8
7/8	11	101	99	98	101	104	100	98	100	102	98	1001	100.1	6
7/8	12	100	103	101	98	99	100	100	99	98	102	1000	100.0	5
												Total 1,200.8		68

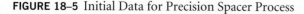

$$k = 12, \qquad \bar{\bar{x}} = 100.067, \qquad \bar{R} = 5.667$$

FIGURE 18–5 Initial Data for Precision Spacer Process

From the R values, calculate the average of the subgroup ranges.

$$\overline{R} = \Sigma R \div k$$

In this case,

$$\overline{R} = 68 \div 12$$
$$= 5.667$$

Next we calculate the UCL and LCL values for the $\overline{x}$-chart.

$$UCL_{\overline{x}} = \overline{\overline{x}} + A_2\overline{R} \qquad LCL_{\overline{x}} = \overline{\overline{x}} - A_2\overline{R}$$

At this point, you know the origin of all the values in these formulas except A_2. A_2 (as well as D_3 and D_4, used later) is from a factors table that has been developed for control charts (see Figure 18–6). The larger the value of A_2, the farther apart the upper and lower control limits ($UCL_{\overline{x}}$ and $LCL_{\overline{x}}$) will be. A_2 may be considered to be a confidence factor for the data. The table shows that the value of A_2 decreases as the number of observations (data points) in the subgroup increases. It simply means that more data points make the calculations more reliable, so we don't have to spread the control limits so much. This works to a point, but the concept of diminishing returns sets in around $n = 15$.

Applying our numbers to the UCL and LCL formulas, we have this:

$$UCL_{\overline{x}} = 100.067 + (0.31 \times 5.667)$$
$$= 100.067 + 1.75677$$
$$= 101.82377$$

$$LCL_{\overline{x}} = 100.067 - 1.75677$$
$$= 98.31023$$

Now calculate the UCL and LCL values for the R-chart.

$$UCL_R = D_4\overline{R} \qquad LCL_R = D_3\overline{R}$$

Like factor A_2 used in the $\overline{x}$ control limit calculation, factors D_3 and D_4 are found in Figure 18–6. Just as with A_2, these factors narrow the limits with subgroup size. With $n = 10$ in our example, $D_3 = 0.22$ and $D_4 = 1.78$. Applying the numbers to the LCL_R and UCL_R formulas, we have this:

$$UCL_R = 1.78 \times 5.667 \qquad LCL_R = 0.22 \times 5.667$$
$$= 10.08726 \qquad\qquad = 1.24674$$

At this point, we have everything we need to lay out the $\overline{x}$- and R-charts (see Figure 18–7).

The charts are laid out with y-axis scales set for maximum visibility consistent with the data that may come in the

Number of Data Points in Subgroup	Factors for $\overline{x}$-Charts	Factors for R-Charts	
		LCL	UCL
(n)	A_2	D_3	D_4
2	1.88	0	3.27
3	1.02	0	2.57
4	0.73	0	2.28
5	0.58	0	2.11
6	0.48	0	2.00
7	0.42	0.08	1.92
8	0.37	0.14	1.86
9	0.34	0.18	1.82
10	0.31	0.22	1.78
11	0.29	0.26	1.74
12	0.27	0.28	1.72
13	0.25	0.31	1.69
14	0.24	0.33	1.67
15	0.22	0.35	1.65
16	0.21	0.36	1.64
17	0.20	0.38	1.62
18	0.19	0.39	1.61
19	0.19	0.40	1.60
20	0.18	0.41	1.59

FIGURE 18–6 Factors Table for $\overline{x}$- and R-Charts

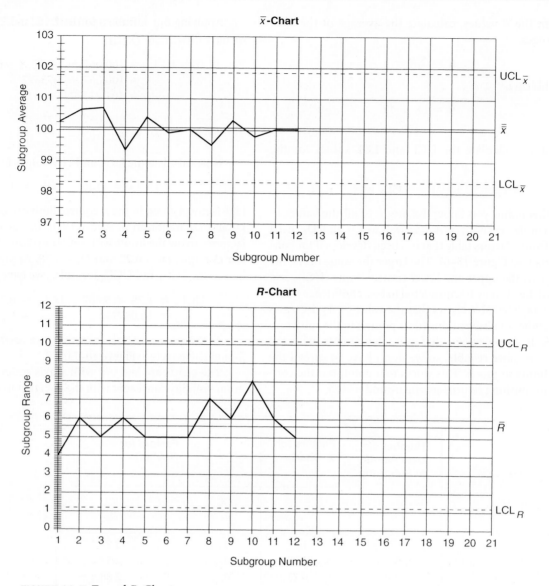

FIGURE 18–7 $\bar{x}$- and R-Charts

future. For new processes, it is usually wise to provide more y-axis room for variation and special causes. A rule of thumb is this:

- (Largest individual value − smallest individual value) ÷ 2.
- Add that number to largest individual value to set the top of chart.
- Subtract it from the smallest individual value to set the bottom of chart. (If this results in a negative number, set the bottom at zero.)

Upper and lower control limits are drawn on both charts as dashed lines, and $\bar{\bar{x}}$ and $\bar{R}$ centerlines are placed on the appropriate charts as solid lines. Then the data are plotted—subgroup averages ($\bar{x}$) on the $\bar{x}$-chart and subgroup ranges (R) on the R-chart. We have arbitrarily established the time axis as 21 subgroups. It could be more or less, depending on the application. Our example requires space for 20 subgroups for a normal 5-day week.

Both charts in Figure 18–7 show the subgroup averages and ranges well within the control limits. The process seems to be in statistical control.

Suppose we had been setting up the charts for a new process (or one that was not as stable). We might have gotten a chart like the one in Figure 18–8.

Plotting the data shows that subgroup 7 was out of limits. This cannot be ignored because the control limits have been calculated with data that included a nonrandom, special-cause event. We must determine and eliminate the cause. Suppose we were using an untrained operator that day. The operator has since been trained. Having established the special cause and eliminated it, we must purge the data of subgroup 7 and recalculate the process average ($\bar{x}$) and the control limits. Upon recalculating, we may find that one or more of the remaining subgroup averages penetrates the new, narrower limits (as in Figure 18–9). If that happens, another iteration of the same calculation is needed to clear

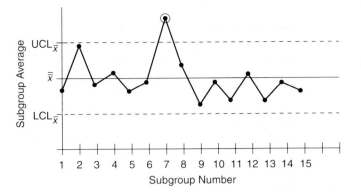

FIGURE 18–8 Chart for an Unstable Process

FIGURE 18–9 The New, Narrower Limits Are Penetrated

the data of any special-cause effects. We want to arrive at an initial set of charts that are based on valid data and in which the data points are all between the limits, indicating a process that is in statistical control (Figure 18–10). If after one or two iterations, all data points are not between the control limits, then we must stop. The process is too unstable for control chart application and must be cleared of special causes.

FIGURE 18–10 The Process Is in Statistical Control

Control Chart Development for Attributes Data (Counted Data)

The *p*-Chart Attributes data are concerned not with measurement but with something that can be counted. For example, the number of defects is attributes data. Whereas the $\bar{x}$- and *R*-charts are used for certain kinds of variables data, where measurement is involved, the *p*-chart is used for certain attributes data. Actually, the *p*-chart is used when the data are the *fraction defective of some set of process output*. It may also be shown as *percentage defective*. The points plotted on a *p*-chart are the fraction (or percentage) of defective pieces found in the sample of *n* pieces. The "Run Charts and Control Charts" section of Chapter 15 began with the example of a pen manufacturer. Now let's take that example to the next logical step and make a *p*-chart.

When we left the pen makers, they seemed to have gotten their defective pens down to 2% or less. If we pick it up from there, we will need several subgroup samples of data to establish the limits and process average for our chart. The *p*-chart construction process is very similar to that of the $\bar{x}$- and *R*-charts discussed in the preceding section. For attributes data, the subgroup sample size should be larger. We need to have a sample size (*n*) large enough that we are likely to include the defectives. Let's use $n = 100$. We want the interval between sample groups wide enough that if trends develop, we will see them. If the factory makes 2,000 pens of this type per hour and we sample the first 100 after the hour, in an 8-hour day we can obtain eight samples. Three days of sampling will give us sufficient data to construct our *p*-chart. After 3 days of collecting data, we have the data shown in Figure 18–11. To that data, we'll apply the *p*-chart formulas shown in Figure 18–12.

Constructing the *p*-chart, we have several things to calculate: the fraction defective by subgroup (*p*), the process average ($\bar{p}$), and the control limits (UCL_p and LCL_p).

Fraction Defective by Subgroup (*p*) The *p* values given in Figure 18–11 were derived by the formula $p = np \div n$. For example, for subgroup 1, $np = 1$ (one pen was found defective from the first sample of 100 pens). Because *p* is the fraction defective,

$$p = 1 \div 100$$
$$= 0.01$$

For the second subgroup:

$$p = 2 \div 100$$
$$= 0.02$$

and so on.

Process Average ($\bar{p}$) Calculate the process average by dividing the total number defective by the total number of pens in the subgroups:

$$\bar{p} = (np_1 + np_2 + \ldots + np_k) \div (n_1 + n_2 + \ldots n_k)$$
$$= 42 \div 2,400$$
$$= 0.0175$$

Date	Subgroup	np	p		Date	Subgroup	np	p
8/11	1	1	.01		8/12	13	4	.04
8/11	2	2	.02		8/12	14	0	0
8/11	3	0	0		8/12	15	1	.01
8/11	4	0	0		8/12	16	3	.03
8/11	5	2	.02		8/13	17	1	.01
8/11	6	0	0		8/13	18	3	.03
8/11	7	3	.03		8/13	19	0	0
8/11	8	2	.02		8/13	20	2	.02
8/12	9	1	.01		8/13	21	4	.04
8/12	10	5	.05		8/13	22	1	.01
8/12	11	0	0		8/13	23	3	.03
8/12	12	2	.02		8/13	24	2	.02

np = number defective in subgroup n = subgroup size = 100 k = # of subgroups

p = fraction defective $\bar{p}$ = process average

FIGURE 18–11 Collected Data for Three Days

---

p = rejects in subgroup ÷ number inspected in subgroup
  = $np \div n$

$\bar{p}$ = total number of rejects ÷ total number inspected
  = $\Sigma np \div \Sigma n$

$$UCL_p = \bar{p} + \frac{3\sqrt{\bar{p}(1-\bar{p})}}{\sqrt{n}}$$

$$LCL_p = \bar{p} - \frac{3\sqrt{\bar{p}(1-\bar{p})}}{\sqrt{n}}$$

FIGURE 18–12 p-Chart Formulas

Control Limits (UCL$_p$ and LCL$_p$)   Because this is the first time control limits have been calculated for the process (as shown in Figure 18–13), they should be considered *trial limits*. If we find that there are data points outside the limits, we must identify the special causes and eliminate them. Then we can recalculate the limits without the special-cause

data, similar to what we did in the series of Figure 18–8 through Figure 18–10 but using the p-chart formulas.

In Figure 18–13, LCL$_p$ is a negative number. In the real world, the fraction defective (p) cannot be negative, so we will set LCL$_p$ at zero.

No further information is needed to construct the p-chart. The y-axis scale will have to be at least 0 to 0.06 or 0.07 because UCL$_p$ = 0.0568. The p values in Figure 18–11 do not exceed 0.05, although a larger fraction defective could occur in the future. Use the following steps to draw a control chart:

1. Label the x-axis and the y-axis.

2. Draw a dashed line representing UCL$_p$ at 0.0568.

3. Draw a solid line representing the process average ($\bar{p}$) at 0.0175.

4. Plot the data points representing subgroup fraction defective (p).

5. Connect the points.

$$UCL_p = \bar{p} + \frac{3\sqrt{\bar{p}(1-\bar{p})}}{\sqrt{n}}$$

$$= .0175 + \frac{3\sqrt{.0175\,(1-.0175)}}{\sqrt{100}}$$

$$= .0175 + \frac{3\sqrt{.01719375}}{10}$$

$$= .0175 + \frac{3 \times .1311}{10}$$

$$= .0175 + .0393$$

$$= .0568$$

$$LCL_p = \bar{p} - \frac{3\sqrt{\bar{p}(1-\bar{p})}}{\sqrt{n}}$$

$$= .0175 - \frac{3\sqrt{.0175\,(1-.0175)}}{\sqrt{100}}$$

$$= .0175 - \frac{3\sqrt{.01719375}}{10}$$

$$= .0175 - \frac{3 \times .1311}{10}$$

$$= .0175 - .0393$$

$$= -.0218 \text{ (set at zero)}$$

FIGURE 18–13 p-Chart Control Limit Calculations

FIGURE 18–14 p-Chart

The p-chart (Figure 18–14) shows that there are no special causes affecting the process, so we can call it *in statistical control*.

Another Commonly Used Control Chart for Attributes Data

The c-Chart The c-charts are used when the data are concerned with *the number of defects in a piece*—for example, the number of defects found in a tire or an appliance. In practice, the data are collected by inspecting sample tires or toasters, whatever the product may be, on a scheduled basis, and each time logging the number of defects detected. Defects may also be logged by type (blemish, loose wire, and any other kind of defect noted), but the c-chart data are the simple sum of all the defects found in each sample piece. Remember, with the c-chart, a sample is one complete unit that may have multiple defect characteristics. The following example illustrates the development of a c-chart.

A manufacturer makes power supplies for the computer industry. Rework to correct defects has been a significant expense. The power supply market is very competitive, and for the firm to remain viable, defects and rework must be reduced. As a first step, the company decides to develop a c-chart to help monitor the manufacturing process. To compile the initial data, the first power supply completed after the hour was chosen as a sample and closely inspected. This was repeated each hour for 30 hours. Defects were recorded by type and totaled for each power supply sample. To develop the initial c-chart, the formulas of Figure 18–15

$$\bar{c} = \text{total number of defects/number of samples}$$

$$\text{UCL}_c = \bar{c} + 3\sqrt{\bar{c}}$$
$$\text{LCL}_c = \bar{c} - 3\sqrt{\bar{c}}$$

FIGURE 18–15 c-Chart Formulas

are applied to the power supply defect data recorded in Figure 18–16.

Calculating the c-chart parameters from the data:

$$\text{Total defects} = 47$$
$$\text{Number of samples} = 30$$
$$\bar{c} = 47/30 = 1.56667$$

$$\text{Largest } c = 3$$
$$\text{Smallest } c = 0$$
$$\text{UCL}_c = 1.56667 + 3\sqrt{1.56667}$$
$$= 4.32167$$
$$\text{LCL}_c = 1.56667 - 3\sqrt{1.56667}$$
$$= -2.18833\,(\text{set at } 0)$$

The c-chart of Figure 18–17 is constructed from these data. Notice that all data points fell within the control limits and there were no protracted runs of data points above or below the process average line, $\bar{c}$. The process was "in control" and ready for SPC. Now, as the operators continue to inspect a sample power supply each hour, data will immediately be plotted directly on the control chart, which, of course, will have to be lengthened horizontally to

Avoid This Control Chart Mistake

Upper control limit, lower control limit, and *process average* are not arbitrary terms, nor are they the same as specifications and tolerances. They are statistically derived from the process's own running data. This cannot be emphasized too strongly. The problem is that if the control limits and process average are not statistically derived from the process, it is impossible to know whether the process is in control, and hence it is enormously difficult to institute or validate process improvements. Yet we find many public and private organizations, and especially the military, using arbitrary or specification limits rather than statistical limits on their "control charts." Using this approach requires less work in setting up the charts, and they may look impressive to the uninitiated, but they are not control charts and can perform none of the functions of a control chart.

Sample	Defects by Type						Number of Defects (c)
	A	B	C	D	E	Other	
1			1	1			2
2		1	1		1		3
3	1						1
4							0
5			1				1
6		1		2			3
7			1			1	2
8			2	1			3
9							0
10	1		1			1	3
11		1					1
12				1	1		2
13	1	1					2
14			2				2
15				1		2	3
16							0
17		1					1
18			1	1			2
19							0
20			1				1
21							0
22						1	1
23		1			1		2
24			2		1		3
25	1						1
26			1				1
27			2			1	3
28							0
29				1		2	3
30			1				1
Sample: 1 power supply. Sample rate: 1 power supply/hour							Total 47

FIGURE 18–16 c-Chart Data

FIGURE 18–17 c-Chart: Power Supply Defects

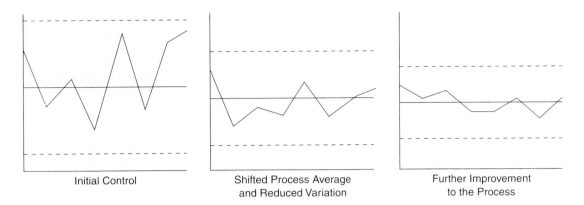

Initial Control

Shifted Process Average
and Reduced Variation

Further Improvement
to the Process

FIGURE 18–18 Succession of Control Charts

accept the new data. This is done with "pages" rather than physically lengthening the chart. Each new page represents a new control chart for the period chosen (week, month, etc.). However, the control limits and the average lines must remain in the same position until they are recalculated with new data. As process improvements are implemented and verified, recalculating the average and limits will be necessary. That is because when a process is really improved, it will have less natural variation. The original average and control limits will no longer reflect the process, and hence their continued use will invalidate the control chart.

The Control Chart as a Tool for Continual Improvement

Control charts of all types are fundamental tools for continual improvement. They provide alerts when special causes are at work in the process, and they prompt investigation and correction. When the initial special causes have been removed and the data stay between the control limits (within $\pm 3\sigma$), work can begin on process improvement. As process improvements are implemented, the control charts will either ratify the improvement or reveal that the anticipated results were not achieved. Whether the anticipated results were achieved is virtually impossible to know unless the process is under control. This is because there are special causes affecting the process; hence, one never knows whether the change made to the process was responsible for any subsequent shift in the data or if it was caused by something else entirely. However, once the process is in statistical control, any change you put into it can be linked directly to any shift in the subsequent data. You find out quickly what works and what doesn't. Keep the favorable changes, and discard the others.

As the process is refined and improved, it will be necessary to update the chart parameters. The UCL, LCL, and process average will all shift, so you cannot continue to plot data on the original set of limits and process average. The results can look like the succession of charts in Figure 18–18.

An important thing to remember about control charts is that once they are established and the process is in statis-

tical control, the charting does not stop. In fact, only then can the chart live up to its name, *control chart*. Having done the initial work of establishing limits and centerlines, plotting initial data, and eliminating any special causes that were found, we have arrived at the starting point. Data will have to be continually collected from the process in the same way they were for the initial chart.

The plotting of these data must be done as they become available (in real time) so that the person managing the process will be alerted at the first sign of trouble in the process. Such trouble signals the need to stop the process and immediately investigate to determine what has changed. Whatever the problem, it must be eliminated before the process is restarted. This is the essence of statistical process control. The control chart is the statistical device that enables SPC on the shop floor or in the office.

This discussion of control charts has illustrated only the $\bar{x}$-chart, R-chart, p-chart, and c-chart. Figure 18–19 lists common control charts and their applications. The methods used in constructing the other charts are essentially the same as for the four we discussed in detail. Each chart type is intended for special application. You must determine which best fits your need.

Statistical Control versus Capability

It is important to understand the distinction between a process that is *in statistical control* and a process that is *capable*. Asking the question "Is our process in control?" is different from asking "Is our process capable?" The first relates to the absence of special causes in the process. If the process is in control, you know that 99.7% of the output will be within the $\pm 3\sigma$ limits. Even so, the process may not be capable of producing a product that meets your customer's expectations.

Suppose you have a requirement for 500 shafts of 2 inch diameter with a tolerance of ± 0.02 inch. You already manufacture 2-inch diameter shafts in a stable process that is in control. The problem is that the process has control limits at 1.97 and 2.03 inches. The process is in control, but it is not capable of making the 500 shafts without a lot of scrap and the cost that goes with it. Sometimes, it is possible to adjust

Data Category	Chart Type	Statistical Quantity	Application
Variables (measured values)	x bar–R (x̄ & R)	Mean value and range	Charts dimensions and their precision, weight, time, strength, and other measurable quantities. Example: Anything physically measurable.
	x tilde–R (x̃ & R)	Median and range	Charts measurable quantities, similar to x̄ & R, but requires fewer calculations to plot. Example: As above.
	x–Rs (also called x-chart)	Individual measured values	Used with long sample intervals; when subgrouping not possible. Example: Products made in batches such as solutions, coatings, etc., or grouping too expensive (e.g., destructive testing). Histogram must be normal.
Attributes (counted values)	p-chart	Percentage defective (also fraction defective)	Charts the number of defects in samples of varying size as a percentage or fraction. Example: Anywhere defects can be counted.
	np-chart (also pn)	Number of defective pieces	Charts the number of defective pieces in samples of fixed size. Example: As above, but in fixed-size samples.
	c-chart	Number of defects	Charts the number of defects in a product (single piece) of fixed size (i.e., like products). Example: Specific assemblies or products (e.g., PC boards, tires).
	u-chart	Number of defects per unit area, time, length, etc.	Charts the number of defects in a product of varying size (i.e., unlike products). Example: Carpet (area), extrusions (length).

FIGURE 18–19 Common Control Charts and Their Applications

the machines or procedures, but if that could have been accomplished to tighten the limits, it already should have been done. It is possible that a different machine is needed.

There are many variations on this theme. A process may be in control but not centered on the nominal specification of the product. With attributes data, you may want your in-control process to make 99.95% (1,999 out of 2,000) of its output acceptable, but it may be capable of making only 99.9% (1,998 of 2,000) acceptable. (Don't confuse that with $\pm 3\sigma$'s 99.73%; they are two different things.)

The series of charts in Figure 18–20 illustrates how *in statistical control* and *capable* are two different issues, but the control chart can clearly alert you to a capability problem. You must eliminate all special causes and the process must be in control before process capability can be established.

MANAGEMENT'S ROLE IN SPC

As in other aspects of total quality, management has a definite role to play in SPC. First, as Deming pointed out, only management can establish the production quality level.[6] Second, SPC and the continual improvement that results from it will transcend department lines, making it necessary for top management involvement. Third, budgets must be established and spent, something else that can be done only by management.

Commitment

As with every aspect of total quality, management commitment is an absolute necessity. To many organizations SPC and continual improvement represent a new and different way of doing business, a new culture. No one in any organiza-

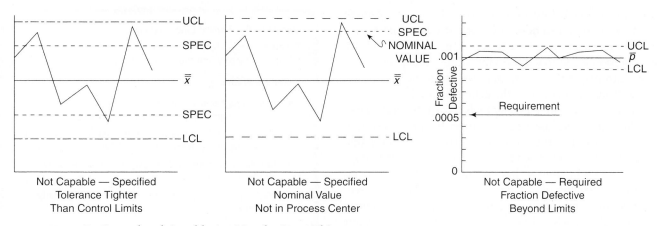

FIGURE 18–20 In Control and Capable Are Not the Same Thing

tion, except its management, can mandate such fundamental changes. One may ask why a production department cannot implement SPC on its own. The answer is that, providing management approves, it can. But the department will be prevented from reaping all the benefits that are possible if other departments are working to a different agenda. Suppose, for example, that through the use of SPC, a production department has its processes under control and it is in the continual improvement mode. Someone discovers that if an engineering change is made, the product will be easier to assemble, reducing the chance for mistakes. This finding is presented to the engineering department. However, engineering management has budgetary constraints and chooses not to use its resources on what it sees as a production department problem. Is this a realistic situation? Yes, it is not only realistic but also very common. Unless there is a clear signal from top management that the production department's SPC program, with its continual improvement initiative, is of vital interest, other departments will continue to address their own agendas. After all, each separate department knows what is important to the top management, and this is what its employees focus on because this is what affects their evaluations most. If SPC and continual improvement are not perceived as priorities of top management, the department that implements SPC alone will be just that, alone.

Training

It is management's duty to establish the policies and procedures under which all employees work and to provide the necessary training to enable them to carry out those policies and procedures. The minimum management involvement relative to SPC training involves providing sufficient funding. More often, though, management will actually conduct some of the training. This is a good idea. Not only will management be better educated in the subject as a result of preparing to teach it, but also employees will be more likely to get the message that SPC is a priority to management.

Involvement

When employees see management involved in an activity, they get a powerful message that the activity is important.

Employees tend to align their efforts with the things they perceive as being important to management. If managers want their employees to give SPC a chance, they must demonstrate their commitment to it. This does not mean that managers should be on the floor taking and logging data, but they should make frequent appearances, learn about the process, probe, and insist on being kept informed.

A major part of SPC is the continual improvement of processes. Deming pointed out that special causes of variation can be eliminated without management intervention. This is essentially true when it comes to correcting a problem. But when it comes to process improvement, management must be involved. Only management can spend money for new machines or authorize changes to the procedures and processes. Without management involvement, neither process nor product improvement will happen.

ROLE OF THE TOTAL QUALITY TOOLS

Some may consider it inappropriate to include tools other than control charts in a discussion of SPC. However, we take the broader view and include several tools:

- Pareto charts
- Cause-and-effect diagrams
- Stratification
- Check sheets
- Histograms
- Scatter diagrams
- Run charts and control charts
- Flowcharts
- Design of experiments
- Five-S
- Failure mode and effects analysis (FMEA)

SPC does not start the moment a control chart is employed. Before SPC can be fully implemented, a lot of work must be done to eliminate the special causes of variation in the process concerned. Consequently, several quality tools will be used before it is time to develop and implement a control chart. When does SPC start? It starts when someone begins cleaning up the process. In the final analysis, this question is not that important because the quality tools come into play either to support SPC or to be part of the SPC package, depending on the definition used.

With SPC, the total quality tools have a dual role. First, they help eliminate special causes from the process so that the process can be brought under control. (Remember that a process that is in control has no special causes acting on it.) Only then can the control charts be developed for the process and the process monitored by the control charts. Their second role comes into play when, from time to time, the control chart reveals a new special cause or when the operator wants to improve a process that is in control. This is dealt with in the section titled "Implementation and Deployment of SPC."

AUTHORITY OVER PROCESSES AND PRODUCTION

Operators who use SPC to keep track of their processes must have the authority to stop the production process when SPC tells them something is wrong. As long as the plots on the control chart vary about the process average but do not penetrate a control limit, the process is in control and is being influenced by the common causes of variation only. Once a penetration is made or the operator sees a run of several plots all on one side of the process average, he or she has good reason to believe that the process needs attention. The operator should be able to stop the process immediately.

A question that frequently arises in the early stages is "Can a line stoppage be justified in terms of cost and, possibly, schedule?" Toyota found early on that the value in stopping the line for any problem was absolute. Not only does it prevent waste and defective products, but also having production at a standstill is a very powerful incentive for finding the cause of the problem and eliminating it—quickly. The word *eliminate* implies that the problem is corrected for good. In a less enlightened factory, the fear of a line stop is so great that the standard procedure is to apply a quick fix to get the line moving again. The emphasis is on keeping production rolling. With this approach, the problem will be investigated and corrected after the line is back in motion. The difficulty is this: the data that might have been available at that moment may have disappeared by the time someone looks for them, and the trail to the root cause may be lost. The odds are good that the same event will recur later on with similar disruption and impact on quality. It will keep recurring until the cause is finally discovered and eliminated. Under SPC and total quality, the emphasis is not on maintaining production regardless but on eliminating any cause of substandard quality the moment it comes up.

Attempting SPC without giving process-stopping authority to the operator is a serious error. Harry Truman once said that war was too important to leave in the hands of the generals. We believe that line stoppages are too

Two Attitudes Toward Line Stoppages
Stopping production lines is seen differently by the traditional factory and the total quality factory.

Traditional Factory

- *Line stops because:* Broken machine, missing or incorrect parts, operator problem, and so on.
- *Reaction:* Find a quick fix; get line moving again. Try to determine and correct the cause later.
- *Result:* Production of defective products and propensity for recurrence.
- *Attitude:* Line stoppages are to be avoided at nearly any cost.

Total Quality Factory

- *Line stops because:* Operator detected an indication of a process problem (e.g., SPC limit penetration or a run).
- *Reaction:* Determine cause and eliminate before restoring production.
- *Result:* Minimizes production of defective product; process becomes more robust.
- *Attitude:* Line stops represent opportunities for improvement.

Source: Stanley Davis.

important to leave in the hands of management. Give the authority to the operator, and the underlying problems will be eliminated.

IMPLEMENTATION AND DEPLOYMENT OF SPC

SPC is not something to go into lightly or approach in a half-hearted manner. It requires the time and commitment of key personnel. It involves training and the expenses that go with it. It may even involve hiring one or more new people with specialized skills. There may be expenses for consultants to help get the organization started and checked out in SPC. The organization may have to invest in some new tools or tooling if what is already on hand turns out to be inadequate. But the single most important issue that must be faced when implementing SPC is the culture change that is implicit in using SPC.

Up to this point, the organization has relied on the quality department to ensure the quality of products. With SPC, the process operator must be the one who ensures product quality, and the quality department must step aside, taking on a significantly different role. Before, if operators could do the assembly steps necessary for their processes, that was adequate. Now their scope of activity must be expanded into new areas, and they must be helped to develop the skills needed to cope with the new requirements. Supervisors and middle managers must give operators the latitude and freedom required to perform the new functions effectively. This sounds easier than it actually is. Many people find it difficult to adjust and adapt to new procedures and attitudes.

Phase	Responsibility	Action
Preparation	Top management Top management Consultant or in-house expert	(1) Commit to SPC (2) Organize SPC committee (3) Train SPC committee
Planning	SPC committee assisted by consultant or expert Consultant or in-house expert QA Management	(4) Set SPC objectives (5) Identify target processes (6) Train appropriate operators and support personnel (7) Ensure repeatability and reproducibility of instruments and methods (8) Delegate responsibility for operators to play key role
Execution	SPC committee, operator, suppliers, customers Operator w/ expert assistance Consultant or in-house expert Operator Operator w/ expert assistance Operator SPC committee and management Operator w/ assistance as required All	(9) Flowchart the process (10) Eliminate the special causes of variation (11) Develop control chart(s) (12) Collect and plot SPC data; monitor (13) Determine process capability* (14) Respond to trends and out-of-limits data (15) Track SPC data (16) Eliminate root causes of any new special causes of variation (17) Continually improve the process (narrow the limits)

FIGURE 18–21 The SPC Implementation Road Map

* If the process is not capable of meeting requirements, it must be changed or replaced; go back to Step 9.

In addition, when SPC is used, functions that were formerly carried out by individuals will increasingly be performed by collaborative teams. Employees learn that solving problems, using the quality tools, and even defining their own processes are best done by teams of people who bring to the table an array of skills, knowledge, and viewpoints that would be impossible for the individual. Interpreting the control charts, finding root causes of any detected special-cause events, and developing ways to actually improve processes are examples of new tasks that come with SPC. All require team activity.

There is no single right way to implement SPC. What is presented here is a general road map for implementation, covering the major steps in the chronological order in which they should be introduced. The detail behind each of the steps must be worked out for each unique application. An SPC implementation is one area in which the retention of an expert consultant has merit. For SPC to provide any benefit, the program must be statistically valid, and it takes an expert to know whether it is or not.

Figure 18–21 summarizes the steps involved in implementing SPC. The implementation steps are divided into three phases: preparation, planning, and execution.

The Preparation Phase

The preparation phase for SPC includes three steps.

Step 1: Commit to SPC Any endeavor that requires spending money, utilizing human resources, changing the organization's culture, hiring employees with new skills, or retaining consultants is something to which top management must be committed. The department that forges ahead without that commitment may find itself cut off in mid-effort, a situation worse than not having started at all.

Step 2: Form an SPC Committee SPC can take a lot of time, especially at first when employees are getting acquainted with it and are getting the processes online. Unlike total quality, however, SPC can be delegated to a cross-functional team that is tasked to oversee implementation and execution. The SPC team leader need not be the resident expert (at the beginning), but a statistics expert must be included on the team and that person must be heard. A typical team will be composed of representatives from manufacturing, quality assurance, engineering, finance, and statistics. In a manufacturing plant, the manufacturing member should be the team leader. The function of the team will be to plan and organize the implementation for its unique application, to provide training for the operators, and to monitor and guide the execution phase. Forming the SPC committee is top management's responsibility.

Step 3: Train the SPC Committee   The newly formed SPC committee must receive basic training before its work starts. In a typical situation, the committee members will have had little or no practical experience with statistics. The training must be done by an expert. It is possible to send employees to training courses or bring the expert to the company. At the conclusion of the training period, the members will not have become experts, but they will know enough to set objectives and to determine which processes should be targeted first. At this point, continued help from a statistics expert remains critical.

The Planning Phase

The planning phase includes the next five steps.

Step 4: Set SPC Objectives   The SPC committee should set objectives for the program. What do we hope to gain from SPC? How will we measure success (at the balance sheet's bottom line, customer feedback, reduction in scrap, lower cost of quality, or perhaps all of these)? If the team waits until the SPC machinery is in place and producing data to decide what gains are expected, consensus may never be reached on how well or how poorly it is working. Set the objectives. Measure against them. As with all objectives, they should be reviewed from time to time to make sure they are still valid and meaningful. Objectives may be added, eliminated, or changed, but they must be in place and understood by all.

Step 5: Identify Target Processes   It is not feasible to attempt to apply SPC to all processes at once. The people involved in designing the SPC application, collecting data and interpreting their meaning, getting the processes under control, and plotting and evaluating control chart data will be in a learning mode for the first several weeks. For that reason, it is important to select just a few pilot processes for the initial implementation. These should be processes that are well-understood and that promise to be relatively easy to bring under control. They should also be important processes, ones that have meaning rather than something trivial. The key point to remember is this: select initial processes from among those that stand the best chance of quick success. With some initial successes under its belt, the organization can go on with confidence to the processes that are the most critical.

Consideration should also be given to the flow from one process to another. For example, if there is a production line with four processes, it makes sense to implement SPC in the order of production flow. Trying to introduce it at the end or in the middle of the four processes may prove difficult. If the first three processes feed their defects into the final process, it will be impossible to eliminate the special causes of variation of the fourth. On the other hand, by starting at the beginning of the flow, putting process 1 under control may eliminate one or more of the special causes affecting processes 2

through 4. The idea is to start implementation at the front of a series of processes, not at the back. Selection of the target processes should be done by the SPC committee, with comprehensive, open communication with the process operators.

Step 6: Train Appropriate Operators and Teams   The operators and teams who will be directly involved with the collection, plotting, and interpretation of SPC data, and those who will be involved in getting the targeted processes under control, will require training in the use of quality tools and in flowcharting, and perhaps in the use of Five-S and FMEA. Some processes may require the use of design of experiments (DOE). If this is the case, the help of a specialist, both to provide training and to assist with the DOE process, may be needed. Training given at this point must make clear the significance and the objectives of the work to be undertaken. Participants will be the process operators and the engineers and quality specialists who support them. Only the employees who will be involved in the initial SPC projects should be included in the first class. As SPC is spread throughout the plant, it will be necessary to train other operators and teams and their support personnel. But by delaying training until it is time to expand beyond the initial processes, the advantage of just-in-time training will be gained. In addition, you will be able to capitalize on lessons learned from the initial projects. The training needed can typically be accommodated in a 1- or 2-day session.

Step 7: Ensure Repeatability and Reproducibility of Gauges and Methods   All measuring instruments, from simple calipers and micrometers to coordinate measuring machines, must be calibrated and certified for acceptable repeatability and reproducibility performance. For SPC to work, the measured data plotted on the control charts must be reliable. A gauge that cannot repeat the same measurement with the same operator consistently or one that is so difficult or idiosyncratic in its use that no two operators can obtain the same data will not work in an SPC environment. The particular application will determine the range of variability that is acceptable in measuring instruments. It must then be verified that each instrument to be used is capable—and that all the people who will be using the instrument are adequately trained in its use. This must be done before Step 10.

Step 8: Delegate Responsibility for Operators to Play a Key Role   As the last step in the planning phase, just before SPC execution is to begin, management should delegate to the process operators' responsibility for maintaining the SPC control charts, collecting and plotting the data, and taking appropriate action. Let the operators know that these functions are theirs, but make certain everyone else knows it, too.

The Execution Phase

The execution phase includes nine steps.

Step 9: Flowchart the Process The first step in the SPC execution phase, taking the broad perspective regarding SPC's boundaries, is flowcharting or characterizing the process to which SPC will be applied. Only when a graphic representation of the entire process exists—including its inputs, its outputs, and all the steps between—can the process be fully understood. Invariably, flowcharting will reveal process features or factors that were not known to everyone. After the flowchart has been completed and everyone agrees that it represents the way the process actually works, a large version should be produced on poster board and permanently placed in open view at the process location. It will provide invaluable information and may even suggest process improvements later on. Members of the SPC team should help, but the development of the process flowcharts should be the responsibility of special teams composed of the process operators, their internal suppliers and customers, and appropriate support members. (Support personnel may include engineers, materials specialists, financial specialists, etc., as needed.)

Step 10: Eliminate the Special Causes of Variation
Now that participants understand the process, it is time to identify and eliminate the special causes of variation. This is best begun through the use of the cause-and-effect diagram, which was discussed in Chapter 15 as one of the seven total quality tools. The cause-and-effect diagram will list all the factors (causes) that might impact the output in a particular way (effect). Then by applying the other tools, such as Pareto charts, histograms, and stratification, the special causes can be identified and eliminated. Until the special causes that are working on the process are eliminated, the next steps will be difficult or impossible to complete. Elimination of the special causes should be a team effort among the process operators, internal process suppliers and customers, engineers, and quality assurance personnel, with additional help from other departments as required. For example, if materials are a factor, the purchasing department might become involved. Be sure to keep the operators at the center of the activity, as this will give them ownership as well as valuable experience.

Step 11: Develop Control Charts With the absence of special causes, it is now possible to observe the process unencumbered by external factors. The statistics expert, or consultant, can now help develop the appropriate control charts and calculate valid upper and lower control limits and process averages. Selection of the control chart type will be determined by the kind of data to be used. (See Figure 18–19.)

Step 12: Collect and Plot SPC Data; Monitor With the special causes removed and with the process running without tweaking (frequent minor adjustments to one or more process factors), the process operator takes the sample data (as specified by the statistics expert) and plots it on the control chart at regular intervals. The operator carefully observes the location of the plots, knowing that they should be inside the control limits, with the pattern varying randomly about the process average if the process is in control.

Step 13: Determine Process Capability Before going further, it is important to determine whether the process is capable of doing what is expected of it. For example, if the process output is to be metal parts with a specified length of between 5.999 and 6.001 inches, but the process turns out as many pieces outside those dimensions as it does within, the process is not capable. The process is capable if its frequency distribution is a bell-shaped curve centered on the specification average—in this case, 6 inches—and with the $\pm3\sigma$ spread coincident with, or narrower than, the specification limits. With the bell curve centered on the specification average and the specification limits coincident with the $\pm3\sigma$ spread of the bell curve, we could expect three nonconforming parts out of 1,000. If the specification limits are inside the $\pm3\sigma$ spread, then the defect rate will be higher; if they are outside (the bell curve is narrower than the limits), the defect rate will be lower.

Two methods exist for determining process capability. The first assumes that the bell curve is centered on the specification average and is called C_p. The second does not assume alignment of the process average and the specification average and is called C_{pk}. Figure 18–22 explains the procedures for calculating these capability indices. As we have already learned, it is possible to have a process that is in control and still not capable of meeting the customer's specifications. When this is the case, it is up to management to replace or upgrade the process capability, which may require the purchase of new equipment.

Step 14: Respond to Trends and Out-of-Limits Data As data are plotted, the operator must respond to any penetration of the control limits or to any run of data above or below the process average line. Either of these is an indication that something is wrong within the process or that some external factor (a special cause) has influenced the process. With experience, operators may be able to handle many of these situations on their own, but when they cannot, it is important that they summon help immediately. The process should be stopped until the cause is identified and removed. This is one of the most important functions of SPC—letting the operator know there is a problem early enough to prevent the production of defective products that must be scrapped or reworked. The only way to respond in such cases is to immediately eliminate the problem. This is another application for team (usually *ad hoc*) participation.

Step 15: Track SPC Data The SPC committee and management should pay close attention to the SPC data that are generated on the production floor. Doing so will give them an accurate picture of their production capability, the quality of their processes, the trends that may develop, and where they should concentrate resources for improvement. A secondary benefit of displaying this level of interest in SPC is that the operators and their support functions will know

Process capability may be calculated in two ways. The first assumes that the process average is centered on the specification average and is denoted as C_p, the process capability index.

$$C_p = \frac{USL - LSL}{6\hat{\sigma}}$$

Where: USL = upper specification limit
LSL = lower specification limit
$\hat{\sigma}$ = estimated process average

$$\hat{\sigma} = \frac{\overline{R}}{d_2}$$

Where: d_2 **is a constant** (see table below)
$\overline{R}$ = process average range

The second method is used when the process average in not assumed to be coincident with the specification average and is denoted as C_{pk}.

$$C_{pk} = \frac{USL - \overline{\overline{X}}}{3\hat{\sigma}}$$

and

$$C_{pk} = \frac{\overline{\overline{X}} - LSL}{3\hat{\sigma}}$$

Where: $\overline{\overline{X}}$ = process average

C_{pk} is taken as the **smaller of the two values**.

For either case, where the capability index
= 1 the specification limits and average are coincident with the process $\pm 3\sigma$ limits and process average.
< 1 the specification limits are tighter than the process spread. The defect rate will be greater than 3 parts per 1,000.
> 1 the process spread is tighter than the specification limits. The defect rate will be less than 3 parts per 1,000.
Note: 1.33 is the preferred minimum capability index.

Table for d_2 Values

# Observations in Subgroup	2	3	4	5	6	7	8	9
d_2	1.128	1.693	2.059	2.326	2.534	2.704	2.847	2.970

FIGURE 18–22 Process Capability Calculation

that management is truly interested in the program, and they will give it the attention and care appropriate to a high-visibility initiative.

Step 16: Eliminate the Root Causes of Any New Special Causes of Variation From time to time, new special causes will come up, even in processes that have long been in control. When this happens, the operator will know it because the SPC data will go out of limits or skew to one side or the other of the control chart centerline. It is important that the root causes of these special causes be eliminated to prevent their recurrence. For example, if the purchasing department placed an order for the next shipment of raw material from a different vendor because its price was cheaper than the current supplier, it is possible that the material coming from the new source might react differently in the process, shifting the process average one way or the other. The root cause may not be the new material. If you scrap it, purchasing is more than likely going to

order the replacement material from the same low bidder, and the problem will probably recur. It would seem that the root cause of the problem is purchasing's tendency to order from the cheapest source. Eliminating this root cause may require a management-approved procedure mandating the use of preferred suppliers. At the very least, there should be an ironclad agreement that purchasing will not order materials from a new supplier without having the material certified by quality assurance and manufacturing personnel. This is a case where the operator initiates the action, a team may identify the root cause, and management involvement may be required to eliminate the problem. This is the way the process is meant to proceed. Wherever the help must come from, it has to be readily available.

Step 17: Narrow the Limits for Continual Improvement With the process under control and the special causes eliminated, continual improvement can be implemented. What this means is that the process average

FIGURE 18–23 Process Improvement

should be centered on the specification average, if that is not already the case and, more frequently, it means the narrowing of the $\pm 3\sigma$ limits (see Figure 18–23). Both of these improvements—centering the process on the specification average and narrowing the limits—will result in fewer parts failing to meet the specifications. Scrappage will be reduced, the process will become more robust, quality will improve, and costs will decrease. The key, of course, is finding ways to improve the processes, but with SPC, one has the understanding of the processes necessary to see and comprehend the problems. Only then can real improvement follow.

INHIBITORS OF SPC

A number of factors can inhibit the implementation of SPC. With SPC, there is not usually the kind of philosophical resistance that is common with some aspects of total quality

management. However, it is true even with SPC that there must be a management commitment because there will be start-up costs associated with implementation. The most common inhibitor of SPC is lack of resources.

Capability in Statistics

Many organizations do not have the in-house expertise in statistics that is necessary for SPC. As SPC is being introduced and decisions are made on where to sample, how much to sample, what kinds of control charts to use, and so on, a good statistician is necessary to ensure the validity of the program. If the organization does not employ such an expert, it should either hire one or retain the services of a consultant for the early phases of the SPC implementation.

The danger inherent in not having statistical expertise is developing an SPC program that is statistically invalid—a fact that can easily escape nonstatisticians. The organization will count on the invalid SPC implementation to control processes when in fact it cannot. A flawed SPC implementation may send messages that make the process control situation worse than it was before. It is important that the initial design of the SPC program be valid. This requires someone with more than a passing knowledge of statistics. If there are any doubts, get help.

Misdirected Responsibility for SPC

Too many companies make the decision to use SPC but then turn it over to the statisticians or the quality assurance department. The value of those departments should not be minimized, but the owner of the process in question should be the person responsible for SPC. This person is the one who can make best use of SPC, and there will be no question about the validity of the data because he or she is the one collecting it. The process operators will require help from the statistician and others from time to time, but they are the appropriate owners of SPC for their processes.

When someone else is responsible for SPC (meaning collecting and logging data, making corrections, stopping out-of-control processes, and getting them fixed), process operators see the entire SPC program as just another check on them, and they are very uncomfortable with it. Management tends to see it the same way, but from their particular perspective—a means of checking up on the operators. Nothing good will come from such a relationship.

Neither is ownership by the statistician the appropriate answer. If the statistician owns SPC, he or she is more apt to find fascination in the numbers themselves than in what they mean in terms of quality. Even if statisticians are tuned in to the objective, the operator will see them and their SPC charts as just another intrusion.

If operators have the responsibility for SPC, they will become familiar with the tasks involved and will see it as a means to help them get the most out of their processes. This is the payoff. All of the others need to observe and review, assisting when needed but never usurping the operator's ownership.

Failure to Understand the Target Process

Unless a process has been flowcharted recently and characterized, the odds are good that the people designing the SPC system for it do not know how the process actually works. Most processes have evolved over many years, changing now and then to meet the requirements of the market or the desires of management or operators. Few are adequately documented. People are usually astonished when flowcharts reveal the complexity of processes they thought to be straightforward. A good SPC system cannot be designed for a process that isn't fully understood.

Failure to Have Processes Under Control

Before SPC can be effective, any special causes of variation must be removed. This was discussed earlier, but it is appropriate to mention it here again as an inhibitor of SPC. Remember, by definition, a process is not in control if any special cause is working on it. The use of control charts assumes an in-control process. Their use will set off visual alarms whenever a new special cause is introduced. But the real work of process improvement can come about only when nothing but the common causes are active. This is why SPC is so powerful. It will show when common causes are the only causes of variation so that improvements to the fundamental process can be made. Will special causes still come up from time to time? Certainly, but this is different from trying to control a process with special causes constantly present, masking both the common causes and each other.

Inadequate Training and Discipline

Everyone who will be involved in the SPC program must be trained not only in data acquisition, plotting, and interpretation for control charts, but also in the use of the seven tools. Not everyone needs to be a statistics expert, but all need to know enough so that with a statistician's help, the program can be designed and operated.

Training should teach that SPC and tweaking do not make a good pair. If tweaking is permitted, SPC data will be meaningless. The process may appear to be more stable than it is if the person doing the tweaking is an expert, or it may show more variation than if left alone. It must be understood that operators and engineers alike are to let the process run essentially hands-off until an out-of-limits condition is detected. Variation between the limits is not to be tweaked out. The only acceptable means of reducing the variation is a real process improvement that will narrow the limits permanently.

Measurement Repeatability and Reproducibility

SPC data are the result of measurement or count. In the case of the variables data (the measurements), the data become meaningless when the measurements are not repeatable. For example, a worn instrument or a gauge with insufficient precision and resolution might yield measurements over an unacceptably wide range when measuring the same object repeatedly. This is not satisfactory. The data taken from all measurements must be accurate to the degree specified, and repeatable, or there is no point in recording them.

Nothing should be taken for granted. Before any gauge is used for SPC, it should be calibrated and its repeatability certified. It is also important that different operators obtain the same readings. This is known as *reproducibility*. Before getting them involved with SPC, certify all gauges and train all operators.

Low Production Rates

Although it is more convenient to implement SPC with processes that have continuous flow, or high rates of product output, it is by no means impossible to apply SPC to low-rate production of the type that is often found in a job shop setting. In a factory that produces several hundred printed circuit boards per day, sampling schemes are relatively easy.

A job shop might produce only a few boards in a day, often with gaps between production days. Sampling there must be done differently. Low-rate production provides an opportunity for taking a 100% sample. It is possible to take a sample from every board. In such an application, a computer-generated random x–y table can designate a specific small area of a board for inspection of solder joints or other attributes. From that, a number representing the fraction defective may be developed. Control charts are easily constructed for fraction-defective data. Low production rates are not a good excuse for avoiding SPC.

SUMMARY

1. SPC originated in the work of Dr. Walter Shewhart at Bell Laboratories in 1931. Although SPC was ignored in the West after World War II, Japan adopted it, subsequently developing it into total quality. SPC is a statistical method of separating special-cause variation from natural variation to eliminate the special causes and to establish and maintain consistency in the process, enabling process improvement. SPC is essential worldwide today to elevate the quality of products and services, while lowering costs, to compete successfully in the world's markets.

2. A total of 99.73% of the output of a process that is in statistical control will fall within the $\pm 3\sigma$ limits of the process. Do not confuse process average and limits with specification average and limits. It is usually desirable to make the process average coincident with the specification average and to make the process spread narrower than the specification limits.

3. Continual improvement of processes requires that special causes be eliminated first. Process improvement narrows the shape of the process's bell curve, resulting in less variation.

4. Continual improvement is a key element of SPC and total quality. SPC enhances the predictability of processes and whole plants. Elimination of waste is another key element of SPC. SPC can help improve product quality, while reducing product cost.

5. SPC makes sampling inspection more reliable. SPC supports process auditing as a substitute for more expensive product inspection. SPC requires a capability in statistics, either in-house or through a consultant. Process operators should be key players in any SPC program. Understanding the process is a prerequisite to SPC implementation. All employees involved in SPC must be trained for their involvement. Measurement repeatability and reproducibility is essential for SPC.

6. Management's role in SPC is similar to its role in total quality overall: commitment, the provision of training, and involvement. The seven tools, augmented by flowcharting, Five-S, FMEA, and DOE, may be used

with SPC. SPC and the operator must have process-stop authority. SPC implementation must be carried out in an orderly, well-thought-out sequence.

7. SPC requires collaborative team activity.

KEY TERMS AND CONCEPTS

Auditing

Authority over processes

Commitment

Continual improvement

Control charts

Control of variation

Elimination of waste

Five M's

Five-S

Flowcharting

FMEA

In-control process

Involvement

Narrow the limits

Natural causes

Out-of-limits data

Predictability of processes

Process capability

Repeatability

Reproducibility

Sampling

Seven tools

Statistical process control (SPC)

SPC committee

Special causes

Target processes

Training

Tweaking

FACTUAL REVIEW QUESTIONS

1. Define the concept of statistical process control.

2. Explain briefly the rationale for SPC.

3. What is meant by variation in processes?

4. Define the following concepts:
   - Continual improvement
   - Predictability of processes
   - Elimination of waste
   - Sampling
   - Auditing

5. What is management's role in the implementation of SPC?

6. Describe how the seven tools are used when implementing SPC.

7. Why is it important to give operators authority over their processes?

8. List the various steps that should be followed when implementing SPC.

9. Why is management commitment so important when implementing SPC?

10. List and briefly explain the major inhibitors of SPC.

CRITICAL THINKING ACTIVITY

SPC Review

1. Review the section "Statistical Process Control Defined." Explain how environment and the Five M's can affect processes used in the following:
   a. A hardware store
   b. A hospital
   c. An accounting firm
   d. A newspaper
   e. A factory
   f. A new-car dealership

2. Explain the relationship that exists between the histogram and the control chart.

3. Contrast the histogram's characteristic of representing a "snapshot" of a process with a control chart.

4. Defend the statement that the operator of the process should be the owner and data plotter of the control chart, as opposed to a person from quality assurance or engineering, for example.

5. Comment on the significance of this statement: "Control chart parameters must be statistically derived and cannot simply be specifications or some arbitrary values that are based on production expectations."

DISCUSSION ASSIGNMENT 18–1

Hi-Sport Manufacturing Co. Inc.

Hi-Sport is a small company that manufactures logo sporting jackets. A key goal of the company has always been excellent quality. This has been achieved largely through rigorous inspection, a process that has come to be known as "inspecting the quality in." As a result, the firm has always had a high reject rate at final inspection. This has necessarily resulted in too many jackets being scrapped or sold below cost as "seconds." It has also resulted in a bothersome percentage of imperfect jackets "slipping through" inspection and ending up in the hands of customers. The impact has been a so-so reputation with customers, and prices that are too high to be competitive with the imports or major U.S. manufacturers.

Management tried and tried to get the production workers to do better, but it seemed that every effort to reduce defects came to nothing. Sometimes it appeared that good ideas and the best of intentions only made matters worse. A few weeks ago the managers retained a manufacturing consultant with statistics and process control credentials. He told them their first priority should be to get their processes under control.

With the consultant's help, they started their program by identifying and eliminating several special causes of variation. These special causes had included machines that needed maintenance and calibration, some employees with insufficient training, and the absence of written work instructions for certain procedures. By the 6-week mark, Hi-Sport's quality had noticeably improved. Management decided it was time to attempt the development of a control chart.

Because rejects were based on pass/fail criteria for various characteristics, the managers needed a control chart that could respond to nonmeasurable attributes. Three common charts meet that requirement: the p-chart, np-chart, and c-chart. The p-chart could help control the percentage of defective jackets. The np-chart could help control the number of defective jackets. The c-chart could help control the number of defects in a jacket. They decided the c-chart would give them what they wanted—namely, using one jacket as the sample and tracking the defects found in the sample.

For the initial chart-development data, one jacket was inspected each hour for 30 consecutive working hours. The data are listed in the accompanying table. The data were recorded in the five most common defect categories, with a sixth column collecting all other types of defects encountered. At the end of the 30th hour, 46 total defects had been recorded from the 30 jacket samples.

Hi-Sport Manufacturing Co. Inc.							
	Defects by Type						Number of Defects
Sample	A	B	C	D	E	Other	
1		1	1		1		3
2		1					1
3							0
4	1		1				2
5					1		1
6		1					1
7	2		1		2		5
8				1			1
9							0
10	1					1	2
11		1		1			2
12							0
13							0
14				1			1
15		1					1
16			1			1	2
17			1				1
18	2					1	3
19							0
20				1			1
21	1						1
22							0
23			2				2
24	1						1
25	2	1		3			6
26	1			1			2
27	1	1		2			4
28			1				1
29				1			0
30			1	1			2

Defects per sample.   Total 46
Sample: 1 jacket. Sample rate: 1 jacket/hour.

SPC Exercise: HI-Sport's Control Chart

1. You are the consultant, and because this is Hi-Sport's introduction to control charts, you will have to help it develop the chart. From the data table, compute c, UCL_c, and LCL_t.

2. Next, construct a control chart. Be sure to include some "headroom" above the upper control limit to allow for any out-of-limit events that may be encountered. Also make the chart long enough horizontally to include all the data points in the table, plus a few more days of real-time data points that will need to be plotted as SPC tracking begins.

3. Now plot the appropriate data from the table on the chart. Is the process in control, or is one or more special causes still lingering? Where do you go from here? Complete your task by (a) providing Hi-Sport with a control chart that reflects an in-control process or (b) abandoning the current data and starting over again by seeking out the special causes that prevented success the first time.

To see how the authors resolved this issue, see the next section.

Authors' Solution to HI-Sport's Control Chart Exercise

In practice, it is not uncommon to encounter a special cause while developing a control chart. This may happen because the special cause is so subtle or infrequently recurring that it has gone unnoticed or simply because there were other special causes, now gone, that had masked this one. Suppose you have collected your data over 5 working days, made the necessary calculations, and plotted the new control chart. To your great consternation, you find that one of your data points is beyond the upper control limit. Have you lost a week's work because there was still a special cause of variation lurking in your process? No. You can salvage it as we do here:

Total defects: 46 (This is the value for c.)

Number of samples: 30 (This is the number of jackets inspected.)

$\bar{c} = 46/30 = 1.533333$

Largest $c = 6$

Smallest $c = 0$

$$UCL_c = \bar{c} + 3\sqrt{\bar{c}}$$
$$= 1.533333 + 3\sqrt{1.533333}$$
$$= 5.248168$$

$$LCL_c = \bar{c} - 3\sqrt{\bar{c}}$$
$$= 1.533333 - 3\sqrt{1.533333}$$
$$= -2.18150 \,(\text{Since this is a negative number, use } 0.)$$
$$= 0$$

The control chart identified as Hi-Sport v1.0 was constructed using these $\bar{c}$, UCL, and LCL values. Note that sample 25 is above the upper control limit, which indicates that it is the result of a special cause. Because the control chart

must be developed from natural (common-cause) variation data only, sample 25 would seem to rule out the entire 30 hours of data. However, if sample 25 is eliminated from the data and if $\bar{c}$ UCL, and LCL are recalculated on the 29 remaining samples, the control chart will remain valid.

Recalculating, $\bar{c}$, UCL, and LCL without sample 25 yields the following:

$$\bar{c} = 40/29 = 1.37931 \quad UCL_c = 4.902632 \quad UCL_c = 0$$

The control chart constructed from these values is shown as Hi-Sport v1.1. Note that with the removal of sample 25 data, $\bar{c}$ (the average number of defects per sample) decreased from 1.533333 to 1.37931. At the same time, the UCL decreased from over 5 to under 5. This is a narrowing of limits, which is good. However, sample 7 is now beyond the upper control limit. The same procedure, deleting sample 7 data, can be repeated. Recalculating the remaining 28 samples yields the following:

$$\bar{c} = \frac{35}{28} = 1.25 \quad UCL_c = 4.604102 \quad UCL_c = 0$$

The corresponding control chart is shown as Hi-Sport v1.2. Note that all sample data points are now inside the control limits and there are no protracted runs below or above the $\bar{c}$ line. With that, Hi-Sport's consultant pronounced the chart ready for use. This was a close call. If you encounter an out-of-limits data point in your initial chart development data, it is OK to simply eliminate the offending sample data from the calculations and proceed. Doing the same again (as was done here) for a second out-of-limits sample is usually acceptable, but if a third one crops up in a set of 30 to 50 data point samples, the process is too unstable for a control chart. Go back to eliminating special causes before collecting all-new data from which to construct your control chart.

c-chart
Defects per Jacket
Hi-Sport v1.0

$UCL_c = 5.248168$
$LCL_c = 0$
$\bar{c} = 1.533333$
OUT OF CONTROL

Sample #7 is out-of-limits on recalculation without sample 25.

Note: Sample #25 was eliminated.

c-chart
Defects per Jacket
Hi-Sport v1.1

$UCL_c = 4.902632$
$LCL_c = 0$
$\bar{c} = 1.37931$
OUT OF CONTROL

Note: Sample #7 was eliminated.

c-chart
Defects per Jacket
Hi-Sport v1.2

$UCL_c = 4.604102$
$LCL_c = 0$
$\bar{c} = 1.25$

You might ask, "If the control chart showed an out-of-limits condition for data sample 7, why not eliminate that special cause before you go on?" If the special cause was known, then certainly it should be eliminated forthwith. (We would still have to eliminate the data sample and recalculate on the remaining data.) The problem is that it occurred several hours (or maybe days) ago and may no longer be apparent. The trail may have become obscured. That is why, when a control chart is in place and an out-of-limits data point is taken, it is important to stop the process immediately to find the cause. The more time that passes between the event and the search, the less likely the cause will be discovered.

DISCUSSION ASSIGNMENT 18–2

The Start of the Japanese Quality Movement

When the U.S. forces occupied Japan at the end of World War II to set up the occupation government, they found the Japanese telephone system to be poor in quality and unreliable. General MacArthur's people knew this would be a major problem for them and for Japan in trying to get the country on its feet again. Bell Laboratories' people were brought in to assist the Japanese telecommunications industry, and starting in May 1946 they taught their Japanese counterparts the principles of modern quality control based on Dr. Shewhart's work.

While the Bell Labs people were in Japan, a copy of Shewhart's book *The Economic Control of Quality of Manufactured Product* was given to the Union of Japanese Scientists and Engineers (JUSE). One of its members (the organization had only 12 at the time) was so taken with Shewhart's ideas that he stenciled by hand a copy of the book onto mimeograph masters, so that it could be reproduced and circulated. These two events were the start of the quality movement in Japan.

Sources: Kaoru Ishikawa, *What Is Total Quality Control? The Japanese Way* (Upper Saddle River, NJ: Prentice Hall, 1985), 15; Mary Walton, *The Deming Management Method* (New York: Putnam, 1986), 12.

DISCUSSION QUESTIONS

1. What was Shewhart's source for the data required for his statistical process control?

2. Shewhart describes two kinds of variation, that resulting from common causes and that resulting from special causes. Define both.

DISCUSSION ASSIGNMENT 18-3

SPC's Effect on Competitiveness

The government invites two companies to bid for a contract to produce 100 flightline avionics maintenance systems. The design is owned by the air force, and the air force will provide all necessary documentation to the successful bidder. Both companies understand the requirements of the contract, and both are equipped and have the know-how to manufacture the devices.

Company ABC, with no SPC experience, develops a conservative proposal, accounting for 25% rework in its manufacturing labor costs, padding materials costs by 10% in anticipation of scrappage, and allowing for inspection sufficient to smoke out most of the defects—calculated at 20% of the basic manufacturing labor.

Company XYZ, which uses SPC in all its manufacturing processes, bids rework and scrap at much lower rates and includes only enough inspection to audit processes and meet the customer's own minimum inspection criteria.

The following chart compares the bids from the two companies:

	Company ABC	Company XYZ
Assembly labor	$200,000	$200,000
Rework labor	50,000 (25%)	8,000 (4%)
Inspection labor	40,000 (20%)	4,000 (2%)
Materials	550,000	505,000
Totals	$840,000	$717,000

With a difference of $123,000, there can be no doubt that Company XYZ will win the contract. Not only is Company ABC's bid 17% higher, but also one would be safe in predicting that its higher-priced product would be inferior to XYZ's product. SPC is the only difference here.

DISCUSSION QUESTIONS

Discuss the following questions in class or outside of class with your fellow students:

1. How would you rate the comparative competitiveness of the two companies?

2. If you work for a company that does not employ SPC, how could SPC help the firm?

ENDNOTES

1. Mary Walton, *The Deming Management Method* (New York: Putnam, 1986), 12.

2. *2010 Initial Quality Study Press Release*, J. D. Power and Associates (Westlake Village, CA: June 17, 2010).

3. Philip B. Crosby, *Quality Is Free: The Art of Making Quality Certain* (New York: McGraw-Hill, 1979), 68.

4. *2010 Initial Quality Study Press Release*.

5. Gregory B. Hutchins, *Introduction to Quality Control, Assurance, and Management* (New York: Macmillan, 1991), 162.

6. Nancy R. Mann, *The Keys to Excellence: The Story of the Deming Philosophy* (Los Angeles: Prestwick, 1989), 21.

CONTINUAL IMPROVEMENT METHODS WITH SIX SIGMA, LEAN, LEAN SIX SIGMA, AND MORE

Even if you're on the right track, you'll get run over if you just sit there.
—*Will Rogers*

MAJOR TOPICS

- Rationale for Continual Improvement
- Management's Role in Continual Improvement
- Essential Improvement Activities
- Structure for Quality Improvement
- The Scientific Approach
- Identification of Improvement Needs
- Development of Improvement Plans
- Common Improvement Strategies
- Additional Improvement Strategies
- The Kaizen Approach
- The CEDAC[1] Approach
- The Lean Approach
- The Six Sigma Approach
- The Lean Six Sigma Approach
- The Theory of Constraints (TOC) and Integrated TOC, Lean, Six Sigma (iTLS) Approach

One of the most fundamental elements of total quality is continual improvement. The concept applies to processes and the people who operate them as well as to the products resulting from the processes. A fundamental total quality philosophy is that all three—processes, people, and products—must be continually improved. This chapter provides the information needed to make continual improvements to the processes and products. (Improvement of employee skills and performance is the subject of Chapters 4, 6, 8, 9, 10, 11, and 12.)

RATIONALE FOR CONTINUAL IMPROVEMENT

Continual improvement is fundamental to success in the global marketplace. A company that is just maintaining the status quo in such key areas as quality, new product development, adoption of new technologies, and process

performance is like a runner who is standing still in a race. Competing in the global marketplace is like competing in the Olympics. Last year's records are sure to be broken this year. Athletes who don't improve continually are not likely to remain long in the winner's circle. The same is true of companies that must compete globally.

Customer needs are not static; they change continually. A special product feature that is considered innovative today will be considered just routine tomorrow. A product cost that is considered a bargain today will be too high to compete tomorrow. A good case in point in this regard is the ever-falling price for each new feature introduced in the personal computer. The only way a company can hope to compete in the modern marketplace is to improve continually.

MANAGEMENT'S ROLE IN CONTINUAL IMPROVEMENT

In his book *Juran on Leadership for Quality*, Joseph Juran writes:

> The picture of a company reaping big rewards through quality improvement is incomplete unless it includes some realities that have been unwelcome to most upper managers. Chief among these realities is the fact that the upper managers must participate personally and extensively in the effort. It is not enough to establish policies, create awareness, and then leave all else to subordinates. That has been tried, over and over again, with disappointing results.[2]

Management can play the necessary leadership role—and that essentially is its role—in continual improvement by doing the following:

- Establishing an organization-wide quality council and serving on it.
- Working with the quality council to establish specific quality improvement goals with timetables and target dates.
- Providing the necessary moral and physical support. Moral support manifests itself as commitment. Physical

support comes in the form of the resources needed to accomplish the quality improvement objectives.

- Scheduling periodic progress reviews and giving recognition where it is deserved.

- Building continual quality improvement into the regular reward system, including promotions and pay increases.

ESSENTIAL IMPROVEMENT ACTIVITIES

Continual improvement is not about solving isolated problems as they occur. Such an approach is viewed as "putting out fires" by advocates of total quality. Solving a problem without correcting the fault that caused it—in other words, simply putting out the fire—just means the problem will occur again. Quality expert Peter R. Scholtes and his colleagues recommend the following five activities, which he sees as crucial to continual improvement (see Figure 19–1):[3]

- ***Maintain communication.*** Communication is essential to continual improvement. This cannot be overemphasized. Communication within improvement teams and among teams is a must. It is important to share information before, during, and after attempting to make improvements. All people involved, as well as any person or unit that might be impacted by a planned improvement, should know what is being done, why, and how it might affect them.

- ***Correct obvious problems.*** Often process problems are not obvious, and a great deal of study is required to isolate them and find solutions. This is the typical case, and it is why the scientific approach is so important in

a total quality setting. However, sometimes a process or product problem will be obvious. In such cases, the problem should be corrected immediately. Spending days studying a problem for which the solution is obvious just so that the scientific approach is used will result in $10 solutions to 10-cent problems.

- ***Look upstream.*** Look for causes, not symptoms. This is a difficult point to make with people who are used to taking a cursory glance at a situation and putting out the fire as quickly as possible without taking the time to determine what caused it.

- ***Document problems and progress.*** Take the time to write it down. It is not uncommon for an organization to continue solving the same problem over and over again because nobody took the time to document the problems that have been dealt with and how they were solved. A fundamental rule for any improvement project team is "document, document, document."

- ***Monitor changes.*** Regardless of how well studied a problem is, the solution eventually put in place may not solve it or may only partially solve it, or it may produce unintended consequences. For this reason, it is important to monitor the performance of a process after changes have been implemented. It is also important to ensure that pride of ownership on the part of those who recommended the changes do not interfere with objective monitoring of the changes. These activities are essential regardless of how the improvement effort is structured.

Improvement Must Be Continual

"Improve constantly and forever the system of production and service. Improvement is not a one-time effort. Management is obligated to continually look for ways to reduce waste and improve quality."

Source: W. Edwards Deming, Cited In Mary Walton, *The Deming Management Method* (New York: Putnam, 1986), 35.

Improvement Is Not Putting Out Fires

W. Edwards Deming said, "Putting out fires is not improvement. Finding a point out of control, finding the special cause and removing it is only putting the process back to where it was in the first place. It is not improvement of the process. [Deming attributed this conclusion to Joseph M. Juran, many years ago.]

"You are in a hotel. You hear someone yell fire. He runs for the fire extinguisher and pulls the alarm to call the fire department. We all get out. Extinguishing the fire does not improve the hotel.

"That is not improvement of quality. That is putting out fires."

Source: W. Edwards Deming, Cited In Mary Walton, *The Deming Management Method* (New York: Putnam, 1986), 67.

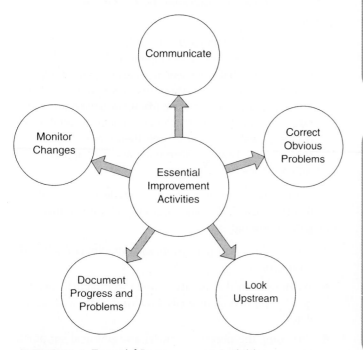

FIGURE 19–1 Essential Improvement Activities

STRUCTURE FOR QUALITY IMPROVEMENT

Quality improvement doesn't just happen. It must be undertaken in a systematic, step-by-step manner. For an organization to make continual improvements, it must be structured appropriately and Quality pioneer Juran calls this "mobilizing for quality improvement."[4] It involves the following three steps:[5]

- *Establish a quality council.* The quality council has overall responsibility for continual improvement. According to Juran, "The basic responsibility of this council is to launch, coordinate, and 'institutionalize' annual quality improvement."[6] It is essential that the membership include executive-level decision makers.

- *Develop a statement of responsibilities.* All members of the quality council, as well as employees who are not currently members, must understand the council's responsibilities. One of the first priorities of the council is to develop and distribute a statement of responsibilities bearing the signature of the organization's CEO. Responsibilities that should be stated include the following: (a) formulating policy as it relates to quality; (b) setting the benchmarks and dimensions (cost of poor quality, etc.); (c) establishing the team and project selection processes; (d) providing the necessary resources (training, time away from job duties to serve on a project team, etc.); (e) launching quality improvement projects; (f) establishing quality measures for monitoring progress and undertaking monitoring efforts; and (g) implementing an appropriate reward and recognition program.

- *Establish the necessary infrastructure.* The quality council constitutes the foundation of an organization's quality effort. However, there is more to the quality infrastructure than just the council. The remainder of the quality infrastructure consists of subcommittees of the council that are assigned responsibility for specific duties, project improvement teams, quality improvement managers, a quality training program, and a structured improvement process.

THE SCIENTIFIC APPROACH

The scientific approach is one of the fundamental concepts that separates the total quality approach from other ways of doing business. Scholtes and his colleagues describe the scientific approach as "making decisions based on data, looking for root causes of problems, and seeking permanent solutions instead of relying on quick fixes."[7]

For putting the scientific approach to work in a total quality setting, Scholtes developed four strategies which are as follows:[8]

- Collect meaningful data.
- Identify root causes of problems.

- Develop appropriate solutions.
- Plan and make changes.

Collect Meaningful Data

Meaningful data are free from errors of measurement or procedure, and they have direct application to the issue in question.[9] It is not uncommon for an organization or a unit within it to collect meaningless data or to make a procedural error that results in the collection of erroneous data. In fact, in the age of computers, this is quite common. Decisions based on meaningless or erroneous data are bound to lead to failure. Before collecting data, decide exactly what data are needed, how they can best be collected, where the data exist, how they will be measured, and how you will know the data are accurate.

Identify Root Causes of Problems

The strategy of identifying root causes is emphasized throughout this book.[10] Too many resources are wasted by organizations attempting to solve symptoms rather than problems. The total quality tools are helpful in separating problems from causes.

Develop Appropriate Solutions

With the scientific approach, solutions are not assumed.[11] Collect the relevant data, make sure they are accurate, identify root causes, and then develop a solution that is appropriate. Too many teams and too many people begin with "I know what the problem is. All we have to do to solve it is . . . ." When the scientific approach is applied, the problem identified is often much different from what would have been suspected if acting on a hunch or an intuition. Correspondingly, the solution is also different.

Plan and Make Changes

Too many decision makers use what is sometimes called the "Ready, fire, aim" approach rather than engaging in careful, deliberate planning.[12] Planning forces you to look ahead, anticipate needs and what resources will be available to satisfy them, and anticipate problems and consider how they should be handled.

Much of the scientific approach has to do with establishing reliable performance indicators and using them to measure actual performance. In his book *Total Manufacturing Management*, Giorgio Merli lists the following examples of useful performance indicators:[13]

Importance of Statistical Thinking

"Statistical thinking is critical to improvement of a system. Only by use of properly interpreted data can intelligent decisions be made."

Source: W. Edwards Deming, Cited In Mary Walton, *The Deming Management Method* (New York: Putnam, 1986), 57.

- Number of errors or defects
- Number of or level of need for repetitions of work tasks
- Efficiency indicators (units per hour, items per person)
- Number of delays
- Duration of a given procedure or activity
- Response time or cycle
- Useability/cost ratio
- Amount of overtime required
- Changes in workload
- Vulnerability of the system
- Level of criticalness
- Level of standardization
- Number of unfinished documents

This is not a complete list. Many other indicators could be added. Those actually used vary widely from organization to organization. However, such indicators, regardless of which ones are actually used, are an important aspect of the scientific approach.

IDENTIFICATION OF IMPROVEMENT NEEDS

Even the most competitive, most successful organizations have limited resources. Therefore, it is important to optimize those resources and use them in ways that will yield the most benefit. One of the ways to do this is to carefully select the areas of improvement to which time, energy, and other resources will be devoted. If there are 10 processes that might be improved, which will yield the most benefit if improved? These are the processes that should be worked on first.

Methodologies for identification of improvement needs were discussed in Chapter 16 (Pareto, the Toyota Practical Problem-Solving model, and others). Another approach is offered by Scholtes and his colleagues. They recommend the following four strategies for identifying improvement needs:[14]

- **Apply multivoting.** Multivoting involves using brainstorming to develop a list of potential improvement projects. Team members vote several times—hence the name—to decide which project or projects to work on first. Suppose the original list contains 15 potential projects. Team members vote and cut the list to 10. They vote again and cut it to 5. The next vote cuts the list to 3, and so on until only 1 or 2 projects remain. These are the first projects that will be undertaken.
- **Identify customer needs.** An excellent way to identify an improvement project is to give the customer a voice in the process. Identify pressing customer needs and use them as projects for improvement.
- **Study the use of time.** A good way to identify an improvement project is to study how employees spend their time. Is an excessive amount of time devoted to a given process, problem, or work situation? This could

signal a trouble spot. If so, study it carefully to determine the root causes.
- **Localize problems.** Localizing a problem means pinpointing specifically where, when, and how often it happens. It is important to localize a problem before trying to solve it. Problems tend to be like roof leaks in that they often show up at a location far removed from the source.

DEVELOPMENT OF IMPROVEMENT PLANS

After a project has been selected, a project improvement team is established. The team should consist of representatives from the units most closely associated with the problem in question, including the process operator. It must include a representative from every unit that will have to be involved in carrying out improvement strategies. The project improvement team should begin by developing an improvement plan. This is to make sure the team does not take the "Ready, fire, aim" approach mentioned earlier.

The first step is to develop a mission statement for the team. This statement should clearly define the team's purpose and should be approved by the organization's governing board for quality (executive steering committee, quality council, or whatever the group is called). After this has been accomplished, the plan can be developed. Scholtes and his colleagues recommend five stages for developing the plan:

1. **Understand the process.** Before attempting to improve a process, make sure every team member thoroughly understands it. How does it work? (This usually requires the development of a process flowchart: see Chapter 15.) What is it supposed to do? Why is that step necessary? What are the best practices known pertaining to the process? The team should ask these questions and others, and pursue the answers together. This will give all team members a common understanding, eliminate ambiguity and inconsistencies, and shine light on any obvious problems that must be dealt with before proceeding to the next stage of planning.

2. **Eliminate errors.** In analyzing the process, the team may identify obvious errors, or potential errors, that can be quickly eliminated. These should be eradicated before proceeding to the next stage. This stage is sometimes referred to as "error-proofing" the process.

3. **Remove slack.** This stage involves analyzing all of the steps in the process to determine whether they serve any purpose and, if so, what purpose they serve. In any organization, processes exist that have grown over the years with people continuing to follow them without giving any thought to why things are done a certain way, whether they could be done better another way, or whether they need to be done at all. Few processes cannot be streamlined.

4. **Reduce variation.** Variation in a process results from either common causes or special causes. Common

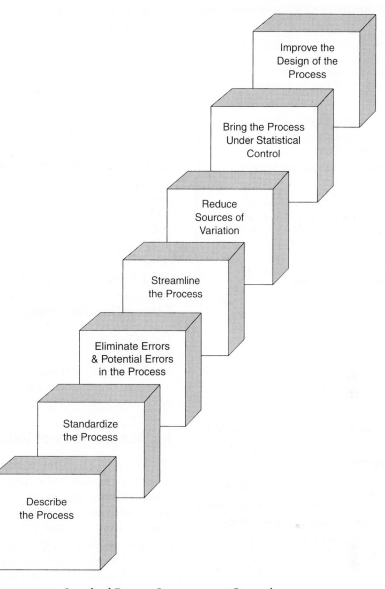

FIGURE 19–2 Standard Process Improvement Strategies

causes result in slight variations and are always present. Special causes typically result in greater variations in performance and may not always be present. Strategies for identifying and eliminating sources of variation are discussed in the next section. See also Chapter 18.

5. ***Plan for continual improvement.*** By the time this step has been reached, the process in question should be in good shape. The key now is to incorporate the types of improvements made on a continuous basis so that continual improvement becomes a normal part of doing business. The Plan–Do–Check–Adjust cycle, discussed in Chapter 16, applies here. With this cycle, each time a problem or potential improvement is identified, an improvement plan is developed (Plan), implemented (Do), monitored (Check), and refined as needed (Adjust).

COMMON IMPROVEMENT STRATEGIES

Numerous different processes are used in business and industry; consequently, there is no single road map to follow when improving processes. However, a number of standard strategies can be used as a menu from which improvement strategies can be selected as appropriate. Figure 19–2 shows several standard strategies that can be used to improve processes on a continual basis. These strategies are explained in the following sections.[15]

Describe the Process

The strategy of describing the process is used to make sure that everyone involved in improving a process has a detailed knowledge of the process. Usually, this requires some inves-

Localizing a Problem

"A vehicle repair operation repeatedly found trucks with rusted fuel pumps. Before they could know what caused the rust, they had to localize the occurrence of the problem. They used stratification analysis of data they collected to localize the problem and found that:

- the problem occurred in vehicles using diesel fuel.
- and of those vehicles, only in ones that operated in a certain geographical area.
- and of those, only ones that got fuel from a specific fueling station.

"This information allowed them to zero in on the fueling site, and they discovered a small hole in a pipe feeding the underground tank. Rain water could seep into the tank through the hole. Repairing the leak and preventing its recurrence solved the problem of rusted fuel pumps."

Source: Joseph M. Juran, *Juran on Leadership for Quality: An Executive Handbook* (New York: Free Press, 1989), 28–29.

tigation and study. The steps involved are as follows:

1. Establish boundaries for the process.
2. Flowchart the process (as it is, not as it should be).
3. Make a diagram of how the work flows.
4. Verify your work.
5. Correct immediately any obvious problems identified.

Standardize the Process

To continually improve a process, all people involved in its operation must be using the same procedures. Often this is not the case. Employee X may use different procedures than Employee Y. It is important to ensure that all employees are using the best, most effective, most efficient procedures known. The steps involved in standardizing a process are as follows:

1. Identify the currently known best practices for the process and write them down.
2. Test the best practices to determine whether they are in fact the best, and improve them if there is room for improvement (these improved practices then become the final best practices that are recorded).
3. Make sure that everyone is using the newly standardized process.

Streamline by Reducing Inventory and Lot Sizes

"Large inventories of work-in-process cause many problems. They slow response time to customers, and are usually costly to maintain, and most deadly of all, hide other problems in the process. One cause of large inventories is slow changeovers from job to job, which also cause large lot sizes. This is true of both manufacturing and nonmanufacturing processes."

Source: Peter R. Scholtes, Barbara J. Streibel, and Brian L. Joiner, *The Team Handbook*, 3rd ed. (Madison, WI: Joiner Associates, 1992), 5–61.

4. Keep records of process performance, update them continually, and use them to identify ways to improve the process even further on a continual basis.

Eliminate Errors and Potential Errors in the Process

The strategy of eliminating errors in the process involves identifying errors that are commonly made or which could be made (potential) in the operation of the process and then getting rid of them. This strategy helps delete steps, procedures, and practices that are being done a certain way simply because that is the way they have always been addressed; and those that could be done incorrectly due to ambiguous or incomplete process procedures; or even faulty process design. Whatever measures can be taken to eliminate such errors are carried out as a part of this strategy.

Streamline the Process

The strategy of streamlining the process is used to take the slack out of the process. This can be done by reducing inventory, reducing cycle times, and eliminating unnecessary steps. After a process has been streamlined, every step in it has significance, contributes to the desired end, and adds value.

Reduce Sources of Variation

The first step in the strategy of reducing sources of variation is identifying sources of variation. Such sources can often be traced to differences among people, machines, measurement instruments, material, sources of material, operating conditions, and times of day. Differences among people can be attributed to levels of capability, training, education, experience, and motivation. Differences among machines can be attributed to age, design, and maintenance. Regardless of the source of variation, after a source has been identified, this information should be used to reduce the amount of variation to the absolute minimum. For example, if the source of variation is a difference in the levels of training completed by various operators, those who need more training should receive it. If one set of measurement instruments is not as finely calibrated as another, they should be equally calibrated.

Bring the Process Under Statistical Control

The strategy of bringing the process under statistical control was explained in detail in Chapter 18. For this discussion, it is necessary to know only that a control chart is planned, data are collected and charted, special causes are eliminated, and a plan for continual improvement is developed.

Improve the Design of the Process

There are many different ways to design and lay out a process. Most designs can be improved on. The best way to improve the design of a process is through an active program of experimentation. To produce the best results, an experiment must be properly designed, using the following steps:

1. Define the objectives of the experiment. (What factors do you want to improve? What specifically do you want to learn from the experiment?)

2. Decide which factors are going to be measured (cycle time, yield, finish, or something else).

3. Design an experiment that will measure the critical factors and answer the relevant questions.

4. Set up the experiment.

5. Conduct the experiment.

6. Analyze the results.

7. Act on the results.

ADDITIONAL IMPROVEMENT STRATEGIES

In his book *Total Manufacturing Management*, Merli lists 20 strategies for continual improvement that he calls "The Twenty Organizing Points of Total Manufacturing Management."[16] Eighteen of these strategies are still valid (see Figure 19–3), and are explained in the following paragraphs:[17]

- *Reduced lead time.* Raw materials sitting in a storeroom are not adding value to a product. Efficient management of the flow of materials is essential to competitiveness. Lead time can be reduced by evaluating the following factors: order processing time, waiting time prior to production, manufacturing lead time, storage time, and shipping time.

- *Flow production.* Traditionally, production has been a stop-and-go or hurry-up-and-wait enterprise. *Flow production* means production that runs smoothly and steadily without interruption. An example illustrates this point. A large manufacturer of metal containers had its shop floor arranged by type of machine (cutting, turning, milling, etc.). All cutting machines were grouped together, all turning machines were grouped together, and all milling machines were grouped together. However, this isn't how the flow of work went. Work flowed from cutting to turning, back to cutting, and on to milling. Arranging machines by type caused a great many interruptions and unnecessary material handling. To improve production efficiency, the machines were rearranged according to work flow. This is often referred to as cellular production. Flow production smoothed out the rough spots and made work flow more smoothly.

- *Group technology.* Traditional production lines are straight. With group technology, processes are arranged so that work flows in a U-shaped configuration. This can yield the following benefits: shorter lead times, greater flexibility, less time in material handling, minimum work in progress, flexibility with regard to volume, less floor space used, and less need for direct coordination.

- *Level production.* This involves breaking large lots into smaller lots and producing them on a constant basis over a given period of time. For example, rather than producing 60 units per month in one large lot, production might be leveled to produce 3 units per day (based on 20 workdays per month). This strategy can yield the added benefit of eliminating the need to store the materials needed for large lots. This, in turn, makes it easier to implement just-in-time manufacturing.

- *Synchronized production.* Synchronized production involves synchronizing the needs of the production line with suppliers of the materials needed on the line. For example, assume that a line produces computers in a variety of different internal configurations. The difference among the configurations is in the capacity of the hard drive installed. Such information as what type of hard drive is needed, in what quantities, at what time, and at what point on the line must be communicated to the hard-drive supplier. The supplier must, in turn, deliver the correct type of hard drive in the correct quantity at the correct time to the correct place on the line. When this happens, synchronized production results.

- *Overlapped/parallel production.* This strategy involves dismantling long production lines with large lot capacities and replacing them with production cells that turn out smaller lots. This allows production of different configurations of the same product to be overlapped or run parallel, that is, concurrently.

- *Flexible schedules.* Production cells and the ability to overlap production or run it parallel allow for a great deal of flexibility in scheduling. The more options available to production schedulers, the more flexible they can be in developing schedules.

- *Pull control.* Pull control is a concept applied to eliminate idle time between scheduling points in a production process, the need to maintain oversized inventories to offset operational imbalances, and the need to plan all target points within a process. With good pull control, work moves through a process uninterrupted by long waiting periods between steps.

- *Visual control.* Visual control is an important aspect of just-in-time manufacturing. It is an information dissemination system that allows abnormalities in a process to be identified visually as they occur. This, in turn, allows problems to be solved as they occur rather than after the fact.

- *Stockless production.* Stockless production is an approach to work handling, inventory, lead time planning, process balancing, capacity utilization, and schedule cycling that cuts down on work in progress. With stockless production, it is necessary to eliminate process bottlenecks, balance the process, and have an even work flow that eliminates or at least minimizes work in progress. Stockless production and just-in-time go hand-in-hand.

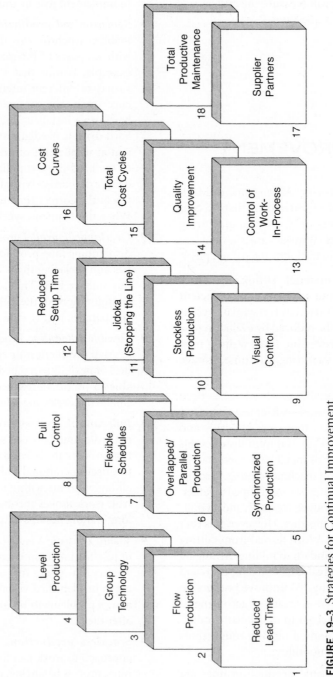

FIGURE 19-3 Strategies for Continual Improvement

348

- **Jidoka.** *Jidoka* means halting an entire process when a defect is discovered so that it won't cause additional problems further down the line. *Jidoka* can be accomplished manually, or the line can be programmed to stop automatically, or both.

- **Reduced setup time.** This strategy consists of any activity that can reduce the amount of time required to break down a process and set it up again for a different production run. Such things as quick changeovers of tools and dies are common with this strategy.

- **Control of work-in-process.** Work-in-process (WIP) often means work that is sitting idle waiting to be processed. Controlling the amount of idle WIP involves organizing for a smoother flow, small lot sizes, process flexibility, pull control, and rapid breakdown and setup.

- **Quality improvement.** In addition to improving productivity using the various strategies discussed in this chapter, it is important simultaneously to improve quality. This book is devoted to an approach for continually improving quality. An important point is that productivity and quality improvements are reciprocally supportive.

- **Total cost cycles.** This strategy involves basing decisions on the total cost cycle rather than isolated pieces of it. It is not uncommon for decisions to be based on reducing the costs associated with part of a process, although another part of the process may have its cost increased by the decision. True improvements have not been accomplished unless overall costs have been reduced.

- **Cost curves.** A cost curve is a graphic representation of a time-based process wherein manufacturing costs accumulate relative to billing. Two types of costs are shown on a cost curve: materials and conversion costs. A cost curve shows graphically how much cost accumulates until the customer is billed for the product. It is a tool to help managers set the optimal point of production.

- **Supplier partners.** This strategy amounts to involving suppliers as partners in all phases of product development rather than keeping them in the dark and revealing your activities to them only through the low-bid process. If tested and trusted suppliers know what you are trying to do, they will be better able to maximize their resources in helping you do it.

- **Total productive maintenance.** Total productive maintenance (TPM) means maintaining all systems and equipment continually and promptly all of the time. In a rushed workplace, one of the most common occurrences is slacking off on machine and system maintenance. This is unfortunate because a poorly maintained system cannot achieve the quality and productivity needed to be competitive. Poor maintenance can result in the following problems: shutdowns from unexpected damage, increased setup and adjustment time, unused uptime,

speeds below the optimum, increased variations, increased waste from defects, and production losses.

THE KAIZEN APPROACH

Kaizen is the name given by the Japanese to the concept of continual incremental improvement. *Kai* means "change" and *zen* means "good." *Kaizen*, therefore, means making changes for the better on a continual, never-ending basis. The improvement aspect of Kaizen refers to people, processes, and products.

If the Kaizen philosophy is in place, all aspects of an organization should be improving all the time. People, processes, management practices, and products should improve continually: "good enough" is never good enough. In his landmark book *KAIZEN: The Key to Japan's Competitive Success*, Masaaki Imai gives an overview of the concept that is summarized in the following paragraphs:[18]

- **Kaizen value system.** The underlying value system of Kaizen can be summarized as continual improvement of all things, at all levels, all the time, forever. All of the strategies for achieving this fall under the Kaizen umbrella (see Figure 19–4). Executive managers, middle managers, supervisors, and line employees all play key roles in implementing Kaizen (see Figure 19–5).

QUALITY TIP ▼

DENSO Manufacturing Tennessee and Kaizen

DENSO Manufacturing, located in Maryville, Tennessee, is part of a larger global company that produces advanced technologies, systems, and components for the automotive industry. The quality standard for DENSO Tennessee is ISO/TS 16949. In addition, the company has achieved ISO 14001 registration and has been recognized for its commitment to recycling and pollution control. The foundation of DENSO Tennessee's quality program is Kaizen. Kaizen is Japanese for good change ("Kai" = change and "Zen" = good). The good change is continual and it involves all personnel—executives, managers, and employees. The company is also committed to the concept of lean manufacturing.

When DENSO Tennessee was awarded the prestigious Shingo Prize for Excellence in Manufacturing, the following accomplishments were noted:

- TS 16949 and ISO 14001 registrations/certifications
- Recycling rate of 95%
- DENSO Global President's Award for Kaizen
- Reduction of the defect rate by 32% during the period considered
- Warranty cost reduction of 60% during the period in question

By applying the principles of total quality, DENSO Tennessee is able to thrive in the global arena in a field that is intensely competitive. By focusing on continual improvement, the company is able to stay ahead of competitors that are, themselves, committed to organizational excellence.

FIGURE 19–4 Elements of Kaizen

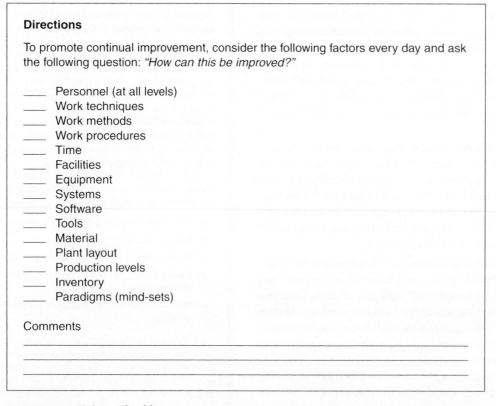

FIGURE 19–5 Kaizen Checklist

- *Role of executive management.* Executive managers are responsible for establishing Kaizen as the overriding corporate strategy and communicating this commitment to all levels of the organization; allocating the resources necessary for Kaizen to work; establishing appropriate policies; ensuring full deployment of Kaizen policies; and establishing systems, procedures, and structures that promote Kaizen.

- *Role of middle managers.* Middle managers are responsible for implementing the Kaizen policies established by executive management; establishing, maintaining, and improving work standards; ensuring that employees receive the training necessary to understand and implement Kaizen; and ensuring that employees learn how to use all applicable problem-solving tools.

- *Role of supervisors.* Supervisors are responsible for applying the Kaizen approach in their functional roles, developing plans for carrying out the Kaizen approach at the functional level, improving communication in the workplace, maintaining morale, providing coaching for teamwork activities, soliciting Kaizen suggestions from employees, and making Kaizen suggestions.

- *Role of employees.* Employees are responsible for participating in Kaizen by taking part in teamwork activities, making Kaizen suggestions, engaging in continual self-improvement activities, continually enhancing job skills through education and training, and continually broadening job skills through cross-functional training.

- *Kaizen and quality.* In a total quality setting, quality is defined by customers. Regardless of how customers define quality, it can always be improved and it should be, continually. Kaizen is a broad concept that promotes quality from the all-encompassing Big Q perspective.

Kaizen Implementation Tools

All of the tools explained in Chapter 15 are used in Kaizen, as are the tools explained elsewhere in this book. In addition, several are specifically thought of as *Kaizen* implementation tools: *Kaizen* Checklists and the *Kaizen* Five-Step Plan.

Kaizen Checklists

Kaizen is about continual improvement of people, processes, procedures, and any other factors that can affect quality. One of the best ways to identify problems that represent opportunities for improvement is to use a checklist that focuses the attention of employees on those factors that are most likely in need of improvement. These factors include personnel, work techniques, work methods, work procedures, time, facilities, equipment, systems, software, tools,

> **Kitchen Kaizen**
>
> Illustrating the mind-set of a Kaizen practitioner, a group leader in the weld shop at Toyota's Lexus plant in Cambridge, Ontario, tells this story: He was at a party and needed to dispose of something. To find a disposal site, he went into the expensive new designer kitchen—granite countertops, the latest top-line appliances, and so on. Locating the trash can, he found that the foot-pedal-operated lid stuck open when he released the pedal. The hostess told him that they had just learned to live with it. The Kaizen mind kicked into operation and he had to solve the problem. Before the party was over, he had found that if a certain part of the lid-raising mechanism was turned around, the lid worked perfectly. Kaizen always produces improvement—even in the kitchen.
>
> *Source: Lexus* magazine, Quarter 1, 2004, 39.

material, plant layout, production levels, inventory, and paradigms (see Figure 19–5).

Kaizen Five-Step Plan

The Five-Step Plan is the Japanese approach to implementing Kaizen.[19] Posters bearing the words *seiri, seiton, seiso, seiketsu,* and *shitsuke* can often be found on the walls of Japanese plants. In English, these words mean "straighten up," "put things in order," "clean up," "standardize," and "discipline," respectively.

- *Step 1: Straighten up.* This step involves separating the necessary from the unnecessary and getting rid of the unnecessary in such areas as tools, work in process, machinery, products, papers, and documents.

- *Step 2: Put things in order.* This step involves putting such things as tools and material in their proper place and keeping things in order so that employees can always find what they need to do the job without wasting time looking.

- *Step 3: Clean up.* This step involves keeping the workplace clean so that work can proceed in an efficient manner, free of the problems that can result when the work site is messy.

- *Step 4: Standardize.* This step was originally aimed at standardizing how the first three of the Five-S's were implemented and maintained, but since then expanded to include standardizing on best practices. Visual management is also a major component of standardization.

- *Step 5: Discipline.* This step involves careful adherence to standardized work procedures. This requires discipline.

Five W's and One H

The Five W's and One H are not just Kaizen tools. They are widely used as management tools in a variety of set-

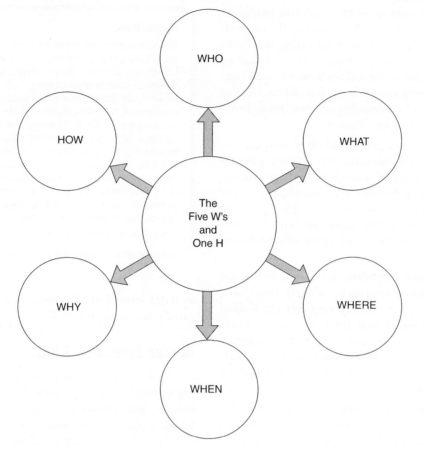

FIGURE 19–6 The Five W's and One H

tings. The Five W's and one H (see Figure 19–6) are Who, What, Where, When, Why, and How. Using them encourages employees to look at a process and ask such questions as the following: Who is doing it? Who should be doing it? What is being done? What should be done? Where is it being done? Where should it be done? When is it being done? When should it be done? Why is it being done? Why do it that way? How is it being done? How should it be done?

Five-M Checklist

The Five-M checklist is a tool that focuses attention on five key factors involved in any process.[20] The Five M's are man (operator), machine, material, methods, and measurement (see Figure 19–7). In any process, improvements can be made by examining these aspects of the process.

THE CEDAC APPROACH

CEDAC is an acronym for *cause-and-effect diagram with the addition of cards*.[21] It was originally developed by Dr. Ryuji Fukuda of Sumitomo Electric, a Japanese manufacturing firm. Its purpose is to facilitate continual improvement in the workplace.

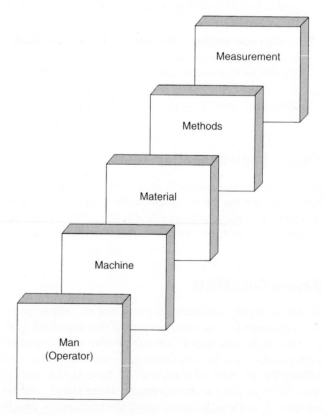

FIGURE 19–7 The Five M's Of Processes

$$Density = \frac{Number\ of\ employees\ with\ mastery^*}{Total\ number\ of\ employees}$$

For example:

Employees with mastery   =   60
Total number of employees   =   100

$$\frac{60}{100} = 60\%\ density$$

*Employees who are skilled at using the improvement system.

FIGURE 19–8 Calculating the Density of Skilled Employees

CEDAC is based on the supposition that three conditions must exist in order for continual improvement to occur. Fukuda explains these conditions as follows:[22]

- *A reliable system.* For continual improvement to occur, there must be a standardized, reliable system. A system that is reliable will yield the same results regardless of who uses it, provided it is applied properly and according to standard procedures.

- *A favorable environment.* Continual improvement will not occur unless an environment favorable to it exists. The keys to creating and maintaining an environment favorable to continual improvement are leadership and education. Leadership manifests itself in the form of commitment, both to the concept of continual improvement and to the allocation of the necessary resources. Education is how employees become skilled in the use of the improvement system. The higher the density of employees who are skilled in the use of the improvement system, the better. Density is expressed as a percentage (see Figure 19–8).

- *Practicing as teams.* Like all endeavors requiring skills, continual improvement strategies must be practiced. Because in a total quality setting work is performed by teams of employees, it is important for team members to practice together.

As teams practice, it is important for individual members to understand that improvements may come only in small increments. This is not merely acceptable; it is also desirable. In a competitive situation, the difference between winning and losing is often quite small.

In the United States, instant replay of sports events and big plays broadcast during the sports portion of the nightly news have accustomed people to last-minute game-winning home runs in baseball, desperation baskets just before the buzzer in basketball, and clock-beating 60-yard touchdown passes in football. What the camera does not show is all of the small, incremental improvements that put these teams in a position to win with one dramatic play in the final seconds

of the game. This is unfortunate because a home-run mentality can mitigate against an organization's ability to make the small incremental improvements that can mean the difference between winning and losing.

The CEDAC system can be divided into two main parts (see Figure 19–9). Each part is subdivided into several related activities. In part 1, a problem is identified. Quality tools such as those explained in Chapter 15 are used, as are additional quality tools, to analyze the problem. Based on

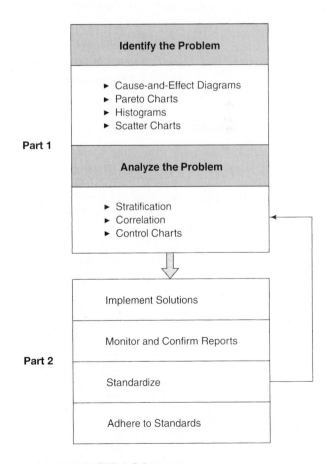

FIGURE 19–9 CEDAC System

Developing a CEDAC Diagram

Figure 19–10 summarizes the main steps in developing a CEDAC diagram.[23] Instructions for these steps are contained in the following paragraphs:

1. *Draw the basic diagram.* The CEDAC diagram should be drawn with the cause side on the left and the effect side on the right. Using CEDAC is a team activity. Consequently, the basic diagram should be large enough to attach to a wall so that it can be reviewed by team members at any point in the process. The cause side is a fishbone diagram with the addition of cards to the left of each spine. The effect side can be any of the various tools explained in Chapter 15 (e.g., a control chart or a Pareto chart). Figure 19–11 is an example of a basic diagram laid out but not yet containing any information. Such a diagram might be as large as 4 × 6 feet or even larger.

2. *Select the focus of improvement efforts.* What is the focus of the CEDAC project? What problem is to be attacked?

the analysis, solutions are implemented in part 2. Results are monitored and confirmed. If the results are positive, the procedures that solved the problem are standardized, and these new standard procedures are followed by all employees. If the desired results are not achieved, the team returns to part 1 to analyze the problem again.

✓ 1. Draw the basic diagram.

✓ 2. Select the focus of the improvements to be made.

✓ 3. Name a project leader.

✓ 4. Establish a way to measure improvements on the effect side.

✓ 5. Establish the improvement goal and projected date of attainment.

✓ 6. Format the effect side of the diagram.

✓ 7. Collect fact cards for the cause side of the diagram.

✓ 8. Develop improvement cards.

✓ 9. Implement proposed improvements, monitor, and measure results.

✓ 10. Select the best improvement cards for standardization.

FIGURE 19–10 Ten-Step Checklist: Developing a CEDAC Program

Fact Cards   Improvement Cards

3 × 5 Card (Typical)

Cause Side

Effect Side

FIGURE 19–11 CEDAC Diagram

Quality tools such as those covered in Chapter 15 can be used to identify the improvement that has the most potential.

3. *Name a project leader.* A CEDAC diagram relates to one specific improvement project and should have its own project leader. This is the person responsible for organizing, facilitating, monitoring, and completing the project.

4. *Establish a measurement method.* Improvements tried as part of the CEDAC process should result in improvements on the effect side of the diagram. These results must be measurable. Does the improvement decrease waste? Improve throughput? Reduce defects? These are improvements that can be measured. Regardless of the focus of the project, establish measures for documenting success or failure.

5. *Establish an improvement goal and date.* The improvement goal and projected target date are established by the project leader. It is important for this person to communicate why the goal and target date are important by relating them to the organization's ability to compete.

6. *Format the effect side of the diagram.* The actual format for the effect side of the CEDAC diagram must be decided on at this point. The preliminary chart prepared in the first step must be finalized. It can be a Pareto chart, a histogram, a control chart, or any other type of quality tool. The actual format selected should be the one that best communicates the necessary facts relating to the project. Figure 19–12 is a format that might be used if the project goal is to reduce throughput time by 50% over a 24-week period or any similar goal.

7. *Collect fact cards for the cause side.* The goal is to reduce throughput time by 50% within 24 weeks. All members of the project team should examine the problem and commit their ideas as to why throughput time is as high as it is to cards (e.g., 3 × 5 cards). These cards are known as *fact cards.* The fact cards should be sorted into general categories (material, manpower, methods, etc.). After all cards have been sorted into categories, the spines on the cause side of the CEDAC diagram are labeled to correspond with these categories. Cards in each category are examined and combined where appropriate. Remaining cards are then attached to the left of the horizontal lines along the spines, as shown in Figure 19–11.

8. *Collect improvement cards.* Each fact card attached to the CEDAC diagram contains a description of some factor that contributes to increased throughput time. Each of these factors should be eliminated. To do this, improvement cards are collected from members of the project team. These cards correspond to the fact cards and contain a recommendation for eliminating the factor described on the corresponding fact card. Improvement cards are attached to the right of the horizontal lines along the spines, as shown in Figure 19–11.

9. *Implement and test improvement ideas.* Improvement ideas should be carefully evaluated for credibility before being attached to the CEDAC diagram. However, after an improvement card is attached, the idea it contains should be implemented and the results monitored and recorded on the effect side of the diagram.

10. *Select cards for standardization.* Improvement ideas that fail to reduce throughput time (see Figure 19–12) should be discarded. Those that work best should be written in as standard procedures in the process in question. After an idea is standardized, it should be adhered to strictly by all personnel.

GOAL: Reduce throughput time by 50% within 24 weeks
(from 16 hours per unit to 8 hours per unit)

FIGURE 19–12 CEDAC Diagram: Effect Side

THE LEAN APPROACH

Lean was originally developed as a manufacturing concept and, as such, is often referred to as *lean manufacturing*. However, as has happened with so many quality management–related concepts, the service sector—impressed with the results enjoyed by practitioners of lean manufacturing—began to adopt and adapt the concept to this sector. Consequently, we use the term *Lean* in this book to convey the message that the concept can be applied with good results in the manufacturing and service sectors. The purpose of adopting Lean as a business improvement method is to produce better products or deliver better services using fewer resources. If the concept had a motto, it would be this: *doing more with less and doing it better.*

Lean Defined

Lean as a concept is based on the Just-In-Time Toyota Production System (TPS) developed at Toyota Motor Corporation by Japanese quality pioneer Taiichi Ohno. Ohno's work incorporated the earlier work of Sakichi Toyoda and Kiichiro Toyoda, the latter being the founder of Toyota Motor Corporation. Lean is a somewhat generic version of the TPS.[24] A Lean operation is one in which a better product is developed or a better service is delivered using *less of everything required* (i.e., human, financial, technological, and physical resources). Lean is about being flexible enough to get the right things, to the right place, at the right time, in the right amounts. At the heart of the concept are the reduction of waste and the improvement of work flow. (For an in-depth study of Just-in-Time and Lean, see Chapter 21).

The reduction of waste approach to Lean implementation grew out of Toyota's desire to eliminate waste in manufacturing processes. Lean focuses on reducing and, ideally, eliminating the following types of waste:[25]

- *Overproduction waste.* This amounts to making more of a product or delivering more of a service than is needed or more than is needed at the moment. In a manufacturing setting, this might mean producing 100 parts when only 50 are needed. In a service setting, it might mean pumping 20 gallons of gas for a customer who wanted only 15.

- *Inventory waste.* This amounts to carrying more inventory than is needed at a given time. The concept of *just-in-time delivery* has the reduction of inventory as part of its broader purpose. In a manufacturing setting, this might mean having more parts stack up at an assembly station than can be used for a given production run. In a service setting, this could mean a bookstore carrying more copies of a given book than it is likely to sell.

- *Motion waste.* This amounts to incorporating unnecessary movement into the production process or into the delivery of services. This was one of the targets of the time and motion studies conducted by Frederick Taylor, who, in 1911, published the classic book *The Principles of Scientific Management.* In a manufacturing setting, this might mean programming too many motions into a CNC milling machine. In a service setting, it might mean having to move around the office several times to obtain everything needed to complete paperwork.

- *Transportation waste.* This amounts to excess movement of parts in a manufacturing setting. In a service setting, it typically means excess movement of people. In a manufacturing setting, this might mean that a part is machined at one side of the shop and must be transported all the way to the other side in order to be finished or incorporated as part of an assembly. In a service setting, it might mean having to transport patients to one end of a hospital for a given test and all the way to the other for another type of test.

- *Overprocessing waste.* This amounts to going beyond customer requirements in ways that create no additional value when producing a product or doing more than the customer wants in a service setting. A manufacturing example would be holding a given part to tighter tolerances than required in the specifications when the application of the part will not be improved by tighter tolerances. The classic service example is the sales representative who holds up a customer by continuing to talk after already making the sale.

- *Defects waste.* This amounts to creating rejected work or causing rework as the result of production or processing errors. In manufacturing, an example of a defect would be a part that is faulty because it does not meet customer specifications. In a service setting, it might mean having to rewrite an insurance policy because of calculation errors in writing the original policy.

- *Waiting waste.* This amounts to people, machines, or processes idling because something that is needed is not yet available. In a manufacturing setting, it might involve an expensive machine and its operator sitting idly because the parts they are to work on have not been delivered. In a service setting, the classic example is the airliner idling on the taxiway waiting for clearance to take off.

- *Underutilization waste.* This amounts to underuse of the talent, skills, and creativity of people and the capabilities of technology. In a manufacturing setting, it might involve failing to include the people who operate processes in brainstorming sessions aimed at improving the performance of those processes. In a service setting, it might mean using a sophisticated word processing system like it is just a typewriter with a visual display monitor.

Tools and Techniques of Lean

The tools and techniques of Lean will be familiar to students of quality management. In fact, most of these tools have already been explained at different places in this book. However, Lean is not just about the application of these tools. It is also about how they are applied and in what order. The tools and techniques most commonly associated with Lean are as follows:[26]

■ *Five-S workplace organization.* The Five-S's come from five Japanese words that translate into English as sort, store, shine, standardize, and sustain. Five-S as a tool is used to ensure a neat, clean, and orderly workplace, one that is conducive to peak performance and continual improvement.

■ *Visual workplace systems.* This tool is used to promote ease of communication. It amounts to using visual aids such as signs, lines, labels, and color coding so that no one has to guess where to go or what to do.

■ *Layout.* This tool is used to achieve the optimum plant layout so that motion and transportation waste are minimized. The idea is to get work that is input for another process as close as possible to that process to reduce unnecessary motion and transportation.

■ *Standardized work (SW).* This tool is used to ensure that processes involving repetitive tasks are being done in the most efficient and productive manner and that all who operate the processes do them in the same way. This prevents the introduction of human and process errors.

■ *Point of use storage (POUS).* This tool is used to ensure that the tools and parts needed at a given workstation are stored conveniently near that station. POUS helps minimize movement and transportation waste.

■ *Batch size reduction.* This tool is used to achieve efficiency for the entire system rather than for a given process within the system. It helps ensure that work flows smoothly and continuously from one process to the next rather than bunching up at any given workstation or any part of a given process.

■ *Quick changeover (QCO).* This tool is used to make process conversions as rapidly as possible. It might involve changing tools quickly in a manufacturing setting or changing a room for a different purpose in a service setting. Regardless, this tool helps eliminate time wasted in making process changes.

■ *Poka-yoke.* This tool is used to error-proof a process to the extent possible. It is Lean's answer to that old maxim "Anything that can go wrong will go wrong." Poka-yoke is especially important for situations where there is the potential for human error. It amounts to asking the question "What could go wrong here?" when setting up a process and then finding ways to eliminate or at least minimize the potential errors identified.

■ *Self-inspection.* This tool involves having personnel check their own work rather than just passing along errors to the next step in the process. In order to apply this tool, individual employees must be trained, provided with inspection standards, given the necessary inspection equipment, and allowed the time necessary to complete inspections.

■ *Autonomation.* The word itself means "automation with a human touch." This tool is used to build automatic alarms/process notifications into the system so that when a problem of any kind arises, a human being is notified and can intervene to solve the problem. For example, a robot that experiences some type of malfunction might shut down, thereby setting off an alarm that will notify a human operator of the need to intervene.

■ *Pull systems/kanban.* This tool is used to provide a visual method—*kanban* is the Japanese word for "sign"—that lets one step in the process know that the next step is ready for its output. The sign or other type of notification is the "pull" that asks for the output.

■ *Cellular and flow.* This tool is used to ensure a steady and consistent flow of work through the system's cells. When the output of one cell in the process sits idly waiting to be used in the next cell, time is wasted. A steady, continuous flow of work is more efficient. This is the opposite of the old "hurry up and wait" phenomenon.

■ *Just-in-time (JIT).* This tool is used to ensure that items are delivered to the next cellular step in the process just in time to be used. JIT is the antidote to work piling up at one station while another station has nothing to work on.

■ *Total productive maintenance (TPM).* This tool is used to ensure that all equipment in a system and all parts of all processes that make up the system are in good condition and ready for use when called on. With TPM, equipment maintenance becomes a normal part of the process. TPM uses process operators in many maintenance procedures.

■ *Value stream mapping (VSM).* This tool uses symbols to describe a value stream. It is implemented in four steps: (1) identify the process groups (of tasks), (2) develop a map of the current state, (3) develop a map of a desired future state, and (4) develop a plan to achieve the future state map. VSM is a continual process, since every process can and should be improved continually. This is the Japanese concept of *Kaizen*.

■ *Change management.* Continual improvement is fundamental to Lean, and improvements do not happen unless changes are made. This tool is used to effectively manage change so that human resistance is minimized. An effective approach to managing change is as follows: (1) create a comprehensive word picture of how things will be different and better after the change (write it from the perspective of the process operators—those who will be affected most by the change and who will have to implement it); (2) communicate the change picture to all stakeholders; (3) give stakeholders opportunities to ask questions, make comments, voice concerns, and vent; (4) ask process operators to identify any roadblocks to successful implementation of the change that you might not have anticipated, and take the steps necessary to eliminate or mitigate these roadblocks; (5) implement, monitor, and adjust; and (6) incorporate the change into the process so that it becomes the normal approach until it is changed as the result of a subsequent process improvement.

- **Teamwork.** This tool is used to ensure that all other aspects of Lean can be implemented effectively. Lean, like all quality management concepts, is by its nature a team-oriented enterprise. The better teamwork is working in the organization, the better the results of Lean will be.

THE SIX SIGMA APPROACH

We touched on Six Sigma in our discussion of histograms in Chapter 15. Now we must take a deeper look at this concept. In 1981, Robert Galvin, who was the president of Motorola, issued a challenge to his company: *Improve performance tenfold over the next 5 years.* Motorola responded and achieved the goal. That led the company to its next challenge. Galvin, by then versed in some work being done in Motorola's Communications Sector with the goal of Six Sigma quality, called for 10 times improvement in each of the next 2-year periods, and achieving Six Sigma quality throughout the corporation by 1992. That required a staggering 100 times improvement in all operations of the company. It was not achieved by 1992, but by that year it was clear that this was the right thing to do. By 1993, many of Motorola's manufacturing operations were operating at or near Six Sigma.[27]

In the first 10 years following Galvin's Six Sigma Challenge, and as a direct result of the Six Sigma Efforts, Motorola claimed to have saved several billions of dollars which went directly to the bottom line as profit. Sales increased by a factor of five, and profits increased by nearly 20% each year.[28] Other companies that have adopted Six Sigma report similar gains.

As the word of Six Sigma spread, other organizations took up the challenge. CEO Jack Welch committed General Electric to Six Sigma (1995). Allied Signal (1994) and Honeywell (1998)—the two now combined under the name of Honeywell International Inc.—were other very large companies that took on Six Sigma. They were soon followed by Ford (2000) and a host of others. A decade into the twenty-first century, rooted in total quality management, Six Sigma enjoys widespread application across many industrial and service sectors. Applicability of Six Sigma is not limited to manufacturing concerns. Albertsons, and parent supermarket chain Supervalu, figure their Six Sigma savings from 2002 through 2008 in the hundreds of millions of dollars.[29] Six Sigma is even finding application in the military. In 2008, the U.S. Army recorded savings of $2 billion from four Six Sigma initiatives involving such disparate projects as[30]

- More efficient meal scheduling
- Streamlining communications through the chain of command
- Reducing the recruiting process from 32 steps to 11
- Better management of clothing outlet inventory

Six Sigma is one of the most innovative developments to emerge out of the total quality movement. Its purpose is to improve processes to the point where the defect rate is 3.4 per million or less, thereby making the company more competitive, profitable, and successful. Originally designed for use in high-volume production settings, it has nonetheless been found equally suited to service organizations, including the military, hospitality industry, supermarkets, and so on. Its benefits include the following:[31]

- Cost reduction
- Productivity improvement
- Market-share growth
- Customer retention
- Cycle-time reduction
- Culture change
- Product/service development

Modern products and services have many built-in opportunities for defects. In manufacturing, for example, most good companies try to operate in the 3-sigma to 4-sigma region. The number of defects from such a company will range between 63 and 2,700 defects per million. The Six Sigma companies expect just 3.4 defects per million.

Motorola won the Malcolm Baldrige National Quality Award in 1988 for its pioneering efforts in the development of the Six Sigma concept. The central core of the Six Sigma concept is a six-step protocol for process improvement. The six steps are as follows:

1. Identify the product characteristics wanted by customers.
2. Classify the characteristics in terms of their criticality.
3. Determine if the classified characteristics are controlled by part and/or process.
4. Determine the maximum allowable tolerance for each classified characteristic.
5. Determine the process variation for each classified characteristic.
6. Change the design of the product, process, or both to achieve a Six Sigma process performance.

It is important to note that the Six Sigma concept is a subset of the broader concept of total quality. Six Sigma is a strategy within the context of total quality that moves the target to a much higher level of quality than organizations have achieved in the past. It is not a concept that supplants or replaces total quality. Rather, it is an innovative way to pursue a higher level of quality under the broad umbrella of total quality.

Six Sigma Belts, Champions, and Executives

Unlike Total Quality Management (TQM), the Toyota Production System and Lean, Six Sigma has a defined organizational hierarchy of Six Sigma expertise and experience for the organization implementing practices and operating Six Sigma projects. These hierarchical levels are named as follows:

- *Executive (CEO, Top Management).* Establish Six Sigma vision for the organization. Empower subordinate Six Sigma leaders. Provide necessary resources for the implementation/projects.

- *Champion.* Trained in Six Sigma methodology and selection of Six Sigma projects that are aligned with business objectives. Executive designates Champions from upper management to identify Six Sigma projects, align and integrate them with the organization's goals and vision. Select and mentor Six Sigma project leader "Belts."

- *Master Black Belt.* Identified by Champions to be cross-functional in-house Six Sigma consultants/facilitators/coaches. Assist Champions in identification of Six Sigma projects. Has extensive project management experience, and thorough mastery of Six Sigma methodology and tools. Guides and mentors Black and Green Belts. Usually full-time Six Sigma employees.

- *Black Belt.* Has significant Six Sigma training. Primarily engaged in leading Six Sigma project execution under the Master Black Belts.

- *Green Belt.* Has Six Sigma training. Project leaders engaged in Six Sigma implementation/projects, operating under guidance from the Black Belts.

If this sounds like a martial arts system, it is for a good reason. In the early days of Six Sigma the folks who were involved in implementation of the practices or execution of the projects needed the aura of authority (and maybe with some intimidation thrown in) carried by a martial arts Black Belt. Motorola could have simply set up the same certification levels, calling them Level 1, Level 2, or Master, Journeyman, and so on, but the Belt nomenclature had a more dynamic ring to it, and it has endured. Although there is no central clearing house for Six Sigma certification, Motorola, the American Society for Quality, the Institute of Industrial Engineers, and many other organizations offer individuals Six Sigma certification.

Key Personnel Preparation and Roles in Six Sigma

One of the strengths of Six Sigma is its emphasis on preparation of the key personnel who will be responsible for its deployment and ongoing operation.[32] This preparation, coupled with well-defined roles for personnel, adds to the potential of this continual improvement method. Advocates of Six Sigma take a four-pronged approach to deploying the concept: (1) understand the concept and all of its component elements, (2) train key personnel who will be the organization's Green and Black Belts, (3) make sure that the organization's Green and Black Belts are provided the environment needed for success by key decision makers who serve as Champions of the Six Sigma deployment, and (4)

provide Master Black Belts to support, guide, instruct, mentor, and assist the Black Belts.

Green Belts are selected personnel in an organization who have completed basic training in the application of DMAIC Roadmap and the various tools associated with it. Black Belts have completed more advanced training in the application of DMAIC and the associated tools. Master Black Belts are Black Belts who have shown themselves to be self-reliant, self-motivated, and excellent problem solvers and who, as a result, have been allowed to complete additional training. Master Black Belts, as a result of their additional training, have a broader array of tools to apply in solving problems. These additional tools become especially important when an improvement project being run by a Black Belt becomes bogged down or hits a roadblock.

Champions, in the long run, represent the most important component in the deployment of Six Sigma. Champions, as the name implies, are key decision makers in an organization who "champion" the cause of effective Six Sigma deployment. They provide an environment in which Six Sigma can be effectively employed. They support the concept and those tasked with applying it. When problems arise between a Black Belt and anyone else in the organization, Champions step in to defuse the situation before it throws the Six Sigma deployment off track. This is especially important when a Black Belt faces resistance from a manager who is higher in the organization.

Mike Carnell and Scot Shank describe an effective Champion as "a hybrid of Henry Kissinger and Xena, the Warrior Princess."[33] By this, they mean that good Six Sigma Champions are both diplomat and warrior and they know when to be which. In addition, Champions must be proficient in: (1) business and operations interface, (2) project selection, (3) pace mediation, and (4) results implementation.[34]

DMAIC Roadmap

The nucleus of Six Sigma is the Define, Measure, Analyze, Improve, and Control or DMAIC Roadmap. Although the five phases of the roadmap concept are constant, the steps, tools, and outputs of each phase can vary slightly, depending on the type of organization and the exigencies of that organization. An excellent model of a DMAIC Roadmap for Six Sigma was developed by Sigma Breakthrough Technologies Inc. The explanations in the remainder of this section are based on this model roadmap.[35] For each phase, there are steps, associated tools, and outputs. The steps and outputs are summarized in the following paragraphs, along with a sampling of some of the tools that might be used.

Define   In this phase of the roadmap, users (1) initiate the project, (2) define the process, (3) determine customer requirements, and (4) define key process output variables. These steps lead to the following outputs: the project charter, the project team, and a list of clear customer requirements. Some of the tools that might be used in this phase include SIPOC maps (see Figure 19–13), value stream maps,

FIGURE 19–13 SIPOC Diagram

affinity diagrams, brainstorming, Murphy's Analysis, customer requirement trees, and surveys.

Measure In this phase, users (1) understand the process, (2) evaluate risks on process inputs, (3) develop and evaluate measurement systems, and (4) measure current performance. These steps result in the following outputs: current state process maps, identified and measured Xs or Key Process Input Variables (KPIVs), verification of measurement systems, and current capability of Ys or Key Process Output Variables (KPOVs). Some of the tools that might be used in this phase include SIPOC/Value Stream Mapping, input/output analysis, detailed process maps, FMEA, data collection plans, data integrity audits, and C&E matrices.

Analyze In this phase, users (1) analyze data to prioritize key input variables and (2) identify waste. These steps result in the following outputs: root causes of defects that are reduced to the vital few, a prioritized list of potential key inputs, and a list of specific wastes. Some of the tools that might be used in this phase include statistical process control (SPC), T-tests, analysis of variance (ANOVA), nonparametrics, chi square regression, Five-S, and multivariable studies.

Improve In this phase, users (1) verify critical outputs, (2) design improvements, and (3) pilot the new process. These steps result in the following outputs: a final list of KPIVs, an action plan for improvement, future state process maps, FMEA, control plans, new process design/documentation, and a pilot study plan. Some of the tools that might be used in this phase include design of experiments, kanban, mistake-proofing, quick changeover, process mapping, process documentation, training plans, SPC, FMEA, and control plans.

Control In this phase, users (1) finalize the control system and (2) verify long-term capability. These steps result in the following outputs: a control system, improvement validated for the long term, identified continual improvement opportunities, handoff of the new process, and team recognition. Some of the tools that might be used in this phase include control plans, process documentation, training plans, SPC, and process capability.

Six Sigma: The Name

The name Six Sigma comes from the concept of standard deviation, a statistically derived value represented by the lowercase Greek letter sigma (σ). The variation of processes and their output products is typically measured in the number of standard deviations from the mean (usually the ideal point). (See the section on histograms in Chapter 15.)

The well-controlled processes of most good companies presently operate between 3 and 4 sigma. This means 99.73% of the output of a process will fall between plus and minus three standard deviations at 3 sigma, or 99.9937% at 4 sigma. If the specification (such as a required dimension with a tolerance) for parts produced by the process should correspond to the $\pm 3\sigma$ values, then a 3-sigma process will yield 2,700 defective parts for every 1 million produced. (See Figure 19–14.)

Let's assume that the specifications describing acceptable product remain constant and that through some improvement we are able to decrease process variation to the point that its new 6-sigma deviation corresponds to the positions of the old 3-sigma values. (See Figure 19–15.) Now if everything else remains constant, the process will yield 99.9999998% acceptable product, or a mere 0.002 defective parts per million. In this case, the process is performing at a

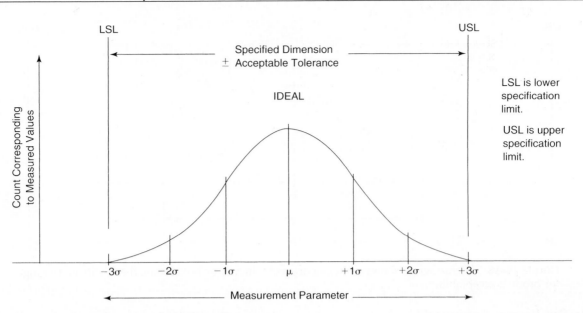

FIGURE 19–14 Histogram of a 3-Sigma Process

Note: Requirements match ±3σ values; 99.73% of product with fall within the specified limits.

6-sigma level. Note that this corresponds to 1 unacceptable part in 500 million produced.

When Motorola embarked on its journey to break out of the normal quality level associated with 3- or 4-sigma processes, it targeted 6 sigma; hence the name Six Sigma. Eventually, other companies began to adopt the Motorola program, and the name has become part of the quality lexicon.

Relationship of Six Sigma to Total Quality

Six Sigma is an extension of total quality management, which has the aim of taking process and product qual-

ity to levels where all customer requirements are met. Depending on which Six Sigma proponent you are listening to, the emphasis may be on improving the bottom line or on meeting customer requirements. Of course, the latter is the best way to accomplish the former. It is important to understand that Six Sigma is not some new field of endeavor separate from the total quality philosophy. Quite the contrary, Six Sigma is a total quality strategy for achieving what all the other total quality strategies attempt to achieve: superior performance that is improved continually, forever.

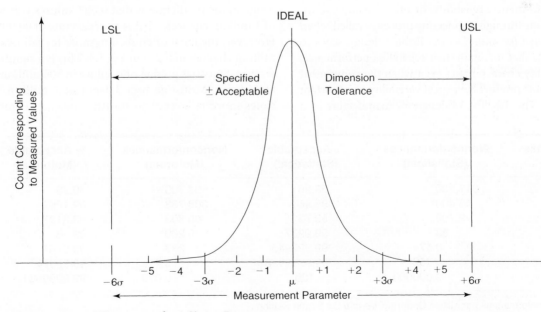

FIGURE 19–15 Histogram of a 6-Sigma Process

Note: Requirements match ±6σ values. Note that requirements are the same as in Figure 19–14, but the process is improved; 99.9999998% of product produced will fall within the specified limits.

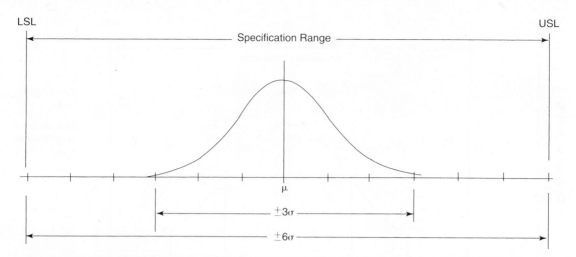

FIGURE 19–16 This histogram shows a 6-sigma process achieved by broadening the specification range for product acceptability.

How Is Six Sigma Achieved?

Six Sigma can be achieved by improving process performance, but improving processes to this degree can be difficult, and in many cases nearly impossible. On the other hand, Six Sigma can be achieved without improving the process at all if the specification describing acceptable product can be loosened enough to correspond to the original process's ±6σ points (see Figure 19–16). Note that in this case the process, which is identical to that of Figure 19–14, was not changed in any way. Instead, the definition of what is acceptable in terms of process input was changed. The specification range has been increased from the values corresponding to the ±3σ points to the values corresponding to the ±6σ points. When we do this, unacceptable product will occur only once in 500 million products.

In order to use this strategy, we must be able to use output that has greater deviation from the ideal value—without sacrificing performance, reliability, or other quality parameters. This is done through engineering processes called *robust design* and *design for manufacture*. Robust design seeks to design products that maintain their reliability, performance, and other quality characteristics even when the component parts of the whole product have great variability of important characteristics. The objective of design for manufacture is to

eliminate the possibility of manufacturing errors by simplifying and "error-proofing" the steps required for manufacturing the product. These techniques—improving processes (both incrementally and in giant leaps) and rendering the processes more efficient and foolproof through the use of robust design and design for manufacture—have been around for a long time and are considered by most to be essential elements of TQM. The difference here is that Motorola did something no one else had done: It set the target at Six Sigma.

Is Six Sigma Really Six Sigma?

In this chapter's discussion so far, we have used numbers relating to acceptable product that are quite different from those found in the Six Sigma literature. For example, at 3 sigma, out of 1 million chances for success, there will be 2,700 failures. That is a success rate of 99.73%. At 6 sigma, the prediction is that 0.002 failures will occur out of 1 million chances. That is a success rate of 99.9999998%. However, the most often seen number for failures out of 1 million chances in Six Sigma is 3.4. This is a significant difference. Statistics predict one failure in 500 million chances at 6 sigma. Motorola uses 3.4 out of 1 million or 1,700 times more failures than statistics project. Figure 19–17

Sigmas	Nonconformances (Statistical)	% Acceptable (Statistical)	Nonconformances (Motorola)	% Acceptable (Motorola)
1	317,400	68.26	697,700	30.23
2	45,400	95.46	308,733	69.1267
3	2,700	99.73	66,803	93.3197
4	63	99.9937	6,200	99.38
5	0.57	99.999943	233	99.9767
6	0.002	99.9999998	3.4	99.99966
7	0.000003	≈ 100	0.019	99.9999981

Nonconformances per Million Opportunities in a Six Sigma Setting

FIGURE 19–17 Sigma Quality Levels, NPMO

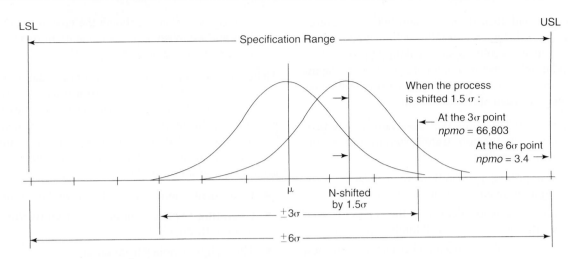

FIGURE 19–18 The $1^1/_2$ Sigma Shift

Note: The process histogram is shifted $1^1/_2$ sigma from its ideal position to account for long-term variation.

illustrates the difference between straight statistics and the Motorola version.

Clearly, the numbers used by Motorola in its Six Sigma program are significantly different from those derived from straight statistics. Which are correct? The answer is that the straight statistics numbers are correct, but the Motorola numbers are better in a practical sense. What Motorola has done is applied a factor to account for slight changes in environmental conditions, different operators, and so on. The reason Motorola considers this valid is that the sigma values of any process are derived from a statistically valid sample of process operation, necessarily taken over a relatively short period of time. The typical histogram is a snapshot of what is going on at the time the data were collected. Should that period be changed from a few weeks to a few years, one would no doubt encounter new variations resulting from the environment, new operators, and other factors. Motorola believes that the short-term view provides an overly optimistic picture of process variation and, consequently, of the process results at a given sigma level. The company concluded, therefore, that the reality of the long term under which the processes operate should be compensated for. Motorola chose to do this by shifting the process average (μ) from the target, or ideal point, by 1.5 sigma to the right, while leaving the normal 6 sigma field and the upper and lower specification limits as they were. (See Figure 19–18.)

Such a shift could take place due to environmental changes or other factors. Drifts and shifts of varying magnitude are the norm in the long term, and Motorola is covering that eventuality by accounting for it before the fact. The values for *nonconformances per million opportunities (NPMO)* are then taken from the right tail of the histogram. Notice in Figure 19–18 that the $+3\sigma$ point intercepts the shifted curve at the equivalent of its $+1.5\sigma$. At 1.5 sigma, there should be 66,803 *NPMO*, which corresponds exactly with Motorola's expectation for 3 sigma. Similarly, the $+6\sigma$ line intercepts the shifted curve at its $+4^1/_2\ \sigma$ point; 4.5 sigma is predicted by statistics to yield 3.4 *NPMO*, the

value used in the Motorola Six Sigma program. Whether in real life the process should shift to the left or the right makes no difference, since the same results occur in either direction. Practically speaking, and pragmatically anticipated by Motorola, the process may shift back and forth by varying magnitudes over time. By introducing the 1.5 sigma shift, Motorola has allowed some long-term variation to enter the picture without causing panic.[36]

We hasten to state that we do not disagree with the route Motorola took with the $1^1/_2$ sigma shift. Smart people determined that this was the appropriate thing to do. Still, we are not completely comfortable with the Six Sigma name if it fails to truly represent 6 sigma. But we will not argue with 3.4 nonconformances out of a million opportunities. This is a quality level that is so far beyond the average that we will gladly accept it, name and all.

THE LEAN SIX SIGMA APPROACH

The name Lean Six Sigma has to be understood before we go any further. Failure to do so will lead to a misunderstanding of the concept itself and its purpose. Clarification is best begun by stating what Lean Six Sigma is not. It most definitely is not some kind of a Lite Six Sigma, like an improvement system designed for those who only want a little improvement or who don't want to be bothered by the details of Six Sigma. What we have here is a wedding between two healthy, robust, powerful systems that stood alone in the two previous sections—Lean and Six Sigma. The Six Sigma part of Lean Six Sigma is still the full-bodied, potent improvement system that we have discussed in the previous section. The Lean part of Lean Six Sigma is still the complete, proven Quality Management system found in the Toyota Production System and Just-In-Time.

The two earlier sections explained the concepts of Lean and Six Sigma, respectively. This section explains a concept that combines the two to form Lean Six Sigma. The two complement each other with their strengths, namely Lean's elimination of waste and Six Sigma's breakthrough methodology for solving performance problems and making improvements, DMAIC, and its infrastructure system of Belts. Lean Six Sigma is nothing more or less than the marriage of Lean and Six Sigma.

Advantages of Lean Six Sigma include:

- Elimination of the Eight Wastes—waiting, overproduction, rework, motion, transportation, processing, inventory, and intellect

- Means of improving process flow whether on the manufacturing floor, in an office, or any other setting

- A structured means for identifying the key factors that determine the performance of all kinds of processes

- Ordered methods for establishing key factors at the best possible level

- Disciplined means of sustaining key factors at the best level

- Synergistic advantage of linking the Lean tools with the Six Sigma tools in a systematic way and in a specified sequence

- Tying all of these to the financial health of the organization

The objective of Lean Six Sigma is to make the organization superior in its day-to-day work and processes, its products and services, and its business results. This has also been the objective of many organizations that have found that Lean alone, or Six Sigma by itself, did not quite provide all the results needed in their quest for a better competitive posture. A lot of those organizations have found that by combining Lean with Six Sigma, significant performance gains relative to processes, products, services, employees, customer satisfaction, and the business bottom line have been realized. Those same organizations would also admit, however great their improvement record has been, that the improvement task is never finished—that continual improvement is a never-ending practice. With technology changing at an ever faster pace and with customer demands and preferences constantly shifting, the need for continually improving processes, employees, products and services will be with us long into the future, if not forever. Given the level of competition in the marketplace of our shrinking world, there will always be the need for improvement of business performance. Lean Six Sigma provides a proven system for achieving continual improvement in every aspect of the organization's business.

THE THEORY OF CONSTRAINTS AND INTEGRATED TOC, LEAN, SIX SIGMA (ITLS) APPROACH

In his 1984 book, *The Goal*, Dr. Eliyahu M. Goldratt introduced a management concept called the Theory of Constraints (TOC). He describes his theory:

> The Theory of Constraints is an intuitive framework for managing an organization. Implicit in the framework is a desire to continually improve performance, and to have a process of ongoing improvement. It starts, as

it must, with clearly defining the goal of the organization and establishing measurements to determine the impact of any action on the goal.[37]

All business organizations have at least one goal, and whether stated or not, that is to make a profit today, this year, next year, and in the future. Ordinarily businesses measure their performance by net profit and return on investment (ROI). The TOC is founded on the premise that an organization's performance against the goal can be determined and managed by the variations of three measures:

- Investment (money invested to be in the business)

- Operating Expense (money spent converting investment to throughput)

- Throughput (money from sales)

The premise giving rise to the theory is that every organization faces constraints, at least one of which limits the rate of goal achievement. Goldratt defines a constraint as "anything that limits an organization from achieving higher performance vis-à-vis its goal."[38] Organizations may have tens, or even hundreds of constraints fitting this description, but a core principal within the TOC is that only one, or just a few, really constrain performance. (Remember the Pareto Principle from Chapter 15.) The constraint may be internal to the organization, such as a machine that cannot produce acceptable parts fast enough, employees who lack the necessary skills, or policies and procedures that are unsuitable for the process as implemented. The constraint may also be external, such as lack of customer demand for the product.

It must be noted here that constraints for the purpose of TOC never include breakdowns. Machines that are considered capable of doing what is needed of them do not become constraints when they occasionally breakdown or go out of calibration or adjustment. This is consistent with TQM which holds that repairing a broken machine cannot be considered an improvement, because it merely restores an earlier level of performance.

The TOC is intended to focus the attention and effort of the organization to the constraint within a value-chain, and uses the following five steps to do that:[39]

1. IDENTIFY the constraint (What is the real or major constraint?)

2. Decide how to EXPLOIT the constraint (Turn it into a positive factor, eliminate, or circumvent)

3. SUBORDINATE AND SYNCHRONIZE everything else to the above decisions. (No other activity should have priority because the constraint is inhibiting achievement of the organization's goal.)

Then to improve the performance of that same value-chain, continue:

4. ELEVATE the performance of the constraint (e.g., add capacity)

5. If in any of the steps the constraint has shifted, GO BACK TO STEP 1.

> **Value-Chain definition:** A chain of activities that add value to a product or service as it passes through each of the sequential steps.

The authors have some difficulty with the Theory of Constraints as a standalone system for continual improvement, although many organizations have used TOC as such with good results. As a consequence of the EXPLOIT and SUBORDINATE steps it is often necessary to utilize buffers. These buffers hold materials or work-in-progress to prevent shutting down production whenever a constraining function cannot keep up with demand. Should the constraint fall behind in its output to the next link of the value-chain, the materials or work-in-process stored in the buffer is used to allow the next link to continue operation. This tactic has been proven to be a major deterrent to continual improvement, because having those buffers available hides problems that should be solved. Therefore, rather than being eliminated once and for all, the same problems keep recurring.

As it turns out, the people who are facing the issues everyday on the firing line of the business world have found that better results are achieved by using the Theory of Constraints methodology concurrently with Lean and Six Sigma than by using any of the three systems by itself or in pairs. The Integrated TOC, Lean, Six Sigma (iTLS) model:[40]

- Focuses on the few yet critical elements that limit global performance of the organization by applying Theory of Constraints tools
- Eliminates waste in the form of "hidden factories" [including buffers] with application of Lean tools
- Reduces undesirable variability to ensure process stability with Six Sigma tools

The iTLS model approaches improvement projects in three successive phases.

1. Apply TOC to focus on processes where changes are necessary.
2. Apply Lean to remove waste from the processes.
3. Apply Six Sigma tools to control process performance and variability.

Should your organization be using Lean, Six Sigma, or Lean Six Sigma, you might do well to consider the addition of TOC.

SUMMARY

1. The rationale for continual improvement is that it is necessary in order to compete in the global marketplace. Just maintaining the status quo, even if the status quo is high quality, is like standing still in a race.

2. Management's role in continual improvement is leadership. Executive-level managers must be involved personally and extensively. The responsibility for continual improvement cannot be delegated.

3. Essential improvement activities include the following: maintaining communication, correcting obvious problems, looking upstream, documenting problems and progress, and monitoring change.

4. Structuring for quality improvement involves the following: establishing a quality council, developing a statement of responsibilities, and establishing the necessary infrastructure.

5. Using the scientific approach means collecting meaningful data, identifying root causes of problems, developing appropriate solutions, and planning and making changes.

6. Ways of identifying improvement needs include the following: using multivoting, seeking customer input, studying the use of time, and localizing problems.

7. Developing improvement plans involves the following steps: understanding the process, eliminating obvious errors and potential errors, removing slack from processes, reducing variation in processes, and planning for continual improvement.

8. Commonly used improvement strategies include the following: describing the process, standardizing the process, eliminating errors and potential errors in the process, streamlining the process, reducing sources of variation, bringing the process under statistical control, and improving the design of the process.

9. Additional improvement strategies include the following: reducing lead time, introducing flow production, using group technology, leveling production through smaller lot size, synchronizing production, overlapping production, using flexible scheduling, using pull control, using visual control, using stockless production, using jidoka, reducing setup time, applying control of Work-in-Process, improving quality, applying total cost cycles, using cost curves, use of supplier partners, applying total industrial engineering, and applying total productive maintenance.

10. *Kaizen* is the name given by the Japanese to the concept of continual incremental improvement. It is a broad concept that encompasses all of the many strategies for achieving continual improvement and entails the following five elements: straighten up, put things in order, clean up, standardize, and discipline. Two important Kaizen tools are "Five W's and One H," and the "Five M Checklist."

11. CEDAC is an acronym for *cause-and-effect diagram with the addition of cards.* (This acronym is a registered trademark of Productivity Inc.) With CEDAC, a cause-and-effect diagram is developed, but fact cards about problems and improvement cards containing ideas for solving the problems are used.

12. Lean is a TQM approach originally designed for manufacturing, but since adapted to any kind of organization. It is intended for smoother, more flexible process flow, reducing waste, and improving the organization's competitive posture. The wastes of overproduction, inventory, motion, transportation, overprocessing, defects, waiting, and underutilization are primary targets of Lean. Compared to a non-Lean company, the Lean organization does more and does it better, while using less.

13. Six Sigma is a statistically based approach that targets the defect rate at 3.4 per million or less. Key elements of Six Sigma include the DMAIC roadmap and an infrastructure of Green Belts, Black Belts, Master Black Belts, and Champions. Like other approaches, Six Sigma aims for quality improvement, but goes further to tie these quality improvement initiatives to the financial elements of the organization.

14. Lean Six Sigma is not a low calorie variation, but a linking of Lean and Six Sigma that synergistically combine the benefits of both.

15. Goldratt's Theory of Constraints (TOC) is a management concept designed to provide continual improvement. It focuses on identifying business or process constraints and exploiting the constraints. The basic TOC has evolved into Integrated TOC, Lean, Six Sigma (iTLS) which combines TOC with Lean and Six Sigma.

KEY TERMS AND CONCEPTS

Black Belts
CEDAC
Champions
Communication
Continual improvement
Cost curves
Customer needs
Defects per million
DMAIC roadmap
Five M's
Five W's and One H
Flexible schedules
Flow production
Green Belts
Group technology
Improvement plans
Improvement strategies
Improvement versus "putting out fires"
iTLS

Jidoka
Just-in-time
Kaizen
Kanban
Key Process Input Variables (KPIVs)
Key Process Output Variables (KPOVs)
Lead time
Lean
Lean Six Sigma
Level production
Localize problems
Look upstream
Management's role in continual improvement
Master Black Belts
Multivoting
Necessary infrastructure
Nonconformances per million opportunities (NPMO)
Obvious problems
Plan–Do–Check–Adjust (PDCA) cycle
Pull control
Quality council
Reduced setup time
Return on Investment (ROI)
Root causes
Scientific approach to problem solving
SIPOC
Six Sigma
Slack
Standardizing processes
Statement of responsibilities
Stockless production
Streamlining processes
Supplier Partners
Synchronized production
Theory of constraints
Total cost cycles
Total industrial engineering
Total productive maintenance (TPM)
Value Stream Mapping (VSM)
Value Chain
Variation and sources of variation
Visual control
Work-in-process (WIP)

FACTUAL REVIEW QUESTIONS

1. Explain the rationale for continual improvement.
2. What is management's role in continual improvement?
3. Describe the five essential improvement activities.
4. If you were an executive manager in an organization, how would you structure the organization for quality improvement?
5. What is meant by using the scientific approach?
6. Describe the steps involved in developing an improvement plan.
7. List and explain three widely used improvement strategies.
8. Explain the following improvement strategies:
   a. Group technology
   b. Synchronized production
   c. Jidoka
   d. Supplier Partners
   e. Total productive maintenance
9. Explain the concept of Kaizen.
10. What is CEDAC and how is it used?
11. What are the primary objectives of Lean?
12. Explain the rationale of Six Sigma's target of 3.4 NPMO.
13. How might a SIPOC map be used in a process improvement project?
14. Define Lean Six Sigma.
15. Explain how Theory of Constraints approaches continual improvement, and how it differs from other approaches.

CRITICAL THINKING ACTIVITY

Which Approach Is Best?

Mark Berry, Sandra Griffith, and Juan Carlos are seniors at Florida Tech University, majoring in industrial technology with a quality emphasis. All three hope to be quality directors after graduation.

"I am going to use the Kaizen approach when I graduate and land my first job," said Mark. "It's simple, easy to use, and effective."

"Not me," replied Sandra. "I like the Six Sigma approach."

"I'm not going to use either of them," said Juan. "I'm going to make myself a master list of improvement strategies and use whatever is best for the individual situation."

Join their debate. What approach do you think is best for promoting continual improvement, and why?

ENDNOTES

1. CEDAC is a registered trademark of Productivity Inc.
2. Joseph M. Juran, *Juran on Leadership for Quality: An Executive Handbook* (New York: Free Press, 1989), 72.
3. Peter R. Sholtes, Barbara J. Streibel, and Brian L. Joiner, *The Team Handbook*, 3rd ed. (Madison, WI: Joiner Associates, 2003), 5–9.
4. Juran, *Juran on Leadership*, 35.
5. Ibid., 42–46.
6. Ibid., 43.
7. Sholtes, Streibel, and Joiner, *The Team Handbook*, 5–9.
8. Ibid.
9. This section is based on Scholtes, Streibel, and Joiner, *The Team Handbook*, 5–10.
10. This section is based on Scholtes, Streibel, and Joiner, *The Team Handbook*, 5–10.
11. This section is based on Scholtes, Streibel, and Joiner, *The Team Handbook*, 5–11.
12. This section is based on Scholtes, Streibel, and Joiner, *The Team Handbook*, 5–11.
13. Giorgio Merli, *Total Manufacturing Management* (Cambridge, MA: Productivity Press, 1990), 143.
14. Scholtes, Streibel, and Joiner, *The Team Handbook*, 5–17.
15. Ibid., 5–67.
16. Merli, *Total Manufacturing Management*, 163.
17. Ibid., 153–165.
18. Masaaki Imai, *Kaizen: The Key to Japan's Competitive Success* (New York: McGraw-Hill, 1986), 1–16.
19. This section is based on Imai, *Kaizen*, 233.
20. Ibid., 237.
21. Ryuji Fukuda, *CEDAC: A Tool for Continuous Systematic Improvement* (Cambridge, MA: Productivity Press, 1989), 3.
22. Ibid., 3–10.
23. This section is based on Fukuda, *CEDAC*, 39–51.
24. This section is based on Andy Carlino and Jamie Flinchbaugh, *The Hitchhiker's Guide to Lean* (Dearborn, MI: Society of Manufacturing Engineers, 2005), 28–42.
25. This section is based on Anthony Manos, Mark Sattler, and George Alukal, "Make Healthcare Lean," *Quality Progress* 39, no. 7 (July 2006): 24–25.
26. Ibid., 26–29

27. Mikel J. Harry and Richard Schroeder, "The Nature of Six Sigma Quality," undated paper, 10.

28. Peter S. Pande, Robert P. Neuman, and Roland R. Cavenagh, *The Six Sigma Way* (New York: McGraw-Hill, 2000), 7.

29. Mark Hamstra, "Supervalu Sees Savings in Six Sigma," *Supermarket News* (January 11, 2010).

30. Retrieved from www.sixsigmacompanies.com/archive/ on September 15, 2010.

31. Pande, Neuman, and Cavenagh, *The Six Sigma Way*, xi.

32. This section is based on Mike Carnell and Scot Shank, "The Champion's Role in Successful Six Sigma Departments." Retrieved from www.isixsigma.com/library/content/c020422a.asp. on January 14, 2008.

33. Ibid.

34. Ibid.

35. This section is based on Ian D. Wedgwood, *LEAN SIGMA: A Practitioner's Guide* (Upper Saddle River, NJ: Prentice-Hall, 2007), 8.

36. Harry and Schroeder, "The Nature of Six Sigma Quality," 10.

37. Eliyahu M. Goldratt, "The Avraham Y. Goldratt Institute," undated paper explaining the Theory of Constraints and the services available from the Goldratt Institute, 1.

38. Ibid., 3.

39. A paper from AGI Goldratt Institute, "The Theory of Constraints and Its Thinking Processes," copyright 2001–2009, 9.

40. Dr. Reza Pirasteh and Celso Calia, "Integration of Lean, Six Sigma & TOC Improves Performance," *Information Week* (April 12, 2010). Retrieved from www.informationweek.com on September 2010.

BENCHMARKING

People seldom improve when they have no other model but themselves to copy after.
—*Oliver Goldsmith*

MAJOR TOPICS
- **Benchmarking Defined**
- **Benchmarking versus Reengineering**
- **Rationale for Benchmarking**
- **Prerequisites to Benchmarking**
- **Obstacles to Successful Benchmarking**
- **Role of Management in Benchmarking**
- **Benchmarking Approach and Process**
- **Making Full Use of Benchmarking Data**
- **Perpetual Benchmarking**
- **Benchmarking Resources**

Benchmarking has become a popular tool among companies trying to become more competitive and striving for world-class performance. The majority of them are actively engaged in benchmarking. Benchmarking is a part of the total quality process, and anyone involved in total quality should have a solid understanding of this subject. This chapter is intended to help readers understand what benchmarking is all about, its benefits, and its pitfalls. The chapter includes sufficient information to enable any enterprise to make rational decisions concerning benchmarking, including whether or not to do it and how to go about it.

Benchmarking was brought to our awareness through Robert C. Camp's 1989 landmark book.[1] In the 20 odd years since then a number of variations have been developed on the benchmarking theme. We have *benchmarking studies*, in which there is no contact with an outside firm—information gained is strictly from the public domain. There is no question that this technique can be useful. It is something that the organization should be doing anyway. Sometimes third-party firms specializing in benchmarking studies are contracted for that work. There is considerable doubt that this is really benchmarking, however.

We also have *competitive benchmarking*, in which a competitor's operation is studied from a distance *without* the cooperation of the target firm. The aim is to learn something that can help improve process or product quality. Competitive benchmarking uses publicly available data, and once again, it is possible to contract this work to specialist third-party firms. This approach, however, doesn't fit our definition of benchmarking.

Also in use are the unstructured plant visits, during which the visitor firm intends to learn something that will help with its processes or products. This is often called benchmarking but has more aptly been named *industrial tourism*. Such visits have some value, but they do not comprise benchmarking.

Many other variations exist, but the form of benchmarking addressed in this book is what has been called *cooperative benchmarking*, *best practices benchmarking*, or *process benchmarking*, in which the focus is radical improvement of key processes. This involves a cooperative effort by two firms, the benchmarking firm wanting to bring a substandard process up to the world-class level of the partner firm's process.

BENCHMARKING DEFINED

Benchmarking has been around since the early 1980s, but it wasn't until the early 1990s that it became a widely accepted means of improving company performance. In 1985, almost no benchmarking activity existed among the Fortune 500 companies. By 1990, half of the Fortune 500 companies were using this technique. Today companies large and small find benchmarking to be an effective component in their total quality effort. If there is a single most likely reason for the slow rise in benchmarking popularity, it is a misunderstanding of the concept—a misunderstanding of what benchmarking is, what it is not, and how to do it. It helps to begin with an examination of what benchmarking is not.

Benchmarking Is Not:	
Cheating	Unethical
Illegal	Industrial espionage
Immoral	

All of these misconceptions about benchmarking assume that one party somehow takes advantage of an unsuspecting competitor by surreptitiously copying the competitor's product or processes. Nothing could be further from the truth. Benchmarking involves two organizations that have agreed to share information about processes or operations. The two organizations both anticipate some gain from the exchange of information. Either organization is free to withhold information that is considered proprietary. In addition, the two companies need not be competitors.

> Benchmarking is the process of comparing and measuring an organization's operations or its internal processes against those of a best-in-class performer from inside or outside its industry.

Benchmarking is finding the secrets of success of any given function or process so that a company can learn from the information—and improve on it. It is a process to help a company close the gap with the best-in-class performer without having to "reinvent the wheel."

A distinction exists between benchmarking and competitive analysis. *Competitive analysis* involves comparing a competitor's product against yours. It compares the features and pricing of the product. Consumers perform competitive analysis when they compare competitors' products as they try to determine which brand of high-definition television or automobile to purchase. Benchmarking goes beyond that to comparing how the product is engineered, manufactured, distributed, and supported. Benchmarking is interested not so much in what the product is and what it costs as in the underlying processes used to produce, distribute, and support it.

Finally, and most important, benchmarking is a tool to help establish where improvement resources should be allocated. If, for example, it is discovered that three of five processes are nearly as good as the best-in-class performers, but two are significantly off the best-in-class mark, the most resources should be allocated to these two. The most benefit for the dollars invested will come from changing those processes to conform more nearly to the best-in-class. Relatively little will be gained by drastically changing a process that is already close to the best there is. Key points to remember about benchmarking are as follows:

- Benchmarking is an increasingly popular improvement tool.
- Benchmarking concerns processes and practices.
- Benchmarking is a respected means of identifying processes that require major change.
- Benchmarking is done between consenting companies that may or may not be competitors.

- Benchmarking compares your process or practice with the target company's best-in-class process or practice.
- The goal of benchmarking is to find "secrets of success" and then adapt and improve them for your own application.
- Benchmarking is equally beneficial for both large and small businesses.

BENCHMARKING VERSUS REENGINEERING

Benchmarking involves partnering with the owner of a best-in-class process so that you might adopt or adapt that process in your operation without having to spend the time and energy to try to design a duplicate of the superior process. Process reengineering requires you to do the latter, on your own. Therefore, in our view, process reengineering should be considered only when it is impossible to use benchmarking. That could happen for a number of reasons, including these:

- No known process available for benchmarking (rare)
- Best-in-class not willing to partner
- Best-in-class inaccessible due to geography or expense

If your subject process is unsatisfactory and you cannot benchmark for any of these reasons, you may have to resort to reengineering. You should be careful to consider the reasons the process is unsatisfactory. It may simply be the wrong process for the job, or it may be out of statistical control. Reengineering will not solve either of those problems. Be sure that the process is appropriate and that it is in control first. If it is still not producing the desired results, suggesting that it is simply not capable, then redesigning it through reengineering is a good approach. One disadvantage with process reengineering is that there is no guarantee that after spending the time and resources, you will have a competitive process. That issue does not exist with benchmarking. With benchmarking, you will have observed a competitive process in action.

When we set out to improve our processes, we normally flowchart them to help us understand how each process really works and to give us a visual impression of the steps, people, and functions involved. Improvement typically comes about by changing or eliminating activity in the process that does not add value or consumes too much time or resources, and so on. There is an alternative way to go about this, and that is to abandon the current process and replace it with a brand new process that provides the same functionality but better, faster, or cheaper. That is process reengineering.

Here is something to think about: if an organization could achieve the same results by either one of these two routes, which one would offer the best chance for success in the workplace? We believe the former—let's call it the continual improvement route—would be more readily accepted by the workforce and would be, therefore, more likely to succeed. Usually, the people most closely related to the process have major input to any continual improvement initiative, and it will not be perceived as something being forced on them by some person or group that fails to understand the process anyway. Whether justified or not, that is the way process reengineering has come across to workers. It tends to be radical and sudden, and seldom is consideration given to the human issues. Many times it is seen as a management tool for laying off workers. It does not have to be that way, but that is, we think, the way process reengineering is widely perceived today.

We say this to lead into our final thoughts on process reengineering. If you find process reengineering to be the approach for one of your processes, never let it be a surprise to your employees. In keeping with the philosophy we have promoted throughout this book, it only makes sense to involve the process owners and their internal suppliers and customers, along with other appropriate employees, in your process reengineering project. Take advantage of their collective brainpower and diverse perspectives, and in the doing, their buy-in will be ensured.

In summary, if you have a very good process to begin with, use continual improvement techniques to make it better. On the other hand, if the process is clearly inferior to some used by other firms, try benchmarking. When you cannot achieve the kind of improvement you need from either of those methods, then process reengineering may be required. But no matter which way you go, be sure to get your people involved.

RATIONALE FOR BENCHMARKING

Never was Yogi Berra's comment, "The future ain't what it used to be," as relevant as it is to modern industry. The future for companies today seems far different from what it seemed in the twentieth century. The first real questions regarding the future and the ability of the United States to sustain its industrial leadership seem to have resulted from the oil crisis of 1974. By then, the United States had lost much of the commercial electronics business to Sony, Hitachi, and Panasonic, but the most important industry in the United States, the automobile industry, seemed secure. However, when the oil embargo struck, Americans quickly traded their big domestic cars for small, more fuel-efficient Japanese models. When the embargo ended, Americans continued buying Japanese cars because consumers found them better than their American counterparts. The Japanese quickly claimed about 30% of the U.S. automobile market (and possibly could have gained much more except for voluntary restraints adopted out of fear that severe trade restrictions would be imposed by Washington). Following these events, North America finally started to wake up to the fact that the world was changing. Whole industries were moving from one part of the world to another, and most of that movement was to Japan. There was good reason to look at the Japanese to see what they were doing differently that allowed them to accomplish this.

What was learned, of course, was that by following the teachings of Deming, Juran, Ishikawa, Taguchi, Ohno, and other quality pioneers, Japan had developed vastly superior practices and processes. These resulted in superior manufactured goods at competitive prices—everything from motorcycles, to cars, to cameras, to electronics of all kinds, and even to ships. It took several years of looking at Japan to realize fully what had happened. For a long time, Western leaders rationalized that Japan's success was due to low labor costs, the Japanese work ethic versus that of Detroit, lifetime employment, and other factors. Such rationalizations simply clouded the real issue: the superiority of the Japanese practices and processes. Now that industrial leaders worldwide are aware that better practices and processes can enhance competitiveness, it makes good business sense to determine where an organization stands relative to world-class standards and what must be done to perform at that level. That is what benchmarking is designed to do.

Twenty years ago, benchmarking was a case of comparing North American industry with that of the Japanese. Today benchmarking is a case of comparing your company with the best in the world. The best in the world for a given comparison may be in Japan or Korea, or it may be next door. It may be your direct competition, or it may be in a completely different industry. In addition to companies all over the world emulating the Japanese, customers all over the world are demanding the highest quality in the products they buy. Business as usual is no longer sufficient. Organizations must be improving always and forever, or they will be out of business soon and forever.

The rationale for benchmarking is that it makes no sense to stay locked in an isolated laboratory trying to invent a new process that will improve the product, or reduce cost, when that process already exists. If one company has a process that is four times as efficient, the logical thing for other companies to do is to adopt that process. An organization can make incremental improvements to its process through continual improvement, but it might take years to make a 4× improvement, and by then, the competition would probably be at 6× or better. Benchmarking is used to show which processes are candidates for continual (incremental) improvement and which require major (one-shot) changes. Benchmarking offers the fastest route to significant performance improvement. It can focus an entire organization on the issues that really count.

Some factors that drive companies to benchmark are commitment to total quality, customer focus, product-to-market time, manufacturing cycle time, and financial performance at the bottom line. Every company that has won the Malcolm Baldrige Award endorses benchmarking (see Discussion Assignment 20–1 later in this chapter). Key points to remember about benchmarking as it relates to continual improvement are as follows:

- Today's competitive world does not allow time for gradual improvement in areas in which a company lags far behind.

- Benchmarking can tell a firm where it stands relative to best-in-class practices and processes and which processes must be changed.

- Benchmarking provides a best-in-class model to be adopted or even improved on.

- Modern customers are better informed and demand the highest quality and lowest prices. Companies have a choice to either perform with the best or go out of business.

- Benchmarking supports total quality by providing the best means for rapid, significant process or practice improvement.

PREREQUISITES TO BENCHMARKING

Before getting involved in benchmarking, an organization should check the prerequisites—those philosophical and attitudinal mind-sets, skills, and necessary preliminary tasks that must precede any benchmarking efforts.

Will and Commitment

Without the will and commitment to benchmark, an organization cannot proceed. Don't waste time or the time of a benchmarking partner in the absence of a commitment and a will to benchmark on the part of the company's top management.

Vision and Strategic Objective Link

Benchmarking requires a strong focus, or it can go off in numerous different directions as benchmarkers get carried away in their enthusiasm. Before benchmarking is started, its objectives must be linked to the company's vision and strategic objectives, providing specific direction and focus for the effort. Failure to do this will almost certainly result in wasted resources and frustration.

Goal to Become the Best— Not Simply Improved

Nothing is wrong with incremental improvement—unless current performance is far below world class. If an organization is not near the world-class level, incremental improvement may only ensure that it remains inferior to the best-in-class forever. Benchmarking requires that the goal be to leap to the head of the field in one radical change, not just to be a few percentage points better than last year.

Openness to New Ideas

If a company is imbued with the "Not-invented-here" Syndrome, it will have a problem with benchmarking. The chief symptom of that affliction is a shortsighted mind-set that is characterized by a reluctance to consider other ways of doing things. Although few will admit it, many people are reluctant to consider ideas or approaches that are not their own. Organizations can be like individuals in this regard. Because the essence of benchmarking is capitalizing on the work and ideas of others, a company must be open to new ideas for benchmarking to provide any value. The benchmarking process may help bring about more receptivity to new ideas by demonstrating that they really work.

Identifying Key Business Processes

Since the organization must devote significant capital and human resources to any benchmarking initiative, it is important that the effort makes a difference and pays dividends. That will only happen if the processes selected for benchmarking activity are those considered to be among your key business processes. Therefore, it is essential that those processes that are critical to your mission be identified. Key business processes are defined as those having maximum impact on the success of the organization. They enable the organization to produce its products or services, effectively monitor the organization's performance, and establish its objectives and plans for the future. Organizations usually have 10 to 15 key business processes. Identifying them is best done by the organization in brainstorming sessions employing the following four steps:

1. Identify the organizations' Critical Success Factors (CSFs). These are the handful of characteristics, functions, capabilities, or limitations that are critical to the success and viability of the organization.

2. Identify the metrics for measuring CSFs. These metrics are called Key Performance Indicators (KPIs), and may include production output and sales data, and supporting management performance data.

3. Identify the processes that drive the CSFs. There will typically be 15 or more processes in this category.

4. Some of these processes may be grouped together, and others ungrouped (if they are completely independent of each other). These are your key business processes. It is from the list of key business processes that you will select your candidates for process benchmarking.

Understanding of Existing Processes, Products, Services, Practices, and Customer Needs

It is mandatory that an organization thoroughly understand its own processes, products, services, and practices and the requirements of its customers so that it can determine what needs to be benchmarked. In addition, it is necessary to have a solid understanding of your process in order to make meaningful measurements against that of the partner.

Processes Documented

It is not enough to understand the processes; they must be completely documented, for three reasons:

- All people associated with the process should have a common understanding of it, and that can come only from documentation.

- A documented starting point is needed against which to measure performance improvement after benchmarking changes have been implemented.

- Your organization will be dealing with people (the partners) who are not familiar with your processes. Process documentation will help the partner understand your organization's processes. With an understanding of where the benchmarking organization is, the partner will be better able to help.

Process Analysis Skills

To achieve an understanding of your own processes, products, and services and to document those processes, you must have people with the skills to characterize and document processes. These same people will be needed to analyze the benchmarking partners' processes and to help adapt those processes to the organization's needs. Ideally, they should be employees, but it is possible to use consultants in this role.

Research, Communication, and Team-Building Skills

Additional skills required include research, communication, and team building. Research is required to identify the best-in-class process owners. Communication and team building are required to carry out the benchmarking both on an internal basis and with the partners.

OBSTACLES TO SUCCESSFUL BENCHMARKING

Like most human endeavors, benchmarking can fail. Failure in any activity usually means that the participant failed to prepare adequately for the venture—failed to learn enough about the requirements, the rules, and the pitfalls. So it can be with benchmarking. In this section, some of the common obstacles to successful benchmarking as drawn from the experiences of dozens of companies are explained.

Internal Focus

For benchmarking to produce the desired results, you have to know that someone out there has a far better process. If a company is internally focused (as many are), it may not even be aware that its process is 80% less efficient than the best-in-class. An internal focus limits vision. Is another firm better? Which is it? Such organizations don't even ask the question. This is complacency—and it can destroy a company.

Benchmarking Objective Too Broad

An overly broad benchmarking objective such as "Improve the bottom-line performance" can guarantee failure. This may well be the reason for benchmarking, but the team will need something more specific and oriented not to the *what* but to the *how*. A team could struggle with the bottom line forever without knowing with certainty that it achieved success or failure. The team needs a narrower target: for example, "Refine or replace the invoicing process to reduce errors by 50%." That gives team members something they can go after.

Unrealistic Timetables

Benchmarking is an involved process that cannot be compressed into a few weeks. Consider 4 to 6 months the shortest schedule for an experienced team, with 6 to 8 months the norm. Trying to do it in less time than that will force the team to cut corners, which can lead to failure. If you want to take advantage of benchmarking, be patient. On the other hand, any project that goes on for more than a year should be assessed; the team is probably floundering.

Poor Team Composition

When a process is benchmarked, those who own the process, the people who use it day in and day out, must be involved. These people may be production line operators or clerks. Management may be reluctant to take up valuable team slots with these personnel when the positions could otherwise be occupied by engineers or supervisors. Engineers and supervisors should certainly be involved but not to the exclusion of process owners. The process owners are the ones who know the most about how the process really operates, and they will be the ones who can most readily detect the often subtle differences between your process and that of the benchmarking partner. Teams should usually be six to eight people, so be sure the first members assigned are the operators. There will still be room for engineers and supervisors.

Settling for "OK-in-Class"

Too often organizations choose benchmarking partners who are not best-in-class, for one of three reasons:

- The best-in-class is not interested in participating.

- Research identified the wrong partner.

- The benchmarking company got lazy and picked a handy partner.

Organizations get involved in benchmarking when they decide that one or more of their processes is much inferior to the best-in-class. The intention is to examine that best-in-class process and adapt it to local needs, quickly bringing your organization up to world-class standards in that process area. It makes no sense to link with a partner whose process is just good. It may be better than yours, but if adopted, it still leaves your organization far below best-in-class. For the same amount of effort, an organization could have made it to the top. Organizations should identify the best and go for it. Only if the absolute best will not participate can taking second-best be justified. Second-best should be used only if it is significantly superior to the process in question.

Improper Emphasis

A frequent cause of failure in benchmarking is that teams get bogged down in collecting endless data and put too much emphasis on the numbers. Both data collection and the actual numbers are important, of course, but the most important issue is the process itself. Take enough data to understand your partner's process on paper, and analyze the numbers sufficiently to be certain that your results can be significantly improved by implementing the new process. Unless the team has been deeply involved in the process, the practical knowledge to successfully adapt and implement it back home may be lacking. Keep the emphasis on the process, with data and numbers supporting that emphasis.

Insensitivity to Partners

Nothing will break up a benchmarking partnership quicker than insensitivity. Remember that a partner is doing your organization a favor by giving access to its process. You are taking valuable time from the partner's key people, and at best, you are disrupting the routine of daily business. If you fail to observe protocol and common courtesy in all transactions, your organization runs the risk of being cut off.

Limited Top-Management Support

This issue keeps coming up because it is so critical to success at all stages of the benchmarking activity. Unwavering support from the top is required to get benchmarking started, to carry it through the preparation phase, and finally to secure the promised gains.

ROLE OF MANAGEMENT IN BENCHMARKING

Management plays a crucial role in the benchmarking process. In fact, without the approval and commitment of top management, benchmarking is not possible. Benchmarking is not something that can occur from the grassroots up without management's direct involvement. Several benchmarking considerations require management's approval before the process can start: commitment to change, funding, human resources, disclosure, and involvement.

Commitment to Change

Benchmarking is a serious undertaking for both benchmarking partners. Unless a firm commitment to change exists—unless the organization fully intends to radically improve its processes to come up to best-in-class standards—benchmarking should not be considered. Unfortunately, too many companies jump into benchmarking without that commitment, with the result that money and personnel are wasted by both parties. In addition, the hopes and expectations of employees are raised, only to be disappointed when nothing comes of it. To obtain any real benefit from benchmarking, an organization must resolve that when a best-in-class process is found, it will do what is necessary to incorporate it as a replacement (or radical improvement) model for its inferior process. That, after all, is what benchmarking is about.

Funding

Only management can authorize the expenditure of funds for benchmarking. These funds will support travel for teams visiting the organizations with best-in-class processes. Teams are usually composed of five to eight people. Visits may last from 2 days to 2 weeks. Travel destinations are inflexible, dictated by the location of the best-in-class firms. Clearly, travel expenses can be high. Management must make the funds available if benchmarking is to be carried out.

Human Resources

In similar fashion to funding, management must make the necessary human resources available for the benchmarking tasks. Although the costs for the human resources are usually far higher than for travel, the availability of personnel is seldom an issue except for the target company.

Disclosure

It may not be immediately obvious, but both companies—the benchmarker and the target—disclose information about their processes and practices. Management may be understandably hesitant to disclose such information to competitors, but what about the case of the noncompetitor benchmarking partner? Even there, management may be reluctant because there can be no ironclad guarantee that information divulged to a noncompetitor will not find its way to the competition. The other side of the coin is that few processes or practices remain secret very long anyway. But if the organization has some unique process that gives it a competitive advantage, the process should be treated as proprietary and not be subjected to benchmarking. In any event, only management can make the decision to disclose information.

Involvement

Management must be actively and visibly involved in every aspect of the benchmarking process. Management should be involved in determining which processes are to be benchmarked and selecting benchmarking partner candidates. Management is in a unique position to establish the communication channels between the companies because top managers tend to affiliate through professional organizations. Dialogue among top-level managers should be encouraged.

It is important for management to stay abreast of benchmarking events and to make certain that the effort supports the objectives and vision of the company. Management's ability to do this is greatly enhanced when it is directly involved. In addition, subordinates will recognize the importance placed on benchmarking by the degree to which management is visible in the process. With management active, all levels will be more productive in their benchmarking activities.

BENCHMARKING APPROACH AND PROCESS

The benchmarking process is relatively straightforward, but steps must flow in a sequence. A number of variations are possible, but the process should follow this general sequence:

1. Obtain management commitment.
2. Baseline your own processes.
3. Identify your strong and weak processes and document them.
4. Select processes to be benchmarked.
5. Form benchmarking teams.
6. Research the best-in-class.
7. Select candidate best-in-class benchmarking partners.
8. Form agreements with benchmarking partners.
9. Collect data.
10. Analyze data and establish the gap.
11. Plan action to close the gap or surpass.
12. Implement change to the process.
13. Monitor results.
14. Update benchmarks: continue the cycle.

These 14 implementation steps are explained in the following sections. Figure 20–2 is provided to help maintain perspective and afford clarity.

Step 1: Obtain Management Commitment

Benchmarking is not something one approaches casually. It requires a great deal of time from key people, and money must be available for travel to the benchmarking partners' facilities. Both of those require management's approval. You expect to gain information from your benchmarking partner for which it will expect payment in kind: namely, information from you about your processes. This can be authorized only by management. Finally, the object of benchmarking is to discover processes to replace yours or at least to make major changes to them. Such changes cannot be made without management's approval. Without a mandate from top management, there is no point in attempting to benchmark. That is why the requirement for management commitment is at the top of the list. If you cannot secure that commitment, proceed no further.

Step 2: Baseline Your Own Processes

When a process is baselined, it establishes the starting point for process improvement. The process baseline documents the current state of the process, its steps, and capabilities. A baselined process will have complete documentation of its inputs and outputs, all of its steps and supporting information, together with process capability data. This is often called process characterization. Process flow diagrams are a key element of baselining, and provide a graphical picture of how the process works, who is involved, and the sequence of activity and of decision points, and so on. Process capability provides information on what can be expected from the process under optimal conditions. (For information on Flow Diagrams refer to Chapter 15.)

If your company is involved in total quality, chances are good that you have already done some baselining of processes because before continual improvement can be used effectively, and certainly before statistical process control can be applied, the processes in question must be understood. That is, the processes must be characterized in terms of process capability, their flowcharts, and other aspects. If this has not been done before, it must be done now. It is critical that you understand your own processes thoroughly before attempting to compare them with someone else's processes. Most organizations think they know their processes well, but that is rarely the case unless a deliberate process characterization has recently been done. It is also important that an organization's processes be completely and accurately documented, not just for its own use but also for the benefit of everyone associated with the process in any way. (See the discussion of flowcharting in Chapter 15.)

Step 3: Identify and Document Both Strong and Weak Processes

Selection of processes or functions to benchmark would seem to be a straightforward decision but is in fact one that gives many would-be benchmarkers a great deal of trouble. If you keep in mind that the purpose of benchmarking is to make a radical improvement in the performance of a process—more improvement than could be made quickly through continual improvement techniques—it follows that most concern should be focused on the weakest processes and the functions that operate them. The processes that are the weakest are the ones that are most detrimental to competitiveness. They offer the most room for dramatic improvement, perhaps many times over. This is where the benchmarking effort should be focused because incremental improvement would not be sufficient to bring them up to the necessary level in the time frame required.

It can be difficult to categorize an organization's processes as weak or strong. A process that creates 50% scrap is an obvious choice for the benchmarking list. On the other hand, a process may be doing what is expected of it and, as a result, be classified as strong. However, it could be that expectations for that process are not high enough. It is possible that someone else has a process that is much more efficient, but you just don't know about it. Never consider a process to be above benchmarking, no matter how highly it is rated. Concentrate on the weak ones, but keep an open mind about the rest. If research identifies a better process, add it to the list.

Above all, document all processes fully—even the strong ones. Keep in mind that as you are looking at one of your benchmarking partner's processes because it is superior to yours, your partner may look at your strong processes for the same reason. If the processes are not well-documented, it will be very difficult to help your partner. It is impossible to compare two processes for benchmarking if both are not fully documented.

Step 4: Select Processes to Be Benchmarked

When you have a good understanding of your own processes and your expectations of them, decide which ones to benchmark. An important point to remember is this: never benchmark a process that you do not wish to change. There is no point in it. Benchmarking is not something you engage in simply to satisfy curiosity. The processes that are put on a benchmark list should be those that you know to be inferior and that you intend to change. Leave the others for incremental change through continual improvement—at least for the time being.

Step 5: Form Benchmarking Teams

The teams that will do the actual benchmarking should include people who operate the process, those who have input to the process, and those who take output from it. These people are in the best position to recognize the differences between your process and that of your benchmarking partner. The team must include someone with research capability because it will have to identify a benchmarking partner, and that will require research. Every team should have management representation, not only to keep management informed but also to build the support from management that is necessary for radical change.

Step 6: Research the Best-in-Class

It is important that a benchmarking partner be selected on the basis of being best-in-class for the process being benchmarked. In practical terms, it comes down to finding the best-in-class-you-can-find-who-is-willing. Because benchmarking is accomplished by process, best-in-class may be in a completely different industry. For example, say that an organization manufactures copy machines. It might consider potential benchmarking partners who are leaders in the copying industry. But if it is a warehousing process that is to be benchmarked, the company might get better results by looking at catalog companies that have world-class warehousing operations. If the process to be benchmarked is accounts receivable, then perhaps a credit card company would be a good partner.

Processes are shared across many industries, so don't limit research to like industries or you might miss the best opportunities for benchmarking. Remember that best-in-class does not mean best-in-your-industry, but best regardless of industry for the process in question. If team members stay up-to-date with trade journals, they should be able to compile a good list of potential benchmarking partners.

Research should cover trade literature, suppliers and customers, Baldrige Award winners, and professional associations. The Internet offers a seemingly endless stream of benchmarking information. Team members will find that the best-in-class processes become well-known very fast.

Step 7: Select Candidate Best-in-Class Benchmarking Partners

When the best-in-class have been identified, the team must decide with which among them it would prefer to work. Consideration must be given to location and to whether the best-in-class is a competitor (remember, the team will have to share information with its partner). The best benchmarking partnerships provide some benefit for both parties. If the team can find a way to benefit its potential partner, the linkage between the two companies will be easier to achieve. Even without that, most companies with best-in-class processes are willing, often eager, to share their insights and experience with others, even if they gain nothing in return. Indeed, Baldrige Award winners are expected to share information with other U.S. organizations.

Step 8: Form Agreements with Benchmarking Partners

After the team has selected the candidate, it contacts the potential partner to form an agreement covering benchmarking activities. It can be useful to have an executive contact an executive of the target company, especially if there is an existing relationship or some other common ground. Often the most difficult part of the process is identifying the right person in the potential partnering company. Professional associations can sometimes provide leads to help the team contact someone in the right position with the necessary authority.

After such a contact has been made, the first order of business is to determine the company's willingness to participate. If it is not willing, the team must find another candidate. When a company is willing to participate, an agreement can usually be forged without difficulty. The terms will include visit arrangements to both companies, limits of disclosure, and points of contact. In most cases, these are informal. Even so, care must be exercised not to burden the benchmarking partner with excessive obligations. Make the partnership as unobtrusive as possible.

Step 9: Collect Data

The team has already agreed to discuss a specific process (or processes). Observe, collect, and document everything about the partner's process. In addition, try to determine the underlying factors, practices, and processes: what is it that makes the company successful in this area? For example, does it employ total productive maintenance, continual improvement, employee involvement, statistics, or various other approaches? Optimally, your process operators should talk directly with your partner's operators. It is important to come away with a good understanding of what its process is (flowchart) and its support requirements, timing, and control. The team should also try to gain some understanding of the preceding and succeeding processes because if you change one, the others may require change as well. If the team knows enough when it leaves the partner's plant to implement its process back home, then it has learned most of what is needed. Anything less than this, and the team has more work to do.

While you are in a partner's plant, try to get a feel for its culture and how it operates. Be open-minded and receptive to new ideas that are not directly associated with the process in question. Observing a different plant culture can offer a wealth of ideas worth pursuing.

Step 10: Analyze the Data; Establish the Gap

With the data in hand, the team must analyze them thoroughly in comparison with the data taken from its own process. In most cases, the team will be able to establish the *performance gap* (the performance difference between the two processes) numerically—for example, 200 pieces per hour versus 110 pieces, 2% scrap versus 20%, or errors in parts per million rather than parts per thousand.

After the team concludes that there is no doubt that the partner's process is superior, other questions arise: Can its process replace ours? What will it cost, and can we afford it? What impact will it have on adjacent processes? Can we support it? Only by answering these questions can the team conclude that implementation is possible.

Step 11: Plan Action to Close the Gap or Surpass

Assume the team concluded that the change to the new process is desirable, affordable, and supportable and that the team wants to adopt the process. In most cases, implementation will require some planning to minimize disruption while the change is being made and while the operators are getting used to the new process. It is very important to approach implementation deliberately and with great care. In some cases, it may be wise to try the new process in a pilot model. This is not the time for haste. Consider all conceivable contingencies and plan to avoid them, or at least be prepared for them. Physical implementation may be accompanied by training for the process operators, suppliers, or customers. Only after thorough preparation and training should an organization implement the change to the new process.

A second aspect of benchmarking should be kept in mind. The objective is to put in place a process that is best-in-class. If the team merely transplants the partner company's process, it will not achieve the objective, although improvements may occur. To achieve best-in-class, an organization must surpass the performance of the benchmark process. It may not be possible to do this at the outset, but the team's initial planning should provide for the development work necessary to achieve it in a specified period of time (see Figure 20–1).

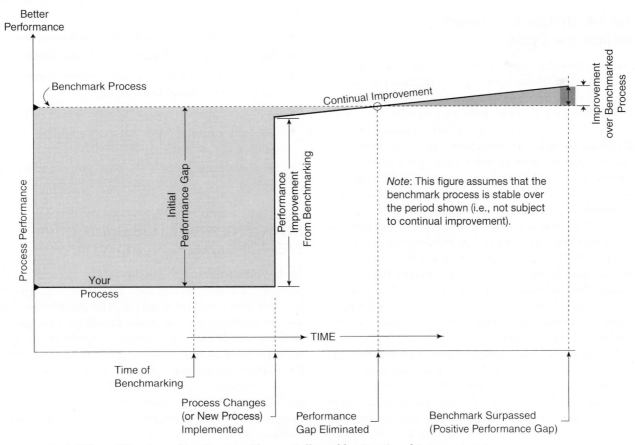

FIGURE 20–1 Effect of Benchmarking Process Change Followed by Continual Improvement

Step 12: Implement Change to the Process

The easiest step of all may be the actual implementation, assuming that the team's planning has been thorough and that execution adheres to the plan. New equipment may or may not be involved, there may be new people, or there may be more or fewer people—but there will certainly be new procedures that will take time to become routine. Therefore, it should not be a surprise if initial performance falls below the benchmark. After people get used to the changes and initial problems get worked out, performance should be close to the benchmark. If it is not, an important factor was overlooked, and another visit to the benchmarking partner may be necessary to determine what it is.

Step 13: Monitor Results

After the process is installed and running, performance should come up to the benchmark quickly. Before long, continual improvement should enable the organization to surpass the benchmark. None of this is likely to happen without constant attention and monitoring. Never install a new process, get it on line and performing to expectations, and then forget about it. All processes need constant attention in the form of monitoring. Statistical process control can be an invaluable tool for this purpose, as can other types of charting.

Step 14: Update Benchmarks; Continue the Cycle

As was explained in Step 11, the intent of benchmarking is not only to catch up with the best-in-class but also to surpass, thereby becoming best-in-class. This is a formidable undertaking because those with best-in-class processes are probably not resting on their laurels. They too will constantly strive for continually better performance. However, you are now applying new eyes and brains to their processes, and fresh ideas may well yield a unique improvement, vaulting your organization ahead of the benchmarking partner. Should that happen, your organization will be sought out as a best-in-class benchmarking partner by others who are trying to bootstrap their performance. Whether that happens or whether the benchmark is actually surpassed, the important thing is to maintain the goal of achieving best-in-class. Benchmarks must be updated periodically. Stay in touch with the best-in-class. Continue the process. Never be content with a given level of performance.

An important consideration, as you either achieve best-in-class or get close, is that limited resources have to be diverted to those processes that remain lowest in performance relative to their benchmarks. Let continual improvement take over for the best processes, and concentrate benchmarking on the ones that remain weak.

> **QUALITY TIP ▼**
>
> **Continual Process Improvement Has No End**
>
> Any process that is "good enough" today will be inadequate tomorrow.
>
> *Source:* David L. Goetsch and Stanley B. Davis.

Three Phases of Benchmarking

The 14-step sequence introduced above represents the three phases of benchmarking: preparation, execution, and postexecution. Figure 20–2 illustrates the benchmarking process or sequence by phase and indicates action responsibility for each step. Figure 20–2 also makes it clear that the final step (14) causes the cycle to start over again at Step 2, confirming the never-ending nature of the benchmarking process for companies that want to achieve or maintain leadership positions. Key points relating to the 14-step sequence of steps for implementing benchmarking are as follows:

- Benchmarking requires top management's commitment, participation, and backing.
- It is necessary that an organization thoroughly understand its own processes before attempting to benchmark.
- The processes that should be benchmarked are those that most need improvement.
- Benchmarking teams must include process operators.
- Benchmark best-in-class, not best-in-the-industry.
- Do not rush into new processes or major changes without thorough, thoughtful planning.
- Do not be satisfied with a zero gap—aim to surpass.
- Carefully monitor new processes or major process changes.
- Benchmarking is not a one-shot process; continue it forever.

MAKING FULL USE OF BENCHMARKING DATA

At the conclusion of the benchmarking project with your partner, data analysis will have produced both quantitative and qualitative information. The quantitative information is effectively the "stake driven into the ground" as the point from which future progress is measured. It is also used as the basis for improvement objectives. Qualitative information covers such matters as personnel policies, training, management styles and hierarchy, total quality maturity, and so on. This information provides insights on how the benchmarking partner got to be best-in-class.

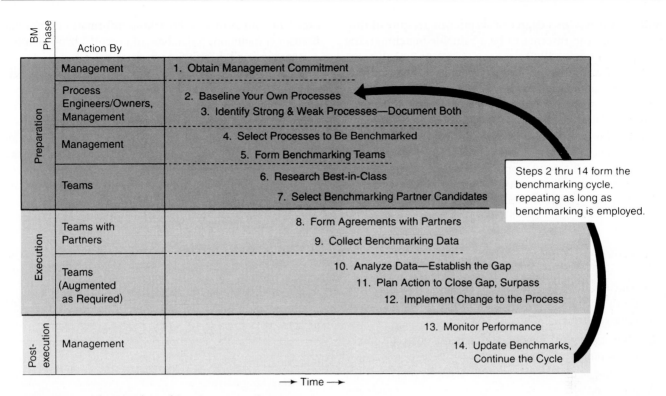

FIGURE 20–2 The Benchmarking Process or Sequence

The quantitative data are clearly the information sought and are always used. However, there may be more value in the qualitative information. It describes the atmosphere and environment in which best-in-class can be developed and sustained. Do not ignore it. Take it very seriously. Study it, discuss it in staff meetings, and explore the possibilities of introducing these changes into your culture.

PERPETUAL BENCHMARKING

If you have been through a series of benchmarking activities and have implemented changes that have significantly improved processes, your organization may develop a tendency to leave benchmarking. After all, there are other things that need attention and resources. But this can be a costly mistake. At this point, the organization not only has greatly improved its processes but also developed some valuable benchmarking experience. Keep in mind that best-in-class continues to be a dynamic and ever-changing mosaic. Processes are constantly being improved and altered. In a relatively short time, an organization can fall behind again. To prevent that from happening, the organization must take advantage of hard-won benchmarking experience and keep the effort moving. This means staying up-to-date with the best-in-class through all the means at your disposal, staying current with your own processes as they are continually improved, and benchmarking the weaker processes. This is a never-ending process.

BENCHMARKING RESOURCES

A number of sources of information can help organizations with their benchmarking efforts. These cover the spectrum from nonprofit associations to cooperative affiliations to for-profit organizations that sell information. In addition, of course, there are consulting firms with expertise and databases covering all aspects of benchmarking.

One of the most promising ventures is the American Productivity and Quality Center (APQC) Benchmarking Clearinghouse (123 N. Post Oak Lane, Houston, TX 77024; phone, [800] 776-9676 or [713] 681-4020; and on the Web at www.apqc.org). The APQC Benchmarking Clearinghouse has been set up to assist companies, nonprofit organizations, and government in the process of benchmarking. It works with affiliated organizations to collect and disseminate best practices through databases, case studies, publications, seminars, conferences, videos, and other media.

A wide range of benchmarking information is available on the Internet. Just ask your search engine to find "benchmarking" or "process benchmarking," and you will probably be rewarded with more information than you can use. This ranges from articles on the subject to promotions for books and consultants. Colleges list the contents of their libraries that are related to benchmarking. We would suggest a word of caution, however. Anyone can put anything on the Internet without verification, so it is always a good idea to approach material from unfamiliar sources with a degree of skepticism. In spite of this, we consider the Internet to be a valuable benchmarking resource center.

Excellent sources of information for benchmarking are trade and professional groups. They can often direct organizations to best-in-class practices, provide contacts, and offer valuable advice. Baldrige Award winners are committed to sharing information with other U.S. companies, and they hold periodic seminars for this purpose.

The trade literature publishes a wealth of relevant information, including lists of companies with best-in-class processes and practices. *Industry Week* is one example of an

excellent source of benchmarking information. Dun and Bradstreet maintains a database of potential benchmarking partners and will share it for a fee.

Consultants and universities that are engaged in benchmarking can help organizations get started by providing initial training, offering advice and guidance, and directing organizations to benchmarking partner candidates.

Again, be cautious, and ensure that any information obtained is current. The very nature of benchmarking makes yesterday's data obsolete. To achieve maximum benefit, organizations must be sure that they are operating on current information.

SUMMARY

1. Benchmarking is a process for comparing an organization's operations or processes with those of a best-in-class performer.

2. The objective of benchmarking is major performance improvement achieved quickly.

3. Benchmarking focuses on processes and practices, not products.

4. Benchmarking is done between consenting organizations.

5. Benchmarking partners are frequently from different industries.

6. Benchmarking is a component of total quality.

7. Benchmarking must be approached in an organized, planned manner, with the approval and participation of top management.

8. Benchmarking teams must include those who operate the processes.

9. Benchmarking is not restricted within industry boundaries, but only to best-in-class processes.

10. It is necessary for the benchmarker to understand its own process before comparing it with another.

11. Because best-in-class is dynamic, benchmarking should be seen as a never-ending process.

12. Management has a key role in the benchmarking process, including commitment to change, making funds available, authorizing human resources, being actively involved, and determining the appropriate level of disclosure.

13. The goal of benchmarking is to become best-in-class, not simply improved.

14. The intent of benchmarking is to replace an inferior process with one rated best-in-class or to radically improve a process, bringing it up to best-in-class performance—and then to surpass best-in-class.

15. A number of obstacles to successful benchmarking exist, including internal focus, overly broad or undefined objectives, unrealistic timetables, improper team composition, failure to aim at best-in-class, diverted team emphasis, insensitivity toward the partner, and wavering support by top management.

KEY TERMS AND CONCEPTS

Benchmarking
Benchmarking partner
Best-in-class
Continual improvement
Customer focus
Internal focus
Key business process
Malcolm Baldrige Award
Performance gap
Process baselining
Process capability
Process characterization
Process flow diagram
Qualitative information
Quantitative information

FACTUAL REVIEW QUESTIONS

1. Define benchmarking.

2. Explain the difference in objectives for continual improvement and benchmarking.

3. List five factors that lead organizations to benchmarking.

4. On which processes should an organization concentrate for benchmarking?

5. Why is it necessary that top management be committed as a prerequisite to benchmarking?

6. What are the reasons for characterizing and documenting an organization's processes before benchmarking?

7. Identify the critical members of the benchmarking team.

8. Explain why it is not enough to simply clone the benchmarking partner's process.

9. Explain the importance of linking the benchmarking objectives with the organization's strategic objectives.

10. Explain how the "Not-invented-here" Syndrome can be a hindrance to benchmarking effectiveness.

11. List and discuss the eight obstacles to successful benchmarking.

CRITICAL THINKING ACTIVITY

A Competitive Crisis

Note: This is a purely fictitious case study in terms of both the company and the numbers.

Empire Communications Products is a company of 420 employees engaged in designing and producing telephone equipment for the wireless telephone industry. It originally spun out of a large communications company several years ago as the wireless phone market began its rapid expansion. Today its major competition is from the North American, European, and Japanese telecom giants, all of which have now recognized the market potential and are competing furiously. Empire Communications has been a respected and successful niche market player, even selling some proprietary products to its big competitors. However, the pressure on profits has become extreme, and the company is searching for ways to cut its costs.

The CEO has had her management steering committee looking into benchmarking as a possible means of making processes more efficient. It has concluded that the company has five key business process areas, each with its own set of processes. The five key business process areas are as follows:

Key Process Area	12-Month Expense	Primary Processes
Engineering (45 employees)	$1,000,000	Research & development
	6,005,000	Design
	300,000	Product improvement
	7,305,000	
Finance (12 employees)	500,000	Accounting
	100,000	Accounts payable
	130,000	Accounts receivable
	730,000	
Human Resources (5 employees)	300,000	Recruiting/hiring
	60,000	Compensation
	260,000	Employee development
	620,000	
Production (350 employees)	1,000,000	Procurement
	30,000,000	Materials
	3,000,000	Warehousing
	3,500,000	Material control
	550,000	Materials preparation
	3,800,000	Production control
	11,100,000	Assembly
	2,050,000	Integration and test
	55,000,000	
Quality Assurance (8 employees)	275,000	Incoming inspection
	500,000	In-process inspection
	150,000	Supplier auditing
	200,000	Internal auditing
	1,125,000	
Total Annual Expenses	$64,780,000	

The steering committee did some research to compare similar expenses with a typical firm in the industry. It found that the company's engineering expenses were close to the average. The same was true of the finance department. Human resources was on average except for expenses for employee development, where it was clear that Empire was spending less for training than the industry at large. What the committee found in the production and quality assurance areas was a major surprise. Empire spent far more than the industry average for warehousing, material control, materials preparation, production control, and even assembly. In quality assurance, Empire's costs were way above the average for inspection. On the other hand, Empire spent significantly less than the average for its materials, integration and test, and supplier audits and internal audits. The comparative data are given here:

Process	Industry Avg.	Empire	Difference
Employee development	450,000	260,000	−190,000
Materials	31,000,000	30,000,000	−1,000,000
Warehousing	975,000	3,000,000	+2,025,000
Material control	180,000	3,500,000	+3,320,000
Materials preparation	85,000	550,000	+465,000
Production control	725,000	3,800,000	+3,075,000
Assembly	10,000,000	11,100,000	+1,100,000
Integration & test	3,060,000	2,050,000	−1,010,000
Incoming inspection	75,000	275,000	+200,000
In-process inspection	200,000	500,000	+300,000
Supplier auditing	1,250,000	150,000	−1,100,000
Internal auditing	2,800,000	200,000	−2,600,000
	$50,800,000	$55,385,000	+$4,585,000

In total, Empire's costs were about $4.6 million above the annual average for its peers. If it could find a way to eliminate the excess cost, the $4.6 million would be added to before-tax profit, virtually doubling its current profit status. That would certainly be welcomed.

Exercise Questions

1. You are a benchmarking consultant. Empire staff has shared this information with you, and it wants to know why you think benchmarking is an appropriate course for it to follow. Is benchmarking likely to help Empire Communications? What will you tell it?

2. Does the pattern of spending more than the average in some areas and under the average in others suggest anything to you (relative to previous chapters)? How will this influence any benchmarking strategy?

3. How would you determine the best process areas for benchmarking?

4. Given the fact that the telecom industry is extremely competitive, is it likely that Empire will find willing benchmarking partners among its competitors? If not, what would you do?

5. Develop a recommendation for Empire Communications for how you propose to lead it through the benchmarking activity and what it should expect to gain from it.

Author's Comments on the Empire Communications Exercise

Question 1. It seems clear that other companies are doing things much differently and, overall, much less expensively than Empire, so benchmarking would seem to be a good avenue for quick, major improvement.

Question 2. Spending less for training *may* mean that some of Empire's employees are not as well-trained as they should be. That will have to be investigated in more depth. Beyond that there seems to be a pattern of over- and underspending that suggests Empire is not doing business like the average firms in production and quality assurance.

The gross differences in warehousing, material control, and production control are probably the result of Empire's use of the traditional manufacturing techniques rather than the lean just-in-time approach, which can be a huge cost saver. If that is the case there will be lots of possibilities for benchmarking.

Empire spends 6.5 times the average for materials preparation. Perhaps it is doing it all in-house rather than having its supplier do it more efficiently. We need to find out exactly what Empire is doing and then look to see where there is a better process to be benchmarked.

Integration and test looks, on the surface, to be a winner. Find out why, and if it turns out to be a superior process, it can be used as an enticement for a prospective benchmarking partner.

Empire appears to have lower materials purchasing expense, but if that is coupled with overspending on incoming inspection and underspending in supplier audits, one gets the impression that Empire is still trying to sort defective materials out at its plant rather than having its suppliers do so before the materials ever get to Empire. That could also help explain why Empire's assembly costs are higher than average (rework due to defective materials).

Almost certainly benchmarking will show Empire new, more efficient ways to do things, but we need to fully understand how Empire works before we go benchmarking.

Question 3. Look for the production processes that indicate the biggest undesirable expense gap and then try to determine which will be easiest to benchmark and implement. Always take the easiest-to-benchmark, financially critical process first.

Question 4. The chances are slim that an outright competitor would become a benchmarking partner, although that does happen. Empire should look at the entire electronics industry (it competes only in telecom), and even outside it if appropriate for the process. Remember, it is best-in-class, not just best-among-competitors, in which we are interested.

Question 5. Your proposal should outline the work to be done internal to Empire: namely, checking out the issues raised by Question 2 and determining where best to start regarding Question 3. After comparing what Empire is doing against what the competition is apparently doing, do the research to find a best-in-class partner. Be sure to tell Empire that any process that is to be benchmarked will have to be thoroughly flowcharted and understood. (It would also be a good idea to point out that even those critical processes that are not on the benchmarking list at present should also be characterized as a first step in an internal continual improvement program.) You will need to talk about the benchmarking team composition, training, and the actual visit to the partner's site. Also, you will need to explain the process of adopting or adapting the new process to the Empire Communications environment and culture. It would be a good idea to go through each of the 14 steps with Empire's Steering Committee.

DISCUSSION ASSIGNMENT 20–1

Benchmarking at Motorola

Motorola, one of the original Malcolm Baldrige Award winners, has found that even after achieving best-in-class, there is much to be gained through continued benchmarking. Every new program, every new product, and every new improvement effort at Motorola is preceded by a search for the best-in-class. In this way, Motorola ensures that every new process introduced will be world class.

DISCUSSION QUESTION

Discuss the following question in class or outside of class with your fellow students:

1. What do you think motivates Motorola to invest in benchmarking?

DISCUSSION ASSIGNMENT 20–2

Benchmarking at Xerox

By the late 1970s, Xerox was losing significant market share to its Japanese competitors. Not only were the Japanese products excellent, but also, to Xerox's dismay, they were sold for less than Xerox could manufacture them. Xerox found that it had nine times as many suppliers as the Japanese companies and made seven times as many manufacturing defects. Lead times for new products were twice as long, and production setup times were five times as long as the competitors'.

Xerox introduced benchmarking in 1980. Its processes and practices were benchmarked against the best in and out of its industry. As a result of these efforts, Xerox saved itself. Today, Xerox is a world-class competitor, capable of holding its own in terms of technology, price, service, and customer satisfaction against any competition. Benchmarking at Xerox has reached into every facet of the company and remains a primary feature of the corporation.

DISCUSSION QUESTION

Discuss the following question in class or outside of class with your fellow students:

1. Using public domain information, such as that available on the Internet, determine where Xerox stands relative to its competitors today.

ENDNOTE

1. Robert C. Camp, *Benchmarking: The Search for Industry Best Practices That Lead to Superior Performance* (Milwaukee, WI: Quality Press/Quality Resources, 1989).

JUST-IN-TIME/LEAN MANUFACTURING (JIT/LEAN)

*Time is money.—**Greek proverb***

MAJOR TOPICS

- **What Do We Call It?**
- **Just-in-Time/Lean Defined**
- **Rationale for JIT/Lean**
- **Development of JIT/Lean**
- **Relationship of JIT/Lean to Total Quality and World-Class Manufacturing**
- **Benefits of JIT/Lean**
- **Requirements of JIT/Lean**
- **Automation and JIT/Lean**

WHAT DO WE CALL IT?

The manufacturing system we will be discussing in this chapter was initially developed by Taiichi Ohno in the 1950s as the successor to Henry Ford's mass production system. Ohno named it the *Toyota Production System (TPS)*. Since it involved making products only when needed from materials that were made available by suppliers only as required, *just-in-time (JIT)* became its generic name. For 30 odd years Toyota Production System or Just-In-Time were the names used for Ohno's remarkably efficient manufacturing system. Then in 1990 three senior managers of MIT's International Motor Vehicle Program (IMVP), Jim Womack, Dan Jones, and Dan Roos, published a book that has had a great influence on the way industries around the world make things. That book, entitled, *The Machine That Changed the World: The Story of Lean Production*, was the result of a five-year, in-depth scholarly study of the Toyota Production System. It detailed in clear terms the superiority of the TPS to the mass production system used by the rest of the world, and virtually unchanged since World War I, and concluded that mass production simply could not compete with the Japanese system. One of IMVP's researchers, John Krafcik, is credited with coining the term "Lean production."[1] The system uses less of everything involved in production: manpower, investment, engineering, inventory, facilities, and so on, thus the term "Lean" fits well. Over the two-plus decades since the book was published, Lean has become the tag for the TPS and JIT, and has reached out across all kinds of industries and organizations to represent a wide variety of adaptations of TPS. In Chapter 19, we devoted several pages to Lean and its role in continual improvement, and even its marriage with Six Sigma and the Theory of Constraints. So this book uses the name Just-In-Time/Lean Manufacturing, or JIT/Lean, for this chapter.

As is so often the case, we find that the same product is being repackaged under other names. This is sometimes done by those searching for clarity of description. Sometimes it is done by those wanting to be seen as having something new and different, when in fact it is not. You may come across the term *focused factory* in reference to a JIT production cell. If you encounter a production system called *demand flow*, or *demand flow technology*, it is JIT with a new label. These are not bad names, and in fact, some may project a clearer picture of the production system than JIT/Lean. But in this book, and in most others, the generic name for pull-system manufacturing, *just-in-time/Lean*, is preferred.

JIT/LEAN DEFINED

When people who should know are asked to define JIT, the typical response is that JIT "is getting your materials delivered just when you need them." Probing a little deeper may elicit a response that suggests JIT manufacturers let their suppliers keep their materials inventory until the manufacturers need it. The first statement demonstrates an inadequate understanding of JIT/Lean, and the second is simply wrong. Even so, many companies under the auspices of JIT/Lean have indeed pushed their warehousing back to the suppliers for a net gain of zero. If these are not the right answers to the question "What is JIT/Lean?" then what is it? Although not exactly what was originally intended, just-in-time/Lean manufacturing, by any of its names, has become a management philosophy that seeks to eliminate all forms of waste in manufacturing processes and their support activities. JIT/Lean permits the production of only what is needed, only when it is needed, and only in the quantity needed. This must apply not only to the just-in-time/Lean manufacturer, but also to its suppliers if the system is to eliminate all possible waste. Those companies that have required their suppliers to do their warehousing clearly have not gotten the point. The supplier should not produce the material until the JIT/Lean manufacturer needs it. In that mode, there is no warehousing and, therefore, no wasted resources for buildings, maintenance, people to care for the material, spoilage, obsolescence, or other related problems.

JIT/Lean is not so much related to supplier activities, although they are important, as to events on the manufacturing floor. For example, assume that a company manufactures motion sensors. There are five discrete processes involved, each carried out by one worker, as illustrated in Figure 21–1a. The traditional production process places a big supply of input materials in the warehouse, doling them out to the production line at the rate of so many pieces per unit time. The electronic assembly and the mechanical assembly processes convert their respective input materials into input materials for the electronic module assembly process. The electronic module assembly and the frame fabrication processes then convert their input materials into input materials for the final assembly process, which, in turn, converts them into completed motion sensors. Each of the five work areas produces at the rate necessary to meet a quota, or to consume all the input materials. The completed sensors are sent to the warehouse for storage until someone buys them.

Figure 21–1a is the simplest possible depiction of this particular combination of the steps required to manufacture the motion sensors. What happens in the traditional manufacturing setting takes on a much more complicated

and convoluted series of events. This is depicted in Figure 21–1b. In Figure 21–1b the materials warehouse sends kits of appropriate materials and parts to the first three assembly/fabrication stations (1, 2, and 3) according to a predetermined schedule. Working to their own assigned schedules, each of the three stations converts the kits into semifinished assemblies or parts and pushes that output to the succeeding stations, 4 and 5. At this point, we may run into a problem. Ideally the output of stations 1, 2, and 3 would go directly to stations 4 or 5, but for a variety of reasons, it is common that the local staging areas for stations 4 or 5 may, at any given time, be unable to accept more input. When that happens, the excess partially built goods, also known as work-in-process (WIP), must be sent to a remote staging area, as shown in the Figure 21–1b. The same thing can happen between stations 4 and 5. A comparison of Figure 21–1a with Figure 21–1b reveals how complicated a simple manufacturing job can become.

FIGURE 21–1a The Traditional Production Process (Simplest Depiction)

FIGURE 21–1b Actual Practices in the Traditional Production Process

FIGURE 21–2 Factory Producing to Forecast Demand (Mass Production)

What is not obvious from Figure 21–1b is the expense involved in this kind of waste in traditional manufacturing. All of that WIP that cannot go straight through the system, as it appears to do in Figure 21–1a, must be transported to a suitable area for storing it; someone has to keep track of its completion status, and where it is; withdrawal from the WIP staging area must be managed; salaries must pay for the extra people involved; overhead costs for the staging area must be absorbed; and carrying costs for the WIP itself has to be paid. Even finished goods may go to a warehouse to await customer orders, adding even more costs. Not one of those costs add value to the product, therefore, it is pure waste. All these functions have costs that add up to making the company uncompetitive and are targets for elimination in a JIT/Lean organization. A similar case can be made for competitive damage caused by time lost in the process, which can easily add an order of magnitude to the manufacturing cycle time.

Just-in-time/Lean approaches the manufacturing process from the opposite end of the line. Rather than pushing materials into the processes and storing them whenever they cannot be accommodated, JIT/Lean controls the line from the output end. Indeed, it can be said that the customer controls the line because nothing is built until there is an order for it. After an order is received for a product, the final assembly process is turned on to put together the required number of units. The assembler pulls the required input materials from the electronic module and frame fabrication processes—only enough to make the required number. Similarly, the electronic module assembly and frame fabrication processes pull input materials from their preceding processes, and so on back up the line. At the top of the line, input materials are pulled from suppliers in the exact quantity needed, and no more.

Following the JIT/Lean procedure, no step in the production process ever overproduces or produces before a demand is made. Therefore, there is no need for a staging area or the people required to move materials into it and out of it, account for it, and so on. No money is tied up in inventory of raw materials, WIP, or finished goods. If there are no stored materials, there is no spoilage or obsolescence. The elimination of these wastes alone makes JIT/Lean the most powerful manufacturing concept to come along since Henry Ford's moving assembly line of 1913. JIT/Lean contributes to the elimination of many more forms of waste, as discussed later in this chapter.

So, the definition of JIT/Lean as used in this book is this:

Just-in-time/Lean is producing only what is needed, when it is needed, and in the quantity that is needed.

RATIONALE FOR JIT/LEAN

Mass production manufacturers set their production schedules based on a forecast of future needs, which, in turn, is based on historical data and trend analysis (see Figure 21–2). The great weakness of this system is that no one can predict the future with sufficient certainty, even with a complete and perfect understanding of the past and a good sense of current trends in the marketplace. One does not have to search long to find examples of failed attempts to correctly project the marketability of products. The Edsel is one of many automobiles that were released with great fanfare to a disinterested public. A new formula for Coca-Cola introduced in the late 1980s is another example of market predictions gone awry. IBM has case after case involving personal computers, such as the unlamented IBM PC Jr. (which failed in the marketplace in spite of the best market research IBM could muster). These failures demonstrate the difficulty of trying to determine beforehand what will sell and in what quantity.

Even products that are successful in the market have limits as to the quantities that buyers will absorb. When production is based on predictions of the future, risk of loss from overproduction is far greater than when production is based on actual demand. The previous section defined JIT/Lean as producing what is needed, only when it is needed, and only in the quantity that is needed (see Figure 21–3). The result of JIT/Lean is that no goods are produced without demand. This, in turn, means no goods are produced that cannot be sold at a price that supports the viability of the company.

So far, we have viewed JIT/Lean from the point of view of the manufacturer and the ultimate purchaser of the product—the producer and the customer. But if we

FIGURE 21–3 Factory Producing to Orders (JIT/Lean)

look at the complete production process, we will find that it contains many producers and customers—internal producers and customers (see Figure 21–4). Each preceding process in the overall system is a producer, or supplier, and each succeeding process is a customer (see Chapter 7). JIT/Lean fits here as well as or better than with the manufacturer-and-purchaser model. No process in the system produces its output product until it is signaled to do so by the succeeding process. This can eliminate waste on a grand scale. It is the elimination of waste that justifies JIT/Lean in any kind of manufacturing operation. Eliminating waste is translated into improving quality and lowering costs. Improving quality and lowering costs translate into becoming more competitive. Although improving competitiveness does not assure survival (the competition may still be ahead of you), being noncompetitive surely guarantees disaster.

Taiichi Ohno, the creator of the just-in-time/Lean system, saw that the mass production system produced waste at every step. He identified seven wastes:[2]

1. Overproducing
2. Waiting (time)
3. Transporting
4. Processing itself
5. Having unnecessary stock on hand
6. Using unnecessary motion
7. Producing defective goods

The elimination of these wastes is at the heart of the rationale for just-in-time/Lean: eliminate these wastes, and you will produce better products at lower cost. If the competition gets there first, your rationale for JIT/Lean is survival.

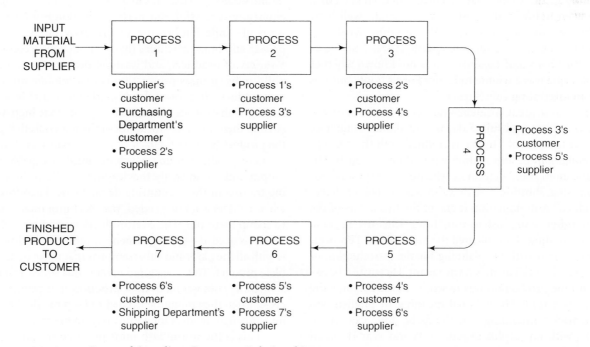

FIGURE 21–4 Internal Supplier–Customer Relationships

DEVELOPMENT OF JIT/LEAN

We have identified Ohno as the creator of the just-in-time/Lean system, and it is true that he was responsible for developing the system as it is now known. However, other names should be remembered, at least to the extent to which they contributed by inspiration. The first is Henry Ford, creator of mass production. Because of Ford's great appreciation of the expense of waste, Ohno said that if Ford were alive today, he would have developed a system much like Toyota's. In his 1926 book *Today and Tomorrow*, Henry Ford talked about the waste of inventory in raw materials, work-in-process, and finished goods in the pipeline to market—and about the efforts taken to reduce the investment in this waste. Between 1921 and 1926, Ford output doubled, but investment in inventory of raw materials, semifinished goods, and finished goods actually declined. Based on 1921 performance, Ford could have had $170 million tied up in this inventory but in fact had (in 1926) less than $50 million. Ford also recognized the waste arising from transportation, waiting (time), and inefficiency on the factory floor. He believed in planning ahead to eliminate the waste before it happened. This is very contemporary thinking, and Ohno may be correct that Henry Ford, had he been living in the past 40 years, might well have developed a Toyota-like system. When Ohno wrote his book on the Toyota Production System, it was titled *Just-in-Time for Today and Tomorrow*. It is not known whether the book's title was a tribute to Henry Ford's book, but it is at least an interesting coincidence.

Ford was a great influence on the Toyoda family—Sakichi, Kiichiro, and Eiji. Sakichi Toyoda, a designer of looms and founder of Toyota, is credited with the concept of *autonomation*, or automation with a human touch. His automatic loom could determine whether a thread was broken or missing, shutting itself down instead of making defective product.[3] Autonomation is one of the two pillars of the TPS, the other being just-in-time/Lean. Kiichiro Toyoda, Toyota's founding chair, planted the seeds of the TPS prior to World War II with his planning for the introduction of the assembly line at Toyota's Kariya plant. He wrote a booklet about how production was to work, and it contains the words *just-in-time*. His original meaning in English was "just-on-time," intending that things be done exactly on schedule, with no surplus produced. World War II halted further work on the system, and after the war, it was Taiichi

Ohno who revived and developed it into the present-day[4] Toyota Production System, which we call JIT/Lean.

Eiji Toyoda, Toyota's president and chairman from 1967 to 1994, and Taiichi Ohno's boss for 35 years, is credited with the JIT/Lean philosophy: "In broad industries, such as automobile manufacturing, it is best to have the various parts arrive alongside the assembly line just-in-time."[5] Eiji Toyoda's greatest contribution may have been his support for Ohno's trial-and-error approach, shielding him from the inevitable controversy of his endeavors. Ohno claims that Eiji never told him to back off or slow down. He absorbed the heat and let Ohno press on unimpeded.[6]

Taiichi Ohno's motivation, like that of the Toyodas, was to eliminate all forms of waste from the production process. He was well-schooled in the Ford mass production system and observed that the system itself created waste in huge proportions. If one was determined to violate the seven wastes, a mass production line would do it. Mass production is prone to *overproducing*; having people or materials *waiting*; *transporting* work-in-process back and forth across the plant; retaining inefficient *processes*; maintaining costly inventories of *stock on hand*; requiring non-value-added *motion* because lines were set up to accommodate product, not workers; and producing *defective* goods because the line must continue to move. The italicized words represent the seven wastes.

Ohno believed that a production system based on just-in-time/Lean could eliminate the wastes. To appreciate fully what is involved here, one must understand that the mass production system as defined by Henry Ford was not irrational. Ford's objective was to produce huge quantities of the same product using an assembly line technology that required little expertise of its workers. The result was a reliable, cheap car that millions of buyers could afford. In that, he and others who used his mass production technology were eminently successful. But mass production is inflexible and wasteful—inflexible because it is driven by the great stamping presses and other machines that do not easily accommodate a variety of products, and wasteful because the underlying philosophy of mass production is that the line must crank out products that spring from market forecasts in a never-ending high-volume stream. To support that high-volume stream, there must be stockpiles of the materials that go into the product because the lack of a single part can shut down the mass production line. Machines must be capable of high output and are so costly they cannot sit idle without creating trauma in the accounting department. Therefore, even when fenders are not needed, the machines must continue to stamp them out. The overproduction will be warehoused until it is needed—perhaps when the press breaks down. So it is with all the parts and subassemblies that make up the complete product. They are stored in large quantities, just in case something goes wrong in their production or transportation cycle, when they might be needed to keep the final assembly line moving—fenders for a rainy day, so to speak.

This is the norm with mass production. The problem with this is that the building space in which these parts and materials are warehoused is expensive. It requires a small army of people to care for the stored materials and parts, and these people add not a whit to the ultimate value of the product. Spoilage occurs by loss, damage, or obsolescence of stored parts—all waste: part waste of inventory, part waste of overproduction.

Mass production advocates emphasize that the lines need to keep moving and that the only way to do this is to have lots of parts available for any contingency that might arise. This is the fallacy of just-in-time/Lean according to mass production advocates. JIT/Lean, with no buffer stock of parts, is too precarious. One missing part or a single failure of a machine (because there are no stores of parts) causes the JIT/Lean line to stop. It was this very idea that represented the power of JIT/Lean to Ohno. It meant that there could be no work-arounds for problems that did develop, only solutions to the problems. It focused everyone concerned with the production process on anticipating problems before they happened and on developing and implementing solutions so that they would not cause mischief later on.[7] The fact is that as long as the factory has the security buffer of a warehouse full of parts that might

be needed, problems that interrupt the flow of parts to the line do not get solved because they are hidden by the buffer stock. When that buffer is eliminated, the same problems become immediately visible, they take on a new urgency, and solutions emerge—solutions that fix the problem not only for this time but for the future as well. Ohno was absolutely correct. JIT/Lean's perceived weakness is one of its great strengths.

Mass production is a *push system* (see Figure 21–5). The marketing forecast tells the factory what to produce and in what quantity; raw materials and parts are purchased, stored, forced into the front end of the production process, and subsequently pushed through each succeeding step of the process, until finally the completed product arrives at the shipping dock. It is hoped that by then there are orders for these goods, or they will have to be either stored or pushed (forced) into the dealers' hands, a widespread practice in the automobile business. The whole procedure, from imperfect forecast of marketability to the warehouse or the dealer, is one of pushing.

What if the market will take only half of the predicted amount or wants none? What if the final assembly process

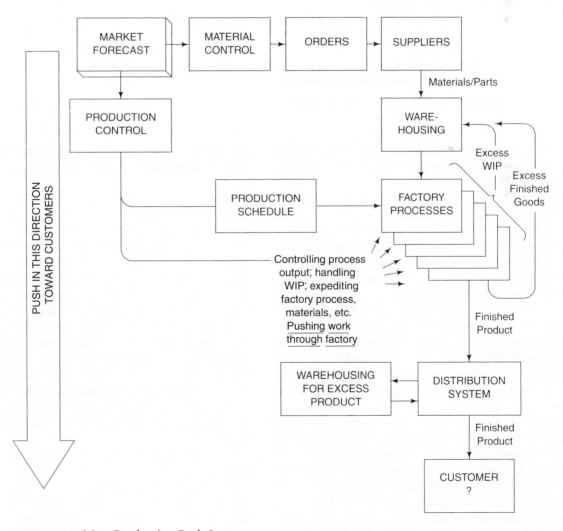

FIGURE 21–5 Mass Production Push System

* The customer in this sense may be the ultimate user of the product, or an intermediary
  such as a distributor, a store, a dealer, etc.

FIGURE 21–6 Just-In-Time/Lean Demand Pull System

can accommodate only two-thirds of the preceding processes' output? These situations present big problems in terms of cost and waste, and they are common.

Just-in-time/Lean, on the other hand, is a *pull system* (see Figure 21–6; the term *kanban* in the figure will be clarified soon). The production schedule does not originate in a market forecast, although a great deal of market research is done to determine what customers want. The production demand comes from the customer. Moreover, the demand is made on the final assembly process by pulling finished products out of the factory. The operators of that process, in turn, place their pull demands on the preceding process, and that cycle is repeated until finally the pull demand reaches back to the material and parts suppliers. Each process and each supplier is allowed to furnish only the quantity of its output needed by the succeeding process.

Figures 21–5 and 21–6 also show a difference in the relationship between the customer and the factory. In the mass production system, no real relationship exists at all. The market forecasters take the place of the customers and place demands on the factory months in advance of production. In the JIT/Lean system, however, the customer's demand is felt throughout the system, all the way to the factory's suppliers, and even beyond that. The JIT/Lean sys-

tem is simpler, eliminating entire functions such as material control, production control, warehousing and stocking, and so on.

The simplicity of JIT/Lean production is most evident on the factory floor. In mass production plants, or even conventional job shops (low-volume, high-variety shops), it is almost never possible to tell from the factory floor how things are going relative to schedules. Parts of any product may be in any number of disparate locations in a plant at any given time—in the machine shop, in the welding shop, on the line, or in storage. Computers keep track of it all, but even then, it is difficult to track a given product through the plant or to track its status at a given point in time. On the other hand, JIT/Lean, being a very visual process, makes tracking easy—even without computers. Parts have no place to hide in a JIT/Lean factory. The only work-in-process is that for which the process has a kanban (see the discussion of kanban in the section titled "Process Problems").

The simplicity of today's JIT/Lean belies the difficulty Ohno encountered in developing the system. Because production must stop for a missing part, a process problem, or a broken machine, methods had to be developed to prevent these occurrences. These preventive strategies are explained in the following sections.

Machine Problems

There are two basic concerns about machines:

1. Is it running and turning out product?
2. If it is running, is the quality of its output product acceptable?

In a mass production environment, question 1 matters most. The tendency is to let the machine run as long as there is product, good or bad, coming out of it. Defective parts will cause problems farther down the line, but the consequences of shutting the machine down to fix it are seen as an even bigger problem. The JIT/Lean factory is more concerned about the second question because allowing a machine to produce defective parts permits the production of waste, and that, above all, is forbidden.

Common sense dictates that machinery should always be maintained properly, but that can be very difficult in a mass production plant. Unfortunately, in many North American factories, machines tend to be ignored until they break down, in keeping with the grammatically incorrect but telling expression "If it ain't broke, don't fix it." Toyota eliminated the machine problem through a systematic preventive maintenance process that keeps all machinery in top shape, modifying it for better reliability or performance, and even predicting when parts should be replaced or adjustments made to maintain the highest-quality output. This has come to be known as *total productive maintenance* or *total preventive maintenance (TPM)*. It has found widespread acceptance in forward-looking companies. Total preventive maintenance, by keeping the machines available for use when they are needed, eliminates a great many line stoppages. We will discuss TPM in more detail later in the chapter.

Process Problems

Process problems can be eliminated when people thoroughly understand the processes, optimize them, and use statistical methods (i.e., SPC) to keep them under control. In addition, the processes are continually improved, most often through the efforts of the same people who work with them every day. Time is allocated for these kinds of efforts in all JIT/Lean factories.

The most difficult conceptual problem with JIT/Lean is the precise control of production and the flow of material or parts through the complete production process. For that, Ohno developed the *kanban* to signal the pulls through the system. Mass production demonstrated that one should not start the control at the beginning of the process. Too many things can go wrong at the bow wave of the flow. Ohno decided that the control had to start at the output end of the factory. From this concept, he introduced *kanban*, which is a Japanese word meaning "card." Ohno used kanban cards to trigger activity and the flow of materials or parts from one process to another. When a succeeding process has used the output of the preceding process, it issues a kanban to the preceding process to produce another.

Although Ohno describes the kanbans as slips of paper in a vinyl pouch—close enough for "card"—kanbans have evolved to a number of forms. A square painted or taped on a workstation may be a very effective kanban. For example, a process produces a subassembly and places it on the marked area of the succeeding process workstation. When the succeeding process uses the subassembly, the marked area—the kanban square—becomes empty and signals the preceding process to make another subassembly and fill the square. The same is done with totable bins. When the parts from a bin have been used, the empty bin is sent back to the preceding process as a signal for more production. Both of these kanban devices work when the part or subassembly in question is the only possible output of the preceding process. Should there be a variety of part or subassembly models, however, the kanban square alone will not provide sufficient information, and the bin with a descriptive card or the kanban card, or its electronic equivalent, must be used. (More information about kanban is provided later in this chapter.)

Lot Size

A final issue to be overcome by JIT/Lean production concerns lot size. Mass production is keyed to the largest possible lot sizes: set up the machines and parts streams to make as many as possible of the same item, like Henry Ford's identical black Model T's, before changing to another model or product. So-called economic lot size is still being taught in many universities. Just-in-time/Lean seeks to build in the smallest possible lots. The modern consumer demands variety. No auto company could survive today with a single car model, with each unit the same in all respects including equipment and color. JIT/Lean accommodates variety by being flexible. That is, the factory is set up so that changes can be rapidly implemented, and at little cost.

Traditionally, it has been a major problem to change models on a production line because breakdown and setup of the machines that have to be changed take a lot of time. Hours and days and even longer for new setups are not uncommon. Ohno saw that the inherent inflexibility of the mass production line was in the setup time for the machines. Too much setup time meant that a manufacturer had to have a second line—or even a new factory—for the other model, or the customers' demand for the second model was simply ignored until the run on the current model was finished. By attacking the problem head-on, Toyota was able to reduce setup times to the point where they were no longer significant. Other companies, using the Toyota approach, found that they could quickly reduce setup times by 90% and even more with some effort.

Omark Industries was one of the first American companies to study the Toyota Production System. Using Toyota's techniques, it reduced the setup time for a large press from 8 hours to 1 minute and 4 seconds.[8] After setup time became irrelevant, it was possible to manufacture in small lots—even lots of one—thereby permitting the intermixing of models on the same line. This meant that customer responsiveness was possible without huge inventories of prebuilt stock in all models. It also meant that one production line (or factory) could do the work of several. This ability is crucial if the factory is to respond to customer demand in a pull system.

The development of just-in-time/Lean production required more than the kanban, a point lost on many Westerners. JIT/Lean came about from the understanding of the seven wastes and the need to eliminate them. The key elimination of nearly all material and parts inventories dictated the requirement for reliability and predictability of the plant's machinery and processes. This led to total productive maintenance and made necessary the use of statistical process control and continual improvement.

With the customer as the driver of production, the control technique for production changed from push to pull, and kanban was introduced as the controlling system. The requirement for small lot sizes, both for elimination of waste and for responsiveness and investment economy, led to the effort to reduce setup time. With all of these factors in place, JIT/Lean was born. Without doubt, JIT/Lean, by any of its names, is the manufacturing system for today. It is adaptable to operations both large and small, high-volume/low-variety, and low-volume/high-variety as well as anything in between. In JIT/Lean, costs, lead time, and cycle time are reduced, quality is improved constantly, and both the customers and the producers and their employees benefit.

RELATIONSHIP OF JIT/LEAN TO TOTAL QUALITY AND WORLD-CLASS MANUFACTURING

The traditional production line pushes product from the front of the line to the final output, and even to the customers, whereas kanban is the controlling agent in a pull system. The two are incompatible. Similarly, implementing JIT/Lean in the absence of a comprehensive total quality system that includes the entire organization can be a problem. The traditional organization is incompatible with JIT/Lean, just as the traditional push production system is incompatible with kanban. In a typical manufacturing company, separate departments exist for engineering, manufacturing, purchasing, accounting, and so on, each with distinct boundaries and agendas. JIT/Lean is no respecter of boundaries. It requires all departments to respond to its needs. If the manufacturing department has embraced JIT/Lean, but the organization as a whole has not at least started a total quality effort, manufacturing personnel will soon encounter obstacles. More often than not there will be outright resistance because JIT/Lean's requirements represent change and departments without a commitment to change will fight it at every step.

As an example, in the defense industry it is common to defray overhead expenses (buildings, utilities, indirect employees' salaries, all fringe benefits, and others) against direct labor dollars as a means of allocating the overhead burden across all contract programs. The more direct labor on a program, the larger the share of the overhead cost that accrues to that program. *Direct labor* is defined as the manufacturing, engineering, purchasing, and other labor charged to specific contract programs. The company may also have more than one pool for overhead defrayment, such as a manufacturing pool and an engineering pool. Virtually all of these companies, and the U.S. Department of Defense, pay a great deal of attention to what they call *overhead rate*. In a typical company in the defense industry, overhead rate is calculated by dividing overhead (indirect) expenses by direct labor cost.

Suppose that for an accounting period there were indirect expenses of $200,000. At the same time, the wages paid for direct labor amounted to $100,000. The overhead rate for the period is $200,000 ÷ $100,000 = 200%. Assume that we had been operating with that 200% rate for some time, and suddenly the manufacturing department discovered JIT/Lean. After the period of time necessary for the implementation to start showing results, manufacturing finds that it can eliminate direct labor positions for production control and material control and also use fewer assemblers on the production floor to get the same number of units out the door each period. A typical early reduction in the direct labor content of the work is 30 to 35%. The next period's overhead expense is almost the same, decreasing slightly for removal of fringe benefits for the employees no longer needed, say, to $188,000. The direct labor is down by one-third to $67,000. This yields an overhead rate of $188,000 ÷ $67,000 = 281%. That kind of an increase in overhead rate, if sustained, can cause the head of manufacturing serious problems. The accounting department uses this overhead rate as proof that JIT/Lean doesn't work. All too often the accounting department blocks further progress in JIT/Lean. One might ask, "But isn't that valid if the overhead rate went out of control?" The answer is nobody should care about the overhead rate. It is simply the ratio of two numbers and carries no meaning without a thorough understanding of the two. What happened to the cost of goods sold in this example? Look at the numbers before and after JIT/Lean:[9]

	Before JIT/Lean	After JIT/Lean
Indirect Expense	$200,000	$188,000
Direct Labor	100,000	67,000
Materials	500,000	500,000
General and Administrative Expense	50,000	50,000
Cost of Goods Sold	$850,000	$805,000

In this example, it cost the company $45,000 less to produce the same goods after JIT/Lean implementation than it did before. Assuming the goods were sold for the same price, that $45,000 becomes pure profit. In the next competition for contracts, the lower cost becomes a competitive advantage (price to the customer can be lowered).

The solution to the overhead rate problem is to change from the obsolete accounting system and adopt an activity-based accounting system or some other more sensible method. In a total quality company, the accounting department is part of the team and would respond to the needs of a production system (JIT/Lean) that is actually improving

company performance. But if the company as a whole is not involved in total quality, the accounting department, with its own walls and agendas, can be a formidable obstacle to progress. The same is true of other departments on whom manufacturing depends. This example could just as easily have been one involving the engineering department and a design philosophy called *concurrent engineering*. Concurrent engineering requires that from the beginning of a new product's design, manufacturing and other departments (and even suppliers) be directly involved with engineering to make sure, among other things, that the product can be manufactured efficiently when it finally goes into production. Traditional engineering departments do not like to have this kind of help from outsiders and will resist—but not in a total quality setting, where the departments all work for the common goal.

For JIT/Lean to bring about the benefits inherent in its philosophy, it must be part of a total quality system. To bring JIT/Lean into a company not otherwise engaged in total quality can be worthwhile (and may even enlighten the leadership), but implementation will be much more difficult, and its results severely restricted.

BENEFITS OF JIT/LEAN

A discussion of the benefits of JIT/Lean must include four very important topics: inventory and work-in-process, cycle time, continual improvement, and elimination of waste. The discussion could be expanded to include such topics as reduced time-to-market, improved employee work life, flexibility, and employee ownership. All of these are definite benefits of JIT/Lean, but this discussion will be confined to the critical four mentioned. These are the usual targets of a JIT/Lean implementation.

Inventory and Work-in-Process

Just-in-time/Lean attempts to drive inventory to zero. But remember that this is a philosophical objective—an aiming point, if you will. In reality, zero inventory makes no sense. Without some inventory, you have nothing from which to produce your goods. The real objective is to minimize the inventory to the maximum possible extent without shutting down production. It is also important to recognize that there are at least three kinds of inventory. First, there is the inventory of raw materials and parts needed to make the product. Traditionally, these have filled warehouses, with enough on hand for several weeks of production, or longer. Second, there is the work-in-process (WIP) inventory of semifinished goods. WIP includes all materials and parts that have been put into the production system, including the various stages from the first process to the last within the factory. WIP may be at a workstation undergoing one of the value-adding production processes, or it may be in storage between processes. In a mass production plant, the stored WIP can be substantial. Job shops—low-volume, high-variety shops not involved in mass production—are notorious for their WIP inventory. Third, there is the finished goods inventory. These finished goods are ready for customers, but the customers are not ready for them. Therefore, they are typically stored in warehouses, although some (most notably automobiles) must be stored in yards, unprotected from the elements.

One might ask, "What is wrong with inventory?" Having materials on hand allows you to produce without worrying about on-time material deliveries. Lots of WIP lets the assembly lines continue when a machine breakdown or some other problem occurs. Having an inventory of stored finished goods means that you can be responsive to customers. If those are positives (and we'll come back to that in a minute), there are also negatives. First, there are the costs of inventorying raw materials and parts, and finished goods. There are the costs of the materials and goods; the labor costs for the storage, handling, and protection of the materials and goods; and the cost of warehouses, real estate, and capital equipment used in the inventorying of the materials and goods. Second, there is the cost of spoilage while in inventory. Spoilage can be due to damage, deterioration, corrosion, obsolescence, and so on. Third, there is the cost of taxes. While the product is in inventory, the manufacturer owns it, it has value, and the various levels of government want their share in the form of taxes.

Now go back to the suggestion made earlier that the three positives associated with inventory might not be so positive after all. The costs discussed earlier are all tangible costs. There are also intangible costs that, while difficult to measure precisely, are nevertheless significant. Foremost among the intangibles is the fact that as long as the manufacturer holds inventory of materials and WIP at high levels, it is not solving the problems and making the continual improvements that can bring efficiency. The very presence of these inventories masks the problems, so they go unnoticed and unresolved—being repeated over and over, consuming unnecessary labor, and preventing product quality improvement. Unmasking the production system's problems through the elimination of inventories is a major strength of JIT/Lean. Many North American and European companies still tend to see the elimination of inventories as a generator of problems. In reality, the problems are already there, and they are costing a great deal in terms of money and quality, but they are just not apparent with big inventories. Through inventories maintained, tons of money is spent, but no value is added, and needed improvements are not made in the production processes. The inevitable net result is loss of competitive position and market share as enlightened competitors use JIT/Lean and total quality to improve their positions.

If a plant could get its production processes under control to the point that they could be relied on to perform as intended, it would be logical to reduce WIP and material and part inventories. However, until the processes are well-understood and in control, reducing inventories substantially will certainly result in production stoppages. One philosophy of reducing WIP and lot sizes is to do so in steps. By incrementally lowering WIP and lot sizes, the problems become apparent in a gradual, manageable stream rather than in a torrent, and they can be dealt with. Once through that process, the next logical step is to work with suppliers to deliver materials and parts in smaller, more frequent lots, until finally there is no need for warehousing at all. This clearly requires that the production processes be capable and reliable and that the suppliers be similarly capable and reliable.

This leaves only the finished goods inventory. As the processes and suppliers become more proficient, and the JIT/Lean line takes hold, production will be geared to customer demand rather than to sales forecasts. The ability of the JIT/Lean line to respond quickly to customer requirements means that it is no longer necessary to store finished goods. The only stored goods should be those in the distribution system, and that level will typically be far less than has been the case under mass production.

JIT/Lean strives for zero inventory of any kind. Achieving zero inventory is not a realistic intent, but by aiming at zero and continually reducing inventories, not only do manufacturers cut costs by significant numbers, but also the whole continual improvement process comes to life, resulting in even more savings and improved product quality.

Cycle Time

Production cycle time is defined as the period bounded by the time materials are sent to the manufacturing floor for the making of a product and the time the finished goods are dispatched from the manufacturing floor to a customer or to finished goods storage. Generally speaking, the shorter the production cycle time, the lower the production cost. That may be reason enough to pay attention to cycle time, but there are other benefits. Short cycles improve a factory's ability to respond quickly to changing customer demands. The less time a product spends in the production cycle, the less chance there is for damage.

We are accustomed to thinking of a mass production line as having the shortest of cycle times, and there have been startling examples of this. Henry Ford's Model T lines (producing up to 2 million cars per year, all the same, all black) achieved remarkable cycle times even by today's standards. For example, Ford's River Rouge facility took iron ore in the front door and shipped completed cars out the back door in four days.[10] When one considers that the Ford cycle included making the steel, in addition to stamping, casting, machining, and assembly, it is all the more amazing. One of his secrets was no variability in the product. Modern lines have the complication of different models and virtually unlimited options.

A modern auto assembly line cannot be compared with Ford's Model T line because the complexity and variability of the contemporary car are so much greater. However, the best lines beat Ford's cycle time for assembly. The differences in JIT/Lean lines and mass production lines are substantial. For example, comparisons between JIT/Lean plants and traditional mass production plants reveal that JIT/Lean plants can assemble automobiles in 52% of the time it takes traditional plants. Because there is very little waiting in a JIT/Lean line, one can assume the cycle time is one-half of that for traditional lines. Interestingly, though not directly related to cycle time, traditional lines produce three times as many defects and require nearly twice the factory space. In addition, JIT/Lean plants can operate with a 2-hour parts inventory, while traditional plants typically need a 2-week supply.[11]

Consider the following example, which helps bridge the issues of inventory and cycle time. The product was a line of very expensive military avionics test systems. The factories (two) were rather typical electronics job shops. Before being converted to JIT/Lean, they were struggling with a production schedule requiring the assembly of 75 large, complex printed circuit boards per day. They rarely met the goal, usually achieving about 50. The attempted solution involved pushing more parts into the front end of the assembly process, hoping that would force more out the other end as finished, tested boards. The computer system revealed that, at any point in time, about 3,500 boards were in the process. At the rate of 50 completed boards per day and 3,500 boards in WIP, simple arithmetic showed that the cycle time for the average board was 13 weeks. Common sense said that 13 weeks was much too long for assembling these boards, but checking with others in the industry revealed that this was a typical cycle time. The company also found that it made absolutely no difference in final output rate to force more materials into the front of the process. This merely increased the number of boards in WIP.

With a production rate of 50 boards a day and 3,500 boards in process, one can imagine the difficulty in keeping track of where the boards were, scheduling them into and out of the various processes, and storing, retrieving, and safeguarding them. Such tasks were nearly impossible. More than 100 people were charged with handling and tracking the boards, adding no value whatever to the product. Further, because the assemblers were being pushed to their limits, quality suffered. The net result was that nearly half of total direct labor was spent repairing defects. That did not add value either. Once again, however, checking with other manufacturers revealed that this was typical. A critical factor was that customer delivery schedules could not be met unless a solution was found. Initially, the company had to subcontract a great many boards, but that was a work-around, not a solution.

The eventual answer was to implement JIT/Lean techniques on the production floor. After a couple of quick pilot runs, in which it was discovered that the most difficult of the boards could be assembled and tested in 8 days (versus 13 weeks), management was convinced, and JIT/Lean was implemented at both plants, following the WIP reduction and lot-size scheme outlined in the previous section. In very short order, the board cycle time fell to about 5 days, and board quality improved dramatically. That enabled the company to eliminate the 100-plus positions that had handled the boards and eventually many other non-value-adding positions as well. The system delivery on-time rate went to 98% (unheard of for this kind of product), customer satisfaction improved, and a respectable profit was made.

The thing to remember about cycle time is this: any time above that which is directly required by the manufacturing process is not adding value and is costing money. For example, assume we use two processes to manufacture a product, and the total time consumed within the processes is 2 hours. It is determined that the actual cycle time is 3 hours. That means that 2 hours of the cycle is adding value and the other hour is not. Invariably, this means a bottleneck is preventing the product from flowing from one process directly into the next without delay. The key is to detect the bottleneck and do something about it. It may be that a plant procedure requires inspection, logging, and a computer data entry. Are these tasks really necessary? Can they be eliminated? If they are necessary, can they be streamlined?

The extra hour may be the result of a problem in one of the processes. For example, it may be that the second process is no longer 1 hour in duration but 2. If the latter is the case, in a traditional production plant, the product flowing out of the first process will stack up at the input of the second process because process 1 will continue to crank out its product at the rate of one unit per hour—whether process 2 is ready for it or not (see Figure 21–7). The surplus product at the input to process 2 will have to be stored for safety and housekeeping reasons, thus obscuring the fact that there is a problem.

As long as the problem persists, WIP will build, output will stay at one unit every 2 hours, but cycle time will increase as backlog builds up in front of process 2; the first unit went through the production system in 3 hours, and one unit per hour was expected after that, but the process is actually achieving one unit every 2 hours. Cycle time increases by 1 hour for each piece—for example, 8 hours later the sixth unit into process 1 will come out of process 2. Such an imbalance would not escape notice for long, and it would be corrected, but by then, several pieces of WIP would be between the processes.

Suppose that the problem in the second process was corrected as the sixth unit was completed. Everything is back to the original 2-hour process time, but by now, there are seven more units through process 1, on which the cycle time clock has already started. If stable from this point forward, the cycle time will remain at 8 hours. We started with a process that had 2 hours of value-adding work and a 3-hour cycle. We now have a 2-hour value-adding process time and an 8-hour cycle. If some means is not taken to cause the second process to catch up, every time there is a glitch in process 2, the cycle time will grow. In a traditional plant, with literally dozens of processes, such conditions could go on forever. As observed earlier, some would hold that having the seven units from the first process sitting on the shelf means that process 1 could be down for a complete shift without causing a problem for the second process—it would merely draw from the seven.

In a JIT/Lean plant, the situation described here would never happen. Process 1 would not produce an additional piece until process 2 asked for it (kanban). At the start, process 1 produces one unit to enable process 2. When process 2 withdraws it, process 1 is signaled to produce another. If for any reason,

Piece #	Process 1 In	Process 1 Out	Wait Time (in Hours)	Process 2 In	Process 2 Out	Cycle Time (in Hours)
1	7 A.M.	8 A.M.	0	8 A.M.	10 A.M.	3
2	8 A.M.	9 A.M.	1	10 A.M.	12 noon	4
3	9 A.M.	10 A.M.	2	12 noon	2 P.M.	5
4	10 A.M.	11 A.M.	3	2 P.M.	4 P.M.	6
5	11 A.M.	12 noon	4	4 P.M.	6 P.M.	7
6	12 noon	1 P.M.	5	6 P.M.	8 P.M.	8
7	1 P.M.	2 P.M.	6	8 P.M.	9 P.M.	8
8	2 P.M.	3 P.M.	6	9 P.M.	10 P.M.	8
9	3 P.M.	4 P.M.	6	10 P.M.	11 P.M.	8
10	4 P.M.	5 P.M.	6	11 P.M.	12 midn.	8
11	5 P.M.	6 P.M.	6	12 midn.	1 A.M.	8
12	6 P.M.	7 P.M.	6	1 A.M.	2 A.M.	8
13	7 P.M.	8 P.M.	6	2 A.M.	3 A.M.	8

FIGURE 21–7 Cycle Time Example

when process 1 completes its second unit, process 2 is not ready to withdraw it, process 1 goes idle. It will stay idle until signaled to produce another—be it a few minutes or a week. No WIP inventory is produced. By process 1 going idle, alarms go off, quickly letting the appropriate people know that something has gone wrong. If there is a difficulty in the second process, causing it to consume too much time, it gets attention immediately. Similarly, if there is a delay getting the output of the first process to the second because of an administrative procedure, that, too, will be dealt with quickly because it will cause problems throughout the overall process until it is solved.

Any contributor to cycle time is apparent in a JIT/Lean environment, and JIT/Lean philosophy calls for continual improvement and refinement. Wait time in storage is simply not a factor in JIT/Lean because nothing is produced in advance of its need by the succeeding process. That single factor can easily remove 80 to 90% of the cycle time in a traditional factory. In the earlier example of the printed circuit board factories, the initial reduction of cycle time from 13 weeks (65 working days) to 8 days was simply the elimination of storage time. That was a reduction of 88%. Further refinement, made possible because of the visibility afforded by JIT/Lean, brought the cycle to 4 days, or only 6%

of the original cycle. Taking it further was restricted by procedural and governmental requirements. In a commercial setting, however, the same boards could probably have been produced in a 2-day cycle with no new capital equipment.

Before JIT/Lean, manufacturers tried to cut cycle time with automation. But that was not the answer. The solution was found in better control of production, and that was obtained with JIT/Lean. JIT/Lean is the most powerful concept available for reducing cycle time.

Continual Improvement

Continual improvement has been discussed in several other chapters and sections of this book. By now, you should have a good understanding of its meaning as applied in a total quality context. Continual improvement seeks to eliminate waste in all forms, improve quality of products and services, and improve customer responsiveness—and do all of this while at the same time reducing costs. A note of caution should be added in regard to interpretation of what constitutes improvement: Problem solving is not necessarily improvement. If a process that had previously been capable of producing 95 out of 100 good parts deteriorates to a level of 50 good parts and the problem is found and corrected to bring the process back to where it had been—that is maintenance not improvement. *Maintenance* is restoring a capability that previously existed. On the other hand, if a process was capable of 95 good parts out of 100 produced and a team developed a way to change the process to produce 99 good parts—that would be improvement. It is important to differentiate between maintenance and improvement. Maintenance is important, and it must go on, but in the final analysis, you end up where you started. *Improvement* means becoming better than when you started. Continual improvement is to repeat that improvement cycle, in W. Edwards Deming's words, constantly and forever.[12]

The discussion of continual improvement in this chapter explains how JIT/Lean supports continual improvement. The traditional factory effectively hides its information through inventories of parts, WIP, and finished goods—people are scurrying about, everybody busy, whether any value is being added or not. The JIT/Lean factory is visual: its information is there for everyone to see and use. Quality defects become immediately apparent, as do improper production rates—whether too slow or too fast. Either of these, for example, will result in people stopping work. While that is not acceptable behavior in a mass production factory, in a JIT/Lean plant it is encouraged and expected.

A true story from Toyota tells of two supervisors, one from the old school and unable to adapt to JIT/Lean and the other ready to try JIT/Lean even if it did seem strange.[13] The first supervisor refused to allow his line to be stopped, whereas the second didn't hesitate to stop his. At first, the line operated by the second supervisor was producing far fewer cars than the other line because it was stopping for every little problem. These problems had been common knowledge among the workers but not among the supervisors. The problems were solved one by one as a result of stopping the line for each. After 3 weeks, the second supervisor's line took the lead for good. The first supervisor believed that stopping the line would decrease efficiency and cost the company money. As it turned out, the reverse was true. By stopping the line to eliminate problems, efficiency and economy were enhanced. The only reason for stopping a line is to improve it, eliminating the need for stopping again for the same reason.

In a mass production plant, the sight of idle workers will draw the ire of supervisors in no uncertain terms. But in a JIT/Lean situation, the rule is if there is a problem, stop. Suppose that a preceding process has responded to a kanban and provided a part to a succeeding process. The succeeding process finds that the part is not acceptable for some reason (fit, finish, improper model, or something else). The succeeding process worker immediately stops, reporting the problem to the preceding process and to supervision. Perhaps an *andon* (a Japanese word meaning "lamp") signal will be illuminated to call attention to the fact that his process is shut down. The problem is to be solved before any more work is done by the two processes, which means that downstream processes may soon stop as well because their demands through kanban cannot be honored until the prob-

lem is fixed and the processes are once again running. This is high visibility, and it is guaranteed to get the proper attention not only to solve the immediate problem but also to improve the process to make sure it does not happen again.

Consider the following example. A few weeks after JIT/Lean was implemented in a New York electronics plant, there was a line shutdown. At the end of this line was a test station that was to do a comprehensive functional test of the product. There was an assembly all set up for test, but the technician had stopped. The line's andon light was illuminated. A small crowd gathered. The problem was that the test instructions were out of date. Over time, the test instruction document had been red-lined with changes and had, up until that point, been used without apparent difficulty. But a company procedure required that any red-lined document be reissued to incorporate the approved changes within 1 year of the first red line. The 1-year clock had expired months earlier, and the technician, with guidance from quality assurance, properly stopped testing. When management asked why the document had not long since been updated, it was found that the documents seldom were updated until the entire job was completed. In many cases, jobs lasted several years. Holding all formal revisions until a job was completed meant that documentation was revised just once, thereby saving considerable expense. Of course, in the meantime, manufacturing was using out-of-date or questionable information. The standard work-around seemed to be that when a system couldn't be completed for delivery, waivers were generated, allowing the tests to be conducted with the outdated red-lined procedures. This had been going on for years but never became apparent to the levels in manufacturing and engineering that could solve it. In this case, it took about 20 minutes to solve the problem. Without JIT/Lean to highlight it, the problem would, in all probability, still exist.

What had happened because of JIT/Lean was a stop at the test station. That also shut off kanbans through the preceding processes. In short order, the line stopped, getting the attention needed to eliminate the problem. If the plant had been operating in the traditional (non–JIT/Lean) way, the assemblies would have piled up at the test station for a while and then the production control people would have carted them off to a work-in-process storage area—out of sight. Eventually, the inventory of previously tested assemblies would have been consumed, and there would have been a "brushfire" from which a procedural waiver would have emerged to enable the test technician to pull the untested assemblies from WIP stores and quickly get them tested so system deliveries could be made. This would have been repeated time and again, just as had been happening surreptitiously in the past.

This is not an uncommon scenario. Fundamentally, it is the result of departments not communicating. Engineering is trying to save money by reducing the number of documentation revisions. Meanwhile, manufacturing may be producing obsolete and unusable product because the documentation is not up-to-date. At best, it results in the continual "firefighting" that saps the collective energy of the organization, leading to quick-fix, work-around "solutions" that let you get today's product out but only make

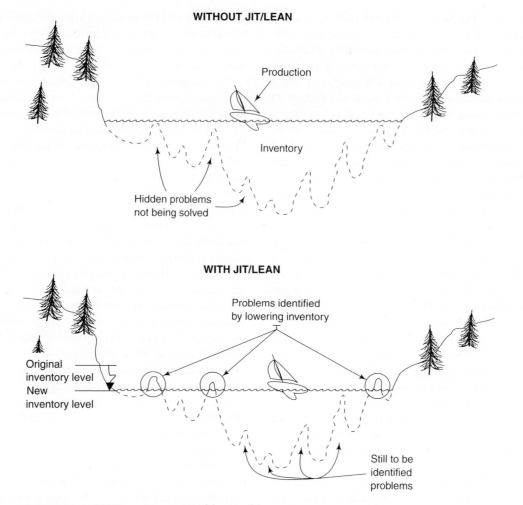

FIGURE 21–8 JIT/Lean Exposes Hidden Problems

each succeeding day that much more difficult. JIT/Lean, by highlighting problems, is quick to dispel the quick-fix mentality, demanding instead that problems be eliminated for today and tomorrow and forever.

The analogy of a lake better illustrates JIT/Lean's ability to reveal real problems (see Figure 21–8). You look out over the lake and see the calm, flat surface of the water and perhaps an island or two. From this observation, you conclude that the lake is navigable, so you put your boat in and cast off. You avoid running into the islands because they can be seen plainly and there is plenty of room to steer around them. However, a rock just below the surface is not evident until you crash into it. It turns out there are lots of rocks at various depths, but you can't see them until it is too late. This is like a traditional factory. The rocks represent problems that will wreak havoc on production (the boat). The water represents all the inventory maintained: raw materials and parts, WIP, and even finished goods. Now if you make the change to just-in-time/Lean, you start reducing those inventories. Every time you remove some, the level of the water in the lake is lowered, revealing problems that had been there all along but that were not eliminated because they couldn't be seen. You just kept running your boat into them, making repairs, and sailing

on to the next encounter. But with the lower water level, the problems become visible and can be eliminated. Clear sailing? Probably not. Other rocks are no doubt just below the new lower surface level, so you have to take some more water out of the lake (remove more inventory), enabling you to identify and eliminate them. Like most analogies, our lake doesn't hold all the way to the logical conclusion of zero inventory because the lake would be dry by then. But remember, true zero inventory doesn't hold either. As was said before, it is a target to aim at but never to be fully reached.

JIT/Lean is by nature a visible process, making problems and opportunities for improvement obvious. Moreover, when problems do occur in a JIT/Lean setting, they must be solved and not merely patched up, or they will immediately reappear. Visibility to all levels, from the workers to the top executive, means that the power to make necessary changes to eliminate problems and improve processes is available.

Elimination of Waste

In the preceding three sections, it was shown how just-in-time/Lean facilitates reduction of inventories and cycle time and promotes continual improvement. This section will show that JIT/Lean is also a powerful eliminator of waste. As discussed earlier in this chapter (in the "Rationale for JIT/Lean" section), Taiichi Ohno created the JIT/Lean system specifically to eliminate the seven wastes he saw in the Ford mass production system. Let's look at them one at a time and see how JIT/Lean helps in their elimination.

1. **Waste arising from overproducing.** Mass production pushes materials into the front of the factory in response to market forecasts. These raw materials are converted to finished goods and pushed through the distribution system. The first real customer input into the process is at the retail level. If customers don't want the goods, they will eventually be sold at prices much lower than anticipated, often below their actual cost. That is waste to the producer. In addition, producing goods for which there is not a matching demand is a waste to society by using resources to no purpose. In a JIT/Lean environment, the customers enter the system at the beginning, pulling goods from the distribution system and, in turn, from the manufacturer. The JIT/Lean factory produces nothing without a kanban, which, in effect, originates with a customer.

The same is true *within* the two kinds of factories. A fender-stamping press in a mass production factory will continue to stamp out fenders even though the final assembly line, which uses the fenders, is stopped. The overproduction must then be handled by people who contribute nothing to the value of the product, stored in buildings that would otherwise be unnecessary, and tracked by people and systems that add no value to the product, but cost a lot of money. In a JIT/Lean factory, the fender-stamping press will shut down unless it receives kanbans requesting more fenders, and there will be no overproduction. Of all the wastes, overproduction is the most insidious because it gives rise to all the other types of waste.

2. **Waste arising from waiting (time).** Wait time can come from many causes: waiting for parts to be retrieved from a storage location, waiting for a tool to be replaced, waiting for a machine to be repaired or to be set up for a different product, or waiting for the next unit to move down the line. JIT/Lean parts are typically located at the workstation, not in some central staging area or warehouse. JIT/Lean sets aside time for tool and machine maintenance, so replacement or repair during a production period is rare. Whereas setup times for machines in mass production plants tend to take hours (or even longer), JIT/Lean factories devote a great deal of attention to setup time, typically reducing it to a very few minutes. In a traditional factory, an operator is assigned to each machine. While the machine is running under automatic control, the operator has nothing to do but wait. In a JIT/Lean factory, the same operator may run five machines, arranged so that he or she can easily see and control all five without much movement. As three machines are running automatically, the operator may set up the fourth and unload the fifth, for example. In this way, the operator's day is no longer mostly wait time.

Perhaps the biggest waste associated with waiting involves not human waiting but inventory waiting. In the traditional setting, raw materials and parts can sit idle for weeks and months before they are needed. Work-in-process may wait weeks to have a few hours of value-adding work done. Finished goods may wait very long periods for customers. JIT/Lean does not allow any of these waits to occur, and the carrying expense is eliminated.

3. **Waste arising from transport.** Mass production factories tend to buy their materials and parts in very large quantities from the lowest price (as opposed to lowest cost or best value) source, regardless of the distance from the source to the factory. JIT/Lean factories of necessity must buy in small quantities (no warehousing) with frequent deliveries, often several times a day. That means that the suppliers should be relatively close to the factory, cutting transportation time and costs.

Transportation within plants can be a very high-cost item, too. Moving things costs money and time and increases exposure to damage. Moving materials in and out of storage areas, to and from the floor, or back and forth across the factory from process to process is waste. None of that happens with JIT/Lean. Production materials are delivered to the point of use in a JIT/Lean factory, so they are not shuttled in and out of storage or put in temporary storage to be moved again before use. Factories are arranged to minimize distances between adjacent processes, whereas the same product manufactured in the traditional factory could log thousands of feet, or even miles, of movement before completion.

4. **Waste arising from processing itself.** Any process that does not operate smoothly as intended but instead requires extra work or attention by the operator is wasteful. An example is the necessity for the operator to override an automatic machine function to prevent defective products. Because one of the basic tenets of JIT/Lean is continual improvement of processes, wasteful processes are soon identified and improved to eliminate the waste. That is far more difficult in the traditional production environment because of its emphasis on output, not process improvement.

5. **Waste arising from unnecessary stock on hand.** Any stock on hand has storage costs associated with it. When that stock is unnecessary, the costs are pure waste. Included in these costs are real estate, buildings, employees not otherwise needed, and tracking and administration. Because JIT/Lean attempts to eliminate stock, unnecessary stock is just not tolerated.

6. **Waste arising from unnecessary motion.** JIT/Lean plants are laid out to minimize motion of both workers and product. Motion takes time, adds no value, makes necessary additional workers, and hides waste. The contrast between a JIT/Lean plant laid out with product orientation and the traditional plant laid out with process orientation is profound (see Figure 21–9). In the traditional plant, there is much motion, with people and product shuttling all over the place. In a JIT/Lean plant, motion is almost undetectable to a casual observer.

7. **Waste arising from producing defective goods.** Defective goods will surely cost money in one of three ways: (a) the product may be reworked to correct the

Traditional Factory Organized by Processes
(illustrating process flow for one product)

JIT/Lean Factory Organized by Product
(illustrating process flow for four products)

FIGURE 21–9 Comparison of Factory Floor Layouts: Traditional versus JIT/Lean

deficiency, in which case the rework labor and material costs represent waste; (b) it may be scrapped, in which case the cost of the materials and the value added by labor has been wasted; or (c) it may be sold to customers who, on discovering that the product is defective, return it for repair under warranty and may be dissatisfied to the extent they will never buy this manufacturer's products again. Warranty costs represent a waste, and the potential for a lost customer is great, portending a future loss of sales.

In a traditional factory, it is possible to produce large quantities of products before defects are discovered and the line corrected. It is not uncommon in mass production for a company to keep the line running, intentionally producing defective products, while trying to figure out what has happened and devising a solution. It is considered less troublesome to fix the defective products later than to shut down the line. In JIT/Lean, however, because line stops are anticipated and because the preferred lot size is one unit, it is improbable that more than one defective unit could be produced before shutting down the line.

Dr. M. Scott Myers, author of the landmark book *Every Employee Is a Manager*, made the case for an eighth waste: the waste arising from the underutilization of talent. Myers believed that the most damaging of the eight wastes is the waste of talent.[14] If all the talents of all employees were brought to bear on the problems and issues of production, the other wastes would probably disappear. This is the rationale for both employee involvement and teamwork. JIT/Lean is designed to make use of the ideas and talents of all employees through team activities and employee involvement, in an environment that fosters the open and free interchange of ideas, all of which are foreign to the traditional production systems. Elimination of waste is an integral focus of just-in-time/Lean by design. No other production system looks at waste except after the fact.

REQUIREMENTS OF JIT/LEAN

For a factory to operate as a just-in-time/Lean production facility, a number of steps must be taken. It is very important that JIT/Lean implementation be a part of a larger total quality program; otherwise, many interdepartmental roadblocks will crop up as time passes. Like total quality, JIT/Lean requires an unwavering commitment from the top because production is more than just the manufacturing department. If these two elements (a total quality program and a commitment from the top) are in place, JIT/Lean implementation should be within reach. The following discussion touches on the issues that must be addressed as the implementation progresses.

Factory Organization

The JIT/Lean plant is laid out quite differently from that to which most people are accustomed. Most traditional factories are set up according to the processes that are used. For example, there may be a welding shop, a machine shop, a cable assembly area, a printed circuit board assembly area, a soldering area, and so on. Each of these discrete processes may be set up in separate parts of the factory (all machining operations done in the machine shop, all cable assembly done in the common cable and harness area, etc.), no matter which of many products it might be for (refer to Figure 21–9). The JIT/Lean plant attempts to set up the factory by product rather than process. All the necessary processes for a given product should be located together in a single area and laid out in as compact a manner as possible.

The chart at the top of Figure 21–9 represents the old process-oriented traditional factory. Each of the processes has its own territory within the plant. Additionally, an area dedicated to warehousing is used for storage of production materials, work-in-process that is waiting for the next process, and perhaps finished goods awaiting orders. There is also an area set aside for shipping and receiving. Materials are received, inspected, processed, and sent to the warehouse area. Finished goods are taken from the warehouse or from final assembly, packed, and shipped. The upper illustration in Figure 21–9

maps the movement from the warehouse through the processes and finally to shipping in a traditional factory.

The lower illustration in Figure 21–9 represents a JIT/Lean factory that is set up to manufacture four different products. The warehousing area is gone. This cannot happen overnight, but an objective of JIT/Lean is to eliminate all inventories. The second thing to notice is that the factory is divided into discrete areas dedicated to the different products rather than to the different processes. Each product area is equipped with the processes required for that product. Parts bins are located right in the work area. These bins may have enough to last from a few hours to a few days or more, depending on the degree of maturity of the JIT/Lean implementation and the nature of the product and its anticipated production life.

Mapped out in the upper illustration of Figure 21–9 is a typical work-flow diagram for one product. Parts and materials are pulled from several locations in the warehousing area and moved to a process A workstation. These materials may be in kit form (all the parts needed to make one lot of a product). The work instructions call for process A first, followed by process D. If process D is busy when the lot is finished by process A, the lot, now WIP, may be stacked up in a queue at process D or taken back to the warehouse for safekeeping. Eventually, process D will process the kit, and it will be sent to process E, perhaps waiting in queue or in the warehouse. This same sequence is repeated through process B, process C, and process F. From there, it goes to shipping. The diagram does not show any trips back to the warehouse between processes, but that could very well happen after every step. The flow-diagram represents a best-case scenario. (This was done purposely to ensure clarity.)

Now observe the flow in the JIT/Lean factory of Figure 21–9. Product 1 is set up to follow exactly the same processing sequence (from parts bins to process A and then to process D, process E, process B, process C, process F, and shipping). In this case, the parts come straight from the bins located in the work cell, not from the warehouse and not in kit form, which is a waste of effort. The work cell is laid out in a U shape for compactness, to keep all the work cell members close to each other. The WIP flows directly from process to process without a lot of wasted movement. Moreover, because this is a JIT/Lean work cell, there will be small lot sizes, with work pulled through the process sequence by kanban. That means there will be no queue time on the floor or in the warehouse. Cycle time for this product in the JIT/Lean work cell can be expected to be less than half of that for the same product in the factory at the top of Figure 21–9. An 80 to 90% reduction would not be unusual.

Before one can lay out a JIT/Lean factory, the processes required for the product must be known. This is usually not a problem. Typically, the greatest difficulty comes in determining how much of a process is needed. How many minutes of a process does the product use? One would think that if the product had been built before in the traditional way, one should know how much process time is required at each step. This may be a starting point, but typically it is not very accurate. With all the wasted motion and waiting time in queues and in the warehouse, the real processing time becomes obscured. However, you can use the best information available and refine it over time. Now that the processes are put right into the product work cell, having just the right amount is important.

In the case of product 4 in Figure 21–9's JIT/Lean factory, it was determined that the product required more capability in process A and process E than was available from single workstations, so they were doubled. Suppose that a product flow of 120 units per hour is anticipated. Each process has the following estimated capability for this product:

A: 75 units per hour	D: 120 units per hour
B: 150 units per hour	E: 70 units per hour
C: 130 units per hour	F: 135 units per hour

Because processes A and E are estimated to be capable of only about 60% of the anticipated demand, there is no point in trying to improve them. Rather, the process capability was doubled by putting in parallel equipment and workstations. This is a beginning. We now can watch for excess capacity that can be removed from the work cell or for bottlenecks that require other adjustment. Work cells are coarsely tuned at first, with fine-tuning taking place during the initial runs. Excess capacity should be removed, just as required added capacity must be brought into the work cell. Bottlenecks will be quickly discovered and corrected. From there on, it is a matter of continual improvement to increase efficiency forever.

Training, Teams, and Skills

Assuming an existing factory is converted to just-in-time/Lean, one would assume that the people who had been operating it would be capable of doing it under JIT/Lean. Naturally, many of the skills and much of the training necessary for the traditional factory are required under JIT/Lean, but JIT/Lean does require additional training. First, the transition from the traditional way of doing things in a factory to JIT/Lean involves profound changes. It will seem that everything has been turned upside down for a while. People should not be exposed to that kind of change without preparation. It is advisable to provide employees with training about why the change is being made, how JIT/Lean works, what to expect, and how JIT/Lean will affect them. Initial training should be aimed at orientation and familiarization. Detailed training on subjects such as kanban, process improvement, and statistical tools should be provided when they are needed—a sort of just-in-time approach to training.

Most factory workers are accustomed to working individually. That will change under JIT/Lean, which is designed around teams. A JIT/Lean work cell forms a natural team. The team is responsible for the total product, from the first production process to the shipping dock. Perhaps for the first time the workers will be able to identify with a product, something that they create, and the processes they own. This doesn't happen in a traditional factory. But with JIT/Lean, it is important to understand that workers must function as a team. Each will have his or her special tasks, but they work together, supporting each other, solving problems, checking work, helping out wherever they can. This may require some coaching and facilitating.

It was enough in the old way of production that workers had the skills for their individual processes. They did not need additional skills because they were locked into one process. This is not the case with JIT/Lean. Specialists are of far less value than generalists. Cross-training is required to develop new skills. As a minimum, work cell members should develop skills in all the processes required by their product. Naturally, there are limits to this. We do not propose that all the members of a work cell become electronics technicians if their cell employs one for testing the product, but the cross-training should broaden their skills as far as is reasonable. Even on the issue of technical skills, it is beneficial to move in that direction. For example, if an operator's task is to assemble an electronic assembly that will be part of an end-item device, there is no reason that operators couldn't test it when they complete the assembly. Go/no-go testers can be built to facilitate testing any electronic assembly, and they can be simple enough to operate that the assembler can easily perform the test. This frees the technician for the more complicated tests downstream and ensures that the assembly is working before it is passed on to the next higher level. It also gives operators a sense of ownership and accomplishment. Over time, they may even be able to troubleshoot an assembly that fails the test.

Requiring multiple skills in JIT/Lean teams is important for several reasons. First, when a team member is absent, the work cell can still function. Second, problem solving and continual improvement are enhanced by having more than one expert on whatever process is in question. New people will have fresh new ideas. Third, if one of the cell's processes starts falling behind, another member can augment the process until it is back on track.

Establishing the Flow and Simplifying

Ideally, a new line could be set up as a test case to get the flow established, balance the flow, and generally work out initial problems. In the real world, this may not be feasible. Normally, the new line is set up to produce deliverable goods. What typically happens is a line is set up and then operated with just a few pieces flowing through to verify the line's parameters. It is very important to maintain strict discipline on the line during pilot runs. Everyone must strictly adhere to procedures. Each operator must stay in his or her assigned work area, with no helping in another process. Only if pilot runs are conducted this way will the information gained be meaningful and valid. This will allow process times to be checked, wait times to be assessed, bottlenecks to be identified, and workers to become synchronized. It is not necessary to have a pull system in place for these preliminary runs because only a few pieces will be involved. In fact, until the flows have been established, kanban is not possible.

The second thing to look for in these pilot runs is how well the line accommodates the work. Are the workstations positioned for the least motion? Is there sufficient space but not too much? Can the operators communicate easily with each other? Is the setup logical and simple? Can any changes be made to make it better, simpler? Don't overlook the processes themselves. Ultimately, that is where most of the simplification will occur.

PRODUCING PROCESS HARNESS ASSY BHA-15	LOCATION BHA-15 SQ. F 1	PART NO. 3371-10130	WITHDRAWING PROCESS PANEL INTEG BPT-1
	CONTAINER TYPE N/A	PART DESCR BETA HARNESS	
	CONTAINER CAPACITY ——	NO. WITHDRAWN 1	RECEIVING LOC BPT-1 WS

FIGURE 21–10 Withdrawal (Move) Kanban (MK)

Kanban Pull System

Having established the flow and simplified it to the extent possible, the company can now introduce the kanban pull system. As the work cell is being designed, the kanban scheme should be developed. For example, will a single or double kanban card system be used? Or, will kanban squares or bins be used? Or, will some combination or a different variation be used?

You may want to use an electronic kanban system, although it might be best to use one of the manual systems initially. After the kinks are worked out the electronic system will be easier to implement. Any kanban plan must be tailored to the application; there is no single, best, universally applicable kanban system.

Readers who are familiar with manufacturing may know that cards have been used in the manufacturing process as long as anyone can remember. They take the form of traveler tags, job orders, route sheets, and so on, but they are not at all the same as kanbans. These cards push materials and parts into a production process, such as PC-board stuffing. When the boards controlled by the card are all stuffed (the electronic components have been inserted into the boards), the entire batch is pushed to the next process—ready or not, here they come. The next process didn't ask for them and may

not be ready for them—in which case, they will stack up in front of the process or be removed from the production floor and stored with other waiting WIP. By contrast, in a JIT/Lean line, the succeeding process signals the preceding process by kanban that it needs its output. Be sure to understand the distinction; with kanban, the succeeding process pulls from the preceding (supplying) process. The kanban always tells the supplying process exactly what it wants and how many. The supplying process is not authorized to make more product until the kanban tells it to do so—nothing waiting, no stored WIP.

Ohno's double card system uses two types of kanbans: the *withdrawal* kanban and the *production* kanban.

■ The *withdrawal* kanban, also called the *move* kanban, is used to authorize the movement of materials or WIP from one process to another (see Figure 21–10). This kanban will contain information about the item it is authorizing for withdrawal, the quantity, the identity of the containers used, and the two processes involved supplying and receiving.

■ The *production* kanban authorizes a process to produce another lot of one or more pieces as specified by the kanban (see Figure 21–11). This kanban also describes

FIGURE 21–11 Production Kanban (PK)

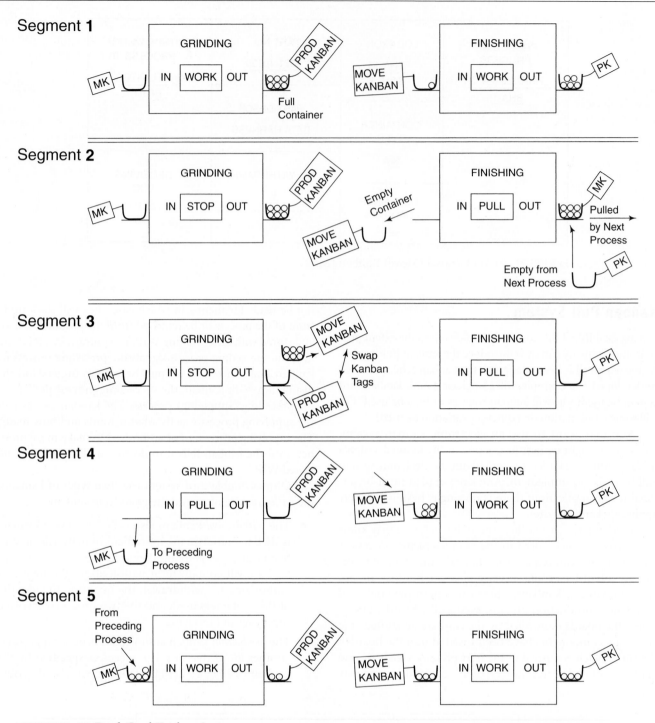

FIGURE 21–12 Dual-Card Kanban System

the piece(s) authorized, identifies the materials to be used, designates the producing process workstation, and tells the producing process what to do with it when it is completed.

Consider the operation of two processes in a manufacturing sequence to see how this works in practice. Figure 21–12 shows a preceding process that does grinding on metal parts. This is the supplier for the parts finishing workstation,

the succeeding process. Figure 21–12 shows five segments, described in the following paragraphs:

Segment 1 reveals that the finishing workstation has containers at both its In and Out areas. The container at the In area carries a move kanban (MK) and has one part left to be used. The container at the Out area has five finished parts in it and is waiting for the sixth. Back at the grinding workstation, the Out container is filled with the six parts authorized by the production kanban (PK) attached. The container at the ln area is empty, and work is stopped until another production kanban appears.

Segment 2 shows that the finishing workstation has completed work on the six parts, emptying the container at its In area. The empty container with its attached MK for six parts is taken back to the grinding workstation, which is ready to supply the parts.

Segment 3 shows that when the empty container is received at the grinding workstation, the move kanban is removed from the empty container and attached to the full container, which is sitting at the process's Out area. This authorizes movement of the six parts to the finishing workstation. At the same time, the production kanban is removed from the full container and attached to the empty one, which is placed at the grinding workstation's Out area. This authorizes the grinding process to grind six more pieces.

Segment 4 shows that the finishing process has now processed two parts. The empty container at the In area of the grinding process has been taken back to the preceding process in order to obtain the parts it needs to grind six new pieces.

Segment 5 shows the finishing workstation halfway through its six pieces, with the grinding process started on its next six pieces. This cycle will repeat itself until there is no more demand pull from the right side (from the customers and the final processes).

The finishing workstation had its Out parts pulled by the next process in segment 2, triggering finishing's pull demand on grinding in segment 3. That, in turn, resulted in grinding's pull from its previous process in segment 4. The pulls flow from the right (customer side), all the way through the production processes to the left (supplier side). When demand stops at the customer side, pulling stops throughout the system and production ceases. Similarly, increase or decrease in demand at the customer side is reflected by automatically adjusted pulls throughout the system.

As suggested earlier, it is not always necessary to use actual kanban cards. In many applications, it is necessary only to use kanban squares, kanban shelves, or kanban containers. In Figure 21–12, for example, the two processes could have used any of these devices. The Out side of the grinding workstation could have the right side of its tabletop marked out in six kanban squares. One part ready for finishing would be placed on each square, like checkers on a checkerboard. The signal to grind six more parts would be the finishing workstation's taking of the parts, leaving the kanban squares empty. In this case, the empty kanban square is the signal to produce more. Marked-off shelf areas, empty containers designated for so many parts, and various other devices can be used. Combinations are the rule.

Kanban is a shop floor control or management system. As such, it has some rules that must be observed:[15]

Rule 1: Do not send defective product to the subsequent process. Instead, stop the process, find out why it was made defective, and eliminate the cause. It will be much easier to find the cause immediately after it happened than it will be after time has elapsed and conditions have changed. Attention to the problem will escalate rapidly as subsequent processes come to a halt, forcing resolution. Only after the problem has been eliminated and the defective part replaced with a good one should the subsequent process be supplied.

Rule 2: The subsequent process comes to withdraw only what is needed, when needed. There can be no withdrawal without a kanban (of some sort). The number of items withdrawn must match the number authorized by the kanban. A kanban must accompany each item.

Rule 3: Produce only the exact quantity withdrawn by the subsequent process. Never produce more than authorized by the kanban. Produce in the sequence the kanbans are received (first in, first out).

Rule 4: Smooth the production load. Production flow should be such that subsequent processes withdraw from preceding processes in regular intervals and quantities. If production has not been equalized (smoothed), the preceding process will have to have excess capacity (equipment and people) to satisfy the subsequent process. The earlier in the production process, the greater the need for excess capacity. Because excess capacity is waste, it is undesirable. The alternative would be for the processes to "build ahead" in anticipation of demand. This is not allowed by rule 3. Load smoothing will make or break the system because it is the only way to avoid these two intolerable alternatives.

Rule 5: Adhere to kanban instructions while fine-tuning. In the previous section, we said that for a kanban system to work, the flow must first be established. Kanban cannot respond to major change, but it is a valuable tool for the fine-tuning process. All the production and transportation instructions dealing with when, how many, where, and so on are designated on the kanban. If the manufacturing process has not been smoothed, one cannot, for example, tell a preceding process to do something early to compensate. Instructions on the kanban must be observed. Adhering to the kanban's instructions while making small, fine-tuning adjustments will help bring about optimum load smoothing.

Rule 6: Stabilize and rationalize the process. The processes need to be made capable and stable. Work instructions and methods must be simplified and standardized. All confusion and unreasonableness must be removed from the manufacturing system, or subsequent processes can never be assured of the availability of defect-free material when needed, in the quantity needed.

Observing the six rules of kanban all the time is difficult, but it is necessary if the production flow in a JIT/Lean system is to mature and costs are to be reduced.

Kanban is often used by itself for shop floor control very effectively, but it can also be used in conjunction with automation, such as bar code and computer augmentation.

Computer-based kanban systems exist that permit the fundamental kanban system in a paperless environment. As with automation in general, such a computerized system must be designed, or tailored, to suit the application. Applying technology simply for technology's sake is never a good idea. Whatever you do, it is best to have the system working in its basic manual form before automating; otherwise, you are likely to automate your problems.

The demand pull system has proven itself far more efficient than the traditional push system. If the advantages of just-in-time/Lean are wanted, there is no alternative but to use a pull system, and kanban, in one form or another, is what is needed.

Visibility and Visual Control

One of JIT/Lean's great strengths is that it's a visual system. It can be difficult to keep track of what is going on in a traditional factory, with people hustling to and fro storing excess WIP and bringing stored WIP back to the floor for the next stage of processing, caches of buffer WIP all over the place, and the many crisscrossing production routes. The JIT/Lean factory is set up in such a way that confusion is removed from the system. In a JIT/Lean factory, it is easy to tell whether a line is working normally or having a problem. A quick visual scan reveals the presence of bottlenecks or excess capacity. In addition to the obvious signals, such as an idle workstation, JIT/Lean encourages the use of information boards to keep all the workers informed of status, problems, quality, and so on.

Each product work cell or team should have one or more boards, perhaps on easels, perhaps on computer screens, on which they post information. For example, if the schedule anticipates the production of 300 subassemblies for the day, the workers will check off the appropriate number each time a succeeding process pulls subassemblies from its output. This keeps the team apprised of how it is doing and presents the information to managers, who only have to glance at the chart to gauge the work cell activity and its kanbans to develop a clear picture of how well the line is doing. Another board charts statistical process control data as the samples are taken in the work cell. Anyone can spot developing trends or confirm the well-being of the process with a quick look at the charts. Every time a problem beyond the control of the work cell or an issue with which the work cell needs help comes up, it is jotted down on a board. It stays there until resolved. If it repeats before it is resolved, annotations are made in the form of four marks and a slash for a count of five (see Figure 21–13). This keeps the concerns of the work cell in front of the managers and engineers who have the responsibility for resolution. The mark tally also establishes a priority for resolution. The longest mark "bar" gets the highest priority. Maintenance schedules for tools and machines are also posted in plain view, usually right at or on the machine, and normal maintenance activity, such as lubrication, cleaning, and cutter replacement, is assigned to the work cell.

FIGURE 21–13 Work Cell Problem Status Board

Consider what happens when these charts are used. Information is immediately available to the work cell. The team is empowered to perform maintenance and solve all problems for which it has the capability. With the information presented to the team in real time, the team solves the problems at once and performs maintenance at appropriate times. This approach minimizes waste, keeps the machines in top shape, and produces a flow of ideas for improvement. The shop floor control loop is as tight as it can get. The operator detects and posts the information. The operator reacts to the information to solve problems or take action.

If a problem is beyond the work cell team's capability, all the people who can bring skills or authority to bear are immediately brought in and presented with the data, and the problem gets solved—quickly. The control loop goes from information to action in one or two steps. In the traditional factory, the operator may not even be aware of a quality problem. It is usually detected by a quality assurance inspector hours or even days after the defect was created. The inspector writes it up. The form may go to the management information system (MIS) department, where, after a period of time, the data are entered into the computer. Sometime later the computer prints a summary report including an analysis of quality defects. The report is sent to management through the company mail or via an intranet system. The report may rest in queue for a length of time before being examined. Managers in traditional plants are kept so busy with meetings and firefighting they hardly have time to read their mail, but eventually they will get around to looking at the report. They will see that the line is (or *was*) having a quality problem and pass the report to the floor supervisor for action. The floor supervisor will attempt to see whether the problem still exists. If it does not, case closed. It happened days or weeks ago, and the operator, who up until now was unaware of the defect(s), can't remember anything that would confirm the problem, let alone suggest a root cause. If the floor supervisor is lucky, the problem may still be there, and the cause may be found. But in the meantime, weeks of production may have been defective.

In this control loop, at least six functions are involved before the loop is closed. That is bad enough, but when the time delay factor is added, finding root causes of problems that come and go is unlikely. Process improvement is much more difficult in this kind of traditional production system. Having had personal experience with both, the authors can attest that the most expensive, most sophisticated computer-based defect analysis system, such as might be employed in the above example, is infinitely inferior to the simple one- or two-step, person-to-person, no-computers-involved control loop of JIT/Lean when it comes to presenting useful information on a timely basis for the purpose of problem solving and process improvement.

Before our plants changed over to JIT/Lean, a mainframe-based defect analysis system was used. The U.S. Navy designated it as a best practice in the industry. Other companies came to see it, and many of them used it as a model for their own new systems. It could analyze data and present it in many different forms. But it had one flaw: time delay. From the time a process produced a defective part until the loop was closed with the operator of the process, several days (at best) had passed. We are not suggesting that the system was unable to make improvements, because it did. But the real revelation came with implementing JIT/Lean and finding what could happen right inside the work cell when workers had the information they needed while it was fresh and vital and were empowered to do something with it. Immediately, defects dropped dramatically, and they continued to drop as continual improvement was established. Before JIT/Lean, these plants were never able to achieve results remotely comparable, even with their megadollar computer-based system.

Every JIT/Lean line develops its own versions of information display techniques. But whatever the variation, everyone has valuable, useful information available at all times. That kind of information is extremely difficult to find in a traditional line and most often comes to light in the periodic (weekly or monthly) computer analysis reports. By then, the trail to the root cause may have been obliterated by the passage of time, other problems, or events. In the JIT/Lean factory, real-time visibility lets people know of the problem right then and there, while the cause is obvious. Coupled with the JIT/Lean philosophy that says that the problem must be solved before going any further, this visibility becomes a driver for elimination of problems and for process improvement.

Eliminating Bottlenecks

Richard Schonberger makes the interesting point that only the bottlenecks in a traditional factory forward work to the next process just-in-time.[16] He explains that in a conventional manufacturing plant, the bottleneck process is one that goes as fast as it can all the time, barely keeping up with demand. If it breaks down, there is real trouble. To keep it running and to attempt to find ways to increase its output, the bottleneck receives attention out of proportion to the rest of the plant, monopolizing the efforts of engineering and management.

In a JIT/Lean plant, all processes are potential bottlenecks in the sense just discussed because there is little excess capacity and there are no buffer stocks to fall back on when a process or machine shuts down. The upside of this is that all processes are constantly under scrutiny—none is ignored. As Schonberger also points out, the fact that all the processes must be watched carefully makes it imperative that the process operators play a major role in the care and monitoring and improving of the processes because there cannot be enough engineers to go around when every process is a potential bottleneck.

For this discussion, though, the bottleneck is put into a slightly different frame of reference. We are talking primarily about the setup stage of a JIT/Lean operation when trying to establish a balanced, rational flow through the production system. In this early stage, it is not uncommon to have some real functional bottlenecks. For example, if the new JIT/Lean line is being established to produce as many as 1,000 parts per day, but the manual assembly process can turn out only 800, there is a bottleneck. One way or the other, the process must be brought up to 1,000 or more. If the process employs two people using hand tools, then the answer is simple: add a third person and the appropriate tools. Then the capacity for that process should be 1,200 per day. The extra capacity will have to be accepted until the process can be improved to bring the daily single-operator output up to 500 each, making it possible to go back to two operators.

Perhaps a machine can produce only 75% of the projected demand. Here the options are a little different. This may be a very expensive machine, too expensive to replicate. Is it possible to put that machine to work somewhere else and put two lower-capacity, less expensive machines in the line, or maybe a single new, higher capacity machine? Can

---

Control Loop Effectiveness

The effectiveness of any control loop is inversely proportional to the number of functions in the loop and the time required to close the loop.

Source: David L. Goetsch and Stanley B. Davis.

the old machine be modified to increase its output? If setup time is a part of the machine's normal day, there is a potential for improvement. Another possibility may be adding a second, smaller machine to augment the existing machine's capacity, although two different machines on the same line making the same part or product is not a desirable solution.

Another kind of bottleneck can exist when a single physical process is shared by two or more JIT/Lean lines. It is preferable to make each JIT/Lean product line independent and self-sufficient, but this is not always possible. An example might be a single-wave solder machine servicing two or more JIT/Lean lines. Because of the cost, size, and maintenance requirements of such a machine, it may not be feasible to put one in each JIT/Lean product line. Rather, all the JIT/Lean lines take their PC boards to a single-wave solder service cell for soldering. The JIT/Lean lines operate independently of each other. Therefore, it is difficult to predict when conflicts might develop. If they all need servicing at the same time, there is a bottleneck. If soldering delays cannot be accommodated, then one or more of the lines must have its own soldering capability.

Technology can often provide solutions to such problems. For example, 20 high-quality drag soldering machines could be purchased for the price of one wave soldering machine. Production rates of drag solder machines are much lower than those of wave machines, but in many applications, they are ideal for placement right in the JIT/Lean line, dedicated to the line's product and controlled by the line. Such solutions are feasible with many other types of machines.

Whether your bottlenecks appear during the setup phase or during production, the best approach is to assign a cross-functional team to solve the problem. The team should have representation from engineering, manufacturing, finance, and any other relevant functional areas. Its job is to list all possibilities for eliminating the bottleneck. This can be done by brainstorming, setting aside those ideas that don't make sense, and finding the most satisfactory solution in terms of quality, expense, efficiency, and timing.

Frequently, the solution to a bottleneck results in some degree of excess capacity in the process, as occurred earlier when the third operator was added. This is not always bad. Although JIT/Lean always works to achieve more and more efficiency—and, taken to the extreme, would have just exactly enough capacity to produce the demanded level and no more—in a practical sense, some excess capacity is desirable. If a line is running at top speed every day, the operators will have no time for problem solving or improvement activities. Some time should be set aside each week for those two items as well as for maintenance and housekeeping. For most applications, 10 to 15% excess capacity is acceptable.

Small Lot Sizes and Reduced Setup Times

For a century, industrial engineers have been taught that the larger the production lot size, the greater the benefit from economy of scale. If one wanted to hold down cost of production, bigger lot sizes were the answer. This was the conventional thinking until the JIT/Lean manufacturing bombshell landed on our shores from Japan in the early 1980s. Under the leadership of Toyota and Taiichi Ohno, Japanese manufacturers concluded that the ideal lot size is not the largest but the smallest. Is it possible that both the manufacturers and the universities could have been wrong all those years? Our conclusion is that the big lot was appropriate as long as mass production systems were used, although they certainly had major problems even then. But once the Toyota Production System came into being, the big lot was not only out of step but impossible to justify.

It stands to reason that if a machine is used to produce different parts that are used in the subsequent processes of production and if the time it takes to change the machine over from one part type to another is 6 to 8 hours, then once the machine is set up for a particular part type, one should make the most of it. It seems to make more sense to run the machine with the same setup for 4 days, setting up for the next part on the 5th day, than to run 1 day, spend the next on setup, and so on. The 1-day runs result in about 50% utilization time for the machine, assuming a single shift for simplicity. The 4-day run yields about 80% utilization.

So what is the problem? If there are four different parts to make on the machine, simply make 20 days' supply in 4 days and then go to the next part. By the time production has used all the 20-day supply of the first part, the machine will have cycled back to make that part again. Perhaps a 30-day supply should be made, just in case the machine breaks down. Would a 40-day supply be better? Where does this stop? If we are willing to risk an occasional breakdown, the 20-day cycle is acceptable. A place to store a 20-day supply of not just one part type but four part types will be needed. Then the capability to inventory, retrieve, and transport these parts

---

Financial Data on the Factory Floor

Work cells develop many kinds of charts for display in their work areas. In a San Antonio plant where employee empowerment was in full bloom, we encountered financial charts in the production areas. The cells determine their contribution per unit produced to several financial factors, including waste, labor cost per unit, and so on, and post a running record of the numbers on a chart in each work cell for all to see. The workers in the cells were obviously tuned in to this and were eager to explain both the data and the methodology used for collecting it. We found this interesting because workers in most factories do not have a clue as to their impact on cost or profit. Seldom do line workers take an interest because management doesn't give them financial information. As a result, a connection between their work and the financial well-being of the company is seldom made. In this San Antonio company, however, with management's encouragement, the production workers themselves proudly keep track of how their cells contribute to the company's financial results. The benefits of this approach can be enormous. With the information constantly in front of the cells' workers, they always have an internal urge to improve. On the other hand, if something goes wrong, the cell is the first to know and react.

will also be needed. That represents land, facilities, and labor that would not otherwise be needed. None of it adds value to the product, so it is pure waste. It is likely that these costs add up to more than the supposed inefficiency of running the machine with a 50% utilization factor, but these costs are more acceptable to accountants. Land, buildings, and people in motion are not as apparent as examples of waste as machines that are not making product. Traditional thinking says, "Because the machine is busy, people are busy, floor space is full, it can't be waste." But it is.

In addition, suppose that a production flaw is found in one of the parts, caused by the machine. Every part made in that lot is suspect. Samples will be tested, and maybe the whole lot will have to be scrapped. This could be 20 days' supply, representing significant cost. The line will be down until new parts can be made—a major disruption.

Suppose the engineering department corrects a design weakness in one of the parts. Is the entire inventory of parts already made scrapped, or do we use them up in production, knowing that they are not as good as the newly designed part? Either is a bad proposition.

Now assume that the 1-day 50% utilization cycle on the machine was employed. The greatest loss we could take would be 8 days' inventory for any of these cases. The 8-day supply can be stored easier than a 20-day supply. This would reduce the cost of warehousing, control, and transportation. Any design changes can be cut-in in 8 days. Everything seems positive except the 50% machine utilization.

Ideally, setup time might be reduced to 30 minutes, producing 1 day's supply of each part every day. Utilization will be 75% and need for any warehousing may be eliminated. This may seem to be out of reach, but manufacturers using JIT/Lean have done far better, often taking setups from many hours to a few minutes. For example, by 1973 Toyota had reduced the setup time for a 1,000-ton press from 4 hours to 3 minutes. Over a 5-year period, Yanmar Diesel reduced the setup time for a machining line from over 9 hours to just 9 minutes.[17] These are not isolated examples.

The general rule seems to be that organizing properly for the setup, making sure the tools and parts that will be needed are in place, and having the right people there at the appointed time will yield an immediate 50% reduction. Then, by analyzing the setup process step by step, a company can usually streamline the process to cut time by half again. Ultimately, the machine itself may be modified to make setup faster and less difficult (e.g., by eliminating the need for adjustment). In any mature JIT/Lean factory, it would be a rare setup that took more than a few minutes, whereas the same setups were previously measured in hours.

The previously supposed advantage of manufacturing in big lots completely disappears when setup times are brought down to the kinds of times being discussed here. Machine utilization can be high to satisfy accounting criteria, and lots can be small to prevent waste and to enable kanban pulling straight from the machine to the next process. Short setup times coupled with kanban have the advantage of flexibility of production. For example, Harley-Davidson used to

> **Small Lot Sizes**
>
> Small lot sizes result in improved product quality, production flexibility, and customer responsiveness. Shortened setup times make small lots possible.

run its motorcycle line in long production runs of the same model. If a dealer placed an order for a model that had just finished its run, it might have been several weeks before that model could be run again, allowing the order to be filled. Harley was one of the first North American companies to adopt the total quality methods—as a means of survival.

For many years now, Harley has been able to mix models on the production line. It no longer has to produce its product in big lots because it was able to reduce setup times all along its line. Now when an order comes in, it is placed in the queue without regard for the model. Customers get their new bikes as they want them configured and far sooner.

Led by Nissan in the United States, auto production lines are beginning to be more flexible as well. Several manufacturers have lines that accommodate two or more models of similar vehicles. The Nissan plant in Canton, Mississippi, which came on-line in 2003, has the capability to intermix five dissimilar models in lot sizes of one on the same line.[18] Flexibility like that can happen only when model-to-model setup is eliminated or made insignificant. Who benefits? The customer gets more choice, higher quality, and lower cost, and the manufacturer becomes more competitive.

Total Productive Maintenance and Housekeeping

This is difficult to comprehend, but many manufacturers spend vast amounts on capital equipment and then ignore the machines until they self-destruct. By contrast, one can find relatively ancient machines in total quality Japanese factories that look like new and run even better. This must become the norm in the United States if U.S. companies are going to compete with the rest of the world. Because a JIT/Lean production line operates very close to capacity in every process, no tolerance exists for machine failure. When the machine is supposed to be running, it had better be, or the whole line will suffer. Companies that have adopted the Japanese philosophy of total productive maintenance have virtually eliminated machine breakdowns. Machines are cleaned and lubricated frequently, most of that work being done by the operators who run the machines. More technical preventive maintenance routines are performed by experts at frequent intervals. The machines are continually upgraded and modified for closer tolerances, faster setup, and fewer adjustments. Not only do the machines last longer, but also during their entire life span they perform as well or better than when new.

The difficulty with TPM is finding the time in which to perform the maintenance, especially in factories in which three shifts are the norm. The third shift is rare in Japan and Europe, so companies there do not share this problem. Regardless of the workday schedule, it is imperative that maintenance time be provided. The operator-performed maintenance is done during the normal shift (one reason to have a bit more than just enough capacity—a half-hour to an hour a day of excess capacity should more than cover operator maintenance needs).

An added benefit of turning some of the maintenance responsibility over to the operators is that the operators develop a sense of ownership for the machines they use and care for. They pay keen attention to the looks, sounds, vibrations, and smells of the machines to spot problems before they develop. For the first time, the operators are in a position to call for maintenance before breakdown occurs. TPM is a must for JIT/Lean production systems.

Housekeeping is another area that is different under JIT/Lean. It is not unusual for the operators themselves to take on the responsibilities formerly associated with janitors. In the better JIT/Lean plants, one will see planned downtime being taken up with cleaning chores—everything spotless, everything in its place. (Remember Five-S from Chapter 15.) It follows that better performance will result from a clean, tidy, and well-organized work area than from one that is dirty and cluttered with tools scattered all over. People like a clean, bright, rational place in which to work. Again, time will have to be made available for this activity.

Process Capability, Statistical Process Control, and Continual Improvement

Process capability, statistical process control (SPC), and continual improvement have already been discussed in detail in this book, but it is important to understand the dependence on them by just-in-time/Lean. Is JIT/Lean a necessary prerequisite for process capability study and improvement, or for SPC, or for continual improvement? The answer is no. At least one of the three is being done in the majority of traditional production plants. Still, there is a connection. The philosophy and discipline of just-in-time/Lean virtually demand that they be used in any JIT/Lean environment. While a traditional manufacturing operation *may* employ one or more of the three, the JIT/Lean manufacturing operation *must*, and it must be all three. The reason may be obvious to you by now. The JIT/Lean plant is fragile. Everything must work when it is supposed to, and it must work close to perfection. There are no warehouses of buffer stock to come to the aid of a broken-down process. There is never much excess capacity to help out in tight spots. All the processes with their machines and people must operate in top form all the time.

This is where process capability, SPC, and continual improvement come in. Even before the JIT/Lean line can be certified for full production, the line has to be balanced or rationalized, and a flow has to be established. Unless it is known what the processes are capable of doing in terms of quality and quantity, it will be difficult to achieve the even flow that is a necessary prerequisite of a kanban system.

Without that, there is no JIT/Lean. In the traditional factory, not knowing the capability of the processes is not such a problem; normally, gross overcapacity exists, so parts are stored for the day things go wrong, and the bad parts are sorted out because there will still be good ones to use. In JIT/Lean, no extra parts can be made, and all have to be good. Workers must have a handle on the processes.

Because one cannot afford (from the time or cost standpoint) to make defective parts, the processes must be in control at all times. The only way to ensure this is through statistical process control. This is not as necessary in a traditional plant, but it is absolutely essential in JIT/Lean. Perfection is difficult to achieve in any circumstance, so it follows that in a complex manufacturing situation, perfection is next to impossible. This is certainly true. We never quite get to the point where all the parts are perfect, but with solid, stable, in-control processes forming the basis of a relentless continual improvement program, we can come very, very close. (Some of the very best American plants target and achieve Six Sigma, 3.4 defects per million.) The best that can be achieved is the minimum that is acceptable for a JIT/Lean factory. In the process of continual improvement, ways are found to do things better, faster, cheaper, and with constantly improving quality. The process never ends, and the diminishing-return syndrome doesn't apply.

Suppliers

In the area of suppliers, JIT/Lean has different priorities from the traditional production system. The most obvious difference is the need for frequent, small-lot deliveries of parts, supplies, and materials, rather than the traditional infrequent, huge-volume deliveries. We are finding more and more JIT/Lean plants in which the suppliers deliver materials directly to the production cells, usually referred to as *point-of-use*. Several systems have been developed to cue the supplier that it is time to replenish materials. One is the *dual-bin kanban* system. Two parts bins are used. Bin capacity may range from a few hours' to a couple of weeks' supply, depending on value, size, usage rate, and intended frequency of replenishment. When the cell has withdrawn all the parts from one bin, the empty bin itself is the signal that it is time to replenish. The supplier routinely checks the bins on the factory floor, and whenever he or she finds a bin empty, it is refilled with the exact number and kind of part designated on the bin label, usually in bar code. The supplier's bin checking must be scheduled frequently enough to ensure that the second bin is never exhausted before the first is replenished. In a variation on the dual-bin kanban scheme, the cell's operators signal the supplier that a bin is empty, either by bar code transmission or by automated electronic purchase order that is triggered by wanding the empty bin's bar code.

Clearly, for this kind of point-of-use materials delivery system to work, the supplier must be 100% reliable, the materials delivered must be of consistently high quality, and both the supplier and the manufacturing organization must be partners for the long haul. Consequently, choosing the suppliers for a JIT/Lean factory is a much more demanding job than it is for a traditional plant. Traditional factories are not so concerned with the delivery being on the dock at the precise date on the purchase order. It was going to be stored for a while anyway. Before that lot was used up, there would be another shipment in the warehouse. Neither do traditional factories concern themselves as much with quality from suppliers. The bad parts could always be sorted out, leaving enough good material to keep the line moving. The primary interest was price. Low price got the order. It quickly becomes apparent that this style of purchasing is incompatible with JIT/Lean.

The JIT/Lean plant must have its materials on the dock exactly on the day specified—in many cases at the hour and minute specified—or production may grind to a halt. Every part delivered must be a good part—there is no inventory cache from which to scrounge more parts to keep things moving. This means that the suppliers' quality must be consistently at or above specified requirements. Delivery and quality performance requirements of JIT/Lean effectively rule out buying for price. There is an often used phrase in JIT/Lean and TQM purchasing: "cost versus price." It suggests a holistic approach to the analysis of purchasing on the basis of total cost and value, not simply vendor price. How reliable is a particular vendor in terms of JIT/Lean deliveries? What kind of quality can be expected from the vendor? Does the vendor use JIT/Lean, SPC, and continual improvement? Are its processes stable and in control? A supplier that gives positive responses in these and other areas may not be the lowest price contender but may well be the lowest cost. Value is what the JIT/Lean purchasing manager must look for, not lowest price on a bid sheet, because in JIT/Lean that turns out not to be the whole story.

When a JIT/Lean factory finds a supplier that delivers excellent materials on time, every time, there is every reason to want to continue to do business with it. More and more companies are turning to supplier partnerships to cement these relationships. What this means is that the two companies agree to work together, not only as supplier and customer but also as unstructured partners. The JIT/Lean manufacturer may, for example, provide training and technical assistance to the supplier to get it started in total quality, JIT/Lean, SPC, and other processes. The JIT/Lean firm may certify the supplier's quality system to the extent that incoming inspections are eliminated, relying on the partner supplier to provide acceptable quality in all its deliveries.

The supplier partner may assign one or more employees to take up residence in the JIT/Lean manufacturer's plant. Duties will include continually checking the kanban bins mentioned above, having them replenished appropriately, and coordinating on-time deliveries of materials, parts, and other supplies provided under the JIT/Lean partnership agreement between the manufacturer and supplier. In addition, the resident supplier employee is empowered to do whatever is necessary to solve supply problems before

they can cause disruption in the JIT/Lean factory. (While this practice has been around for two decades in the United States, and much longer in Japan, it is now sometimes referred to as *JIT II*. In the authors' view, it is simply a logical variation of the materials element of just-in-time/Lean that can work very well in numerous situations.)

The supplier may also be called on to assist in the design phase of a new product, bringing its unique expertise to the design team. Such relationships usually carry a multiyear agreement, so the supplier can count on the business as long as its performance remains high.

There may be preferential bidding treatment—say, an advantage of 10% or more over nonpartnership rivals. Effectively what happens is that the JIT/Lean manufacturer extends its factory right back into the supplier's premises. They operate to each other's requirements, and both are locked to each other. The results of this kind of arrangement have been excellent.

This kind of relationship is a far cry from the early ill-conceived attempts of some manufacturers to get into JIT/Lean before developing a full understanding of the concept. In those days, some companies would determine that by using JIT delivery of parts and materials, money could be saved. That part had some merit, but the execution was flawed. The companies simply told their suppliers to deliver a week's supply of materials once a week, rather than their customary 60 days' supply every 2 months. The suppliers' reaction is easy to imagine. They were being told, in effect, to store the materials in their own warehouses (the capacity for which they didn't have) and to trickle the deliveries from the warehouses in small quantities weekly. This was simply a case of moving the storage facility from the manufacturer's plant to the suppliers'. A GM or a Ford has the power to do that to a supplier, but the suppliers, being smaller and with less influence, couldn't force the same back to their own suppliers, so they got caught in an intolerable situation. Only when the suppliers revolted and cried long and loud that this was not JIT—"and by the way, if you want me to store your goods for you, you're going to pay the tab anyway"—did the would-be JIT/Lean manufacturers see the error of their ways.

The new approach is working well because both parties benefit enormously. If a company wants JIT/Lean, then it must have the best possible suppliers, and both must want to work together for the long haul.

AUTOMATION AND JIT/LEAN

Automation has not been discussed a great deal in this book. We have stuck to the fundamentals. One should not read into this, however, that JIT/Lean and automation are mutually exclusive. Rather, it is more meaningful to discuss the processes that use humans and manual machines than the same processes powered by robots. If the fundamentals where humans apply are understood, the same fundamentals will be useful in an automated plant. All the same rules apply. We are not anti-automation.

We are, however, against "automation for the sake of automation." Many companies have made the costly mistake of thinking that automation will solve manufacturing problems. During the 1980s, manufacturers in the United States invested billions of dollars in automation. Cadillac built what was at the time the most highly automated auto assembly plant in North America and probably in the world. It turned into a nightmare of high-tech problems that took years to sort through. The plant that was to produce six cars per hour, after a year of operation, could do only half that and the quality of manufacture was, to put it charitably, questionable. Two years later, Toyota opened a new plant in Kentucky. Visitors to that plant, expecting to see a high-tech automated production line, were disappointed to find very little in the way of robotics.[19] The difference in the philosophies of the two companies becomes obvious. Executive managers at GM believed that by spending enough money, they could buy their way out of the trouble they were in. Toyota knew what it was capable of doing in one of its other low-tech plants that was operating successfully in Japan and simply cloned it down to the last detail in Kentucky. No razzle-dazzle; just good common sense.

Automation may be advantageous in many applications, but if you have not solved the problems in the human-operated versions of those same applications, you are not ready to automate them effectively. If you try, you will automate your problems and will find the robots far less adept at working around them than the humans they replaced.

It is frequently found that the need for automation is decreased or eliminated by converting to JIT/Lean. We certainly found that to be the case in two electronics plants. We were well into a program to build a factory of the future. The building was ready, much of the automation was on hand, and the rest—several million dollars' worth—was on order when we started the conversion to JIT/Lean. Within months, it had become obvious to everyone, including the designers of the new factory, that we were getting more out of JIT/Lean for almost no investment than could be projected for the new automated plant. The outstanding orders for automation equipment were cancelled and penalties were paid, and we walked away from the whole idea. We had learned in those few weeks of exposure to JIT/Lean that world-class manufacturing equates to JIT/Lean in a total quality environment, not to a factory full of robots and automatic guided vehicles. JIT/Lean and automation are compatible, but one should look long and hard at the need, and the company's readiness for it, before automating processes.

Having said that, automation clearly has its place in harmony with JIT/Lean. There are many examples of very successful automated plants, especially for high-volume manufacturing. Automation and JIT/Lean are completely compatible. Probably the best example of that is in today's auto industry. Two such plants have recently come on-line in Alabama and Georgia. Hyundai opened its first American plant in Montgomery, Alabama, in May 2005, making 300,000 vehicles per year there. The Alabama-produced Sonata sedan has been ranked in the top three in J. D. Power and Associates' mid-size sedan category in 2008, 2009, and 2010. This plant is one of the first designed from the ground up as a highly automated JIT/Lean auto production facility. A tour of the plant will convince the fervent skeptic that it has taken the auto industry into a new era in which JIT/Lean and automation are superbly blended. Where traditional auto plants tended to be dark, noisy, grimy, smelly, hot, and frantic in the hustle and bustle, Hyundai's Montgomery plant is none of that. No matter where you are in the plant, the atmosphere is almost soothing, and it is certainly one of the most pleasant factories of any type that the authors have ever visited. It is a place where the 2,300 employees genuinely seem to enjoy working. And it doesn't end there. An hour from Montgomery, up Interstate 85 in West Point, Georgia, Kia Motors opened a sister plant of the same size and capacity, using the same automation technology and, of course, JIT/Lean. The first Kia Sorento rolled off that line in November 2009.

Regardless of factory age, and although employing large numbers of workers, the auto industry is a big user of automation whether in North America, Japan, or Korea. And all those plants use JIT/Lean successfully. Remember, JIT/Lean was originally designed for an auto producer, and as automation has been integrated, and as automation capabilities have evolved, JIT/Lean has been there doing its job. In these plants, JIT/Lean is at least as valuable as it is in plants with less automation. Its pull system prevents overproduction of any manufacturing element, and supplies materials at the front end of the process when needed, and does it without the massive inventories of the pre-JIT/Lean era. Whether the processes are operated by humans or robots makes no difference in this regard.

SUMMARY

1. JIT/Lean is a management philosophy that seeks to eliminate all forms of waste. As a production system, JIT/Lean produces only what is needed, when it is needed, in the quantity needed.

2. Taiichi Ohno is credited with the development of the Toyota Production System and JIT/Lean.

3. The root justification for JIT/Lean is improved product quality with lower costs.

4. JIT/Lean began as a means of reducing the seven wastes. Over time, the JIT/Lean system came to be a pull system whose small lot production is supported by reduced setup times. Total productive maintenance and statistical process control were integrated to provide the necessary production reliability and predictability. Continual improvement provides the vehicle for the relentless attack on all wastes.

5. JIT/Lean is at its best as a part of a total quality system. Results can be severely restricted when JIT/Lean is operated without the total quality umbrella.

6. Inventory reduction, shortened cycle time, continual improvement, and elimination of waste are all inherent benefits of JIT/Lean.

7. JIT/Lean has a different set of requirements from traditional production systems: providing training in new skills; rationalizing production flow for the pull system; empowering operators to take advantage of JIT/Lean's visibility features; guarding against bottleneck vulnerability through TPM, process capability study, SPC, and continual improvement; producing small lots and shortening setup times; and establishing close working relationships with superior suppliers.

8. JIT/Lean is successfully employed around the world in situations where automation is nonexistent and equally successful in the most highly automated plants on the planet.

9. World-class manufacturing employs JIT/Lean as an integral part of a total quality system, producing the highest quality products at competitive prices. It is not related to the presence or absence of automation.

KEY TERMS AND CONCEPTS

Automated electronic purchase order

Automation

Autonomation

Bar code

Bottlenecks

Buffer stock

Continual improvement

Cycle time

Demand flow

Dual-bin kanban

Electronic Kanban

Focused factory

Internal/external customers

Just-in-time (JIT)

JIT/Lean

JIT II

Job shop

Kanban

Lean production

Line stops

Lot size

Manufacturing process

Marketability

Mass production

Overhead/overhead rate

Point of use

Production flow

Production smoothing

Productivity gap

Pull production

Push production

Setup time

Seven wastes

Staging

Statistical process control (SPC)

Supplier partnerships

Total productive maintenance (TPM)

Toyota Production System (TPS)

Value-adding labor

Work-in-process (WIP)

FACTUAL REVIEW QUESTIONS

1. Define JIT/Lean.

2. Explain the difference between the traditional production system and JIT/Lean in terms of placement of production control.

3. Describe the bases for production scheduling for mass production systems and for JIT/Lean.

4. Explain how a JIT/Lean process knows when and how much to produce.

5. What two fundamental advantages are provided by JIT/Lean?

6. List the seven wastes.

7. Identify the two pillars of the Toyota Production System.

8. Explain how traditional mass production contributes to the seven wastes.

9. Explain how JIT/Lean impacts each of the seven wastes.

10. Discuss JIT/Lean's vulnerability to parts shortages, breakdowns, and bottlenecks from the perspective of the mass production advocate and the JIT/Lean advocate.

11. Explain the push system and what triggers it to start.

12. Explain the pull system and how it is started.

13. Why is superior machine maintenance and improvement critical to JIT/Lean?

14. Describe how kanban supports the pull system.

15. What are the advantages of reduced setup time?

16. Why does this book recommend that JIT/Lean be a part of a total quality system?

17. Describe JIT/Lean's objectives relative to inventory and WIP.

18. Discuss the relative complexity of the two production systems.

19. Explain cycle time, and list its constituent elements.

20. Why is a JIT/Lean production line-stop considered a positive phenomenon?

21. Explain how inventory can deter problem solving.

22. Describe the difference in plant organization and layout between the two production systems.

23. Explain how JIT/Lean can cause immediate cycle time reduction.

24. To whom is credit given for the development of the JIT/Lean system?

25. Discuss the relative value of JIT/Lean in production environments of little or no automation versus those that are highly automated.

CRITICAL THINKING ACTIVITIES

1. Study the operations of an electric utility company, and determine where the production of electricity stands vis-à-vis push or pull systems. Using charts and narrative, explain your finding.

2. Study the operation of a supermarket, and list the JIT/Lean features in use. Look for special JIT/Lean practices such as supplier partnerships, and describe how they operate in a supermarket environment.

3. Develop a chart contrasting the philosophies of mass production and JIT/Lean.

4. Mass production was the most successful production system from the time of Henry Ford's Model T until the 1960s. There is no question that this system permitted the manufacture of a wide range of goods at much lower prices than had been possible before then. Given this success, how do you explain that JIT/Lean is supplanting mass production?

5. You are the president of a new division of a major auto producer. Your organization has been chartered to design and build a line of cars to compete with intermediate-size Asian and European imports. The division is to be located in a historically agricultural state that has availability of unskilled labor but no experience in auto manufacturing. Your key staff and mid-level managers will be handpicked from among other divisions. The corporate headquarters staff has not been able to come to terms with how the new division should be set up. The options seem to be these: (a) set up as a total quality organization, using JIT/Lean in the factory or (b) because the corporation has little experience with either, set up like the other divisions in a traditional hierarchy and production system, converting to total quality and JIT/Lean little by little as time and experience permit. You believe that in the long run, total quality and JIT/Lean are necessary to compete, especially with the Japanese and Koreans. But you and the people who will make up the division's management team are

experts in mass production. Going the traditional route looks like an easier start-up path. Going directly to total quality or JIT/Lean has unknowns.

The CEO is leaning toward letting you make the call, but he wants you to convince him and the senior staff. You have to prepare a briefing for the corporate staff for that purpose. Which course will you choose? Explain the advantages and possible pitfalls of both, and make the argument that supports your choice.

DISCUSSION ASSIGNMENT 21–1

Have the American Automakers Finally Caught up with the Japanese in Terms of Product Quality?

For over 35 years the U.S. auto industry has taken a beating from the Japanese manufacturers. It was only in the 1980s that we discovered what the Japanese were doing that we were not, namely using Ohno's JIT/Lean system of production and putting top priority on continually improving processes and products. In the face of plummeting market share in the late 1970s and early 1980s, Ford closed nine factories, and GM shut down 20. Chrysler was staggering on the brink of bankruptcy. The industry was facing a full-scale invasion from Japan. Although foreign cars had been around forever, they had historically accounted for a very small share of the American market. But in the 1980s, car buyers discovered that the cars from Japan were so superior to competing American brands that the auto industry got its first true taste of foreign competition—and found it a bitter taste indeed. Suddenly the U.S. automakers found themselves in a market that demanded better quality and value for the dollar. What had been good enough to keep Detroit going was no longer good enough.

Ford realized sooner than the others that it would have to find out how the Japanese were able to produce such reliable, efficient, high-quality cars for the prices being charged. Ford managers were dispatched to Japan to study the methods of the leading Japanese automakers. Expecting to find the answer in a high degree of automation, they were surprised to find less than existed in their own plants. Nor was it that the Japanese worker was superior. Ford made a startling discovery. The difference was, it rightly concluded after long study, not automation or technology, or the Japanese workers, or lower wages, but how the workers were managed. American managers believed that once a production system achieved stability, it should be maintained at that point. Japanese managers, on the other hand, believed that production stability was just a starting point, and from that point onward, continual improvement must be applied. The Japanese also believed in a harmonious relationship between managers and workers. That too was contrary to Detroit's historic adversarial relationship between management and labor. Japanese managers actively encouraged all workers to suggest ways to improve processes. Detroit's managers

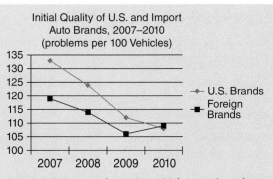

Initial Quality of U.S. and Import
Auto Brands, 2007–2010
(problems per 100 Vehicles)

Source: J. D. Power and Associates IQS for 2007 through 2010.

FIGURE 21–14

adamantly prohibited workers from suggesting changes. In Detroit, the worker's job was to follow instructions—period.[20] All the Japanese automakers were practicing JIT/Lean using Taichi Ohno's model, and quality and productivity were improved incrementally every year. It has been estimated that the cars of Japan equaled the quality of American cars by 1970. Ten more years of continual improvement in Japan, while the U.S. automakers smugly held to the status quo, created an enormous quality and productivity gap with the American industry by the 1980s.

During the 1980s, the U.S. automakers had some gut-wrenching decisions to make, but it came down to this question: "Are we going to stay in the auto business?" In other words: survival. Thirty years later the press release for the 2010 Initial Quality Study (IQS) by J. D. Power and Associates states that the U.S. auto brands, as a whole, surpassed the imports in initial quality for the first time."[21] In its study, J. D. Power has the U.S. brands at a quality level of 108 problems per 100 vehicles, while the imports achieved 109. Very close indeed, but during the four-year period 2007 through 2010 the IQS has had the U.S. brands on a converging trajectory to the Import brands. See Figure 21–14.

DISCUSSION QUESTIONS

Discuss the following questions in class or outside of class with your fellow students:

1. What steps were taken by the U.S. auto industry to close the gap with the Japanese?

2. How are the rankings of the import brands affected by the inclusion of those from Europe?

3. What can you say about the IQS performance of the Korean brands, Hyundai, and Kia? You will find the following Web site helpful: www.jdpower.com.

DISCUSSION ASSIGNMENT 21–2

Taiichi Ohno's JIT/Lean system, with the elimination of practically all inventories, and using demand pull (kanban) to coordinate the flow of materials and assemblies through the production process, has been resisted by some on the basis that if even the smallest part in the system failed to appear or perform when needed, the entire process must come to a halt. Ohno proclaimed that this "weakness" of JIT/Lean was in fact its power since it removed all safety nets, and, with the production line stopped, forced the entire organization to focus on resolving the root cause of the problem so that it never recurs.

CourseKar Industries manufactures golf carts. Their product is reasonably successful, but competing manufacturers sell their carts for less than CourseKar can, and yet have fewer product warranty and reliability problems. As a result, CourseKar's market share has been slipping, and the Board of Directors is calling for action. Management knows that its competition has been using JIT/Lean production techniques for several years. But while they find JIT/Lean appealing for eliminating waste and improving quality and productivity, they are concerned that conversion to JIT/Lean, with its precariousness of having little or no inventory of materials on hand would be too great a risk. In order to lower production costs and improve quality, management is leaning toward a hybrid JIT/Lean system instead. This system will employ the principles and methodology of JIT/Lean, but will maintain buffer stocks of materials and assemblies to prevent every part delivery problem or malfunction on the line from shutting down the production process.

DISCUSSION QUESTIONS

Discuss the following questions in class or outside of class with your fellow students:

1. If something as trivial as a missing screw or a broken tool can stop a JIT/Lean production line, how could Ohno consider that to be a power of the concept?

2. Discuss what would likely happen if a needed screw or a working tool is missing from a traditional mass production line.

3. Discuss the implications of a JIT/Lean production system that employs buffer stocks or materials and parts.

4. Discuss the potential for a nonmanufacturing organization to benefit from employment of JIT/Lean.

ENDNOTES

1. James Womack, Daniel T. Jones, and Daniel Roos, *The Machine That Changed the World* (New York: HarperCollins, 1990), 13.

2. Taiichi Ohno, *Just-in-Time for Today and Tomorrow* (Cambridge, MA: Productivity Press, 1990), 2.

3. Retrieved from www.businessdictionary.com/definition/autonomation.html on October 26, 2010.

4. Ohno, *Just-in-Time for Today and Tomorrow*, 28–29.

5. Ibid., 9.

6. Ibid., 75.

7. Womack, Jones, and Roos, *The Machine That Changed*, 62.

8. David Lu, *Kanban—Just-in-Time at Toyota* (Cambridge, MA: Productivity Press and Japanese Management Association, 1986), 6.

9. Materials and general and accounting expenses are held constant for this example to keep it simple, although both could be expected to decrease under JIT/Lean.

10. C. E. Sorensen, *My Forty Years with Ford* (New York: Norton, 1956), 174.

11. Womack, Jones, and Roos, *The Machine That Changed*, 83.

12. W. Edwards Deming, *Quality, Productivity and Competitive Position* (Cambridge, MA: MIT Center for Advanced Engineering Study, 1982), 30.

13. Lu, *Kanban*, 73.

14. M. Scott Myers, *Every Employee Is a Manager* (San Diego, CA: Pfeiffer, 1991), 72.

15. Lu, *Kanban*, 87–92.

16. Richard I. Schonberger, *World-Class Manufacturing* (New York: Free Press, 1986), 67.

17. Kiyoshi Suzaki, *The New Manufacturing Challenge: Techniques for Continuous Improvement* (New York: Free Press, 1987), 43.

18. David Welch, "How Nissan Laps Detroit," *BusinessWeek* (December 22, 2003): 58–60.

19. Maryann Keller, *Rude Awakening: The Rise, Fall, and Struggle for Recovery of General Motors* (New York: Morrow, 1989), 206–209.

20. Robert L. Shook, *Turnaround: The New Ford Motor Company* (Upper Saddle River, NJ: Prentice Hall, 1990), 81–83.

21. *2010 Initial Quality Study Press Release*, J. D. Power and Associates (Westlake Village, CA: June 17, 2010).

IMPLEMENTING TOTAL QUALITY MANAGEMENT

All glory comes from daring to begin. —***Anonymous***

MAJOR TOPICS
- **Rationale for Change**
- **Requirements for Implementation**
- **Role of Top Management: Leadership**
- **Role of Middle Management**
- **Viewpoints of Those Involved**
- **Implementation Variation Among Organizations**
- **Implementation Approaches to Be Avoided**
- **An Implementation Approach That Works**
- **Getting On with It**
- **What to Do in the Absence of Commitment from the Top**
- **Implementation Strategies: ISO 9000 and Baldrige**

This chapter is intended to serve three purposes:

1. To summarize in one chapter some of the salient points made elsewhere in the book concerning the key elements and philosophy of total quality.

2. To develop a logical "road map," or structure for implementation, in order for the student of total quality to better understand the scope and magnitude of total quality implementation.

3. To provide a practical, hands-on, how-to guide for implementing total quality in any organization, in the sincere hope that this book will have inspired some who are in positions of leadership to take this next step.

Total quality management has been accurately described as a journey, not a destination. It is the fervent hope of the authors that many who study the material presented in this book will embark on that journey. This chapter is offered as your guide.

Six decades ago Japan was in a state of crisis. Japan's industry had been decimated by World War II, and its economy was in shambles. It was struggling to rebuild its economy and put people to work. This involved more than just getting the factories running again. Even if they could manage to get production flowing, who would buy the goods that were produced?

The vast majority of Japanese people had all they could do to put clothes on their backs and food in their bellies. Japan had to look beyond its own shores for markets. The most obvious market was the United States, the economy of which had burgeoned during the war. However, the U.S. market posed two problems for the Japanese, which were as follows: convincing Americans that they should buy goods from the nation that attacked Pearl Harbor, and overcoming the American association of Japanese goods with inferior quality. Before World War II, Japan had been notably unsuccessful in American markets because of the perception of poor quality in its goods.

Enter Dr. W. Edwards Deming, an American statistician who had been in Japan in 1947 at the request of the Supreme Commander of Allied Powers to help prepare for a census to be taken in 1951. He had met some of the Japanese people who formed the Union of Japanese Scientists and Engineers (JUSE). As JUSE wrestled with the problems confronting Japanese industry and the economy, they were introduced to the 1931 McGraw-Hill book *The Economic Control of Manufactured Product* by Dr. Walter Shewhart of Bell Laboratories, the originator of the control chart. From their acquaintance with Deming, they thought he might help them apply Shewhart's techniques. JUSE wrote Deming in March 1950, asking him to give a series of lectures to plant managers, engineers, and research workers. Deming gave his first lecture on June 19, 1950. Some 500 people attended. Always unwilling to invest his time on a lost cause, Deming insisted that the top executives of Japanese industry get involved. JUSE arranged for that first high-level meeting on July 5, 1950. The top 21 Japanese company presidents attended. Deming told them that they could compete in the world's markets within 5 years if they followed his teachings. They did it in *4* years.

This chapter sets the stage for implementation of total quality in any organization. Had Japan not been in such dire straits after World War II—industry in shambles, people needing jobs, the nation with no money with which to import food—perhaps people there would not have listened to and acted on Deming's recommendations. They were *seeking a route to survival.* Your organization may or may not be in a similar fix. When an organization is truly facing the possibility of going out of business, there is a better chance that its management can be convinced to embrace the principles of total quality. On the other hand, when an organization is doing pretty well, then taking on the work that is involved in becoming a total quality organization is more difficult to sell—unless you are at the top of the organization chart.

Change is always difficult, and changing a culture that has been ingrained for many years is a monumental undertaking. When change is seen as the last hope for survival, it gets easier. People are more receptive to change when they realize that they will surely be out of jobs unless change is made. Is it worth the trouble? Unquestionably. Is survival ensured with change? No. But the other side of the coin is that going out of business is virtually ensured if you don't change. Every enterprise, no matter what the type, will be pressured more and more as total quality pervades industry, education, health care, government, merchandising, and services. Managers should consider whether they would prefer to be ahead of the quality groundswell or engulfed by it—out of control, fighting for survival with the odds against success much higher.

This chapter provides insights to help you implement total quality. No one best way fits the needs of all organizations. What you will find in this chapter are not prescriptions, but suggestions and examples of what has worked, with the idea that you may find the inspiration that will lead you to success in your own organization.

RATIONALE FOR CHANGE

What's wrong with the traditional way we do business?

1. *We are bound to a short-term focus.* If the organization of which you are a part is similar to most in the West, it is driven by short-term objectives. This is true whether you are in industry, education, health care, services, or government. For more than 60 years, we have been the victims of Keynesian economics. Everything we do has to have a measurable payback in the next quarter or the next year, or it cannot be justified. Whether Keynes had that in mind or not, it

has become a reality of Western management and business. It is the sentiment "Don't tell me how good it will be in 5 years. What are you going to do for me today?"

2. *The traditional approach tends to be arrogant rather than customer focused.* Western organizations have tended to be arrogant. They think they know more about what their customers need than their customers do. Or worse yet, they don't care about their customers' needs. To illustrate this point, go into a typical government office and try to get something done—get new license plates for your car or have some legal papers executed. Often you will find that the employees, whose salaries come from your taxes, are rude, inefficient, and totally disinterested in you or your needs. The same thing has happened in industry.

3. *We seriously underestimate the potential contribution of our employees, particularly those in hands-on functions.* The person who knows the most about a job—and the one who is most likely to know how to solve problems—is the person who is doing that job and facing the job's problems day in and day out. This truth is proven over and over, yet the typical traditional manager does not believe it. This factor alone is responsible for much of the poor job performance and ill will that exists between management and labor, the folks who have to do the work. People generally want to do a good job; but faced with processes that are not capable and management that will not listen, they soon determine the only way to get ahead, or stay employed, is to "live with it and don't make waves." The result is that the brainpower we employ is largely wasted. Think about it: if you are in a 100-person organization and only two or three people can make changes to the procedures you work by and the processes you work with, 97% or 98% of the idea potential and creativity is silenced—but you still pay for it.

Let us bring home this point. Konosuke Matsushita, the head of Matsushita, the giant Japanese company that produces electronic equipment under the Panasonic brand name, writes:

> We are going to win and the industrial West is going to lose out; there's not much you can do about it because the reasons for failure are within yourselves.
>
> Your firms are built on the Taylor Model. Even worse, so are your heads. With your bosses doing the thinking while the workers wield the screwdrivers, you're convinced deep down that this is the right way to run a business. For you, the essence of management is getting the ideas out of the heads of the bosses and into the hands of labor.
>
> We [in Japan] are beyond the Taylor Model. Business, we know, is now so complex and difficult, the survival of firms so hazardous in an environment increasingly unpredictable, competitive and fraught with danger, that their continued existence depends on the day-to-day mobilization of every ounce of intelligence.[1]

Considering what Matsushita, Sony, Hitachi, and other Japanese consumer electronic firms did to the American

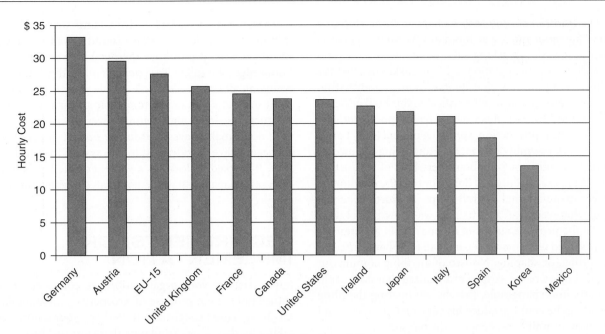

FIGURE 22–1 Hourly Production Labor Costs in U.S. Dollars, 2005

Source: U.S. Department of Labor, U.S. Bureau of Labor Statistics, December 2007.

Note: EU–15 is the average for Austria, Belgium, Denmark, Finland, France, Germany, Greece, Ireland, Italy, Luxembourg, the Netherlands, Portugal, Spain, Sweden, and the United Kingdom.

competition, his remarks, while chilling, seem reasonable. The Japanese certainly won that battle, but the war is not over yet. Many Western organizations have also concluded (if belatedly) that our traditional management system (the Taylor Model) wastes brainpower in unthinkable amounts and is no longer appropriate; they have adopted the total quality model. If yours has not, now is the time.

4. *The traditional approach equates better quality with higher cost.* Philip Crosby wrote a book titled *Quality Is Free.*[2] The title was probably intended to catch the potential buyer's interest with its shock value. When the book was published in 1979, not many traditional managers would buy the idea that quality is free. In the ensuing years, however, that title has proven to be *understated.* Organizations that have successfully changed themselves into total quality enterprises have found not only that quality is free but also that it brings unforeseen benefits. Sadly, though, many traditional managers still believe that if you want better quality, you have to pay more for it. But the marketplace has found that if you want better quality, you simply pick the supplier that has demonstrated superior quality at the same price. That is why the Japanese cars have been so successful. Unfortunately, it is also the reason so many of our industries—radios, televisions, VCRs, and stereo equipment, just to name a few—have been lost. Better quality was to be had from other suppliers—for the same cost—and that is where the buyers went.

This issue of better quality from foreign competitors for the same cost is not a matter of lower wage scales in those countries. With few exceptions, wage scales in most of the developed nations do not differ widely. December 2007 data from the U.S. Department of Labor include hourly labor costs in U.S. dollars for production workers in several countries for the year 2005, the last year for which data are available (Figure 22–1). You will note that France, Canada, the United States, Ireland, Japan, and Italy all have hourly production labor costs between $20 and $25, with the United States and Japan separated by $1.89. For most of the past 15 years, Japan's hourly production labor costs have been higher than those of the United States. The figure also shows that if any geographic entity was being adversely affected by high labor costs in 2005, it was Europe. Eight European countries and Australia and Canada (not all shown on Figure 22–1) had higher hourly labor costs than did the United States. Of course, there are a number of countries, including Korea, Taiwan, and Mexico, whose hourly production labor costs are significantly less than ours. But the point we want to make here is that whether in the United States or Japan, the cost of producing comparable quality products should be about the same. The same product would likely cost a little more if produced in Europe and a little less if produced in Korea, and that is borne out by product pricing with which we are all familiar. It is important to keep in mind that for manufactured goods like automobiles, televisions, washing machines, and so on, labor costs represent only 10 to 15% of the product's cost to the manufacturer and can be significantly less than that in factories with automation. That means that it takes a large difference in labor cost to yield a meaningful change in the ultimate cost of the product. The fact is that, when Japan is able to produce a $20,000 car that is of superior quality compared to an equivalent domestic offering, it is simply because that company has embraced total quality methods and honed them for 40 to 50 years.

5. *The traditional approach is short on leadership and long on "bossmanship."* Far too many Western managers see their jobs as simply telling subordinates what to do and when to do it. It is their station in life to make sure that the procedures are followed, that quotas are met, and that no one makes waves. It is easy to be critical of this kind of "leadership," but for 95 years, it is what we have been taught. It is a product of mass production, springing out of Henry Ford's Highland Park assembly line in 1913 and being adopted in one form or another by just about every kind of production activity. What exactly did Ford do? Prior to 1908, all automobiles were manufactured in craft shops. In North America, Europe, wherever, craft production was how things were made. All the people engaged in the making of an automobile were skilled craftsmen. All parts had to be hand-fitted by filing, cutting, or shaping. No two of anything coming out of a craft shop were the same. Ford realized that if he could make parts interchangeable, thereby eliminating the filing and bending, he could produce his cars a lot cheaper—and achieve unit-to-unit consistency in the bargain.

For example, in 1908 a Ford assembler/fitter (notice the latter designation) spent 514 minutes to complete his task before repeating the same steps on the next car. His work included getting the parts, filing or shaping them to fit, and bolting them on and adjusting and aligning as necessary. It also included maintaining his tools. These were multiple tasks—tasks requiring a craftsman's skills. At about that time, Ford finally achieved perfect part interchangeability. Ford assemblers then went to a single task, with the cycle time dropping to 2.3 minutes—the assembler's assigned task took only 2.3 minutes to complete before the assembler was ready to repeat it again on the next car. Productivity went up in a dramatic fashion. Having to do only one simple task over and over meant that the assembler (he was no longer a fitter) got to be an expert at it very quickly. Ford took it to the next step in 1913 with his introduction of the moving assembly line. Now the assembler no longer had to move. The work came to him. Assembler cycle time dropped to 1.19 minutes.

We cannot give Ford all the credit for part interchangeability because Cadillac apparently beat him to that goal by 2 years, achieving it in 1906. But Ford must be credited with the moving assembly line and what has been called the *interchangeable worker.*[3] Ford no longer needed skilled craftsmen. He could hire unskilled assemblers direct from the farm or immigrants who couldn't speak or read English. Within just a few minutes, they would be as expert as the assembly line demanded. This division of labor down to its simplest terms paid big dividends for Ford and for society in general. For the first time, the possibility of owning an automobile was not restricted to the wealthy. When the Model T was introduced in 1908 with its interchangeable parts, it cost far less than competing cars. In the early 1920s, Ford's interchangeable workers produced 2 million identical cars each year, and the cost was reduced by another two-thirds. Ford's production techniques soon found their way into virtually all manufacturing activities in North America and Europe.

Mass production had arrived—and with it the elimination of skills. Soon industry found ways to divide labor in other areas to minimize the need for worker skills and knowledge. We called it *specialization.* In this kind of environment, all you needed were simple work instructions, the right tool, and the requisite muscle to turn it. Follow the instructions—over and over and over again. Don't improvise; don't make waves; just follow orders. Supervisors and managers have been trained in this system for nearly a century. It worked, at least for a while. For the last half of that period the Japanese have demonstrated a better approach.

REQUIREMENTS FOR IMPLEMENTATION

Some parts of your organization are concerned that the future holds little promise of prosperity unless fundamental changes are brought about. Perhaps your competition is taking market share. You know that your product quality is not good enough. There is strife within your firm, bickering among departments, endless "brushfires." The total quality approach is working for others. Maybe total quality is what is needed. What has to happen for total quality to take place? What are the requirements for its implementation?

Commitment by Top Management

First and foremost, for total quality to become *the way we do business,* an unwavering and unquestioned commitment is required at the top. The CEO, general manager, or whatever title the top person has must commit not only resources but also a considerable amount of his or her own time. Top executives should plan on a third to half their time being used in the total quality effort. Certainly, less than a quarter of their time is not sufficient. Some say, "But the president is so busy. Why can't he delegate the implementation?" Neither in personal experience nor in the recorded experiences of the many companies of which we are aware is there a single success story of a delegated total quality implementation. People expect the boss to put his or her efforts on the most important issues. If they fail to see that effort as being total quality, the subliminal message is that total quality is not number one. Some departments will press on—for a while—until they get at cross purposes with other departments that are marching to the beat of a different drummer. Who has the authority to solve the impasse? Only the boss, and he or she is not involved in the process.

For an organization to completely embrace total quality from the mailroom to the executive office, a profound change is required in the corporate culture. Changing a culture is very difficult even when everyone is willing, and it is almost never the case that everyone will be willing. Some see danger in change, danger to their personal position, the threat of loss of power or prestige, perhaps even loss of employment. Some just like everything the way it is and see no reason to change. Some will be unwilling to put in the work required. Some cannot believe that total quality makes sense. If the message from the top is not crystal clear and if the person at the top is not seen as being totally involved, that will be all the encouragement some will need to "toss wrenches into the gears."

But there is another reason the person at the top must be involved: the change to total quality is a learning experience. If the boss is not involved in it day to day, he or she will never know enough about what is happening to make rational decisions affecting the change. For example, suppose department heads have been meeting over the course of a month or two, wrestling with the issue of how the organizational structure needs to change to accommodate total quality. These people have aired the problem, have developed suggestions for change, and generally understand the issue. However, a change as far-reaching as creating a new organizational structure is beyond the scope of the department heads. Only the person at the top can do that. How do the department heads get that person to understand everything that has happened in these meetings? They have been at it for weeks. A 1-hour briefing is not going to get the boss up to speed. In this setting, the naysayer's impassioned plea for the status quo takes on a credibility that would have been impossible if the boss had been involved in the meetings from the start. The boss hears from one side that the proposed change must be put in place if total quality is ever going to provide the promised benefit. From the other side, he or she hears that the proposed change would be disruptive at best, and possibly disastrous. The span of control will be too wide, allowing things to drop through the cracks. Perhaps the system currently in place is not perfect, but at least it is familiar—and it works. What would you do? If you were the boss and heard these arguments, would you risk the company and make the change? The easy thing to do is do nothing: tell the department heads that you understand where they are coming from and that maybe sometime later it will be an appropriate thing to do, but in the meantime, they'll have to figure ways to work around the structure.

What happened in this example goes on all the time. The boss is given a briefing from which he or she is expected to know as much as the briefer. It cannot be. The briefer has been directly involved in weeks of discussion and has the benefit of long and thoughtful consideration and deliberation. The boss got a few minutes of encapsulated data and has had no opportunity to consider them. Should he or she decide against the change, the decision will make an immediate and lasting impact on the proponents. They won't make that mistake again. Wasted weeks of effort, and for what? Only to be told that the boss thought the organization had better stay the way it is and make the best of it. Total quality will probably come to a screeching halt then and there. Does this happen in the real world? Yes, it does!

Commitment of Resources

The other part of the commitment is resources. Total quality implementation need not be expensive, but everything has a cost. In this case, the cost will certainly include some training. It may also include some consultant expense. The dollars must be there when they are needed. The difficulty is that it will not be easy to project a payback; so many factors can affect a company's performance that it may be impossible to know with certainty that X dollars invested in training yielded Y dollars in performance gains. This area conforms to Deming's truth that some things are not measurable. Accountants don't like to hear that.

The test for commitment of money should be one of reasonableness. Does it make sense to do this? Is the timing right? Is the money available? Can we afford it? Is it the right thing to do? If the answer to these questions is yes, you should not worry unduly about trying to capture the payback. Chances are good that it would cost more to figure out what the payback should be than the project itself will cost, and you can never be certain of the data.

Organization-wide Steering Committee

The third thing needed for company-wide implementation is a top-level steering committee. It may be called by a number of names, but it should be chaired by the person filling the top position in the organization's structure, and its membership should comprise that person's direct subordinates. In a typical corporate setting, this would be the president as chair, with all of the vice presidents filling the membership. The function of this group is to establish how total quality is to be implemented and then to see that it happens. As the conversion process starts, it will be necessary to set up cross-functional teams, to establish the teams' objectives, and to monitor results. Ultimately, this group will find itself operating as a team rather than just as the staff. It will set the vision and goals for the organization, establish teams to pursue the goals, monitor the teams' progress, and reward them for their achievements. The important point, from the outset, is that implementation requires management. Otherwise, it can easily set off in too many directions at once, some of

---

QUALITY TIP ▼

It Isn't Easy, but It's Worth Doing

In a review of an earlier edition of this book on the Amazon.com Web site, the reviewer chastised the authors for making TQM sound like it was difficult to achieve. We are quite sure the writer of the review had never been through a TQM implementation because if he had, he would more likely have agreed that it is not easy. The task is sometimes more than an organization is prepared to take on or to complete. Even so, it is shortsighted not to try, for it is certainly possible to accomplish with support from the top and a well-planned approach. The easy part will come after total quality is in place and performance and quality are improving, while simultaneously costs and time required are declining. Take our word for it—few TQM implementations take place without a lot of hard work and determination, none without a supporting commitment from the top. Yes, it is difficult, but the reward makes the endeavor sweet.

Source: David L. Goetsch and Stanley B. Davis.

which may not even be in concert with the company's objectives. This cannot be allowed to happen. The energy that is going to be unleashed throughout the organization must be channeled. The steering committee does that.

Another important aspect of the steering committee is symbolic. If the employees observe the top-management group functioning like a team and doing things differently from the way things used to be done, they will get a strong message that this time something really is happening. If, on the other hand, they see the staff operating just as they always have, they will know that failure is simply a matter of time. Why bother to get involved? Do not minimize the difficulty of doing this. The typical staff is made up of stars, not team players. They have insulated their respective departments with walls that can defy all efforts to penetrate them. Their interests usually lie in their own departments rather than in the long-term vision and objectives of the company. What is worse, they don't have a common language—having backgrounds as diverse as engineering, finance, management information systems, human resources, quality assurance, manufacturing, purchasing, and so on. In many cases, they do not trust each other. Is it any wonder that we have problems? The person with the biggest challenge is the one who has to forge this crowd into a cohesive, mutually supportive team. But it must be done. The upside is that almost invariably, once they really start to function as a team, staff members will never want to go back to the old ways again.

Planning and Publicizing

So far, we have secured commitment from the top and established the steering committee. At this point, the real work has only begun. We've just said we're going to do it and determined who is going to manage it. Now we have to get down to the details. The steering committee must develop the vision statement and guiding principles, set the goals and objectives, put the TQ implementation plan in place, and then develop an award and recognition program and other publicity efforts. All these matters will be discussed next.

Vision Statement and Guiding Principles   Where would the organization like to be 5 or even 10 years down the road, and what are the guiding principles for operating the business? The vision statement is a long-range strategic view. Total quality needs a long-range vision because total quality is achieved only over a relatively long period, although there will be visible improvements practically from the outset. We are really talking about fundamental changes in the way we do things and how people work together; about involving customers and suppliers in ways never before considered and putting values on matters that may never have been discussed. Not everything will come together overnight, so the vision must be of a distant target to provide a consistent course into the future. Without that, the company will find itself taking turns and detours with every new quarter or year. That will destroy the effort. Consistency is the watchword.

Toyota Motor Sales USA Inc.:
To be the most successful and respected car company in America.
Rollins College:
To be one of the nation's leading colleges, emphasizing academic excellence, responsible citizenship, personal growth, and ethical leadership.
Park Place Lexus:
To be the unparalleled retail automotive group in the United States.

FIGURE 22–2 Sample Vision Statements from a Manufacturer, a College, and a Car Dealership
Sources: Toyota, www.toyotamotors2alesus.com, retrieved September 23, 2011; Rollins College, www.rollins.edu, retrieved September 23, 2011; Park Place Lexus, www.quality.hist.gov/PDF_Files/Park_Place_Lexus_Profile.pdf, retrieved September 23, 2011.

The vision statement need not be lengthy—in fact, the shorter, the better. But it must represent the best collective thoughts of free and open discussion by the steering committee. If your organization is part of a larger entity (such as a division within a company) that has a vision, then you need only tailor yours to support that one. The total quality vision statement will usually include a recognition that only the customers make the final judgment of success or failure. If not stated in words, that idea must be implicit. Sample vision statements from a variety of businesses are found in Figure 22–2.

The guiding principles are the second element of the vision and usually accompany the vision statement in a single document. The guiding principles establish the rules of conduct for the organization and its members. These principles may be concerned with honesty, ethics, respect, fairness, quality, suppliers, customers, community, environment, roles of management and employees, and so on. This can sound very lofty indeed, and that is not a bad thing. People want to be associated with organizations with lofty ideals. They want to be proud not only of their own contribution but also of the company. Sample guiding principles are listed in Figure 22–3.

A well-written vision statement with its attending guiding principles has the following properties:

1. Is easily understood by all stakeholders (employees, customers, suppliers, and others)
2. Is briefly stated yet clear and comprehensive in meaning
3. Is challenging yet possible to accomplish, lofty yet tangible
4. Is capable of stirring excitement and unity of purpose among stakeholders
5. Sets the tone for how the organization and its employees conduct their business
6. Is not concerned with numbers

The vision statement must be crafted in such a way that all employees can relate to it and, in so doing, execute their work in a manner and direction that is consistent with its meaning and objectives.

Evonik Industries AG (Formerly Degussa)
Focus on our customers.
Operate according to Responsible Care principles that protect employees, environment and the community.
Respect diversity in culture, gender, nationality and race.
Treat people fairly, with consistency and respect different opinions.
Be open, honest, and share information.
Encourage learning, develop people, foster teamwork.
Set clear goals, empower employees and encourage open feedback.
Take responsibility, and lead by example.

Support innovation and initiative, learn from mistakes, strive for excellence.
Act with passion for our business.

PepsiCo Inc.
Care for customers, consumers and the world we live in.
Sell only products we can be proud of.
Speak with truth and candor.
Balance short term and long term.
Win with diversity and inclusion.
Respect others and succeed together.

FIGURE 22–3 Sample Guiding Principles

Sources: Evonik Industries, www.degussa-usa.com/north_america/en/company/visionmissionguidingprinciples, retrieved September 1, 2008; PepsiCo Inc., www.pepsico.com/PEP_Citizenship/pepsicovalues/index.cfm, retrieved September 1, 2008.

Goals and Objectives The broad strategic goals and objectives established by the steering committee must harmonize with the vision statement. These goals and objectives are for the total organization rather than necessarily aimed at the individual operating departments. They flow from the vision statement and are frequently part of the organization's strategic plan. To achieve the vision, these are the objectives that must be achieved. From these goals and objectives, supporting specific tactical objectives will be developed for departments, teams, and even individuals. The vision points the company in the desired direction and girds employees with the principles they must use in pursuit of the vision. The broad goals and objectives represent the strategic targets along the way to achieving the vision. Finally, a lower tier of specific tactical objectives describes what must be done as

the company goes about achieving broad objectives and the vision. At both levels, objectives should be stated relative to total quality implementation. A word of caution: don't try to include every possibility and contingency. A few well-crafted goals are what you want. It may be that not all of your goals are measurable, but all should be defined such that you at least know when a goal has been achieved. See Figure 22–4 for the hierarchy and Figure 22–5 for sample objectives.

Total Quality Implementation Plan The plan is driven by the vision, goals, and objectives. It spells out as precisely as possible the route the implementation will take. No two total quality implementations will be the same. Your own organization—after considering your vision and objectives, studying the material, perhaps consulting with

FIGURE 22–4 Hierarchy of Vision and Objectives

Maytag Corporation
- **Broad objective** (Strategy):
  Premium brand leadership
    Specific objective (Tactic):
    Extend the product offerings of our Maytag and Jenn-Air brands.
- **Broad objective** (Strategy):
  Continuous reinvestment in new product introductions and innovation
    Specific objectives (Tactic):
    A new Maytag dishwasher.
    A new Hoover deep carpet cleaner.
    A new Jenn-Air laundry line.

FIGURE 22–5 Sample Broad and Specific Objectives

Source: Maytag Corporation, *First Quarter Report*, 1995.

someone who has been there, and deliberating among the steering committee members—is best equipped to chart its own course. You may want to set up some pilot projects in two or three departments. Proceed slowly and monitor closely. Another organization may establish the total quality initiative by setting teams to work at understanding functional processes. A manufacturing organization may start by introducing just-in-time concepts on the assembly floor—probably in pilot programs at first. At this point, everyone is learning. Don't fret about the mistakes, but do learn from them. Soon a couple of successes will be achieved, and then things will tend to fall into place more readily.

One thing the implementation plan must provide for is training. Before the top executive and the steering committee can function as a total quality team, they will require training. This can be obtained through a variety of sources: seminar courses are available, a consultant could be brought in, or self-teaching is possible (but is probably the least desirable approach). After the steering committee has been trained, it will be ready to start its work. Before the first pilot program is initiated, however, the people who are to be involved must be trained. That degree of training is usually minimal—perhaps as little as a half day. Don't let them venture forth without some training.

A common mistake in U.S. industry has been to go into an across-the-board training program before total quality is introduced. This is wrong on several counts. First, it is a very expensive approach. Second, not everyone needs the training at one time. Third, most of those trained will have forgotten what they learned before getting a chance to apply it. It is better to train only as needed, a kind of just-in-time approach to training.

Many companies have successfully used the approach of cascading training. First the steering committee members are trained. They go off and do their planning to get ready for total quality. Then just prior to the first implementation, members of the steering committee train the total quality project leaders, who, in turn, train the team members.

Awards and Recognition Program   How will you recognize team achievement? An awards and recognition

program should be in hand before the implementation starts. The typical award/recognition program found in the United States is out of step with the total quality concept. Our society is oriented toward individuals. Our award programs recognize individual achievement. Even in team sports that is true. Consider the Heisman trophy. There may be a *best college football player* out there, but unless he is a member of a team that supports his efforts in superlative fashion, he will never win that trophy. Virtually all team sports, amateur or professional, have most valuable player awards. Many manufacturing plants have similar programs to recognize exceptional performance by individuals who are nominated by their peers. For a time, this approach was well-received, and perhaps it still has its place. But as total quality started to be a way of life, people began to view such systems as counterproductive. When trying to do things through teams, don't create superstars. We are not suggesting that exceptional individual accomplishment should go unrecognized, but the focus of the reward system should be on the teams.

These award and recognition programs usually operate on two levels. At one level, the employee review establishes pay raises, frequently associated with an annual or semiannual performance review. The other is like the one mentioned earlier: a kind of spot award for having achieved something special. Both now need to be oriented toward the team rather than the individual. It is very difficult to do that in the former case. This is an area of continuing study in many U.S. firms. The obstacle is that as individuals, we do not want to be penalized for the team's actions. Of course, we would not complain if the team carried us above our own limitations. The perceived problem is far smaller than it appears; it is not likely that any individual will be penalized because he or she happened to be assigned to a team of poor performers. Teams themselves tend to weed out the poor performers far more effectively than management ever could. Still, not many American or Canadian workers are paid on the basis of their teams' performance. Until that happens, we are sending the wrong message to them. This will be a good project for the human resources department.

Spot awards are easily set up to recognize team accomplishments. These need not be extravagant. Some companies provide a dinner for two to each of the winning team's members. Movie tickets are also popular. Some use cash awards. Some simply stress recognition, usually in a forum where all peers are present. Some companies have periodic awards banquets or similar affairs. The possibilities are endless, but employees must see the award process as being fair and equitable, and in tune with the organization's stated intentions.

Publicity Approach   An approach for publicizing total quality activities and results is important. All the employees need to know what is going on—all the time. Every employee survey of which we are aware has placed communications at or very near the top of the problem list. It used to be that we tried to give employees *only as much information as they needed*. Now we know that if there is information, virtually all employees need it. They may not act on it directly in their daily job function, but failing to provide sufficient information to employees with which to make life's decisions is an unconscionable lapse in caring about people. In addition, only when employees are fully informed can they understand many management decisions and consequently support management when they otherwise might be hostile. When it comes to total quality implementation, every employee will be affected in dramatic ways. It is absolutely essential that they understand what is going on and why. There should be no sugarcoating; tell it straight. Let employees know ahead of time what is planned and how they will be affected. When results come in, good or bad, let them know about it. It will be far better to admit a failure in a project than to let the employees find out about it through the underground communications that *always* fill an information void. The failure can be used to demonstrate that there will be no recriminations.

Almost limitless possibilities exist for communicating: a company newspaper or newsletter, all-employee meetings, videos playing in the lunchroom, special total quality bulletins, the intercom system, and so on. Some companies make a very big deal of it and hold picnics, fairs, or even circuses for the express purpose of communicating about total quality. Pick your methods, and use them vigorously.

Infrastructure That Supports Deployment and Continual Improvement

With commitment from the top, a high-level steering committee, a set of plans for at least the early phases of implementation, and the means of providing the required training, the only thing we may lack is the infrastructure that will support the deployment of total quality throughout the organization and continual improvement on a never-ending basis. Actually, most of what we talked about in the previous section—the vision and its harmonized objectives, the awards and recognition program, and certainly communication—can be considered a part of the supporting infrastructure. Three other infrastructure features—your operating procedures, organizational structure, and union situation—can offer support for your total quality implementation efforts, or they can get in your way. These considerations will be discussed next.

Procedures   Virtually all organizations should operate in accordance with published procedures. You will undoubtedly find that many of your procedures, having been developed in another culture, do not support total quality and represent an opportunity for improvement. Be aware of this always, and never accept the old excuse "We've got to do it this way because that's what the procedures say." Don't buy it. If there is a better way, change the procedures.

Organization   The typical Western organizational hierarchy does not fit with total quality (see Figure 22–6). Such organizations are arranged in departments that effectively raise all kinds of barriers to efficient operation. Communication among them is only the most notable of the problems. As total quality implementation progresses, you may find it necessary to alter your organization; it is an

FIGURE 22–6 Typical Traditional Organization

FIGURE 22–7 Total Quality Organization

absolute certainly that you will run into walls that have been built up around the departments over the years.

There are a number of ways to eliminate the walls. Some firms have simply designed new organizational structures. Others develop minicompanies oriented toward specific products or customers by drawing cross-functional talent from the functional "home" departments—the engineering department or the accounting department, for example (see Figure 22–7). Both approaches seem to work well. All members of the team (whether 6 or 600) must see their prospects as tied to the project team, not to the home department. This is what *organizational reengineering* is about.

Union Considerations In organizations with organized labor, the union is an inherent part of the infrastructure. The natural bent of the labor unions makes it difficult for them to accept the changes necessary for maximum benefit of total quality. Many unions as we know them today are another product of the mass production era. Just as much of U.S. and European management is out of step with the realities of today's worldwide business environment, so are these unions. Fundamentally, the traditional unions embrace the concept of division of labor to a fault. Henry Ford's assembler of 1913, tightening the same two bolts over and over again—never touching the third bolt—epitomizes their view of the worker. By making sure management could not require him to service bolt 3, the union guaranteed a job for another assembler. This is not confined to the assembly line. In an engineering laboratory of an electronics firm with organized labor, an engineer is forbidden to place a scope probe on a circuit test point. That is the job of the union's technician. So the engineer tells the technician where to probe and looks over the technician's shoulder to see the response on the oscilloscope screen. Does the engineer need the technician to do this probing? Not at all. Does the technician in this role add value to the process? No. Would they both prefer to work under different rules? Certainly, the engineer would. But the union assures the technician of a job where one might argue none would exist without the union.

These kinds of work rules are incompatible with total quality. Division of labor becomes a thing of the past. People are asked to do multiple tasks and to consider matters that would never have been brought up before—such as "Is this part perfect?" They are expected to stop the process when a problem occurs. Their ideas and suggestions are not only solicited but also expected. Work is done in teams, and people are shifted from function to function to pick up peak demands or to fill in for someone who is absent. These are very difficult concepts for some unions.

But over the past few years, unions have been coming around to the point of tolerance, at least. In shops where these techniques have been successfully applied, such as the Japanese automakers' transplants in the United States, their unions have become supporters of total quality. An Illuminating example is the NUMMI plant in Fremont, California, which was jointly operated by Toyota and General Motors (GM) from 1984 to 2009. The Fremont plant had been operated earlier by GM, and when GM closed the plant in 1982, it had the worst record in the GM family—an unmanageable workforce, rampant absenteeism, and a quality record that was an embarrassment. When the plant reopened in 1984 under joint management by Toyota and GM, the same equipment was in place, and the workforce was composed of the same people who had been laid off a few years earlier. But everything else was different. The United Auto Workers (UAW) had signed a contract that permitted the plant to be run according to the Toyota model. Work was to be performed by teams. Employee participation was expected. Division of labor was a thing of the past. NUMMI had four job classifications in contrast to some GM plants with 183.[4] The UAW went along with the rules changes in return for a no-layoff policy. Everyone, it appears, turned out winners—the workers, the companies, the union, and, most important, the customers. In a very short time, the cars rolling off the NUMMI line, Toyota Corollas and Geo (later Chevy) Prizms, were receiving the top quality ratings in GM—virtually defect free. The Prizm had the best initial quality rating of all cars produced in the

United States or Europe in 1995, and it was only marginally led by five very expensive Japanese models. Lest you attribute this to a fluke, the Corolla has consistently been rated at or near the top of the J.D. Power and Associates studies. For 2007, J.D. Power and Associates ranked the MUMMI–produced Tacoma the best midsized pickup for initial quality.

The absence of a union shop might make total quality implementation easier, but the presence of a union is certainly no excuse for living with the status quo. Unions have found that the benefits outweigh the disadvantages and may even be able to help in the company's quest for total quality. The union must be a part of the team. In fact, many companies place the top union official on the total quality steering committee.

ROLE OF TOP MANAGEMENT: LEADERSHIP

Every organization must have a leader. That is what we pay our top managers to be. Yet, our expectations are infrequently met. For some inexplicable reason, Westerners have difficulty defining leadership. Leaders are described as people that command or guide a group or activity—not a very illuminating definition. In management circles, the debate goes on about who should be called a leader or whether so-and-so has leadership ability. Somehow the point has been missed: if a person is in charge of any group, that person must lead.

From this perspective, every supervisor, manager, director, vice president, president, and CEO must be a leader. The problem is that most of them have never been told what their job is, and few figure it out for themselves. Their job is to *lead*. You may be thinking that this is rather obvious. It is not. The way our society has traditionally organized its enterprises, the farther up the organizational structure you climb, the less leadership is demanded. When new floor supervisors in a factory have just been promoted from a position on the line, they intuitively know that they have to help the less experienced people, and usually they do so. That is a major role of leadership. On the other hand, when a company president becomes the CEO, he or she is likely to spend less time in a leadership role in the company, making it more competitive, than in lobbying Washington to do something about "unfair foreign competition."

Any person in charge of any group is a leader. That person may or may not be an *effective* leader. Too many times he or she is not. But someone put the person in a leadership position—it did not happen by self-proclamation. Who did it? Management, of course. Which brings us back to these questions: What is a leader? What skills, what natural abilities, what aura are prerequisites of leadership? While some individuals seem to possess qualities that are useful in leadership, we have all known excellent leaders who did not look the part. It helps to be attractive and to have charisma, but these traits are not necessary, nor are they a guarantee of leadership ability. So what is it that separates the good leaders from the ineffective?

1. *Leaders pull rather than push.* They are out in front leading the effort, not back in the office (foxhole) yelling, "Charge!" Wess Roberts says it well: "A Chieftain can never be in charge if he rides in the rear."[5] What this really means is that the leader is *visibly involved in the effort he or she is leading.* The antithesis of this is the general manager who gathers the people together and says, "We are going to be a total quality organization, and I'm putting Jim in charge of getting it done." That is abdication of leadership. A corollary to this definition of leadership is this: if you're not personally involved in an effort, you cannot be leading it.

2. *Leaders know where they want to go.* They set the vision for their organizations and chart the course to achieve the vision. Moreover, they make the choices of how to achieve the vision and *stick with it.* They provide the constancy of direction and purpose necessary for success in the long run. They keep their eyes on the prize and are not buffeted by the tempests that are often confronted. A second corollary is this: if you don't know where you're going, you cannot lead the expedition.

3. *Leaders must be courageous and trustworthy.* There are snares and obstacles along any new pathway. Leaders cannot turn back every time they encounter one. If the goal is worth going after, they must stay the course—even at the risk of enduring hardship along the way. Short-term objectives must be sacrificed if they become obstacles to achieving the vision—and in our society, that takes courage. In similar fashion, leaders can be trusted to come to your aid when one of those obstacles springs up in your area. You have to know beyond any doubt that if, when following their marching orders, something goes wrong, they will be there to protect you and won't "hang you out to dry." When people see courage flagging or subordinates taking the heat when things get tough, they will vote the leader out of the leadership office regardless of "rank." The third corollary is this: if you don't have faithful followers, you cannot be a leader.

4. *A leader's most important role after forming the vision and setting the course is helping people to do their jobs with pride.* This is about training and nurturing. It is about giving employees the necessary tools, both physical and intellectual. It is about encouraging when something is difficult and praising when something is accomplished. It is about, as the army commercial says, helping your people to be all that they can be. The role of the leader is not to dictate but to facilitate. It is not to know it all but to find out what others know and put it to use. It is not to "keep people in line" but to involve them to the fullest extent of their capabilities. The fourth corollary is this: a group that is not trained and equipped for a task cannot be led to accomplish it.

ROLE OF MIDDLE MANAGEMENT

The middle manager is not in a position to initiate the kind of cultural change required by total quality. The middle manager must deal with the facilities, equipment, and processes put in place by higher management. He or she must operate within budget constraints for training self and subordinates. The middle manager is to a greater or lesser extent stuck with the infrastructure established by higher management. The manager in the middle cannot commit company resources, establish the corporate vision, or set up recognition and publicity programs. Nor can the middle manager arbitrate interdepartmental friction. These are the very reasons that no successful total quality program can exist without the full backing and involvement of the top levels. This is not to say that the middle manager (and let's include all levels between the hands-on workers and the department heads) fails to play a role in total quality—far from it. These are the people who will carry the brunt of the work as the path to total quality unfolds.

From personal experience, and from the experience of others, it is clear that the middle-management levels present the greatest obstacles to success in total quality. It always seems easier to sell total quality to the top managers and the hands-on people than to the middle managers. There are several reasons for this:

- A good many people in these positions have been there a long time, recognize that they will progress no further, and see total quality's sweeping changes as threats to maintaining their status quo. Many times their insecurity is well-founded because Western hierarchies typically have far too many layers, and total quality makes that obvious.

- Many middle managers moved into those positions after long apprenticeships in the hands-on level. They feel that they know more about their subordinates' jobs than the subordinates themselves do. One of the basics of total quality is that the expert in any job is the person doing it day in and day out—not the one who did it 10 years ago.

- Most of the middle managers came up doing only what they were told to do, making no waves, playing the company game. That they were successful at it is demonstrated by their eventual promotions to their current stations. They may really believe that is the way it should be.

- Middle managers as a group tend to study less than managers at the top. Often the events that are reshaping the world's industry pass them by, and they simply do not know what total quality is about. People seldom support any concept they do not understand.

There are also many bright, forward-thinking people in the middle manager levels. These are the ones who will become total quality leaders, while the others fade away. The people in this category will take on a role similar to the top managers—the role centers on leadership. We can take the previous section, "Role of Top Management"; strip away functions that apply only to top managers, such as creating the vision and broad objectives and committing resources; and apply the rest directly to the middle manager. The middle manager must be a facilitator, enabling his or her people to do their jobs better, easier, and with increased satisfaction. He or she must help, teach, encourage, praise, and, most important of all, *listen* to these people. He or she must build trust and work for the success of the team.

Middle managers will often function as project team leaders, seeking to define and characterize processes and finding ways to improve them, or will take on a wide variety of special total quality projects. With their teams, they will find new ways to do things and new things to do. They will find themselves on the firing line, for it is at this level that products are produced and information is collected and analyzed. This is, in other words, where the action is, the *raison d'être* for the enterprise. How effective middle managers are in adapting to total quality, and how successful their leadership is, will have the greatest possible impact on the company's ultimate success.

VIEWPOINTS OF THOSE INVOLVED

The journey into total quality will be accompanied by fundamental changes in the culture of the organization. That being so, it is helpful to examine the perspectives of people at various levels and at various milestones along the way. This is presented not so much as a warning as an attempt to raise the sensitivity level of the manager of a total quality effort. Naturally, no two cultures will show identical reactions, but we believe these to be typical.

Factory or Office Worker

Initial reaction: Here we go again. Another company buzzword.

After some experience: Hey, maybe there's something to this total quality.

Six months later: I'd never go back. We're proud of what we do. We're a team.

Middle Management (Unenlightened)

Initial reaction: We've been through "zero defects" and "do it right the first time." This, too, shall pass.

After some experience: They are having lots of problems. They must be nuts to think involving lower levels will do anything but cost money.

Six months later (the still unenlightened): They're just trying to do away with our jobs.

Six months later (the newly enlightened): It's hard to deny success. I'm beginning to understand.

Middle Management (Enlightened)

Initial reaction: Time will tell whether top management is really behind this.

After some experience: We're finding problems we never knew we had. Our team is excited.

Six months later: We're operating better than ever, but we've just scratched the surface. Total quality is the way to go.

Top Management

Initial reaction: How much will this cost, how difficult will the cultural transition be, and will the employees buy in?

After some experience: Most of the staff (now steering committee) are on board. Lower levels seem to be developing enthusiasm, but there is some resistance in the middle levels. Overall, we're making progress, but it is sure taking a lot of attention.

Six months later: Definite progress in several areas. Almost everyone involved and excited. A few holdouts in the middle. Fewer crises to deal with. More time to put into total quality.

The Customer

After the first year: Far better delivery performance. Quality improved. If they can maintain this kind of improvement, they've got my business.

It is our experience that once a total quality effort gets off to a good start and the successes begin to add up, a kind of critical mass develops that causes the whole effort to gain momentum and enthusiasm. From that point on, it is as difficult to slow the effort as it was initially to get it started. Nearly everyone becomes a proponent of total quality.

IMPLEMENTATION VARIATION AMONG ORGANIZATIONS

People who are about to undertake the leadership of total quality implementation in their organizations invariably look to the published literature or the experiences of others for the recipe that will result in success for them. Unfortunately, that magic, succeed-every-time formula does not exist. Our

organizations and their cultures are all different, they are staffed with people who are all different from each other, and their business situations are always unique. Therefore, the implementation plan that worked well for XYZ company will never fit exactly with the needs of ABC company. However, in the literature and the experiences of other organizations you will certainly find the ideas and techniques that can be tailored to your own situation. You will find that the approaches to implementation that have been successfully used cover the spectrum of possibilities. The point is this: there is no *one right way*. For a given organization with its special strengths and weaknesses, its peculiar business situation, and its unique culture, there may well be some *wrong ways*. There will also be more than one *right way*.

We have already discussed some of the starting tasks: making a commitment at the top, forming a steering committee of the top management staff, and defining the organization's vision and broad objectives. These are musts. There are some other necessary steps.

1. ***Train the steering committee.*** The basics of this training should include these things:
   - Deming's Fourteen Points and Seven Deadly Diseases (see Figures 22–8 and 22–9)
   - The seven tools and the add-ons (see Chapter 15)
   - Team building

2. ***Identify organizational strengths and weaknesses.***
   - What are we really good at?
   - What needed strengths do we lack?

3. ***Identify the probable advocates of total quality.***
   - Which departments are most likely to be advocates of total quality?
   - Who will resist total quality?

4. ***Identify customers, both external and internal.***
   - Who are the organization's real, ultimate customers?
   - Who are the internal customers of the various departments or processes?
   - Who are the customers of the individual employees?

5. ***Develop a means for determining customer satisfaction (external/internal).***
   - Establish the current baseline against which you will measure improvement.

By completing these tasks, the steering committee will be able to make rational judgments about how the journey should be started. For example, if you conclude that one of your weaknesses is in data collection and analysis, it would probably not be advisable to start into total quality with a wholesale leap into process improvement. If you cannot establish the baseline data and collect and analyze data as changes are implemented, how will you know whether you are doing the right things? If that is a weakness, you will have to overcome it before you can do much with your complex processes. On the other hand, if this is one of your

1. **Create constancy of purpose for improvement of product and service.** Dr. Deming suggests that the role of any company should be to stay in business and provide jobs. Research, innovation, and continual improvement are mandatory in order to do that.
2. **Adopt the new philosophy.** No longer put up with poor quality and bad attitudes. These must be unacceptable.
3. **Cease dependence on mass inspection.** Quality cannot be inspected into a product. All inspection can do is cull out most of the defective ones, which will be reworked or thrown out. That is too expensive, and not satisfactory. Quality comes from relentlessly improving the processes that make the product.
4. **End the practice of awarding business on price tag alone.** Buying materials for your products on the basis of lowest price is fraught with problems. Instead, you should seek quality and value and establish long-term relationships with your good suppliers.
5. **Improve constantly and forever the system of production and service.** It is management's responsibility to constantly improve processes, products, and services, while reducing waste.
6. **Institute training.** We have neglected this extremely important function to the extent that too many Western workers do not know how to do their jobs.
7. **Institute leadership.** Find out what leadership is, and do it. It is not giving orders or threatening. It is leading, helping, facilitating.
8. **Drive out fear.** Too many workers continue to do their jobs poorly because they are afraid to ask or suggest. Fear has a huge economic and quality impact.
9. **Break down barriers between staff areas.** We must get people working as a team for the goals of the enterprise, not working to protect and maximize department objectives. Structures must support the whole, not isolate into fiefdoms.
10. **Eliminate slogans, exhortations, and targets for the workforce.** They do no good and are often seen as putting down the workforce, treating members like children. If the teams want to create their own slogans, let them.
11. **Eliminate numerical quotas.** Quotas send the signal to the people that volume is what counts, not quality or processes. They force people to achieve the quotas no matter what the cost in terms of waste or company reputation.
12. **Remove barriers to pride of artisanship.** Everyone wants to do a good job, but too often we do not provide people with the leadership, training, tools, or processes necessary. These barriers to pride of artisanship must be eliminated.
13. **Institute a vigorous program of education and retraining.** Every employee from top to bottom will have to be educated in total quality, the statistical tools, and teamwork.
14. **Take action to accomplish the transformation.** Make this everyone's job, from the top executive to the hands-on labor. Everyone must be involved, and the top levels must be committed to support and facilitate the effort.

FIGURE 22–8 Deming's Fourteen Points

strengths, you might make your first venture the establishment of one or more process teams, the task of which will be to flowchart a key process, understand how it works, characterize it to baseline its present capability, and then set about refining the process. In one high-tech company that used this approach, the steering committee identified the key processes and established cross-functional teams for each one. The committee capitalized on their data and analysis strengths to get the movement started. Each of the key process teams established lower-level process teams as required. Because everything we do is associated with some process, this company soon found that total quality had permeated its operations. Its Baldrige-based score, a score derived using the criteria for the Malcolm Baldrige Quality Award, more than doubled in a year and a half, placing it at the world-class level.

If you have a manufacturing group that you believe will advocate total quality, you might start by introducing just-in-time/Lean production techniques on the factory floor. Manufacturing has led the way to total quality in a great many companies. On the other hand, you may have some particular problem that has not been solved by the traditional methods. The approach used by many organizations is to enter total quality with the establishment of cross-functional teams (perhaps including the steering committee itself) applying total quality techniques to analyze and solve

1. **Lack of constancy of purpose.** You must have a long-range plan and stick to it. Otherwise, you are buffeted by every new influence, and no one knows where he or she is supposed to be headed.
2. **Emphasis on short-term profits.** The focus must be on the long-range vision, not this quarter's numbers, which often lead to counterproductive decisions.
3. **Evaluation by performance, merit rating, or annual review of performance.** We need to promote teamwork, not individual contribution. Everything about most evaluation systems in use today is counterproductive and demoralizing to employees.
4. **Mobility of management.** Managers need to stay in jobs long enough to learn them and then offer stability over a longer period. Total quality is a long-term project, and there must be continuity to see it through.
5. **Running a company on visible figures alone.** Dr. Deming rightly claims that the most important figures are unknown and unknowable. What numbers do you assign to a delighted customer, or to a team of employees who are fired up to solve process problems? Running by the numbers, especially short-term numbers, can take you in the wrong direction.
6. **Excessive medical costs.** (U.S. only) When the average American automobile's price includes $1,500 for medical insurance costs for the workers who built it, we are fighting an uphill battle to be competitive with the rest of the world.
7. **Excessive costs of warranty, fueled by lawyers who work on contingency fees.** (U.S. only) No comment needed. It is a competitiveness issue.

FIGURE 22–9 Deming's Seven Deadly Diseases

problems. This problem-solving team approach is probably the most common introduction to total quality. It is important that the problems to be attacked and the team structures be controlled by the steering committee—especially at first. In the beginning, everyone will lack experience. At the same time, enthusiasm can build very quickly. The combination of inexperience and overenthusiasm can produce chaos and, if unchecked, will surely fail to produce the desired results. During the first 6 months or so, nothing should be done that is not directed by the steering committee. In fact, the steering committee needs to stay on top of all total quality activities forever, at least to the point of receiving regular input from all the teams. Nevertheless, the steering committee must remain receptive to suggestions for problems to be solved. Some of those *ad hoc* problems probably should be on the list of early candidates.

Another valid approach, if you are strong in the statistical area, is starting total quality by implementing the use of the seven tools. You know by now that the application of these tools is not restricted to the manufacturing floor. They may be applied wherever processes are at work, and that is everywhere. Before this can happen, the people affected will require a few hours of instruction on the use of the tools.

The customer satisfaction approach is another valid entry. For this, the employees will have to identify their internal customers and determine their basis for customer satisfaction. Then teams can be deployed to find ways to improve their processes in light of their internal customers' expectations. Results can be seen almost at once with this approach because little time elapses between complet-

ing a process and getting the output of that process to the internal customer. This approach also works with external customers and is very important, but the cycle time in the external customer loop is much longer, so the information feedback is slower. Many times it does not exist at all except in customer satisfaction's impact to orders and the bottom line.

> ## QUALITY TIP ▼
>
> ### The Eighth Deadly Disease
>
> We would like to be presumptuous enough to add an eighth Deadly Disease to Deming's list of seven: *Executive incentive programs that involve stock that may be sold in less than 5 years after retirement.* Stock-option programs are the vehicle through which many executives acquire wealth, presumably by being wise managers, thereby enhancing the stock's value. However, there can be enormous pressure to make decisions that drive up the stock's price in the short term, sacrificing the long term, when executives are able to dispose of their stock holdings for personal gain while still employed by the company or within 1 or 2 years after retirement. The result can be that the corporate vision is abandoned, and with it the company's best prospects for the future. Executives may engage in schemes such as massive downsizing, selling off units, even selling out to another company, and many other stratagems that can quickly, if temporarily, raise the stock price. If they could not sell the stock until the fifth anniversary of their retirement, the incentive would be to make decisions compatible with the company's long-term interests (i.e., its vision).
>
> *Source:* David L. Goetsch and Stanley B. Davis.

Although there is no one right way to implement total quality, the fundamentals apply in all cases. You have to approach it in a structured manner that takes advantage of your strengths, culture, and business situation and the personalities involved. Your first steps should be careful, deliberate, and well-monitored. Study the data and listen to the people. Use the feedback you gain to help make the mid-course corrections that will assuredly be required. Build on your successes and learn from your failures. Keep your eye on the vision, and never let Deming's Fourteen Points be out of mind. Communicate, communicate, and communicate some more.

IMPLEMENTATION APPROACHES TO BE AVOIDED

Before we immerse ourselves in the right way to approach a total quality implementation, let's dispense with some wrong approaches. There are surely more examples of inappropriate total quality implementation than there are of superlative ones. Not surprisingly, however, we do not learn about most of the failures without being directly involved. Still, there is a lot of information around from which we can identify approaches to be avoided.

The following discussion gives you some ideas of implementation approaches that you should avoid.

- *Don't train all your employees at once.* It became popular in the mid-1980s to play numbers games with the number of employees who had received training in total quality, the seven tools, SPC, and so on. Some organizations (including government) spent megadollars training thousands of employees from the top of the organization to the bottom as a first step. Then they found that the vast majority of those employees would have no use for the training for months or years. By that time, not having applied their new skills, the employees had forgotten most of the training. People find it discouraging to be trained in a new subject but unable to do anything with it. The right way to do it is to train small groups of your people just-in-time—just as they need it.

- *Don't rush into total quality by putting too many people in teams.* Another early total quality numbers game was keeping score by the number of teams that were deployed or the percentage of employees on teams. Management wanted numbers, and because it was often difficult to develop meaningful numbers in terms of increased profitability, customer satisfaction, reduction of waste—all attributable to total quality—the number of teams was something—but no one knew what. The one thing that was certain in these cases was that aside from the teams themselves, no one knew what they were doing, except spending money. This was a throwback to the early days of American quality circles. The idea then was to get everyone into quality circles and let the circles pick projects on which to work. This is not at all like Japanese quality circles. Taiichi Ohno

started quality circles at Toyota as production process teams.[6] He postulated that rather than having assembly line operators work as individuals, as they do in a mass production factory, small teams possessing the skills demanded by their broader process(es) could be more efficient. In addition to the normal assembly process, Ohno also assigned quality checking, routine machine maintenance, and housekeeping duties to the teams. He also allocated time for them to discuss their work and develop ways to improve their processes. This was the genesis of the Japanese kaizen, continual incremental improvement.

The people in early quality circles in the United States didn't necessarily work together, they had none of the additional duties, and they were not focused on kaizen. They did take an hour or so a week to meet and discuss problems, but few of the problems they discussed had much relevance to quality improvement. Teams should be formed deliberately as needed to take on specific issues or problems as directed by the steering committee. Don't worry about how many teams you have, only about results.

- *Total quality implementation must not be delegated.* One approach has been for top management to commit the organization to total quality and then to delegate the implementation to the quality assurance department. Beyond demonstrating colossal ignorance of the meaning of total quality, this also reveals something about the leadership at the top. In this case, top management sees it as another program to be endured, and since it is about quality, who better than the QA director to run it? One very competent, nationally known quality assurance professional and advocate of total quality got caught in this trap. He tried very hard for 2 or 3 years to make a successful total quality implementation, but everyone in the company knew the top management was not involved, so the roadblocks held and the program was a failure. A successful total quality implementation requires both complete commitment and active, personal, day-in, day-out involvement by top management and staff.

- *Don't start an implementation before you are prepared.* Sometimes higher level managers find it difficult to acknowledge that they don't know something. It should be obvious that plunging into anything as technically and sociologically complex as total quality without having a grasp of the subject will guarantee failure. A lot of plants can be found throughout the United States where the walls are plastered with control charts, where weekly meetings are held to review the data, and where phrases such as "employee involvement" abound. Yet in these same plants, there is no real continual improvement, no real involvement. What has happened is that the traditional department heads, without any total quality leadership, have given the boss what he or she wanted—charts and buzzwords. Be sure to become educated on the subject of total quality before attempting to implement. This must include the top manager and his or her immediate subordinates.

AN IMPLEMENTATION APPROACH THAT WORKS

We have just discussed implementation approaches that have demonstrated through practice that they should be avoided. Experience has also provided a wealth of information on successful implementations and the techniques that made them that way. Much can be learned from successful implementations, but we must always be mindful that we will not be able to duplicate another's success by following exactly the same path; there are simply too many variables.

Our 20-step total quality implementation process will work for any organization with a little tailoring here and there to accommodate the specific organization.

We have said that no two total quality implementations will be the same. However, every implementation will require certain steps, and these steps must be taken in a logical order. Refer to Figure 22–10. Our implementation model has three phases:

- Preparation
- Planning
- Execution

The preparation phase is necessary for any organization, and the steps are listed in the appropriate order. With the skills honed and the critical information developed in the prepara-

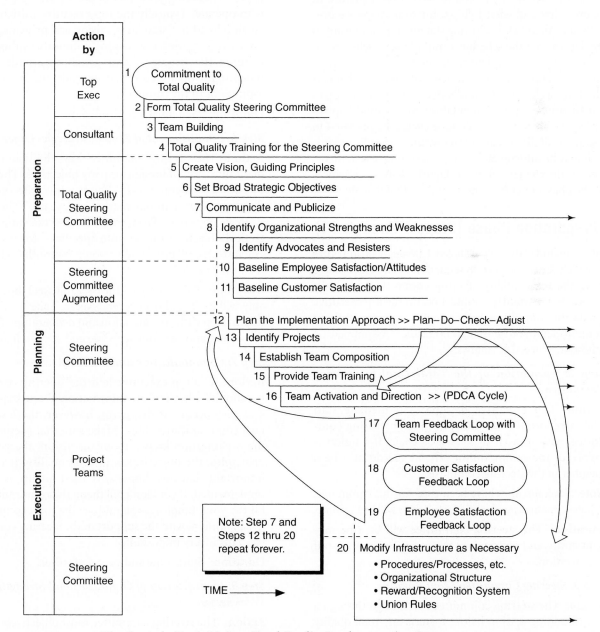

FIGURE 22–10 The Goetsch–Davis 20-Step Total Quality Implementation Process

tion phase, we can enter the planning phase. It is here that the unique strengths and weaknesses and other characteristics of the organization are accommodated by tailoring. Then we go into the execution phase, carrying out the planning just completed. At this point, we find ourselves in a continuous loop between planning and execution as we go further along the total quality pathway. Even when we can say that we have fully implemented total quality, this loop will continue to operate, making continual improvement and superior competitiveness a reality. As we go step-by-step through this 20-step implementation process, continue your reference to Figure 22–10 so that you develop a clear picture of how the steps interrelate and how they should be sequenced in time.

We have discussed things that must be done and other things you need to consider for your journey into total quality. Now these things must be put into a time-phased sequence: a schedule. You need to have a clear picture of what comes first and what follows, for some steps are prerequisites for others. The following statement is not meant to be a disclaimer, but the schedule cannot have a well-defined time scale. Only you can determine the time you require to do these things, how long certain steps will take. For that reason, the time scale must be undefined; however, when you apply it to your own implementation, you should apply a more precise scale to target milestone events. Be prepared to allow some flexibility because even within a specific organization, it may be difficult at first to project time requirements for some of the changes. Refer to Figure 22–10 for clarification of the phases of entry and execution of total quality.

The Preparation Phase (Steps 1 through 11)

This phase includes the steps labeled 1 through 11 in Figure 22–10, which are carried out in sequence. Even before Step 2 (forming the total quality steering committee) can take place, one all-important event must occur: the top executive must make the commitment of time and resources. Without that commitment, you should go no farther. Assuming that commitment, proceed as follows:

Step 2: Formation of the Total Quality Steering Committee

Action: Top executive designates immediate staff (direct reports) to be the total quality steering committee, with himself or herself as chair. If a union is involved, the senior union official should also be a member of the steering committee.

Note: Several names have been used for this committee. Whatever name you choose, the function will be the same.

Duration: The steering committee will be a permanent entity and will replace the former executive staff organization.

Step 3: Steering Committee Team Building

Action: The steering committee needs to go through a team-building session before it starts any total quality work. This will usually require an outside consultant.

Duration: This usually requires 1 to 3 days, preferably done away from the work environment.

Step 4: Steering Committee Total Quality Training

Action: The steering committee will require training in total quality philosophy, techniques, and tools before it starts any total quality work. Usually requires an outside consultant.

Duration: Two or 3 days of intensive training. This should be followed through in the long run with self-study and appropriate seminars.

Step 5: Creation of the Vision Statement and Guiding Principles

Action: The first real total quality work effort is creating the organization's vision statement and putting on paper the guiding principles under which the company is to operate. Typically the top executive initiates discussion by using "strawman" vision and principles. The objective is getting the steering committee's thoughts, refining the language, and concluding with short, meaningful documents that embody the hopes and aspirations of the company.

Duration: Plan on at least 1 full day.

Step 6: Establishment of Broad (Strategic) Objectives

Action: The steering committee flows the vision statement into a set of broad company objectives. These are by nature on a grand scale—for example, "Become the dominant player in our market in 5 years." These are strategic objectives. From these flow a set of supporting tactical objectives that go into specifics—for example, "by introducing new products on a 9-month cycle over the next 3 years."

Duration: This will take at least a full week but probably will be spread over several weeks. Take the time to do this step with consideration and deliberation, but on the other hand, set your schedule and stick to it.

Step 7: Communication and Publicity

Action: The top executive and the steering committee should communicate information about steps 2 to 4 as they occur. At this point, however, there should be a communication blitz. Make sure that everyone in the organization knows about the vision, the guiding principles, the objectives, and total quality. It is very important that they know why total quality is being implemented. If you don't tell them, the rumor mill will fill the void. Employees should see the top executive as the champion, with the support of the steering committee. This is very important.

Duration: Starts now and goes on forever.

Step 8: Identification of Organizational Strengths and Weaknesses

Action: The steering committee must objectively identify the strengths and weaknesses of the organization.

This information will help guide it to the best total quality implementation approach and may also highlight deficiencies that must be corrected.

Duration: Plan on a full day.

Step 9: Identification of Advocates and Resisters

Action: (May be parallel to or after Step 8.) The steering committee should try to identify those in key slots who are likely to be total quality advocates and those who are likely to resist total quality. This will help in selecting the early projects and team members.

Duration: Should require no more than an hour or two if the members independently prepare their assessments prior to the meeting.

Step 10: Baseline Employee Satisfaction/Attitudes

Action: (May be parallel to or after Step 8.) With the help of the human resources department or an outside consultant, the steering committee should attempt to gauge the current state of employee satisfaction and attitudes. Although there are sophisticated devices for determining this information, it is probably only necessary to make an objective judgment. Having that established, you will later be able to determine whether your total quality changes are working effectively, as shown by improving satisfaction and attitudes.

Duration: Allow a week to do it in-house and at least a month if you have an outside firm do it. Should be repeated annually.

Step 11: Baseline Customer Satisfaction

Action: (May be parallel to or after Step 8.) The steering committee, perhaps augmented by the department that works closest with customers, should attempt to obtain objective feedback from customers to determine their level of satisfaction. Depending on the size of the customer base, the selection of customers to be surveyed may be random. Be certain that someone doesn't pick only those known to be favorably disposed. Having this information will allow you to judge the effectiveness of your total quality efforts as seen by the ones who make the final determination—your customers.

Duration: Allow 2 months if you send out survey forms and 2 weeks if you do it by phone. Should be repeated annually.

The Planning Phase (Steps 12 through 15)

Step 12: Plan the Implementation Approach—Then Use Plan–Do–Check–Adjust (PDCA Cycle)

Action: Now is the time for the steering committee to start planning the implementation of total quality. This step becomes continuous because after initial projects are under way, information will be fed back to this step to accommodate course correction, adjustment, and so on. In addition, this step will continue to spin out new

projects and teams. Also, once total quality is in motion, this step effectively shifts to operate within the PDCA cycle, as originated by Walter Shewhart.[7]

Duration: Never ends. This is the step from which the total quality process is managed, not only at the implementation stage but for as long as the process exists.

Step 13: Identification of Projects

Action: The steering committee is responsible for selecting the initial total quality projects, based on the strengths and weaknesses of the company, the personalities involved, the vision and objectives, and the probability of success. The early projects must be selected to assure success in order to set a foundation of positive experience from which to move to the more difficult challenges later on. The steering committee should be open to suggestions for projects from all sources.

Duration: Initial projects selected over a few days. Process continues forever.

Step 14: Establish Team Composition

Action: After the projects have been selected, the steering committee establishes the composition of the teams that will execute them. Most teams will be cross functional, having representation from multiple departments or disciplines, as appropriate for the project at hand. This is one step where it is handy to know who the advocates are.

Duration: This task goes on forever.

Step 15: Provide Team Training

Action: Before a new team can go to work, it must be trained. Training should cover basics of total quality and tools appropriate to the project. Training may be done by a member of the steering committee.

Duration: At least one-half day, followed by facilitation. As new teams are formed, the need for training will continue until eventually all employees are trained and experienced.

The Execution Phase (Steps 16 through 20)

Step 16: Team Activation and Direction (Use PDCA Cycle)

Action: The steering committee gives each team its direction and activates it. Teams work on their assigned projects using the total quality techniques they have learned. They use the plan–do–check–adjust cycle as their total quality process model.

Duration: Project teams, depending on the project, may have life spans of weeks, months, or longer. Measurable results must continue to flow, however, to ensure that the team is being effective.

Step 17: Team Feedback Loop to the Steering Committee

Action: Through this step, the project team closes the loop with the steering committee by providing feedback information on progress and results. This feedback is usually in the form of presentations to the steering committee. Early on, this loop should be tight, with feedback coming in frequent packets—perhaps weekly. As the project gets on track and stabilizes, monthly feedback is appropriate. Never let it go longer than that. The steering committee uses this feedback to determine if adjustments or changes in direction are required. Any changes desired are fed back to the project team, which carries out the new instructions. Both the team and the steering committee use the PDCA cycle.

Duration: Specific projects may have finite lives of weeks, months, or longer, but this process across all the projects goes on forever.

Step 18: Customer Satisfaction Feedback Loop

Action: Special project teams are deployed to obtain customer feedback information, covering both external and internal customers. Formal external customer surveys should be conducted annually, and other customer satisfaction data (sales results, warranty data, customer service input, data from customer visits, etc.) are collected and processed on a continual basis. Internal customer satisfaction is baselined for key processes and monitored continually. (This latter may be done by the project team assigned to the process in question.) All of this information is fed back to the steering committee on a regular basis, certainly no less frequently than quarterly. This information is digested in the steering committee's PDCA cycle and influences direction changes issued to the project teams and also the formation of new project teams.

Duration: Forever.

Step 19: Employee Satisfaction Feedback Loop

Action: Another special project team periodically takes the pulse of employee attitude and satisfaction. Formal surveys may be done annually, and in between, it is necessary for the steering committee and other managers only to stay close to the employees to develop rather accurate information on attitude and satisfaction. This information is fed to the steering committee as another stream of data on which to evaluate progress and determine any necessary course corrections.

Duration: Forever.

Step 20: Modify Infrastructure as Necessary

Action: Feedback to the steering committee from steps 17, 18, and 19 (from project teams, customers, and employees) will guide the steering committee to address necessary changes in the corporate infrastructure—procedures and processes, organization structure, awards and recognition programs, union rules, and so on. Many times the changes will have to be made by the steering committee itself (e.g., those involving organization structures). On other occasions, it is appropriate to authorize the project teams to make the changes *that are needed* (e.g., those involving the processes on which they are working).

Duration: Because we are talking about continual improvement, this goes on forever.

We have now walked through the various implementation phases. In this exercise, we have followed the process from the time the top executive decided to embrace total quality through working teams. Starting with Step 12 and going through Step 20, we have a closed-loop system that will continue for as long as the total quality process is in use. The feedback to the steering committee provides the information it needs to manage the process. The steering committee, in turn, issues new instructions, establishes new teams, and so on to keep efforts going in the direction that will achieve the objectives and remain in harmony with the vision.

Step 7 (communication and publicity) also goes on forever. We cannot overemphasize the importance of keeping employees informed. Many companies have found that through innovative communication, it is possible to stimulate the kind of enthusiasm throughout the ranks that really produces advocates.

Our coverage of this material is necessarily concise. For a complete in-depth treatment of the Goetsch–Davis 20-step total quality implementation process, you are invited to read our companion book, *Implementing Total Quality* (Prentice Hall, 1995).

GETTING ON WITH IT

Whether an organization can go through this kind of an implementation without the help of a consultant will depend on the internal availability of one or more experts. Students who study total quality in college can become these internal experts. Rather than trying to muddle through, it would be far better to enlist the aid of a consultant to get you through the implementation and into execution. It is certainly possible to pay a lot of money for such services, but it is by no means necessary. Most consultants would prefer to work with you on a part-time basis (simultaneously servicing other clients). A typical 6-month implementation would probably require I person-month or less of consulting services. This could be a wise investment for your organization because the "muddle through" method is almost sure to fail, after which it will be doubly difficult to recover, to try again.

Virtually every type of enterprise can benefit from total quality. Starting on the journey now may put you ahead of your competition. Failure to start now may leave you behind and doomed to failure as the whole world embraces the principles of total quality.

WHAT TO DO IN THE ABSENCE OF COMMITMENT FROM THE TOP

We have said repeatedly throughout this book that no entity can truly become a total quality organization without complete, unwavering, participative commitment from the very top. For those of you who have that commitment, your path is clear—you know what to do and how to proceed. However, many of you will not be so fortunate, and you face a dilemma. Should you try to push total quality from where you are, or should you forget it and wait for top management to come around? There can be no hard and fast answer to this. So much depends on where you are in the organization and whether the top managers are outwardly hostile to total quality or merely unknowledgeable. Even the geographical structure of the organization is a factor.

If your top management is hostile to total quality, it would not seem prudent for you to push the subject much beyond trying to enlighten them. Even that could be hazardous, depending on your relationship with the management group. Certainly, any overt total quality initiatives on your part in defiance of management's wishes would not be in your best interest. If enlightenment does not work, it may be time to consider moving on to different employment. That is not always a reasonable option, but long-term prospects for your current employment are not bright either, given top management's attitude toward total quality.

If your top managers are simply ambivalent toward total quality, perhaps because they do not know much about it, you have a whole different ball game. Assuming your position gives you some latitude of operation, you may be able to construct a mini-implementation within your department that can improve performance in many areas. To do this, you must be the head of a department or must be able to influence a department head who will work with you. Because departments can range in size from just a handful of people to a complete stand-alone facility far removed from the home office, the magnitude of accomplishment of a departmental total quality implementation can vary greatly. The head of a stand-alone facility can look at the implementation almost as if he or she headed the company. The more common situation, where the department is one of many, proximally located, will not offer the same freedom of action, but it is still worth pursuing. Generally speaking, all processes contained within the department, even though they have extradepartmental suppliers and customers, are good candidates for a total quality effort. You should concentrate your efforts there first. After you have gained some successes that have been noticed by top management and other departments, you can begin to push for expansion into the cross-functional processes, requiring other departments to join you in total quality initiatives.

Recognizing that *departmental total quality* is a contradiction in terms (i.e., it cannot be *total quality* until every aspect of the organization is involved and committed to it), implementing total quality in a single department is better than not doing it at all. If the implementation is well-done, the gains will be significant enough to attract the attention of other departments and of top management. Your department may provide the seeds for the larger organization to become involved.

Getting started in a single department is not much different from the process we have just studied for a company-wide implementation. The numbers of people involved in every step may be smaller, but most of the steps are required. The following list briefly addresses each of the 20 steps for applicability in a departmental implementation:

- **Step 2.** Unless it is a very large department, such as a stand-alone plant or something similar, you may not require a steering committee. For a large department, we would recommend one.

- **Steps 3 and 4.** If you have a steering committee, you will need to give the members some training. Because you are doing this on your own without top management's involvement, don't expect a lot of support money at this point.

- **Steps 5, 6, and 7.** Setting the vision, mission, and guiding principles for your department is a good idea. If these exist at the company level, yours should flow directly from them and support them. If the company has no vision, mission, or guiding principles, be sure to have yours approved by top management before proceeding. Once that is done, communicate them to every department employee.

- **Steps 8 and 9.** This is just as important at the department level as it is for the larger organization. The identification of department strengths and weaknesses and of those likely to help you will be of invaluable assistance in selecting your initial projects.

- **Steps 10 and 11.** We believe that it will be important for you to know your employee attitude index within the department. In terms of baselining customer satisfaction, you will probably be looking at internal customers in other departments, but the same considerations apply. In this case, it should be easy to survey for the information.

- **Step 12.** Must be done. No matter what the scale, the implementation approach should always be thoroughly planned.

- **Step 13.** You should identify your initial projects based on your department's strengths and weaknesses, where your support is, and, very important, the processes and activities that are contained completely within your department. Try to pick initial projects that can yield measurable gains without significant expense.

- **Steps 14, 15, and 16.** Follow the same procedure as for the larger organization, but recognize that you may have to improvise in the training step in the absence of dollar support.

- **Steps 17, 18, and 19.** These steps follow the same procedures as for the larger organization except that customer feedback will probably be from your internal customers in other departments. If you elect not to use a steering committee, the feedback path will be directly to you.

- **Step 20.** Although you may find it advantageous to make some intradepartmental infrastructure changes, you will probably have to secure approval of top management before the fact.

As in the earlier discussion, steps 12 through 20 become a repeating cycle even within a departmental implementation. Eventually, it will become clear whether your implementation has piqued the interest of top managers, encouraging them to spread the implementation to other departments, or whether total quality will go no further in the organization. Another possibility is that your peers may join you department by department. This is far from the ideal way to implement total quality in any organization, but it is preferable to discarding total quality out of hand.

IMPLEMENTATION STRATEGIES: ISO 9000 AND BALDRIGE

Organizations that are not ready to undertake a full total quality implementation but that want to move in that direction can use the criteria of several different award and certification programs as a starting point. The two programs that we recommend are ISO 9000 and the Malcolm Baldrige Award.

ISO 9000 as a Starting Point

If an organization has not yet committed to total quality but is in a business that could benefit from ISO 9000 registration, going through the preparation steps will automatically provide a start into total quality. Although ISO 9000 and total quality are not equivalent, as we discussed in Chapter 14, any total quality organization should apply the kinds of procedures, checks, and management involvement required by ISO 9000. ISO 9000 is a subset of total quality, but it is close to TQM.

ISO 9000 registration requires, for most organizations, a lot of work. If starting without any written procedures, if processes are not well-documented, and if there is no quality system or quality manual, an organization faces an uphill battle. But the work required is work that must be done for total quality anyway. ISO 9000 preparation can get an organization started on a total quality implementation.

Self-Assessment Based on Baldrige or Similar Criteria

The Malcolm Baldrige National Quality Award program, which operates under the auspices of the National Institute of Standards and Technology (NIST), was established in 1987 by legislation (P.L. 100–107) and is intended to:

- Promote awareness of the importance of quality improvement to the national economy.
- Recognize organizations that have made substantial improvements in products, services, and overall competitive performance.
- Foster sharing of best-practices information among U.S. organizations.

From 1988 through 2010, 91 organizations have received the coveted Baldrige Award. Competitors for the award are evaluated according to criteria organized into seven categories. The categories are weighted in value, with a maximum score being 1,000. The list of evaluation criteria, which is updated periodically, is shown in Figure 22–11. Each of the seven categories is broken down into two or more subcategories, so that the evaluation covers the 17 areas of the organization's operations considered most meaningful to an evaluation of world-class ranking. Each subcategory is further broken down two more levels to enable the evaluation of the actual processes used.

Competing for the Baldrige Award can be quite expensive, but at the time of this writing, at least 45 states sponsor quality programs based on the Baldrige. The state competitions offer most of the benefits at a much lower cost. (The most significant difference lies in the prestige of the national award.) Most states also offer self-assessment criteria derived from the Baldrige. These, or the Baldrige criteria themselves, can be used by organizations wishing to assess themselves against world-class standards without going through the actual competition.

Virtually all of the Baldrige competitors, both the winners and those who have not won, say that the real value of the Baldrige Award is not in the award but in the preparation. Consequently, more and more organizations are going through the preparation phase without any intention of competing for the prize. What does this do for them? It shows them how they stack up against a world-class standard and provides them with a list of needed improvements. If an organization has not yet committed to total quality, conducting a Baldrige-based self-assessment will provide a scorecard for comparison against the best in the world. More than that, it will clearly identify the areas that most need to be improved, thus providing the impetus for implementing total quality, and putting all your people to work on the areas of need. Do that in the context of the 20-step total quality implementation process.

Do not get the idea from this discussion that an organization can implement total quality without the order, discipline, and planning suggested by this book. Ultimately, organizations will need everything presented here from

---

QUALITY TIP ▼

Seeing It as It Is

As a word of caution, a self-assessment score would probably not hold up against an assessment by qualified outside assessors. Much of our consulting effort has been involved in these assessments. Whenever we have conducted a Baldrige-type assessment, we have always required the executive team to conduct a self-assessment first. Without exception, the self-assessment score is higher than our assessment team's score—usually by 200 to 300 points. Many executives think their organizations' performance is better than it really is. The facts emerge from the middle and lower levels of the organization; hence, the difference in scores.

Source: David L. Goetsch and Stanley B. Davis.

1. **Leadership** (120 points)

   Examines how the organization's senior leaders guide and sustain the organization; the organization's governance; and how the organization addresses its ethical, legal, societal, and key community responsibilities.

2. **Strategic Planning** (85 points)

   Examines how the organization develops strategic objectives and action plans; how these objectives and action plans are deployed; how they are changed if required; and how progress is measured.

3. **Customer Focus** (85 points)

   Examines how the organization engages its customers for long-term marketplace success, including how the organization listens to the voice of the customers, builds customer relationships, and uses this for improvement and innovation.

4. **Measurement, Analysis, and Knowledge Management** (90 points)

   Examines how the organization selects, gathers, analyzes, manages, and improves its data, information, and knowledge assets; how it manages its information technology; and how it reviews and uses reviews to improve its performance.

5. **Workforce Focus** (85 points)

   Examines the organization's ability to assess workforce capability and capacity needs and build a workforce environment conducive to high performance in alignment with the organization's vision and objectives.

6. **Operations Focus** (85 points)

   Examines how the organization designs, manages, and improves its work systems and work processes to deliver customer value and achieve organizational success and sustainability; and readiness for emergencies.

7. **Results** (450 points)

   Examines the organization's performance and improvement in all key areas—product and process outcomes, customer-focused outcomes, financial and market outcomes, workforce-focused outcomes, and leadership and governance outcomes. Also examines performance levels relative to those of competitors and other organizations providing similar products and services.

FIGURE 22–11 Seven Categories of Criteria for the Malcolm Baldrige National Quality Award

Source: National Institute of Standards and Technology, October 2011.

cover to cover. By using ISO 9000 or quality award assessment criteria, an organization can get started. But the full-fledged implementation we have described will be needed if an organization is to realize the full benefit of total quality.

Addresses for ISO 9000 and Quality Awards Information

For ISO 9000, ANSI/ISO/ASQ Q9000:

American Society for Quality
PO Box 3005
Milwaukee, WI 53201-3005
Phone: (U.S. & Canada) 800-248-1946
Web: www.asq.org

For the Malcolm Baldrige National Quality Award:

Baldrige Performance Excellence Program
(Malcolm Baldrige National Quality Award)
100 Bureau Drive, Stop 1020
Gaithersburg, MD 20899-1020
Web: www.nist.gov/baldrige/
E-mail: nqp@nist.gov

You may also contact the ASQ, as listed above.

SUMMARY

1. The traditional way of doing business presents the following problems:
   - We are bound to a short-term focus.
   - The traditional approach tends to be arrogant rather than customer focused.
   - We seriously underestimate the potential contribution of our employees, particularly those in hands-on functions.
   - The traditional approach equates better quality with higher cost.
   - The traditional approach is short on leadership and long on bossmanship.

2. The requirements for implementation are as follows: commitment by top management, creation of an organization-wide steering committee, planning and publicizing, and establishing an infrastructure that supports deployment and continual improvement.

3. The role of top management can be summarized as providing leadership and resources. The role of middle management is facilitation.

4. Although implementation must vary with each organization, the 20 fundamental steps offered in this chapter must be followed, generally in the order given. Tailoring to the organization's specific culture, values, strengths, and weaknesses is done in the *planning* phase, steps 12 through 15.

5. Implementation approaches that should be avoided are as follows: don't train all employees at once, don't rush into total quality by putting too many people in too many teams too soon, don't delegate implementation, and don't start an implementation before you are prepared.

6. Implementation phases are as follows: preparation phase, planning phase, and execution phase.

7. Going through the ISO 9000 registration steps will give an organization a good start on implementing total quality. ISO 9000 is an international standard for providers of goods and services that sets broad requirements for the assurance of quality and for management's involvement.

8. The Malcolm Baldrige National Quality Award evaluates candidates for the award according to criteria in seven categories: leadership; strategic planning; customer focus; measurement, analysis, and knowledge management; workforce focus; operations focus.

KEY TERMS AND CONCEPTS

Advocates
Baseline customer satisfaction
Baseline employee satisfaction/attitudes
Commitment by top management
Communicate and publicize
Customer feedback
Customer focused
Employee feedback
Evaluation criteria
Execution phase
Infrastructure
Interchangeable worker
ISO 9000
Leadership
Malcolm Baldrige National Quality Award
National Institute for Standards and Technology (NIST)
Organization
Organization-wide steering committee
Planning and publicizing
Planning phase
Preparation phase
Production labor costs
Resisters
Short-term focus
Strategic (broad) objectives
Strategic planning
Tactical (specific) objectives
Team activation—PDCA cycle
Team composition
Team training
Union considerations
Vision statement and guiding principles
World-Class Standard

FACTUAL REVIEW QUESTIONS

1. What is meant by the statement "We are bound to a short-term focus"?

2. How does the traditional approach to doing business equate quality with higher cost?

3. Differentiate between leadership and bossmanship.

4. List and explain the requirements for total quality implementation.

5. Describe the necessary components of an infrastructure that supports goal deployment and continual improvement.

6. What is the role of top management in the implementation of total quality?

7. What is the role of middle management in the implementation of total quality?

8. List the implementation steps that follow after the vision statement and broad objectives have been developed.

9. List and briefly explain implementation approaches that should be avoided.

10. Implementation of total quality happens in phases. Explain each phase in the order it occurs.

11. What is ISO 9000 registration, and how does it relate to total quality?

12. List the various categories of criteria for the Malcolm Baldrige National Quality Award.

CRITICAL THINKING ACTIVITY

1. The chart below was developed from the J.D. Power and Associates *Initial Quality Studies* for the years 2004 through 2007. Using Jaguar as an example, we see that in 2004, the Jaguar nameplate was ranked 3rd in initial quality with 98 problems per 100 cars, improved to 2nd in 2005, and dropped to 5th in 2006 and then to 6th in 2007. When you compare the ratings of the American nameplates (marked with asterisks), do you find a trend of overall improvement in rankings? What do the rankings and number of problems suggest for the American, Japanese, Korean, and European cars? Who (by nameplate or geographic area) seems to have the best record over this four-year period, and which nameplates seem not to "get it"?

   Note: Lexus, Honda, Infiniti, Toyota, Acura, Nissan, and Mazda are Japanese nameplates. Hyundai and Kia are Korean. Jaguar, Mercedes Benz, Audi, BMW, and Volvo are European nameplates.

2. E-Z Open Manufacturing Company is a leading maker of manual can openers. In the year just closed, E-Z Open controlled 17.2% of the manual can opener market in North America. That placed the company in the number two sales position for manual can openers. The company in the number one position, Saf-T Products Co., had a 22.3% share of the North American market. E-Z Open was eager to expand its market with a new rechargeable battery-operated can opener. Saf-T also has an electric can opener, but it is a countertop model that must be plugged in to operate. E-Z Open thinks it has a more desirable product with a battery-operated model because it will not tie up kitchen counter space, nor will it be encumbered by an electric cord. In addition, both the manual and the electric models now have removable cutter heads that can easily be cleaned. (Difficulty in keeping can openers clean has been a problem since the first rotary cutter models appeared 80 years ago.)

   Already well into the early work of a TQM implementation, E-Z Open is gearing up for a big year. It is at the point where it needs a vision statement, guiding principles, a mission statement, and a set of broad objectives. You have been retained as a consultant to help develop all of these. The company will hold an off-site meeting of the steering committee in 2 weeks, and you are to attend. It has asked you to provide the "strawman" documents to kick off the meeting. Your task is to develop the initial versions of each of the documents except the objectives.

3. E-Z Open Manufacturing's organization structure is straight out of the 1950s. The president is the senior executive, and he has a secretary and five department heads reporting to him. The departments are product development, manufacturing, finance, marketing, and human resources. Each is headed by a vice president (VP). Quality assurance is headed by a manager who reports to the manufacturing VP. The VP of product development has 35 people working on designs for a new family of small kitchen appliances, which the company hopes will render the firm immune to the dreaded can opener demand cycle.

Initial Quality Study Nameplate Ranking, 2004–2007 (ranked by problems per 100 vehicles)

Nameplate	2004	2005	2006	2007
Lexus	1/87	1/81	2/93	2/94
Cadillac*	2/93	5/104 tie	7/117 tie	25/135
Jaguar	3/98	2/88	5/109	6/112 tie
Honda	4/99	12/112	6/110	4/108
Buick*	5/100 tie	4/100	23/134	14/127
Mercury*	5/100 tie	16/120	16/129 tie	8/113
Hyundai	7/102	10/110 tie	3/102	12/125 tie
Infiniti	8/104 tie	9/109	7/117 tie	9/117
Toyota	8/104 tie	7/105	4/106	6/112 tie
Mercedes Benz	10/106	5/104 tie	27/139	5/111
Audi	11/109 tie	8/106	18/130	26/136
BMW	11/109 tie	3/95	29/142	21/133
Volvo	14/113	31/140 tie	20/133 tie	16/129
Acura	15/117	15/116	10/120 tie	17/130
Chevrolet*	16/119	20/127 tie	14/124	15/129
Chrysler*	17/120	19/121	10/120 tie	27/151
Dodge*	18/121 tie	24/130	19/132	30/156
Lincoln*	18/121 tie	13/113	12/121 tie	3/100
Pontiac*	20/122	22/129	20/133 tie	21/133
Ford*	23/130	20/127 tie	15/127	10/120
Saturn*	30/149	27/136	16/129 tie	19/132
Kia	31/153	31/140 tie	26/136	12/125 tie
Nissan	32/154	16/120 tie	12/121 tie	19/132
Mazda	33/157	35/149	31/150	34/163
Hummer*	37/173	10/110 tie	36/171	33/162

1st number is the rank for that year.
2nd number is the number of problems per 100 vehicles.
The chart does not include all makes.
*American nameplate.

Source: Adapted from J. D. Power and Associates *Initial Quality Studies*—2004 through 2007.

Manufacturing is aware of the new-product development effort and is concerned that it might face problems getting these products into production. Finance figures that the company cannot build mixers with the tools used for making can openers but has no clue as to the investment size. Meanwhile, marketing, gleeful that it will soon have something new to sell, keeps sending ideas for still more new products into product development. Quality assurance is totally occupied inspecting can openers and is out of the loop for the new products. You have gotten a sense for this, and you think the infrastructure is an impediment to the growth the firm is anticipating. What would you have the company do?

4. Using your place of work as the model, how does (or could) TQM benefit it in general, and in particular, what improvements would you expect from following the 20-step implementation process? (If you are a full-time student, and not employed, skip this question.)

5. Using your college as the model, explain how implementing a total quality program might benefit both the institution and its students. Include specific areas for improvement.

DISCUSSION ASSIGNMENT 22-1

McDonnell Douglas Corporation

McDonnell Douglas is now part of the Boeing Company, but that does not diminish in any way the turnaround that took place at McDonnell Douglas between 1992 and 1997. Times were not good for the company in the early 1990s. With the military buildup a thing of the past, the huge military division watched as sales plummeted. The commercial aircraft division struggled to be competitive with Boeing and Airbus. Waste and inefficiency were rampant. McDonnell Douglas stock sat at $9 a share in 1992—the lowest in anyone's memory. The company, once the nation's largest defense contractor, and the world's number two supplier of commercial aircraft, was in serious trouble.

The senior management staff under the leadership of John McDonnell, then board chair, decided to try total quality management. They got off to a very rocky start but learned from their mistakes and by 1992 were making good progress. Starting that year, executives were measured on three items: cash flow, return on net assets, and TQM, with the latter being tied to improvement on a Baldrige self-assessment score. In 1992, the self-assessment score was 200 (on the 0–1,000 scale). Over the next 3 years, the score increased by 100 points per year. This took the company from being a so-so performer in the traditional ranks to being a high midlevel performer in the TQM realm.

McDonnell Douglas found that as its Baldrige self-assessment score improved each year, its key business performance indicators tracked in parallel fashion. By 1995, its stock valuation reached $70 per share, profits were several times greater than in 1992, cash was up, and debt was down—all in a vastly smaller market. TQM literally turned around this giant company to the extent that the Boeing Company considered it imperative to merge in order to save Boeing. (The merger became final on August 1, 1997.)

DISCUSSION QUESTIONS

Discuss the following questions in class or outside of class with your fellow students:

1. Explain how the use of TQM could contribute to the improvement noted in McDonnell Douglas Corporation's key business performance indicators.

2. What was John McDonnell's motive in making improvement in the company's Baldrige self-assessment score a part of executive performance evaluations?

Source: From a paper delivered by John McDonnell, board chair, McDonnell Douglas Corporation, at the Florida Sterling Awards for Quality, June 1995, Orlando, Florida.

ENDNOTES

1. Helio Gomes, *Quality Quotes* (Milwaukee, WI: ASQ Quality Press, 1996), 34.

2. Philip B. Crosby, *Quality Is Free: The Art of Making Quality Certain* (New York: McGraw-Hill, 1979).

3. James Womack, Daniel T. Jones, and Daniel Roos, *The Machine That Changed the World* (New York: HarperCollins, 1990), 30.

4. Maryann Keller, *Rude Awakening: The Rise, Fall, and Struggle for Recovery of General Motors* (New York: Morrow, 1989), 131.

5. W. Roberts, *Leadership Secrets of Attila the Hun* (New York: Warner, 1991), 107.

6. Womack, Jones, and Roos, *The Machine That Changed*, 56.

7. Mary Walton, *The Deming Management Method* (New York: Perigee, 1986), 87.

INDEX